Geology

OCR and Heinemann are working together to provide better support for you

Heinemann is an imprint of Pearson Education Limited, a company incorporated in England and Wales, having its registered office at Edinburgh Gate, Harlow, Essex, CM20 2JE. Registered company number: 872828

www.heinemann.co.uk

Heinemann is a registered trademark of Pearson Education Limited

Text © Pearson Education Limited 2008

First published 2008

14
10 9

British Library Cataloguing in Publication Data is available from the British Library on request.

ISBN 978 0 435692 11 7

Edited by Jo Egre
Designed by Wearset Ltd, Boldon, Tyne and Wear
Project managed and typeset by Wearset Ltd, Boldon, Tyne and Wear
Illustrated by Wearset Ltd, Boldon, Tyne and Wear
Cover photo © Martin Bond/Science Photo Library
Printed in Malaysia (CTP-PPSB)

Acknowledgements
We would like to thank Lucie Johnson, Amy and Charlotte Mugglestone, Graeme Richards and Ian Smith for their invaluable help in the development and trialling of this course.

The authors and publisher would like to thank the following for permission to reproduce photographs:

p3 NASA/Roger Ressmeyer/Corbis; p4 T Frances Stratton; p4 M Corbis; p4 B StockTrek/Getty Images; p5 StockTrek/Getty Images; p11 Geopix; p15 Geopix; p16 Leverett Bradley/Corbis; p20 T Cumulus; p20 M Cumulus; p20 B D. Falconer/PhotoLink/Getty Images; p21 Frances Stratton; p23 Frances Stratton; p26 National Geophysical Data Center/NOAA; p27 Geopix; p31 Cumulus; p37 L Frances Stratton; p37 R NASA/Science Photo Library; p38 US Geological Survey/Science Photo Library; p39 Irina Efremova/Dreamstime; p40 T Masao Hayashi/Duno/Science Photo Library; p40 B Nathan Jaskowiak/Shutterstock; p41 Georg Gerster/Science Photo Library; p46 Frances Stratton; p48 Frances Stratton; p49 T Frances Stratton; p49 B Frances Stratton; p50 Frances Stratton; p51 Frances Stratton; p52 Malcolm Fry; p53 TL Frances Stratton; p53 TR Frances Stratton; p53 B Frances Stratton; p55 L Frances Stratton; p55 R Frances Stratton; p56 Frances Stratton; p57 L Frances Stratton; p57 R Frances Stratton; p59 T Frances Stratton; p59 B Frances Stratton; p61 Frances Stratton; p66 TL Siede Preis/Getty Images; p66 BL Charles Smith/Corbis; p66 TR Cumulus; p66 BR Siede Preis/Getty Images; p67 B Frank Mugglestone; p71 TR Frank Mugglestone; p71 BL Frances Stratton; p71 BR Frank Mugglestone; p74 Frances Stratton; p75 TR Alfred Pasieka/Science Photo Library; p75 B Frances Stratton; p75 B Frances Stratton; p76 T Frances Stratton; p76 B Frances Stratton; p77 Frances Stratton; p77 BL Frances Stratton; p77 BR Frances Stratton; p78 TL Frances Stratton; p78 TM Frances Stratton; p78 TR Frances Stratton; p78 BL Frances Stratton; p78 BR Frances Stratton; p79 Frances Stratton; p80 L Frances Stratton; p80 M Frances Stratton; p80 R Frances Stratton; p83 Geopix; p88 Frances Stratton; p89 Frances Stratton; p90 Frances Stratton; p91 Frances Stratton; p92 TL Frances Stratton; p92 Frances Stratton; p92 BL Frances Stratton; p92 BR Frances Stratton; p93 TL Frances Stratton; p93 TR Frances Stratton; p93 B Frances Stratton; p95 TL C. Sherburne/PhotoLink/Getty Images; p95 TR PhotoLink/Getty Images; p95 B C. Sherburne/PhotoLink/Getty Images; p96 Frances Stratton; p97 TL Dorian Weisel/Corbis; p97 TM Frances Stratton; p97 TR Frances Stratton; p97 RM Dorian Weisel/Corbis; p97 RB Frances Stratton; p99 T Geopix; p99 B Frances Stratton; p100 Frances Stratton; p101 PhotoLink/Getty Images; p102 TL Frances Stratton; p102 R Frances Stratton; p102 BL Frances Stratton; p103 T Geopix; p103 B InterNetwork Media/Getty Images; p105 TL Frances Stratton; p105 TR Frances Stratton; p105 B Frances Stratton; p107 Frank Mugglestone; p108 T Frank Mugglestone; p108 M Frank Mugglestone; p108 B Frank Mugglestone; p110 T Frank Mugglestone; p110 M Frank Mugglestone; p110 B Frank Mugglestone; p111 L Frances Stratton; p111 R Frances Stratton; p113 Frances Stratton; p114 Frances Stratton; p115 Frances Stratton; p116 Frances Stratton; p117 T Frank Mugglestone; p117 M Frank Mugglestone; p117 B Frances Stratton; p118 T Frances Stratton; p118 M Frances Stratton; p118 B Frances Stratton; p119 Frances Stratton; p121 Frank Mugglestone; p123 TL Frances Stratton; p123 R Frances Stratton; p123 BL Frank Mugglestone/Frances Stratton; p124 StockTrek/Getty Images; p126 T Frances Stratton; p126 B Frances Stratton; p127 T Frances Stratton; p127 B Frances Stratton; p128 T StockTrek/Getty Images; p128 B Frances Stratton; p130 T Frank Mugglestone; p130 B Frances Stratton; p131 L Frances Stratton; p131 R Frances Stratton; p132 T Carl and Ann Purcell/Corbis; p132 B Frances Stratton; p133 Frances Stratton; p135 Frank Mugglestone; p137 T Frances Stratton; p137 B StockTrek/Getty Images; p140 Charles Smith/Corbis; p141 Frank Mugglestone; p141 Frances Stratton; p144 Frances Stratton; p145 Frances Stratton; p146 L Frances Stratton; p146 R Frances Stratton; p149 T Cumulus; p149 B Joyce Photographics/Science Photo Library; p151 Frances Stratton; p162 Cumulus; p165 Deborah Armstrong; p173 Frances Stratton; p175 Frances Stratton; p176 T Cumulus; p176 B Cumulus; p177 Geopix; p179 Cumulus; p181 Cumulus; p182 T Mark Karrass/Corbis; p182 B Kevin Burke/Corbis; p186 Cumulus; p187 Frances Stratton; p189 T Frances Stratton; p189 B Frances Stratton; p194 PhotoLink/Getty Images; p197 David R. Frazier/Science Photo Library; p200 T Frances Stratton; p200 B Paul Glendall/Alamy; p201 Jeremy Walker/Science Photo Library; p203 Martial Colomb/Getty Images; p204 Wernher Krutein/Corbis; p206 InterNetwork Media/Getty Images; p209 T Deborah Armstrong; p209 B Deborah Armstrong; p212 Andrew Ward/Life File/Getty Images; p213 L Frances Stratton; p213 M Frances Stratton; p213 R Cumulus; p214 Stockbyte/Getty Images; p217 T Irish Geological Survey; p217 B Irish Geological Survey; p220 Frances Stratton; p221 T Frances Stratton; p221 M Frances Stratton; p221 B Frances Stratton; p223 T Ismael Montero; p223 M Alan Sirulnikoff/Science Photo Library; p223 B Visual&Written SL/Alamy; p225 LT Frances Stratton; p225 LB Frances Stratton; p225 RT Frances Stratton; p225 RB Frances Stratton; p227 T Frances Stratton; p227 B Frances Stratton; p228 Siede Preis/Getty Images; p232 Elmer Frederick Fischer/Corbis; p234 T Siede Preis/Getty Images; p234 B Steve Bowman/Corbis; p239 TL Frank Mugglestone; p239 TR Frances Stratton; p239 TM Frances Stratton; p239 B Frances Stratton; p240 Siede Preis/Getty Images; p241 Robert Yin/Corbis; p243 Siede Preis/Getty Images; p246 Frances Stratton; p251 T Jim Wehtje/Getty Images; p251 B Siede Preis/Getty Images; p252 Gregory Ochocki/Science Photo Library; p253 T Marty Snyderman/Corbis; p253 B Frances Stratton; p254 T Derek Siveter; p254 M Dee Berger/Science Photo Library; p254 B The Natural History Museum, London; p255 T Manfred Kage/Science Photo Library; p255 B Dr Jeremy Burgess/Science Photo Library; p259 Frances Stratton; p260 T Kaz Chiba/Getty Images; p260 B Danil Calilung/Corbis; p262 Frank Mugglestone; p263 Frances Stratton; p264 L Tom McHugh/Photo Researchers/Photolibrary; p264 R Tom McHugh/Photo Researchers/Photolibrary; p266 Frances Stratton; p267 Frances Stratton; p273 RT Edward Kinsman/Science Photo Library; p273 RB Edward Kinsman/Science Photo Library; p273 L Geological Survey of Canada/Science Photo Library; p275 Frances Stratton; p276 Frances Stratton; p279 Frances Stratton; p281 Frances Stratton; p289 Frances Stratton; p294 T Michael McCoy/Science Photo Library; p294 M Cumulus; p294 B Sheila Terry/Science Photo Library; p295 Doug Allen/Science Photo Library.

The authors and publisher would like to thank the following for permission to use copyright material:

p22 case study: 'Is Istanbul next?' precis from issue 2201 of New Scientist, 28 August 1999, p5; p47 Fig 2 (3rd diagram): Paterson, M.S., Geological Society of America, Bull. 69, pp465–476, 1958; p47 Fig 2 (4th diagram): Griggs, D.T., Turner, F.J. and Heard, H.C., in Rock Deformation, eds D.T. Griggs and J. Hardin, Geological Society of America, Mem. 79, 1960; p153 Fig 2: http://www.tulane.edu/~sanelson/eens212/regionalmetamorph.htm; p210 Fig 1: adapted from issue 2572 of New Scientist, 10 October 2006, pp42–45; p217 Fig 2 and Fig 3: reproduced with permission from the Geological Survey of Northern Ireland © Crown Copyright; p233 Fig 3: adapted from an image by the UC Museum of Paleontology, www.ucmp.berkeley.edu; p235 Fig 3: http://www.starfish.ch/reef/reef.html; p251 Fig 2, p252 Fig 1, p253 Fig 3 and p261 Fig 3: Rhona M. Black, The Elements of Palaeontology, 1989 Cambridge University Press; p265 case study: precis from issue 2568 of New Scientist, 9 September 2006, pp35–39; p268 Fig 1: http://upload.wikipedia.org/wikipedia/commons/thumb/5/5f/Diplodocus_size_comparison.png/800px-Diplodocus_size_comparison.png; p287 Fig 2: Copyright © 1994–2001 Russell E. McDuff and G. Ross Heath. All rights reserved.

Every effort has been made to contact copyright holders of material reproduced in this book. Any omissions will be rectified in subsequent printings if notice is given to the publisher.

Geology

AS
A2

OCR and Heinemann are working together to provide better support for you

Debbie Armstrong, Frank Mugglestone,
Ruth Richards and Frances Stratton

with Stephen Davies, Malcolm Fry
and Tony Shelton

Series editor: Frances Stratton

www.heinemann.co.uk

✓ Free online support
✓ Useful weblinks
✓ 24 hour online ordering

01865 888080

Official Publisher Partnership

Contents

How to use this book

In this book you will find a number of features planned to help you.

- **Double page spreads** filled with information about each topic in the specification.

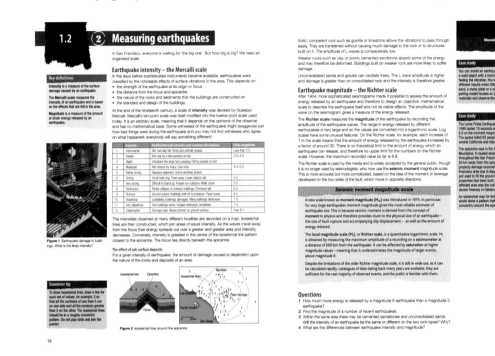

- **End of module examination questions**. These have been selected to show you the types of question that may appear in your examination.

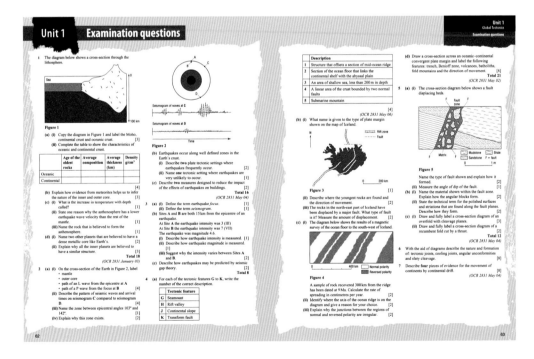

Within each double page spread you will find other features to highlight important points.

- **Key Definitions**. These are the terms that appear in the specification. You must know the definitions and how to use them.
- **Terms in bold**. These draw attention to terms that you are expected to know. These are important terms used by geologists.

- **Examiner tips**. These are selected points to help you avoid making common errors in the examinations.

- **Worked examples**. These are examples to show you how calculations should be set out.

- **How Science Works**. This book has been written in a style that reflects the way that scientists work. Certain sections have been highlighted as good examples of How Science Works.

- **Case Studies**. In some spreads there are case studies describing specific examples.
- **Questions.** At the end of each topic are a few questions that you should be able to answer after studying that topic.

Examiner tip

Worked example

How science works

Case study

The examination

It is useful to know some of the language used by examiners. Often this means little more that just looking closely at the wording used in each question on the paper.
- Look at the number of **marks allocated** to a part question – ensure you write enough points down to gain these marks. The number of marks allocated for any part of a question is a guide to the depth of treatment required for the answer.
- Look for words in **bold**. These are meant to draw your attention.
- **Labelled diagrams and drawings** often communicate your answer better than trying to explain everything in sentences.

Look for the **action word**. Make sure you know what each word means and answer what it asks. The meanings of some action words are listed below.
- *Define*: only a formal statement of a definition is required.
- *Explain*: a reasoned answer is required using geological background.
- *State*: a concise factual answer without supporting argument.
- *List*: a number of points with no elaboration. If you are asked for **two** points then give only two!
- *Describe*: state in words, using diagrams where appropriate, the main points of the topic. It requires more technical terms than a list where single words will be sufficient.
- *Discuss*: a detailed account of the points involved in the topic.
- *Calculate*: a numerical answer is required. In general, working should be shown.
- *Sketch*: often used for diagrams where you are simplifying the geology of a fossil or fold or from a photo. Sketches should be fully labelled using technical terms and label lines must end exactly at the feature to be labelled. Scales are vital to make sense of a diagram.

Finally, when you first read the question, do so very carefully and do not ignore the introductory sentence. Once you have read something incorrectly, it is very difficult to get the incorrect wording out of your head! If you have time at the end of the examination, read through your answers again to check that you have answered the questions that have been set.

The Earth is one of a number of planets circling the Sun, but it is the only one which appears to support life today in our Solar System.

The table below summarises our current knowledge of the planets in the Solar System.

Planet	Description	Distance from Sun (AU)*	Atmosphere	Mean Temp (°C)	Vol. (Earth = 1)	Density (gm/cm³)	No. of Moons
Mercury	Heavily cratered surface with signs of volcanism; a weak magnetic field similar to the Earth's, so has an iron-rich core	0.4	Thin, mainly helium and sodium	−183/427	0.05	5.43	0
Venus	Desert surface has craters, shield volcanoes and structures resembling lava flows	0.7	Dense, carbon dioxide and clouds of sulfuric acid	457/482	0.88	5.24	0
Earth	67% oceans – landmasses with volcanoes, high mountains, extensive rivers and lakes; desert areas and ice caps; few impact craters	1.0	Nitrogen and oxygen, with variable amounts of water vapour	15/20	1.00	5.515	1
Mars	Large shield volcanoes; features which look as if they may have been formed by running water. No running water on the surface today but water is trapped in polar ice caps and may also be trapped underground	1.5	Thin, mainly of carbon dioxide	−87/−5	0.149	3.933	2
Asteroid belt	Fragments of carbonaceous, silicate and metallic material						
Jupiter	Small rocky or metallic core. Enormous pressures in the core generate large amounts of heat, radiation and a powerful magnetic field	5.2	Hydrogen and helium cloud belts and a large red spot, which is a giant whirling storm of rising gas	−150	1316	1.33	>60
Saturn	Rings composed of icy debris; a rocky core covered by liquid hydrogen	9.5	Hydrogen	−180	755	0.70	>30
Uranus	Icy rings and a rocky core	19.2	Mostly hydrogen, with some helium and methane	−197	52	1.30	>20
Neptune	Faint ring system; a magnetic field, so probably has a rocky core	30.1	Mostly hydrogen, with some helium and methane	−200	44	1.76	>10

*AU = Astronomical Units – by definition the Earth is 1 AU from the Sun – 149.6 × 10⁶ km

Figure 1 The Solar System

The Solar System

The terrestrial planets

As you can see from the table, the four planets closest to the Sun share some characteristics as well as some important differences. Collectively Mercury, Venus, Earth and Mars are known as the terrestrial ('Earth-like') planets. They are formed of materials similar to those of the Earth – the only planet that we have really detailed knowledge of.

The gas giants

The remaining four planets: Jupiter, Saturn, Uranus and Neptune are collectively described as the gas giants. The International Astronomical Union redefined the term planet in August 2006, so Pluto is now classified as a dwarf planet.

Origins of the Solar System

Space exploration has contributed greatly to our knowledge. In particular, the Hubble telescope has enabled astronomers to observe the early stages of star formation. The Big Bang was the event that led to the formation of the Universe about 14 billion years ago. It was the point in time when all matter and energy were created. At that moment, all matter was compressed into a space billions of times smaller than a proton. Both time and space were set to zero.

The Solar System is believed to have formed around 4500 million years ago. The Solar System formed when a giant molecular cloud of gas and dust collapsed (the nebula hypothesis) – possibly when it was hit by a shockwave from a nearby exploding star (a supernova). The material eventually formed a rotating disc and as material was drawn towards the centre it triggered nuclear reactions which resulted in the formation of the Sun. Other material in the disc of dust particles began to stick together by a process called accretion. This formed progressively larger objects, finally resulting in the formation of planets.

Space exploration

Much of our knowledge about the planets has come from space exploration missions. Space exploration began in the 1960s with early missions to the Moon, Venus and Mars.

Earth's moon

The first soft landing missions were sent to the Moon with the first manned landing in 1969. The Apollo missions brought back 20 kg of rock and soil. These rocks were much older than expected, with the oldest rocks dated to 4400 Ma. The **Moon** has a solid crust, mantle and core and the surface is made up of:

- the maria – dark areas composed of basalt lava flows, which were generated by impacts of meteorites
- the highlands – light coloured areas composed of a plagioclase-rich rock anorthosite.

Mars

So far, the exploration of Mars has occurred in three stages:

- In the 1960s the space probes Mariners 3 to 7 flew by Mars, taking as many pictures as possible. They identified huge volcanoes including Olympus Mons, the largest volcanic structure in the Solar System.
- As knowledge and technologies grew, we began putting spacecraft in orbit around Mars for longer-term, global studies. These orbital missions started in the 1970s and in 2005 the Mars Reconnaissance Orbiter was capable of taking photos showing objects just 10 cm across.
- In 2007 spacecraft landed on the surface to move around and explore. This will tell us more about the geology of the planet, the presence of water, and maybe even clues about whether Mars was ever a habitat for life.

Venus

Venus is similar in size, mass, composition and distance from the Sun to the Earth. Spacecraft have landed on Venus and mapped it using radar, so that the data on temperature and pressure are actual measurements. Venus has no oceans and is covered by thick, rapidly spinning clouds that trap surface heat, creating a scorched greenhouse-like world with temperatures hot enough to melt lead. The clouds reflect sunlight, making Venus the brightest planet in our sky.

The asteroid belt

Asteroids are large, rocky objects left over from the formation of the Solar System and lie between Mars and Jupiter. They are thought to be the remains of a planet that failed to form when the rest of the Solar System was created. While most asteroids may be only the size of pebbles, Ceres, the largest, has a diameter of about 914 km. Collisions between asteroids result in fragments being broken off. These fragments then travel through the Solar System and some are captured by the Earth's gravity and fall to the Earth's surface as **meteorites**.

Key definitions

The **Solar System** is the Sun, planets, their moons, comets and asteroids.

The **Sun** is a star composed of hydrogen and helium. It is the largest object in the Solar System and contains more than 99.8% of the total mass.

A **planet** is a sizable object orbiting a star.

A **moon** is a natural satellite orbiting a planet.

Asteroids are rocky objects which failed to form a planet.

Meteorites are fragments of rock, which fall to Earth from space.

A **comet** is composed of ice and dust. The outer layer melts into water vapour as it gets closer to the Sun.

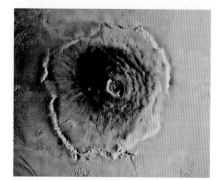

Figure 2 Olympus Mons on Mars

Questions

1 Research the space missions to the Moon, Mars and Venus to find out the latest information that is being collected.

2 Mauna Loa is the largest volcano on the Earth, with an estimated volume of 26000 km³. Olympus Mons is 27 km high and has a diameter of 600 km. Assuming that Olympus Mons is conical in shape, calculate its volume. How much larger is it than Mauna Loa? *Hint:* The volume of a cone can be calculated using the formula $\frac{1}{3}\pi r^2 h$.

3 Why does the surface temperature on Mercury vary between −183 °C and 427 °C?

Meteorites

Most meteorites come from the asteroid belt, but a few are thought to come from the Moon and perhaps Mars. Meteorites can be identified as coming from the Moon because they have a composition and age similar to rock samples brought back from the Moon. Hopefully, future missions to Mars will be able to confirm which meteorites come from there.

The table below summarises the main types of meteorites found on the Earth.

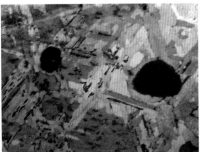

Figure 1 Cross-section of an iron nickel meteorite

Type	Characteristics	Interpretation
Iron	Composed of an alloy of iron and nickel 6% of known meteorites are of this type	Thought to represent the core of a small planet-like object, which formed early in the history of the Solar System
Stony	Composed of silicate minerals including olivine, pyroxene and plagioclase feldspar 93% of known meteorites are of this type	Thought to represent the mantle of a small planet-like object, which formed early in the history of the Solar System
• Carbonaceous chondrites	A type of stony meteorite which contains water and organic compounds	Similar in composition to the Sun but with fewer volatiles

Evidence for impact craters

There is clear evidence that asteroids have collided with many planets and moons in the Solar System. The impact forms distinctive craters, which you can see, on the surface of the Moon, with a pair of binoculars. The craters all have a circular depression with a rim of broken rock and they cover most of the Moon's surface.

The Earth's surface does not show such extensive craters though there are some, including the 50 000-year-old Meteor Crater in Arizona. There is no reason to assume that the Earth is less prone to impacts than the Moon so there must be another reason. The key difference is the amount of activity affecting the Earth's surface. The Earth's crust is subjected to weathering, erosion and long-term recycling by plate tectonics, all of which destroy craters.

The graph below shows the relationship between the size of impacts and their frequency. The K-T impact event of 65 Ma was the one that contributed to the extinction of the dinosaurs. So what are your chances of being killed by a meteorite impact? You are much more likely to be killed in a car accident in the next 2 years (1 in 5000) than by a meteorite like the one which formed Meteor Crater (1 in more than 750 million!).

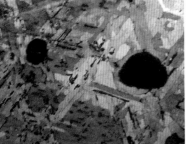

Figure 2 Craters of the Earth's moon

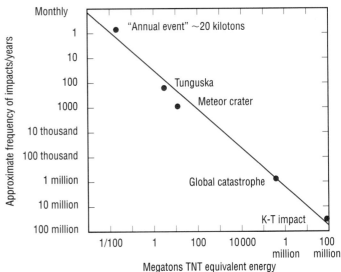

Figure 3 Meteor Crater in Arizona and frequency of meteorite impacts

The diagrams in Figure 4 show the later stages of the formation of a crater. The impact causes:

- material to be ejected and quartz grains to be violently shocked and even melted
- rock strata to be tilted
- material at depth to be brecciated (broken up)
- the ejected material falls back to the surface but the sequence of rocks is inverted because material closer to the surface is ejected first and falls back to the surface earlier.

The explosive energy of the Meteor Crater event has been likened to a 40 megaton explosion. The meteorite which made it was composed almost entirely of nickel-iron, suggesting that it may have originated in the interior of a small planet. It was 45 m across, weighed roughly 300 000 tons, and was travelling at a speed of 12 km per second. It would have devastated an area about 80 km in diameter.

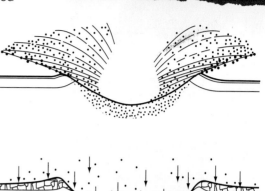

Figure 4 Ejecta around a crater

Volcanic activity in the Solar System

Volcanic activity is clearly seen on Mars with the huge shield volcanoes like Olympus Mons. It is not surprising that Venus has volcanoes as well. These inner planets have a core and rocky mantle like the Earth, so volcanic activity as a result of heat from the core is to be expected.

It was when fly-bys of the outer gas giants took place in the 1980s that volcanism was discovered on their moons. The most interesting of the moons is Io, which is extremely volcanic with evidence of lava flows covering craters formed earlier in its history. Io is too small to have its own heat source for the volcanic activity and the heat is thought to be generated by tidal heating – the result of the enormous gravity field of Jupiter.

Dating the planets

The generally accepted age for the Earth and the rest of the Solar System is about 4550 million years (plus or minus about 1%). Unfortunately, the age cannot be measured directly from material on the Earth as the surface was initially molten. Then the processes of erosion and crustal recycling destroyed the original surface.

The oldest rocks, which have been found so far on the Earth, date to about 3800 to 3900 Ma. Some of these rocks are sedimentary, and include minerals as old as 4200 Ma. Rocks of this age are rare, but have been found on North America, Greenland, Australia, Africa and Asia.

The method used to date the rocks is radiometric dating, which uses the decay of radioactive isotopes. To determine the age of an object, we need to know two important values:

- the rate at which the radioactive isotope decays – the half-life – which is determined in a laboratory
- the amount of the radioactive isotope compared to the amount of the isotope that it decays to.

One of the methods used by geologists studying the planets is radiometric dating by Rubidium-87 (^{87}Rb), which decays to Strontium-87 (^{87}Sr), with a half-life of 4.88×10^{10} years.

Dating rocks is a complex process, so radiometric dates are quoted with a degree of uncertainty, which is usually less than 1%. For example, a lunar (from Earth's Moon) basalt from the Sea of Tranquillity has been dated as 3650 ± 50 Ma.

Figures 5 and 6

Figure 5 Map showing the area which would be affected if a meteorite 45 m across impacted on the centre of London

Figure 6 Volcanic eruption on Io

Questions

1 How do meteorites provide evidence for the internal structure and composition of the Earth?
2 Research the evidence for the Tunguska event of 1908.
3 Research volcanic activity on Venus, Mars and the moons of Jupiter. Describe the type of activity and the relative scale of the volcanoes.

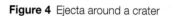

Compared with the other planets in the Solar System, ours is medium in size but quite dense. During the formation of the Earth (see spread 1.1.1), dense metallic elements concentrated at its central **core**, sinking beneath the lighter minerals which developed into the surrounding **mantle**. These two 'spheres' make up over 99% of the Earth. The veneer of cold, solid rock, the **crust**, is a very thin skin of the least dense rock, which cooled against the 'atmosphere'. The main layers are separated by named boundaries where there are distinct changes in composition and physical properties. We will never visit the centre of the Earth so all the information that we have about the deep layers of the Earth is deduced by analysis of data from earthquakes, meteorites and density measurements.

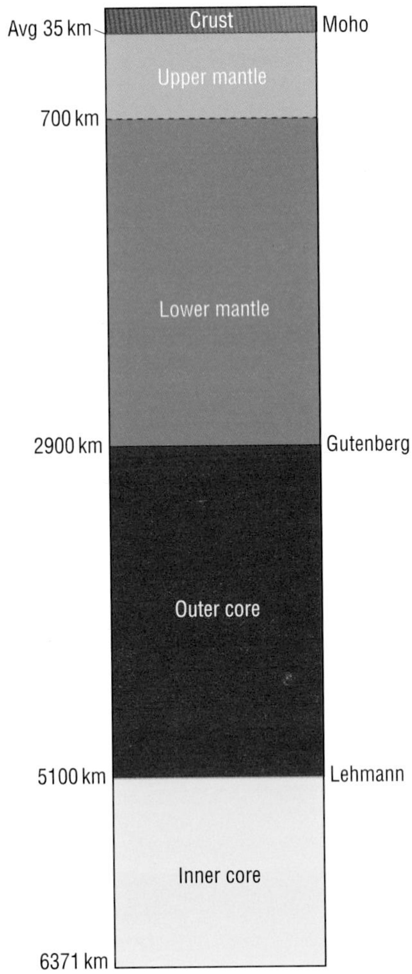

Figure 1 Layers of the Earth

The inner core from the centre of the Earth – 6371 km to approximately 5100 km

- The inner core is believed to be made of a solid material, due to the extreme pressure which is estimated at 3 600 000 atmospheres, compared to 1 atmosphere at the surface.
- Earthquake waves, both P and S waves, move through the inner core, with the S waves being generated by the P waves. This provides good evidence of a solid layer.
- The composition of the core is a mixture of iron and some nickel, based on meteorite evidence and the fact that iron nickel has the correct density of more than 12 g/cm^3.

The Lehmann Discontinuity at 5100 km

The Lehmann boundary is a phase boundary between materials of the same composition but in different states, so it is not a distinct boundary. It is a zone of about 100 km where the rocks change from all liquid in the outer core through a liquid-solid mix to all solid in the inner core.

The outer core from 5100 km to 2900 km

- The outer core is liquid iron nickel. Seismic or earthquake waves provide clear evidence that the outer core is liquid because S waves cannot pass through liquid and they do not pass through the outer core.
- P waves slow down due to the reduction in rigidity.
- The pressure in the outer core is less than that of the inner core, allowing a liquid to exist.

The Gutenberg Discontinuity at 2900 km

This is a very distinct and clear boundary marking a change of material from metallic iron nickel to stony silicate material. It also changes state between the liquid outer core and the solid mantle. Therefore at this boundary the P wave velocity decreases and the S waves stop altogether.

The lower mantle from 2900 km to 700 km

- The lower mantle is solid because S waves can travel through it.
- P waves increase in velocity steadily as the increasing pressure causes the rocks to become more rigid – less compressible.
- It is made of the same type of silicate material as the stony meteorites.

The upper mantle from 700 km to an average of 35 km

- The upper mantle also consists of solid silicates but they are less dense than the lower mantle.
- The main rock is peridotite.

Part of the upper mantle lies within the asthenosphere, while part is within the lithosphere.

The crust

The nature of the crust underneath the continents is different from that under the oceans.

		Oceanic areas	Continental areas			
CRUST	Composition	Rich in Fe and Mg	Rich in Al and Si		**LITHOSPHERE**	
		Basalt (pillow lavas)	Granitic rocks			Rigid
		Dolerite (dykes)	Igneous, metamorphic and sedimentary rocks – deformed			
		Gabbro in layers				
	Density	2.9 g/cm³	Average 2.7 g/cm³			
	Age	Oldest oceanic crust is 200 Ma	All ages, up to 4000 Ma			
	Thickness	5–10 km average 7 km	Up to 90 km under highest mountains; average 35 km			
						— Moho —
UPPER MANTLE		Peridotite of lithosphere upper mantle				
		Peridotite of asthenosphere upper mantle			**ASTHENOSPHERE**	
		5–200 km deep	75–300 km deep			Rheid

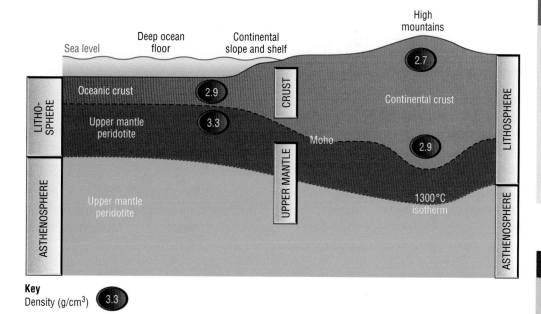

Figure 2 Cross-section through the upper mantle and crust

The asthenosphere

Most of the mantle behaves as a solid with the ability to flow, very slowly over millions of years. This type of material is known as a **rheid**. The upper mantle is made of a rock called **peridotite**. At depths between 75 and 670 km, but especially between 75 and 250 km, the temperature is high (>1300 °C) enough for about 5% of crystals in the peridotite to partially melt. This causes a film of melted minerals to surround each solid crystal, allowing the mantle material to flow more easily. This upper part of the upper mantle shows plastic properties even though it is still solid. It has also lost some of its rigidity and therefore P and S waves will slow down, which is why it is sometimes called the *low velocity layer*.

The lithosphere

Nearer the surface, the mantle is cool enough to prevent **partial melting**. This zone is always rigid and brittle. The lithosphere cannot flow, but it can be carried by the underlying asthenosphere. It is brittle, so has broken into plates. The outermost skin of the lithosphere is the oceanic or continental crust, divided from the mantle lithosphere by the Moho.

Examiner tip

Plate tectonics divides the upper mantle (with its thin skin of crust) into two layers according to their physical properties, so we can understand how the layers behave. The rigid lithosphere ('rock sphere') made of crust and upper mantle moves above the plastic asthenosphere ('weak sphere').

Key definitions

A **rheid** is a solid material that flows.

Peridotite is an ultramafic igneous rock composed of the minerals olivine and pyroxene with a coarse crystal size.

Olivine is a dense, ferromagnesian silicate mineral.

Partial melting is where a proportion of the minerals will have a lower melting point, allowing them to melt while the rest remains solid.

Examiner tip

It is important to use crust and lithosphere in the right context. They are not the same, although some textbooks and websites use the terms loosely. Crust is oceanic and continental crust, while lithosphere is crust plus part of the upper mantle.

Questions

1 Draw a scale drawing on 1 side of A4 paper of the Earth showing the core, mantle and crust. How thick should the crust be on your diagram?
2 What is the difference between the crust and the lithosphere?
3 Explain how a solid rock can undergo plastic flow.
4 Where will the continental crust be thickest?

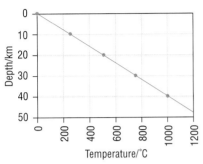

Figure 1 Graph to show the increase in temperature with depth – the geothermal gradient

Direct methods of observation

We can find out about distant planets and moons, but though the interior of the Earth is tantalizingly close by cosmic standards, how can we get there? Finding out about the Earth is a challenge as we can only see a very small part of it. First-hand observation and sampling of rocks and structures allows us to touch rocks from a maximum depth of about 250 km. As it is 6371 km to the centre of the Earth, the only part of the Earth that can be observed directly is the top 3.9%!

The crust beneath our feet

Most of the land surface of the Earth is now very well mapped, even though there may be some debate about detail and interpretation. Analysis of surface geology maps will suggest what lies below the surface, especially in areas where older crustal rocks have been brought to the surface during earth movements and exposed by erosion. From this we know that the upper continental crust is varied, showing a range of sedimentary, igneous and metamorphic rocks, with an overall granitic composition.

Mines and boreholes

We have direct access to the higher levels of the crust by means of mines for coal, metal ores and diamonds. Problems of drainage, ventilation, high working temperatures and lifting the ore to the surface limit the depth of a mine. The deepest mines, for gold in South Africa, penetrate nearly 4 km of the crust.

Boreholes penetrate a little deeper. A Russian research borehole in Siberia reached a depth of almost 13 km. The deepest oil well penetrates 10 km into the crust, the depth below which oil is not found. Samples of rocks and microfossils can be brought up from boreholes and remote sensing undertaken.

Geothermal gradient

The geothermal gradient is the rate of increase in temperature per unit depth in the Earth. In deep boreholes and mines the temperature of the rock increases with depth and can cause serious problems. The average geothermal gradient of the Earth is about 25 °C/km. However, in volcanically active areas, the temperature may increase by about 30 to 50 °C/km. If the rate of temperature change were constant, temperatures deep in the Earth would soon reach the point where all known rocks would melt. However, we know that the Earth's mantle is solid because S waves pass through it. The temperature gradient is lower in the mantle for two reasons:

- Radioactive heat production is concentrated within the crust of the Earth, where radioactive elements such as uranium are found.
- The mechanism of thermal transport changes from conduction within the rigid lithosphere plates, to convection in the asthenosphere and upper mantle, and this transports the heat differently.

Volcanoes bringing magma from depth

The magma that feeds volcanoes through vents originates in the lower crust or upper mantle and so carries up samples of the rocks from these layers. Basalt lavas which erupt at mid-ocean ridges are formed by partial melting of the upper mantle. We can estimate the composition of the upper mantle from the chemical analysis of these basalts and their volatiles.

Occasionally, the igneous material in a volcanic pipe includes diamonds and other minerals, which have a compact crystal structure. Diamonds crystallise under the high

---

Deep mining

The deepest mine in the world is the Western Deep Levels gold mine in South Africa, currently 3585 m deep. The mine today has 800 km of tunnels and employs 5600 miners. The mine is a dangerous place to work and an average of five miners die in accidents each year. The journey to the rock face can take 1 hour from the surface.

The mine is so deep that temperatures can rise to dangerous levels due to the effect of the geothermal gradient. Mining companies use giant air conditioning equipment on the surface to send cool air down to the miners, to cool the mine from 55 °C down to a more tolerable 28 °C. Work is underway to extend the mine deeper to some 3.9 km underground by 2009.

A lucrative gold deposit has been located at a depth of 5 km, but the temperature at this level is estimated to be a blistering 70 °C, and they are trying to find an economic way to mine it. The trend in underground mining is towards increased automation, especially for ultra-deep mining. Work is being done on developing robot machines with computer guidance – even operating the machinery from the surface.

pressure conditions of the upper mantle, at depths of up to 250 km. The enclosing igneous rock, called **kimberlite** after the Kimberley diamond mine in South Africa, also includes **xenoliths** of peridotite. The magma carries up fragments of country rock torn from the walls of these very deep volcanic vents. Kimberlite pipes are the result of explosive volcanism from deep mantle sources. Within 2 km of the surface, the highly pressured magma explodes upwards and expands to form a conical vent a few hundred metres to a kilometre across.

Ophiolite suites – ocean crust on land

During the collisions of plates, sections of oceanic crust may be broken off a descending oceanic plate and thrust onto the edge of the continental plate, instead of being carried down into the mantle. They may then be exposed by erosion. The section of ancient oceanic crust can be examined on land without the need to drill a borehole through the ocean floor. The peridotite at the base of an ophiolite sequence is from the upper mantle. If the structure of an ophiolite sequence is returned to its original undeformed orientation, its total thickness is usually about 7 km, the thickness of the oceanic crust.

Ophiolites can be seen in the Lizard Peninsula in Southwest England and the Troodos Massif in Cyprus. These ophiolite sections are millions of years old, but they are similar to the modern-day oceanic crust and upper mantle, see Figure 2.

Key definitions

Kimberlites are fine-grained, ultramafic igneous rocks.

A **xenolith** is a fragment of 'foreign' rock included in an igneous rock, which has come from a different source.

An **ophiolite** is a section of oceanic crust and upper mantle broken off and attached to the edge of a continent during plate movement.

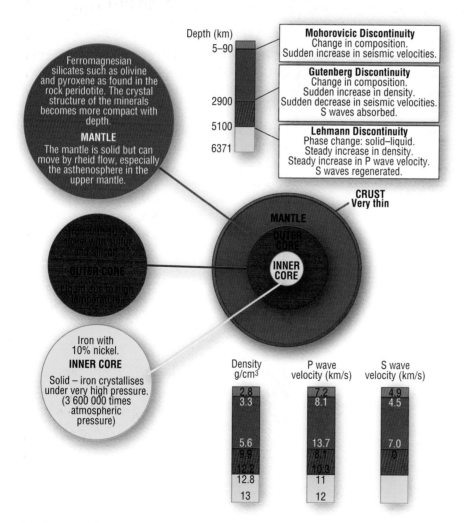

Figure 2 Summary of the structure of the Earth

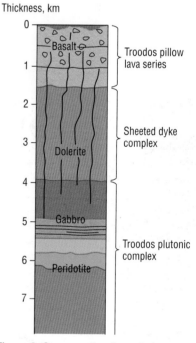

Figure 3 Cross-section through the Troodos ophiolite, Cyprus

Questions

1 The crust is thin under the oceans – why not drill boreholes there to sample the full crustal sequence? Research one of the deep drilling projects.

2 How do we know that the upper mantle is made of peridotite?

3 Plot a graph to show the geothermal gradient where the average is 30 °C/km.

Indirect methods of observation

You have just seen that we have very limited direct access to actual rocks inside the Earth. Instead, we rely on the remote sensing methods provided by seismic waves, density data and meteorite evidence to infer the nature of the deeper layers of the Earth.

Seismic (earthquake) waves

Vibrations from large earthquakes are detected as seismic waves by seismographs all around the world. Analysis of many earthquakes over the last 100 years has helped geologists to build up a detailed picture of the inside of the Earth.

P and S waves are seismic waves that travel through the layers of the Earth, so are called body waves. They travel:
- faster if the rock becomes more rigid and more incompressible
- slower if the rock becomes more dense.

If the rock loses its rigidity completely, S waves slow down until they stop. So S waves cannot travel through a liquid.

In 1909, Andrija Mohorovičić found that seismic velocities changed suddenly from 7.2 to 8.1 km/s at the **Mohorovičić Discontinuity**, or **Moho**, a few kilometres beneath the Earth's surface. Therefore, the rigidity, incompressibility and density of the rocks on either side of the boundary must be different.

He also found that, for one earthquake, two pulses were received at one seismograph and suggested that the waves travelled by two routes – one above the boundary and one below the boundary. If the seismograph is far enough away, the wave following the deeper, longer path arrives first, travelling through the more rigid and incompressible rocks below the Moho.

The velocity of P and S waves varies as they pass through the layers, as can be seen on the graph, and they can be used to show different physical properties and locate the boundaries between layers:

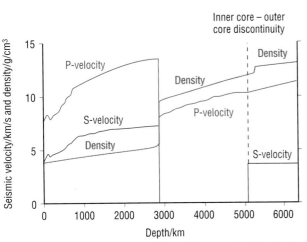

Figure 1 Change of density and P and S wave velocity with depth

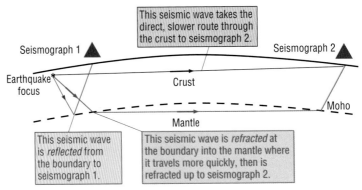

Figure 2 Finding the Moho

- Both P and S waves slow down in the asthenosphere because the 1 to 5% partial melting reduces the rigidity.
- Both P and S waves speed up through the mantle as the pressure increases and the rock becomes more incompressible.

- P waves suddenly slow down at the Gutenberg Discontinuity as they enter the liquid outer core where the rigidity is low. S waves stop completely as they cannot be transmitted in a liquid.
- P waves start to speed up at the Lehmann Discontinuity as they enter the solid inner core. S waves are propagated at 90 degrees to the P waves.

Where P and S waves cannot pass – the shadow zone

In 1906, Richard Oldham noticed that, for large earthquakes, the P and S waves were not recorded by seismographs located within a zone, which lay at large distances from the focus. This is called the **shadow zone**.

Seismic waves are refracted at the **Gutenberg Discontinuity** – which marks the edge of the Earth's **core**. The wave reaching the surface 102 degrees from the focus is not affected. The waves that should have arrived between 103 and 142 degrees are refracted at the discontinuity creating a zone where there are no P or S waves. Beyond the shadow zone, from 142 degrees, S waves are not received and P waves arrive late as they travel more slowly through it.

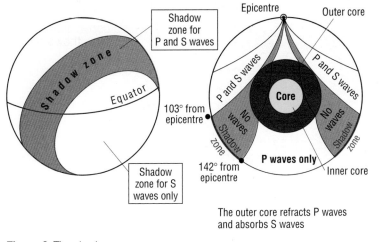

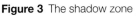

Figure 3 The shadow zone

In 1936, Inge Lehmann suggested that the inner core might be solid due to the very high pressure. The phase boundary between the inner and outer core is named after her. It is a wide zone of a mixture of solid and liquid rather than a distinct boundary. She predicted that S waves can be generated in and travel through the inner core. It was possible to do this using information from 'earthquakes' generated by the testing of hydrogen bombs, set off at a precisely known time and location.

Density

The average density of the Earth is 5.5 g/cm³. The density of the rocks making up the continental crust is 2.7 g/cm³ and that of the oceanic crust 2.9 g/cm³. The density of the core must therefore be high. The graph in Figure 1 shows the changes in density with depth, with a clear increase at the core boundary where the composition is believed to become iron and nickel.

Extra-terrestrial visitors – meteorites

The Earth shares a common origin with the other planets and the debris left over from the formation of the Solar System. Frequently, small (and sometimes large) fragments of debris fall to Earth as meteorites, although most burn up as they pass through the atmosphere. The meteorites are not the same as our crustal rocks, which have been influenced by weathering, metamorphism and other changes, but they could be similar in composition to the mantle and the core of the Earth. Of the two main types, iron meteorites are the denser, which suggests that they are similar to the Earth's core; the less dense stony meteorites are probably similar to the mantle (see spread 1.1.3).

Figure 4 Part of a 20-tonne iron meteorite from Greenland with a composition of 89% iron, 8% nickel, 2% sulfur

Questions

1 Explain why seismic waves travel through the Earth on curved paths.
2 Define a discontinuity.
3 Using the main differences between the chemical composition and physical state of the core and mantle, explain why the Gutenberg Discontinuity is a major boundary within the Earth.
4 Compare the P wave shadow zone with the S wave shadow zone.

The Earth is magnetic

From meteorite and other evidence, we know that the core of the Earth is made of iron and nickel, two of the three main magnetic elements. Can this help to explain the Earth's magnetism?

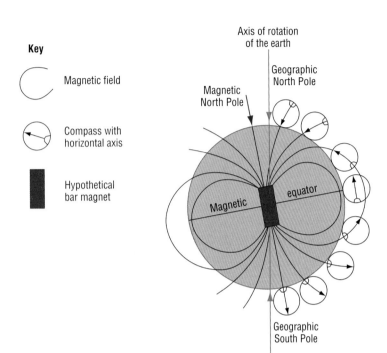

Key

⌒ Magnetic field

⊘ Compass with horizontal axis

▮ Hypothetical bar magnet

Figure 1 The Earth's magnetic field and inclination at different latitudes

Ancient mariners used needles of a material they called lodestone (*'leading stone'*) – known to us as the mineral magnetite (Fe_3O_4) – as compasses because it aligns itself in a north–south direction. As William Gilbert observed in 1600, the Earth behaves 'like a giant magnet'. Its field is represented by a bar magnet lying approximately along the axis of the Earth's rotation.

Origin of the Earth's magnetic field

The outer core is hot and molten, and believed to be made of iron and nickel. The temperature is probably higher near the inner core boundary, so convection currents will exist within the outer core.

A convecting mass of molten iron will generate electricity. The generation of electricity induces magnetism, which generates more electricity, and more magnetism, and so on. The balance between generation and destruction allows the Earth to show a continuous, if weak, magnetic field. The effect is called the 'self-exciting dynamo'. The outer core temperature is well above the **Curie point** at which materials lose their magnetism. So the Earth's magnetism cannot be permanent and must be constantly generated.

The circulation of the convection currents is affected by the rotation of the Earth and therefore the position of the magnetic poles is close to the geographic poles.

Variations in the field

The 'self-exciting dynamo' sometimes runs down as convection in the core changes. The magnetic field gradually fades away over a period of several thousand years. It then increases again but with the poles the opposite way round. The evidence for these reversals is found in the rocks as **remanent magnetism**.

Magnetic reversals and palaeomagnetism

The iron-rich magnetic minerals in lavas align themselves with the Earth's magnetic field and as they cool through the Curie Point, retain this magnetisation permanently. They act like 'frozen compasses', showing the direction to the poles at the time of their formation. Minerals in lavas erupted when the polarity was normal are aligned north–south, and in lavas erupted when polarity was reversed are aligned south-north. The age of the lavas, and therefore the date of each magnetic reversal, is known from radiometric dating and from fossils in interbedded sediments.

Aerial surveys show many reversals in the remnant magnetism in basalts of the ocean floor. Sensitive magnetometers show normal field strength over the zones of normal polarity. Above the zones of reversed polarity, measurements are weaker because of the opposing effects of the reversed remnant and the normal modern polarity.

Key definitions

Palaeomagnetism is ancient magnetism preserved in the rocks.

A **magnetic anomaly** is a value for the Earth's magnetic field that is different from the expected value.

Magnetic inclination is the angle of dip of the lines of a magnetic field. It is the angle with the horizontal made by a compass needle.

Remanent magnetism is magnetism shown by rocks due to the alignment of their magnetic minerals according to the Earth's magnetic field at the time of their formation.

Earth's magnetic decline

By sifting through ships' logs recorded by Captain Cook and other mariners dating back to 1590, researchers have been able to study the behaviour of the magnetic field. The data show that the overall strength of the planet's magnetic field was virtually unchanged between 1590 and 1860. Since then, the field has declined at a rate of roughly 5% per 100 years.

Every 300 000 years on average, the north and south poles of the Earth's magnetic field swap places. The field must weaken and go to zero before it can reverse itself. The last such reversal occurred roughly 780 000 years ago, so we are long overdue for another magnetic flip. Once it begins, the process of reversing takes less than 5000 years, experts believe.

The field's strength is now declining at a rate that suggests it could virtually disappear in about 2000 years. Researchers have speculated that this ongoing change may be the prelude to a magnetic reversal, during which the north and south magnetic poles swap places.

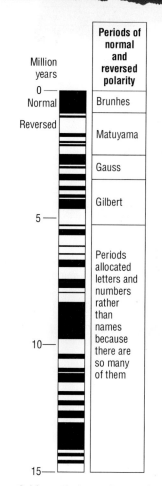

Figure 2 Magnetic reversals over the last 15 million years

Magnetic inclination

We can also find the latitude of a volcano at the time that it erupted its lavas by using the **magnetic inclination** of the frozen compasses. Following the lines of the Earth's magnetic field, a freely suspended compass needle lies exactly vertical at the magnetic poles. This is how the magnetic poles are located. At the magnetic equator, the needle is exactly horizontal. We can now measure the inclination of a rock of known age to find its latitude when it formed.

Apparent polar wandering curves

Geologists studying palaeomagnetic pole positions have found evidence suggesting that the magnetic poles wandered all over the globe. This is called **apparent polar wandering**. Polar-wandering is a topic that has been viewed differently by geologists over the years. Some geologists believed that the continents moved, and some believed that the poles moved. One discovery was that the path of apparent polar wandering measured in North America was different from the path in Europe. Rocks of the same age in Europe and North America suggested that the north pole was in two positions at the same time. The Earth's magnetic and geographical poles are close so it is likely that the magnetic pole has always been near the north pole. Therefore the continents must have moved on the surface of the earth. Europe and North America show different poles because they were in different positions than they are today.

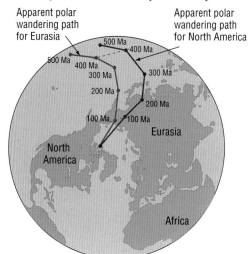

Figure 3 Polar wandering curves for North America and Europe. The curves are the same between 400 Ma and 200 Ma when the continents were joined

Questions

1 Why is palaeolatitude important?
2 Why is it not possible to find palaeolongitude?
3 What is palaeomagnetism?
4 Describe how rocks become magnetised

An earthquake is a vibration in the rocks of the crust and upper mantle caused by a sudden dislocation of the rocks along a fault. The vibrations are called earthquake waves or seismic waves.

A **seismic wave** is a wave that travels through the Earth, generally as the result of a tectonic earthquake, but sometimes from an explosion such as a nuclear bomb. Particles of a rock vibrate, transmitting energy from one particle to the next, away from the source of the earthquake.

Body waves travel through the interior of the Earth. They follow paths bent by the varying density and rigidity of the layers within the Earth. This effect is similar to the refraction of light waves. There are two types of body wave – P waves and S waves.

P waves

P waves take their name from:
- Primary – travel fastest and arrive first.
- Push – are longitudinal or compressional waves so the vibration of the rock particles is back and forth, like sound waves. P waves can travel through any type of material.
- Pressure – the particles alternately move together (compression) and apart (rarefaction) in the direction of travel of the wave, which is therefore a longitudinal wave.

The properties of a rock, which govern how quickly the wave travels, are:
- **Density (ρ)**: the denser a material, the harder it is for a wave to pass through it and the more the wave is slowed down.
- **Incompressibility (k)**: P wave energy causes rapid compression, then the material rebounds (springs back) and passes the energy along. The faster the material rebounds, the faster seismic waves can travel through it. A material with high incompressibility will rebound quicker and P waves will travel faster.
- **Rigidity (μ)**: is the same as shear strength or how much a material resists a bending force. A liquid has zero rigidity.

The velocity of P waves depends on all three properties. Their values change at, for example, the Gutenberg Discontinuity where P waves slow down and refract from their original path, resulting in the **P wave shadow zone** between 103° and 142° (see spread 1.1.5).

Velocity of P and S waves

The formula for the velocity of a **P wave** is

$$V_p = \sqrt{\frac{(k + {}^4/_3\,\mu)}{\rho}}$$

The formula for the velocity of an **S wave** is

$$V_s = \sqrt{\frac{(\mu)}{\rho}}$$

S waves

S waves take their name from:
- Secondary – travel slower than P waves – about 60% of the P wave velocity and so arrive second, after the P waves.
- Shear – the movement of the particles is sideways, in a shearing motion, at right angles to direction of travel of the wave. This is a transverse wave. The ground moves alternately to one side and then the other.
- Several times larger in amplitude than P waves.

Modelling P waves

Lay a Slinky™ on a flat smooth table. Each loop represents a particle of rock. Stretch the slinky slightly and send pulses along it by pushing one end gently but sharply.

The coils alternately get closer (compression) and further apart (rarefaction) in the same plane as the movement or propagation of this pressure wave. The loops oscillate but do not move along the coil.

Modelling S waves

Lay out the Slinky™ again. This time move the end from side to side, at right angles to its length. Try variations in movement.

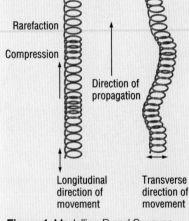

Figure 1 Modelling P and S waves

Try big and small movements, slow and quick movements, stretch the coil a bit more. Is there any difference in the speed at which the wave travels?

S waves can be generated by P waves.

If two slinkies are arranged at right angles and a P wave created in one, then an S wave will form in the slinky at right angles.

The S wave velocity depends only on density and rigidity. S waves do not travel in liquid. This can be shown using the formula for V_s and setting $\mu = 0$ (a liquid has no rigidity). Hence S waves do not travel through the molten outer core, resulting in the **S wave shadow zone** from 103 degrees round to 103 degrees. S waves can be generated in the inner core by P waves.

Surface (L) waves

Surface waves travel just below the Earth's surface. They travel more slowly than body waves. Because of their low frequency, long duration and large amplitude, they can be the most destructive type of seismic wave. There are two types of surface waves: Rayleigh waves with vertical movement and Love waves (L waves) with horizontal movement.

L waves take their name from:
- Long – the wavelength of the wave is longer than for the P and S waves.
- Last – they arrive last of the three main waves.
- Love – type of long wave named after the scientist who identified them.

The oscillation is in a circular motion so the waves lose energy quickly with distance away from the epicentre. L waves are confined to the surface layers of the Earth and these **surface waves** are the ones which cause damage to buildings.

Locating earthquakes

The focus

The **focus** is the point within the Earth at which the earthquake originates. It occurs along a fault plane as one section of crust moves alongside another. Seismic waves radiate out from the epicentre in all directions at the same time.

Depth of focus

Earthquakes are classified by their depth of focus:
- shallow-focus   0–70 km
- intermediate   70–300 km
- deep-focus   300–700 km

Earthquakes do not originate at depths greater than 720 km because deeper, warm rocks are not brittle enough to fracture so faults do not occur.

The epicentre

The **epicentre** of an earthquake is the point on the Earth's surface directly above the focus. The epicentre is marked on surface maps to represent the position of the focus. The epicentre is where the greatest amount of damage is likely to occur.

Finding the epicentre

Locating the epicentre is important because it indicates the position of the focus. It is highly unlikely that a seismometer will happen to be positioned on the epicentre, so a map showing areas of equal seismic intensities is compiled, either from observations of humans or readings from seismometers, at different locations across the area. The epicentre is located in the centre of the area of greatest intensity.

Questions

1 Draw a table showing the differences between P, S and L waves.
2 Why does the velocity of seismic waves increase with depth?
3 Why are seismic waves refracted at the Gutenberg Discontinuity?
4 How do we know that the outer core of the Earth is liquid?
5 Why do earthquake waves travel in curved paths through the mantle instead of straight lines?

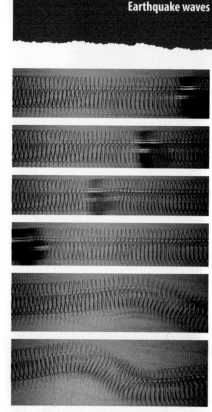

Figure 2 Photos showing P and S waves travelling through Slinkies

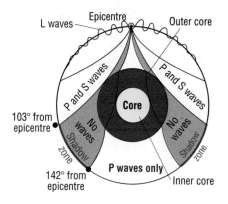

The outer core refracts P waves and absorbs S waves

Figure 3 Body and surface waves

Key definition

An **isoseismal line** (line of 'equal shaking') is a line on a map that joins up points of equal intensity, separating zones of different intensities.

In San Francisco, everyone is waiting for 'the big one'. But how big is big? We need an organised scale.

Earthquake intensity – the Mercalli scale

In the days before sophisticated instruments became available, earthquakes were classified by the noticeable effects of surface vibrations in the area. This depends on:

- the strength of the earthquake at its origin or focus
- the distance from the focus and epicentre
- the nature of the rocks and sediments that the buildings are constructed on
- the standard and design of the buildings.

At the end of the nineteenth century, a scale of **intensity** was devised by Guiseppi Mercalli. Mercalli's ten-point scale was itself modified into the twelve-point scale used today. It is an arbitrary scale, meaning that it depends on the opinions of the observer and has no mathematical base. Some witnesses of the earthquake might exaggerate just how bad things were during the earthquake and you may not find witnesses who agree on what happened; everybody will say something different!

	Intensity	Modified Mercalli intensity scale summary descriptions	Likely magnitude
1	Instrumental	Not normally felt. Birds and animals uneasy	Less than 3.5
2	Feeble	Felt only by a few persons at rest	3.5–4.0
3	Slight	Vibrations like large lorry passing. Felt by people at rest	
4	Moderate	Felt indoors by many. Cars rock	4.0–5.0
5	Rather strong	Sleepers wakened. Some windows broken	
6	Strong	Small bells ring. Trees sway. Loose objects fall	5.0
7	Very strong	Difficult to stand up. People run outdoors. Walls crack	5.5
8	Destructive	Partial collapse of ordinary buildings. Chimneys fall	6.0
9	Ruinous	Ground cracks, buildings shift off foundations. Pipes break	6.5
10	Disastrous	Landslides, buildings damaged. Many buildings destroyed	7.0
11	Very disastrous	Few buildings stand, bridges destroyed, landslides	7.5
12	Catastrophic	Damage total. Waves formed on ground surface	Over 8.1

The intensities observed at many different localities are recorded on a map. Isoseismal lines are then constructed, which join areas of equal intensity. As the waves travel away from the focus their energy spreads out over a greater and greater area and intensity decreases. Conversely, intensity is greatest in the centre of the isoseismal line pattern closest to the epicentre. The focus lies directly beneath the epicentre.

The effect of sub-surface deposits

For a given intensity of earthquake, the amount of damage caused is dependent upon the nature of the rocks and deposits of an area.

Key definitions

Intensity is a measure of the surface damage caused by an earthquake.

The **Mercalli scale** measures the intensity of an earthquake and is based on the effects that are felt in the area.

Magnitude is a measure of the amount of strain energy released by an earthquake.

Figure 1 Earthquake damage to buildings. What is the likely intensity?

Examiner tip

To draw isoseismal lines, draw a line for each set of values, for example, 5 so that all the numbers of less than 5 are on one side and all the numbers greater than 5 on the other. The isoseismal lines should be in a roughly concentric pattern. Do not play dotto and join the points!

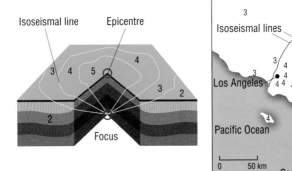

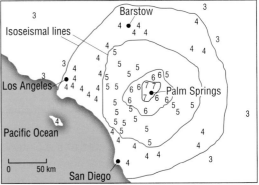

Figure 2 Isoseismal lines around the epicentre

Solid, competent rock such as granite or limestone allows the vibrations to pass through easily. They are transferred without causing much damage to the rock or to structures built on it. The amplitude of L waves is comparatively low.

Weaker rocks such as clay or poorly cemented sandstone absorb some of the energy and may therefore be deformed. Buildings built on weaker rock are more likely to suffer damage.

Unconsolidated sands and gravels can oscillate freely. The L wave amplitude is higher and damage is greater than on consolidated rock and the intensity is therefore greater.

Earthquake magnitude – the Richter scale

After 1904, more sophisticated seismograms made it possible to assess the amount of energy released by an earthquake and therefore to design an objective, mathematical scale to describe the earthquake itself and not its visible effects. The amplitude of the wave on the seismogram gives a measure of the energy released.

The **Richter scale** measures the **magnitude** of the earthquake by recording the amplitude of the earthquake waves. The range in energy released by different earthquakes is very large and so the values are converted into a logarithmic scale. Log scales have some unusual features. On the Richter scale, for example, each increase of 1 in the scale means that the amount of energy released by the earthquake increases by a factor of around 30. There is no theoretical limit to the amount of energy which an earthquake can release, and therefore no upper limit for the numbers on the Richter scale. However, the maximum recorded value so far is 8.9.

The Richter scale is used by the media and is widely accepted by the general public, though it is no longer used by seismologists, who now use the **seismic moment** magnitude scale. This is more accurate but more complicated, based on the idea of the moment or leverage developed on the two sides of the fault, which move in opposite directions.

Seismic moment magnitude scale

A new scale known as **moment magnitude (M_w)** was introduced in 1979. In particular, for very large earthquakes moment magnitude gives the most reliable estimate of earthquake size. This is because seismic moment is derived from the concept of **moment** in physics and therefore provides clues to the physical size of an earthquake – the size of fault rupture and accompanying slip displacement – as well as the amount of energy released.

The **local magnitude scale (M_L)**, or **Richter scale**, is a quantitative logarithmic scale. M_L is obtained by measuring the maximum amplitude of a recording on a **seismometer** at a distance of 600 km from the earthquake. It can be affected by **saturation** at higher magnitude values – meaning that it underestimates the magnitude of larger events, above magnitude 6.

Despite the limitations of the older Richter magnitude scale, it is still in wide use, as it can be calculated rapidly, catalogues of data dating back many years are available, they are sufficient for the vast majority of observed events, and the public is familiar with them.

Case study

You can model an earthquake by hitting a solid object with a hammer and feeling the vibration. You will get very different results when hitting concrete, sand, a metal plate or a wood block. Try putting model houses on your different materials and observe the effect.

Case study

The Loma Prieta Earthquake, California, 1989 lasted 15 seconds and measured 6.9 on the moment magnitude scale. The quake killed 62 people throughout central California and injured 3756.

The epicentre was in the Santa Cruz Mountains. It caused severe damage throughout the San Francisco Bay Area, 95 km away from the epicentre. Major property damage occurred in the San Francisco area due to **liquefaction** of soil used to fill the ground on which properties had been built. The worst affected area was the collapsed double-decker freeway in Oakland.

An isoseismal map for this earthquake would show a pattern that is not concentric around the epicentre.

Questions

1 How much more energy is released by a magnitude 5 earthquake than a magnitude 3 earthquake?
2 Find the magnitude of a number of recent earthquakes.
3 Within the same area there may be cemented sandstones and unconsolidated sands. Will the intensity of an earthquake be the same or different on the two rock types? Why?
4 What are the differences between earthquake intensity and magnitude?

Earthquakes occur when solid, brittle, competent rocks suddenly fracture and move relative each other. The energy released is transmitted through the rocks as seismic waves.

The elastic rebound theory

- Two parts of a body of rock are under **stress** due to opposing forces acting on the rock.
- The opposing forces are often due to tectonic plates moving in opposite directions.
- The body of rock is slowly deformed and put under **strain**.
- The energy applied to the deformed rock is stored as potential or **strain energy** within the rock.
- The deformation continues until the stress overcomes the strength of the rock and it fractures.
- The two parts of the rock move relative to each other and there is displacement along the fracture or **fault**.
- The strain energy which had been stored in the rock is released, causing the ground to vibrate as an earthquake.

Weak or plastic (incompetent) rocks such as mudstone, shale and hot metamorphic rocks steadily deform under stress by bending or moving by plastic flow, and therefore do not fracture.

Detecting waves – the seismometer

A **seismometer** detects and records ground motion. It is made up of two parts. One is attached to a large mass and does not vibrate with earth movements, while the other is allowed to move freely with the vibrations. The relative movement between the two is recorded. The recording is called a **seismogram**. Nowadays seismometers measure and record ground motion digitally. Modern seismometers can measure movements smaller than one nm (one millionth of a millimetre). They use the same principles but are based on the relative movement between a coil of wire and a magnet, which induces a current.

Key definitions

Stress is the force per unit area acting on or within a body.

Strain is the change in shape of a body in response to stress.

Undeformed crust

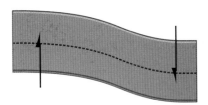

Crust deforms due to stress and is under strain

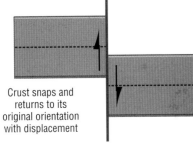

Crust snaps and returns to its original orientation with displacement

Fault occurs as the rock snaps

Figure 1 The elastic rebound theory

Key definitions

A **seismograph** is a device which receives and records seismic vibrations.

A **seismometer** is a device which receives seismic vibrations and converts them into a signal which can be transmitted and recorded.

A **seismogram** is the paper or electronic record made by a seismograph.

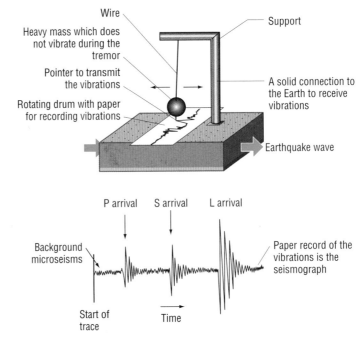

Figure 2 Seismometer and seismogram

The data from seismometers can be collected automatically and analysed by remote computers. A seismometer is a sensor placed in the ground to detect vibrations of the Earth. The **seismometer** together with the unit recording the signal is called a seismograph. The seismometer senses the ground vibration and converts this to a signal that can be recorded. The terms seismograph and seismometer are often used interchangeably.

A seismic station will normally have an array of seismometers arranged to pick up vibrations in the vertical and two principal horizontal directions.

Detecting waves – the seismogram

One earthquake shock will produce three vibrations on the seismogram, the P, S and L waves. Plotting the arrival times for these waves at seismographs, which are at increasing distances from the epicentre, gives a time-distance curve, from which the speed of the wave can be calculated.

The time gap between the arrival of P and S waves increases with distance from the epicentre. If you know the time gap, you can read off from the graph the distance of your seismometer from the epicentre. You now know how far away the epicentre is, but it could be in any direction. Using the distances from at least three seismograms, you can determine the location of the epicentre.

Now that you know the distance between the epicentre and the seismometer you can calculate the magnitude of the earthquake. The magnitude depends on the amount of energy released at the focus, whereas the amplitude on the seismogram depends on the distance away from the epicentre. To calculate the magnitude, the amplitudes shown on seismograms at successive distances from the epicentre are compared. It was this kind of calculation which led Richter to design his scale.

The shadow zone

From 103° to 142° from the epicentre, the seismograph receives no vibrations. Beyond 142°, the seismogram shows P but no S waves. The seismogram shows that the P waves are late arriving because they are slowed down by the liquid outer core. However, they do not arrive as late as would be expected if the whole of the core were liquid, suggesting that there is a solid inner core, due to the immense pressure at those depths.

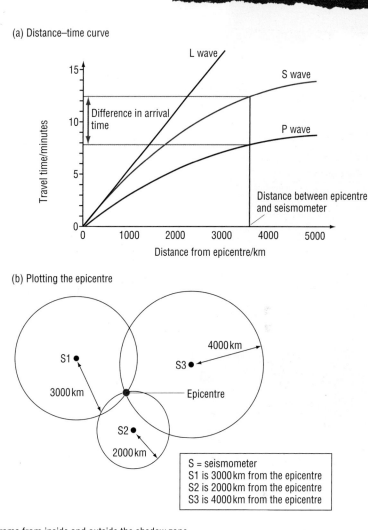

(a) Distance–time curve

(b) Plotting the epicentre

S = seismometer
S1 is 3000 km from the epicentre
S2 is 2000 km from the epicentre
S3 is 4000 km from the epicentre

(c) Seismograms from inside and outside the shadow zone

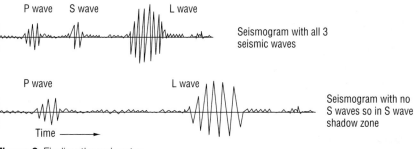

Seismogram with all 3 seismic waves

Seismogram with no S waves so in S wave shadow zone

Figure 3 Finding the epicentre

Questions

1 From the time-distance curve, calculate the distance from the epicentre for a P–S arrival gap of three minutes.

2 Summarise the elastic rebound theory in 12 words.

3 Compare the usefulness of isoseismal lines and seismographs as methods for locating epicentres.

The physical effects of earthquakes

When the crust suddenly fractures, elastic energy is released and transferred by high amplitude L waves travelling through the surface layers of the Earth. The most destructive effects of this energy are felt at the epicentre.

Ground movement

Earthquake vibrations travel through the ground, causing little permanent damage if the intensity is low. Stronger, larger amplitude earthquakes cause shear, or lateral, movement of the ground surface, which is more damaging. Earthquakes of intensity 12 on the Mercalli scale make 'the ground surface move as a series of waves, with cracks opening at the crest and closing at the troughs', adding a highly destructive, vertical component. The upward acceleration of the ground may be greater than that of gravity, in which case loose objects can be thrown bodily upwards.

Figure 1 Ground subsidence

Damage to structures

Movement of the ground separates one part of the structure from another. For example:
- Bricks and stonework separate along the mortar, causing walls to collapse.
- Floors separate from supporting walls, causing them to 'pancake' on top of each other.
- Bridges built in sections separate from their supporting piers.
- Sections of gas, water and drainage pipes separate from each other and leak.

Buildings sway when their foundations move sideways but the top storeys lag behind. If the dimensions of a building are such that its natural frequency matches the frequency of the earthquake's vibration, the amount of sway increases automatically – and disastrously – by resonance.

Liquefaction

The vibration in the bedrock is transmitted into superficial deposits at the surface. In wet sand, and other unconsolidated deposits, the water separates from the solid particles and rises to the surface. Houses built on alluvial deposits can suddenly find themselves standing on water and large amounts of damage are caused. Liquefaction helps salad cream come out of the bottle when you shake it vigorously.

Figure 2 Collapsed building in Mexico City after the 1985 earthquake

Landslips

On steep slopes made unstable by high rainfall, the vibration may trigger landslides and mudflows, partly assisted by liquefaction. Not only do these cause loss of life by burial, but also hamper rescue attempts.

Aftershocks

The main movement along the fault releases most of the energy, but subsequent movements, minutes or hours or even days afterwards, cause aftershocks. Structures weakened by the main shock may collapse during this period, causing further damage and added difficulties for rescue workers.

Tsunamis

A tsunami is a water wave which is set up at the same time as an earthquake but it is not a seismic wave. A tsunami is caused by the bodily displacement of a large volume of water by the movement of a large section of crust on the sea floor.

In open water, the tsunami has an amplitude of about a metre, a wavelength of several hundred kilometres and a speed up to 700 km/hr. When the tsunami approaches the shallow waters of the coast, the height of the wave increases dramatically, surging across low-lying coastal areas with devastating effect. A more immediate warning is given as the sea drains away from the shore-line immediately before the tsunami strikes.

Tsunamis also result from the displacement of water by large landslides, for example, when the flanks of a volcano collapse into the sea.

Figure 3 Landslip of a road

Early warning of tsunamis

The catastrophic effects of tsunamis can be mitigated by a good early warning system, by maintaining a barrier of trees and other vegetation along the coastal strip to absorb the wave's energy, and by building houses back from the shore-line, preferably raised above ground level. The earthquake arrives well before the tsunami, giving several hours' warning for distant epicentres. However, whilst tsunamis are associated with high magnitude earthquakes, not all strong earthquakes are followed by tsunamis. Mid-ocean detectors are needed, connected to effective communications on land. Countries which can afford this expensive system are well protected. The Indian Ocean Tsunami Warning System has been set up by UNESCO after 230 000 people died following the Sumatran earthquake of 2004.

The social and economic effects of earthquakes

Earthquakes themselves seldom kill, but the effects of collapsing dwellings, fire and disease can cause hundreds of thousands of casualties. Housing and industrial buildings are damaged, communications dislocated and services disrupted, often for many years after the earthquake. The local economy suffers at just the time when money is needed for rebuilding. Each country responds differently, depending on its wealth, infrastructure, climate and geography. These are some of the considerations.

Before the earthquake	Frequency and magnitude of earthquakes in the area
	Quality of forward planning and training
During the earthquake	Population density and the number of people affected
	Magnitude of the earthquake and the proximity to the epicentre
	Amount of damage caused
The rescue	Quality of the emergency services – fire, search and rescue teams, policing the area
	Availability of medical services and supplies
	Availability of emergency food and water, shelter and sanitation
	Viability of communications
The aftermath	Healthcare, hygiene and sanitation
	Restoration of water and electricity
	Rebuilding costs, materials and labour
	Employment opportunities

Figure 4 Photo of the displacement in the expansion joint in the back wall of the UC Berkeley football stadium. Some of this displacement is due to creep along the Hayward fault, while some is due to differential settling. Approximately 32 cm of offset is observed at the top of the stadium. The seismic safety rating for the stadium is poor!

Case study

As the ground beneath the Japanese city of Kashiwazaki shook on July 16, 2007 with a 6.8 magnitude earthquake, barrels toppled and a transformer caught fire at the largest nuclear power plant in the world. Nearly 1300 litres of radioactive coolant leaked into the Sea of Japan.

Accusations flew almost immediately with some people criticising the Tokyo Electric Power Company, which operates the plant. Others blamed lax regulations governing the quake-proofing of nuclear plants, or claimed its location was poorly chosen.

Questions

1 Research a large recent earthquake and describe the effects that it had. You will need to know the magnitude and location. Compare the earthquake that you have researched with others in the group.

2 An earthquake occurs on one side of the Pacific. How long does it take a tsunami wave to reach the other side? (Research the appropriate data to use.)

3 There have been earthquakes in Britain. Describe the effects of these earthquakes.

Most methods of predicting earthquakes (and volcanic eruptions) look for *change*, but first you must identify normal patterns. This involves expensive long-term monitoring. Some countries have better warning systems than others.

Case study

'Is Istanbul next?' precis from Issue 2201 of *New Scientist*, August 28, 1999, page 5.

Since the 1999 Izmit earthquake in Turkey, geologists are warning that things could be even worse next time. They say this quake leaves Istanbul vulnerable to a direct hit.

In 1997, Turkish and American geologists charted a series of 10 earlier quakes, each with a Richter magnitude greater than 6.7, which occurred in a progression from east to west along the 1500-kilometre North Anatolian fault. They explained the progression by showing that each quake increased stress in the zone where the next quake occurred. The team concluded that 'the port city of Izmit is most vulnerable.' They were right.

There is a well-defined seismic gap extending 150 km west of Izmit that includes Istanbul. It has all the right ingredients for a quake with a magnitude of more than 7. However, not all experts think the next quake will be under Istanbul.

Seismic gap theory

Historical records for a particular fault show the period of elapsed time between earthquakes. If the pattern is regular, the date for the next earthquake may be predicted. The theory is applied to sections of a fault which have been quiet for some time – the **gap** between active areas – where the fault is locked and the stress steadily builds up, ready for a high magnitude event. Those sections of the fault which move frequently dissipate their elastic energy in many small, less destructive earthquakes.

Unfortunately, patterns are not regular enough to be useful within the human time frame. It assumes that movement, frictional forces and other properties are constant, which they are not. However, if the gap theory suggests that an earthquake is due, it is time to monitor the area more closely.

Stress

Many minute cracks develop within a rock under stress, increasing its volume and allowing the inward percolation of water and gases. The microcracks and water change the properties of the rock in ways which may be detectable.

Changes in ground levels

The area around the focus may tilt due to deformation and swell slightly due to the microcracks. Tiltmeters, using laser technology and GPS, measure the slope of the ground level very accurately. Strain gauges in boreholes measure deformation and therefore any increase in stress.

Detailed measurements of gases

Radon, a radioactive decay product of uranium in granite, percolates up through the microcracks. As a heavy gas, radon accumulates in water wells in which it is easily detected by its radioactivity. If the amount of radon increases, new pathways are opening up for the gas, and an earthquake may be imminent.

Changes in water levels in wells

Groundwater percolates into the microcracks, lowering the level of water in wells. The levels return to normal as the water is replenished, before the earthquake occurs.

Physical properties

The number of foreshocks increases before a main event. P wave velocities decrease, then increase again before the quake. Water increases the electrical conductivity of the ground, lowering its resistivity.

Coloured lights in the sky immediately before an earthquake may be caused by changes in the electrical properties of quartz and other minerals under stress.

Magnetism and animal behaviour

Research in China confirms that animals show disturbed behaviour just before an earthquake. Pigs squeal and dogs bark (as they do for other reasons too), ground-living birds perch in trees and animals such as snakes leave their 'burrows'. Animals may be able to detect slight changes in the Earth's magnetic field or feel the very small vibrations of foreshocks.

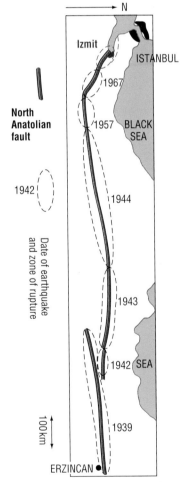

Figure 1 The Anatolian Fault, Turkey

Social consequences of earthquake prediction

It is one thing to predict an earthquake, but quite another actually doing something about it. One problem is the uncertainty of predicting the exact date, place and magnitude of the event. Another is human nature. Consider *your* reaction to the suggestion that you (and a million other people) should evacuate your homes because there *may* be an earthquake within the next week.

Reducing the impact of earthquakes

Earthquakes themselves rarely kill. Fatalities and injuries are caused by falling buildings, fires and later disease often caused by lack of clean drinking water. Improved building practices, although expensive, reduce the risk to people.

Planning

First the risk is assessed by forecasting the likely number and magnitude of future earthquakes. Local authorities may ban buildings from the fault line itself, from areas of alluvial deposits which may suffer liquefaction, and from areas liable to landslides. They also plan emergency procedures for when the earthquake does happen.

Building design

It is too expensive to stop all damage to buildings. Instead, they are designed to protect people, from total collapse, falling structures and broken glass. Wooden structures are flexible and accept a certain amount of strain. For larger buildings, steel-reinforced concrete is safer than bricks and masonry (see spread 1.2.4). Foundations may be reinforced by pumping liquid cement into a network of micropiles drilled into the ground.

Ground or base isolation systems

The building rests on large rollers, rubber pads, springs or sliders coated with non-stick Teflon. The inertial mass of the building keeps it stationary whilst the ground moves beneath, or allows the building to move without damage. Older buildings can have this system inserted for future protection (for example, the Utah State Capitol).

Resisting shear forces

Each part of the structure is connected to other parts to prevent collapse. Diagonal bracing by cables or rigid girders strengthens the framework. Large open spaces are not included, and floors are fixed to the walls to add rigidity and prevent pancaking. Shear walls, extending the full height of the building without any openings, add to the rigidity.

Absorbing sway

Tall buildings are designed to sway, absorbing the energy through flexible supports and materials made, for example, of rubber. Hydraulic systems, sometimes computer-controlled, dampen the movement, like shock absorbers in a car. Flexible connections between different parts of the building help to counter movements.

Services

Broken gas mains and power lines can cause fires, and fractured water mains prevent the fires from being put out. These problems can be avoided by using flexible piping to allow for movement.

Questions

1 Choose three methods of predicting earthquakes and research how they have been used.

2 Should geologists issue warnings of likely earthquakes? Discuss in groups and prepare arguments for and against.

3 What other building designs can you find which help to reduce damage during earthquakes?

Utah State Capitol

The State Capitol in Salt Lake City, Utah, is a magnificent domed building, constructed in 1915 right above the 300 km long Wasatch Fault, which is likely to generate a large earthquake. The Capitol is a large, open-spaced building supported by external, but no internal, columns.

Improvements can be made to the structure to reduce the effects of a magnitude 8 earthquake, at a cost of about £100 million:

- Replace a slice from the base of each column with a base isolation unit made of laminated layers of rubber and steel plates around an energy-absorbing lead core.
- Insert sliders made of Teflon-coated pads resting on stainless steel plates under the columns that bear less load, allowing sideways movement of 60 cm so that the building will slide backwards and forwards without damage.
- Build new concrete load-bearing walls to add strength of the building. To carry the extra weight the soil will be reinforced with micropiles.

Figure 2 San Francisco office building retro-fitted with flexible steel girders

If you have studied a map of the South Atlantic, you may have noticed the similarity of the coastlines of Africa and South America. For 300 years, since reasonably accurate maps became available, scientists have suggested that the two continents may at one time have fitted together. In 1915, **Alfred Wegener**, in his book *The Origin of Continents and Oceans*, set out evidence for **continental drift**, using continental fit, the distribution of rocks and ancient glaciations. In his time, most Earth scientists did not believe in continental drift because they could see no mechanism by which continents could be moved. It is only since the 1950s that evidence from palaeomagnetism and exploration of the sea floor has led to widespread acceptance of continental drift.

Key definitions

Continental drift is the large-scale horizontal movement of continents during geological time.

Tillites are ancient glacial deposits preserved within a rock sequence.

Evaporites are minerals formed by the evaporation of saline water, for example, halite (rock salt) and gypsum.

The evidence for continental drift

A large landmass called Gondwanaland is believed to have existed about 250 Ma. This huge continent included what are now South America, Africa, Antarctica, India and Australia. As a single continent, it had the same rocks and fossils and was glaciated at the same time. Gondwanaland broke up in the Jurassic about 167 Ma, the fragments drifting apart to form the continents. The evidence for its former existence can still be seen in the rocks of South America and Africa.

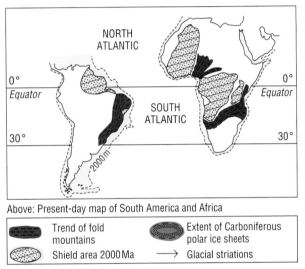

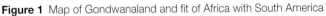

Above: Present-day map of South America and Africa

- Trend of fold mountains
- Shield area 2000 Ma
- Extent of Carboniferous polar ice sheets
- → Glacial striations

Below: Reconstruction of Gondwanaland 250 Ma

Figure 1 Map of Gondwanaland and fit of Africa with South America

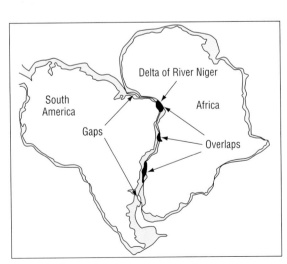

Figure 2 Gaps and overlaps

Fit of the continents

Using the present coastline of Africa and South America does not give an exact jigsaw fit. This is not surprising because:

- Sea level is constantly changing, so a coastline is a temporary feature.
- Deposition and erosion has occurred since the two continents drifted apart 167 Ma.
- Where there has been erosion of the continents, there is a gap.
- Where there has been deposition of sediment, there is an overlap.

There is a much better fit if you use the edge of the continental shelf or a specific depth, like 1000 m, or 500 m.

Rock types

To prove that two rocks on either side of an ocean were once part of the same outcrop, they must have the same:

- distinctive characteristics – of mineral composition and physical features
- age determined by radiometric dating.

Examples of matching rocks include Precambrian cratons (see spread 1.3.4), Carboniferous coals and **tillites**, Permian red sandstones and **evaporites** and Upper Triassic flood basalts.

Mountain chains

Fold mountain chains are linear features hundreds of kilometres long. The map of Gondwanaland shows how one Precambrian fold mountain chain crosses from Africa to South America and back to Africa as a continuous belt – so the two continents must have been joined together in the Precambrian. The trend of fold mountains provides a way to match geology across continents.

Fossils

If Africa and South America have always been separated, they should have a different fossil record, especially for animals and plants which lived on land or on shallow sea floors. Such animals and plants would be unable to spread across a wide ocean. During the Carboniferous, land-based reptiles (*Mesosaurus*) and plants (*Glossopteris*) are found in both Africa and South America.

Glaciation

In both South America and Africa, there are sedimentary deposits of angular, poorly sorted and scratched pebbles (clasts) in a fine-grained matrix. This is a fossil boulder clay or tillite deposited by an ice sheet that existed during the Carboniferous about 300 Ma. Glacial striations are used to trace the movement of the glaciers to one common source area in central southern Africa.

Gondwanaland probably occupied a position near the south pole, as ice sheets cannot extend to the equator. Africa and South America are now much further north, so this is clear evidence that the continents have moved.

Palaeomagnetism

Iron-rich minerals in some rocks hold a record of the Earth's magnetic field at the time of their formation. A large number of rocks are collected then dated, and the direction of palaeomagnetism measured. This data is then plotted as an **apparent polar wandering curve**. The curves for South America and Africa suggest that, before 160 Ma, one north pole was in two positions at the same time. In fact, the magnetic pole cannot significantly change position. Instead, if we assume the north pole remained fixed, it must be the continents that have moved. If the two continents are re-positioned next to each other, the two curves match up, and there is then one position for the pole. The curves diverge only after the continents started to drift apart.

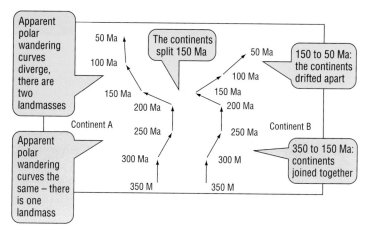

Figure 3 Polar wandering curves for two continents

Case study

In Britain, coal, coral limestones, desert sandstones and evaporite deposits all suggest tropical or equatorial climates during Carboniferous and Permian times. We assume that the world's climate belts have followed the same pattern throughout geological time, as they are all created by the relationship of the Earth to the Sun and by atmospheric circulation. Therefore Britain must have moved from tropical latitudes 250 Ma to its present-day temperate climate belt.

Key definitions

An **apparent polar wandering curve** is depicted by a line on a map, which joins up the apparent positions of the magnetic north pole over time.

Examiner tip

'Continental drift' applies only to the continental landmasses. It is part of, but not the same as, the theory of plate tectonics. Continental drift uses evidence from the continents, while sea floor spreading uses evidence from the oceans. Together they provide evidence for plate tectonics.

Questions

1 Why do we fit the continents together along the edge of the continental shelves and not the modern coastline?
2 Which of the lines of evidence did Alfred Wegener not know about?
3 What evidence is there that Britain has drifted north over geological time?

Before the development of sonar in the 1940s, we knew very little about the ocean floor. Accurate maps of the world's ocean floors were produced in the 1950s by ships sailing backwards and forwards taking soundings. The maps were surprising, showing areas of high mountains forming ridges on the ocean floors and also deep trenches. The topography of the ocean floor is more extreme than the land surface, with trenches 12 km deep compared to the highest mountains, such as Everest at 8 km high.

Developing the theory of sea floor spreading

In the early 1960s, geologist Harry Hess proposed the hypothesis of sea floor spreading, in which basaltic magma from the mantle rises to create new ocean floor at mid-ocean ridges (MORs). On each side of the ridge, the sea floor moves away from the ridge. As Hess formulated his hypothesis, Robert Dietz independently proposed a similar model. Dietz's model had a significant addition, assumed the sliding surface was at the base of the lithosphere, not at the base of the crust. As the continents drift apart, the oceans become wider. Sea floor spreading provides the mechanism that allows the movement of continents. It is the process of oceanic crust being continuously created at the MOR and spreading away from the ridge. Hess and Dietz succeeded where Wegener had failed. They provided a mechanism for the movement of continents on the soft, plastic asthenosphere, with convection currents as the driving force.

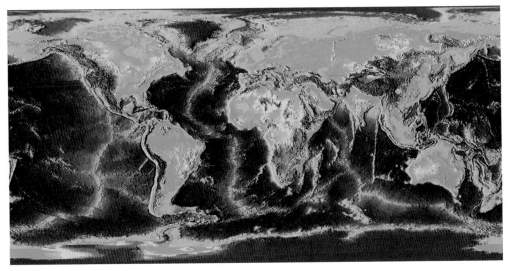

Figure 1 Topographic map of the world's oceans

Evidence for sea floor spreading

As more research has been done on the ocean floor, data are constantly improving. New technologies have allowed the deep sea floor to be filmed from submersibles capable of working in the high pressures at depth. These submersibles have also measured water and rock temperatures and collected samples. Drill ships have taken cores of sediments and underlying igneous rocks, and analysis of these has given the age of the ocean floor. Ships have measured the variations in gravity and magnetism that occur in the ocean basins. Satellite measurements and visual images can help still further, giving us detailed information about the oceans. Satellite altimetry is an essential tool for mapping the ocean floor spread has added detail to the original maps, which filled in the areas between echo sounding lines by extrapolation.

Mid-ocean ridges

In all the oceans' basins are large mountain chains running down the centre, called **mid-oceanic ridges** (MOR). They are clearly seen on the oceans map. In the middle of the MOR is an axial rift, a deep valley with steep-sided mountains either side. Occasionally the MOR rises above sea level, forming islands such as Iceland on the Mid-Atlantic Ridge. Closest to the ridge the crust is hot and expanded, so forming the ridge itself. Away from the ridge, the crust cools and contracts, creating the flatter areas of the ocean basins.

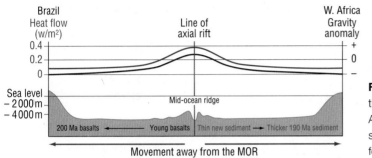

Figure 2 Cross-section through the Mid-Atlantic Ridge to show symmetrical pattern of features

Figure 3 Pillow lavas where magma has cooled quickly on the outside but was still molten inside

High heat flow and volcanic activity with gravity anomaly

The average heat flow of the ocean basin floors are shown on the graph above. MORs show the highest heat flow directly above the axial rift. This suggests that convection currents in the mantle are rising under ocean ridges, bringing magma close to the surface. This forms fissure volcanoes in and near the axial rift. The eruptions are of non-explosive, low viscosity, basaltic lava. If the basalt cools quickly under water, the outside rapidly solidifies while the inside remains liquid for longer, producing pillow lavas. Gravity anomalies show a similar pattern to the heat flow, with a positive anomaly peaking in line with the axial rift. The broad positive anomaly at the MOR means there is an excess of mass due to the large volcanoes and the rising magma.

Transform faults and earthquakes

Shallow-focus earthquakes occur along the length of the MOR, caused by the rising magma. They also occur along linear transform faults, which have large horizontal displacements, are perpendicular to the ridge and can be thousands of kilometres long. The transform faults divide the MOR into sections, with movement taking place in opposite directions, causing many small, shallow earthquakes. Sea floor spreading proceeds section by section, with periods of activity alternating with periods with no eruption or movement.

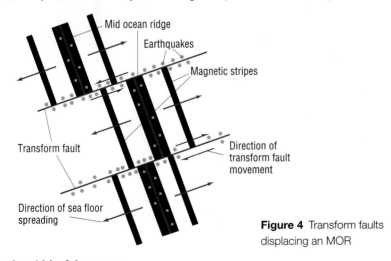

Figure 4 Transform faults displacing an MOR

Measuring the width of the oceans

Satellites can be used to measure the exact location of a series of fixed receivers on the surface of the Earth. The positions of these relative to each other is recorded and their relative movement can be calculated. When this is used in Iceland it proves that the two halves of the island are moving away from each other at a rate of about 2.5 cm per year.

Key definitions

A **magnetometer** is towed behind a ship to measure changes in magnetism. It can detect the strength and direction of the magnetic field.

A **gravimeter** can be towed behind a ship to measure changes in gravity. As a satellite orbits the Earth it collects a continuous profile of geoid height across an ocean basin. Profiles from many satellites, collected over many years, are combined to make high resolution, gravity anomaly images. The satellite-derived gravity measurements can be compared and combined with gravity anomaly measurements made by ships. One milligal (mgal) is about one millionth the normal pull of gravity (9.8 m/s^2). Typical variations in the pull of gravity are 20 mgal, although over the deep ocean trenches they exceed 300 mgal.

Questions

1 Describe the changes as you go away from the MOR.
2 Explain how sea floor spreading causes continents to drift. Use the terms convection, asthenosphere, lithosphere and partial melting.
3 Research the work of the submersibles such as Alvin to describe some of the features that they discovered on the deep sea floor. Hydrothermal vents or black smokers and the organisms that live around them are a good start.

Magnetic anomalies

The Earth's magnetic field undergoes complete reversal, so that north becomes south, and vice versa. This may happen up to four times in a million years. The sea floor acts as a tape recorder for these changes in the Earth's magnetic field. As new magma is erupted at a mid-ocean ridge (MOR), the iron particles line up parallel to the Earth's existing magnetic field. As the rocks cool down, they remain permanently magnetised by the field. The result is a striped magnetic anomaly pattern on the sea floor, showing normal (black) and reversed (white) polarity of the Earth. They form a symmetrical pattern parallel to the MOR. These zones are not all of the same width, varying with the length of time during which the magnetic field stayed in one direction, and with the amount of lava erupted during any particular period.

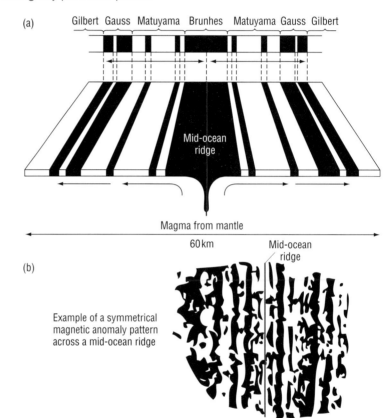

Figure 1 Magnetic reversals over the last 5 Ma. **a** theoritical model **b** actual map showing localised variation in lava produced

The important observation is that the pattern of reversals is symmetrical on either side of the MOR. The only possible interpretation for this symmetry is that the crust on the two sides of the ridge is moving apart. Basalt erupts at the ridge to form new oceanic crust, which then spreads away from the ridge equally on both sides. Ocean floor basalts can be radiometrically dated to give a series of absolute dates from which the rate of spreading can be calculated. This is conclusive proof for sea floor spreading.

Dating sediments

The thin oozes and other fine-grained sediments on the ocean floor can be dated from core samples by using pelagic microfossils, which sank to the sea floor after death. At the base of the core is the sediment which was deposited first and therefore shows the date when sedimentation started on that part of the newly formed basalt sea floor. Measuring the distance from the MOR to sediments of known maximum ages is another method of finding the rate of sea floor spreading.

Case study

Drill ships, such as the JOIDES *Resolution*, collect core samples of sediments that provide evidence of sea floor spreading.

Distance east of MOR (km)	Sediment thickness (m)
0	0
22	315
34	268
41	194
56	259
76	416
102	537

The sea floor is uneven, so thickness will vary locally.

The thickness of the sediments increases away from the ridge. This is because the ocean floor's age is greater away from the ridge, because the sediments have had longer to be deposited so are thicker. Sediment forms very slowly (1 mm per 1000 years) from the remains of microscopic plankton such as radiolaria or foraminifera. The age pattern is symmetrical, ranging from zero at the MOR, where there is no sediment, to 200 Ma furthest away from the ridge, where it can be up to 2000 m thick.

The structure of the ocean crust

Whenever you drill into the oceanic crust, the overall structure is always the same. This is because all the igneous rocks form as a result of the magma rising up at the MOR, cooling and the rocks then moving apart symmetrically:

- Basaltic pillow lava is the material from volcanoes that cooled rapidly under water, forming fine crystals.
- Dolerite dykes are the vertical feeder pipes from the magma chamber supplying the volcanoes. The dolerite cools fairly slowly, so the crystals are medium sized.
- Gabbro cools slowly, forming coarse crystals in the magma chamber.
- Peridotite is part of the upper mantle within the lithosphere, where the magma originates by partial melting.

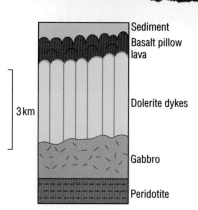

Figure 2 Structure of the ocean crust and lithosphere

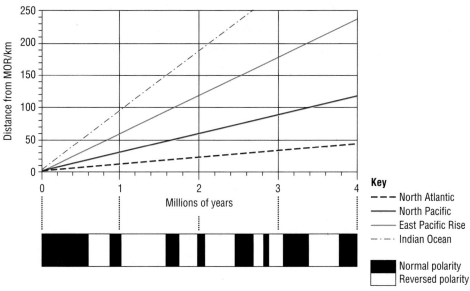

Figure 3 Spreading rates of oceans

Examiner tip

- If movement is 1 cm/yr on both sides of a ridge, the rate of spreading of the ocean is 2 cm/yr. Remember to double your answer.
- A change in gradient on a graph shows a change in the spreading rate for the ridge.
- Make sure of the zeros! There are 6 zeros in a million and 5 zeros to convert km to cm.
- If you remember that distance = velocity × time, you should be able to do any calculation given two items of data.

Worked example: rate of spreading

$$\text{Annual rate of spreading (cm/yr)} = \frac{\text{Distance moved in cm}}{\text{Number of years taken}}$$

The fastest rate of spreading at the moment is 16.8 cm/yr at the East Pacific Rise between the Nazca and Pacific plates. Rates can also vary along the same boundary. The South Atlantic is spreading at about 4 cm/yr and the North Atlantic at only 2 cm/yr along the Mid-Atlantic Ridge.

Below the graph, the diagram shows a magnetic anomaly pattern across an MOR. Basalts erupted 3 Ma are now 30 km from the middle of the ridge. It has taken 3 000 000 years for the basalt to move 3 000 000 cm, at an average rate of 1 cm/yr.

Questions

1. Using the graph of sea floor spreading, calculate the average rate of spreading of one side of the North Pacific and North Atlantic oceans. Which of the four oceans is spreading fastest?
2. Plot the sediment data to show the thickness away from the MOR. Insert a line of best fit.
3. The age of the oldest sediments at the edge of the Atlantic is 190 Ma. If the distance across the Ocean is 3800 km, what is the average rate of sea floor spreading?

Major features of the Earth

Continents drift and oceans spread. Before we can interpret the evolution of these major features of the Earth, we need to describe them in more detail.

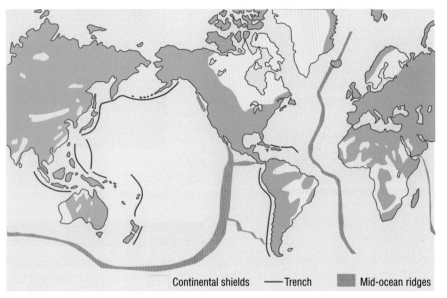

Figure 1 Map showing the main features of the Earth

Continental shields —— Trench [Mid-ocean ridges]

Under the oceans

If you were to travel from Britain to America over the present sea floor, you would pass across a gently sloping **continental shelf**, a steeper **continental slope** down to the **abyssal plain** of the deep ocean floor, then up the sides of the **mid-ocean ridge** with its **median rift valley** at the top, down to the abyssal plain on the other side and back up onto a continent again. From South America into the Pacific, you would cross a narrow continental shelf and down into a very deep **oceanic trench**. Beyond this, on the abyssal plain you would pass a number of **seamounts** rising as submarine mountains.

Ocean basins make up 60% of the Earth's surface. At present, sea water fills the basins and overflows onto the continental shelves so that about 70% of the Earth's surface is covered by water.

Key definitions

Mafic describes igneous rocks with 45 to 52% silica, such as basalt.

Pelagic is applied to organisms living in, and sediment deposited from, the main body of sea water.

Planktonic is applied to organisms that float in sea water.

Clastics are sediments made up of fragments of pre-existing rock.

Continents are situated on crust with an average thickness of 35 km and a mean composition close to that of granite.

Ocean basins are situated on crust with an average thickness of only 7 km, formed mainly of rocks with a basaltic composition.

Continental shelf Although below sea level at the present time, the shelf is part of the continent
Continental slope Steeper (average 4 degrees) slope of the continental margin between the edge of the continental shelf at about 200 m and where it merges into the abyssal plain at 1500–3500 m deep. Deep submarine canyons cut across the slope in places. Sediments are transported down the slope by submarine avalanches called turbidity currents
Abyssal plain This is the deep ocean basin 3–5 km deep. It is flat with the mafic rocks of the oceanic crust below it. It is covered by thin beds of fine-grained, slowly deposited, pelagic sediment derived from wind-blown dust, volcanic ash and the skeletons of microscopic planktonic organisms (i.e. foraminifera and radiolaria). Thicker deposits of coarser sediment are carried in by turbidity currents. The area is aseismic, meaning there are no earthquakes
Mid-ocean ridge Elongated submarine ridge in the middle of the ocean, rising 2 or 3 km above the abyssal plain and up to 1000 km wide. Built up of basalt extruded at the divergent plate boundary where two oceanic plates move apart by sea floor spreading. An axial rift valley, a deep valley with steep mountainous sides, splits the summit of the ridge. There are frequent shallow-focus earthquakes due to rising magma and movement along transform faults
Deep-sea trench Very deep (up to 11 km), narrow (up to 150 km), elongated submarine valley occurring at the edges of the oceans alongside fold-mountain belts and island arc systems. There are shallow-focus earthquakes Many trenches occur around the edge of the Pacific
Seamount Submarine basalt volcano rising at least 1000 m above the ocean floor without reaching sea level. Seamounts may occur singly, in groups or in chains Some seamounts are topped by a coral atoll A seamount with an eroded flat top is called a **guyot**

Table 1 Topographic features of the oceans

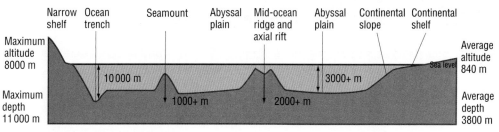

Figure 2 Cross-section of continents and oceans

Over the land

The continental land surface together with the continental shelf and slope make up 40% of the Earth's surface. The continental shelf is often uncovered when sea level drops during an ice advance. The view of the world shows large areas of shelf around Britain and much of this was once dry land. You could have walked to France just 9000 years ago!

The continents show a huge variety of rock types, structure and age, unlike the rocks of the oceanic crust. Continents may be divided into structural areas with similar characteristics.

Continental shelf
This is the area of sea floor around the edge of continental landmasses, which gently slopes to a depth of 150–200 m before giving way to the steeper continental slope
The shelf is formed of continental crust and is covered with beds of clastic sands and clays or carbonate (limestone) deposits. Marine organisms thrive in the shallow, sunlit waters. There are few earthquakes
Fold mountains
Fold mountain ranges, or the eroded roots of former mountain chains, form linear belts along the margins of the continents. They are made of very thick sequences of sedimentary rocks, which have been strongly folded and faulted by compressive forces, and metamorphosed by the high pressures and temperatures. Extrusive and intrusive igneous rocks are common
The high mountain ranges form two main linear belts several 1000 km long; one situated on the western side of North and South America, e.g. the Rockies and Andes and the other, the 'Alpine-Himalayan belt', which formed in the last 60 Ma
Their width is generally 300–800 km and they contain the world's highest mountains, e.g. Everest 8 km high Earthquakes at all depths are common as fold mountains are formed on destructive plate margins. Depth of focus increases with distance away from the trench
Continental shield or craton
The continental shields are stable blocks of rocks that form the ancient cores of the continents, e.g. the Canadian, Scandinavian and Australian shields. They are made of highly deformed crystalline Precambrian metamorphic and igneous rocks; contain the worlds oldest rocks, e.g. the Isua gneisses of Greenland, dated at 3950 my; are often on a very large scale of thousands of kilometres; have no earthquakes – aseismic areas as they are in the centre of plates away from plate boundaries; are areas of low relief due to long periods of erosion; make up large sections of rigid continental crust, although this may not be obvious due to a cover of younger sedimentary rocks
Major rift valley and rift system
A rift valley is a linear strip of crust that has slipped down along normal faults, which dip towards the valley (graben structure). Normal faults are formed by extension of the crust, which is either pulled apart by tension or gently arched upwards by rising magma. The crust subsides due to gravity, between the fractures, to form the valley. Magma may rise up the faults, leading to volcanic activity alongside and within the rift valley. Shallow-focus earthquakes are common along the fault lines
The East African Rift Valley is part of a major rift system that continues to the Red Sea. This system represents the initial stages of the continent splitting to form a new ocean

Table 2 Features of the continent

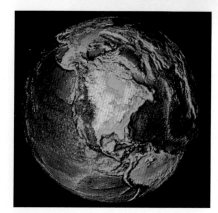

Figure 3 The Earth from space, showing elevation of land and oceans

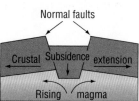

(a) Original crust and mantle

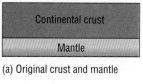

(b) Tension caused by extension and gentle uplift due to rising magma underneath. Normal faults develop

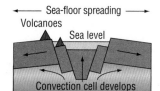

(c) Continued extension. Formation of volcanoes and perhaps flood basalts. Incursion of the sea. Sea-floor spreading starts.

Figure 4 Formation of a rift valley

Questions

1 Compare the origin of the two types of valleys – rift valleys and deep ocean trenches.

2 Compare the origin of the two types of mountain ranges – mid-ocean ridges and fold mountains.

3 Explain why the continental shelf may be dry land or below sea level.

An earthquake is a vibration in the rocks of the Earth's crust and upper mantle, caused by a sudden dislocation of the rocks along a fault. Analysing earthquakes and earthquake distribution enables us to interpret the forces which caused the dislocation. The pattern of earthquakes in ocean basins is different from that of the continents, showing that they have different tectonic settings.

Where are the earthquakes?

Earthquakes are mainly confined to active seismic zones around the world, where stresses are acting in the crust and upper mantle. Between these zones are **aseismic** areas with no stresses to cause dislocation and therefore no earthquakes. Aseismic areas are generally the continental shields of old stable rocks and the ocean basins. Britain is, at the present time, an aseismic area (other than the minor tremors we occasionally feel).

Distribution of modern-day earthquakes

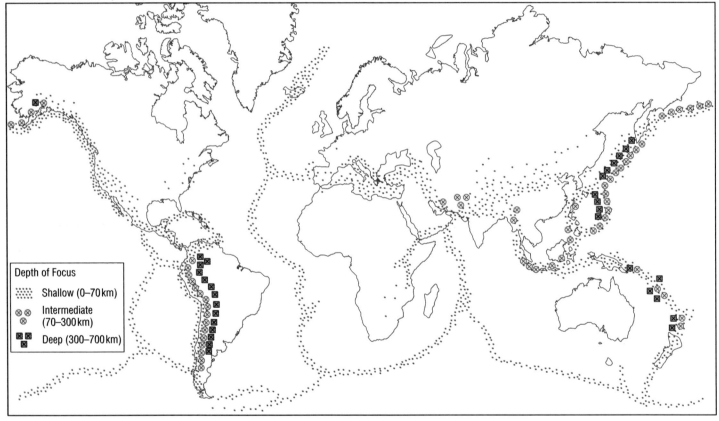

Figure 1 Simplified map of world earthquake zones divided into shallow, intermediate and deep

Key definition

Earthquakes are classified by their **depth of focus**, or the depth at which the stress acts:

* shallow-focus   0–70 km deep
* intermediate   70–300 km deep
* deep-focus   300–700 km deep

Earthquakes do not originate at depths greater than 720 km, because deeper rocks are not brittle enough to fracture.

Depth of focus

The world map of earthquakes shows that there are separate zones of shallow-focus and deep-focus earthquakes. The **depth of focus** is related to the plate boundaries.

Mid-ocean areas

Mid-ocean ridges (MORs): shallow-focus earthquakes

The high heat flow and eruption of basaltic pillow lavas at the MOR indicates rising magma. When magma moves, it vibrates to produce harmonic waves (similar to the wave patterns in some musical instruments), which are detected as small, shallow-focus earthquakes. It is the same phenomenon that makes old pipes rattle and bang as water flows through them.

Axial rift system: shallow-focus earthquakes

Extension of the crust at the rift valley along the centre of the MOR causes formation of normal faults. Movement along the faults, usually subsidence, causes earthquakes.

Transform fault: shallow-focus earthquakes

The oceanic crust spreads away from the MOR in sections between transform faults. Horizontal movement along the transform faults causes earthquakes.

Subduction zones

Where an oceanic plate is subducted beneath a continental plate, the depth of origin of earthquakes ranges from shallow to deep.

Deep-ocean trench and fold mountains

Earthquakes are shallow under the deep-ocean trenches and along the oceanic sides of fold mountains, such as the Pacific coast of the Andes. The trench marks the line at the surface where two plates meet. Further inland, towards the fold mountains, the foci of earthquakes get progressively deeper along a zone that slopes away from the trench at about 45 degrees. This marks the top of the boundary between the two plates where one moves beneath the other. This zone is called the **Benioff** zone.

The earthquakes are due to friction between the two plates as they slide past each other or get stuck and then suddenly move.

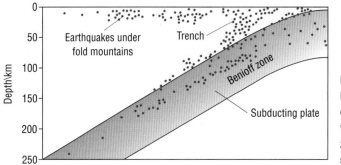

Figure 2
Benioff zone. Dots are earthquake foci and they mark the Benioff zone at the top of the subducting plate.

This active zone is present underneath the full length of the mountain range. It is hardly surprising that Peru and Chile experience many devastating earthquakes. The Benioff zone is also present under island arc systems.

When an area of sea floor spreading reaches the edge of a continent, the denser oceanic rocks are forced down under the light continental rocks in the process of **subduction** ('leading down'). The inclined boundary between the plates, starting at the trench and ending where the descending plate melts, is an active zone of stress and displacement, causing progressively deeper earthquakes. This is called the **subduction zone**. Rising magma under island arcs causes shallow-focus earthquakes.

Collision zones

Where two continents collide, such as India and Asia, there will be shallow and medium earthquakes along deep faults. Compression is taking place as the Indian plate is still being pushed north from the Indian Ocean MOR.

Where plates slide past each other at conservative plate margins, shallow earthquakes are common.

Questions

1 Why are there no deep earthquakes under the Mid-Atlantic Ridge?
2 Why are there no earthquakes deeper than 720 km?
3 Explain why shallow-focus earthquakes are more common than deep-focus earthquakes.

How science works

Earthquakes are confined to the lithosphere, the brittle part of the crust and the upper mantle. As these are shallow earthquakes, the lithosphere must be thin under the MOR. The underlying, less rigid asthenosphere moves steadily without sudden displacements and therefore does not produce earthquakes. Most of the earthquakes are of low magnitude, with hundreds of earthquakes of magnitude less than Richter 2 every day. Sometimes there are larger earthquakes of around magnitude 5, but as population is very low in these areas they rarely cause problems.

Examiner tip

Subduction and Benioff zones are two related zones occupying the same position under fold mountains and island arcs, so the terms are sometimes used synonymously.

However, the Benioff zone marks a plane along which earthquakes are generated.

The subduction zone is where the downward movement of an oceanic lithospheric plate, beneath another plate, is 'destroyed' by partial melting as it descends into the mantle.

The moving Earth

We have discussed a number of different ideas so far in isolation – sea floor spreading, continental drift, subduction zones. Is there one theory which will pull all the threads together?

We can take South America as an example:

- South America is moving away from Africa. Does that mean that the two continents will meet up again round the other side of the world?
- The Pacific Ocean is spreading from the East Pacific Rise. Does that mean that the surface of the Earth is getting bigger?
- Along the west coast of South America, there is an active belt of earthquakes, fold mountains and volcanoes. Compression has folded and faulted the rocks.
- Along the east coast of South America there is no active belt. The continental crust meets the oceanic crust as part of the same plate.

The ideas behind plate tectonics

In 1962, Harry Hess recognised that the surface area of the Earth could not get any bigger and suggested that, while the sea floor is created at the MOR, it is consumed at the oceanic trenches along the subduction zone. The ocean floor acts as a 'conveyor belt' of oceanic crust from the MOR to the trench. The Pacific Ocean and South American plates are colliding with each other so strongly that fold mountains are formed. The continental crust of South America is not merely drifting over the oceanic crust of the Pacific basin but colliding with it. The South Atlantic is spreading from the east and so South America is moving in the same direction as one unit.

In 1965, Tuzo Wilson suggested that the surface of the Earth is divided into a small number of sections, which are much thicker than just the crust. Some of these *tectonic plates* are capped by oceanic crust, some by continental crust, but most by both. We should not think about the uppermost layer of the Earth in terms of the crust, but of these thicker sections. It is the *lithospheric plates* that are moving, not just the crust.

A unifying theory – plate tectonics

The plate tectonic theory gives a coherent explanation for many of the major global geological events such as earthquakes, volcanoes, faults, folds and fold mountains. It brings together a number of earlier hypotheses, which attempt to explain the distribution of the continents and oceans.

The uppermost layer of the Earth is divided into a number of sections, which are constantly in motion relative to each other, carried by moving material beneath:

- The sections are the rigid **lithosphere plates**.
- The moving material is the plastic **asthenosphere**, which is partially melted and acts as a rheid – a solid that can flow.

The **plate boundaries** or **margins** between the lithospheric plates are zones of geological activity along which the relative motion is taken up. By comparison, areas within the plates are geologically inactive (aseismic).

Identifying plate margins

New crust is formed along the MOR and destroyed along subduction zones, because plates are moving apart or coming together. Where plates meet there will be displacement and therefore earthquakes, which suggests a way of marking out the boundaries between them. The interior parts of the plates will not be involved in any interactions and will be aseismic.

Examiner tip

Make sure you know the difference between continental drift, sea floor spreading and plate tectonics. Exam questions usually ask for one of these and giving the wrong evidence will reduce your marks. Evidence for continental drift is only the evidence on land. Evidence for sea floor spreading is found only in the oceans. Plate tectonics describes what is happening at plate boundaries. Modern plate boundaries are active areas with earthquakes and volcanoes.

Key definition

The **lithosphere plate** is a layer or shell of the crust and upper mantle, in which the rocks are rigid and brittle.

The **lithosphere** is divided into plates, which are carried by the moving, underlying **asthenosphere**. The base of the lithosphere is taken as the 1300 °C isotherm and varies from 5 km at a MOR to 300 km below fold mountains on a continent.

A **continental plate** carries a continent but will also have oceanic crust.

An **oceanic plate** has no continental material.

Examiner tip

Seven large and several small lithospheric plates have been identified as the aseismic areas outlined by active earthquake zones.

Learn the names, types and approximate geographical position of the seven major plates: Pacific, South American, North American, African, Eurasian, Indian-Australian and the Antarctic plates.

The map of plates in Figure 1 shows that earthquake zones mark plate boundaries.

There is plenty of other evidence to help map the plate margins:
- earthquake zones outline the lithospheric plates
- changes in heat flow
- chains of volcanoes
- trenches and rift valleys
- changes in gravity
- fold mountain belts

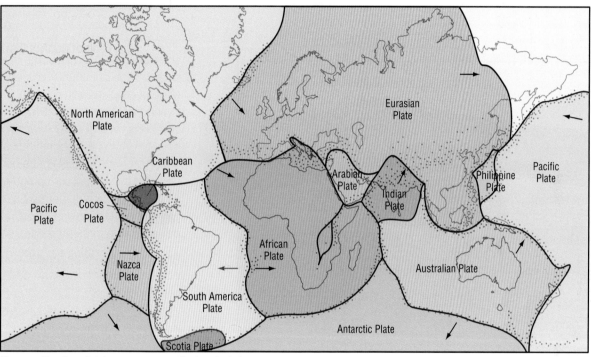

Key ⟶ Direction of plate movement ⦂ Earthquake foci

Figure 1 Present-day plate tectonic map of the world

Types of crust

Most plates are a combination of oceanic and continental crust, so the term 'oceanic' or 'continental' applies to that part of the plate at a plate margin. The Eurasian plate that we live on starts at the Mid-Atlantic Ridge where it is oceanic, then extends as a continental plate across Europe and Asia.

	Oceanic crust	**Continental crust**
Thickness of lithosphere	About 5 km under the MOR, thickening to 200 km away from the ridge	Up to 300 km thick under major mountain ranges; about 75 km under the continental platform
Density (g/cm³)	2.9	2.7
Age	0–200 Ma	0–3960 Ma
Average composition	Lithospheric mantle (peridotite of the upper mantle) capped by basaltic oceanic crust with a thin layer of sediments at the top	Lithospheric mantle (peridotite of the upper mantle) capped by granitic crust, which is deformed and contains a mix of igneous, metamorphic and sedimentary rocks
Examples	Pacific, Cocos and Nazca plates	Arabian Plate is almost entirely capped by continental crust Most other plates carry continental crust

Questions

1 Outline the theory of plate tectonics in 20 words.
2 What is the difference between plate tectonics and continental drift?
3 Apart from earthquakes, what other geological feature marks the position of plate boundaries?
4 Is it possible to see plate boundaries on land?

At **divergent** plate margins, plates are moving apart. In the present-day mid-Atlantic, the edges of two oceanic plates are involved.

When South America separated from Africa 180 million years ago, the divergent plate margin was in the centre of the supercontinent of Gondwanaland. This supercontinent split along a major rift system, probably similar to the one now seen in East Africa.

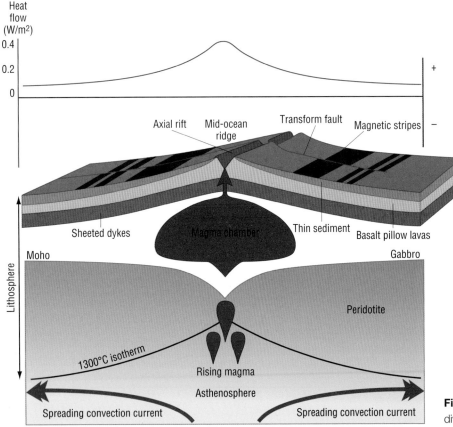

Widespread extrusions of plateau basalts accompanied the split. The rift valley widened and subsided below sea level, allowing the ocean to flood in. As the separation continued, the continental crust stretched and became thinner, leaving wide continental slopes on the edge of each section of plate. The thinned continental crust finally split completely and the gap was filled with basalt, forming the beginnings of the oceanic crust. The one plate had become two. Sea floor spreading started as new crust was generated at the MOR, giving the alternative name of **constructive** plate margin.

At all mature divergent plate boundaries, oceanic plates move apart and create new crust.

Figure 1 Section across a divergent plate margin

Examples of divergent plate boundaries

Divergent plate boundaries are locations where plates are moving away from one another. Rising convection currents in the mantle push up and move along the bottom of the lithosphere, flowing sideways beneath it. This lateral flow causes the lithosphere plate above to be dragged along in the direction of the flow. In the area where the convection current is moving up, the overlying plate is stretched, thins, breaks and pulls apart, forming a mid-ocean ridge (MOR). Extensional forces stretch the lithosphere and produce a deep axial rift.

When the plates start to move apart, pressure is reduced, allowing the peridotite mantle material below to partially melt. The magma accumulates below the ridge and some finds its way up through feeder dolerite dykes until it reaches the surface or sea floor and becomes a fissure lava flow.

The Mid-Atlantic Ridge is a good example of a divergent plate boundary. For most of its 7000 km length, it is a submarine feature. However, Iceland is above sea level, probably because there is a hot spot under Iceland as well as the ridge.

The East African Rift Valley may become a new ocean in time. The northern part of this rift system, in the Red Sea between North Africa and Arabia, is now a divergent plate margin where new basaltic ocean crust is being formed. This split started in the Eocene about 40 Ma and accelerated during the Oligocene about 23 Ma. The sea is still widening and it is likely that it will become an ocean, perhaps in another 50 Ma.

At the volcanic vents, the lava erupts as globules, which cool rapidly in the cold sea water to form fine-grained basalt in rounded masses of **pillow lavas**.

In the feeder pipes from the volcanoes, magma which does not reach the surface cools as medium-grained **dolerite**, forming sheeted dykes. Below the dykes, the magma cools slowly to solidify in layers of coarse-grained **gabbro**.

All of this mafic material adds on to the trailing edge of the spreading plate, creating new oceanic crust.

Case study

Iceland lies on the Mid-Atlantic Ridge and is the only landmass where we can walk across the ridge and see evidence for sea floor spreading. You can:

- observe volcanoes and high temperature water due to the magma below the surface
- observe the faults of the axial rift
- feel earthquakes
- discover the youngest rocks in the centre of the island, and
- measure the movement as Iceland gets bigger.

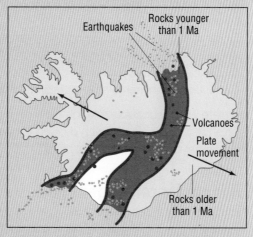

Figure 2 Map of Iceland and photo across the MOR

Case study

An eruption of Yemen's Jabal al-Tair volcano killed at least eight people in October 2007. The volcano sits on an island in the Red Sea, at the boundary between the African and Arabian plates where they are moving apart.

The victims were soldiers caught by surprise when the volcano suddenly blasted out lava. Clouds of ash rose high into the sky while the ground shook with a swarm of earthquakes. It is the first eruption recorded at the volcano since 1883.

The boundary continues into East Africa as the East African Rift Zone, and there is volcanic activity in Kenya and Tanzania.

Evidence of divergent plate boundaries

- Dating of the basalts, sediments and magnetic anomalies on the ocean floor clearly shows that the age of the crust increases with distance from the MOR (see spread 1.3.2). The two plates on either side, which carry the oceanic crust, must therefore be moving apart. The centre of spreading is the axial rift where tension forms a rift valley.
- The MORs are among the largest mountain ranges in the world. They are made of mafic igneous material derived from the ultramafic magma of the upper mantle.
- Heat flow is higher than average across the ridge, peaking at the median rift, confirming that hot magma is rising beneath it. This upwelling of magma and expansion of the hot rock may help to increase the height of the ridge, where there are eruptions of basalt.
- As the magma moves, it makes harmonic tremors, which are detected as shallow-focus earthquakes.
- Fissure volcanic eruptions of mafic lava often form basalt pillows.
- Shallow focus earthquakes also occur due to displacement along transform faults.

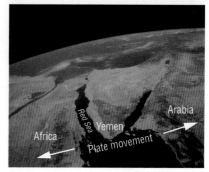

Figure 3 Photo of the northern part of the Red Sea

Black smokers

Smokers are hot springs occurring in narrow zones on the flanks of MORs. High speed jets of very hot solutions (350 °C) are emitted from a series of small vents. These hot waters are rich in sulfur, with copper, iron, zinc and gold dissolved from the rocks below, giving the water its characteristic black colour.

On cooling, and helped by the action of bacteria living in this warm, mineral-rich environment, minerals are precipitated around the vent in the form a chimney, a few metres tall. Iron, copper and zinc sulfides are made from the elements listed above, and have the potential to form ore deposits, especially if the oceanic crust is carried onto land by plate movement to form ophiolites.

Questions

1 How would you identify the location of MORs?
2 What is the importance of black smokers?
3 Draw a cross-section of the oceanic crust to show the layered structure.
4 Draw a cross-section of a divergent plate margin to show all the evidence.

When two plates move towards each other a collision takes place. There are two types of plates, oceanic and continental, so there are three types of convergent plate margins:

- Oceanic–continental: collision of the Nazca and South America plates, forming the Andes.
- Oceanic–oceanic: the collision of the Pacific plate and the Eurasian plate in Japan.
- Continental–continental: the collision of India with Eurasia, forming the Himalayas.

The plate which subducts may be older and therefore colder, or it may be slower. It is always the oceanic plate which descends because it is made of dense basalt compared to the lighter granitic continental plate.

Evidence for convergent plate boundaries

There are many processes operating at plate boundaries that do not occur elsewhere. This means that looking at the distribution of these features allows us to identify modern plate boundaries. We can use the same ideas to identify ancient plate boundaries. The presence of intermediate volcanic rocks, ophiolites, batholiths and folded and faulted rocks forming an ancient fold mountain belt in Scotland tells us that this was an active plate boundary 350 million years ago.

Heat flow anomalies

Heat flow measurements at both oceanic–oceanic and oceanic–continental margins show the same pattern. There is a negative anomaly at the trench where cold lithosphere is subducting and a positive anomaly at the island arc or volcanic belt where magma is being intruded.

Volcanic activity

As the subducting plate heats up there is partial melting along the top surface of the descending oceanic crust, producing a basaltic magma. This is less dense than the surrounding material and so rises to form volcanoes in an island arc or chain in a continent. However, basaltic magma is at a temperature of 1200 °C, and as this rises through silicic continental crust it causes partial melting and some mixing of magma may occur to give the intermediate rock, andesite.

Batholiths

Where continental crust is melted by magma most of the material will remain separate as the viscosity of the magmas is very different. The melted silicic material can form large granite batholiths deep in the continental crust below fold mountains.

Trenches

Trenches form above the point where the oceanic plate is being subducted. They are long, narrow, linear features that form the deepest parts of the Earth's surface, arranged parallel to the edge of the plate.

Fold mountain belts/orogenic belts

Fold mountains form on the edges of the continents parallel to the subduction zone. They are compressional features made of folded and faulted sediments that have been scraped off the descending plate onto the non-subducting plate. The high pressures and temperatures at convergent plate margins mean that rocks are regionally metamorphosed.

Figure 1 Convergent plate margins (volcanoes) around the Pacific – the Ring of Fire and earthquakes

What's in a name?

It's easy to get confused!

Divergent margins are also called **constructive** because new material is added to the crust.

Convergent margins are also called **destructive**. Oceanic crust is consumed along the subduction zone, giving the alternative name of **destructive plate margin**.

Benioff zone

As the oceanic plate descends, the sloping plane of the boundary is marked by increasingly deep-focus earthquakes along the **Benioff zone** (named after the scientist who identified it). At higher levels in the crust, where the subduction is beginning, the earthquakes are generated along the boundary itself partly due to friction. Further down, the foci occur within the plate itself as the interior part of the plate remains colder and more rigid, while the edges of the plate heat up and move more easily.

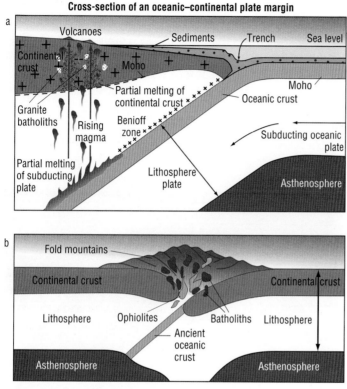

Figure 2 Cross section of **a** convergent plate margin
b continental–continental plate margin

Figure 3 Fold mountains of Himalayas

Convergent continental–continental plate margin

Two continental plates of similar composition and density meet under the Himalayas. The Indian plate has spent the last 100 million years as an island, drifting north away from Africa and Antarctica when it was part of Gondwanaland. Movement was initially slow but increased in the last 60 million years, with a maximum rate of 19 cm per year, until it collided with continental Asia.

The smaller Indian plate was forced under the larger Asian plate, producing shallow and intermediate earthquakes along the boundary. However, subduction soon stopped because there is no difference in density, and the plates crumpled together instead. The sediments deposited in the ocean which occupied the decreasing space between the advancing plates were intensely compressed and metamorphosed. They now form the fold mountains of the Himalayas. The remains of the subduction zone sank beneath the collision zone without having the opportunity to form magma to feed volcanoes.

The continental crust increased in thickness and its base began to melt, creating viscous, silicic magma which slowly rose through the overlying crust to form granite batholiths. No lava was erupted.

The Indian plate is less dense than the surrounding mantle into which it was forced, and the additional buoyancy elevated the mountains – the Himalayas – to a greater than average height.

Questions

1 Summarise the main differences between divergent and convergent margins.

2 Why are there no volcanoes at continental–continental margins?

3 Why do intermediate and silicic magmas not mix easily?

4 Why does the oceanic plate move down beneath a continental plate?

Oceanic–oceanic convergent plate margin

The slower or older/colder oceanic plate is carried downwards at the trench, into an area of higher temperature. The geothermal gradient increases with depth, so as the plate is subducted the temperature increases.

- Partial melting of the basaltic oceanic plate begins as the lower temperature minerals begin to melt.
- The melted minerals separate and, being less dense than the surrounding oceanic crust, begin to rise as magma with an intermediate composition.
- The magma erupts at the surface to form volcanoes which erupt intermediate and mafic lava such as andesite and basalt (see spread 2.2.1).
- The volcanoes create an arc of volcanic islands, reflecting the curving shape of the convergent plate boundary beneath.
- The rocks of the island arc are metamorphosed by the increase in temperature and pressure. Some of these rocks are metamorphosed sediment scraped off the descending plate.

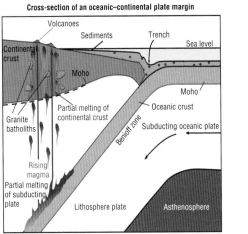
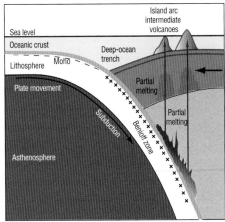

Figure 2 Cross-sections of convergent plate margins, oceanic–oceanic and oceanic–continental

Oceanic–continental convergent plate margin

All the processes operating at oceanic–oceanic plate margins are the same here. However, the presence of continental crust makes it more complicated.

- The magma rising from the subducting oceanic plate is at a high enough temperature to cause partial melting of some of the continental crust that it passes through. This means that some of the silicic magma formed may reach the surface to form explosive rhyolitic volcanoes and some will mix with the rising mafic magma to create large volumes of intermediate magma that form the enormous strato volcanoes of the Andes.
- Large batholiths will also be formed from melted continental crust and intruded deep in the core of the fold mountains.
- Compression of the continental crust and the sediments scraped off the subducting plate will form fold mountain chains. These are intensely folded and faulted, creating fold mountains with major thrusts, nappes and overfolds (see 1.4.6). The continental crust shortens laterally and therefore extends vertically as high mountains with deep roots, adding to any uplift caused by the oceanic plate forcing its way under the continental plate.

Japan: a convergent oceanic–oceanic plate margin

Along the length of the coast of Japan
- there is a deep ocean trench;
- there are shallow- to deep-focus earthquakes;
- there is an arc of volcanic islands. The islands are made of volcanic, not continental, material.

Figure 1 Photo of volcano Mt Fuji in Japan – steep sides tell us it is intermediate in composition

The Andes: a convergent oceanic–continental plate margin

The denser Nazca oceanic plate subducts beneath the continental South American plate. The Andes are fold mountains over 5000 m high and 7000 km long, with some of the world's largest volcanoes. There is normally a volcano erupting somewhere in South America. The area is prone to large earthquakes, often with the epicentre close to the Peru–Chile trench which extends right the way down the west coast. They show a clear pattern, with the shallow-focus earthquakes close to the trench and deeper-focus ones inland.

Figure 3 Photo of the Andes

- Many of the rocks in the deeper part of the mountain chain will be regionally metamorphosed by heat and pressure. Gneiss and migmatite in the core of the mountains grade outwards through schist and slate.
- Segments of the former oceanic crust may be broken off at the top of the subduction zone, trapping an ophiolite suite within the fold mountains (see spread 1.1.4).

Conservative plate margins

In some places plates slide laterally past each other. The San Andreas Fault, along with its many associated faults, is the best known example. There is no subduction and therefore the earthquakes which occur are shallow-focus. There are no volcanoes or other features to mark the plate boundary. The movement of one plate alongside the other is unremitting, so California will continue to suffer from severe earthquakes well into the future.

The difficulty when trying to predict this movement is that parts of the fault are creeping, making many small movements, while other sections are stuck. In these areas there are seismic gaps where no earthquakes have occurred to release the stress. The frictional strength is overcome as stress builds up and the rocks suddenly move to produce a major earthquake.

The San Andreas Fault zone has seismically active sections where small earthquakes are frequent, and locked sections where there is no known recent movement. The strain builds up over many years in the locked sections, until there is a sudden 'break'. The last big earthquake on a locked section was at San Francisco in 1906. It registered 8.6 on the Richter scale. Many parts of the city were completely flattened and approximately 700 people were killed. This part of the fault has not moved since. If the fault had locked for 100 years (until 2006) then 5 m of sudden movement would be possible (5 cm x 100 years = 500 cm).

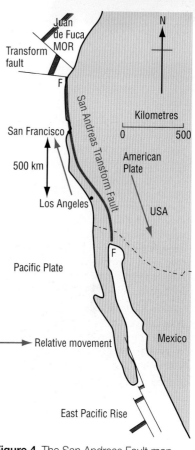

Figure 4 The San Andreas Fault map

San Andreas Fault zone

The San Andreas Fault is a transform fault which occurs on land. It connects two volcanically inactive oceanic rift systems in the Gulf of California to the south and in the Pacific just north of San Francisco. San Francisco is actually on the Pacific plate and not the American!

- Length is over 1300 km.
- Plates move past each other at a relative rate of 5 cm per year, with the Pacific plate moving faster.
- The East Pacific plate is moving northwest and the North American plate west-northwest but at a slower rate.
- The fault started at least 200 million years ago.
- In the last 140 million years, the displacement (of Jurassic rocks) has been 560 km.

Figure 5 The San Andreas Fault

Questions

1 What are the differences between a divergent and a conservative plate margin?
2 What is the relationship between a subduction zone and Benioff zone?
3 Why is the San Andreas Fault called a transform fault instead of a transcurrent fault?
4 Calculate how long it will take for Los Angeles to reach the position where San Francisco is now – 450 km to the north – if the rate of movement is 5 cm per year.

When Wegener proposed his theory of continental drift, his biggest problem was finding a mechanism by which the continents could move. His theory was largely ignored, partly because of limited knowledge about the interior of the Earth, but also because it was difficult to see how the continents could move over the top of the oceanic crust. So to explain the theories of continental drift, sea floor spreading and plate tectonics, we need to find a mechanism by which the lithospheric plates can move.

Convection cells

The interior of the Earth is hot. This heat is partly left over from the formation of the Earth, but is also due to ongoing decay of radioactive heat-producing elements. If more heat is generated in some areas than others, it is possible for convection currents to be set up, as originally suggested by the English geologist Arthur Holmes in 1928. Slow-moving convection currents within the asthenosphere, or possibly within the whole mantle, move the overlying lithospheric plates with them. Convection cells are set up when hot, lower density material rises upwards. This then flows sideways and starts to cool down. As the material cools, it becomes denser and sinks back down.

Where a convection current rises to the surface at a divergent plate margin or hot spot there is:

- high heat flow
- rising magma
- eruption of lava.

Near the surface of the Earth, the current stops rising and spreads out laterally on either side of the MORs, resulting in sea floor spreading away from the ridge. It is this part of the convection cell that carries the rigid lithosphere across the Earth's surface, like a giant conveyor belt. Beneath the lithosphere, partial melting in the asthenosphere reduces friction and acts as a lubricant for the movement of the lithosphere.

Where two of these lateral currents meet at subduction zones, either one or both start to sink, as they are now much cooler and therefore denser. There is:

- a deep ocean trench
- low heat flow
- evidence of compression.

In other words, subduction zones are convergent plate margins. This descending flow of material eventually replaces the mantle material, which rises under the MORs.

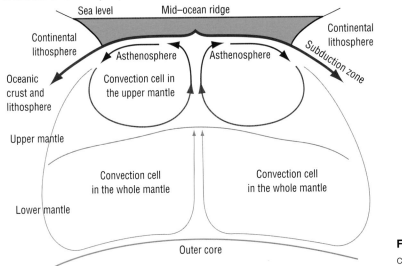

Figure 1 Convection cell in the mantle

Other possible mechanisms for plate movement

Ridge push at MORs

In this model, rising magma injected along the MORs at divergent plate margins forcibly pushes the lithospheric plates apart. The sheeted dykes found on either side of the ridge axis are evidence for this process. Some geologists argue that this model is flawed because tensional forces are dominant along ridges and it would be more accurate to describe this process as gravitational sliding off the raised ridges (they are huge mountain ranges!).

Ideas of mantle convection

Mantle convection is quite different from heating liquid in a pan – the missing factor is pressure. Computer simulations of mantle convection have not yet included all the variables of temperature, pressure, volume of the mantle, the uneven distribution of radioactive elements, plate tectonic movements and melting, so research into mantle convection is ongoing.

Mantle convection may carry the plates like a conveyor belt, with divergent plate margins above where the convection cells rise. Convection may cause the lithosphere to split at MOR, and then carry the lithosphere laterally towards the subduction zone. The descending cell at the trench would drag the lithosphere down into the mantle.

Another model takes the lithosphere as the cold upper layer of the convection cell. Because of its greater density, the lithosphere tends to sink. Subduction occurs not because the plate is pulled down by the descending mantle, but because the plate is the dense sinking limb of the cell, driven by slab-pull.

The whole mantle may convect as a single layer driven by heat from the outer core. There could be jet-like plumes of low-density material that rise from the core-mantle boundary region to form hot spots. The mantle may form two separate convecting layers. The upper layer consists of upper mantle, asthenosphere and lithosphere which subducts to depths of 700 km before becoming undetectable by seismic activity. Below 700 km, the mantle may form separate cells which convect at a very slow rate independently of the upper mantle.

Slab pull at subduction zones

Recently, attention has focused on the idea that gravity pulls subducted oceanic lithosphere down into the mantle at convergent plate boundaries. This may be the main driving force for lithospheric plate movement. In this model, the weight of cold, dense lithosphere sinking downwards at ocean trenches pulls the rest of the oceanic lithosphere with it.

Recycling the Earth

We have already seen that no area of oceanic crust is older then 200 Ma, because in geological terms oceans are temporary features that open and close due to the shifting balance between their formation at MORs and destruction at subduction zones. The complete cycle of opening and closing of an ocean is called a Wilson Cycle, after the Canadian geologist J Tuzo Wilson, who suggested the idea in 1967.

If you travel along a 'moving walkway', for example, in an airport, there is no danger of running out of floor because the belt is continuous and returns back to the beginning, out of sight, underneath the walkway. Similarly, the Earth will never run out of basalt because the material brought to the surface at a divergent plate margin is returned to the depths of the mantle along the subduction zone of the convergent margin. The melted material is then carried as the return current, gaining heat from the underlying core over which it passes, back to the 'start' of the convection cell where it rises once again under the MOR. Slab pull probably limits the maximum size of an ocean and one complete Wilson Cycle takes about 500 million years to complete!

Case study

In Britain, the 400 Ma Caledonian mountain belt marks an ancient convergent plate margin. Scotland was part of North America and England and Wales were part of Europe (Gondwanaland), separated by a large ocean called the proto-Atlantic Ocean or Iapetus. In Greek mythology, Iapetus was the father of Atlantis!

The evidence for an ancient plate margin includes:
- extensive intermediate volcanic lavas and pyroclasts in N. Wales, the Lake District and southern Scotland
- folded and faulted rocks in an ancient fold mountain belt
- regionally metamorphosed rocks
- granite batholiths
- fossils of different genera of trilobites that must have been two separate faunas on either side of the Iapetus Ocean.

After the collision, for the next 300 Ma, Europe and North America were joined together as part of the supercontinent Pangaea. Around 100 Ma, the present-day North Atlantic Ocean started to open as a result of rifting in a different direction to that of the Iapetus Ocean.

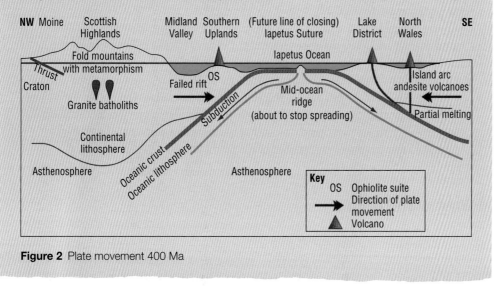

Figure 2 Plate movement 400 Ma

Questions

1 Describe models of convection in the rheid mantle.
2 How different would the future development of the Earth be if the convection in the mantle stopped completely?
3 Explain the difference between ridge push and slab pull.

So far we have only considered volcanoes that are found along active plate margins. There are a number of volcanoes located in the centre of plates for which we must also find an explanation. The most notable example is the island chain of Hawaii in the middle of the large Pacific Plate.

Magma from the deep

The 'Big Island' of Hawaii is built of five – three of them active – shield volcanoes. Mauna Loa (4100 m) is the highest and Kilauea is the most active volcano on Earth, producing daily eruptions of lava. The actual height of the Hawaiian volcanoes, from the sea floor to their summits, is greater than the height of Everest, so the volume of lava that built them was immense. The volcanoes sit on oceanic crust that is only about 5 km thick, so where did all the lava come from?

Hawaii is located on a **hot spot** above a rising **mantle plume**. Mantle plumes are stationary, long-lived areas of high heat flow within the mantle. They consist of a long, thin conduit and a bulbous head that spreads out at the base of the lithosphere. As the plume head reaches the lithosphere, the reduction in pressure causes widespread partial melting of ultramafic mantle producing huge volumes of mafic magma. The mafic magma accumulates beneath the lithosphere until it is able to punch a hole through to form a shield volcano.

A geophysicist, W Jason Morgan, proposed the theory of mantle plumes in 1971. He suggested that, along with mantle convection cells, mantle plumes are another way in which the Earth loses heat energy. The Earth's core is considerably hotter than the mantle. There is little evidence that any material moves across the Gutenberg boundary, so heat must be transferred across the boundary by conduction. As heat is transferred across the boundary, the material in the lowest part of the mantle becomes hotter, less dense and more buoyant. These overheated portions of the mantle will start to rise as low density **diapirs** that become mantle plumes. So it is possible that mantle plumes originate from as deep as the core–mantle boundary.

Evidence for mantle plumes

Mantle plumes are just one of a number of hypotheses that have been suggested to explain hot spot volcanoes within plates. There are several lines of evidence that geologists have used to support the theory.

- **Seismic tomography** and heat flow: Using a network of seismometers geophysicists can use seismic wave velocities to construct three-dimensional computer generated images of heat flow within the Earth. Seismic waves slow down when they travel through hotter, low density material. There are 32 regions in the mantle where P waves travel slower than average and these have been interpreted as rising mantle plumes. Changes in S wave velocities indicate that the plumes extend to the core–mantle boundary.
- Geochemistry: Chemical and isotopic analyses of basalts erupted at hot spots show them to be different from basalts erupted at mid-ocean ridges (MORs) or island arcs. This suggests that the magma originates from a different source area of the mantle. It seems that subducted oceanic crust that has sunk down as far as the core–mantle boundary forms a major component of the plume material.

Moving island chains

All the islands of the Hawaiian-Emperor chain are made of basaltic shield volcanoes. Apart from those on the 'Big Island', the others are extinct. Towards the northwest, they get progressively older and more eroded, continuing as a 6000 km line of submarine guyots and seamounts, which extend to the Aleutian Islands.

Key definitions

A **hot spot** is a volcano within a plate, which is the surface expression of a mantle plume.

A **mantle plume** is a stationary area of high heat flow in the mantle, which rises from great depths and produces magma that feeds hot spot volcanoes.

A **diapir** is a body of lower density, buoyant material rising upwards in the same way as hot wax does in a lava lamp.

Examiner tip

The terms hot spot and mantle plume are often used synonymously. Technically, the plume refers to the hot rising mantle material, which results in the high heat flow values, which can be recorded as a 'spot' on a map.

Key definition

Seismic tomography is a computer imaging technique, based on seismic wave velocities.

Case study

Although the Mid-Atlantic Ridge is a large volcanic mountain range marking the position of a divergent plate margin, it does not normally reach above sea level. Where islands do appear above the surface, the amount of lava produced is much higher than normal, suggesting the presence of a hot spot and mantle plume.

So Iceland lies on an MOR and also on a hot spot – two reasons for its large amount of volcanic activity. The Icelandic magmas are said to be 'evolved', implying there has been plenty of time for them to develop as they rise through the mantle, producing silicic and intermediate lavas as well as mafic basalts.

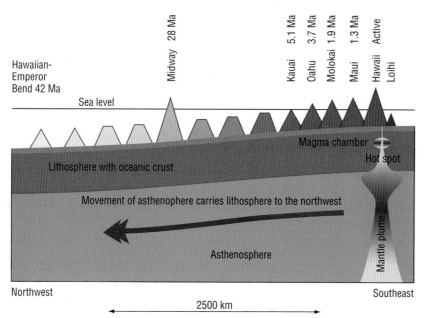

Figure 1 Cross-section through the Hawaiian-Emperor chain

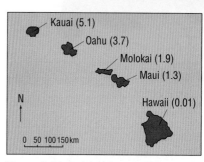

Figure 2 Map showing part of the Hawaiian island chain

There are two possible explanations for this pattern:
- The position of the mantle plume has moved towards the southeast.
- The Pacific Plate has moved towards the northwest over a stationary plume.

The second suggestion is more likely. A volcano builds when a vent or series of vents is created through the lithosphere. Plate movement then carries the volcano off the mantle plume so it becomes extinct and a new vent and volcano form over the stationary plume. Eventually a chain of volcanoes form, each one younger then the one before. The position and ages of these seamounts show the direction and rate of plate movement. In the case of Hawaii, the age of volcanic islands and seamounts show the hot spot is 80 million years old. A new, submarine volcano, Loihi, is growing 30 km south of Kilauea, showing the mantle plume is still active today. At the Hawaiian-Emperor Bend, the chain of seamounts turns north towards the Aleutian Trench, indicating that there was a change in the direction of plate movement 42 Ma.

Worked example: using hot spots to calculate rates of sea floor spreading

If the age of a volcanic island is known from radiometric dating and its distance from the active hot spot is measured, then it is possible to calculate the rate of plate movement and hence the rate of sea floor spreading. You can use the formula: speed = distance ÷ time.

Study the map showing part of the Hawaiian island chain. Using the points on Hawaii and Maui, calculate the rate of sea floor spreading. Give your answer in cm/year.

Distance between Hawaii and Maui = 15 mm on map. Using the scale 15 mm = 225 km.

Age difference between Hawaii and Maui = 1.3 − 0.01 = 1.29 million years.

$$\text{Speed} = \frac{\text{distance}}{\text{time}} = \frac{225 \text{ km}}{1.29 \text{ million years}} = \frac{225 \times 1000 \times 100 \text{ cm}}{1\,290\,000 \text{ years}} = \frac{22\,500\,000}{1\,290\,000} = 17.4 \text{ cm/year}$$

Examiner tip

Make sure you learn the formula: speed = distance ÷ time. When asked to do calculations, check if the units asked for are kilometres per million years (the easiest!), centimetres per year or millimetres per year.

Case study

There are numerous examples of oceanic hot spots from around the world – Hawaii, the Canary Islands, the Azores, St Helena and Ascension, to name a few.

Due to the thickness of the crust, mantle plumes do not manifest themselves as obvious hot spots in continental areas, but they do exist. The Yellowstone 'super-volcano' in North America is a hot spot.

Mantle plumes have also been implicated in the break up of large continents and in the formation of continental flood basalts. These are huge volumes of basalt erupted in continental areas over a short time period. They include the 65 Ma Deccan Traps in India, the 250 Ma Siberian Traps in Russia and the Karoo basalts and Ferrar dolerites of South Africa and Antarctica.

Questions

1 Explain the difference between a hot spot and a mantle plume.
2 Explain why the Hawaiian-Emperor chain gets older towards the northwest.
3 By using the points on Oahu and Molokai, shown on the map of part of the Hawaiian island chain, calculate the rate of sea floor spreading. Give your answer in cm/year.

Beds and bedding planes

A **bed** is a layer of sedimentary rock that has been laid down under a specific set of environmental conditions. Usually the youngest beds will be found on top of older beds, though sometimes the strata have been inverted. Several beds are known as **strata**. A bed may be just a few millimetres thick or it could be several metres thick. Each bed is laid down parallel to the surface of deposition, which means it is roughly horizontal. A bed may be laid down by a single event over just a few hours, such as when a river floods and deposits a layer of mud over the flood plain. However, a bed can form very slowly over a period of hundreds of thousands of years, such as on the deep ocean floor where sedimentation is extremely slow.

A **bedding plane** is the line that separates each bed and is parallel to the surface of deposition. The bedding plane is usually an even line but where the surface of deposition is irregular it is uneven.

Where erosion has occurred between beds being laid down, then the bedding plane may cross-cut older beds.

Beds will be different from each other in a variety of ways:
- **colour** – small changes in shade or major differences, for example, between a red and a green bed;
- **grain size** – the grains can vary between a fine clay and coarse pebbles or there could be minor changes between a fine sand and a medium sand;
- **grain shape** – will vary between angular and rounded;
- **sorting** – will vary between well sorted and poorly sorted;
- **composition** – each bed will contain different amounts of minerals, such as quartz, mica or clay and the cement or the matrix will vary;
- **bed thickness** – some beds will be very thin, called **laminations**, or they can be very thick, known as **massive**.

Dipping beds

Beds are often tilted or folded by Earth movements, so that they are no longer horizontal. Understanding **dip** means that we can work out where a bed may occur under younger beds. Dip is measured as the maximum angle between a horizontal line and the dipping bedding place.

Stress and strain

Stress is the term used to describe the forces applied to a rock by Earth movements or the weight of overlying rocks. **Strain** is the term used to describe the deformation caused by the applied forces. The strain is a change in volume or a change in shape – or both. Rocks behave in different ways to stress, depending on their physical properties:
- Competent rocks stay the same thickness when they are deformed and react in a brittle way. Sandstones, limestones and most igneous rocks are competent.
- Incompetent rocks will vary in thickness when they are deformed, as they behave in a plastic way. Mudstones and shales are typical incompetent rocks.

Key definitions

A **bed** is a unit of sedimentation, which can vary considerably in thickness.

A **bedding plane** marks the break between beds. It represents a break in sedimentation, a change in the composition or grain size, or a change in colour of the sediments.

The **dip** is the maximum inclination of a bed measured from the horizontal using a clinometer.

The **strike** is the direction at right angles to the dip. There is zero dip in this direction. It is a bearing measured from north using a compass.

The **apparent dip** is a dip that is measured to be less than the maximum inclination.

Figure 1 Photo of dipping beds and diagram of dip and strike

Key definitions

Strain is: $\dfrac{\text{the change of length of line}}{\text{the original length of line}}$

Stress is the force applied to rocks.

Case study

If you put a bar of chocolate in a fridge for a while and then take it out and try to break it into pieces, you will find that it is difficult to break and when it breaks it will do so suddenly with a sharp noise. The chocolate is behaving as a brittle material like a competent rock.

By contrast, if you put a bar of chocolate into your pocket on a warm day, you may be surprised to find that the bar has deformed to the shape of your pocket. In this case, the bar has been deformed because it has become more plastic or ductile.

Rocks will behave similarly in the right circumstances. At the Earth's surface, rocks are cold and brittle but at depth within the Earth they are more likely to behave in a plastic or ductile manner.

The factors affecting stress and strain

There are three main factors which affect the stresses applied to a rock and the resulting strains. The important thing to remember is that all of these factors operate together:

- The higher the temperature, the more plastic the rocks will be. At high temperatures, rocks will fold, not fault, even if the original rock is competent. Cold rocks will behave as brittle materials and therefore fracture.
- The strength of rocks increases with confining pressure and therefore rocks at depth are more difficult to deform. The weight of the overlying rocks causes the confining pressure.
- Time is crucial in determining the type of deformation that occurs. If the pressure is applied for a short period of time, then the rocks may well behave in a brittle manner, whilst pressure applied over an extended period of time can result in plastic deformation.

The relationship between forces and geological structures

Tensional forces usually result in the fracturing of rocks and crustal extension. If the forces result in a displacement of the rocks on either side of the fracture plane, then the structure is described as a fault. If there is no displacement, then the structure is described as a joint.

Compressional forces can result in either the fracturing or the folding of rocks. When rocks are cold they will tend to fracture and faults are formed. If the rocks are warm then they are more likely to fold. In both cases, the deformation will result in a shortening of the Earth's crust.

Shear forces result in the deformation of rocks in one plane – usually horizontally. These may result in faults or folds.

Using fossils and ooliths to measure strain

In order to measure the amount of strain that a rock has undergone, we can use bilaterally symmetrical fossils or ooliths. Undeformed fossils are used to establish the original shape and then the amount and direction of deformation can be analysed. Ooliths were originally spherical in shape and after deformation they become ellipsoid.

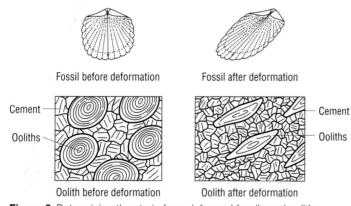

Fossil before deformation   Fossil after deformation

Cement — Ooliths   Cement — Ooliths

Oolith before deformation   Oolith after deformation

Figure 3 Determining the strain from deformed fossils and ooliths

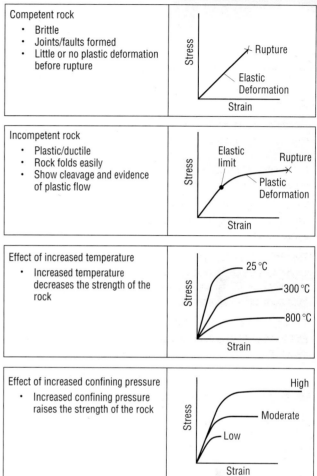

Figure 2 The relationship between stress and strain

Key definitions

Tension is the force trying to pull rocks apart – the Earth's crust will be lengthened.

Compression is the force trying to push rocks together – the Earth's crust will be shortened.

Shear forces are the forces which act along a plane in the rock and promote sliding along that plane.

Competent rocks are strong and brittle and tend to joint and fault.

Incompetent rocks are weak and plastic and tend to fold and develop cleavage.

Questions

1 Measure the apparent dip in Figure 1.
2 Use Figure 3 to identify the direction of compressive stress.

Angular unconformities

All unconformities represent a break in time – a period when no sediment was deposited. This may be the result of a change in the environment or the result of earth movements and erosion. An angular unconformity occurs where the rocks above the unconformity have a different dip, and possibly strike, to the rocks beneath the plane of the unconformity.

How an unconformity forms

Stage 1: Deposition of beds of rock, with the oldest at the bottom and the youngest at the top.

Stage 2: Beds of rock are tilted by earth movements as a result of compressive forces folding the rocks.

Stage 3: Erosion of the older beds of rock. This could be a time gap of thousands of years or many million years.

Stage 4: Deposition of younger overlying beds of rock. They are deposited unconformably on the underlying series. The eroded surface is the plane of unconformity. Fragments of the underlying beds may form conglomerate, which is a sedimentary rock formed of pebbles. This will be the first bed of the younger rocks called a basal conglomerate.

Stage 5: Uplift and erosion expose the unconformity. Often all the rocks will be folded again, so that the younger rocks are tilted as well.

How to recognise an unconformity

Angular unconformities can be recognised on a map in several ways:

- There is a difference in strike and dip of the beds below and above the plane of unconformity (see map in Figure 1).
- The presence of a basal conglomerate – rounded fragments left on the erosion surface are incorporated into the younger sediment.
- Older beds and structures (e.g. faults, fold axial plane traces and igneous intrusions) are cut off by the younger rocks above the plane of unconformity. The structures do not stop at the plane of unconformity, but continue beneath it.
- The rocks above the unconformity are younger than those beneath the unconformity.

Youngest rocks | Oldest rocks | 1

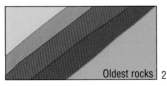

Oldest rocks | 2

Oldest rocks | 3

Oldest rocks | 4

Youngest rocks | Basal conglomerate
Plane of unconformity
5

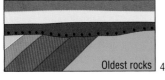

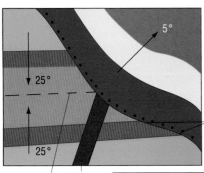

5°

25°

25°

Plane of unconformity

Dyke
Fold axial plane trace

Map showing a fold, a dyke and beds cut off at an unconformity

Figure 1 Development of an angular unconformity is shown in cross sections 1–5. The map shows the unconformity covering older rocks

Plane of unconformity

Younger rocks

Older rocks

Figure 2 Photo of an angular unconformity

Joints

Joints are produced by tensional forces. These forces may be the result of folding, cooling or unloading of rocks. They give rocks a distinctively 'blocky' appearance when they outcrop at the Earth's surface. Joints will only form in competent rocks, which are brittle and break when put under tension. Competent rocks include sandstone, limestone and granite. Joints will not occur in incompetent rocks such as mudstone or clay. Joints in sedimentary rocks are normally found perpendicular to the beds.

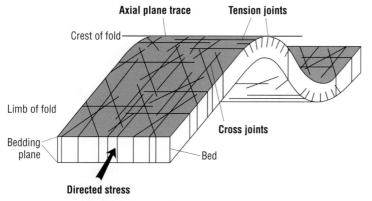

Figure 3 Tectonic joints in folded rocks

Joints produced by folding

Tectonic joints are produced by the tension created in rocks when they are folded by Earth movements. Compressive forces fold the rocks but cause some of the rocks around a fold to be under tension. The rocks fracture because the outer surface of the bed is stretched more than the inner surface. The rock is competent so it does not change in thickness as it is bent, so brittle fractures form.

Two types of tectonic joints are common:
- tension joints, parallel to the axial plane trace of the fold
- cross joints, at an angle to the axial plane trace of the fold.

As you can see from the photo, tension joints and cross joints show no displacement across the fracture plane. Where there are a number of joints with a similar orientation, they are described as a joint set.

Joints produced by cooling

Cooling joints are caused by tensional forces set up in an igneous rock as it cools steadily and contracts. The joints will be perpendicular to the cooling surfaces of thick basalt lava flows, dykes and sills, so will often be vertical. The igneous rock is insulated and then cooled with evenly spaced cooling centres. As the rock cooled and crystallised it shrank slightly and this resulted in a series of column-like structures, which are polygonal in plan.

Joints produced by unloading of rocks

Unloading joints often form in granite, an igneous rock which cooled deep below the surface where the pressure is high. The weight of the overlying rocks 'compressed' the rock – this is called the load pressure. When the granite is exposed at the surface, as a result of uplift and erosion, the lack of load pressure from overlying rocks allows them to expand. Joints form roughly parallel to the Earth's surface. Most of these joints are approximately horizontal, but they can also be vertical.

Questions

1 Draw your own set of fully labelled diagrams to show the development of an angular unconformity.
2 Why do joints form mainly in competent rocks and not in incompetent rocks?
3 The Giant's Causeway is a world-famous site of columnar jointing. Research this and other areas where columnar jointing is common.

Tension joints at fold crest

Cross joints

Figure 4 Tectonic joints in folded rocks

Vertical hexagonal columnar joints with lava flow on top

0   30 cm

Figure 5 Columnar joints at the Giant's Causeway

Faults are brittle fractures where there is displacement, which can be horizontal, vertical or a combination. Faults are very common structures in the Earth's crust. They are of great importance as areas of weakness where earthquakes take place when stored stress is released. They range from a few centimetres to hundreds of kilometres in length, and are formed by tension, compression or shear forces.

Fault characteristics

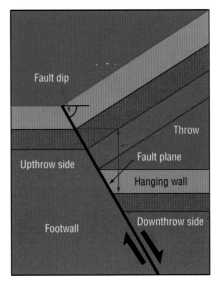

Figure 1 Diagram of fault characteristics

Key definitions

A **fault** is a fracture in a rock along which there has been an observable amount of displacement.

The **fault plane** is the surface along which movement takes place.

Throw is the amount of vertical displacement measured vertically between the top of the same bed seen on both sides of the fault.

Fault dip is the angle between the fault plane and the horizontal.

Hanging wall is the side that lies above the fault plane.

Footwall is the side that lies below the fault plane.

Downthrow is the side of the fault that has moved down.

Upthrow is the side of the fault that has moved up.

Figure 2 A normal fault

Examiner tip

- Fault movement of upthrow and downthrow is usually shown on diagrams of faults by means of a half arrow symbol.
- On geological maps, the downthrow side of a fault is shown by means of a tick on the downthrow side of the outcrop of the fault plane.

Faults can be described using a set of technical terms:
- Fault plane: the plane of fracture, along which the rocks have been displaced
- Throw: the vertical displacement of rocks along the fault plane
- Fault dip: the maximum inclination of the fault plane as measured from the horizontal
- Hanging wall: the rocks that lie above the fault plane if the fault is not vertical
- Footwall: the rocks that lie beneath the fault plane if the fault is not vertical
- Upthrow: side of the fault where the movement is upwards in relation to the other side
- Downthrow: side of the fault where the movement is downward in relation to the other side.

Fault planes are not always simple fractures. There is often a relatively narrow zone of shattering along the fault. This area of the fault zone may become a route for mineralising fluids or water.

Fault types

Faults are divided into those with largely vertical movement, dip-slip faults, and those with largely horizontal movement, strike-slip faults.

Dip-slip faults

Dip-slip faults are where the movement along the fault plane is parallel to the dip of the fault plane. There are two main types: normal faults (the result of tension) and reverse faults (the result of compression). These faults often have a steep dip and their outcrop pattern is usually straight.

Normal faults

The Earth's crust is being stretched and close to the surface, where the rocks are cold and brittle, they fracture to form a normal fault. In a normal fault the hanging wall is the downthrow side. Extension of the crust is the result of the tensional (pulling apart) forces. This causes a lengthening of the crust and in cross-section there is clearly a gap created in the formerly continuous beds of rock. The downthrow side of the fault sinks under the influence of gravity. The principal stress direction forming these faults is vertical forces due to the weight of overlying rocks, with the minimum stress being horizontal tensional forces.

Graben and horst

Where two normal faults face each other, that is dip towards each other, then a graben or rift valley is formed. The graben is the area that forms the downthrow between the two faults. Rifts occur at the centre of mid-ocean ridges and form the East African Rift Valley system.

Where two normal faults face away from each other, that is dip away from each other, a horst structure is formed. The horst is the block uplifted between two faults.

Reverse faults

These faults are formed by compressional forces, which cause a shortening of the Earth's crust. In a reverse fault the hanging wall is the upthrow side. Reverse faults can be recognised because there is an overlap of the strata created by the fault movement, causing a repetition of the formerly continuous bed. The principal stress direction forming these faults is horizontal compressional forces, with the minimum stress being vertical. This suggests that these faults form relatively close to the Earth's surface where there is less overlying rock.

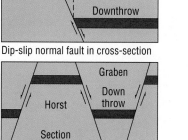

Dip-slip normal fault in cross-section

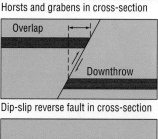

Horsts and grabens in cross-section

Dip-slip reverse fault in cross-section

Dip-slip thrust fault in cross-section

Figure 3 Faults types cross-sections

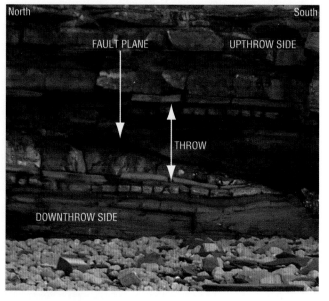

Figure 4 A thrust fault

Thrust faults

Thrust faults are a type of reverse fault, where the fault dip is less than 45 degrees. They are formed by compressional forces. These structures are often associated with major fold mountain systems and have displacements which can be measured in kilometres (in some cases hundreds of kilometres). In northwest Scotland the Moine Thrust brings Precambrian rocks over 560 Ma to rest above Cambrian rocks less than 560 Ma. This fault formed in the Caledonian orogeny. Thrusts can result in inverted strata, particularly when they form on the limb of a fold.

Questions

1 Study the photo of the normal fault in Figure 2 and state the downthrow side, the dip of the fault plane and the throw. Measure the angle of dip in the fault of Figure 4.
2 What is the difference between a fault and a joint?
3 Draw labelled cross-section diagrams to show the difference between normal and reverse faults.

Strike-slip faults

These are the faults where the fault plane is vertical and the movement along the fault is horizontal – parallel to the strike of the fault plane. These faults are often large-scale structures, with large displacements. There are two main types: tear fault and transform fault.

Tear fault

A tear fault is the result of shearing forces applied to the rocks. A large-scale example is the Great Glen Fault in the Highlands of Scotland. This fault is thought to have a displacement of around 100 km and was produced as part of the formation of the Caledonian mountains. One piece of evidence used to recognise this fault is the existence of two granite bodies on either side, which are similar in composition, age and structure. These granites are now located at either end of the Great Glen on opposite sides of the fault.

When describing a tear fault, the terms dextral and sinistral are used. These terms reflect the sense of movement along the fault plane. If the block of rock on the opposite side of the fault has moved to the right then it is described as dextral (right-handed) and if it has moved to the left then it is described as sinistral (left-handed).

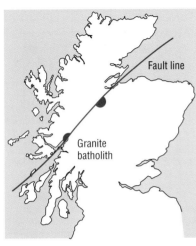

Figure 1 The Great Glen fault displacing a granite batholith

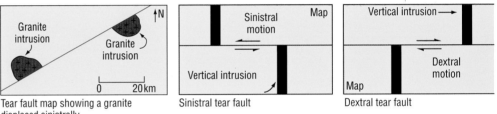

Tear fault map showing a granite displaced sinistrally

Figure 2 Tear fault maps

Transform faults

Transform faults are associated with plate margins and often described as conservative plate margins. They are common at right angles to a mid-ocean ridge (MOR). They can be thousands of kilometres long and can be seen on the map on page 26. They are the result of different rates of movement within a plate and allow the rigid plates to adjust for these differences in the rate of movement. Superficially they resemble tear faults but when the movements along the fault plane are considered, they are clearly a different type of fault. The diagram shows how a transform fault can be distinguished from a tear fault.

Figure 3 A dyke displaced by a tear fault (red line)

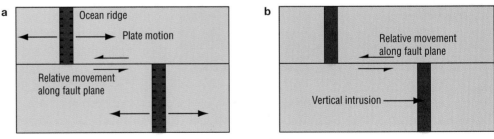

Figure 4 Distinguishing **a** a transform fault from **b** a tear fault.

Features associated with fault planes

Slickensides

Slickensides are scratch marks found on fault planes. They are left by the grinding of pieces of rock along the fault plane as the fault moves. They are best seen where the fault plane is coated in a mineral precipitated from a fluid that moved along the fault plane. The two surfaces are polished with linear grooves and ridges parallel to the direction of movement. Therefore the striations show the direction of the last movement along the fault plane.

Fault breccia

This rock is found along fault planes and consists of fragments broken from the rocks on either side of the fault plane (which is often a zone rather than a simple plane). The fragments are large and angular and made of hard, competent rock. They may be cemented by minerals precipitated in the fault zone at a later stage.

Examiner tip

On geological maps and in the field, faults can be most easily recognised where rocks of different ages or types have been brought together. The fault may stand out as a feature because the rocks on either side erode at different rates. Fault planes are sometimes lines of weakness that can be exploited by erosion, and valleys along a fault may result, such as the Great Glen.

Figure 5 Photos of fault breccia and slickensides

Figure 6 Fault zones

Key definitions

Slickensides is the polishing and striations found on a fault plane indicating the direction of relative movement.

Fault breccia is composed of fragments produced by rocks fracturing during faulting.

Questions

1 The photo above shows a number of faults close together. What forces produced these structures? Draw a fully labelled sketch with appropriate measurements to show structural features from Figure 6.
2 Explain why small earthquakes regularly occur along transform faults at MORs.
3 Research information on two large-scale faults: the Great Glen fault in Britain and the San Andreas Fault in California. What do they have in common and how do they differ?

A fold is a flexure in rocks, where there is a change in the amount of dip of a bed. All folds are produced by **compressive** forces acting horizontally, so are usually formed at convergent plate margins. Hard, brittle rock may fold and not break if the stress is applied slowly and continuously over a long period of time. They can be small-scale structures found over a few metres in a single outcrop or on an enormous scale over tens of kilometres. There are two broad categories:

- An upfold is **anticlinal** or an **antiform**, with dips pointing outwards. It is an anticline if the ages of the rocks are known, and an antiform if describing the shape only.
- A downfold is **synclinal** or a **synform**, with dips pointing inwards. It is a syncline if the ages of the rocks are known, and a synform if describing the shape only.

Describing folds

gentle   the inter-limb angle is between 180 and 120 degrees
open   the inter-limb angle is between 120 and 70 degrees
closed   the inter-limb angle is between 70 and 30 degrees
tight   the inter-limb angle is less than 30 degrees
upright   the axial plane is vertical
inclined   the axial plane dips
symmetrical   symmetrical about the axial plane
asymmetrical   not symmetrical about the axial plane

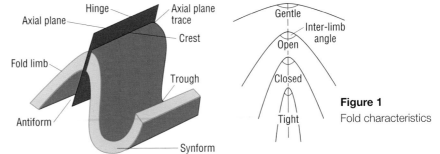

Figure 1
Fold characteristics

The axial plane bisects a fold but in a cliff face, quarry or cross-section diagram can only be seen as a single line. The axial plane trace can usually only be seen on a map in the centre of a fold. In some cases folds can be seen in 3D in the field, and you can walk along the axial plane trace.

Recognition of folds

An anticline is an upward closing fold, where the oldest rocks are in the core of the fold. Conversely, a syncline is a downward closing fold, where the youngest rocks are in the core of the fold.

An anticline has the dip arrows pointing out from the axial plane trace.

A syncline has the dip arrows pointing in to the axial plane trace.

Symmetrical folds are symmetrical about the axial plane and have limbs of the same length and thickness.

Asymmetrical folds are not symmetrical about the axial plane, and have limbs of different length or thickness.

In an upright fold the axial plane is vertical, whereas in an inclined fold, the axial plane is inclined.

Case study

Take a piece of modelling clay and form it into a bar. On one surface mark a series of circles – these will show the strain in the rocks (as we saw with ooliths in spread 1.4.1). Bend the bar into a fold. The circles towards the outside of the fold will be elongated parallel to the shape of the fold, while those near the inside of the fold will be elongated at right angles to the pressure.

An alternative process can be demonstrated using a pack of cards. Draw two bedding planes across the pack and then produce a fold – the fold is formed by a series of small movements as each card moves slightly with respect to those adjacent to it. This process is called shear folding and is common in incompetent rocks. In practice, both of these processes operate together.

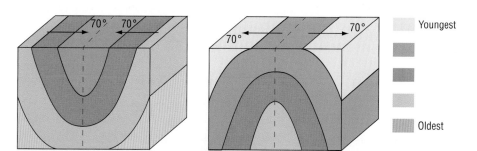

Figure 2 Symmetrical syncline and anticline

Figure 3 The fold is a symmetrical anticline formed by gentle compression

Figure 4 An inclined anticline formed by large compressive forces

Questions

1 Describe how you would tell the difference between a symmetrical anticline and an asymmetrical syncline.
2 Make a detailed labelled sketch of Figure 3 using technical terms and measurements.
3 By using as many as possible of the technical terms given in the text, fully describe the fold in the photo in Figure 4.

Domes and basins

The outcrop of a dome or basin on a geological map is circular or oval. These structures are anticlines and synclines, which dip in all directions. Domes have beds which dip outwards in all directions and basins have beds which dip inwards in all directions.

If the top of a dome is eroded away, the result will be a series of concentric strata with the oldest rocks exposed at the centre.

Because the strata dip towards the centre, the rocks in a basin will have the youngest rocks in the centre.

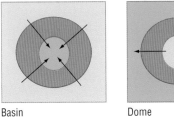
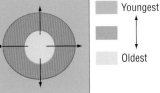

Basin   Dome

Youngest

Oldest

Figure 1 Domes and basins

Overfolds

These structures are characterised by having both fold limbs dipping in the same direction, but by different amounts. They result from compressional forces. The axial plane is inclined. Overfolds can be either anticlinal or synclinal.

One of the limbs of the fold is the correct way up, while the other is inverted – turned upside down. This can be identified by observing way-up structures in the rocks. One example of a way-up structure, which can be used to determine if the fold limb is the correct way up or not, is graded bedding, where the heaviest/largest particles are at the bottom of a bed.

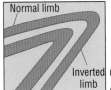

Normal limb

Inverted limb Cross-section
0 2 m

Figure 2 Overfold

Increasing the pressure

Most of the folds covered in this spread develop as pressure increases. The sequence starts with:
- an asymmetrical fold
- more pressure forms an overfold and the steeper limb will be inverted
- still more pressure makes a recumbent fold which again has an inverted limb
- if the pressure increases still more then the recumbent fold may break, forming a nappe with a thrust fault on one limb.

Figure 3 Photo of recumbent fold

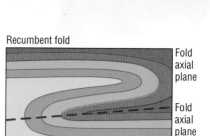
Recumbent folds

These folds are a step further than overfolds, as they are formed by high compressive forces. In this case, the axial plane of the fold and its limbs are close to horizontal and always less than 30 degrees. The photo in Figure 3 shows a series of anticlines and synclines, stacked up on each other. The rocks are usually incompetent or plastic, in order to absorb such high levels of stress. Recumbent folds are generally a feature of fold mountain ranges. They can be recognised by:

- Both the limbs and the axial plane will be at very low angles.
- One limb of the recumbent fold is inverted.

Nappe

Nappes form some of the world largest tectonic features. They are huge recumbent folds that have broken along **thrust planes**. Movement along the thrust plane is horizontal and part of the fold has been moved forward along the thrust. The top of the fold can be tens of kilometres away from the lower part of the fold. These are large-scale structures found in fold mountain ranges such as the Alps.

Isoclinal folds

Isoclinal folds can be recognised by parallel limbs that are nearly vertical and in very tight folds. The axial planes are usually vertical. They can be recognised on maps by outcrops of repeated and parallel beds.

Structures on photographs

Recognising minor structures as well as folds and faults is important. When compression creates folds some beds will fracture while others bend. This means that on a photograph of a fold or fault you are likely to have joints and often mineral veins or cleavage. You always have beds and bedding planes. The thickness of a bed of clay may change between the limbs and the core because the clay is plastic and will be forced out of some areas.

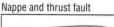
Recumbent fold

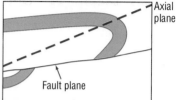
Nappe and thrust fault

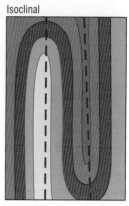
Isoclinal

Figure 4 Fold types

Questions

1 Draw simple cross-sections to show the differences between a basin and a dome.
2 Describe the characteristic features of overfolds and recumbent folds.
3 Identify, describe and draw labelled sketches of the folds shown in the photos below.

Figure 5 Folds for question 3

Cleavage is a feature of rocks containing platy minerals. Platy minerals include clay minerals and micas, with a long thin shape. When these align, they form a series of planes along which the rock tends to split.

The origin of cleavage

Incompetent sedimentary rocks such as mudstone contain many clay minerals. When these rocks are heated and compressed, the minerals begin to recrystallise. They usually recrystallise as micas or mica-like minerals with a distinctive platy form. Recrystallisation causes a change in the rock so it is no longer a mudstone but altered by low grade metamorphism to a slate.

These platy minerals are recrystallising and growing in an environment where there is a strong stress field, so they will tend to grow in the direction of least resistance. This is at right angles to the stress field which means that all of these platy minerals form roughly parallel to each other. They are also parallel to the axial planes of the folds, which result from the applied stress.

On the normal limb of the fold, the bedding dips at a lower angle than the cleavage. On the inverted limb, the opposite is true, that is the dip of the bedding is steeper than the dip of the cleavage.

Key definitions

Cleavage is **planes of weakness** in a rock along which the rock will split.

Cleavage forms in **incompetent sedimentary rocks** such as shale or clay made from clay minerals.

Incompetent means that the rocks are plastic and do not fracture.

Cleavage forms **perpendicular** to the maximum pressure that forms a fold, so is at an angle to the bedding planes.

Examiner tip

Cleavage is only found in incompetent rocks. Competent rocks, such as igneous rocks or limestones often have a crystalline structure. This does not allow particles to change direction under pressure. Similarly, sandstones have rounded grains that simply rotate under pressure.

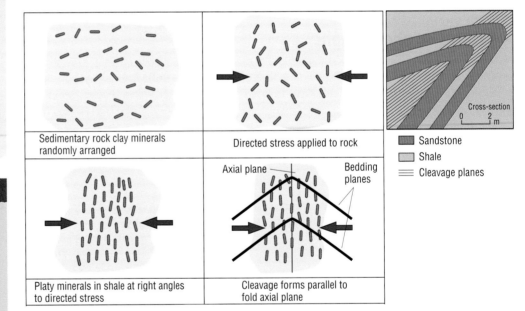

Sedimentary rock clay minerals randomly arranged

Directed stress applied to rock

Platy minerals in shale at right angles to directed stress

Cleavage forms parallel to fold axial plane

Axial plane

Bedding planes

Cross-section
0   2
└──┘ m

■ Sandstone
□ Shale
≡ Cleavage planes

Figure 1 The formation of slaty cleavage

Slate

Few materials share such high levels of resistance to weather, pollutants and freeze-thaw weathering. Slate is impermeable and splits into thin sheets along cleavage planes, which makes it ideal as a roofing and paving material as well as for floors and work surfaces.

Case study

Strands of spaghetti make a useful simulation for cleavage. Clay minerals are so small that you need a very high powered microscope to be able to see them. The spaghetti strands have a broadly similar shape, so react in the same way as clay minerals. In the photos, the particles are clearly aligned at right angles to the pressure.

Figure 2 Spaghetti and cleavage

The photo shows part of a fold in which the competent beds have been folded and slaty cleavage has developed in the rocks. The rocks in this case are muddy sandstones. The beds are dipping towards the left-hand side and the cleavage is nearly vertical. The cleavage is formed by platy minerals in the rock, which formed when the clay minerals were altered by heat and pressure and recrystallised as micas. The mica minerals are aligned perpendicular to the pressure forming the fold and parallel to the fold axial plane.

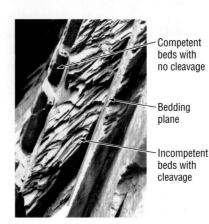

Competent beds with no cleavage

Bedding plane

Incompetent beds with cleavage

Figure 3 Cleavage planes at an angle to the beds

	Bedding	Jointing	Cleavage
How to recognise structures on photographs and diagrams	Differences in colour or composition between beds	Fractures along which there is no displacement	Rock splits easily along parallel planes, making slates
	Differences in grain size between beds	Often perpendicular to bedding	Often parallel to the axial plane of folds
	Structures within the beds and along the bedding planes	Possible mineralisation along the joints	Planes very close together – a few mm
Type of rock they form in	All types	Only develops in **competent** rocks, such as sandstones or limestones	Only develops in **incompetent** rocks, such as shales, which contain platy clay minerals and micas

Questions

1 Draw an overfold and a recumbent fold and add cleavage planes in the correct places.
2 Explain why sandstone composed only of quartz will not develop cleavage.
3 Create a summary table of structures produced by compression and those formed under tension.

Geological structures can be used to prove that one rock is older or younger than another. This is called age relationships. In some areas there are no fossils or minerals suitable for radiometric dating, and so using cross-cutting structures can be the best way of deducing these age relationships. We can use beds, faults, folds and unconformities to put together the geological history of an area.

Geological maps show us what is going on at the surface where the different rocks outcrop. Cross-sections may be seen in quarry faces, coastal cliffs or road cuts, or they may be calculated from the evidence from surface outcrops. A block diagram shows surface features like a map on the top and cross-sections on the sides.

(a) Block diagram

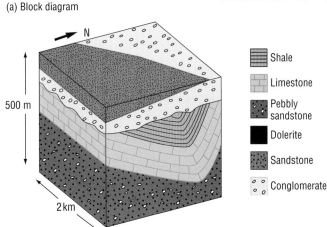

Shale

Limestone

Pebbly sandstone

Dolerite

Sandstone

Conglomerate

Using cross-cutting relationships to deduce the age relationships

In the block diagram (Figure 1a) there is a clear sequence of events shown:

1 The first event is the lower sequence of rocks, which were laid down with the pebbly sandstone first, followed by the limestone and then the shale.
2 These beds were folded into a synclinal fold.
3 The area was eroded, leaving an uneven top.
4 The conglomerate was laid down unconformably horizontally on top of the eroded sandstone.
5 The sandstone, which is the youngest rock, was laid down.
6 The area was tilted to the southeast, followed by more erosion.

(b) Cross-section

Bed 4

Plane of unconformity

Bed 3

Bed 2

Bed 1

Fault

In the top map view of the block diagram, only the unconformable beds can be seen to outcrop, while in the cross-section the older beds are visible.

A different cross-section (Figure 1b) shows:

1 Beds 1 to 3 have been folded into a syncline.
2 They are then cut by a fault, which is the younger structure because it cross-cuts the beds and fold.
3 Finally, an unconformity developed after erosion and bed 4 was laid down. This cuts across the fault, which means that the unconformity is the youngest feature.

(c) Map

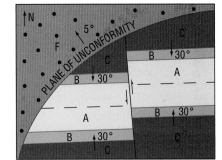

On the map of a different area (Figure 1c), the same ideas can be seen, though they look very different:

1 The beds formed first, with C being the oldest, then B and A.
2 A symmetrical synclinal fold formed with both limbs dipping north and south at 30 degrees and the axial plane trace trending west–east.
3 The fold was cut by a strike-slip fault that has displaced the axial plane trace of the fold, without the outcrop width of the fold changing. The fault is sinistral.
4 Erosion followed and bed F was laid down as an unconformity. This cuts across all other features, so is the youngest structure.

Figure 1 Cross-cutting relationships in block diagram and cross-section

Examiner tip

To identify folds on maps from outcrop patterns:
- If the dip arrows point inwards and the youngest beds are in the centre, it is a syncline.
- If the dip arrows point outwards and the oldest beds are in the centre, it is an anticline.
- If the width of beds outcrop is the same on both limbs of the fold, it is symmetrical.
- If the width of beds outcrop is different on both limbs of the fold, it is asymmetrical.

Recognising strike-slip faults from outcrop patterns on maps

Faults can easily be identified on maps where they displace the beds. It is difficult or impossible in most cases to identify specific dip-slip faults. However, it is straightforward to identify a strike-slip fault where it has cut across a fold. There are two key methods:

- If the axial plane of the fold is displaced, horizontal movement must have taken place. This is also true if a vertical dyke is displaced by the fault.
- If the outcrop width of the beds on either side of the fault is the same, no vertical movement has taken place.

Determining upthrow and downthrow of faults on maps

The downthrow side of a fault is normally where the younger rocks are found. It is more complicated if the rocks have been folded. When the movement of the fault is vertical, as in a normal fault, then the axial plane trace of a fold will not be displaced. There is a rule you can apply:

- If a fault displaces the axial plane trace of a syncline, the width of the centre bed of the outcrop will be wider on the downthrow side.
- If a fault displaces the axial plane trace of an anticline, the width of the centre bed of the outcrop will be narrower on the downthrow side.

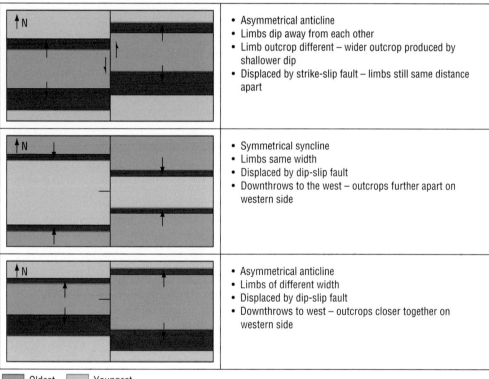

- Asymmetrical anticline
- Limbs dip away from each other
- Limb outcrop different – wider outcrop produced by shallower dip
- Displaced by strike-slip fault – limbs still same distance apart

- Symmetrical syncline
- Limbs same width
- Displaced by dip-slip fault
- Downthrows to the west – outcrops further apart on western side

- Asymmetrical anticline
- Limbs of different width
- Displaced by dip-slip fault
- Downthrows to west – outcrops closer together on western side

⬛ Oldest ⬜ Youngest

Figure 2 Recognising faults and determining upthrow and downthrow of faults using maps

Questions

1 Draw a diagram to show a map view of a symmetrical anticline that has been displaced by a vertical fault at a right angle to the axial plane trace.

2 Draw a diagram to show a map view of a strike-slip fault that has cut across a dyke. The movement should be sinistral.

3 Draw your own cross-section to show at least five events, which should include beds, folding, faulting and unconformities. You could have two different faults or unconformities. Write a geological history for your cross-section.

4 Draw a field sketch of the faulted fold in the photo to show the geological features. Use technical terms to label it and indicate the age relationships of the structures.

Figure 3 Photo showing a faulted fold in incompetent rock

1 The diagram below shows a cross-section through the lithosphere.

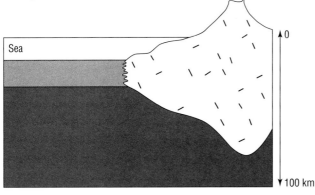

Figure 1

(a) (i) Copy the diagram in Figure 1 and label the Moho, continental crust and oceanic crust. [3]

(ii) Complete the table to show the characteristics of oceanic and continental crust.

	Age of the oldest rocks	Average composition	Average thickness (km)	Density g/cm³
Oceanic				
Continental				

[4]

(b) Explain how evidence from meteorites helps us to infer the nature of the inner and outer core. [3]

(c) (i) What is the increase in temperature with depth called? [1]

(ii) State one reason why the asthenosphere has a lower earthquake wave velocity than the rest of the mantle. [1]

(iii) Name the rock that is believed to form the asthenosphere. [1]

(d) (i) Name two other planets that are believed to have a dense metallic core like Earth's. [2]

(ii) Explain why all the inner planets are believed to have a similar structure. [3]

Total 18

(OCR 2831 January 03)

2 (a) (i) On the cross-section of the Earth in Figure 2, label
- mantle
- outer core
- path of an L wave from the epicentre at **A**
- path of a P wave from the focus at **B** [4]

(ii) Describe the pattern of seismic waves and arrival times on seismogram **C** compared to seismogram **D**. [4]

(iii) Name the zone between epicentral angles 103° and 142°. [1]

(iv) Explain why this zone exists. [2]

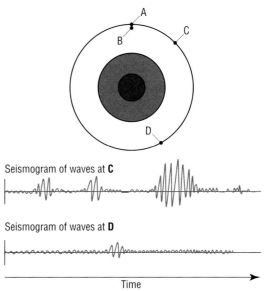

Seismogram of waves at **C**

Seismogram of waves at **D**

Time

Figure 2

(b) Earthquakes occur along well defined zones in the Earth's crust.

(i) Describe **two** plate tectonic settings where earthquakes frequently occur. [2]

(ii) Name **one** tectonic setting where earthquakes are very unlikely to occur. [1]

(c) Describe **two** measures designed to reduce the impact of the effects of earthquakes on buildings. [2]

Total 16

(OCR 2831 May 04)

3 (a) (i) Define the term earthquake *focus*. [1]

(ii) Define the term *seismogram*. [1]

(b) Sites **A** and **B** are both 15 km from the epicentre of an earthquake.
At Site **A** the earthquake intensity was 3 (III)
At Site **B** the earthquake intensity was 7 (VII)
The earthquake was magnitude 4.6.

(i) Describe how earthquake intensity is measured. [1]

(ii) Describe how earthquake magnitude is measured. [1]

(iii) Suggest why the intensity varies between Sites **A** and **B**. [2]

(c) Describe how earthquakes may be predicted by seismic gap theory. [2]

Total 8

4 (a) For each of the tectonic features **G** to **K**, write the number of the correct description.

	Tectonic feature
G	Seamount
H	Rift valley
J	Continental slope
K	Transform fault

	Description
1	Structure that offsets a section of mid-ocean ridge
2	Section of the ocean floor that links the continental shelf with the abyssal plain
3	An area of shallow sea, less than 200 m in depth
4	A linear area of the crust bounded by two normal faults
5	Submarine mountain

[4]
(OCR 2831 May 06)

(b) (i) What name is given to the type of plate margin shown on the map of Iceland.

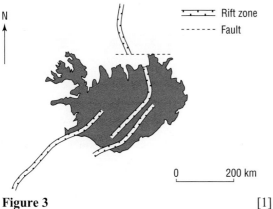

Figure 3 [1]

(ii) Describe where the youngest rocks are found and the direction of movement. [2]

(iii) The rocks in the north-east part of Iceland have been displaced by a major fault. What type of fault is it? Measure the amount of displacement. [2]

(c) (i) The diagram below shows the results of a magnetic survey of the ocean floor to the south-west of Iceland.

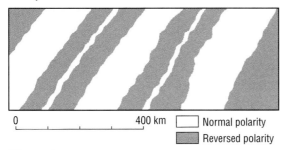

Figure 4

A sample of rock recovered 300 km from the ridge has been dated at 9 Ma. Calculate the rate of spreading in centimetres per year. [2]

(ii) Identify where the axis of the ocean ridge is on the diagram and give a reason for your choice. [2]

(iii) Explain why the junctions between the regions of normal and reversed polarity are irregular. [2]

(d) Draw a cross-section across an oceanic–continental convergent plate margin and label the following features: trench, Benioff zone, volcanoes, batholiths, fold mountains and the direction of movement. [6]

Total 21

(OCR 2831 May 02)

5 (a) (i) The cross-section diagram below shows a fault displacing beds.

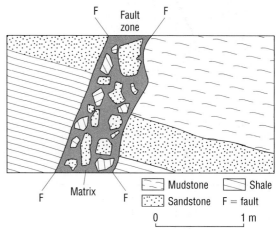

Figure 5

Name the type of fault shown and explain how it formed. [2]

(ii) Measure the angle of dip of the fault. [1]

(b) (i) Name the material shown within the fault zone. Explain how the angular blocks form. [2]

(ii) State the technical term for the polished surfaces and striations that are found along the fault planes. Describe how they form. [2]

(c) (i) Draw and fully label a cross-section diagram of an overfold with cleavage planes. [3]

(ii) Draw and fully label a cross-section diagram of a recumbent fold cut by a thrust. [2]

Total 12

(OCR 2831 May 04)

6 With the aid of diagrams describe the nature and formation of: tectonic joints, cooling joints, angular unconformities and slaty cleavage. [8]

7 Describe **four** pieces of evidence for the movement of continents by continental drift. [8]

(OCR 2831 May 04)

Rocks, and the minerals from which they are made, are vitally important. They provide a great many of the raw materials for things we need and use in our everyday lives, from bricks to metals. They also contain a record of the history of our planet. This record can be read if we understand something about rocks and the processes that form them.

Rocks seem permanent and unchanging. In fact they are changing slowly all the time. Igneous, metamorphic and sedimentary rocks, although different from one another, have all been produced by processes that occur as part of the rock cycle over millions of years. The Earth is 4500 million years old and some rocks have been round the rock cycle several times.

Key definitions

Extrusion is the emission of magma onto the Earth's surface where it forms a lava flow.

Weathering is the breakdown of rocks *in situ*.

Erosion is the removal of weathered material, usually by the physical action of transported fragments.

Transport is the means by which weathered material is moved from one place to another by water, wind, ice or gravity.

Deposition is the laying down of sediment that occurs when a transporting agent loses energy.

Burial occurs when sediment is covered by younger layers of sediment accumulating on top if it.

Diagenesis defines all processes that take place in sediments at low temperature and pressure at or near the Earth's surface.

Recrystallisation is the solid state process that changes minerals into new crystalline metamorphic minerals.

Metamorphism is the changing of rocks in the Earth's crust by heat and/or pressure and/or volatile content. It is isochemical and occurs in the solid state.

Partial melting is the incomplete melting of rock in the lower crust or upper mantle.

Magma accumulation is magma collecting within a magma chamber.

Crystallisation occurs during the cooling of magma or lava so that solid mineral crystals form.

An **intrusion** is igneous rock formed below the Earth's surface. The magma can be forced into pre-existing rocks, for example, either along bedding planes and joints, or by cutting across the existing rocks.

Uplift is the return of buried rocks to the Earth's surface by tectonic forces.

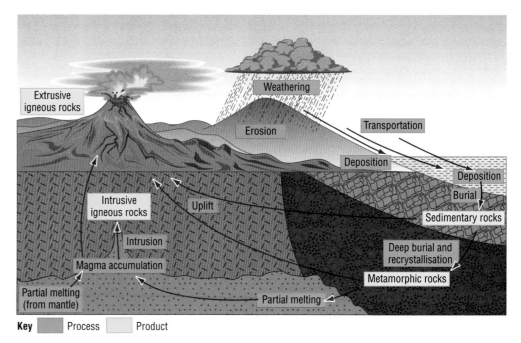

Figure 1 The rock cycle: a sequence of processes that links all three rock groups

Processes at the Earth's surface

Igneous processes

Magma, a hot melt from within the Earth's crust or upper mantle, may be erupted onto the surface as lava flows. If the eruption is more explosive, solid fragments called pyroclasts are produced. This process forms **extrusive** igneous rocks. The lava and solid fragments begin to cool at the surface. The lava becomes rock when crystals form from the magma and it becomes solid. The process is called **crystallisation**.

Sedimentary processes

Weathering takes place when rock is exposed to the Earth's atmosphere and water. Rain, temperature changes and plants among other things, start to break it down *in situ* by mechanical, chemical and biological processes. Fragments and soluble compounds that are produced by weathering are removed by **erosion**, which wears down the Earth's surface by the mechanical action of the weathered fragments. The fragments and soluble compounds are transported from one place to another by gravity, running water, ice, wind and the sea. The fragments are often reduced in size by collisions during **transport**.

Transporting agents lose energy sooner or later. The velocity of the wind may be reduced or a river may flow into a calm sea or lake. When this happens, **deposition** takes place.

Processes below the Earth's surface

Sedimentary processes

Deposition of sediment usually, although not always, occurs in lakes, oceans and seas. **Burial** occurs as sediment is covered by more and more layers of sediment deposited on top:

- As the sediments are buried more deeply they become compacted. This means that the grains of sediment are moved into closer contact, due to the pressure of the sediment above them.
- Water that circulates between the grains of sediment deposits minerals in the spaces between the grains. These and other changes that occur in buried sediments are part of the process of **diagenesis**.
- The growth of minerals in pore spaces and the compaction of grains result in the formation of sedimentary rocks.

Many sedimentary rocks are buried even more deeply as more material is deposited above them. Pressure and temperature increase as they move to greater depths inside the Earth.

Earth movements

Rocks can be exposed at the Earth's surface if they are **uplifted** by tectonic processes. Earth movements push rocks up by folding or faulting, so that rocks formed deep below the surface are now at the surface. Erosion over millions of years will expose rocks. In Cornwall, the granite that forms Dartmoor crystallised at least 10 km below the surface and erosion over 200 Ma has removed all the overlying rocks.

Metamorphic processes

Metamorphism is the process by which rocks in the Earth's crust are changed by the effects of heat and/or pressure. The process is described as isochemical. This means that the chemical elements in the metamorphic rock are the same as those in the parent sedimentary rock. Metamorphism involves **recrystallisation**, a solid-state process by which existing minerals are changed into new crystalline metamorphic minerals.

No melting takes place during metamorphism.

Igneous processes

Melting is caused at depths where temperatures are high enough, but different minerals have different melting points so that part of the rock may melt whilst some is still solid. This is known as **partial melting** and occurs in the lower crust and upper mantle. It is the process by which magma forms.

Figure 3 Partial melting takes place along grain boundaries, rather like the melting of ice cubes in a glass

Magma begins to form where crystal grains melt along their contacts

Because it is hot and expanded, magma has a lower density than the rocks surrounding it and this causes it to rise and join with other rising magma. This **magma accumulation** creates underground magma chambers.

As the magma rises it forces its way into pre-existing rocks, either along bedding planes and joints or by cutting across the existing rocks. This is **intrusion**. The magma cools, because temperatures within the Earth decrease with decreasing depth below the surface. **Crystallisation** may take place below the surface rather than above it and igneous rocks formed below the Earth's surface are also described as intrusions, or as intrusive igneous rocks. The rock cycle is completed when lava and pyroclasts are extruded at the Earth's surface to form extrusive igneous rocks.

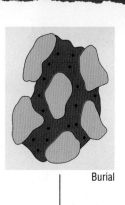

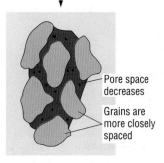

Burial

Pore space decreases

Grains are more closely spaced

Figure 2 Grains move closer together as they are more deeply buried, becoming more compact and with less pore space between them

Questions

1 Write a definition of the term *rock cycle*.
2 Describe how sediment becomes sedimentary rock.
3 Describe how the formation of metamorphic rocks differs from the formation of igneous rocks.

Minerals are used to help classify sedimentary, igneous and metamorphic rocks. However, before dealing with the classification of rocks, we need to know exactly what rocks and minerals are.

Rocks and minerals

All **rocks** are composed of minerals. A **mineral** is a naturally occurring chemical compound having a definite composition and crystalline structure. The rock forming minerals are those that form most of the rocks. There are other minerals, such as the metallic minerals, which are important for their economic value. Most rock forming minerals are silicates, the main exception being calcite, which forms the sedimentary rock limestone and the metamorphic rock marble.

Quartz   Feldspar

Mica   0   5
mm

Quartz, feldspar and mica are all minerals that are essential components of the rock granite

Figure 1 Thin section diagram showing that rocks are made of minerals

Well formed crystals of quartz, a common rock forming mineral.

Feldspar is commonly white or pink and has vitreous lustre

Quartz found in rocks almost always has no regular crystalline shape and looks like grey broken glass

Metallic lustre is common in some ore minerals but not in rock forming minerals

Figure 2 Characteristics of minerals

Characteristics of rock forming minerals

Minerals have physical characteristics that can help geologists to recognise them.

Habit

The habit, or shape of some mineral crystals, can be very distinctive. Cubic crystals such as halite and fluorite are easy to recognise. Garnet is a complex shape based on a cube forming a dodecahedron. The hexagonal shape of quartz can be seen in the photo. Some mineral crystals grow in pairs and are said to show twinning. This can be a feature of feldspars.

Colour

Colour can be used to identify some minerals, but this is not very reliable as some minerals can occur in several different colours. Colour is used to distinguish between the two micas – muscovite is pale grey and biotite is black. Quartz can be purple, pink, grey, yellow, white or clear, so colour is not diagnostic. Streak is the colour of the powder of a mineral. Most silicates have a white streak, which does not help to distinguish between them. Galena is a lead grey colour and the streak is the same colour, while iron pyrite is brassy yellow but the streak is black.

Key definitions

A **thin section** is a thin (0.03 mm) slice of rock that is translucent, mounted on a glass slide and viewed through a microscope.

Rock is an aggregate or mixture of one or more minerals.

Minerals are naturally occurring inorganic crystalline compounds with a definite chemical composition.

Hardness

The hardness of minerals is measured on Mohs' scale of hardness. It measures resistance to scratching. Hard minerals scratch softer ones.

Mohs' scale of hardness		
Hardness	**Reference mineral**	**Common objects**
1 (soft)	Talc	Scratched by fingernail
2	Gypsum	
3	Calcite	Scratched by 2p coin
4	Fluorite	Scratched by steel nail
5	Apatite	
6	Feldspar	Can just be scratched with steel nail
7	Quartz	Scratch glass
8	Topaz	
9	Corundum	
10 (hard)	Diamond	

Cleavage and fracture

Some minerals have cleavage planes, which are planes of weakness in their atomic structure. Cleavage may be termed perfect, good or poor depending on how easily it splits along a cleavage plane. In minerals like muscovite, cleavage is perfect in one direction so that the mineral splits into thin sheets. There may be more than one direction of cleavage and the angles made between cleavage planes can also help in identification. Calcite has cleavage in three directions not at right angles.

Minerals that break along an irregular surface tend to fracture. They do not have cleavage because the bonds between atoms are strong. This is fracture. Sometimes the fracture is a series of concentric curved cracks, rather like a broken glass bottle, which is called conchoidal fracture. A mineral with cleavage planes may also fracture if it breaks along a direction that is not a cleavage plane.

Lustre

The surface appearance of a mineral is described as its lustre and depends on its ability to reflect light. Minerals that are shiny like metal have metallic lustre. Minerals that are dull are described as earthy. Most rock forming minerals have vitreous lustre, like glass.

Specific gravity

Specific gravity is the ratio of the mass of a mineral compared with the mass of an equal volume of water. Because it is a ratio it has no units. Quartz has a specific gravity of 2.65, meaning that the mass of a volume of quartz is 2.65 times the mass of the same volume of water. Pale coloured minerals have S.G. of around 2.7; barite has S.G. 4.5; mafic minerals S.G. 3.3 and metallic minerals S.G. of 5.0 and over.

Reaction with acid

Calcite reacts strongly with dilute HCl. This is a very good way to distinguish it from other pale coloured vitreous minerals.

Mica has perfect cleavage in one direction

Calcite has perfect cleavage in three directions not at right angles

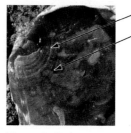

A conchoidal fracture is a series of concentric curved cracks

Figure 3 Cleavage and fracture

Questions

1 Describe one difference between rocks and minerals.
2 Describe how calcite can be distinguished from quartz.
3 Research the diagnostic properties of the rock forming minerals listed on the next page.

Pressure, temperature and rocks

The temperatures and pressures in the rock cycle produce the three broad classes of rocks. Igneous, sedimentary and metamorphic rocks are all formed under different pressure and temperature conditions in the rock cycle. The boundaries are actually zones where one rock grades into another. This can be seen with shale, a sedimentary rock, and slate, a metamorphic rock, which form at very similar temperatures and pressures.

- The boundary between the diagenesis of sediments and metamorphism, which occurs under conditions of higher temperature and pressure, is gradational.
- The boundary between metamorphic and igneous rocks is where partial melting occurs. Metamorphic rocks recrystallise in the solid state but igneous rocks crystallise from magma.

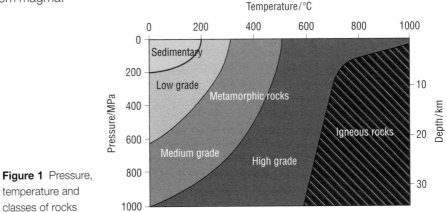

Figure 1 Pressure, temperature and classes of rocks

Igneous, sedimentary and metamorphic rocks

Rocks are classified according to the way they are formed.

Sedimentary rocks

These rocks form at relatively low pressure and temperature at shallow depths below the Earth's surface. Existing rocks exposed at the Earth's surface are broken down by weathering and erosion. The rock cycle diagram (see 2.1.1) shows that broken fragments of these rocks and ions in solution are transported usually to the oceans by rivers. The energy of the water decreases when it spreads out, where rivers enter the oceans, and the fragments of rock are deposited on the ocean floor.

Over millions of years more and more fragments are deposited, buried and compacted into layers to make sedimentary rocks for example sandstone. Many **sedimentary rocks** are made up of **clasts** (fragments or grains) held together by cement, rather than interlocking crystals. The grain size of clasts can vary considerably. Other sedimentary rocks are biologically formed from the remains of organisms, or chemically formed by the precipitation of ions from sea water. Sedimentary rocks may contain fossils of plants, animals or the traces of animal activity. They are usually built up in layers, or beds.

Igneous rocks

Igneous rocks are formed from magma (liquid rock) within the Earth. They may form at high or low pressures depending on depth, but they all form at high temperatures. Magma eventually cools to form igneous rocks composed of interlocking crystals. The mineral crystals do not usually have any preferred alignment. There are two main types of igneous rocks.

- Intrusive (hypabyssal or plutonic) igneous rocks – these have medium crystal size if the magma cooled fairly slowly at intermediate depths, for example dolerite, or coarse crystal size if the magma cooled slowly at greater depth inside the Earth's crust, for example granite. The minerals are hard **silicates**, such as quartz and feldspar, and separate mineral crystals can be seen in the rock.

Key definitions

A **clast** is a fragment of broken rock.

Sedimentary rock is a rock composed of fragments that have been deposited compacted and cemented

Igneous rock is a rock that has crystallised from a magma.

Silicates are the most important and abundant group of rock-forming minerals, with an atomic structure containing SiO_4 arranged as tetrahedra.

- Extrusive (volcanic) igneous rocks - these have a fine crystal size because the magma reached the Earth's surface. Erupted as lava or ejected as fragments, it cooled rapidly, producing rocks such as basalt or pumice. Individual crystals cannot usually be seen.

Metamorphic rocks

Within the Earth rocks may be subjected to heat or pressure – or both. This causes their texture and mineral composition to change. Minerals in the original or parent rock recrystallise in the solid state to form new minerals. This means that **metamorphic rocks** are composed of interlocking crystals, but they often show preferred alignment if they have been affected by pressure. There are three main types of metamorphism: burial, contact and regional. If they contain flat crystals, rocks affected by pressure as part of burial or regional metamorphism show **foliation**. Foliated layers commonly contain mica. Metamorphic minerals tend to be hard silicates but marble is composed of calcite, a carbonate mineral.

	Igneous	Sedimentary	Metamorphic
Texture	Crystalline. Minerals interlocked in a mosaic	Fragmental. Made of grains/fragments or fossils cemented together	Crystalline. Minerals interlocked in a mosaic
Mineral alignment	Crystals have no preferred alignment	Grains not usually lined up	Crystals aligned, show foliation if affected by pressure
Main minerals	Quartz. Plagioclase and potash feldspar. Hornblende (amphibole). Augite (pyroxene). Olivine. Micas, muscovite and biotite	Quartz. Potash feldspar. Calcite. Mica, mainly muscovite. Clay minerals. Rock fragments	Quartz. Plagioclase and potash feldspar. Micas, muscovite and biotite. Garnet. Calcite. Al_2SiO_5 polymorphs
Formation	Crystallised from magma	Deposition of rock and mineral particles	Recrystallisation of other rocks
Features	As igneous intrusions – dyke, sill, batholith or lava flow, no beds	In beds	Large areas or zones – no beds
Fossils	None	May be present	Usually none, deformed if present
Ease of breaking	Hard and does not split	May be soft and crumbly but some sedimentary rocks are difficult to break if well cemented	Hard but may split in layers
Thin sections	Quartz / Potash feldspar / Biotite	Quartz grains / Cement — 1 mm	Garnet / Quartz / Muscovite — 0 2 mm

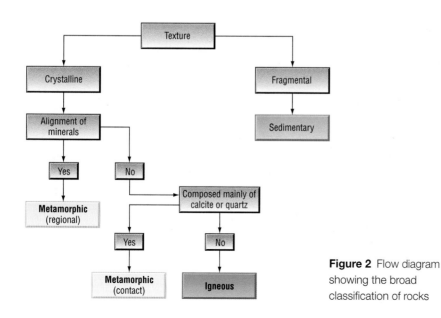

Figure 2 Flow diagram showing the broad classification of rocks

Questions

1 A rock specimen has crystalline texture and shows preferred mineral alignment. Name the class of rocks to which it belongs.

2 A rock specimen contains calcite and well preserved fossils. Name the class of rocks to which it belongs.

3 Name two minerals that are found in igneous rocks only and one that is found in metamorphic rocks only.

A geological timescale

The **geological column** is a table arranged in order of time. It is the time framework used by geologists.

Era	System		Age (Ma)
Cenozoic	Neogene		
	Palaeogene		65.5
Mesozoic	Cretaceous		
	Jurassic		
	Triassic		251
Palaeozoic	Permian		
	Carboniferous		
	Devonian		
	Silurian		
	Ordovician		
	Cambrian		542
Precambrian*			
			4500

*Precambrian is a traditional term that is widely used to refer to rocks older than Cambrian. It is not an era or system name.

Figure 1 The geological column

All the divisions in the first column are **eras**. They are geological time units. All the divisions in the second column are **systems**. They refer to rocks formed during a particular interval of time.

Key definitions

The **geological column** is a table that contains all the eras and systems in the correct time sequence.

An **era** is a major unit of time that contains several periods/systems.

A **system** refers to rocks laid down in a named time period and is shorter than an era.

Case study

William Smith was the son of an Oxfordshire farmer. As a boy, he picked up stones covered with shells from the ploughed fields. It developed into a hobby – fossil collecting. William qualified as a surveyor at the time when canals were being built to transport coal. Work took him to coal mines and excavations for the new canals.

It gave him a great opportunity to add to his fossil collection. When he saw large numbers of fossils on a rock surface he recognised it as a collection of creatures that had lived for a short time on the sea floor. He realised that a series of layers had been deposited and that fossil groups in the lower layers were older than those in the upper layers. Arranging the fossil faunas in his collection according to the layers in which they were found, he discovered that they were not all the same. Some fossils were present in many layers but others in only a few. He was the first to recognise that fossil faunas succeeded one another in a definite order.

Within 25 years of his discovery, all but one of the geological systems was defined, with fossils being used to establish time relations. In 1831, he was presented with a medal by the Geological Society and described as 'the father of English geology'.

Dating principles

The geological column shows the relative ages of rocks and dates from absolute dating.

Relative dating

Relative ages use comparisons rather than years. The Jurassic system is pre (earlier than) Cretaceous and post (later than) Permian. The main relative dating principles are:

- The law of superposition states that sedimentary layers are deposited one on top of the other, so that the higher layers are younger than the lower ones.
- The law of original horizontality states that all sedimentary rocks were originally laid down in a nearly horizontal position.
- The law of cross-cutting relationships states that faults or igneous intrusions must be younger than the rocks they cut through.
- The principle of included fragments states that any sedimentary rock that has fragments of another rock in it must be younger than the included rock fragments.

Relative dating is something you do every time you look at a sequence of rocks in the field, on a photograph or on a geological map. You decide which rock is the youngest and which is the oldest using these principles.

Dating using fossils

A few fossils are very distinctive in particular systems. Ammonites, like the one in the photographs, are restricted to the Jurassic only. Therefore we can use fossils to say that a rock belongs to a particular system. If we understand the sequence of fossils we can say whether one rock is younger or older than another.

Figure 2 Younger and older. As you walk to the left you are walking into older and older rocks along the base of the cliff

Figure 3 Mesozoic ammonite and Palaeozoic trilobite

Absolute dating

Absolute dates of rocks for all the geological systems can be obtained using the principle of radioactive decay. Radiometric dating methods are used to put actual dates on the geological column. For example, it is now known that the Cambrian system contains rocks that are between 542 and 488 millions of years (Ma) in age.

Questions

1 Describe the difference between relative and absolute dating.
2 Name the system that is pre-Permian and post-Devonian
3 Explain how relative dating principles are used to obtain a correct time sequence for igneous and sedimentary rocks.

Classification of igneous rocks

Igneous rocks make up about 95% of the Earth's crust. You will see sedimentary rocks at the surface in most places in the United Kingdom while deeper in the crust the rocks are all igneous and metamorphic.

The classification of igneous rocks can be complex with internationally agreed classifications based on chemical analysis or proportions of the minerals present. These methods require time-consuming microscopic analysis of thin sections or expensive measurements. Neither of these methods helps to identify igneous rocks in the field. Therefore, the older simple system based on observation of the physical characteristics remains in common use. You will be using observations of the mineral composition, the crystal size and the silica percentage and colour of the rocks.

Crystal grain size

The easiest way to classify igneous rocks is by observing crystal grain size. The grain size can tell us a great deal about the cooling history of the rocks and this link to their origin is covered on the next pages. For the purpose of classification, igneous rocks are divided on the basis of the average crystal size. This means looking at all the crystals in a specimen and ignoring any very large crystals called phenocrysts. If no crystals can be seen, even using a hand lens, the rock has a glassy texture showing it cooled too quickly for any crystals to form.

- Fine grained crystals are less than 1 mm in size so that individual crystals cannot be identified by eye.
- Medium grained crystals are 1 to 5 mm in size and can be seen by eye.
- Coarse grained crystals are greater than 5 mm in size and can be seen and identified by eye.

Silica percentage

Chemical analyses give the overall chemical composition of a rock, rather than which minerals are present. The majority of SiO_2 in igneous rocks is not present as quartz (SiO_2), but is contained within other silicate minerals such as feldspar and olivine.

It is easier to link the SiO_2 percentage to colour as a short cut to identification. The mafic rocks are rich in dark-coloured ferromagnesian minerals such as olivine and augite. Silicic rocks are rich in the light-coloured minerals quartz and feldspars. But colour can be misleading in rocks such as obsidian, which looks black but is clear in thin section and is a silicic rock.

Mineral composition

Igneous rocks usually contain many different rock forming minerals but only a few essential minerals are used in classification.

Felsic minerals

The **felsic minerals** are quartz and feldspar, which are both rich in silica. The term felsic comes from the words feldspar and silica.

Case study

You cannot see the silica content in the field, and measuring SiO_2 percentages requires laboratory work. Most modern analyses are carried out using an X-ray fluorescence analyser (XRF), where a beam of fast-moving electrons is directed onto a sample. The X-rays that are given off by the different kinds of atoms are detected. The mass % is given as oxides of SiO_2, TiO_2, Al_2O_3, FeO, MnO, MgO, CaO, Na_2O, K_2O and P_2O_5. Silica is by far the most abundant oxide found during chemical analyses – its content varies between 40 and 75%.

Quartz	Recognising quartz in igneous rocks	Mineral characteristics of quartz
An important essential mineral only found in silicic or intermediate rocks. The magma must be oversaturated with silica so that excess silica is left after the other rock forming minerals crystallise to form the quartz	It is very different from looking at an individual crystal – it looks grey in colour and has an amorphous shape as all the crystals grew in an enclosed space. If you look at it with a hand lens you will see the glassy appearance and lack of any smooth cleavage surfaces. You will also find that quartz crystals resist scratching with a steel nail	Hardness 7 Colour white, grey or transparent No cleavage Vitreous lustre (glassy) Composition SiO_2

Examiner tip

Learn the classification table using name and description cards with specimens or photos. If you know the table then you can answer nearly all the questions on igneous rocks.

Silica percent is not the same thing as the mineral quartz. Quartz is made entirely of silica (SiO_2) but the silica percent includes the silica in all the rock forming minerals. A rock with no quartz will contain silica because it is contained within silicate minerals such as olivine.

Feldspars	Recognising feldspars in igneous rocks	Mineral characteristics of feldspars
The feldspars are the most common rock forming mineral in igneous rocks. They form about 60% of the minerals in these rocks so are essential to igneous classification. The main types of feldspar are potassium feldspar and plagioclase feldspar. Potassium feldspar (orthoclase) is only found in silicic and intermediate igneous rocks so is a good mineral to use for classification. It is often found as large phenocrysts as well as in the groundmass of granite.	The pink colour of most K feldspar makes it very easy to identify. Grey or white feldspar is plagioclase. If you look at it with a hand lens you will see the glassy appearance and smooth cleavage surfaces. Feldspar crystals can just be scratched with a steel nail	Hardness 6 Colour pink for K, white or grey for plagioclase Good cleavage in two directions Vitreous lustre (glassy) Composition $KAlSi_3O_8$

Mafic minerals

These are minerals that contain both magnesium and iron, so the term **mafic** comes from the words magnesium and ferric (iron). These minerals are also referred to as ferromagnesian.

Biotite and muscovite mica	Recognising biotite and muscovite mica in igneous rocks	Mineral characteristics of biotite and muscovite mica
The micas are biotite, found in silicic or intermediate rocks, and muscovite, found in silicic rocks only	Shiny black crystals of biotite can be easy to identify though the silvery flakes of muscovite are more difficult to pick out and need a hand lens. Micas can be scratched with a copper coin and are the only minerals in igneous rocks that are soft enough for this test	Hardness 2.5 Colour of biotite is black and muscovite silvery One perfect cleavage that makes flakes Vitreous lustre (glassy)

Hornblende, augite and olivine	Mineral characteristics of hornblende (amphibole)	Mineral characteristics of augite (pyroxene)	Mineral characteristics of olivine
Hornblende is one of a group of minerals called amphiboles, which are particularly common in intermediate rocks. They are not easy to identify in hand specimen and can easily be confused with augite. Augite belongs to the pyroxene group of minerals and is one of the main minerals in mafic and ultramafic rocks. Olivine is found in some mafic and ultramafic rocks. It will only form when the magma is undersaturated in silica.	Hardness 5.5 Colour black Two cleavages at 120°, forming six-sided crystals Vitreous lustre (glassy)	Hardness 5.5 Colour black to dark green Two cleavages at 90°, forming eight-sided crystals Vitreous lustre (glassy)	Hardness 6.5 Colour light green No cleavage Vitreous lustre (glassy)

Using all the methods described, an igneous classification table can be created that makes the identification and description of igneous rocks possible.

Key definition

Mafic minerals are dark coloured, silica poor and rich in magnesium and iron.

SILICA CONTENT

Grain size	Mode of origin	>66% Silicic	52–66% Intermediate	45–52% Mafic	<45% Ultramafic
		Colour ———————————————————————→
		Light			Dark
Glassy	Volcanic extrusive	Obsidian**			
Fine <1 mm	Volcanic extrusive	Pumice Rhyolite	Andesite	Basalt	
Medium 1–5 mm	Minor intrusion Hypabyssal			Dolerite	
Coarse >5 mm	Major intrusion Plutonic	Granite Diorite Granodiorite		Gabbro	Peridotite
		Quartz	Quartz (rare)		
		Potassium feldspar	Potassium feldspar		
		Plagioclase feldspar (Na)	Plagioclase feldspar	Plagioclase feldspar (Ca)	
		Biotite	Biotite	Augite	Augite
		Muscovite	Hornblende	Olivine	Olivine

** NB Obsidian is an exception to the rule, being silicic but dark in colour

Questions

1. Give one difference and one similarity for each of the following pairs of igneous rocks:
   (a) basalt and dolerite;
   (b) andesite and rhyolite;
   (c) granite and gabbro.
2. Why is obsidian black?
3. Describe how you would distinguish between silicic and mafic igneous rocks.

Crystal grain size

Examining crystals in igneous rocks is one of the quickest ways to identify rocks in the field or from samples. The rate of cooling is the main factor that controls crystal size. The general rule is **the slower the rate of cooling, the larger the crystal size**.

However, there are other factors that can be important. Where an intrusion is large, the inside of the intrusion will cool more slowly than the outer part. This is because it is better insulated and it will lose heat more slowly.

If a large intrusion cooled at a depth of 1 km, it could have a range of crystal grain sizes from fine at the edges to coarse in the centre.

Crystal grain size and depth of cooling

The table shows how size of crystal is related to speed of cooling and where cooling takes place.

	Glassy	Fine	Medium	Coarse
Crystal grain size	No crystals	Crystals are <1 mm so individual crystals cannot be seen by eye	1–5 mm in size, so individual crystals can be seen by eye but are difficult to identify	Crystals are >5 mm, so can be seen and identified in hand specimens
Rate of cooling	Forms very quickly – in hours, usually in the sea as water is the quickest way of cooling magma	Forms due to rapid cooling over weeks or months	Fairly slow cooling over a few thousand years	Cools very slowly over millions of years
Where	At the surface – they are always volcanic **extrusive**	At the surface in **extrusive** volcanic rocks as lava flows. In chilled margins at the edges of minor intrusions	Below the surface, in minor intrusions, ~1 km down (**hypabyssal**)	Found in major intrusions at great depth >10 km down, as batholiths or **plutonic** rocks

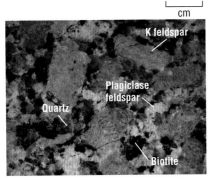

Figure 1 Photo of granite labelled to show grey quartz, pink K feldspar, white plagioclase and black biotite

Case study

It can be difficult to see individual minerals in a hand specimen so a very thin slice 0.03 mm of a rock is sawn, ground and glued to a microscope slide. Using an ordinary microscope, just the outline of the crystals can be seen but in polarised light the minerals have very distinctive colours. Photos taken through a microscope are called photomicrographs. Often drawings of photomicrographs are used to illustrate the rock texture, as in Figure 2.

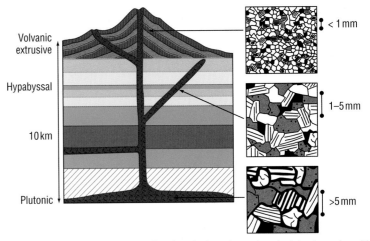

Figure 2 Cross-section through volcanic, hypabyssal and plutonic rocks with photomicrograph drawings of fine, medium and coarse crystal grain size

Glassy texture

If lava flows into the sea, cooling can be very rapid – in minutes on the outside of the flow. The inside could still be molten. This is why some pillow lavas show a layered structure with glass on the outside and fine crystals inside. Where cooling is rapid, there may be no time for crystals to form. Obsidian forms in this way. It looks black because light will not pass through it but in a thin section it is a clear glass.

Figure 4 Obsidian arrow head which appears black but would be clear glass in thin section

Figure 3 Photomicrograph of a plutonic mafic igneous rock in polarised light

```
0          0.5
|          |
     mm
```

Pegmatites

A pegmatite is an igneous rock that has exceptionally large crystals. The crystals are normally larger than a few centimetres and can often be tens of centimetres or even metres long. Pegmatites form in the last stages of crystallisation from the water-rich residual magma. The pegmatite crystals of quartz, K feldspar and muscovite grow in a supersaturated solution. Pegmatites can produce large crystals in a short (geologically) period of time.

Figure 5 Photo of a pegmatite

Examiner tip

Drawings of igneous crystal grain sizes are often used in exams or you may be asked to draw one. In igneous rocks the crystals are interlocking angular shapes so drawing rounded grain shapes is not correct.

How to grow a giant crystal

By allowing a saturated solution of copper sulfate to evaporate slowly to dryness, you will get a number of small copper sulfate crystals. Choose a large crystal and tie cotton around it and suspend this seed crystal in a saturated solution of $CuSO_4$. You will need to keep the solution topped up with $CuSO_4$, but with patience over a few weeks, a large crystal several centimetres in size can be grown.

Questions

1 Explain how you would distinguish between a hypabyssal and a plutonic rock.
2 Use hand specimens or photos of rocks to measure the crystal grain size for a variety of rocks. What difficulties did you find in measuring accurately?
3 What is the largest crystal ever found in an igneous rock?

Igneous rocks generally consist of interlocking crystals, which gives them a crystalline texture. Pyroclastic rocks will have a fragmental texture as they consist of fragments of glass, crystal and rock, as a result of explosive volcanic activity.

Igneous textures reveal a great deal about how a rock was formed, so are invaluable in helping determine the cooling history.

Equigranular texture

An equigranular texture simply means that all the crystals are of equal size but may all be fine, medium or coarse. The relationship of crystal size to cooling is the larger the crystal size, the longer the time of cooling:
- Fine grained crystals formed by rapid cooling at the surface are extruded.
- Medium grained crystals formed by slow cooling below the surface are hypabyssal.
- Coarse grained crystals formed by very slow cooling deep below the surface are plutonic.

Usually the crystal grain size can be related to the depth of cooling but there are exceptions:
- An intrusion that cooled 2 km below the surface will have medium grained crystals but will also have fine grained chilled margins at the edges which cooled rapidly.
- A lava flow that cooled at the surface will have fine grained crystals but if it is very thick then the centre of the flow may be medium grained.

Vesicular and amygdaloidal

Vesicular texture is where gas bubbles are trapped in lava as it cools rapidly, leaving holes where the gas was present. The holes, called vesicles, are usually oval or ellipsoid in shape and are also elongated parallel to the direction of flow. The gas rises so most vesicles are found near the top of the lava flow or sometimes at the edge of an intrusion. Vesicular texture is common in basalt and pumice.

Amygdaloidal texture is where vesicles are later infilled by minerals deposited from groundwater. A vesicular rock will be very porous so that groundwater can flow through it. The groundwater contains dissolved minerals such as calcium carbonate, so calcite will be precipitated into the holes. This can happen millions of years after the vesicular rock formed. The most common minerals are calcite or quartz but other minerals can be found. Each infilled hole is called an amygdale, though large ones, partially filled with crystals growing in towards the centre, are called geodes. It is common in basalt.

> **Examiner tip**
>
> Texture is the general character or appearance of a rock, shown by the arrangement of the minerals with the crystal shape and size. It does not refer to the roughness or smoothness of the rock's surface.

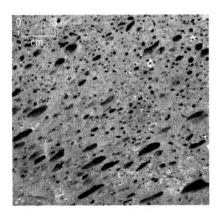

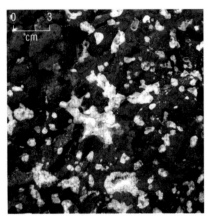

Figure 2 Vesicular and amygdaloidal basalt with white calcite crystals in the amygdales

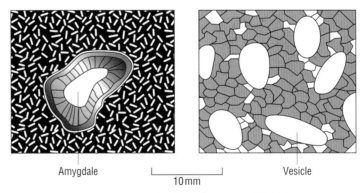

Amygdale |— 10mm —| Vesicle

Figure 1 Photomicrographs of vesicular and amygdaloidal texture

Flow banding

Flow banding occurs where layers of dark and light minerals form due to the separation of minerals within a silicic lava flow. They will be aligned parallel to the flow direction, though they are often contorted because the lava was viscous so flowed slowly. Flow banding is usually seen in **rhyolite**.

Porphyritic

A porphyritic texture forms where a rock has two stages of cooling and results in two distinct sizes of crystals. Large crystals are called phenocrysts and form first by cooling slowly. They are surrounded by a finer grained groundmass, which cooled more quickly. Porphyritic texture can be found in any igneous rock but it is common in porphyritic basalt and porphyritic granite, though each has formed at different depths.

In a porphyritic basalt the phenocrysts, often plagioclase feldspar, start to form slowly in the magma chamber below the volcano. When an eruption occurs, magma and plagioclase crystals are erupted to the surface where rapid cooling forms the fine grained crystals of the groundmass. Sometimes the phenocrysts will be aligned parallel to the direction of flow of the lava.

The phenocrysts in a porphyritic granite, often of potassium feldspar, start to form very slowly at great depths – perhaps 30 km. The magma and feldspar crystals move up within the crust by diapiric action to form a batholith at a depth of about 15 km. The rest of the magma then cools very slowly to form the coarse grained crystals of the groundmass.

Figure 3 Flow banding in a silicic rock with dark layers that are glassy with no crystals and lighter layers with very fine crystals

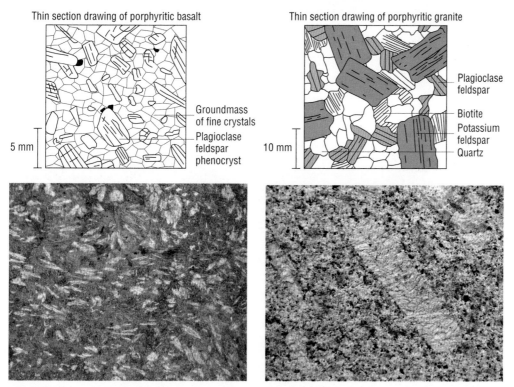

Figure 4 Thin section drawings and photos. Porphyritic texture in basalt (with phenocrysts aligned in direction of flow) and granite

Questions

1. Describe the difference in the rates of cooling in hypabyssal and plutonic rocks.
2. How does glassy texture form?
3. Explain why the large white crystals in a porphyritic basalt will have a different origin and composition to the large white crystals in an amygdaloidal basalt.

Identifying silicic and intermediate igneous rocks

Look for the following characteristics to identify an igneous rock in the field or hand specimen, or by using drawings or photos:

- crystal grain size to tell you the rate of cooling
- mineral composition and colour to help with the silica content
- igneous textures to tell you about the origin.

Silicic igneous rocks

High-silica magma contains 66 to 75% silica and is mainly generated by melting of the Earth's crust at convergent plate margins. Rocks formed from high-silica magma tend to have a lot of quartz and other high-silica minerals such as plagioclase and potash feldspar and muscovite and biotite micas. The colour should be light. Silica-rich magmas are very viscous, much stiffer than toothpaste, so little magma reaches the surface and granite is the most common silicic rock. These magmas solidify at relatively low temperatures, typically 600 to 900 °C.

Having identified that a rock belongs to the group of silicic rocks, look at the crystal grain size to identify the actual rock.

Examiner tip

Medium grained silicic rocks do exist, but they are not required for this specification. If they are equigranular they are called microgranite, if they are porphyritic they are called quartz porphyry.

	Obsidian	Pumice	Rhyolite	Granite and granodiorite
Crystal grain size	Glassy	Glassy shards and fine crystals	Fine crystals	Coarse crystals
Texture	Glassy with conchoidal fracture	Vesicular	Flow banded	Porphyritic or equigranular

0 5 mm

0 4 mm

0 5 mm

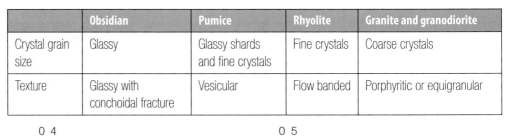

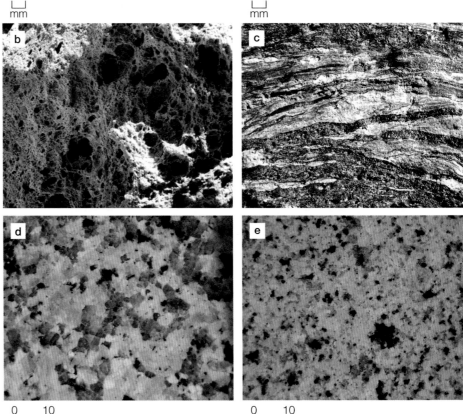

Figure 1 Photos showing characteristic minerals, crystal grain size and textures for:

a obsidian;
b pumice;
c rhyolite;
d granite;
e granodiorite

0 10 mm

0 10 mm

Intermediate igneous rocks

Intermediate magma contains 52 to 66% silica. The most common igneous rock formed from this type of magma is andesite, a fine grained volcanic rock. The coarse grained plutonic rock is diorite. They usually contain abundant plagioclase feldspar, together with dark ferromagnesian minerals such as the pyroxene augite and the amphibole hornblende, but little or no quartz. The magma is less viscous than a silicic magma but still very sticky (viscous). It solidifies at a higher temperature than a silicic magma. Andesites are common at convergent plate margins.

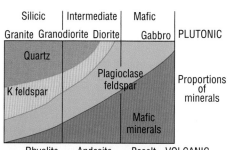

Figure 2 The distribution of rock forming minerals in igneous rocks

Figure 3 Lava showing a grey colour typical of intermediate rocks

	Andesite	**Diorite**
Crystal grain size	Fine	Coarse
Texture	Vesicular, amygdaloidal, porphyritic or equigranular	Equigranular or porphyritic

Chemical analysis of igneous rocks

In the early days of chemical analysis, rocks were broken down into different oxides and the amount of each oxide was weighed. For this reason, chemical analyses of igneous rocks have always been reported as weight percentages of oxides, rather than as separate elements. The table shows the variation of the eight main oxides in the four groups of igneous rocks.

As you saw in spread 2.2.1:

Weight % oxides	**Silicic**	**Intermediate**	**Mafic**	**Ultramafic**
SiO_2	70.8	62.5	49.0	41.7
Al_2O_3	14.6	17.6	18.2	0.9
Fe_2O_3	1.6	2.1	3.2	2.9
FeO	1.8	2.7	6.0	5.7
MgO	0.9	0.9	7.6	47.7
CaO	2.0	2.3	11.2	0.7
Na_2O	3.5	5.9	2.6	0.1
K_2O	4.2	5.2	0.9	0

Questions

1 Using the table of chemical analysis and spread 2.2.1 decide:
   (a) Which mineral contains potassium?
   (b) Which mineral contains most of the Al_2O_3?
   (c) Which mineral contains most of the MgO?

2 Name the rock with a coarse crystal grain size and a composition of SiO_2 73.9%, Al_2O_3 14.3%, Fe_2O_3 1.5%, MgO 0.8%, CaO 0.4%, Na_2O 3.5%, K_2O 4.5%.

3 Describe how you would distinguish between a gabbro and a basalt, and a granite and granodiorite.

Identifying mafic and ultramafic igneous rocks

Mafic igneous rocks

The first thing to look for in identifying a mafic rock is the colour, which should be dark due to the abundant ferromagnesian minerals. The minerals will be the pyroxene augite, and sometimes olivine with Ca-rich plagioclase but no quartz. Low-silica magma contains only 45 to 52% silica. This type of magma is easy to recognise from the analyses by low amounts of silica and large amounts of MgO and FeO. The magma has low viscosity so it easily reaches the surface, making basalt the most common mafic igneous rock. It solidifies at high temperatures above 1000 °C. Most low-silica magma is produced by melting of the Earth's mantle.

Once you have identified that a rock belongs to the group of mafic rocks, then look at the crystal grain size to identify the actual rock.

	Basalt	Dolerite	Gabbro
Crystal grain size	Fine	Medium	Coarse
Texture	Vesicular or amygdaloidal, or porphyritic or equigranular	Porphyritic or equigranular	Equigranular

Figure 1 Photos showing the differences between the mafic rocks: **a** vesicular basalt; **b** porphyritic dolerite; **c** equigranular gabbro

Case study

Geologists get very excited when the diamond miners bring up chunks of peridotite along with the diamonds. They might not be as valuable as the diamonds but they can tell us a great deal about the mantle. Kimberlite pipes are Precambrian volcanic pipes that brought magma up from great depths in the mantle – at least 250 km. The force of the eruption ripped fragments of mantle rock from the sides of the vent.

Using density to distinguish between the groups of igneous rocks

A simple practical activity using a displacement may be used to measure the specific gravity of rocks:

- Weigh a dry rock for each of the four igneous groups. (Avoid vesicular or amygdaloidal textures.)
- Fill a can so that water is just dripping out of the overflow.
- Carefully lower a rock into the can and catch the overflowing water in a measuring cylinder.
- Repeat for each of the rocks and calculate the densities.
- $\text{Density} = \dfrac{\text{weight of dry rock}}{\text{water displaced cm}^3}$

The answers should show a pattern of increasing density from about 2.7 g/cm³ for silicic rocks to 2.9 g for mafic and 3.3 cm³ for ultramafic.

Ultramafic rocks

These rocks contain less than 45% silica and consist almost entirely of ferromagnesian minerals. The most common ultramafic rock is peridotite, which forms much of the upper mantle. This is mainly olivine with some pyroxene and a small amount of Ca-rich feldspar. Some ultramafic rocks are monomineralic, meaning they consist of only one mineral.

Ultramafic rocks have extremely high melting points. Ultramafic magma does not exist on Earth at present, although in the Precambrian ultramafic lavas did exist, indicating that the Earth was hotter than at present. We can find ultramafic rocks from the mantle, where fragments have been brought up to the surface by volcanoes. The most famous of these are the kimberlite pipes of South Africa. Other peridotites are found as ophiolites in mountain ranges where a slab of oceanic crust has broken off at a subduction zone.

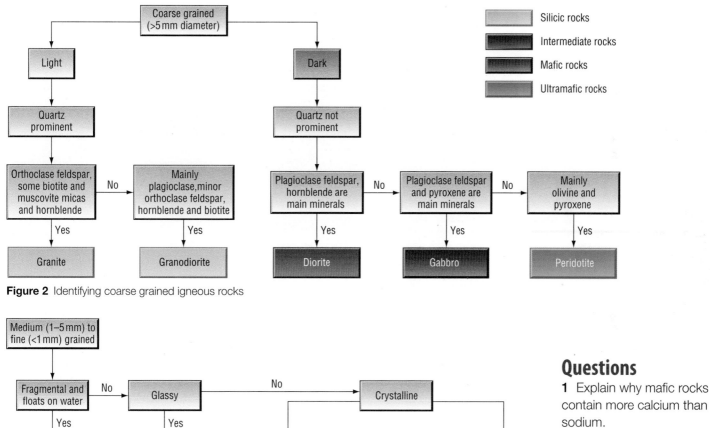

Figure 2 Identifying coarse grained igneous rocks

Figure 3 Identifying medium and fine grained igneous rocks

Questions

1 Explain why mafic rocks contain more calcium than sodium.
2 Describe the relationship between vesicular and amygdaloidal texture.
3 Describe how you would distinguish between basalt and dolerite, and gabbro and peridotite.
4 Look on the Internet for granite kitchen work surfaces. Are they really all granite? Can you identify the actual rock that is often called 'black granite'?

2.2 ⑥ Where does magma come from?

The Earth is solid for most of the crust, mantle and core and only the outer core is liquid. The geothermal gradient means that temperatures increase as you go further into the Earth. If the average geothermal gradient of 30°C per kilometre is applied to the melting of mafic rock, then you would expect molten rock at a depth of just 40 km. This does not happen due to another key variable – pressure. As the pressure increases with depth, rock needs higher temperatures to melt. Another variable is the presence of water in a rock, which decreases the temperature needed to melt.

Most magma is generated at active plate margins as one of the plate tectonic processes. You will need to remember the types of plate margins from spread 1.3.7 and 1.3.8.

Magma at divergent plate margins

Divergent plate margins are rarely seen at the surface, as mid-ocean ridges (MOR) are on the deep ocean floor. Iceland is one of the few places where rifting and magma can be seen. Oceanic crust is thin below an MOR with mantle rocks just 5 km below the surface. Partial melting of the ultramafic peridotite of the upper mantle produces mafic magma.

Key definitions

A **divergent plate margin** is where two plates are moving apart and magma is rising up between them.

A **convergent plate margin** is where two plates are colliding and magma is formed above a subduction zone or deep in the crust.

A **hot spot** is formed by a fixed mantle plume bringing magma to the surface.

Partial melting occurs where some of the minerals in a rock melt to form a magma.

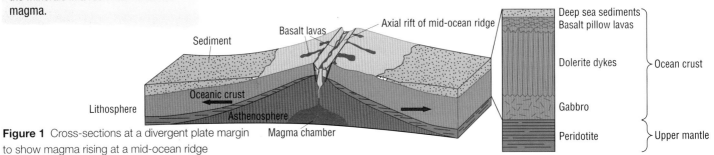

Figure 1 Cross-sections at a divergent plate margin to show magma rising at a mid-ocean ridge

Plate margin	Origin of magma	Composition of magma	Extrusive volcanic activity	Intrusive activity
Divergent (Mid-Ocean Ridge)	Partial melting of peridotite in asthenosphere	Mafic	Frequent eruptions submarine, fissure or shield Mainly non-viscous basalt lava, few pyroclasts Effusive non-violent eruptions	Dolerite dykes and sills below volcanoes
Convergent ocean–ocean	Partial melting of subducting oceanic plate	Mafic to intermediate	Regular but infrequent eruptions strato-volcano Lots of basalt lava with some pyroclastics and andesite Violent eruptions	Dolerite dykes and sills below volcanoes
Convergent ocean–continent	Partial melting of subducting oceanic plate Partial melting of continental crust and mixing of magmas	Intermediate and silicic	Irregular and infrequent eruptions Strato-volcano and lava domes Little lava, mainly andesite with some rhyolite, large amounts of pyroclasts Very violent eruptions of ash, agglomerate and ignimbrites	Dolerite dykes and sills below volcanoes Batholiths
Convergent continent–continent	Partial melting of deep continental crust	Silicic	None	Batholiths
Hot spots	Partial melting of peridotite in asthenosphere	Mafic	Frequent eruptions at shield volcano Mainly non-viscous basalt lava Effusive non-violent eruptions	Dolerite dykes and sills below volcanoes

Magma at hotspots

A similar process is operating at hot spots where mantle plumes rise from deep in the mantle and partial melting of mafic material results. Convection in the mantle slowly transports heat from the core to the Earth's surface. Mantle plumes carry the heat upwards in narrow, rising columns of hot material, which spreads out when the plume head meets the base of the rigid lithosphere. At this shallow depth lower pressures allow partial melting of mantle peridotite to form enormous volumes of basaltic magma. This basalt may erupt onto the surface over very short timescales (less than 1 million years) to form flood basalts.

If the plume provides a continuous supply of magma in a fixed location, it forms a hot spot. As the lithosphere moves over this fixed hot spot due to plate tectonics, the eruption of magma onto the surface forms a chain of volcanoes parallel to the movement of the plate. The Hawaiian island chain in the Pacific Ocean is a good example.

Magma at convergent plate margins

When two plates collide, magma will be generated. As a plate is forced down, the geothermal gradient increases and partial melting results. The reasons are different, depending on the type of plate margin.

Magma generated at an oceanic–continental plate margin

Where plates converge and the oceanic plate subducts, partial melting of the oceanic plate will produce magma. If the plate subducts and the magma rises quickly at shallow depths then it will be basalt. Often the magma rises through silicic continental crust and this may partially melt. The rising mafic magma may be at temperatures in excess of 1000°C and silicic material melts at just 800°C. The result is mixing of the mafic and silicic melts to give intermediate magma. The two components have different viscosities so mixing is difficult. Some of the magma will reach the surface to form intermediate volcanoes. Most will be intruded to form granite batholiths.

Magma generated at a continental–continental plate margin

Where two continental plates converge, neither continent will subduct. However, the high pressures and weight of sediments, which have been deformed to form fold mountains, combine to force the base of the crust down. As a result, the Moho is at its deepest below the highest fold mountains. Partial melting at the base of the continental crust will produce silicic magma. As continental crust is silicic and starts to melt at 800°C, this is the temperature below the mountains due to the geothermal gradient. As the magma rises it intrudes to form granite batholiths. There are no volcanoes present as the silicic magma is too viscous to rise to the surface.

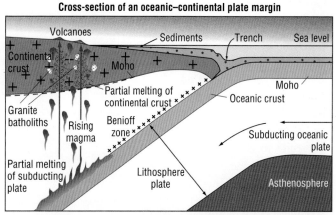

Cross-section of an oceanic–continental plate margin

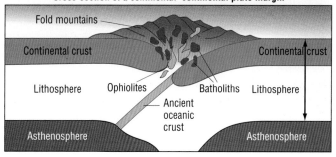

Cross-section of a continental–continental plate margin

Figure 2 Magma forming at convergent plate margins: oceanic–continental and continental–continental

Figure 3 Mountains and granite batholith

Questions

1 Draw your own simple cross-sections (not 3D) to show magma rising at a divergent plate boundary and an oceanic continental convergent plate boundary.
2 Describe how you could distinguish rhyolite from andesite.
3 Why are rhyolite and andesite lavas that are 430 Ma in age found in what is now North Wales?

What is magma? It is a mixture of minerals melted and mixed together with volatiles and water. The initial composition of magma may be mafic or silicic, but the concept of differentiation shows how different rocks can be produced from a single magma.

Bowen's Reaction Series

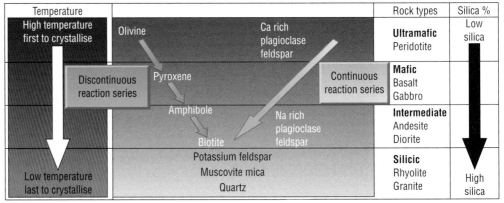

Figure 1 Bowen's Reaction Series

Bowen's Reaction Series

Norman L Bowen was an American geologist who, during the 1920s, carried out a series of experiments to find the temperatures at which minerals in igneous rocks crystallised. He used powdered rock that he heated until it melted and then cooled it down to a specific temperature and observed which minerals crystallised out. The result was Bowen's Reaction Series, which gives us the order in which minerals crystallise from a magma.

Norman L Bowen was an American geologist who, during the 1920s, carried out a series of experiments to find the temperatures at which minerals in igneous rocks crystallised. He used powdered rock that he heated until it melted and then cooled it down to a specific temperature and observed which minerals crystallised out. The result was Bowen's Reaction Series, which gives us the order in which minerals crystallise from a magma.

Discontinuous Series

The left-hand side of the diagram is called the Discontinuous Series. All these minerals are mafic minerals rich in iron and magnesium with silica. In a mafic magma, olivine will be the first mafic mineral to form at a high temperature (>1500 °C). As the temperature lowers, pyroxene (augite), then amphibole (hornblende) and finally biotite will form. If cooling takes place slowly then the early formed, high temperature minerals react with the magma to form the next mineral down in the series. For example, olivine reacts with the magma to form pyroxene if there is enough silica present. If the magma is cooled quickly when it is erupted from a volcano, then the reaction will not have time to occur and olivine is preserved. Often the reaction of one mineral with the next will be incomplete and a reaction rim will be seen around the edge of a crystal.

Continuous Series

The right-hand side of the diagram is the Continuous Series, showing the crystallisation of plagioclase feldspar. Plagioclase is calcium (Ca) rich at the high temperature end and sodium (Na) rich at low temperatures, with intermediate compositions of 50% Ca and 50% Na at temperatures in between. Plagioclase is continuously reacting with the liquid to form a more Na-rich crystal as the temperature decreases. Sometimes individual crystals of plagioclase will show zoning. The centre of the crystal is Ca-rich plagioclase and towards the edges the crystal is richer in Na-rich plagioclase and poorer in Ca.

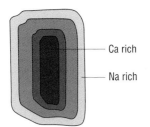

Figure 2 Zoned crystal of plagioclase feldspar. The crystal started growing when the temperature was high, at which Ca forms, and as the magma cooled the plagioclase crystal continued to grow with new layers forming, gradually becoming richer in Na

Plagioclase feldspar	Found in silicic rocks		Found in intermediate rocks		Found in mafic rocks
Found in all igneous rocks but has a continuous range of composition so that different forms are found in each of the groups of rocks. There is no observable difference between plagioclase feldspars in hand specimen, as all the minerals are white or grey with a vitreous lustre.	$NaAlSi_3O_8$ ⟶				$CaAl_2Si_2O_8$
	100% Na	75% Na	50% Na	25% Na	0% Na
	0% Ca	25% Ca	50% Na	75% Ca	100% Ca
	Sodium rich				Calcium rich

Knowing that Ca-rich plagioclase is only found in mafic and ultramafic rocks, while Na-rich plagioclase is found in silicic and intermediate rocks, means that they are used in classification of igneous rocks.

Low temperature minerals

When the two reaction series converge at a low temperature, minerals remain that will not react with the remaining liquid. This final group of minerals to crystallise are the felsic minerals rich in silica. These are potassium feldspar followed by muscovite mica and finally quartz at a temperature of about 700°C.

The importance of Bowen's Reaction Series

1 Figure 1 shows the igneous rock types that form at high and low temperatures. The pattern is clear:
   - Mafic rocks form at high temperatures as they contain olivine, pyroxene and Ca-rich plagioclase.
   - Silicic rocks form at low temperatures and contain quartz, muscovite, K feldspar and some Na-rich plagioclase and biotite.

2 The reaction series matches with the stability of minerals when exposed to weathering at the Earth's surface:
   - The minerals at the low temperature end of the reaction series are the most stable at the Earth's surface, because they formed in conditions closest to the low temperature surface environment. As a result the most common mineral in sedimentary rocks is quartz.
   - The high temperature minerals are most unstable and quickest to weather at the surface.

The processes of magmatic differentiation

Magmatic differentiation is a number of processes that cause a magma to evolve into magmas of different compositions. This leads to different igneous rocks being produced from a single parent magma. A mafic magma may crystallise to form ultramafic, basic, intermediate and even silicic rocks.

Fractional crystallisation

As olivine and pyroxene form at high temperatures, they use iron and magnesium from the magma. The high temperature plagioclase crystals are rich in calcium. The result is that the magma becomes depleted in iron, magnesium and calcium. The remaining liquid becomes enriched in silica, potassium, sodium and water because the early formed minerals are poor in these elements. Over time, the composition of the magma changes from the original.

Gravity settling

Generally crystals will be denser than the liquid in which they are suspended, so will settle out:
- Early formed minerals with a higher density than the surrounding liquid, such as olivine, sink to form a layer at the base of the intrusion.
- Gravity settling removes the crystals from the remaining liquid so they do not react with the remaining magma.
- A layer of dense, early formed minerals at the base of an intrusion or magma chamber is a **cumulate layer**.

Filter pressing

During the crystallisation of magma, there is a point where crystals and liquid exist together as a slushy mass. Due to the weight of the overlying crystals, the liquid gets squeezed out forming a separate layer above. This liquid is depleted in the elements incorporated into the early formed crystals and enriched in the elements which form felsic minerals.

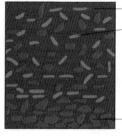
Magma
Plagioclase crystals
Olivine crystals

Figure 3 Gravity settling of dense olivine

Questions

1 Why will you never get olivine and quartz in the same rock?
2 If you were to melt a basalt containing augite, olivine and plagioclase feldspar (Ca-rich), which mineral melts first?
3 Which of the minerals in Bowen's Reaction Series would you expect to weather at the Earth's surface the most easily? Why?

The results of magmatic differentiation

What happens when molten rock becomes solid? As a magma crystallises, the crystals that form will have a different composition to the molten rock. When the crystals separate from the rest of the magma as they grow, the chemistry of the magma changes. A single magma could form ultramafic, mafic, intermediate and silicic rocks if there is enough time for differentiation to take place. If the parent magma is mafic then in theory it will produce:

- peridotite at the base of the intrusion, rich in dense olivine;
- gabbro forming the main part of the intrusion;
- diorite may exist towards the top of the intrusion;
- granite may form veins or a thin layer at the top of the intrusion.

In most cases intrusions are complex, with multiple injections of magma that may vary in composition. It is unusual to have a single volume of magma that crystallises in one period of cooling.

Major layered intrusions

These are large mafic or ultramafic igneous intrusions that cooled slowly below the surface so there was time for them to form distinct layers. Most of the world's platinum and chromium comes from layered intrusions, giving an added incentive to understand how they formed. Gravity settling is the key process in the formation of layers of magnetite, chromite and platinum.

The Palisades Sill

The Palisades Sill in New Jersey, USA outcrops along the Hudson River and is over 300 m thick. It was intruded into Triassic sediments at a depth of about 3 km, so that it cooled slowly and has now been exposed by erosion. The sill can be divided into three sections, each shows a different igneous process at work.

1 The only parts of the sill to cool rapidly are the upper and lower edges, which were in contact with the cold country rock. These chilled margins have fine grained crystals and most importantly have the same composition as the original magma because they cooled before any differentiation took place. The rock is a basalt.

2 As the main part of the intrusion began to crystallise, the early formed olivine crystals began to sink by gravity settling. Olivine has a density of 3.8 gm/cm^3 compared to 3.0 gm/cm^3 for a mafic magma. The olivine crystals form a layer 10 m thick at the base of the intrusion – just above the chilled margin.

3 Crystallisation was taking place from both the top and bottom of the sill as the crystals grew in the cooler areas. The main rock forming the intrusion is medium grained dolerite. The last part of the magma to crystallise is about 200 m above the base of the intrusion and is coarse grained gabbro because it cooled slowly. As a result of fractionation, the composition is lower in mafic minerals than the original composition because the magma is depleted in iron and magnesium by the time this rock forms. It is richer in plagioclase as the last part of the magma to crystallise is enriched in silica.

		% olivine	% pyroxene	% plagioclase feldspar	% silica
1	Chilled margin (original composition of magma)	3	50	47	51.8
2	Olivine-rich layer	25	38	34	48.2
3	Last formed part of the sill	0	30	65	52.9

The table shows the chemistry of the sill in each of these sections. The percentages do not add up to 100% because there are small amounts of other minerals present.

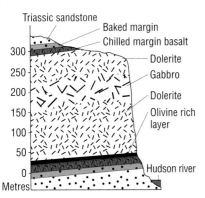

Triassic sandstone — Baked margin — Chilled margin basalt — Dolerite — Gabbro — Dolerite — Olivine rich layer — Hudson river

Metres 300 250 200 150 100 50 0

Figure 1 A cross-section of the Palisades Sill

How science works

Did the Palisades Sill form from a single injection of magma? Research is still going on and different theories have suggested two, three or even four separate injections of magma – but in every theory, fractionation is still a key process.

The Skaergaard Intrusion

The Skaergaard Intrusion in Greenland is one of the most studied in the world. It was intruded during the Tertiary, when the North Atlantic was opening, as a magma chamber for basalt volcanoes. Magma was probably intruded in a single injection into a huge conical intrusion.

The Skaergaard is divided into three major units:

1 The Marginal Border Series is a fine grained chilled margin that cooled rapidly. It is no longer the same composition as the original magma, as it has been contaminated by country rock. Crystals grew inwards from the sides of the intrusion.

2 The Layered Series shows rhythmic layering, most easily explained by crystal settling interrupted by periodic large-scale convection. A sequence of denser (olivine or pyroxene) crystals beneath lighter plagioclases is deposited by gravity settling. Then filter pressing causes the expulsion of the differentiated liquid. Then convection mixes the magma, and the process is repeated. Each cycle is more evolved due to the removal of the crystals in the rhythmic layers, resulting in **cumulates** forming from the floor upwards.

3 The Upper Border Series is thinner, but mirrors the 2500 m Layered Series with layers that crystallized from the top down.

Worked example: cooling rates

A mafic magma is at a temperature of 1450 °C when it is intruded. The geothermal gradient is 30 °C per kilometre. What will be the difference in temperature between the country rock and an intrusion at a depth of 5 km?

$1450 - (30 \times 5) = 1300 °C$

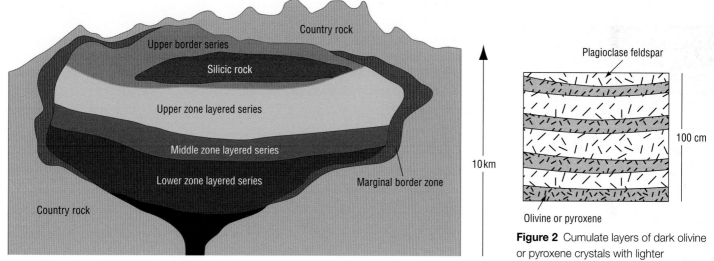

Figure 3 Possible interpretation of the structure of the Skaergaard Intrusion

Figure 2 Cumulate layers of dark olivine or pyroxene crystals with lighter plagioclase

Hekla Volcano

Hekla is a large volcano in Iceland near the central rift zone. The magma should be entirely mafic as Iceland is on a divergent plate margin, yet it erupts intermediate lava. The graph shows the longer the time between eruptions the more silicic the magma that is erupted. If there is a long interval between eruptions, fractionation in the magma chamber causes more mafic minerals, which crystallise at high temperatures, to be found at the bottom and felsic minerals at the top. Each eruption takes magma from the top of the magma chamber and then as the eruption progresses from lower in the magma chamber.

The 1947 eruption occurred after an interval of 102 years and initially erupted lava with a silica content of 63%, which formed a silicic rhyolite and as with all the eruptions ended up as intermediate andesite with a silica content of 54%.

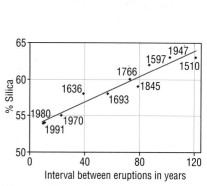

Figure 4 Time intervals between Hekla eruptions and the silica content

Questions

1 Describe the properties of minerals that will sink due to gravity settling.
2 Why will convection operate in large intrusions such as the Skaergaard?
3 There was an eruption of Hekla in 2000: what was the silica percentage of the initial melt?

Intrusive igneous rocks are those that crystallise below the Earth's surface, so intrusion is a process that cannot be observed. You can only see intrusive rocks after the rocks that used to lie above them have been eroded away. Most of the intrusive rocks that we see are millions of years old.

Intrusions are described as concordant where they are intruded along a bedding plane and discordant where they cross cut a bedding plane. When magma is moving up through **country rocks**, the intrusions will follow any line of weakness. This could be a fault, joint or bedding plane. Igneous intrusions are often found below areas of volcanism. The dykes extend from the magma chamber to the vents and are the feeders for the overlying lavas.

Minor intrusions

The word minor suggests that these intrusions are small, but many are not. Certainly some are small with dykes that are just a few centimetres wide but hundreds of metres long. Many minor intrusions are huge, such as the Palisades Sill, described in spread 2.2.8, which is 300 m thick, outcrops for 60 km and underlies thousands of km². The 100 m thick Whin Sill underlies a large area of northeast England and outcrops along the line of Hadrian's Wall:

- Most sills and dykes are made of the medium grained, mafic rock **dolerite**, except along the margins where chilling by the country rocks produces a finer grained basalt.
- Sills and dykes that have granite as a source will be made of porphyry or microgranite, which are both medium grained silicic rocks.

Sills

Sills are sheet-like intrusions that are concordant and parallel to the beds. Some sills occasionally cut across the beds in steps from one bed to another, to form **transgressive sills**:

- Sills are generally irregular with a variable width and a sinuous outcrop.
- They are usually intruded along bedding planes.

Sills are intruded when the fluid pressure is so great that the underlying magma actually lifts the overlying rocks. This means that sills usually form at shallow depths in the Earth where the weight of overlying rocks is not too great.

Dykes

Dykes are sheet-like intrusions that are **discordant** and often vertical:

- They range in size from a few centimetres to more than 100 m thick, and commonly are 1 to 2 m across.
- As most dykes are vertical they form straight lines in outcrop, forming long, thin features.
- They are often intruded along zones of weakness in the country rock, such as faults or joints.
- Dykes are common as feeder vents under volcanoes, so may have a radial pattern.

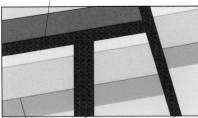

Concordant intrusion

Bedding plane   Discordant intrusions

Figure 1 Concordant and discordant intrusions

Key definitions

Minor intrusions cool at hypabyssal depth below the surface and include sills and dykes.

Major intrusions are plutonic and cool deep below the surface and include batholiths.

The **contact** is where the igneous rock meets the country rock.

Country rock is any rock that the igneous rock is intruded into.

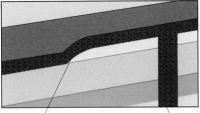

Trangressive sill   Dyke

Figure 2 Transgressive sill and dyke

0   1
m

Figure 3 Photo of a dyke with chilled and baked margins visible

Major intrusions batholiths

The most common form of **major intrusion** is a batholith, which can be very large:

- The Peru–Chile batholith in the Andes of South America is 4500 km long.
- The batholith that extends from Dartmoor in Devon to Lands End in Cornwall and to the Scilly Isles is over 235 km long.
- Most batholiths are discordant where they are intruded into the country rock.
- The outcrop for many batholiths is roughly **circular** in shape with steep sides.
- Batholiths are normally **granite** in composition although they can be composed of granodiorite or even diorite, all of which are coarse grained.
- They cool very slowly at depths of 5 to 30 km as plutonic rocks.

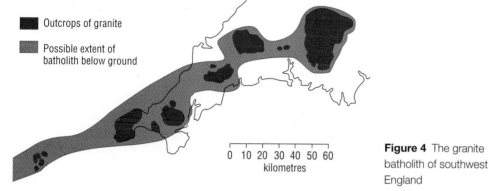

Figure 4 The granite batholith of southwest England

Figure 5 Photo to show xenoliths in granodiorite

Formation of granite magmas

Most batholiths are intruded at convergent plate margins where they form the core of fold mountains, which have resulted from plate collision. High temperature mafic magmas will rise up through the crust and the heat from these will partially melt continental crust. **Partial melting** produces silicic magma, which rises because it is less dense than the rock from which it was melted. Silicic magma is viscous and rises through the crust slowly. It is difficult for it to mix with other magmas because the viscosities are so different. Batholiths are huge bodies of magma usually produced by repeated intrusion of magma in the same area. As the magma moves up it generates more magma by stoping and assimilation.

Stoping and assimilation

At shallow depths of about 10 km, the crust is cold and brittle and batholiths may intrude by **stoping**. Magma moves upwards along joints, faults and bedding planes, separating masses of country rock. Eventually, pieces of country rock are detached and settle into the magma where they are known as **xenoliths**. No new space is created during stoping, as the magma simply fills the space formerly occupied by the country rock. As the xenoliths fall into the magma most will be **assimilated** as they gradually melt to become more magma.

Questions

1 Describe how you would identify a sill from a dyke on a map.

2 The island of Mull in northwest Scotland has a coastal section where 375 dykes were intruded in 20 km with a total width of 763 m. Calculate the average width of dyke for Mull and Arran and state the area where crustal extension was greatest.

3 The amount of granite in the crust is far greater than the quantity of granite that could be produced by partial melting. Explain how granite can be formed in other ways.

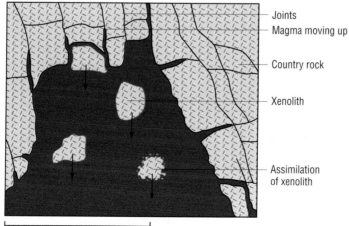

Figure 6 Cross-section of part of the top of a batholith showing stoping and formation of xenoliths

Extrusive volcanic rocks are those that cool **at** the Earth's surface while intrusive rocks cool **below** the surface. To distinguish between these two methods of formation, you will need to make observations of the characteristics of the rock, particularly crystal grain size. In general, extrusive rocks will have fine grained crystals compared to medium or coarse grained crystals for intrusives. Looking at the field relationships between igneous rock and the country rock is another key method. Chilled and baked margins are good indicators of intrusive rocks. Most igneous textures can be found in any rocks, but flow banding and vesicular texture nearly always indicate an extrusive origin.

Key definitions

A **chilled margin** is where the igneous rock has cooled rapidly so it has fine crystals.

A **baked margin** is in the country rock where it was heated by the intrusion and altered.

A **metamorphic aureole** is a large area around a batholith where the rocks have been metamorphosed.

Chilled margin

- The edge of the igneous intrusion, which is closest to the cold country rock, cools more rapidly than the rest of the intrusion and forms the **chilled margin**.
- The chilled margin may be only a few centimetres to several metres wide.
- The chilled margin has **fine grained** crystals because it cooled **quickly**.

Baked margin

- The area of country rock adjacent to a minor intrusion gets altered by the heat from the intrusion and is called the **baked margin**.
- The rocks are recrystallised by the heat, so they have been contact metamorphosed.
- The rocks in the baked margin have a sugary texture and become harder and lighter in colour.
- The baked margin may be a few centimetres to a few metres wide, depending on the size of the intrusion. The larger the intrusion, the wider the baked margin.

Metamorphic aureole

Batholiths, as major intrusions, heat a much larger zone of country rock so that a **metamorphic aureole** can be hundreds of metres to several kilometres wide. The rocks in the aureole are altered by contact metamorphism to produce new metamorphic rocks. If the batholith is intruded into a country rock of shale, then a clear sequence of changes takes place:

- Closest to the intrusion, where the heat is greatest for longer, the rocks will be totally recrystallised to form hornfels.
- Further away from the intrusion the rocks will be recrystallised to form a rock containing the metamorphic mineral andalusite.
- In the zone just inside the metamorphic aureole, where the heat was least, recrystallisation is partial so that a spotted rock forms. There is more detail on contact metamorphism in spread 2.4.4.

The width of a metamorphic aureole will depend on the size and temperature of the intrusion, the dip of the sides of the intrusion and the composition of the surrounding rocks.

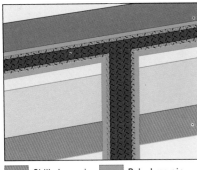

| | Chilled margin | | Baked margin |

Figure 1 Chilled and baked margins of a dyke and sill

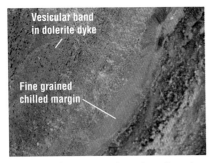

Vesicular band in dolerite dyke

Fine grained chilled margin

Figure 2 Chilled margin at the edge of a dyke

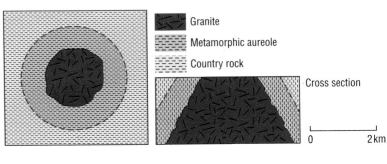

Granite

Metamorphic aureole

Country rock

Cross section

0   2 km

Figure 3 A map and cross-section of a granite batholith

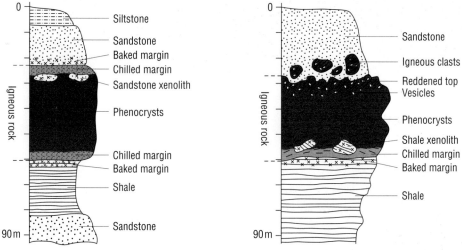

Figure 4 The differences between sills and lava flows

Figure 5 The top of a dolerite sill with sedimentary beds overlying

How would you distinguish intrusive sills from extrusive lava flows?

In the field it can be very difficult to be sure if a mass of rock is an ancient lava flow now covered in more recent sediments or a sill intruded between two beds of rock.

Sills have:	Lava flows have:
Two chilled margins due to contact with cool country rock, both above and below	Only one clear chilled margin below, while the top may be chilled or made of scoria
Two baked margins, both above and below, because the sill heats all the country rock around it	One baked margin below the lava flow and none above, as when it formed there was only air above
Xenoliths from rocks above and below the sill as the sill rips up material	No xenoliths from above the sill but possibly some from below
May show differentiation of magma if the sill is thick and cools slowly	May have flow banding or phenocrysts, may be aligned parallel to the direction of flow
Medium average crystal grain size as hypabyssal and cooled slowly	Fine average crystal grain size as volcanic and cooled rapidly
Dolerite as the most common rock	Basalt as the most common rock
Rare vesicles	Vesicles common in the upper part, may become amygdales when infilled by minerals
No fragments of the sill in overlying rocks	Lava fragments in overlying sedimentary rocks as a result of erosion and redeposition
A regular upper surface	Irregular upper surface made up of scoria or rubble
No weathering of the upper surface	A reddened surface or even an ancient soil if the flow was chemically weathered

Questions

1 Describe three important ways of distinguishing a sill from a lava flow.
2 Compare a baked margin with a metamorphic aureole.
3 Describe the differences between basalt and gabbro, and rhyolite and granite to show the relationship between the rock types and their origins.
4 Research and write a case study of the Carboniferous Whin Sill and the Tertiary lava flows of the Antrim Plateau and Giants Causeway in Northern Ireland.

Volcanoes are proof that the Earth is active and that the plates are in constant motion. The word **volcano** comes from the little island of Vulcano in the Mediterranean near Sicily. In mythology Vulcano was the chimney of the forge of Vulcan, the blacksmith of the Roman gods. When volcanoes erupt they produce huge volumes of gases, as well as a mix of pyroclasts and lavas, depending on the type of volcano.

Volcanic gases

All atmospheric gases, except photosynthetic oxygen, were released by volcanic eruptions. The gases are dissolved in the magma while it is under pressure at depth, then as the pressure decreases near the surface the gases are released by an eruption. The main gas is water vapour in the form of steam, which accounts for about 70% of all the gas released. The other main gases are CO_2 (12%), N (7%) and SO_2 (7%), with trace amounts of H, CO, S, Ar, Cl and F. These gases can combine with hydrogen and water to produce numerous toxic compounds, such as HCl, HF, H_2SO_4 and H_2S. Rain can be very acid close to volcanoes. Fumaroles are often a sign of gas escaping and activity below the surface.

Lava flows

Lava flows from recent eruptions can be very distinctive but ancient lavas are more difficult to recognise as they usually lack the surface features of rubbly blocks and flow patterns.

Mafic lavas

These low viscosity flows of basalt are thin and widespread over many kilometres because they are fluid. They cool to form:

- aa lava flows with a rough blocky, jagged surface, or
- pahoehoe flows with a smooth or ropy surface.

The pahoehoe flows are less viscous than the aa flows and as the lava cools it becomes even more viscous so that a pahoehoe flow may become an aa. Erupting lavas have temperatures in the range 1000 to 1200°C, but most do not flow very fast. Lava in a lava tube may move rapidly but most flows are at walking pace with scoria falling down from the top to the front of a flow. If they cool underwater, pillow lavas may form.

Key definition

A **volcano** is a vent at the surface of the Earth through which magma and other volcanic materials are ejected.

Case study

Carbon dioxide is a common but little-noted hazard of eruptions. It can be a problem in confined spaces and low-lying areas. The 1973 eruption at Heimaey, Iceland resulted in toxic levels in many buildings. The only fatality during the eruption was a looter who was overcome by carbon dioxide whilst attempting to steal from a pharmacy.

Lake Nyos is a crater lake in Cameroon, Africa. Gas is still seeping into the lake from the magma below and the lake is supercharged with carbon dioxide. In 1986, the lake vented several cubic kilometres of carbon dioxide, which is denser than air. It flowed down adjacent valleys and suffocated about 1800 people and their animals.

Case study

There has been some limited success in stopping lava flows. A lava flow threatened the port and town of Heimaey in Iceland. It was prevented from destroying the harbour by spraying cold sea water onto it, though many of the houses were already destroyed.

On Mt Etna they tried breaching the sides of a lava channel to divert the flow, by constructing barriers and bombing the lava flow. In Hawaii, twenty bombs were dropped in the path of a lava flow to save the city of Hilo. This diverted the lava away from the city.

Figure 1 Basalt lava flows on Hawaii showing **a** high temperature lava flowing in a lava tube **b** cooling lava forming a pahoehoe flow **c** cold lava where it flowed across a road **d** aa flows on the side of Mt Teide, Tenerife

Intermediate and silicic lavas

Viscous flows of andesite are irregular and tend to be limited to the area around the cone. Silicic flows of rhyolite are rare as they are very viscous so they tend to be thick but small in area. Very sticky lava can form lava domes within the crater and often shows flow banding.

Pyroclastic material

Magma can be forcefully or explosively ejected into the atmosphere as particles called **pyroclasts**.

- Ash is the smallest particles, less than 2 mm, and forms the **pyroclastic** rock **tuff** when consolidated.
- Lapilli are particles between 2 mm and 64 mm and forms a lapilli tuff.
- Bombs and blocks are the coarsest particles, over 64 mm, and form the pyroclastic rock **agglomerate** close to the crater of the volcano.
- Nuée ardentes are the gaseous magma that forms the fast moving pyroclastic flows that can flow several kilometres and cool to form the rock **ignimbrite**.

Pumice has already been described as a silicic igneous rock. It is so light that it can travel a long distance from the volcano like the pyroclasts. When Krakatoa erupted, pumice fell on ships several kilometres from the volcano and floated on the sea looking like snow.

Figure 2 Pyroclastic rocks from Tenerife and a large block from Hawaii

Questions

1 Describe the characteristics of the rocks that make lavas – basalt, andesite and rhyolite.
2 How do aa and pahoehoe flows differ when they are both basaltic?
3 Explain how a nuée ardente forms and why it is so dangerous.

When an eruption occurs you would expect all the area around the volcano to be equally affected. In reality the pattern is nearly always very uneven so that you could be 3 km in one direction from the volcano and be unaffected or 10 km in the other and have substantial damage. These differences are caused by the variables – energy of the volcanic blast, grain size of the pyroclasts, velocity and direction of winds, gradient of the sides of the volcano and magma viscosity.

Distribution by grain size

Coarse bombs and blocks are dropped close to the vent and therefore found in a circular pattern around the vent. The finer pyroclastic material will be carried further away from the volcano and could cover hundreds or even thousands of kilometres. The ash gets finer and thinner with distance away from the vent.

Distribution by wind

Where the wind blows in a prevailing direction during an eruption, the ash will be deposited mainly on the leeward side of the volcano. The ash cloud can be carried by the wind over huge distances and, if it gets up to the jetstream, can go right around the world. The higher the wind velocity, the further the ash particles can be carried.

Key definitions

An **isopachyte** is a line joining points of equal thickness of a deposit such as ash. The maps may be called isopach maps.

Lahars are mudflows of wet ash and volcanic debris that can flow rapidly down a mountainside.

Viscosity is a measure of a fluid's resistance to flow and controls the stickiness of a magma, which in turn depends on the silica content.

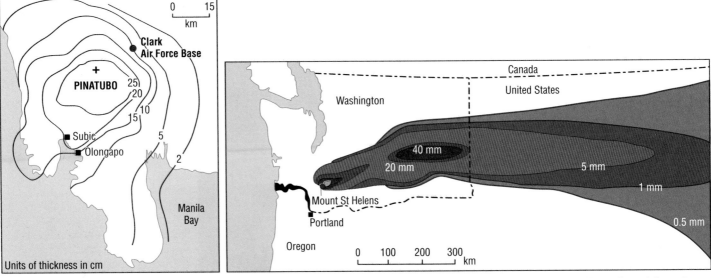

Figure 1 Isopachyte maps showing thickness of ash deposits around Mt Pinatubo 1991 and Mt St Helens 1980, where wind has affected the pattern of ash deposits. Wind was blowing from west to east

Examiner tip

If you are given a series of thicknesses then do not play dotto and join the points. Instead draw a line for each set of values, e.g. 5 m thickness so that all the numbers of less than 5 are on one side and all the numbers greater than 5 on the other. The isopachytes should be in a roughly concentric pattern.

Isopachyte maps are helpful in interpreting the distribution of ancient pyroclastic deposits, so that hazard maps can then be created.

Case study

The 1991, the Mt Pinatubo eruption was the second largest this century (after Katmai in 1912), and deposited a huge volume of pyroclastic material on steep slopes. The ash from the 1991 eruption covered houses, roads and fields. It was thickest in the valleys. The Philippines have a tropical climate with regular heavy rainfall. The combination of all this unconsolidated material and heavy rainfall has generated hundreds of lahars, some of which have been enormous.

Evacuation meant that only 200 people were killed directly by the 1991 eruption. Many times more have been killed or injured by lahars since the 1991 eruption. These lahars will continue to be a problem for decades.

Distribution by energy of blast

The most obvious relationship is that the greater the energy of the blast, the further away from the volcano the pyroclasts will be found. However, it is likely that the blast energy will be directed in one direction, so that even very close to the volcano there could be very little effect if the blast was in a different direction. The best recent example of this was the 1980 eruption of Mt St Helens, which produced a lateral blast due to a landslide on the northwest side of the volcano. This reached about 12 km from the summit, with the shockwave travelling at speeds above 1000 km/h. Pyroclastic flows of gas and rock, reaching up to 800 °C degrees, raced down the mountainside at speeds up to 320 km/h. Everything in the blast zone – natural or man-made – was obliterated within seconds. In a zone 13 to 27 kilometres from the summit, millions of trees were flattened.

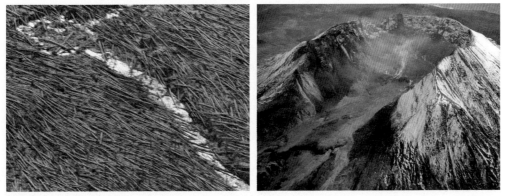

Figure 2 Trees felled by the blast from Mt St Helens and north flank of the volcano showing collapsed side

Lahars

A volcanic disaster occurred at a Colombian volcano called Nevado del Ruiz in 1985. The lahar began when hot ash and pyroclastic flows erupted, just after 9:00 pm, from the vent of the volcano and rapidly melted the snow and ice. The water and ash surged down, picking up sediment and rocks, forming lahars. These travelled 74 km down river valleys to the town of Armero. The lahar, moving at speeds of up to 50 km/hr, entered Armero at 11:30 pm as a wall of muddy water nearly 40 m high. Armero was inundated and 23 000 people were killed, about 5000 injured, and more than 5000 homes destroyed, covered by 2–5 m of mud.

Scientists were monitoring Nevado del Ruiz at the time of the eruption. Likely lahar pathways were identified on maps, and nearby communities were warned of the danger, but not in time for the people of Armero. The town was built directly on top of the 1845 mudflow deposit.

Distribution of lavas by viscosity

The viscosity or resistance to flow of lava is important because it determines how the lava will behave. It controls the length of lava flows, the velocity of the flow and the shape of the volcano.

Highly viscous rhyolite and andesite lava means that:
- The volcano will have steep sides.
- Eruptions are infrequent.
- Lava flows move slowly, are short in length and tend to be thick.
- Trapped gases may escape explosively.
- There are explosive eruptions, and tuffs and pyroclastic flows form.
- A degassed viscous lava or one that is hotter than usual may form a lava flow.

Basalt lava with low viscosity means that:
- The volcano will have shallow sides, but wherever the slopes are slightly steeper the flow will speed up.
- Eruptions will be frequent.
- Lava flows easily, forming long flows in channels and tubes.
- Gases are easily released.
- Eruptions are rarely pyroclastic and are usually quiet.
- Cooler basalt lava is quite viscous.

Case study

Viscosity of lavas

Substance	Viscosity (Pa s)
Air (at 18 °C)	1.9×10^{-5} (0.000019)
Water (at 20 °C)	1×10^{-3} (0.001)
Pahoehoe lava	100 to 1000
Aa lava	1000 to 10 000
Andesite lava	10^6 to 10^7
Rhyolite lava	10^{11} to 10^{12}

Figure 3 Damage caused by lahars

Questions

1 Draw a cross-section through a strato-volcano and show where the coarse and fine pyroclasts will be found.
2 Explain the relationship of viscosity to the composition of lavas.
3 Research the distribution of ash from recent large volcanic eruptions.

One of the world's most studied volcanoes is the Hawaiian shield volcano of Mauna Loa on Big Island, Hawaii. It is taller than Everest if measured from the sea floor and 150 km wide at the base. It is made almost entirely of basalt lava flows. Yet even Mauna Loa is dwarfed by the fissure eruptions that created the flood basalts of the Deccan Traps in the west of India. They consist of more than 2000 m of flat-lying basalt lava flows and cover an area of nearly 500000 km^2 (more than twice the size of the British Isles).

Mafic volcanoes have many features in common, even though their shapes vary:
- The viscosity of the magma is low because the silica content is low, consequently the basalt lavas are fluid and can be fast flowing.
- The gas content of the magma is high but the low viscosity allows the gas to escape so that eruptions are quiet and non-explosive (0 or 1 on the VEI scale).
- Eruptions are frequent, sometimes daily, but usually every few years.
- The activity is described as effusive and classified as Hawaiian.
- They occur at divergent plate margins or hot spots.

Shield volcano

A **shield volcano** is characterised by gentle slopes of less than 10 degrees. They are composed almost entirely of thin basalt lava flows built up from a central vent and fissure eruptions on the flanks of the volcano. The low viscosity of the magma allows the lava to travel down the sides of the volcano on a gentle slope, but as it cools and its viscosity increases, its thickness builds up on the lower flanks, forming a somewhat steeper lower slope. Most shield volcanoes have a roughly circular or oval shape in map view. Very little pyroclastic material is found within a shield volcano.

Figure 1 Low viscosity basalt lava, flowing in a lava tube at a temperature of 1200°C, seen though a break in the top of the lava tube

Key definitions

Shield volcanoes have gentle slopes of less than 10 degrees and a roughly circular shape around a central vent.

Fissure eruptions are where magma reaches the surface along long, linear cracks or fissures.

Submarine eruptions are where magma comes from a vent or fissure on the sea floor.

Low viscosity is where magma is fluid and flows freely.

Effusive is the term used to describe the fluid, non-explosive, basalt lava.

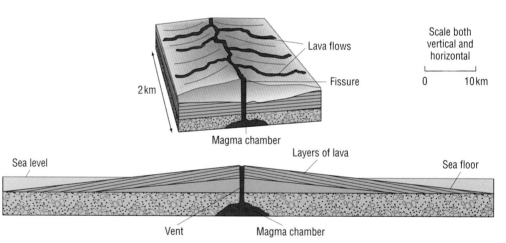

Figure 2 Cross-sections of a shield volcano and a fissure eruption

Examiner tip

When drawing a shield volcano think about the angle of slope of the sides of the volcano. If you draw a steep angle it is impossible for it to be a shield volcano as the basaltic fluid lava cannot form a steep sided volcano. It should be less than 10 degrees, and even the strato-volcanoes are usually only about 30 degrees.

Fissure eruptions

Iceland has a number of fissures parallel to the axial rift of the mid-ocean ridge and these can erupt huge quantities of fluid lava that spreads out over a large area. Lava erupted from the 30 km long Laki fissure in 1783–84, and covered an area of 560 km^2. The lavas from these **fissure eruptions** build up to form plateaus. Vast quantities of volcanic gases, particularly SO_2, are released, which are believed to affect the climate. The eastern United States recorded the lowest ever winter average temperature in 1783–84, about 4.8 °C below average. Europe also experienced an abnormally severe winter.

Figure 3 Lava erupting as a fissure eruption. A fissure on Kilauea, Hawaii in the foreground, and steam rising from other fissures in the distance

Figure 4 Columnar jointing in a lava flow at the Giant's Causeway in Northern Ireland

Columnar jointing

Where lava flows are more than 3 m thick, the inside of the flow will cool steadily and slowly, perhaps over weeks instead of the hours or days for the outside of the lava flow. Hexagonal columns form in the centre of these thick lava flows as it contracts during cooling. The cooling originates at equally spaced centres and proceeds in all directions from these centres. Contraction causes tension cracks to start to form half-way between each cooling centre.

Submarine eruptions

When lava is erupted underwater the outer skin cools very rapidly while the inside is still molten. Pressure of more lava behind causes the front to break through to form a new pillow shape. Pillow lavas are recognised by their characteristic rounded shape. Each pillow has a rounded top and a sagging bottom, so pillow lava can be used as a way-up structure to identify the youngest rocks. Vesicles may be present towards the outer, upper edge of the pillows and the spaces between pillows may be infilled with fine glassy materials.

Figure 5 a Lava flowing into the sea in Hawaii **b** Pillow lavas in Iceland mean that the eruption took place underwater

Volcanic Explosivity Index (VEI)

The Volcanic Explosivity Index, or VEI, was proposed in 1982 as a way to describe the relative size or magnitude of explosive volcanic eruptions. It is a 0 to 8 index of increasing explosivity. Each increase in number represents an increase of around a factor of ten.

VEI	Classification	Description	Height of eruption column	Volume of pyroclasts erupted	Frequency of eruption	Example	Occurrences in last 10 000 years
0	Hawaiian	Non-explosive	<100 m	<10 000 m³	Daily	Kilauea	Many
1	Hawaiian/ Strombolian	Gentle	100–1000 m	>10 000 m³	Daily	Hekla, Iceland 2000	Many
2	Strombolian/ Vulcanian	Explosive	1–5 km	> 1 000 000 m³	Weekly	Unzen, Japan 1990	3477
3	Vulcanian/ Pelean	Severe	3–15 km	>10 000 000 m³	Yearly	Nevado del Ruiz (1985)	868
4	Pelean/ Plinian	Cataclysmic	10–25 km	>0.1 km³	≥10 yrs	Soufrière Hills (1995)	278
5	Plinian	Paroxysmal	>25 km	>1 km³	≥50 yrs	Mt St Helens (1980)	84
6	Plinian/ Ultra-Plinian	Colossal	>25 km	>10 km³	≥100 yrs	Krakatoa 1883	39
7	Plinian/ Ultra-Plinian	Super-colossal	>25 km	>100 km³	≥1000 yrs	Tambora (1815)	4
8	Plinian/ Ultra-Plinian	Mega-colossal	>25 km	>1000 km³	≥10 000 yrs	Toba (73 000 BP)	None

Questions

1 On a world map, identify the areas where mafic volcanoes are found. Label Iceland and Hawaii.

2 Describe how you could use pillow lavas as way-up indicators.

3 Research the dangers of living in the active areas of Iceland and Hawaii.

These are the volcanoes that make the news. They are spectacular eruptions that may be heard many kilometres away and may affect large areas with ash falls.

Where are the explosive volcanoes?

All these volcanoes occur at convergent plate margins and particularly around the edge of the Pacific where the oceanic plate is subducting. The chains of volcanoes above the subduction zone are called the 'Ring of Fire' and there is usually at least one erupting somewhere in the world.

Strato-volcanoes are so named because they consist of layers of lava and pyroclastic deposits. The lava has a wide range of compositions with silica between 71 to 50% and the rocks will be mainly andesite with some basalt and rhyolite. Rhyolite lava flows are rare because the silicic magma is so viscous that most of it cools below the surface as intrusive granites.

Intermediate and silicic volcanoes have many features in common, even though the shape and size of these volcanoes varies:

- The viscosity of the magma is high because the silica content is high. The **andesite** and especially **rhyolite** lavas are thick and sticky and move slowly. This means that the angle of the sides is steep, at about 30 degrees.
- The gas content is high but the high viscosity does not allow the gas to escape so that eruptions are explosive when the gas finally does break through. These volcanoes range from 2 to 8 on the VEI scale.
- At least 50% of the material erupted is pyroclastic, which can include the incandescent gaseous cloud containing droplets of magma and ash called nuée ardente.
- Eruptions are infrequent, sometimes hundreds of thousands of years between eruptions, or more often tens of years.
- The activity is described as explosive and classified as Strombolian, Vulcanian or Plinian – all named after Italian volcanoes.
- They occur at convergent plate margins where subduction is taking place.

Strato-volcanoes

Strato-volcanoes form the largest percentage, over 60%, of the Earth's individual volcanoes. These volcanoes ideally have a conical shape but in many cases the outline is irregular due to slope failure, caldera collapse or explosive damage. New cones build up near the site of an older cone and create complex volcanoes. Each eruption can last hours, days or years and though the viscous lava rarely flows much further than the volcano base, the ash will cover vast areas.

When the lava is silicic it may be so viscous that it hardly flows at all, piling up in the vent to form volcanic domes. Lava domes are bulbous and very steep sided and form slowly with new lava pushing up from below. Silicic magmas have high gas content and this can result in nuée ardente pyroclastic flows.

Each volcano has an eruptive cycle:

- A period of no activity when the volcano may appear dormant. During this time the magma chamber is filling with magma, differentiation may be taking place and pressure is building up. These viscous magmas allow gas pressures to build up to high levels.
- Once the pressure exceeds the weight of overlying rock, including old lava plugging the vent, there will be an explosion. This blasts away part of the top of the volcano where the vent was blocked and allows the gas-rich, pyroclastic material to escape. This creates the layers of ash (tuff), blocks (agglomerate) and nuée ardente pyroclastic flows (ignimbrites).
- The final stage is when lava reaches the surface and forms a layer on top of the pyroclasts. As gas pressure decreases, the lava supply reduces until it cools in the vent, plugging it ready for the next cycle.

Key definitions

A **Hawaiian eruption** has large amounts of very fluid basaltic magma from which gases escape, but few pyroclasts.

A **Strombolian eruption** is more explosive with less fluid basalt and andesite lava. It has regular explosions of gas and pyroclastic material.

A **Vulcanian eruption** is violent with viscous andesitic lava and large quantities of pyroclastic material from large explosions.

A **Plinian eruption** is extremely explosive with viscous gas-filled andesitic and rhyolite lava and tremendous volumes of pyroclastic material blasted out.

Case study

Redoubt Volcano, Alaska began erupting on December 15, 1989. Ten hours later, the crew of KLM Flight 867 struggling to restart the plane's engines, as 'smoke' and a strong odour of sulfur filled the cockpit and cabin. For 5 long minutes the plane, bound for Anchorage, Alaska, with 231 terrified passengers aboard, fell in silence towards the rugged, snow-covered mountains (3000 m high). All four engines had shut down when the aircraft inadvertently entered a cloud of ash blown from 150 miles away. Only after the crippled jet had dropped from an altitude of 8504 to 4054 m (a fall of more than 4 km) was the crew able to restart all the engines and land the plane safely at Anchorage. The plane required $80 million in repairs, including the replacement of all four damaged engines.

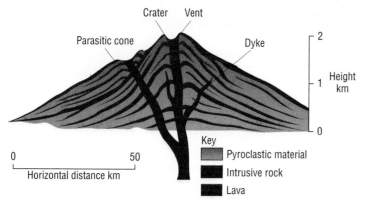

Figure 1 Cross-section of a strato-volcano showing layers of lava and pyroclasts

Figure 2 Puerto Varas Osorno, Chile, showing the conical cone and grey andesite lava flows

Calderas

A caldera is a large (1–20 km) circular volcanic depression caused by violent explosions followed by collapse of the top of the volcanic cone. Figure 3 shows three stages in the formation of a caldera.

1 A series of violent explosive Plinian eruptions of pyroclastic flows, ash and pumice take place, removing large volumes of magma.
2 The magma chamber starts to empty as the magma is erupted and the top of the volcano begins to collapse down into the weakened area below. This compresses the remaining magma so that eruptions are even more violent.
3 Finally the entire cone of the volcano collapses and this may cause tsunamis if the volcano is coastal or is an island, such as Krakatoa.

Where is the magma chamber?

The size of a magma chamber can affect the eruption. If the chamber where the magma is stored is small then the eruption is likely to be short. Most magma chambers are probably areas where the crust or mantle is partially melted rather than a great lake of magma below the surface. One way to think about a magma chamber is to picture a water-filled sponge. The sponge would represent the solid rock and the water the magma. Beneath Yellowstone, on average, the magma chamber is about 90% solid rock containing 10% liquid in its pores.

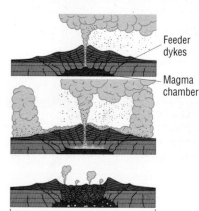

Figure 3 The formation of a caldera

Finding the magma chamber

One way to locate a magma chamber is to put seismometers all around a volcano and record the seismic waves generated by earthquakes. When seismic waves encounter molten material they either slow down (P-waves) or are stopped (S-waves). If material is partially melted then both P- and S-waves will slow down. Some of the waves travel directly under the volcano and seismometers on the opposite side of the volcano from where the earthquake originated will not receive or will get delayed P- and S-waves. The magma chamber creates a shadow zone allowing its size and depth to be calculated. Below Yellowstone, the magma chamber has a volume of approximately 15 000 km³ and is about 60 km long and up to 40 km wide. The top of the magma chamber is about 5 to 6 km deep and the bottom about 16 km deep.

Figure 4 Geysers

Geysers and hot springs

Geysers are hot springs from which a column of hot water and steam is explosively discharged at intervals. The largest geysers erupt to a height of 200 m. This happens if the vent is constricted allowing the pressure to build up. Hot springs are common in volcanic areas as groundwater is heated by the magma at depth. Convection causes the gas-rich, superheated water to rise. As it rises, the pressure decreases and flash boiling results and the water may explode upwards. The water drains back into the ground and is reheated for the cycle to begin again.

Questions

1 Explain why eruptions of mafic magma are quiet, while eruptions of silicic magma are explosive.
2 How does a crater differ from a caldera?
3 Why do strato-volcanoes form at convergent plate boundaries and shield volcanoes at divergent plate boundaries?
4 Research where an explosive volcano is erupting today and describe the type of activity.

⑮ Predicting volcanic eruptions

Until recently, volcanologists had to risk their lives by going into volcanoes to collect data, such as levels of gas emissions. Improvements in remote sensing and technology of equipment designed to give continuous data sent direct to laboratories, is making it easier and safer to obtain high-quality data.

Volcanologists can only predict eruptions if they:
- have a good knowledge of the eruptive history of a volcano
- have instrumentation on and around a volcano well in advance of an eruption
- can continuously monitor and interpret data coming from the equipment.

Even then, volcanologists can only offer probabilities that an event will occur. They can never be sure how severe a predicted eruption will be, exactly when it will occur or how long it will last.

Methods of predicting volcanic activity

Historic pattern of activity
Some volcanoes erupt regularly, so by studying the frequency of eruptions it may be possible to predict when an eruption is due. For example, 'during the past 4000 years the Soufrière volcano has had an average of one explosive eruption every 100 years'. Analysing the composition, distribution and volume of dated pyroclastic deposits and lavas helps to predict the pattern and size of future eruptions.

Ground deformation
Swelling of the volcano suggests that magma is moving up under the volcano. The rate of swelling is measured using tiltmeters and GPS that can accurately measure both vertical and horizontal movements to a millimetre. Thermal monitoring using infrared band satellite imagery can also detect magma movement to just below the volcano's surface. Localized ground displacement on steep volcanoes may indicate slope instability, which could lead to mass movement.

Gas emissions
As magma nears the surface and its pressure decreases, gases escape. This is like what happens when you open a bottle of fizzy drink and carbon dioxide escapes. Sulfur dioxide is one of the main components of volcanic gases, and increasing amounts being released suggests that magma is nearing the surface. There may also be changes in gas composition in the ratio of CO_2/SO_2. Changes in fumarole gas composition, or in the emission rate of SO_2 and other gases, may indicate variation in magma supply rate or a change in magma type.

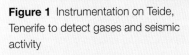

Figure 1 Instrumentation on Teide, Tenerife to detect gases and seismic activity

Key definitions

An **active** volcano has shown eruptive activity within recorded history. Currently there are about 600 active volcanoes and each year 50 to 60 actually erupt.

An **extinct** volcano has not shown any historic activity and is usually deeply eroded.

A **dormant** volcano is one that has not shown eruptive activity within recorded history, but shows geological evidence of activity within the geologically recent past.

Case study

The deformation of Mt St Helens prior to the May 18, 1980 eruption showed the north side of the volcano bulging upwards as magma was building up beneath.

Case study

On May 13, 1991, an increasing amount of sulfur dioxide was released from Mt Pinatubo in the Philippines. This was a volcano that had not erupted for 600 years. By May 28, sulfur dioxide emissions had increased to 5000 tonnes, 10 times the earlier amount. Mt Pinatubo later erupted on June 12, 1991. Before the Mt Pinatubo eruption, sulfur dioxide emissions dropped to a low level. The successful prediction of its eruption led to 300 000 people being evacuated, which saved thousands of lives and millions of dollars worth of military equipment at the nearby Clark Air Force Base.

Changes in groundwater
Borehole and well measurements are increasingly used to monitor changes in a volcano's subsurface gas pressure and thermal regime. Increased gas pressure will cause water levels to rise and suddenly drop right before an eruption, and the increased local heat flow can reduce flow in aquifers.

Seismicity

Earthquakes commonly provide the earliest warning of a volcano preparing to erupt, and earthquake swarms immediately precede most volcanic eruptions. Seismic observations use seismographs to monitor increased seismicity of three types:

- Short-period earthquakes are caused by the fracturing of brittle rock as magma forces its way upwards.
- Long-period earthquakes are believed to indicate increased gas pressure in a volcano's magma chamber.
- Harmonic tremors are the result of magma vibrating in the vent as it moves upwards.

Risk analysis

Studies of the geological history of a volcano are essential to make an assessment of the types of hazards and the frequency at which these hazards have occurred in the past. Geologists examine sequences of pyroclastic deposits and lava flows and their age and characteristics to determine the past behaviour of a volcano.

This information is then combined with knowledge about the present topography of the volcano to make volcanic hazard maps. These are used by public officials to create contingency plans for evacuations, rescue and recovery if another eruption is predicted. It can go wrong, such as in 1976 when an eruption of the Soufrière volcano, Guadeloupe was predicted and 70 000 people were evacuated for 3 months – and nothing happened! Forecasts of likely future eruption scenarios provide local officials with information for land use planning or even to change patterns of habitation, to construct artificial barriers for protection from lahars and lava flows and to construct evacuation routes.

Hazard maps show zones of danger expected from specific hazards for each volcano:

- Lava flows generally move slowly so rarely kill, but they destroy property and agricultural land.
- Blast damage can be very destructive for areas close to volcanoes, with people in the danger zone killed, trees flattened and buildings destroyed.
- Ash falls can affect areas far from volcanoes, causing damage to property as the weight of ash causes roofs to collapse.
- Pyroclastic flows are very hot and travel rapidly, but are mostly confined to valleys. They are responsible for many deaths as they are unpredictable.
- Lahars (mudflows) can be generated by pyroclastic flows or debris avalanches that become 'wet' from rivers or rain, by hot volcanic products that land on snow, by eruptions out of crater lakes or when eruptions occur under ice. They can move rapidly, and may be very destructive and though limited to valleys may affect areas far from the volcano.

Case study

In December 2000, scientists predicted an eruption within two days at Popocatépetl, on the outskirts of Mexico City. Their prediction used increasing long-period earthquakes as an indicator of an imminent eruption. The government evacuated tens of thousands of people; 48 hours later, the volcano erupted as predicted. It was Popocatépetl's largest eruption for 1000 years, yet no one was injured.

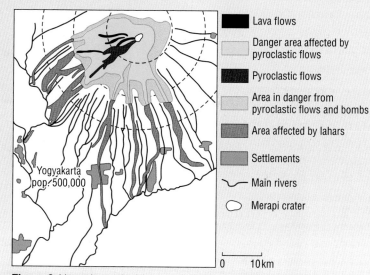

Figure 2 Hazard map for Merapi, the most active volcano in Indonesia, which produces more pyroclastic flows than any other volcano on Earth

Key:
- Lava flows
- Danger area affected by pyroclastic flows
- Pyroclastic flows
- Area in danger from pyroclastic flows and bombs
- Area affected by lahars
- Settlements
- Main rivers
- Merapi crater

Yogyakarta pop. 500,000

0   10km

Figure 3 Geologists measuring the lava dome on Mt St Helens

Around the world, some densely populated places such as Japan and Indonesia, have large numbers of people living in the danger zones of volcanoes. Would you want to live with the threat of lava flows, ash falls, pyroclastic flows, explosions, blasts and lahars?

It might seem crazy to live near an active volcano and even to move back into an area that has already been devastated by an eruption, but that is what people do. Vesuvius famously destroyed Pompeii and Herculaneum in the 79 AD eruption, and now about 3 million people live in the area and could be seriously affected by a future eruption. So why choose to live there? Geologists agree that it is not a matter of if Vesuvius will erupt again, but when, and how violently. The Italian government is even offering 30 000 Euros to anyone living in one of the 18 towns in the immediate area, who is willing to move out of the danger zone!

Benefits brought by volcanoes

Geothermal power

The heat from a magma chamber, lava flows or from areas of hot springs can be used as an energy source. In areas such as Iceland geothermal power is the main source of electricity and used for heating homes and businesses. It means plentiful, cheap power that is both renewable and sustainable, as Iceland sits on the Mid-Atlantic Ridge where volcanic activity is common. Geothermal power is used in volcanic areas around the world, including Italy, Kenya and New Zealand for:

- electricity generated directly from steam in volcanically active areas
- electricity generated by water pumped down and heated from hot rocks
- space heating for greenhouses, public buildings and homes
- hot water supply for swimming pools, cooking and domestic use.

Figure 1 A geothermal swimming pool in Iceland

Fertile soils

Agriculture around volcanoes is often very intensive. Lava and some volcanic ash weathers rapidly in tropical conditions and forms a deep, fertile, soil layer. The soils are rich in the trace elements lacking in old soils where soluble minerals will have been leached out. The coffee plantations in Costa Rica produce high grade beans with a distinctive flavour from being grown on the rich volcanic soils.

After an eruption, the area covered in lava looks very inhospitable yet vegetation starts to colonise in just a few years. Lava and ash are both porous and can hold water very well and this helps to create fertile conditions.

Figure 2 Trees are already established on this cinder cone from the 1909 eruption on Tenerife

Somewhere to live

Volcanic tuff formed from ash is a useful building material. It is easy to cut and carve and light in weight, so dwellings can be cut directly out of the rock – they are cool and dry to live in. The tuff is also quarried and cut into blocks to build houses and public buildings. Tuff is used in the manufacture of cement and has been used since Roman times.

Figure 3 A local Tenerife business operates out of buildings excavated in the tuff

Volcanoes and the atmosphere and oceans

Volcanoes have been active ever since the Earth formed 4500 Ma and without volcanic gases the Earth would have no atmosphere:

- Volcanoes supply large volumes of gases to the atmosphere and initially created the Earth's atmosphere of carbon dioxide, sulfur dioxide and nitrogen – the oxygen came later from plants.
- All the water now in the oceans originated as volcanic gas in the form of water vapour. Juvenile water is still being added to the water cycle by volcanic eruptions.

Minerals

Volcanic activity concentrates some elements, which can then be of economic value:

- Much of the world's sulfur is mined from around active volcanoes.
- Black smokers are hydrothermal vents on the mid-ocean ridges that produce a variety of sulfide metals deposits rich in nickel, copper, silver, zinc, mercury, manganese and lead.
- Bacteria found living in the springs of Yellowstone are now used in DNA and AIDS testing.

Figure 4 Sulfur crystals growing at a fumarole

Volcanic activity as a cause of climate change

Volcanic gases probably cause the global cooling that is seen for a few years after a major eruption. As volcanoes erupt, they blast huge clouds into the atmosphere. These clouds are made up of particles and gases, including sulfur dioxide. Millions of tons of sulfur dioxide gas can reach the stratosphere from a major volcanic eruption. There, the sulfur dioxide converts to tiny persistent sulfuric acid (sulfate) particles, known as aerosols. These sulfate particles reflect energy coming from the Sun, preventing its rays from heating the Earth, and causing global cooling. Following eruptions, these aerosol particles remain in the stratosphere for three to four years.

When Mt Pinatubo erupted in the Philippines in June 1991, an estimated 20 million tons of sulfur dioxide and ash particles blasted more than 20 km high into the atmosphere. Gases and solids injected into the stratosphere circled the globe for three weeks and could be clearly seen on satellite images.

Large-scale volcanic activity may last only a few days, but the massive amount of gases and ash can influence climate patterns for years.

Figure 5 Eruption of Pinatubo showing ash and gas cloud

Case study

The eruption of Tambora in Indonesia in 1815, resulted in an extremely cold spring and summer in 1816, which became known as the year without a summer. The Tambora eruption was 7 on the VEI scale. New England and Europe were hit exceptionally hard with snowfalls and frost throughout the summer. Sea ice migrated across Atlantic shipping lanes, and alpine glaciers advanced down mountain slopes. All but the hardiest crops were destroyed and farmers were forced to slaughter their starving animals.

Case study

In 1883, the Indonesian volcano Krakatoa erupted violently in the second largest eruption in history – 6 on the VEI scale. Ash reached an altitude of 40 km. It generated twenty times the volume of pyroclasts released by the 1980 eruption of Mt St Helens. Fine particles from the eruption had drifted all the way to the Atlantic in three days and in thirteen days had circled the globe. In the year following the eruption, average global temperatures fell by about 1 °C. Weather patterns were chaotic for years, and temperatures did not return to normal until 1888. It caused intense, beautiful red sunsets, which provided inspiration for many famous artists. The eruption injected a large amount of sulfur dioxide gas high into the stratosphere, which was subsequently transported by high-level winds all over the planet. Ash from Krakatoa has been found in ice cores from Greenland.

Questions

1 Describe ways in which volcanic gases cause global cooling.
2 Describe how people living in New Zealand and Iceland benefit from volcanic activity.
3 Draw up a table of advantages and disadvantages of living close to a volcano.

All rocks are formed below the Earth's surface. When rocks are uplifted near to the surface, and when they are exposed at the surface, temperature, pressure and chemical conditions are different from those where they were formed. When this happens, rocks change. **Weathering** is the *in situ* chemical alteration and mechanical breakdown of rocks by exposure to the atmosphere, water and organic matter.

Chemical weathering

Rocks decompose when the chemical structure of their minerals breaks down. Chemical weathering reactions, all of which involve water, produce ions that are removed in solution leaving an insoluble residue, usually clay minerals. Carbonation and hydrolysis are important reactions because they affect two common rock forming minerals, calcite and feldspar.

Carbonation

Carbon dioxide gas in the atmosphere reacts with rainwater and pore water in the soil to form carbonic acid. The air in soil pore spaces is rich in carbon dioxide due to decomposing plant litter. This makes groundwater more acidic than rainwater. Carbonation is most important in the weathering of limestone.

$$CaCO_3 + H_2CO_3 \rightarrow Ca^{2+} + 2\,HCO_3^-$$
calcite + carbonic acid = calcium + hydrogen carbonate ions in solution

Limestone generally contains insoluble impurities. They are left behind as clay residues.

Hydrolysis

The reaction between water and silicate minerals, especially feldspars, is important because they are the most common rock forming minerals. **Hydrolysis** is speeded up if the water contains carbonic acid. H^+ ions from water and carbonic acid react with the minerals' ions. The products include a residual clay mineral, silica, carbonate or bicarbonate (K, Na or Ca, depending on the original mineral) in solution.

Mechanical weathering

Exfoliation

Exfoliation is sometimes known as 'onion-skin weathering', because curved sheets peel off from rocks affected by it. In hot deserts there is a marked difference between hot daytime and cold night-time temperatures. Different minerals expand and contract by different amounts during heating and cooling, causing the rock to disintegrate.

Frost shattering

Water enters cracks, joints and bedding planes. In climates where daily temperatures fluctuate above and below 0°C, water freezes and expands by 9%. This exerts pressure on rocks, leading to eventual failure. It produces a residue of angular fragments called scree.

Pressure release

Atmospheric pressure at the Earth's surface is much lower than pressures within the Earth, even at quite shallow depths. When this pressure is released from rocks due to the erosion of the rocks above them, they expand producing fractures, which are more widely spaced the further they are from the surface. Rocks that are well jointed or have many bedding planes are less likely to be affected by this form of weathering.

Key definitions

Weathering is the *in situ* chemical alteration and mechanical and biological breakdown of rocks by exposure to the atmosphere, water and organic matter.

Carbonation is the reaction between carbonic acid and minerals.

Hydrolysis is the reaction between minerals and water, causing the minerals to decompose.

Exfoliation occurs when sheets of rock split off due to differential expansion and contraction of minerals during diurnal heating and cooling.

Frost shattering is caused by the expansion of freezing water in fractures which forces rocks apart.

Pressure release is the expansion and fracturing of rock due to removal of overlying rocks.

Figure 1 Weathering processes: exfoliation and frost shattering

Biological weathering

Root action

Tree roots can grow along bedding planes and joints and force them apart mechanically. They keep surfaces open so that water can penetrate and so make chemical weathering easier. When trees sway in the wind, their roots can prise open fractures in rocks.

Figure 2 Root action

Burrowing

Burrowing animals include worms, reptiles and mammals. Their activity brings rock material from shallow depths up to the surface, where more weathering can affect it. The burrows allow atmospheric gases and water to penetrate, making chemical weathering more likely. Fragments that may have been produced by other forms of weathering are usually reduced in size by burrowing organisms.

Climate and weathering		
Climatic zone		**Weathering**
Arctic	mean annual temp ~2 °C mean annual rainfall ~10 cm	Mainly mechanical (frost shattering)
Temperate	mean annual temp ~10 °C mean annual rainfall ~ 50 cm	Mechanical, chemical and biological (frost shattering, carbonation, hydrolysis, root action)
Warm arid	mean annual temp ~20 °C mean annual rainfall ~10 cm	Mainly mechanical (exfoliation)
Humid tropical	mean annual temp ~20 °C mean annual rainfall ~200 cm	Intense chemical, some biological with greatest amount of residue (carbonation, hydrolysis, root action)

Questions

1. Describe how carbonation produces soluble products.
2. Explain why the weathering sequence of silicate minerals is similar to Bowen's Reaction Series.
3. Explain how climate affects weathering processes.

What happens to weathered material?

The answer is that some will remain where it is and the rest will be transported away. Transport can be due to:

- gravity – moves loose weathered sediment down slopes
- wind – lifts and transports finer grained sediment
- rivers – lift and transport sediment of all sizes, including heavy and large grains
- the sea – moves sediment of all sizes
- ice – depending on climatic conditions, can carry large amounts of rock debris.

The grains of sediment are involved in the process of **erosion.** They come into contact with rocks over which they are travelling, perhaps in a desert, in the bed of a stream or along the coast. These rocks are subjected to **abrasion.** They may be sandblasted by wind blown sediments in deserts, ground down by boulders rolling along a riverbed or chipped away by shingle carried by the sea when waves crash into cliffs.

Transported grains are not only in contact with the Earth's surface, but are also in contact with each other. **Attrition** is the wearing down of the transported sediment by rolling, rubbing and crushing together of sedimentary grains during transport. The more contact there is between grains and the longer they have been in transport, the smaller and more rounded they become. Harder minerals, like quartz, survive better than less hard minerals, like mica, which may be completely crushed.

Methods of transport

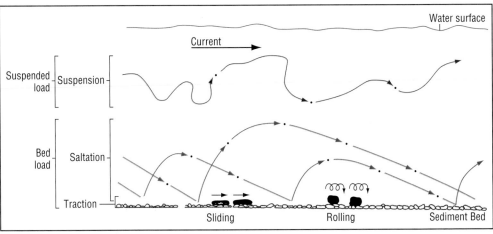

Key ● Sedimentary particles

Figure 1 Methods of sediment transport in water

Figure 1 shows all the methods of sediment transport in water. Most methods also apply to wind transport, though wind does not transport material in solution. Ice carries sediment embedded within it. Larger grain sizes can be transported when the velocity of the current is greater. Bed loads consist of larger grains that are moved by **traction** and smaller grains that bounce along the bed by **saltation.** Finer grains do not touch the bed and so are the suspended load. Dissolved material transported in **solution** is invisible and so cannot be shown. Grains become smaller the longer they have been transported.

Clay sized particles require high velocities for erosion because they are flat and platy in shape and are cohesive so tend to stick together. If you have ever tried washing sticky mud off boots, it's a lot more difficult than washing off sand. The clay particles remain in **suspension** even at very low current velocities because they are small, have low mass and are buoyant.

Key definitions

Erosion is the wearing away of the land surface and removal of sediment by means of transport.

Abrasion is the wearing away of the Earth's surface by the action of wind, water or ice dragging sediment over or hurling it at a surface.

Attrition is the wearing down of sedimentary grains due to collisions with other grains during transport.

Solution is the transport of ions dissolved in water, particularly K, Ca and Na.

Suspension is the transport of material in water or air, without it touching the Earth's surface.

Saltation is the transport of material by bouncing.

Traction is the transport of material by rolling and sliding along a surface.

Examiner tip

Sometimes candidates get weathering and erosion confused. They both result in the breakdown of rocks, but in weathering there is no movement of material, it all happens in place (*in situ*). However, in the case of erosion, there is always a method of transport involved.

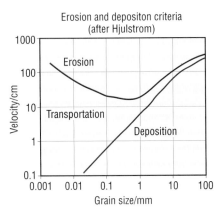

Figure 2 Relationship between current velocity of water and sediment transport

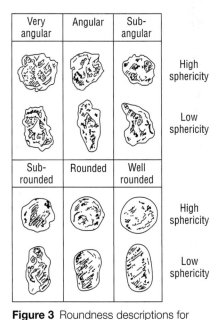

Figure 3 Roundness descriptions for grains of sediment of high and low sphericity

Grain shape and roundness

Grains get rounder the longer they have been transported, and the degree of **roundness** can be described using Figure 3.

The shape of grains depends on the type of rock or mineral from which they are made, rather than on transport. There are many ways to describe **shape**. One way is to compare the grain to a sphere. Figure 3 shows grains that have high and low degrees of sphericity.

Figure 4 Grain shapes

Grain size

Measurement and classification of the grain size of sediments is made using the Wentworth–Udden scale. As the range of grain sizes found in nature is large, a logarithmic scale is more practical than a linear scale.

The **grain size** is obtained from the average diameter of the grains of sediment being studied. The diameter in mm is not always easy to remember, so the phi (Ø) scale is also used. This scale also has advantages when making a statistical analysis of sediment grain sizes.

Diameter/mm	Phi Ø	Sediment name
>2	−2 to −8	Gravel, pebbles, cobbles, boulders
2	−1	Sand – very coarse
1	0	Sand – coarse
0.5	1	Sand – medium
0.25	2	Sand – fine
0.125	3	Sand – very fine
0.0625	4	Silt
0.039	8	Clay

The Wentworth–Udden scale

Questions

1 Describe one difference and one similarity between the processes of weathering and erosion.
2 Explain why quartz grains that have been transported in water for a long time are more rounded than those transported for a short time.
3 Use the graph of current velocity and transport to answer:
  (a) which sediment grain size requires the least energy for erosion to take place?
  (b) what is the sediment size being deposited, if the velocity is 100 cm/s?
4 Describe a situation when very high velocities occur. Research the type of material carried by a high velocity river.

- The sizes, size range and roundness of sediments are all related to how the sediments were transported, because wind, water and ice vary in terms of energy and viscosity.
- Fine grained, well rounded sediments have been transported for a longer time than coarse grained angular fragments.
- The shape of grains depends on the type of rock or mineral from which they are made.
- Sedimentary deposits in which all the grains are of similar size have been transported in higher energy conditions than those where there is a wide range of sizes.
- How sediments were transported is related to environmental factors, such as climate.

So the answer to the question is – quite a lot.

One method of interpreting sediments is by analysing the grain shape – the more rounded the sediment, the longer the time of transport. Angular shapes suggest rapid deposition with little transport. A second method involves analysing the grain size distributions of sediments and investigating how well sorted they are.

Sorting

A sedimentary deposit of grains that are all the same size would be described as very well sorted. One with a wide range of sizes would be termed very poorly sorted. The range of terms used to describe sorting is shown on the photos of sediments.

Sorting provides information about how sediments were transported. Wind does not transport very coarse grains. It deposits well sorted sands as energy and velocity decrease. Finer grains are blown further, forming deposits elsewhere.

Rivers flowing with high energy may transport coarse as well as medium and fine grained sediment. As energy levels fall, larger heavier grains are deposited first, medium sized grains are transported further and finer grains are deposited last. Poorly sorted sediment has usually not been transported far because the transporting medium lost energy quickly. A desert stream that rapidly dries up due to infiltration or high rates of evaporation will deposit the sediment very quickly. A meltwater stream from a glacier will lose energy as melting stops after the summer thaw has ended and sediment will be deposited over a short period of time.

Grain size analysis of sediments

Sand and gravel sized sediments are analysed using a sieve bank, a stack of sieves arranged so that the one with the biggest holes (4 mm or 2 Ø) is at the top and the one with the smallest (0.0625 mm or 4 Ø) is at the bottom. The sieve stack is rotated and shaken. The sediment trapped on each sieve is weighed. If you use 100 g of sediment it makes calculations very simple.

Results are plotted as histograms. Different methods of transport produce different grain size distributions, shown in the graphs below.

The energy of the transporting medium is the key factor that affects the degree of sorting.

Grain size data is plotted as cumulative frequency curves. They show the total percentage of sediment that fails to get through a given sieve size. This kind of graph allows a direct comparison between different samples of sediment, because they can all be plotted on the same graph.

Well sorted sediments have almost vertical curves. Poorly sorted sediments have curves that stretch across a wide range of sizes. The degree of sorting can be quantified. The coefficient of sorting (p) can be measured from cumulative frequency graphs using the following equation:

$$\text{coefficient of sorting } (p) = \frac{\varnothing_{84} - \varnothing_{16}}{2}$$

where $\varnothing_{84}$ is the Ø value of the cumulative mass of 84% of the sample and $\varnothing_{16}$ is the Ø value of the cumulative mass of 16% of the sample.

Figure 1 Sediment sorted into well sorted, moderately sorted and poorly sorted

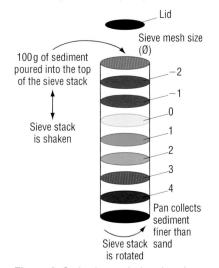

Figure 2 Grain size analysis using sieves

Worked example: calculating the coefficient of sorting

The dashed red lines on the cumulative frequency graph have been drawn:

- at 84% and the value of phi is 3 for the glacial sediment
- at 16% and the value of phi is −1.7 for the glacial sediment
- using the equation above

$$\frac{3 - (-1.7)}{2} = \frac{4.7}{2} = 2.35$$

The table shows how the coefficient allows sorting to be expressed numerically.

	Value	Degree of sorting
Coefficient of sorting	<0.50	Well sorted
	0.50–1.00	Moderately sorted
	>1.00	Poorly sorted

- The value of 2.35 tells us that the till is very poorly sorted.

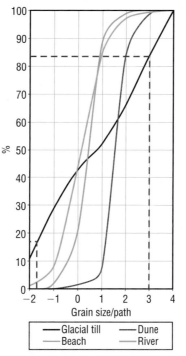

Figure 4 Cumulative frequency curves of the four sediments

Characteristics of sediments related to transport

This table summarises the characteristics of sediments transported by wind, ice, rivers and the sea. Gravity has also been included, but this material is too varied and often too coarse to be analysed using sieving.

Transport	Grain size	Composition	Roundness	Sorting
Wind blown dune sand in a high energy environment	Fine to medium sand	All quartz sometimes red due to iron oxide	Well rounded	Very well sorted, so that most of the sediment is in one sieve, as fine sand is easiest for the wind to carry
Ice – deposited as glacial till in a low energy environment	Varies from very coarse (boulders) to very fine (clay)	Varied – any rock fragments and clay	Angular to sub-angular	Very poorly sorted, so material in every sieve
River deposit of sand in channel Usually high energy with fast currents	Coarse to fine sand, may be coarser nearer to source	Quartz and mica with rock fragments	Angular near to source but sub-angular to sub-rounded downstream	Poorly sorted near to source of river Moderately sorted downstream gives wide range of sediment size in sieves
Beach or offshore bar in the sea High energy	Medium sand Sometimes coarse (pebbles and gravel) close to shore and on beaches	Nearly all quartz with some shell or rock fragments	Sub-rounded to rounded	Moderately sorted with sediment mainly in a few sieves
Gravity Low energy	Varies from very coarse (boulders) in rock falls to very fine in soil creep	Varied – any rock fragments	Angular to very angular	Very poorly sorted Larger fragments sometimes found at the base of a slope

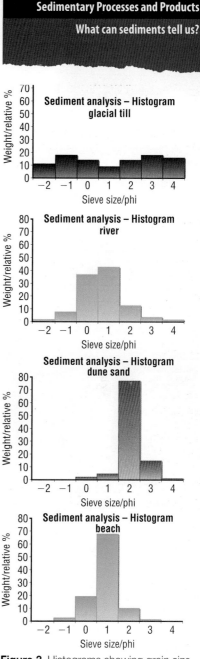

Figure 3 Histograms showing grain size distributions of four sediments

Questions

1 Draw diagrams to show well sorted, moderately sorted and poorly sorted sediments.

2 Explain why transport by ice gives grains different characteristics than grains transported by wind.

3 Calculate the coefficient of sorting for the dune, beach and river sediments on the cumulative frequency graph.

4 Explain the advantages and disadvantages of qualitative and quantitative methods of grain size analysis.

Three groups of sedimentary rocks

Most sedimentary rocks are formed from **clasts** produced as a result of weathering and erosion. Clasts can range in size from boulders to clay and include solid fragments called **pyroclasts** that have been ejected from volcanoes. The erosion, transport and deposition of clasts are by mechanical processes and they are described as **mechanically formed** sedimentary rocks.

The products of chemical weathering always include ions in solution. They are transported in solution in rivers and the sea. A change in the chemical environment can lead to their deposition, for example, where sea water is evaporated and $CaCO_3$ crystals are precipitated. The weathering transport and deposition of these rocks is by chemical processes and they are called **chemically formed** sedimentary rocks.

Biologically formed sedimentary rocks result when organisms, such as sea creatures or trees, extract ions that are in solution in sea water or groundwater and turn them into organic tissue, such as shells or wood. When the organism dies, its remains will be deposited and may be buried to form sedimentary rocks. Often the remains are transported and become broken up. Shell fragments are an example of this. Rocks composed of these fragments are described as **bioclastic**.

Key definitions

A **clast** is a rock fragment or grain resulting from the breakdown of larger rocks.

A **pyroclast** is a fragment of rock formed by a volcanic explosion.

A **bioclastic** is a biologically formed sedimentary rock composed of fragmented organic material.

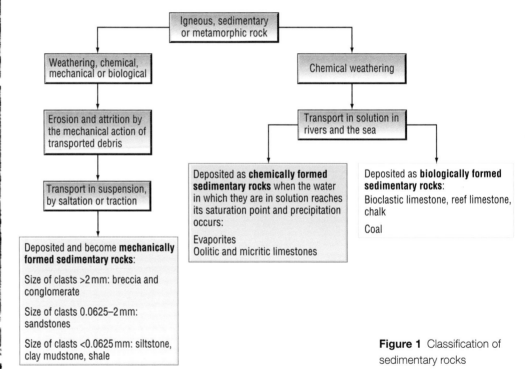

Figure 1 Classification of sedimentary rocks

Figure 2 Mechanically formed sedimentary rocks **a** large boulder 3100 mm in conglomerate **b** breccia **c** sandstone and conglomerate

Classification

Classification of sedimentary rocks involves examining them in the field, in hand specimen, through photos and thin sections. The three groups are classified more precisely by using grain size, grain shape, mineral composition and fossil content.

Grain size is used to divide up the mechanically formed sedimentary rocks. Here are some examples:

All photos show rocks that are poorly sorted.

Grain shape is used to distinguish between conglomerate, which has rounded clasts and breccia which has angular clasts.

Grain size is not so useful in classifying chemically and biologically formed sedimentary rocks, but mineral composition and **fossil** content are. A rock containing more than 50% calcium carbonate is limestone. This is usually in the form of the mineral calcite. It is easy to recognise as it reacts strongly with dilute hydrochloric acid (HCl). There are several different types of limestone, based on their fossil content and type of grain.

Figure 3 Biologically formed sediment and sedimentary rocks

Examiner tip

Make sure that you can distinguish clastic from non-clastic sedimentary rocks. Clastic rocks are mechanically formed and contain fragments (clasts) which can be any size. None of them are chemically or biologically formed.

Descriptions of the main groups of sedimentary rocks				
Group	Processes of formation	Characteristics	Sediment, chemical or biological composition	Rock names
Mechanically formed	Transported terrestrial sediment formed by weathering, erosion and transport	Clastic (subdivided by grain size and composition)	Boulders, cobbles, pebbles, gravel Sand Silt, clay	>2 mm – conglomerates and breccias 2–0.0625 mm – sandstones <0.0625 mm – mudstone, shale, clay, siltstone
	Transported volcanic material	Pyroclastic	Ash and lapilli Blocks and bombs	Tuff Agglomerate
Biologically formed	Formed by activity of living organisms	Biogenic and bioclastic	Reef organisms Shell fragments of calcareous organisms Terrestrial plant matter Calcareous algae (coccoliths) Micro organism oozes	Crinoidal, reef, bioclastic limestone, Coal Chalk Chert
Chemically formed	Formed by evaporation of water and precipitation of minerals	Chemical	Evaporite minerals (subdivided by composition) Ooliths Calcareous (lime) mud Iron minerals	Evaporites dolomite, gypsum, halite, K salts Oolitic limestone Micritic limestone Ironstones

Questions

1 Describe how mechanically formed sedimentary rocks are classified.
2 State one characteristic that identifies the biologically formed rock, limestone.
3 Describe how the mechanically formed sedimentary rocks shown in the photos were transported.

Using observations to identify rocks

You have seen that sedimentary rocks can be classified by observing grain size, grain shape and mineral composition. Now these observations are used to identify some mechanically formed sedimentary rocks. The flow diagram shows how the observation of characteristic features can be used to identify these rocks.

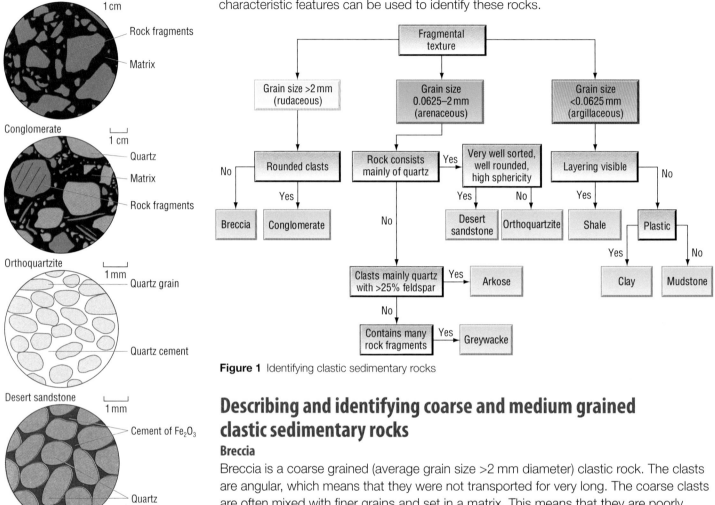

Figure 1 Identifying clastic sedimentary rocks

Breccia
1 cm
Rock fragments
Matrix

Conglomerate
1 cm
Quartz
Matrix
Rock fragments

Orthoquartzite
1 mm
Quartz grain
Quartz cement

Desert sandstone
1 mm
Cement of Fe$_2$O$_3$
Quartz

Arkose
1 mm
Pink feldspars with cleavage planes
Matrix
Rock fragments
Grey quartz grains are sub rounded to sub angular

Greywacke
1 mm
Rock fragments
Quartz
Clay matrix
Mica

Figure 2 Thin section diagrams of clastic sedimentary rocks

Describing and identifying coarse and medium grained clastic sedimentary rocks

Breccia

Breccia is a coarse grained (average grain size >2 mm diameter) clastic rock. The clasts are angular, which means that they were not transported for very long. The coarse clasts are often mixed with finer grains and set in a matrix. This means that they are poorly sorted, making it possible to infer that the transporting medium lost energy quickly. Breccias commonly form as scree, alluvial fans and wadi deposits. Volcanic breccias are pyroclastic rocks from a volcanic vent.

Conglomerate

Conglomerate is another coarse grained clastic rock. The clasts are rounded, which means that they have been transported for a longer period of time than the angular clasts in a breccia. The large clasts may be surrounded by a finer grained matrix and be poorly sorted. In some conglomerates, the clasts are held in place by mineral cement. Conglomerates commonly form as beach and river channel deposits.

Sandstones

Sandstones are a very important group of sedimentary rocks, as they are one of the main oil reservoir rocks and aquifers for water supply, as well as being used as a building stone. They may be well cemented, in which case they will have a low porosity, or be poorly cemented, in which case they will have a high porosity. The main component is quartz but other minerals low on Bowen's Reaction Series, such as muscovite, mica and K feldspar, are also common. Sandstones are found in virtually all sedimentary environments.

Orthoquartzite

Orthoquartzite is a sandstone (average grain size 0.0625 to 2 mm diameter). It consists only of quartz grains held together by quartz cement, so it is white of grey in colour. The grains are well sorted and well rounded, indicating transport over a long period. This indicates extensive weathering so that less stable minerals are not present. Orthoquartzites commonly form in beach and shallow marine deposits.

Desert sandstone

Desert sandstone is red in colour due to iron oxide coating the quartz grains. It is very well sorted, with very well rounded, medium sand-sized (1 mm) grains having high sphericity, sometimes referred to as 'millet seed sand'. The grains have a frosted appearance when examined using a hand lens. Unlike orthoquartzite, desert sandstone is not composed entirely of quartz due to the iron oxide coating around the grains. The clasts are cemented together by silica or iron minerals. These rocks commonly form in arid environments as wind blown sands.

Arkose

Arkose is a medium to coarse grained sandstone that contains at least 25% K feldspar. The other main mineral is quartz, though rock fragments and mica are also present. Arkose is often pink in colour due to the feldspars and is usually moderately sorted. The grains will be sub-angular to sub-rounded, showing that the sediment has not been transported very far. It is commonly formed in alluvial fan environments in arid areas.

Greywacke

Greywacke sandstones are fine to coarse in grain size. They are dark coloured and poorly sorted, with angular to sub-angular clasts that mainly consist of rock fragments (lithic clasts) with some quartz and K feldspar. More than 15% of the rock is clay matrix. They commonly form as turbidite deposits, so often show graded bedding.

Figure 3 Desert sandstone. Each grain is < 1 mm

Sandstones				
	Orthoquartzite	**Desert sandstone**	**Arkose**	**Greywacke**
% Quartz	90%–99%	90%+	50%–70%	50%
Minerals	Almost all quartz. Contains only very small amounts of other minerals	Quartz and hematite	Mainly quartz, but at least 25% feldspar. Some rock fragments and mica	Many rock fragments, mica and clay
Sorting	Well sorted	Well sorted	Poorly sorted	Poorly sorted
Roundness of grains	Well-rounded to sub-rounded	Very well-rounded	Sub-angular	Angular to sub-angular

Questions

1 Describe the texture of the breccia shown in the diagram.
2 Describe one similarity and one difference between arkose and greywacke.
3 Explain the characteristic features of desert sandstone.

Fine grained clastic sedimentary rocks

Argillaceous rocks are very fine grained. This makes observation of their characteristic features difficult. Rather than just using optical microscopes, X-ray diffraction techniques are necessary to study them in detail. The fine grained clastic rocks are the most abundant, accounting for about 75% of all sedimentary rocks. Fossils are common in these fine grained rocks, while they are very rare in the coarser clastic rocks.

Mudstone

Mudstones are dark grey, very fine grained clastic rocks. They contain **clay minerals**, mica and quartz, but you will not be able to identify individual minerals even with a hand lens. The minerals do not have any preferred alignment and so mudstones are not layered. Also, mudstone does not have **plasticity**.

Clay

Clay is very fine grained, more compacted than mudstone and contains 40% water. The grains are clay size (average grain size up to 0.0039 mm) and mainly consist of clay minerals. Clay may have a variety of colours, including dark brown, red and green, depending on the carbon or iron content. The higher the organic content, the darker the clay. Clay is plastic and can be moulded. It forms layers, with distinct bedding planes.

Shale

Shale is a dark coloured, fine grained clastic rock that has distinctive layers, due to the alignment of minerals. The clay minerals are flat and platy and align parallel to the beds at 90 degrees to the pressure from the weight of overlying rocks. The rock easily splits along the layers or laminations and for this reason it is described as **fissile**. It is composed of clay minerals, mica and quartz. Shale is not plastic but hard, brittle and impermeable.

All of these argillaceous clastic rocks and sediments are deposited in low energy environments, commonly marine but also on the flood plains of rivers or in lakes. They may contain fossils. None of them has significant amounts of cement between the grains.

Describing and identifying non-clastic sedimentary rocks

Non-clastic is the term used to describe rocks that do not contain rock fragments, so is used for the biologically and chemically formed sedimentary rocks (see spread 2.3.4).

Limestones

Limestones fall into two groups:
- chemical limestone formed from the precipitation of $CaCO_3$ from sea water
- biological limestone formed from organic remains such as shell fragments.

Most limestone contains more than 90% $CaCO_3$, usually in the form of calcite, so observing its mineral composition is a good method of identification. Modern limestone is composed of aragonite, a form of $CaCO_3$ that is unstable in rocks and changes to calcite. Calcite reacts vigorously with dilute HCl and has three cleavage directions, not at right angles, making it easy to identify.

Key definitions

Clay minerals are a group of sub-microscopic platy aluminium silicates related to mica.

Plasticity is the ability of a material to permanently change shape without fracturing.

Fissile refers to the tendency of a rock to split into thin layers.

Figure 1 Shale is fissile and splits into thin sheets

Oolitic limestone

These are chemically formed limestones containing sub-spherical sand sized grains about 1 mm in diameter, called ooliths. In cross-section, ooliths show concentric layers of calcium carbonate surrounding a nucleus, which may be a grain of sand, shell fragment or pellet. The ooliths are surrounded either by a fine grained calcite mud **matrix** (**micrite**) or a crystalline calcite cement (**sparite**).They form in tropical or sub-tropical seas, in shallow water agitated by high energy waves.

Fossiliferous limestone

These biologically formed limestones are composed of fossils or fragments of fossils. They can be described as bioclastic if they are made of fossil fragments, but they are not clastic. They may have a micrite matrix or sparite cement. One common type is a crinoidal limestone that is made up of stem sections or single ossicles with rare plates formed from the calyx or arms of a crinoid. Reef limestones contain fragments of corals as well as many brachiopod or bivalve shells. Many other limestones can be described as shelly, made almost entirely of bivalve or gastropod shells. Fossil rich limestones can form in a range of environments from low energy freshwater lakes or lagoons, such as the gastropod Viviparus limestone of the Jurassic, to marine beds, such as the Ostrea bed full of bivalves, also of the Jurassic. If the fossils are whole then the rock is likely to have been formed in a low energy environment, while broken fossils suggest high energy.

Chalk

This is a biologically formed limestone composed of coccoliths, the calcareous disc or oval shaped platelets that form part of the skeletons of single-celled algae. The chalk is white as it is pure calcium. Chalk is commonly formed in low energy, deep water shelf environments.

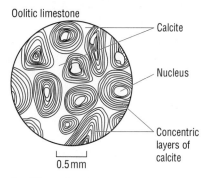

Oolitic limestone
- Calcite
- Nucleus
- Concentric layers of calcite

0.5 mm

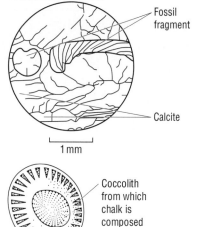

Fossiliferous limestone
- Fossil fragment
- Calcite

1 mm

- Coccolith from which chalk is composed

0.001 mm

Figure 2 Diagrams of non-clastic sedimentary rocks

Figure 3 Shelly limestone from the Jurassic that is over 90% whole and broken shells of the bivalve Ostrea

Questions

1 Draw a scale diagram to show the characteristic features of chalk.
2 Explain why fossiliferous limestones are not described as clastic sedimentary rocks.
3 If the shelly limestone in the photo is 24% whole fossils and 76% broken fossils, describe the possible conditions of deposition of this rock.

What are sedimentary structures?

When sediments are deposited they form a series of horizontal layers or beds. Each bed is separated from the next by surfaces called bedding planes. Sedimentary structures are features found on bedding planes or within a bed. They are produced by a variety of sedimentary processes and in a range of environments. They can provide evidence for the environments in which they form and some of them can be used to indicate whether beds are the right way up.

Where sedimentary structures are found	Use as way-up indicator	Use as palaeo-current indicator	Use as palaeo-environmental indicator
Within beds			
• cross bedding	Yes	Yes	Sometimes – large-scale desert dunes
• graded bedding	Yes	No	Sometimes – in turbidity currents
• imbricate structure	No	Yes	Yes – river channels
• salt pseudomorphs	Yes	No	Yes – arid evaporation
On bedding planes			
• ripple marks	Yes	Yes – if asymmetrical	Yes – beach or shallow sea or dune
• desiccation cracks	Yes	No	Yes – arid evaporation
• flute casts	Yes	Yes	Yes – turbidity currents on deep ocean floor

Cross bedding

Sand grains will be moved by wind, river or marine currents in high energy environments. The sand particles are deposited to form dunes or sand bars. The currents are unidirectional – they flow in one main direction over a period of time. The result is a gentle slope on the windward/upstream side (side from which currents flow) and a steep slope on the lee side where the sand grains avalanche down the slope to settle at a maximum angle of 37 degrees from the horizontal. This is the maximum angle of rest.

Dunes or bars constantly migrate down current, but only the lee side or slip face is preserved. A new dune migrating on top of an original dune cuts off the first set and produces a new cross-bedding set.

Wind blown sand in deserts is found in large dune structures so the cross bedding is measured in metres. Beach and shallow sea sand bars produce cross bedding that is about 10 to 15 cm high, while the smallest scale is in rivers at about 3 to 10 cm high. Cross bedding can be used as a **palaeocurrent** indicator, as the cross-bedding planes always dip down in the direction of current flow.

Cross bedding is the right way up when it is concave upwards. The cross-bedding pattern flattens out at the base but is cut off at the top. This is due to erosion, which can only occur at the top.

Cut off at top due to erosion

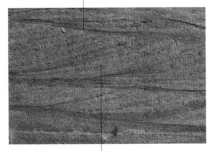

Cross bedding flattens at base and is concave upwards

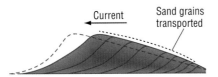

Figure 1 Cross bedding

Graded bedding

The largest and heaviest particles are on the bottom of the bed and finer particles are at the top. So in each layer, the grains become progressively finer towards the top, but there is an abrupt change in grain size at each bedding plane. This makes graded bedding useful as a **way-up structure**.

Graded bedding can form when the velocity of a turbidity current decreases, depositing the largest and heaviest particles first, followed by progressively smaller and lighter particles as the current velocity decreases further. Turbidity currents that flow onto the abyssal plain from the continental slope, or rivers that flow into lakes, bring sediment into the calm water where it settles out to form a distinct bed. Graded bedding is found in sandstones, greywacke or conglomerates.

Graded bedding

Size of grains varies from coarse at the bottom to finer at the top

Current direction

Imbricate structure

Pebbles are rolled along a stream bed and then pile up against each other. Flat (disc and blade shapes) pebbles stack against each other so that their long axes are roughly parallel. This orientation provides maximum resistance to movement. The pebbles are inclined (dip) in an upstream direction, the tops of the pebbles pointing downstream.

Imbricate structure
In river sediments, imbricated pebbles 'lean' in the direction of the current

Salt pseudomorphs

Cubic halite crystals grow at the surface of a bed due to evaporation of salty water in arid environments. The crystals may become partly embedded in sediment deposited by evaporating saline water. The sediment dries out in the heat. When the dried-up lake fills with water again the halite crystals are dissolved leaving cubic-shaped moulds. These are then infilled by sediment, which takes on the shape of the halite crystals. Hence the name pseudomorph, meaning imitation form.

Salt pseudomorphs
Halite forms cubic crystals which may be infilled by sediment if the halite has dissolved

Figure 2 Graded bedding, imbricate structure and salt pseudomorphs

Key definitions

Palaeocurrent indicator is a sedimentary structure that allows the direction of an ancient current to be deduced.

Palaeo-environmental indicator is a sedimentary structure formed in specific environmental conditions in the ancient past.

A **way-up structure** allows geologists to work out whether rocks are in their original orientation or whether they have been inverted by folding.

Questions

1 Draw a diagram to show cross bedding in rocks that have been inverted.
2 State the current direction that produced the imbricate structure in the photo.
3 Apart from scale, describe one other way in which cross bedding formed in wind blown dunes could be distinguished from cross bedding formed in a river channel.
4 Draw a diagram of a recumbent fold showing one bed with graded bedding. Label the inverted limb.

Ripple marks

Ripple marks form as sand grains are transported by saltation in high energy conditions:

- Symmetrical ripple marks are formed by oscillating currents, so they are most common on beaches where tidal action moves sediment up and down the beach.

Symmetrical ripple marks formed by the tides on a beach

Ripple marks

← Current direction →

Symmetrical ripple marks

Ripple marks have pointed crests and rounded troughs – a way-up indicator

Current direction →

Asymmetrical ripple marks

Up ↑

- Asymmetrical ripple marks are formed by currents that travel in one direction, so they are common in river, shallow sea and desert environments where the wind acts in the same way as water. These ripple marks can be used as palaeocurrent indicators.

Desiccation cracks

These cracks only form in clay-rich sediments. Loss of water due to evaporation by solar heating causes mud to contract, forming polygonal-shaped blocks separated by cracks. Each crack has a V-shaped cross-section with a wide top and a narrow base, which makes them good way-up indicators. The cracks are wider at the top because evaporation of water from the mud is greatest near the surface, which receives most solar heat energy.

Cracks are only preserved if they are infilled by sediment, usually silt or mud of a different colour. Desiccation cracks are good palaeo-environmental indicators of arid areas with high evaporation rates, such as playa lakes.

Desiccation cracks

Plan view shows polygonal blocks separated by cracks

Cracks infilled by fine sediment

Cracks narrow downwards – way-up indicator

Flute casts

A flute cast is a structure found at the base of a bed. Flute casts are formed as a result of erosion caused by turbulent flow, often associated with powerful turbidity currents. They can form in any environment where water flows with high energy over soft mud. They form parallel to the current and are deeper and pointed at the upstream end. This makes them good palaeocurrent indicators. They are infilled by overlying sediments.

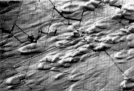

Flute casts

Base of a bed showing flute casts

Deeper, pointed end is upstream

Direction of current →

Wider, shallower downstream end

Deeper, pointed upstream end

Turbulent flow erodes soft mud

Figure 1 Ripple marks, desiccation cracks and flute casts

Palaeocurrents

Measurements made on sedimentary structures can be used to show palaeocurrent information in the form of a rose diagram:

- This method works well for flute casts, by measuring with a compass the orientation of each structure. The direction of flow tells us the direction of the turbidity current that formed the structures.
- Cross-bedding dip directions can also be measured as the sediment is only preserved on the leeward slope of a dune or sand bar. Measuring sets of cross bedding over a large area gives data that can then be plotted to show the current direction. The wind direction that formed the sand dunes of the Triassic can be identified using this method.

Interpreting a rose diagram

A number of measurements of cross bedding were taken in a series of sandstones to help determine the current direction that formed the cross-bedded sandstones.

Orientation (degrees from north)	Number of cross-bedding readings
1–30°	10
31–60°	14
61–90°	2
91–120°	8
121–150°	5
151–180°	3
181–210°	0
211–240°	0
241–270°	0
271–300°	0
301–330°	0
331–360°	3

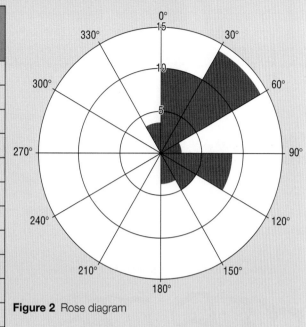

Figure 2 Rose diagram

Figure 4 Cross bedding in a desert sandstone

The data are plotted on the rose diagram by shading in the appropriate area. In this case the current direction is northeast. If the data are for a trend, the second half of the diagram is completed by repeating the data for 1 to 180 degrees. When a compass is used to measure the direction of dip it could be placed either way so the readings for 1 to 30 degrees will be the same as those for 180 to 210 degrees.

Way-up indicators

Way-up indicators are needed where rocks have been inverted by folding, making it difficult to identify the bottom and top of a bed.

	Correct way up	Inverted	Identification
Graded bedding	Younger rock / Older rock		In graded bedding the heaviest/largest particles settle out first, so the sequence is coarse to fine upwards
Cross bedding	Younger rock		Each cross bedding plane is concave upwards. Truncated cut off planes are at the top
Ripple marks	Younger rock / Older rock		Each ripple has a crest that points up
Desiccation cracks	Silt infilling / Clay	Older rock / Younger rock	Cracks are wide at the top and narrow downwards. They are filled by younger sediment

Figure 3 Way-up structures

Questions

1 Explain why desiccation cracks are wider at the top than the base.
2 Name the sedimentary structures that are useful in determining palaeocurrent directions.
3 Draw a recumbent fold and show graded bedding in one bed. Explain why sedimentary structures can help to put the beds in age order in areas where the rocks are deformed.

⑨ **Turning sediments into rocks – diagenesis**

Sandstone is not the same as sand. **Diagenesis** is the group of processes which change sand from a sediment into sandstone, a sedimentary rock. It takes place at low temperatures and pressures, at or near the Earth's surface. The main processes involved in diagenesis are compaction and cementation. Sediments are lithified, meaning they become sedimentary rocks. Diagenesis may continue after sediment has been converted to a rock, so **lithification** is part of diagenesis.

Compaction

Mud and sand

As layers of sediment accumulate, one on top of another, their mass produces load pressure. This acts vertically and affects the sediments below causing compaction to take place. Grains become more closely packed and this reduces the **porosity** of the sediment.

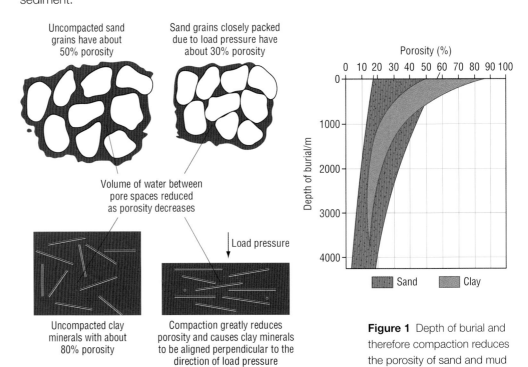

Figure 1 Depth of burial and therefore compaction reduces the porosity of sand and mud

Mud and clay are much more affected by compaction than sandstones. The original thickness of sediment can be reduced by as much as 80% in mudrocks. The compacted sediment becomes mudstone, or if the minerals show preferred alignment, it becomes shale. The diagram shows how porosity varies with depth of burial and therefore compaction in sand and mud.

Plants and coals

Where plant remains fall into swamps, the process of decay uses up the available oxygen. Anaerobic bacteria change the plant material into **peat**. Woody material (lignin), resins and waxes are preserved. If peat is buried beneath other sediments it is subjected to increased pressure and temperature, which expels water and volatiles such as CH_4 and CO_2. This reduces volume and increases the proportion of carbon it contains. As diagenesis continues, the peat gradually takes on the properties of coal. These gradual changes result in different types of **coal**, which are ranked according to the proportion of carbon they contain.

Cementation

Sandstones

Sands and many biologically formed types of sediments have greater **permeability** than muds. Groundwater containing minerals in solution flows through the pore spaces and where conditions are right the minerals are precipitated forming a **cement**, which binds grains together to form sandstones and limestones. The most common cementing minerals are:

- quartz, from pressure solution, e.g. in orthoquartzites
- calcite, from solution of carbonate shells, e.g. in fossiliferous limestone
- iron minerals, often hematite or limonite

Key definitions

Cement is the minerals precipitated between grains in sedimentary rocks binding them together.

Reducing pore space means reducing space for water or oil

When a rock becomes compacted the grains are pushed together making the pore spaces where water or oil can be stored much smaller. If the sediment is then cemented by minerals, then both porosity and permeability will be reduced.

Unconsolidated sand	Sandstone compacted but not cemented	Well cemented sandstone
57% porosity	35% porosity	3% porosity

This means that most aquifers where water is stored and reservoir rocks for oil and gas are in younger rocks that are most likely to have a high porosity.

However, using porosity can be very useful. A dam built on uncemented sandstone would leak water. A tunnel through a porous rock is likely to let in water, which could be dangerous.

Limestones

Modern limestones are composed of aragonite, an unstable form of $CaCO_3$. It changes to become the more stable form, calcite. Some ancient corals had hard parts composed of calcite. The details in these fossils are better preserved than in fossils of creatures that had hard parts composed of aragonite that converted to calcite during diagenesis. Pore spaces between shell fragments may be filled by coarse grained sparite. Spaces left when the soft parts of organisms decay are also filled by calcite crystals that grow from the internal surfaces of the fossil fragments. Parts of crinoid fossils, made from large single crystals of calcite, develop large overgrowths of calcite. These textures are illustrated in this spread.

	Increasing rank	Composition	Characteristics
	Peat Thickness of peat before compaction	Water/Gas	Spongy plant debris
	Lignite Relative thickness of lignite from compaction of peat	Carbon / Water/Gas	Contains recognisable woody material in brown, crumbly coal
	Bituminous coal Relative thickness of bituminous coal from compaction of lignite	Water/ Gas / Carbon	Black in colour and has bright and dull layers
	Anthracite Relative thickness of anthracite from compaction of bituminous coal	Carbon	Hard with bright metallic lustre

(left axis: **Increasing depth of burial**)

Figure 2 Diagenesis and coal

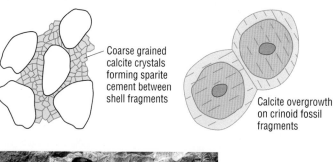

Coarse grained calcite crystals forming sparite cement between shell fragments

Calcite overgrowth on crinoid fossil fragments

Calcite crystals filling fossil shells

Figure 3 Textures in limestone cements

Questions

1 Name the sediments that are most affected by compaction.
2 Describe the processes that change sand into orthoquartzite.
3 Describe the conditions in which plant remains are preserved.

Glacial environments exist in arctic climates. At the present day they are restricted to polar regions and high mountains where the temperature averages are close to zero. There have been at least three ice ages when arctic climates were more extensive – the late Precambrian, the Ordovician and the Permo-Carboniferous. We know this because the rocks and sediments produced are the same as those now forming in polar regions. Ancient glacial deposits occur in places that are far from the modern poles, as a result of plate movements.

Glacial processes and products

Vast amounts of sediment were eroded and transported by the actions of ice, water and wind during the Quaternary. Material deposited from beneath glaciers and ice sheets is known as till or boulder clay and covers much of the surface in northern England and the Midlands. Following the melting of ice sheets and glaciers, large volumes of sand and gravel were transported along river valleys or deposited along the edges of the ice sheets. In some areas, large ice-dammed lakes formed in which clays and sands were laid down.

Boulder clay

Where rocks obstruct the movement of a glacier, the pressure of the ice on the upstream side of the rock causes local melting of the ice. The water flows to the downstream side of the rock where it freezes in any fractures that exist in the rock. This allows the ice to pluck large fragments away as it refreezes and the ice moves on due to gravity.

Fragments of rock at the base of a glacier scratch striations on underlying rock surfaces. Abrasion during transport produces fine grained, crushed rock fragments.

When ice melts, it deposits poorly sorted material in the form of boulder clay (till), which may become lithified to form tillite. Boulder clay or **till** is composed of the unsorted materials of glacial erosion. The main characteristics are:

* poor sorting
* angular fragments
* large clasts randomly orientated and scattered throughout clay
* clasts may be striated
* may contain **erratics**.

Boulder clay deposited from melting ice sheets covers very large areas.

Fluvio-glacial deposits

These are sediments that have been transported by glacial meltwater streams before being deposited on an outwash plain some distance away from the melting ice. They are mainly composed of gravels and sands but can contain coarser pebbles. They are sorted by fast flowing braided streams and may show cross bedding and sometimes graded bedding. Most of the finer mud and silt is carried further away, often to lakes, where it is deposited as varves.

Varves

When glacier ice melts, lakes are formed. During the spring thaw, streams transport fine sand, silt and clay. The sand and silt size grains settle to the floor of the lake first. The very fine grains remain in suspension, settling when the lake freezes in winter. This produces fine-grained laminated sediments called **varves,** in which the silty layer represents summer deposition and the clay layer represents winter deposition. Each pair of varves represents one year's deposition. They have been counted and used to date events at the end of the last ice age.

Case study

During the Quaternary there was widespread glaciation separated by more temperate climatic conditions (interglacials). There have been at least seven glacial-interglacial cycles, although only the last three or four of these resulted in ice sheets spreading across Britain. During the ice ages, an ice sheet 1 km thick existed and glaciers developed in upland areas.

The climate of the interglacials was temperate, similar to that of today and at times warmer. During the warmer interglacials, hippopotamuses, elephants, hyenas and lions lived in southern Britain. During the cold glacial episodes, woolly mammoths, woolly rhinoceros and reindeer roamed over much of southern England.

During glaciations, sea level was up to 120 m lower and the English Channel and most of the North Sea were land.

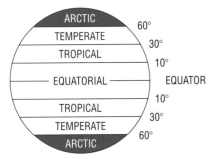

Figure 1 Location of arctic climates

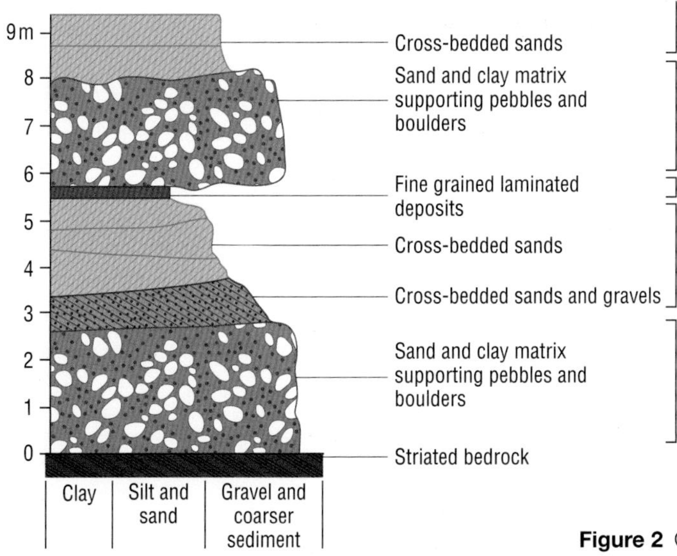
9m
8
7
6
5
4
3
2
1
0
Cross-bedded sands
Sand and clay matrix supporting pebbles and boulders
Fine grained laminated deposits
Cross-bedded sands
Cross-bedded sands and gravels
Sand and clay matrix supporting pebbles and boulders
Striated bedrock
Clay
Silt and sand
Gravel and coarser sediment
Fluvio-glacial sand and gravel
Till deposited from melting ice
Varves in lake
Fluvio-glacial sand and gravel
Till deposited from melting ice

Figure 2 Glacial sequence

Evidence for glacial deposits from fossils

Glacial sequences indicate cold climates, i.e. deposition in polar regions or during ice ages. Glacial deposits contain few fossils because the climate was generally too harsh for most forms of life.

Oxygen isotope ratios can be measured using shells of marine microfossils. The ratios show ocean water temperature. Pollen grains are preserved in lake sediments. Some plants such as pine tolerate cold more than others such as oak and this affects their abundance in pollen samples from lake sediments.

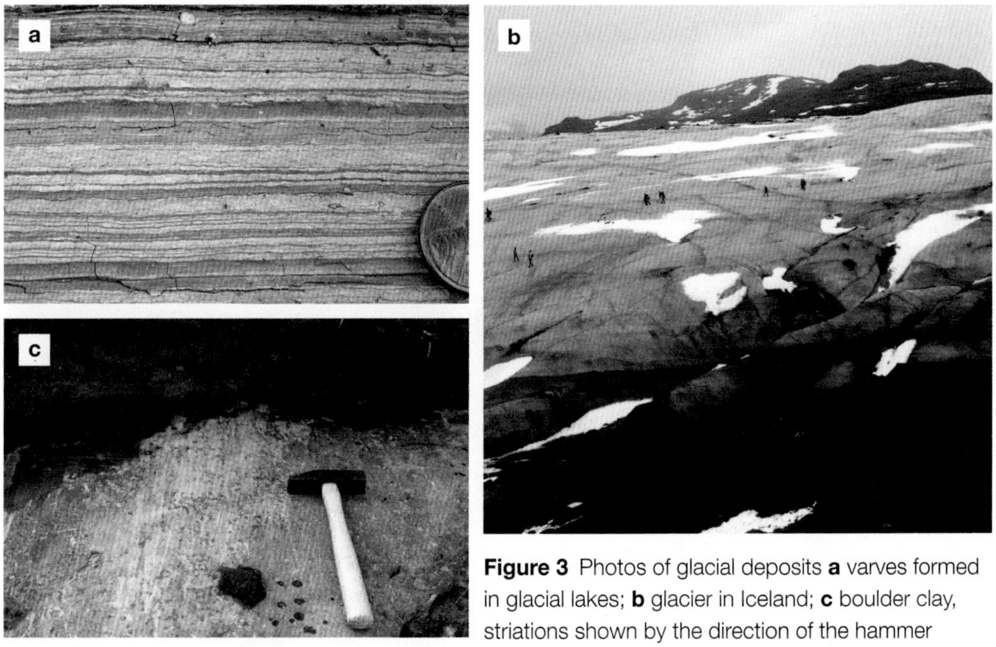
a
b
c

Figure 3 Photos of glacial deposits **a** varves formed in glacial lakes; **b** glacier in Iceland; **c** boulder clay, striations shown by the direction of the hammer

Questions

1 Explain why boulder clay is poorly sorted.
2 Describe the sequence of events shown in the glacial sequence diagram.
3 Explain how freeze–thaw weathering may have produced the ice wedge cast shown in the photo.
4 Research the sediments that were laid down in Britain under glacial conditions during the Quaternary.

Key definitions

Till is a poorly sorted sediment ranging from boulders to clay size, deposited from ice and not reworked by water.

Erratics are clasts of a different rock type from that found locally and therefore transported from another area.

Fluvio-glacial deposits are sediments produced by meltwater streams flowing from a glacier.

Varves are fine grained banded deposits from glacial lakes containing coarser pale material deposited in summer and finer dark material deposited in winter.

Examiner tip

Ancient glacial deposits can be recognised by:

- striations – the scratches formed by rocks carried in moving ice. They can be used to tell the direction of movement of ancient ice ages;
- tillite – the rock formed from very poorly sorted and varied material dropped by the ice;
- varves – the annual lake clays and silts in distinctive thin layers;
- fluvio-glacial sands and gravels.

Fluvial environments include all parts of rivers, from the smallest streams to huge rivers all the way to the estuaries where rivers meet the sea. Rivers are the transport systems for sediment, moving enormous quantities of mud, sand and rock down to the sea. You will remember that as the particles are transported they get smaller and rounder due to attrition and abrasion.

Rivers are generally high energy environments, with only the flood plain where there is not a strong current flowing. However, when heavy rainfall causes flooding, the energy level will rapidly rise so that even small streams will carry large boulders. In dry conditions, very little water will flow and the energy levels will be low.

River

The Mississippi River carries roughly 550 million metric tonnes of sediment into the Gulf of Mexico each year. The water of the Mississippi is usually a murky brown colour due to the sediment from its $3\,250\,000$ km² basin – enough to extend the coast of Louisiana 91 m each year.

Case study

Although gradient decreases downstream, the flow velocity generally increases. This is due to three main factors:

- Velocity (ms⁻¹) increases continuously due to gravity induced acceleration.
- Flow resistance is high in the upper parts of a stream due to boulder-strewn, broad, shallow channels.
- Total volume of water increases downstream as tributaries join the main channel.

The higher the velocity, the more sediment can be transported. Rivers on flat areas are carrying huge quantities of fine sediment in suspension, giving them a brown colour.

Velocity and deposition

Streams flow downhill from a source area to a lake or the sea. The gradient down which the stream flows is steeper in upper mountainous areas and shallower across the flood plain near the mouth of the stream. The velocity of water in a river is slower near a stream bed or bank than it is in the centre where flow is faster. This is due to friction with the channel floor and sides. The current tries to flow in a straight line so the bank is eroded where the current hits the outside of a river bend.

Where velocity is reduced, deposition takes place. Reductions in velocity occur:

- where there is a sudden change in slope
- on the inside of meander bends
- where a tributary joins a river
- where rivers enter lakes or seas that do not have strong currents.

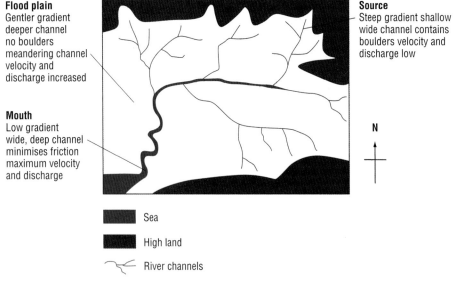

Flood plain
Gentler gradient deeper channel no boulders meandering channel velocity and discharge increased

Mouth
Low gradient wide, deep channel minimises friction maximum velocity and discharge

Source
Steep gradient shallow wide channel contains boulders velocity and discharge low

N

- ▬ Sea
- ▬ High land
- ⤳ River channels

Figure 1 Map and photo of fluvial environments. Photograph shows muddy channels flowing to the NW into the sea

Characteristic products of sedimentation in fluvial environments

Alluvial fan breccias, conglomerates and arkoses

Where mountain streams flow onto a flat valley floor or plain, there is a marked decrease in gradient and reduction in stream velocity and energy. Large volumes of sediment are deposited to form alluvial fans.

Breccias form from angular and coarse scree fragments. Conglomerates composed of rounded pebbles form in the streams. Arkose is formed from sand sized material deposited rapidly in fairly arid conditions, as it contains more than 25% feldspar, which shows little sign of weathering. The usual source of the feldspar is granitic rock upstream.

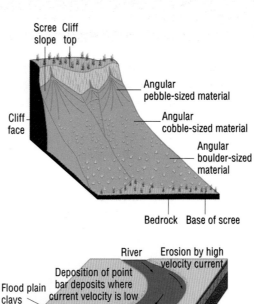

Figure 2 Fluvial deposits

Channel conglomerates and sandstones in meandering rivers

Meandering streams flow in channels with looping curves. The bank on the outside of a meander bend is eroded and deposition occurs on the inside of the meander on **a point bar**. As a result, the channel migrates laterally.

Meandering rivers and braided rivers result in **upward fining** cycles of sediments, as shown in the graphic log opposite. Conglomerates form from the **channel lag** and may show imbricate structure if the clasts are disc or blade shaped. Sandstones form as the point bar deposits on the insides of meander bends in the channels. They are often cross bedded and moderately well sorted with sub-rounded grains. They can contain muscovite as well as quartz, so may be described as micaceous sandstones. The sandstones have rare masses of lignite, which are fossil tree trunks washed into the rivers. The clays and mudstones formed in the low energy environment of the **flood plain**.

Flood plain clays and silts

At times of high flow, rivers flood the surrounding flat area adjacent to the channel, forming a flood plain. Clays rich in organic material are deposited from the suspended load of the river and may contain fossil plants. Siltstone is also common on the flood plain and may show very small-scale cross bedding. The mudstones may show evidence of sub-aerial exposure to the elements, with desiccation cracks and the development of soils. Any fossils will be terrestrial in origin, for example, vertebrate footprints or plant fossils.

Questions

1 Describe the fluvial environments in which the sedimentary rocks shown in the graphic log were deposited.
2 Describe the texture of sediments deposited in alluvial fan environments.
3 Explain with the aid of diagrams how meandering river channels migrate laterally.
4 Research the sediments that were laid down in Britain under fluvial conditions during the Triassic.

Key definitions

Upward fining describes a series of layers in which average grain size decreases upwards as energy decreases.

A **channel lag** is a coarse grained sediment deposit left in a channel after finer grained particles have been transported away.

A **point bar** is a deposit of sand or coarser grained sediments on the inside of a meander bend.

A **flood plain** is flat land adjacent to a river over which it spreads when in flood.

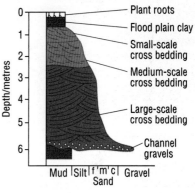

Figure 3 Graphic log of a fluvial sequence

Examiner tip

Ancient river deposits can be recognised by:
● the limited lateral extent – as the channels move the sandstone in lenses, cross cutting into older beds
● lignite plant fossils in sandstones but generally the lack of fossils
● the mix of conglomerate, sandstone and shales all together.

Many, but not all, of the hot deserts on Earth are in tropical latitudes. Outside these latitudes, there are extensive deserts in continental interiors where there is a wide diurnal temperature range due to a lack of cloud cover. When rainfall does occur it is often torrential. The bare, sun-dried ground allows rapid run-off, causing **flash floods** that give streams high energy for short periods. Perhaps surprisingly water is one of the main agents of erosion and transport in deserts. The other is the wind, which moves sand and finer grained sediment, leading to the formation of dunes.

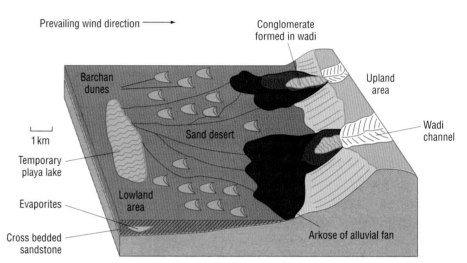

Figure 1 Geography of a hot desert environment

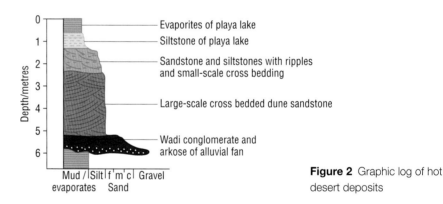

Figure 2 Graphic log of hot desert deposits

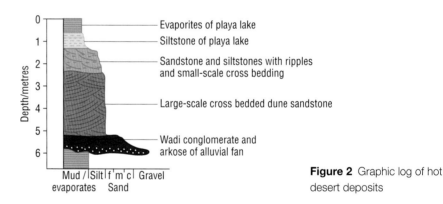

Figure 3 a Poorly sorted clasts in a wadi conglomerate – grain size varies from cobbles to fine sand. Haematite coating the grains gives the rock a red colour.
b Flash flooding in the Arizona desert

Processes and products in hot desert environments
Wadi conglomerates

Desert stream channels are known as **wadis**. Their source is usually in mountains, so they have steep gradients. Together with the intensity of the rainfall, this gives the streams very high energy and so they can transport coarse grained fragments. Energy is quickly lost when the rain stops and because water sinks into the porous rocks of the channel. Deposition is rapid, leaving poorly sorted conglomerates. Grains may be sub-rounded if they have been transported on several occasions. Grains that have only been briefly transported, perhaps during one flash flood, may be angular. Desert conditions often lead to grains having a red coating of oxidised iron minerals.

Desert sandstones

Sand grains are transported by high energy winds and affected by attrition. This makes them:

- very well sorted
- very well rounded
- high sphericity
- frosted due to the collisions between grains.

They are composed entirely of quartz grains because other minerals present in the source rocks have been removed by mechanical and chemical weathering. Quartz remains because it is unreactive and hard. The frosted surfaces of the grains are due to attrition during transport. Because of their shape and size they are sometimes described as 'millet-seed sand'.

Desert sandstones are formed from these sands. The grains are coated with oxidised iron minerals so that they have a red colour and desert sandstones often have silica cement. They show large-scale cross bedding on a scale of metres rather than centimetres because they are often deposited in large dunes. The dunes may be crescent-shaped barchan dunes or straight seif dunes. The dunes move in the direction of the prevailing wind and sand is blown up the windward side and slips down the leeward side. It is this face that can be preserved to make the cross bedding. Some dunes are 200 m high.

Playa lake evaporites

Due to the hot climate, infrequent rainfall, high rates of evaporation and infiltration, desert streams tend not to flow all the way to the sea. Hot deserts are often regions of inland drainage where streams flow into temporary **playa lakes.** Stream water flowing into the lakes contains ions of calcium, sodium and potassium in solution. They are products of the weathering of rocks upstream. When the water evaporates in the hot sun, all of the dissolved ions become more concentrated. The least soluble are the first to precipitate out to form layers of **evaporite minerals**. The most soluble will be in the centre of the playa lake.

Evaporites			
Solubility	**Mineral name**	**Properties**	**Order of precipitation**
Less soluble	Calcite	White; hardness = 3; rhombic crystals and good cleavage; vigorous reaction with dilute HCl	Precipitated first
	Gypsum	White; hardness = 2; crystals or may form nodular layers	
	Halite	Cubic 'hopper' crystals; cubic cleavage; salty taste	
More soluble	K minerals		Precipitated later

Fine grained sediment is also deposited from suspension to form mudstones in playa lake environments. These may contain desiccation cracks, ripple marks and salt pseudomorphs, as well as lenses of evaporites, usually gypsum.

Questions

1 Explain why halite is found near the middle of dried-up playa lakes.

2 Describe the formation of salt pseudomorphs.

3 Describe and explain the sequence of environments shown in the graphic log.

4 Research the sediments that were laid down in Britain under hot, arid conditions during the Triassic.

Key definitions

A **flash flood** is a brief but very high energy flow of water over a surface or down a river channel, usually caused by heavy rainfall.

A **wadi** is a river channel in a hot desert region in which flow may occur very occasionally.

A **playa lake** is a temporary lake formed by storm run-off in deserts having inland drainage.

Evaporites are sedimentary rocks resulting from the evaporation of saline water.

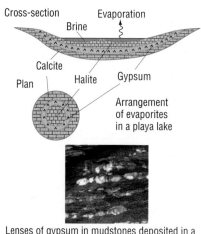

Figure 4 Cross bedded desert sandstone

Lenses of gypsum in mudstones deposited in a playa lake

Figure 5 Playa deposits

Examiner tip

Ancient desert deposits can be recognised by:

- red colour formed by iron oxide
- well sorted and well rounded sandstones with large-scale cross bedding
- evaporites and clays formed in playa lakes
- sedimentary structures – desiccation cracks and salt pseudomorphs.

Deltas occur where a river flows into a sea or lake and deposits its load of sediment. There must be little wave or tidal action to allow the sediment to build up at the mouth of the river and not be washed away. It is the decrease in energy that causes deposition of sediments, with the coarsest grains settling out first.

The build up of sediment causes the river channels to become blocked so that the river switches its course and splits into **distributary** channels.

Deltas are just above sea level and in between the distributary channels there are usually swamps. In equatorial and humid tropical climates vegetation grows very rapidly and is abundant. Plant remains require anaerobic conditions if they are to be preserved, and swamps provide these conditions. This is why ancient plant remains are preserved as coal in equatorial deltaic sequences.

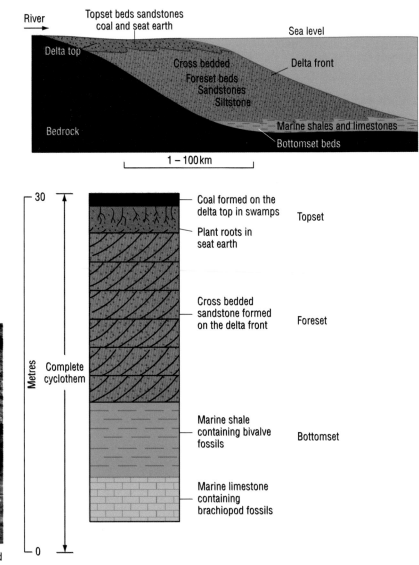

Figure 1 Satellite photo of the Mississippi Delta showing sediment flowing into the Gulf of Mexico through distributary channels

Figure 3 Photo of a river channel containing course grained sands and gravel cutting through older beds

Figure 2 Cross-section through a delta

The delta top

The delta top is dominated by distributary channels with areas of swamps, bays or flood plains in between. The channels change course frequently, a process known as delta switching that leads to lateral changes in the pattern of sedimentation.

Sediments deposited on the delta top are called the **topsets**. Coarse grained sands and gravels are deposited in the channels. They make up the bulk of sediments in the delta top and form channel sandstones, which may contain cross bedding.

Clays are deposited in areas between the channels. In the swamps, anaerobic conditions allow peat formation. Diagenetic processes lead to the formation of coal. Soils in which the trees grew may be preserved as **seat earth**.

The delta slope

As the river meets the sea, the coarsest sand grains are deposited first and the finest silt last. Deposition occurs on the delta slope and as the front of the delta advances into the sea, a vertical succession forms.

Sediments deposited on the delta slope are called the **foresets**. Coarse sand, often cross bedded, is deposited at the top. Lower down there are likely to be finer sands and silts. Marine fossils may be found.

Offshore deposition

This takes place in the area of low-energy deeper water at the bottom of the delta slope. These sediments are called **bottomsets**. They consist mainly of clays and silts, which are thinly bedded and lack sedimentary structures. They lithify to form shales, which may contain marine fossils.

Deltaic sequences

The sequence produced in a delta is a coarsening upwards sequence. It is repeated many times and each cycle is known as a **cyclothem**. It starts with marine shales and silts then fine to coarse sandstones, and finally coals, sandstones, seat earth and clay. Limestones are sometimes found at the base of the succession, representing normal marine conditions before the deltaic conditions begin.

Bioturbation and trace fossils are common, with marine fossils in the bottomsets and non-marine fossils in the higher parts of the deltaic sequence. Plant fossils are often found and sometimes, if the surface of the delta is exposed, soils and coal may form. There is often very rapid deposition of mud covering the plant material before it decays. Many of the swamps are anaerobic, which increases the chances of the plant material being preserved to form coal.

The cyclothem or part of it may be repeated many times in succession, due to subsidence or emergence, leading to marine transgressions and regressions. These are caused by:
- changes in sea level
- local isostatic changes, due to the mass of sediment causing the sea floor to sink
- changes in position of the delta lobes, due to migration of the channels
- changes in the rate of sedimentation, allowing the delta to build out or be inundated by the sea.

Questions

1 Name the climatic zone where coal is likely to form.
2 Explain why there are many layers of coal in deltaic sequences.
3 Explain why deposition takes place where rivers enter the sea.
4 Research the sediments that were laid down in Britain under deltaic conditions during the Upper-Carboniferous Coal Measures.

Key definitions

Foresets are the inclined layers formed on the delta slope, commonly consisting of cross bedded sandstones.

Bottomsets are the lowest horizontal layers of a delta, commonly consisting of shales.

A **cyclothem** represents layers repeated due to cyclic sedimentation.

Bioturbation is the disturbance of sediment by the activities of organisms (e.g. burrowing).

Seat earth is a sandy or clay-rich fossil soil found beneath a coal seam. It represents the soil in which coal forming plants grew and frequently contains carbonised traces of plant roots.

A **distributary** is a stream channel that takes water away from the main stream channel.

Topsets are the uppermost horizontal layers of a delta commonly consisting of channel sandstones, coal and seat earth.

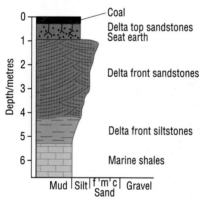

Figure 4 Graphic log of a deltaic sequence

Examiner tip

Ancient deltaic deposits can be recognised by:
- beds of coal with plant fossils and seat earth containing roots below
- channel deposits of sandstone in lenses cross-cutting into beds of coal, forming washouts
- marine sandstones with cross bedding
- shales with marine fossils.

Most shallow sea areas receive large amounts of clastic sediment transported from the land by rivers. Shallow seas extend from the extreme low water level of the **spring tide** to the edge of the continental shelf about 200 m below sea level. The extent of these shallow seas varies greatly and around the coast of Britain there are large areas.

The **littoral zone** is defined as the area between the high water and low water marks and this includes beaches. It is covered by the sea for part of the time and this high energy tidal area accumulates sediment.

Most sand and finer grained sediment deposited on beaches and in shallow seas has been transported to the sea by rivers. Coarser grained sediment may have been supplied by the erosion of coastal cliffs. Pebbles and cobble sized sediments are usually found at the back of a beach, to where they have been transported by high-energy waves during storms. Transport in shallow seas may be by **longshore drift** or by **rip currents**. The currents are uni-directional and take water and sediment along the coast or back out to sea. Tides are bi-directional.

Key definitions

Spring tides are the tides with the greatest range, and occur about every two weeks.

The **tidal range** is the vertical difference in height between extreme high and extreme low water.

The **littoral zone** is the area between extreme low and extreme high water of the spring tide.

Longshore drift is the combination of littoral drift and beach drift.

A **rip current** is a narrow fast current flowing seaward, away from the coastline.

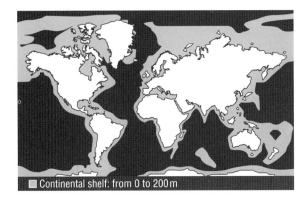

Continental shelf: from 0 to 200 m

Cross-section of a continental shelf

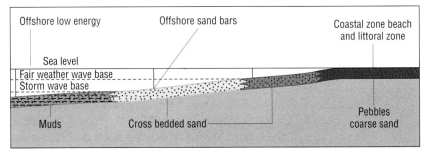

Offshore low energy | Offshore sand bars | Coastal zone beach and littoral zone

Sea level
Fair weather wave base
Storm wave base

Muds | Cross bedded sand | Pebbles coarse sand

Figure 1 Map showing the extent of the continental shelf and a cross-section showing where the sediment is deposited

Conglomerate with rounded pebbles formed on a beach

Sandstone formed lower on beach

Fine sandstone formed in a shallow sea

Fine sandstone forming a ripple mark | Clay infilling tops of ripple marks

Figure 2 Shallow sea sediments

Beach environments

Beaches are mainly composed of sand and gravel, though some may contain mud. Sand grains are regularly picked up and moved around by waves and this makes them well sorted. The grains are usually rounded as a result of attrition whilst being transported by waves and tides. The rocks commonly formed are light coloured orthoquartzites, as they are made entirely of quartz.

A few specially adapted burrowing organisms such as bivalves can survive in these extreme environments, which vary between being land and being covered by the sea, according to the tides. Tracks, trails and burrows of beach organisms as well as broken shells may be found scattered through the sand or in shell banks.

The bi-directional movement of water by tides leads to the formation of symmetrical ripple marks with crests that are parallel to the crests of the waves.

In high-energy areas, beach gravel, pebbles or cobbles are deposited. These are less frequently worked than the beach sands because they are only affected by the highest tides and highest energy storm waves. They are less well sorted than beach sands. Traces of life are rare in this environment, though there may be some shell fragments washed in. The rocks commonly formed are conglomerates. The fact that they formed on a beach is usually shown by the presence of shell fragments.

Shallow seas

The material deposited in marine sediments has its origin on the land:
- Rivers carry a suspended load of clay minerals, a dissolved load of salts, and some bed load of sand.
- Wind carries atmospheric dust, which can be deposited anywhere in the sea.

Below the littoral zone is the shallow water of the continental shelf, where the average water depth is 130 m. Here sediments are mainly affected by the currents. In general, sediment size decreases as depth and distance away from the coast increases.

Continental shelves are dynamic areas with a number of key variables that increase variety in sediment deposition:
- Sediment supply controls the rate of sedimentation. It can be very low where little sediment is entering the sea, perhaps from a low lying landmass or an area with little weathering and erosion. Where erosion is high and large rivers are transporting sediment, the rate of deposition is high.
- Changes in sea level have a huge effect on the areas close to shore. A rise in sea level causes the sea to flood the land and the zones of sediment move inland so that mud may be deposited on top of sand. This is called a marine **transgression**. Submerged forests around the coast of Britain are evidence of the rise in sea level since the last glacial period. Fossil forests are where trees were submerged and preserved by replacement of the woody tissue by silica or calcite. A drop in sea level means that the sea retreats, causing a marine **regression** and renewed erosion on land takes place bringing more sediment to the sea.
- Sediment transport can be increased by changes in a current direction or rate of flow. Many offshore sand bars can move several hundred metres in a year, causing a danger to shipping.

The sea water contains suspended sediment, reducing daylight penetration closer to shore. The abundance of life is closely linked to the availability of sunlight. The area of the continental shelf where the water depth is less than 100 m has abundant life.

Glauconite is a distinctive green potassium iron silicate mineral found in some sandstones formed in shallow seas. Uni-directional currents (e.g. littoral drift and rip currents) form asymmetrical ripple marks in sandstones. Mudstones and clays form in areas of lower energy offshore and commonly contain a wide range of fossils.

Questions

1 Explain why you would not expect to find whole fossils in a beach conglomerate.
2 Describe one similarity and one difference between sandstones formed in a river channel and in a shallow sea.
3 Explain why both symmetrical and asymmetrical ripples are found in shallow seas.
4 Research the sediments that were laid down in Britain as the Greensands under shallow sea conditions during the Cretaceous.

```
0   10
L___l
  cm
```

```
0   2
L___l
  cm
```

Figure 3 Sandstone with vertical burrows and Cretaceous Gault Clay with fossils

Clear, blue, shallow seas are the tropical island paradise shown on many travel posters of places such as the Maldives and the Bahamas. What they all have in common is a lack of terrigenous sediment – no sand or mud at all. These islands are cut off from areas where there is a supply of sediment by deep water. Most of them are just a few metres above sea level and rivers are very rare. As a result the seas have no suspended sediment and a wide range of organisms thrive.

The rocks that form in clear, non-clastic, shallow marine environments are biologically and chemically formed limestones. All limestones consist largely of calcium carbonate so react with dilute hydrochloric acid. They often contain visible **macrofossils** but **microfossils** and fossil fragments are also common.

Although most limestones are formed from the remains of organisms living in the sea, some are composed of calcium carbonate that has been directly precipitated from sea water by chemical processes.

Bioclastic or fossiliferous limestone

As much as 75% of a bioclastic rock may be composed of the remains of invertebrate skeletons from organisms such as crinoids, bivalves, brachiopods, gastropods or a mixture of fossils. The rest of the rock is formed of calcite mud and ordinary **detrital** mud. The rock itself is commonly grey in colour, such as the Carboniferous Limestones of Derbyshire. They are hard, well jointed and in thick, massive beds. They may contain the broken remains of stem segments (ossicles) of crinoids and so are called crinoidal limestones.

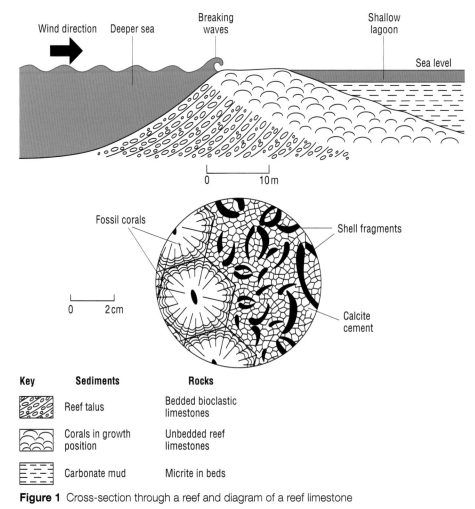

Figure 1 Cross-section through a reef and diagram of a reef limestone

Key	Sediments	Rocks
	Reef talus	Bedded bioclastic limestones
	Corals in growth position	Unbedded reef limestones
	Carbonate mud	Micrite in beds

Figure 2 Photo of the Great Barrier Reef and a coral limestone

132

Bioclastic limestones are also common from the Middle Jurassic. They are often crumbly and fossils such as *Ostrea*, a bivalve, can be picked out whole. These limestones are often cream in colour. Skeletal remains are broken into fragments during transport by the action of marine currents or waves.

Reef limestone

Corals provide the main framework of a reef, but other organisms also live on and around reefs. Carbonate secreting algae encrust the reef, cementing it together. Crinoid, brachiopod echinoid, bivalve, gastropod and trilobite remains can all be found in reef limestones. Reef limestones are typically unbedded because reefs form by growing upwards.

Reef building corals live in warm, shallow, high-energy, well oxygenated tropical waters. Water temperatures need to be between 25 and 29 °C. Reef building corals do not grow well at depths greater than 25 m. Although reefs and atolls occur in the middle of oceans, the corals only live in the shallow water near landmasses. In the Pacific, volcanic islands are colonised by corals and as the islands sink the coral may grow up at the same rate so that the coral forms a barrier reef around the island. Eventually the island sinks and a ring of coral called an atoll forms.

Chalk

Chalk is white, hard, often massive and well jointed. It is a biologically formed limestone composed of coccoliths, the tiny calcareous disc or oval shaped platelets measured in microns (10^{-6} m) that formed part of the skeletons of single-celled algae. It may contain the microfossils of foraminifera such as *Globigerina*. There may also be macrofossils of echinoids, belemnites, brachiopods and bivalves. Chalk is formed in low-energy, deep water shelf environments (<200 m), but only where very little sediment was being supplied from the land. Flint nodules are common in chalk.

Oolitic limestone

These rocks are formed from ooliths (see spread 2.3.6 for a description of oolitic limestone). They form in shallow seas where tiny grains of sand, shell fragments or pellets are rolled in carbonate mud by tidal currents and wave action. Around this nucleus concentric layers of calcium carbonate, in the form of aragonite, are precipitated from the sea water. The ooliths are therefore formed by chemical processes in warm tropical climates. Most ooliths form in water less than 2 m deep, a depth where wave agitation and tidal movements are active.

Oolitic limestones are typically white but may be yellow or orange if iron stained. Current and wave action means they are often cross bedded.

Fossils are common but the main organisms such as brachiopods and bivalves are those which were attached to the sea floor to withstand the high-energy conditions. Some organisms, such as irregular echinoids and bivalves, survived by burrowing. Many fossils are broken by the high-energy conditions.

Micrite

Micrite is a fine, hard crystalline limestone formed from calcite mud, which has undergone diagenesis. The calcite mud is produced by chemical precipitation from sea water or by carbonate secreting algae. There are normally no fossils visible.

Questions

1 Describe the formation of ooliths and how the oolitic limestone forms.
2 Explain why reef limestones contain many fossils other than corals.
3 Research the sediments that were laid down in Britain as the Carboniferous Limestone under shallow carbonate sea conditions.

Figure 3 Photo of beds of chalk in a quarry

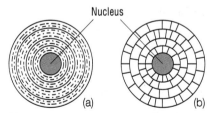

Figure 4 Internal structure of **a** modern ooliths and **b** ooliths in oolitic limestone (both about 1 mm in diameter)

Examiner tip

Ancient shallow sea carbonate deposits can be recognised by:
- composition of calcium carbonate
- abundant fossils in most limestones
- light colour due to lack of terrigenous sediment.

Evaporites form in shallow marine environments or on land in playa lakes in hot deserts (see spread 2.3.12). Normal sea water contains a variety of ions in solution, giving it a salinity of about 35 **parts per thousand** (ppt) or 3.5%. As sea water evaporates, the brine produced first becomes saturated, then **supersaturated**, at which point crystals of evaporite minerals begin to crystallise in reverse order of solubility.

- Small quantities of calcite and dolomite (carbonates) are precipitated (<1%)
- followed by gypsum and anhydrite (3%)
- then a large quantity of halite (78%)
- finally the potassium salts.

Formation of evaporites in barred basins

The basin is a bay with a restricted entrance. In hot arid conditions, water evaporates from the basin, causing lowering of the surface, drawing more water in through the narrow channel at the entrance.

Evaporation of surface water increases the salt concentration, especially at the end of the basin, away from the normal sea water entering over the bar:

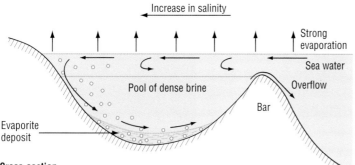

Cross-section

- Carbonates are precipitated near to the entrance due to their low solubility.
- Further away from the entrance, gypsum crystals precipitate at the surface due to evaporation and dissolve as they fall through the water below, increasing the density of water at the bottom of the basin.
- Dense **brine** sinks from the surface to the bottom of the basin and the concentration of gypsum is increased further as crystals fall from the surface and dissolve. Eventually the water in the basin is saturated in gypsum. When this occurs, gypsum crystals can form and sink to the sea floor without dissolving.
- The process is repeated for the other evaporite minerals.

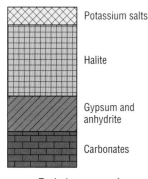

Typical sequence of minerals in a barred basin evaporite deposit

Figure 1 Evaporite deposition in a barred basin

Permian salt deposits in Europe contain 490 m of evaporites, and in some places more. This would mean evaporating a 29 km high column of sea water. Obviously these great thicknesses could not have built up by evaporating a fixed volume of sea water because there are no ocean basins 29 km deep. Instead, if the water supply is regularly topped up within a shallow **barred basin**, large volumes of evaporites could build up over time. Repeated evaporite cycles are recorded from some deposits, meaning that a basin evaporated then was flooded and evaporated again. Incomplete cycles are formed when normal sea water floods into the basin before complete evaporation has taken place.

Formation of evaporites in sabkhas

Sabkhas are low lying coastal sand flats in hot arid regions. Very gentle slopes mean that during extreme high tides the whole coastline is under water.

Processes operating in a sabkha environment

- Very strong evaporation occurs so that as the sea water approaches the coast salinity increases.
- Much of the calcium carbonate in the sea water is removed by shelled organisms living offshore.
- Evaporation of groundwater from the supratidal area draws sea water into the sediment along the shore.

Key definitions

Parts per thousand is sometimes written as ppt.

Supersaturated describes a solution that contains more dissolved substance than does a saturated solution.

Brine is a concentrated solution of salts formed by partial evaporation of sea water.

A **barred basin** is a bay partly isolated from the open ocean by a bar.

Evaporite conditions occurred in Britain in the Upper Permian Zechstein deposits in northeast England. The Zechstein was a large saline sea that extended from the North Sea area over much of northern Europe as far as Poland. The western margin of this sea overlapped the northeast coast of England, depositing thick evaporites.

Five major evaporite cycles are recognised, some with the complete sequence of carbonates, through anhydrite to thick halite capped by potassium salts.

Fossils are absent because the water was too saline to support life.

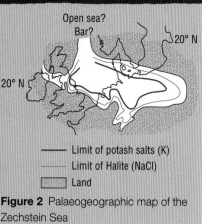

Key:
- Limit of potash salts (K)
- Limit of Halite (NaCl)
- Land

Figure 2 Palaeogeographic map of the Zechstein Sea

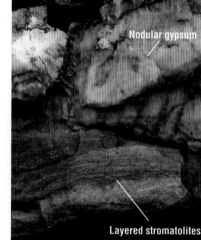

Nodular gypsum

Layered stromatolites

Figure 4 Photo of part of a sabkha succession

- Evaporites develop above the high water line as groundwater is evaporated. Algae grow on the shore between high and low tide levels and are preserved as stromatolites. Evaporite minerals are found above the stromatolites in sabkha sequences.
- The first mineral to crystallise out within the sediments is gypsum ($CaSO_4.2H_2O$).
- Anhydrite ($CaSO_4$) crystallises out next, forming nodules in the sediment.

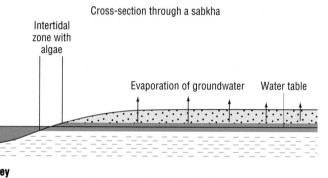

Cross-section through a sabkha

Intertidal zone with algae

Evaporation of groundwater   Water table

Sabkha succession

10 cm

Supratidal sediments with nodules of anhydrite

Intertidal stromatolites

Lagoon or shallow sea deposits

Key
- Supratidal flats with gypsum, anhydrite and halite
- Lagoon or shallow sea
- Stromatolites
- Lagoon clays

Figure 3 Evaporite deposition in a sabkha

When the Mediterranean dried up

Buried beneath the Mediterranean sea floor are immense deposits of evaporites, nearly 2 km thick. The Mediterranean is in a region where evaporation greatly exceeds precipitation. Today water enters the Mediterranean from the Atlantic, replacing water lost through evaporation. If water were not constantly flowing in through the Straits of Gibraltar, the Mediterranean Sea would dry up.

Beginning about 6 Ma, the opening between the Mediterranean and the Atlantic was blocked by tectonic uplift from the African Plate pushing into the Eurasian plate, combined with a drastic drop in sea level caused by an ice age. The sea dried up over about 1000 years. The Mediterranean sea floor became a desert 3000 m below sea level and would have looked like the Dead Sea on a larger scale. A single drying up of the Mediterranean would only form salts or evaporites 100 m thick. However, the salts are 1000 to 2000 m thick. This tells us that periodically, waters would cascade over the Gibraltar sill, partially filling the basin only to evaporate again, perhaps as many as 40 times.

About 4.5 Ma, tectonic movements opened the Atlantic Ocean access again. A very large waterfall 1 km high allowed the Atlantic to pour in through the Gibraltar Straits and refill the Mediterranean over about 100 years.

Questions

1 Explain why halite is rarely found in sabkha deposits.
2 Describe the sedimentary structures that are found in evaporite sequences.
3 Salt deposits often form salt domes due to the low density. Explain this process.
4 Research the events and sediments formed when the Mediterranean Sea dried up 25 Ma.

Deep sea sediments, found at depths greater than about 500 m, cover roughly two-thirds of the sea floor. The main deep sea sediment is carbonate ooze, which covers nearly half the ocean floor. A deep marine basin is the area in the centre of an ocean, far from land, where organisms to be fossilised are rare. Deep basins consist of several regions:

- The continental shelf is next to the land and extends out to the top of the continental slope.
- The continental slope has a steeper gradient and in many places is cut by submarine canyons eroded by turbidity currents.
- The continental rise has a gentle gradient because it is where turbidity currents deposit much of their load.
- The abyssal plain continues out across the ocean floor.
- At convergent plate margins there is a trench where sediments carried by turbidity currents are deposited.

Key definitions

A **turbidity current** is a high velocity current that flows down gentle gradients because the sediment dispersed within it makes it denser than sea water.

A **turbidite** is an upward fining deposit of greywacke deposited from a turbidity current.

A **Bouma sequence** is an idealised sequence of sediments and sedimentary structures seen in a turbidite deposit.

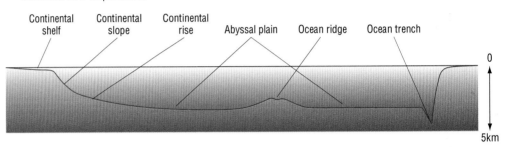

Figure 1 Cross-section through a deep marine basin with the vertical scale exaggerated

Ocean margins

Most deposition on the abyssal plain takes place from **turbidity currents**. Sediment brought to the sea by rivers accumulates on the continental shelf. If an earthquake causes the material to slip down the continental slope, it will become a turbidity current.

The density of the turbidity flow means that it flows with high velocity down the gentle gradients (average gradient of the continental slope is 4 degrees). A turbidity current transports huge volumes of clastic material from the continental shelf. The sediment includes coarse and medium grained particles, as well as large quantities of mud. Much of the sediment is deposited in submarine fans on the continental rise or in ocean trenches. However, some can be spread over a distance of thousands of kilometres across the abyssal plain. The heavier coarse grains are deposited first. As the current loses energy, finer sand and silt settles out. During times when turbidity currents do not flow, fine mud (interturbidite) is deposited from suspension to form shale. The overall product is an upward fining sequence called a **turbidite**, shown in the diagram and described in the table.

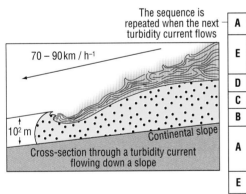

Figure 2 Deposition from turbidity currents

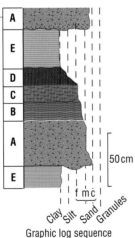

Graphic log sequence

	A turbidite sequence all laid down from a turbidity flow over a few days or weeks	Structures	Interpretation
E	Shale, which may contain pelagic marine fossils such as graptolites	Parallel laminations	Interturbidite
D	Fine sandstone, then siltstone	Ripples, cross bedding	Low velocity
C	Sandstone (greywacke)	Cross bedding	
B	Coarse, then medium sandstone (greywacke)	Parallel laminations, graded bedding	Decreasing current velocity
A	Coarse bed of pebble to granule size conglomerate in a sandy matrix	Graded bedding, erosional base	High velocity

Sedimentary structures in turbidite deposits

- Graded bedding is a very common sedimentary structure in greywackes, due to the coarse particles settling out faster than the finer particles.
- Flute casts are hollows eroded by turbidity currents before being filled in by sediment, so are found at the base of the greywacke beds.

Turbidite deposits show lateral changes. The thickness of the deposits changes as they get thinner with distance across the abyssal plain, as most of the material is deposited close to the foot of the slope. The grain size decreases away from the source of the sediment as the fine sediment is less heavy and so can be carried further. The ratio of sand to mud also decreases.

With these characteristics and sedimentary structures such as flute casts, the flow direction of ancient turbidity currents can be determined.

Figure 3 Turbidite sequence

Case study

One of the largest turbidity currents of modern times was triggered by the Grand Banks earthquake of 1929, though it was not recognised as a turbidity current at the time. A thick sequence of sediment had been deposited on the edge of the Grand Banks, off Newfoundland, Canada, by the St Lawrence River. A series of submarine telegraph cables had been laid along the continental slope, continental rise and abyssal plain. After the earthquake, the cables were broken in sequence down the slope to the abyssal plain and the times at which these breaks occurred were known exactly.

The breaks were caused by a mass shown by calculation to have moved at up to 100 km/hour and to have travelled at least 700 km. The turbidity current was triggered when a sediment slide near the epicentre of the earthquake flowed downslope as a density current. It formed a sheet-like turbidite deposit over an estimated 100 000 km² of ocean floor.

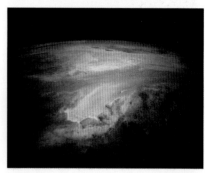

Figure 4 Wind transport of fine sediment seen from space

Ocean basins

The abyssal plains are between 3 and 5 km below sea level. Although they are remote from land, they are covered in sediment. They are flat because sediment covers the underlying topography. Some of the deposits are mud carried by turbidity currents. Some are clay and silt sized particles transported by the wind. The wind blown sediment is deposited to form pelagic clay.

Many of the sediments are biogenic, including calcareous and siliceous oozes. When planktonic organisms die, their tests slowly sink to the sea floor to be preserved as microfossils.

Carbonate oozes contain skeletal remains of coccolithophores (see spread 2.3.6) and foraminifera. They are usually only preserved at depths shallower than 4 km. This depth is known as the **carbonate compensation depth** (CCD). The depth varies across the oceans and has varied during the Earth's history. Below the CCD, any carbonate material dissolves before it reaches the sea floor, due to higher CO_2 content and lower temperature of the water.

Siliceous oozes form from the skeletons of **diatoms** in deposits nearer the poles and **radiolaria** in deposits nearer the equator. Silica dissolves at a slow rate in sea water. Oozes accumulate where the rate of deposition is greater than the rate of solution. Sedimentation rates on the abyssal plains are estimated at 1 mm per 1000 years, up to 3 cm per 1000 years.

Key definitions

Plankton are minute organisms living in the surface layers of the ocean, that are transported by currents.

A **diatom** is a planktonic plant that secretes siliceous material.

Radiolaria are planktonic animals with a siliceous test.

Calcareous ooze is pelagic clay containing >30% biogenic skeletal material made of calcite.

Siliceous ooze is pelagic clay containing >30% biogenic skeletal material made of silica.

The **carbonate compensation depth** is the depth in the oceans at which the rate of solution of solid $CaCO_3$ equals the rate of supply.

Questions

1 Name the features eroded into the sea floor by turbidity currents.
2 Explain the relationship between changes in energy level and the rocks shown in the graphic log sequence.
3 Explain why the depth of the CCD may change.
4 Research the rocks formed in deep sea deposits of the Silurian of Wales.

Examiner tip

Ancient deep marine deposits can be recognised by:
- sequences of greywackes and shales
- sedimentary structures such as flute casts and graded bedding
- only pelagic fossils.

Metamorphism is the **isochemical** process by which rocks are changed by either heat or pressure, or both heat and pressure. The chemical composition of the parent rock will be the same as the metamorphic rock produced.

The rock undergoes the very slow process of solid-state recrystallisation without melting. Different temperatures and pressures cause new minerals to grow in rocks that have the same composition. The minerals produced are directly related to pressure and temperature conditions. The lower temperature limit for metamorphism is between 200 and 150°C. Below these temperatures, changes are part of diagenesis. There is no lower pressure limit. The upper temperature limit is where melting occurs. This happens at around 800°C.

The process of metamorphism may result in:
- destruction of fossils, beds and sedimentary structures
- hardening of the rock
- change in colour
- alignment of minerals
- growth of new metamorphic minerals.

Key definition

Isochemical means that no elements are added or removed, with the exception of volatiles such as water and carbon dioxide.

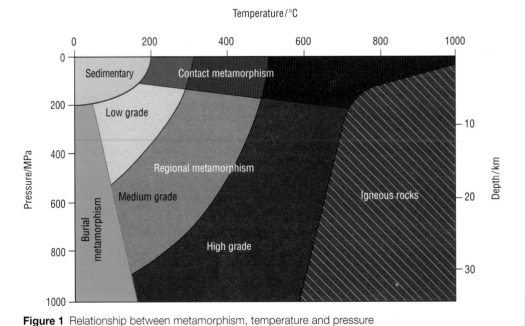

Figure 1 Relationship between metamorphism, temperature and pressure

Case study

Making a brick – it's metamorphism!
- Take a mass of soft, grey-coloured, sticky, crushed clay mixed with water and a little limestone.
- Stir well.
- Press into a brick shape.
- Put in the furnace at 1400 °C for 2 days.
- Cool slowly and you will have a hard, red brick.

Temperature

Temperature is a key variable in metamorphism:
- High temperatures occur near to igneous intrusions, where the magma heats the surrounding rocks.
- Temperature also increases with depth, due to the geothermal gradient.

As temperature increases, the rate of metamorphic reactions also increases. This is because many of the chemical reactions require heat to take place. Higher temperatures increase the rate at which ions diffuse between minerals, though it is still a slow process because the ions have to move through solid rock during metamorphism. The whole process is greatly speeded up by water, which allows the ions to diffuse more rapidly.

Pressure

Pressure steadily increases with depth and is applied to rocks in three different ways:

- Pore pressure is the pressure exerted by fluids between the grains in a porous rock. The presence of water speeds up reactions by acting as a catalyst and increasing the rate and ease of ion exchange. In an experiment where two dry solids were heated together for 2 hours at 1300°C, only 10% reacted. When the same solids were heated in water for the same time, the reaction was completed at only 600°C.
- Load pressure is the weight of overlying rocks and physically brings minerals into contact with each other over very long periods of time.
- Tectonic stress or pressure is caused as the rocks undergo folding or faulting and very high pressures are exerted, but usually over relatively short periods of time.

In all cases the higher the pressure, the greater the degree of metamorphism. Reactions that depend on pressure only are less common than temperature dependent reactions.

Time

Time is very important because metamorphic reactions take place very slowly. These reactions usually take millions of years to occur. Pressure and temperature conditions that produce metamorphism have to exist over long periods of time, in order for the reactions to occur.

Types of metamorphism

Contact metamorphism

Contact metamorphism occurs adjacent to igneous intrusions, which increase the temperature in the surrounding **country rock**. The metamorphism is important on a local scale, producing a metamorphic aureole. Temperatures are generally high but pressure is low. As pressure is not a significant factor, the minerals are not aligned in contact metamorphic rocks.

Burial metamorphism

Burial metamorphism occurs in conditions of medium to high pressure and relatively low temperature. To some extent, burial metamorphism overlaps with diagenesis, and grades into regional metamorphism as temperature increases. It affects rocks deeply buried by the weight of overlying sediments. It also occurs at subduction zones where sea floor sediments and basalts are buried. Rocks buried at the deepest levels almost always contain the blue mineral glaucophane. They are called blueschists.

Regional metamorphism

Regional metamorphism affects larger areas than contact metamorphism, extending over hundreds or thousands of square kilometres. It is caused by low to high temperature and low to high pressure at convergent plate margins. It can result from either subduction or continental collision. Pressure is significant and so minerals have a preferred alignment. Regionally metamorphosed rocks occur in the cores of fold mountain belts where mountain ranges have been eroded.

> **Key definition**
>
> **Country rock** is the rock into which an igneous rock has been intruded.

Questions

1 Describe the temperature and pressure conditions associated with each of the three types of metamorphism.
2 Describe the effects on the surrounding rocks of an igneous intrusion that cooled in 500 years.
3 Explain why it is more difficult to know the pressure at which metamorphic rocks form than the temperature at which they form.

All metamorphic rocks are formed from parent rocks, the original rocks that existed prior to metamorphism. The composition of these rocks affects the mineralogy of the metamorphic rocks, so they have a kind of 'family likeness'.

Foliated rocks produced by regional metamorphism

These rocks have all been affected by pressure, to some degree, during regional metamorphism. Any platy minerals they contain take on a preferred alignment known as **foliation**. All the rocks described in this spread are foliated. (For an explanation of how foliated textures form, see spread 2.4.4.) The most common platy mineral is clay so the rocks described below all have shale as the parent rock.

Slate

The parent rock of slate is shale (for a photo of shale, see spread 2.3.6). Shale is composed of clay minerals and fine quartz particles. Because clay minerals are rich in aluminium, so are the metamorphic minerals in slate. This is mainly composed of clay minerals and mica (although chlorite and quartz may also be present). Shale is fine grained (grains <1 mm diameter) and shows **slaty cleavage.** Traces of original bedding may still be preserved as relict bedding.

Figure 1 Shale and slate

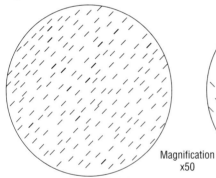

Shale, composed of clay minerals aligned by compaction during diagenesis

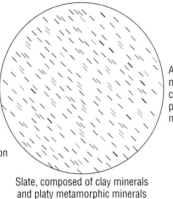

Magnification x50

Alignment of minerals has changed due to pressure during metamorphism

Slate, composed of clay minerals and platy metamorphic minerals mica and chlorite

Slate is a fine grained metamorphic rock that has slaty cleavage i.e. it splits into thin sheets

Schist

The parent rock of schist is shale. Schist is produced by higher temperatures and pressures than those producing slate. It is medium grained (1 to 5 mm) and crystalline. Although it can occur in a variety of colours, it always has a shiny appearance where the flat surfaces of muscovite and biotite mica crystals are visible. Schist is typically composed of mica and garnet. The garnets often form large crystals called **porphyroblasts**. The mica crystals are all aligned at right-angles to the maximum pressure, forming the texture **schistosity.**

Gneiss

The parent rock of gneiss is shale. Gneiss is formed by the highest temperatures and pressures during regional metamorphism. It is a coarse grained (>5 mm), crystalline rock with **gneissose banding**. Gneiss is typically composed of quartz and feldspar in the light bands and biotite mica (and other mafic minerals) in the dark bands.

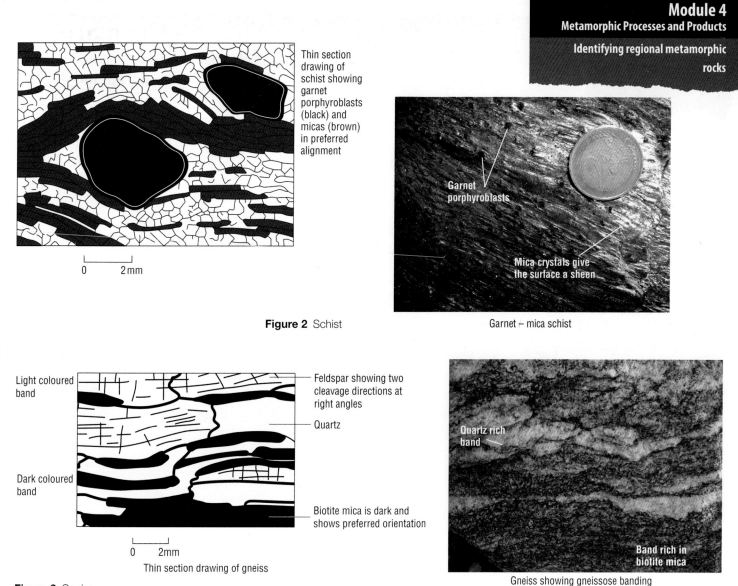

Thin section
drawing of
schist showing
garnet
porphyroblasts
(black) and
micas (brown)
in preferred
alignment

0   2mm

Figure 2 Schist

Garnet – mica schist

Garnet
porphyroblasts

Mica crystals give
the surface a sheen

Light coloured
band

Dark coloured
band

Feldspar showing two
cleavage directions at
right angles

Quartz

Biotite mica is dark and
shows preferred orientation

0   2mm

Thin section drawing of gneiss

Figure 3 Gneiss

Quartz rich
band

Band rich in
biotite mica

Gneiss showing gneissose banding

Summary table of rocks produced by regional metamorphism only					
Parent Rock	Metamorphic rock	Colour	Texture	Mineral composition	Type of metamorphism
Shale, composed of clay minerals	Slate	Grey or purple or green or black	Slaty cleavage, fine grain size (<1 mm)	Clay minerals and muscovite mica, with some chlorite and quartz	Low grade regional
Shale	Schist	Silvery sheen	Schistosity, medium grain size (1–5 mm)	Muscovite and biotite mica Quartz Garnet Kyanite	Medium grade regional
Shale	Gneiss	Dark and light bands	Gneissose banding, coarse grain size (>5 mm)	Biotite mica Mafic minerals Quartz K feldspar Sillimanite	High grade regional

Questions

1 Which metamorphic rock would you associate with high grade regional metamorphism?
2 With the aid of labelled diagrams, describe the differences between schist and slate.
3 With the aid of labelled diagrams, describe one similarity and one difference between schist and gneiss.

The parent rock, for all the metamorphic rocks described in spread 2.4.2, was shale but this does not mean that shale is the only parent rock. The chemical composition of the minerals that make up shale is more varied than that of limestones, which are composed of calcite ($CaCO_3$), or of sandstones, some of which can be almost pure SiO_2 in the form of quartz. There is a much wider range of metamorphic minerals that can recrystallise from clay minerals. This means that shale can be the parent of different metamorphic rocks, but limestone and sandstone cannot.

Unfoliated rocks produced by contact or regional metamorphism

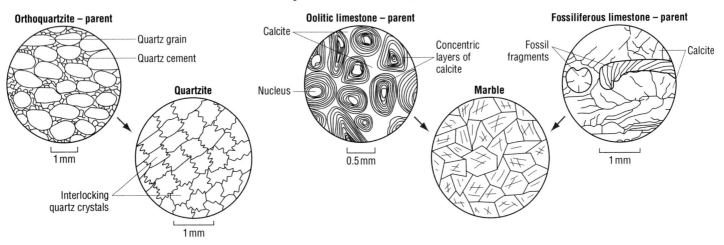

Figure 1 Thin section drawings of quartzite, marble and their parent rocks

Because these rocks do not contain platy minerals such as mica they do not show foliation. They can be produced by either regional or contact metamorphism.

Quartzite
The parent rock of quartzite is orthoquartzite, sandstone composed of quartz grains held together by quartz cement. Quartz grains in the sandstone recrystallise, forming interlocking quartz crystals. The quartz crystals are equidimensional so there can be no foliation. This texture is described as **granoblastic**. Any sedimentary structures or fossils in the parent sandstone are destroyed. The colour of quartzite is white or grey, unless there were other minerals in the original rock. For example, if any iron oxide was in the parent rock, there will often be a pink colour.

Marble
Limestones are made essentially of one mineral, calcite, which is stable over a wide range of temperatures and pressures. As a result, metamorphism of limestone only causes the original calcite crystals to grow larger. Calcite grains and fossil fragments in the limestone parent rock recrystallise to form an interlocking mosaic of calcite crystals. The crystals are equi-dimensional, so there can be no foliation. Marble has granoblastic texture, but the crystals of calcite make it look sugary in texture. Calcite will react with dilute HCl. Fossils are destroyed during metamorphism.

Marble from pure limestone is white. Impurities in the parent limestone give some marble a range of coloured streaks:
- If there are clay minerals in the limestones, then a number of green or red minerals such as garnet may form.
- If there are sand grains present, a chemical reaction between calcite and quartz will produce wollastonite, which can be light green, pinkish, brown, red or yellow.

> ### Key definition
>
> Granoblastic describes the texture of metamorphic rocks that contain interlocking equi-dimensional, crystals.

Rocks produced by contact metamorphism

Spotted rock

Because contact metamorphism involves only increased temperatures, it cannot produce foliation. During contact metamorphism, spots may form in the rock where the heat has only partially recrystallised the rock. A spotted rock contains the same minerals as shale or slate. If slate is the parent rock of spotted slate, it will show foliation, but this was produced due to pressure during regional metamorphism (see spread 2.4.2). The randomly orientated spots may contain biotite, andalusite and graphite, but they are usually too indistinct to be identified in hand specimen.

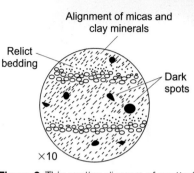

Figure 2 Thin section diagram of spotted slate showing clay minerals and mica aligned at 90° to maximum pressure. The remains of the sedimentary bedding can just be seen as relict bedding

Summary table of unfoliated rocks					
Parent rock	Metamorphic rock	Colour	Texture	Mineral composition	Type of metamorphism
Limestone composed of calcite (CaCO₃)	Marble	White	Granoblastic Medium grain size (1–5 mm) grain size increases with metamorphic grade	Calcite (reacts with dilute HCl)	Contact or regional
Sandstone composed of quartz (SiO₂)	Quartzite	White or grey	Granoblastic Medium grain size (1–5 mm), grain size increases with metamorphic grade	Quartz	Contact or regional
Slate or shale composed of some clay minerals, mica and quartz	Spotted rock	Grey or purple or green or black with darker spots	Slaty cleavage if slate parent rock Fine grain size (<1 mm)	Clay minerals and mica Poorly formed minerals (mica, andalusite, graphite) in spots	Contact

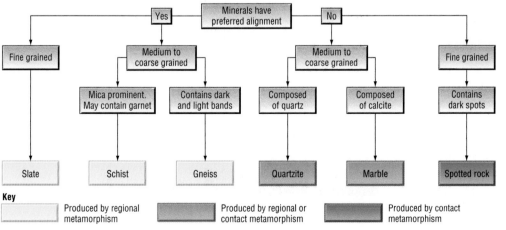

Figure 3 Identifying metamorphic rocks

Questions

1 Explain why marble is not always white.
2 Explain why limestone and sandstone produce the same metamorphic rocks in both contact and thermal metamorphism.
3 State two pieces of evidence indicating that quartzite is a metamorphic rock.

143

Metamorphic rocks are classified mainly based on their **texture**. This is because grain size and orientation tell us a lot about the conditions of metamorphism.

If rocks are subjected to directed pressure, a preferred orientation of the minerals develops at 90 degrees to the pressure. If the minerals are flat or platy, foliation is produced (see spread 2.4.2). Because it results from pressure, foliation is a characteristic of rocks formed by regional metamorphism.

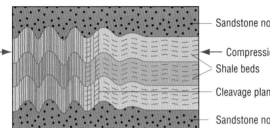

Sandstone no cleavage
Compression
Shale beds
Cleavage planes
Sandstone no cleavage

Foliation produced by the alignment of flat minerals e.g. mica

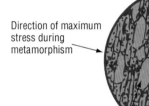

Direction of maximum stress during metamorphism

Direction of maximum stress during metamorphism

Flat minerals like mica align so that their long axis is at 90° to the direction of pressure

Slaty cleavage

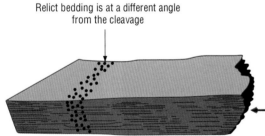

Relict bedding is at a different angle from the cleavage

Slaty cleavage developed at 90° to maximum stress

Figure 1 Foliation and slaty cleavage

Slaty cleavage

Rocks with slaty cleavage will split into thin sheets along the cleavage planes. It occurs in fine grained rocks formed by low grade regional metamorphism:

- It can only form in rocks consisting of platy minerals such as clay minerals, chlorite and micas.
- At the microscopic scale, these minerals become aligned at 90 degrees to the direction of maximum pressure during metamorphism.
- Slaty cleavage may be at any angle to bedding, but is usually parallel to axial planes of the folds.
- It cannot occur in rocks with rounded grains, such as quartz in sandstones.

Bedding and fossils may not be completely destroyed by metamorphism, leaving traces or **relict structures**. Fossils may be deformed due to the high levels of compressive stress. Slates are common in North Wales and the Lake District.

Schistosity

Found in schists (medium grained rocks formed by regional metamorphism), schistosity results from the alignment of flat, platy minerals, commonly muscovite mica, at 90 degrees to the direction of maximum pressure during metamorphism. Light coloured muscovite mica is concentrated into thin parallel bands, giving the rock a characteristic shiny appearance (micaceous sheen) where flat surfaces of mica are visible.

Garnet porphyroblasts are often present and they disrupt the alignment of mica minerals.

Schists are found in the Highlands of Scotland in **Dalradian** rocks.

Key definitions

A **relict structure** is a structure such as bedding present in the parent rock, which is partially preserved in a metamorphic rock.

Dalradian is the name of a group of rocks formed in late Precambrian times, found in Scotland.

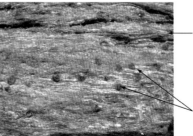

Schistosity caused by alignment of micas

Garnet porphyroblasts

Figure 2 Porphyroblastic texture in a schist

Gneissose banding

Found in gneisses (coarse grained rocks formed by regional metamorphism), gneissose banding is formed when light (usually quartz and feldspar) and dark coloured minerals (usually biotite mica and mafic minerals) are separated into bands. The mica-rich layer is foliated and the pale layer has granoblastic texture. The bands may be contorted or folded but are roughly at 90 degrees to the maximum pressure direction (for a thin section drawing and photo showing gneissose banding, see spread 2.4.2).

Porphyroblastic texture

This texture occurs in both regional and contact metamorphic rocks. Porphyroblasts are large crystals that grow during metamorphism and are surrounded by a finer grained groundmass. Metamorphic rocks that contain these large crystals are described as porphyroblastic. Garnet porphyroblasts found in schists may contain **inclusions**. Pyrite porphyroblasts can develop in slate, often forming clear cubic crystals.

Gneiss – dark and light bands

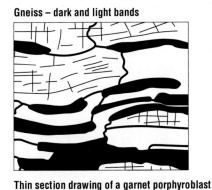

Thin section drawing of a garnet porphyroblast

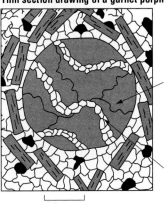

Garnet porphyroblasts commonly have curved cracks when seen in thin section

Inclusions of early formed minerals enclosed by a garnet porphyroblast

2 mm

Figure 3 Gneissose banding

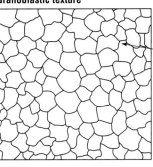

Figure 4 Pyrite porphyroblast in slate

Granoblastic texture

This is an **unfoliated** texture and is formed by thermal metamorphism. Pressure is not a factor in the formation of a granoblastic texture. The main characteristics are randomly orientated, equidimensional crystals usually in rocks with few, and sometimes only one, mineral. Hornfels is an example of a fine grained rock with granoblastic texture. Marble and quartzite are also granoblastic. Because of their medium grain size and white colour, their texture is sometimes described as sugary.

Granoblastic texture

Equidimensional crystals with no preferred alignment

Figure 5 Granoblastic texture

Examiner tip

How to tell the difference between the igneous texture porphyritic and the metamorphic texture porphyroblastic:
- **porphyritic** is where large crystals – phenocrysts – form first in the magma so grow larger than the groundmass, which cools later.
- **porphyroblastic** is where large crystals such as garnet grow **after** the groundmass has developed and they may distort the groundmass crystals.

Questions

1 Name two metamorphic rocks that are unfoliated.
2 With the aid of labelled diagrams explain how a garnet porphyroblast affects the alignment of micas in a schist.
3 Explain why slaty cleavage commonly has a different orientation from relict bedding.

Contact metamorphism occurs when the country rock is affected by heat from a large igneous intrusion. Because temperature differences between the surrounding rock and the intruded magma are greater at shallow levels in the Earth's crust where pressure is low, contact metamorphism is described as high temperature, low pressure metamorphism. High temperature, not pressure leads to the formation of altered, recrystallised, unfoliated rocks in a zone surrounding the intrusion. This zone is the **metamorphic aureole**. Around a large igneous intrusion, such as a batholith, the metamorphic aureole may be up to 10 km wide. Temperature decreases with distance from the contact with the intrusion and for this reason the effects of contact metamorphism are greatest near to the contact and decrease with distance. **Metamorphic grade** increases in all directions towards the intrusion.

Key definitions

A **metamorphic aureole** is a region surrounding an igneous intrusion in which the country rocks have been recrystallised and changed by heat from the intrusion.

A **metamorphic grade** is a measure of the intensity of metamorphism. Although increases in temperature only result in increasing grade in contact metamorphism, grade is also used to describe regional metamorphism where both temperature and pressure vary.

Contact metamorphism of shale

The chemical composition of minerals in shale is varied and so a range of different metamorphic rocks is formed, depending on the temperature and therefore the distance away from the intrusion:

- Close to the contact with the intrusion, temperatures are high and so high grade metamorphism occurs. Shale is completely recrystallised to form a fine grained, hard, splintery, granoblastic metamorphic rock called **hornfels**.
- Further away from the contact, where the heat is less intense, medium grade metamorphism occurs. Clusters of a new metamorphic mineral andalusite, form porphyroblasts. This partly recrystallised rock is andalusite slate or rock.
- In the outer part of the metamorphic aureole, temperatures are lower. Some recrystallisation occurs, causing clusters of dark minerals to grow in separate spots. Iron, carbon or biotite mica will form the spots. The rock in this outer part of the metamorphic aureole is called spotted rock and is formed by low grade metamorphism.

Andalusite porphyroblasts

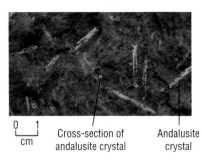

0 1
cm

Cross-section of andalusite crystal   Andalusite crystal

A metamorphic aureole showing contact metamorphism of shale

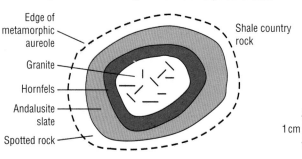

Edge of metamorphic aureole

Shale country rock

Granite

Hornfels

Andalusite slate

Spotted rock

Shale with spots of partial recrystallisation

1 cm

Black spots of iron or carbon

Figure 1 Metamorphic aureole showing contact metamorphism of shale and photo of a spotted rock and andalusite rock

Factors controlling the width of metamorphic aureoles

Volume of the magma

The size of intrusions ranges from batholiths down to minor intrusions (see spread 2.2.9). Dykes and sills are not large enough and do not produce enough heat to develop a metamorphic aureole. Because the volume of magma is small it cools quickly and there is only sufficient heat to change the rock for a few centimetres on either side. This narrow zone of bleached and hardened rock is known as a **baked margin**.

Larger intrusions cool slowly and heat the surrounding rocks over long periods of time (10^4–10^6 years), allowing a wide metamorphic aureole to develop.

Temperature of the magma

The volume of magma in an intrusion affects the maximum temperature reached at any point and also the time it takes for temperatures to rise in the country rocks. Metamorphism will not occur unless the temperature rises above 200 °C for an extended period of time. A small intrusion produces little metamorphic change because the rock has little time to warm up and there is not enough time for metamorphic reactions to occur before the rock cools down. With larger intrusions there is time for metamorphic reactions to take place and for new minerals and recrystallisation to occur, because temperatures remain high for much longer periods of time.

Composition of the magma

Mafic magma may be intruded at a temperature of 1200 °C, whilst silicic magma may be intruded at 850 °C. Silicic magmas contain more volatiles. When they enter the country rock they speed up metamorphic reactions. This compensates for the lower temperature of the magma, because metamorphic aureoles surrounding silicic intrusions are of similar size to those around mafic ones.

Composition of the country rock

Rocks largely composed of one mineral, such as limestone and orthoquartzite, show much less variation than clay-rich rocks such as shale. Quartzite and marble have larger crystals the nearer they are to the igneous intrusion and are uniform. Metamorphic aureoles formed in sandstone country rocks are typically narrower than those formed in clay-rich rocks. If the country rock is permeable and contains groundwater, heat will be able to move by convection, allowing a wider aureole to develop.

Dip of the contact

The dip of the sides of the intrusion has a major effect on the width of the metamorphic aureole. A shallow angle of dip gives a wide aureole and a steep angle of dip gives a narrow aureole. If the sides of the intrusion dip at different angles, then the metamorphic aureole will be asymmetric.

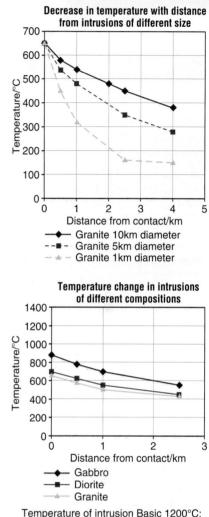

Figure 2 Graph showing the effects of temperature and composition of magma

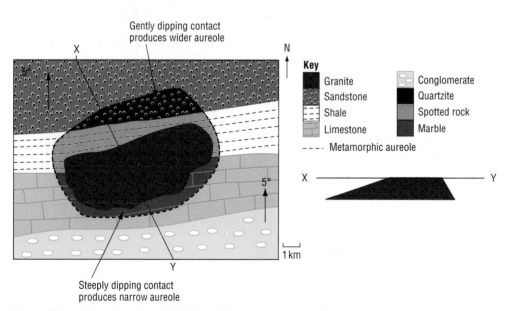

Figure 3 Map of an intrusion with dipping sides

Questions

1 What is the term for the zone surrounding a granite batholith?
2 Hornfels forms at 460 °C. Using Figure 2, state how far away from each intrusion hornfels will form.
3 Explain the relationship between metamorphic rocks and metamorphic grade.

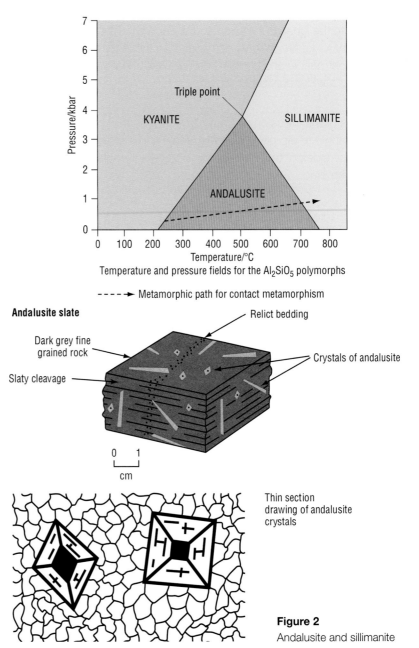

The thermal gradient and index minerals in a metamorphic aureole

When a batholith is intruded into beds of shale, increases in metamorphic grade are marked by the appearance of an index mineral:

- Index minerals are metamorphic minerals, which are stable under specific temperature and pressure conditions. They indicate the metamorphic grade.
- In contact metamorphism, biotite is the low grade mineral found in spotted rocks.
- The Al_2SiO_5 polymorph andalusite indicates medium grade and is found in andalusite rich rocks.
- Sillimanite, another Al_2SiO_5 polymorph, indicates high grade and is found in hornfels.
- Because contact metamorphism is caused by temperature only, an increase in grade represents a thermal gradient.

Some of the minerals that crystallise at low grades are stable at higher grades, so more than one index mineral can be found in one rock.

Figure 1 Sketch map showing index minerals and metamorphic grade

Temperature and pressure fields for the Al_2SiO_5 polymorphs

----► Metamorphic path for contact metamorphism

Figure 2
Andalusite and sillimanite

Case study

The Skiddaw granite is part of a major intrusion in the English Lake District. The intrusion is an oval dome shape measuring 10 km × 6 km, with a wide metamorphic aureole.

The zones around the granite are:
- Unmetamorphosed country rock – Skiddaw slates are fine grained parent rocks showing slaty cleavage, formed by regional metamorphism before the intrusion.
- Outer zone of spotted slate – where the grain size is slightly coarser than in the country rocks and small round dark spots are visible. The spots contain biotite and organic material.
- Middle zone – Andalusite slate is medium grained and generally crystalline, containing andalusite porphyroblasts.
- Close to the intrusion – the parent slate has been completely recrystallised to hornfels that can contain sillimonite.

The Al₂SiO₅ polymorphs in contact metamorphism

The Al_2SiO_5 **polymorphs** andalusite and sillimanite are found in contact aureoles – andalusite is the low to medium temperature, low pressure polymorph found in andalusite slate, whereas sillimanite is the high temperature polymorph found in hornfels. With increasing metamorphic grade, contact metamorphism follows a path from andalusite to sillimanite on the Al_2SiO_5 polymorph phase diagram. Kyanite, the high pressure, low temperature polymorph, is not found in contact metamorphic rocks due to the lack of pressure.

Formation of quartzite and marble

When orthoquartzite, a sandstone composed entirely of quartz, is affected by contact metamorphism, all sedimentary structures including cross bedding and graded bedding are destroyed. The quartz grains in the sandstone recrystallise to form an interlocking mosaic of crystals giving it a granoblastic texture. Near to the contact with the igneous intrusion, in the zone of high grade metamorphism, the crystals are larger than they are further away from the contact where temperatures are not as high. The resulting rock is white or pale grey in colour and known as metaquartzite.

Where limestones are affected by contact metamorphism, all sedimentary structures and fossils are destroyed. The grains and cement composed of calcite will recrystallise to form an interlocking mosaic of crystals giving it a granoblastic or sugary texture. This metamorphic rock is called marble. Crystals are larger near to the contact with the igneous intrusion and smaller further away, due to the thermal gradient. If the parent limestone is composed purely of calcite, the resulting metamorphic rock is white in colour. Impurities in the limestone may give streaks of different colours in the marble.

Examiner tip

Make sure that you know the products of contact metamorphism. Do not write about slate (unless it is spotted slate or andalusite slate formed when the country rock was slate), schist and gneiss, if you are answering a question on contact metamorphism.

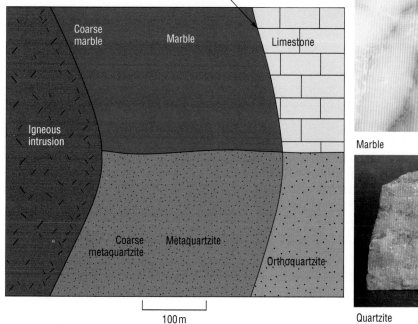

Marble

Quartzite

Figure 3 Sketch map and photos showing contact metamorphism of limestone and orthoquartzite

Questions

1 Explain why andalusite is not formed by the contact metamorphism of pure limestone.
2 Draw a cross-section through a metamorphic aureole and through shale country rock. Label the rock types that would be present on your cross-section.
3 Explain why there are no relict structures in quartzite.

Most regional metamorphism is accompanied by deformation, so these metamorphic rocks will have foliated textures.

Regional metamorphism and plate tectonics

Regional metamorphism results from both heat and pressure generated at convergent plate margins during subduction and continental collision.

The geothermal gradient and plate tectonics

- Along subduction zones magmas are generated, rise and intrude into the crust. Temperatures are high near the surface result so the geothermal gradient may be in the range of 50 to 70 °C/km, and contact metamorphism results.
- Compression occurs at a subduction zone where the oceanic crust starts to subduct and the edge of the non-subducting plate is deformed. The geothermal gradient is normal at 25 °C/km.
- Along a subduction zone, relatively cool oceanic lithosphere is pushed down to great depths. This produces a low geothermal gradient of 10 to 15 °C/km.

Convergent plate margins with subduction zones

- When oceanic and continental plates collide, high pressure is produced as the oceanic plate is subducted.
- The result is high pressure, low temperature burial metamorphism and the formation of blueschists.
- Further away from the subduction zone, magma is rising from the melting oceanic plate and pressures are lower, so high temperature, low pressure metamorphism occurs.
- High temperatures lead to the formation of igneous intrusions and metamorphic aureoles.

Paired metamorphic belts will form at convergent margins with subduction zones. The zone closest to the trench will have high pressure due to compressive stress and low temperature as no magma is rising. The zone further away has high temperature due to rising magma and low pressure.

Convergent plate margins continental–continental

Fold mountains form at these margins (see spread 1.3.7) where the Earth's crust is deformed, thickened and there is extensive intrusive igneous activity. The Himalayan mountain range began to form about 50 Ma when India collided with Asia. The Himalayas are still growing as the plates are still moving towards each other. High temperatures and pressures acting over such long periods create broad (>100 km^2) and often complex orogenic belts affected by all grades of regional metamorphism.

At the deepest part of the orogenic belt the pressures and temperature will be highest, giving high grade regional metamorphism. Away from the collision zone and higher in the crust the grade of metamorphism will be low.

Case study

Paired metamorphic belts include areas in New Zealand, Indonesia, Washington State in the United States, Chile, and the coast of South America. All these areas lie around the Pacific at convergent plate margins, where subduction has occurred.

Case study

The Dalradian sedimentary rocks were deposited in late Precambrian and Cambrian times in an ancient ocean called Iapetus, which existed between Scotland and England. Continental–continental plate movements caused the ocean to close and the 13 km of sediments that had been deposited in the ocean were deformed and regionally metamorphosed to form the Caledonian orogenic belt. The area of metamorphism extends both south and north of the Great Glen Fault into the Highlands of Scotland. The metamorphic zones are displaced by the fault.

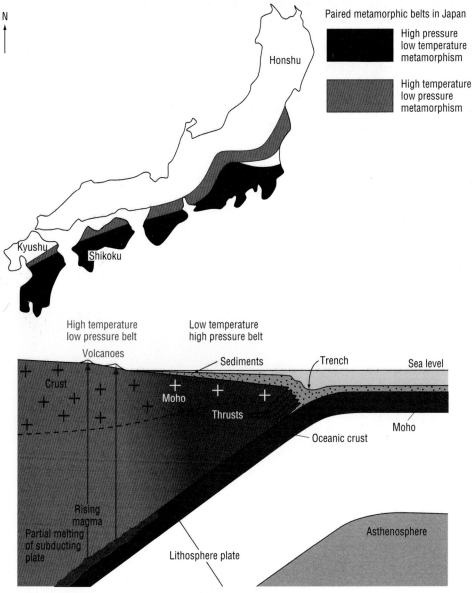

Figure 1 legend:

Paired metamorphic belts in Japan

High pressure low temperature metamorphism

High temperature low pressure metamorphism

Figure 1 Paired metamorphic belts in Japan

Migmatite is a coarse grained mixed rock with some of the characteristics of gneiss and some of the characteristics of granite, formed by partial melting of the rock during the highest grade metamorphism, at the high temperature boundary between metamorphism and igneous activity.

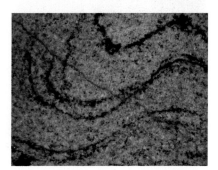

Figure 3 Migmatite

Grades of regional metamorphic rocks

Regional metamorphism of shale produces the following rocks (they are all described in spreads 2.4.2 and 2.4.3):

- low grade: slate
- medium grade: schist
- high grade: gneiss

Regional metamorphism of orthoquartzite and limestones produces the same products as contact metamorphism – quartzite and marble. Each of these rocks is composed of only one mineral, quartz and calcite, respectively. The minerals are equi-dimensional, so they cannot align under pressure.

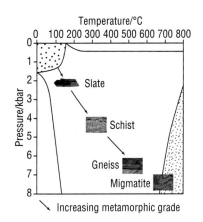

Figure 2 Regional metamorphic rocks and their relationship to pressure and temperature

Questions

1 Describe the formation of a paired metamorphic belt.

2 Describe two general changes that would occur in a mudstone during regional metamorphism.

3 Draw up a table with the following headings: metamorphic grade; parent rock; metamorphic rock; mineral composition; texture. Complete it using the information in this spread and spreads 2.4.2 and 2.4.3.

Mapping the Dalradian Supergroup

- In 1893, George Barrow mapped a sequence of highly deformed regionally metamorphosed rocks in the south-eastern part of the Scottish Highlands. The metamorphism and deformation occurred during closure of the Iapetus Ocean and the Caledonian orogeny about 400 Ma ago. These Precambrian rocks are known as the Dalradian Supergroup.

- As you already know, clay-rich sedimentary rocks such as shale produce a variety of metamorphic minerals, as temperature and pressure conditions change. When Barrow mapped rocks like these, he noticed that there was a pattern to the occurrence of metamorphic minerals. He used the first appearance of some of these minerals, which he termed **index minerals**, to draw **isograds**. Some of the minerals that crystallise at low grades are stable at higher grades so more than one index mineral can be found in one rock.

- He was able to map **metamorphic zones** using index minerals and isograds, which define the boundaries of the zones. Although he did not do all the mapping personally, the system he devised was named after him and the zones are called **Barrovian zones.**

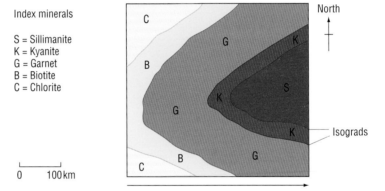

Index minerals

S = Sillimanite
K = Kyanite
G = Garnet
B = Biotite
C = Chlorite

0   100 km

Increasing grade

Figure 1 Index minerals, isograds and metamorphic zones

Index minerals and metamorphic zones

	Metamorphic grade				
	low		**medium**		**high**
Rock type	Slate		Schist		Gneiss
Index minerals and metamorphic zones	Chlorite	Biotite	Garnet	Kyanite	Sillimanite

The chlorite zone represents low grade (low pressure and low temperature) regional metamorphism. The rock is slate where most of the rock has recrystallised but some clay minerals may still exist.

Schists develop as a result of increasing temperatures and pressures and can be found in both the biotite and garnet zones. The grain sizes increase with metamorphic grade. Schists formed at lower temperatures and pressures are composed of quartz, muscovite mica and biotite mica. Medium grade metamorphism results from higher temperatures and pressures and many schists formed at this grade contain garnet, and less commonly, kyanite porphyroblasts.

Kyanite is typically found in gneisses and the kyanite zone represents high grade regional metamorphism. The sillimanite zone represents high grade regional metamorphism with very high temperatures and pressures. The rocks are gneisses. Estimates based on the sillimanite zone indicate a maximum temperature of about 700 °C and maximum pressure of about 7 kb. This pressure exists at a depth of about 25 km below the surface of the continental crust. It gives a geothermal gradient of about 28°C km^{-1}.

Quartz and plagioclase feldspar are stable throughout the whole range of grades. This makes them no use as index minerals.

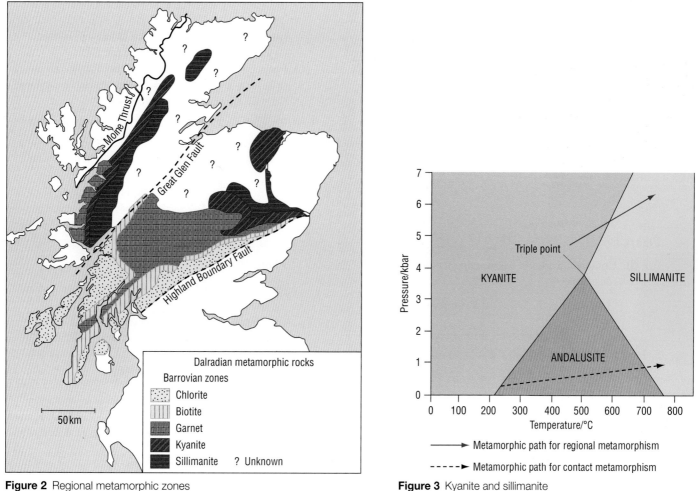

Figure 2 Regional metamorphic zones

Figure 3 Kyanite and sillimanite

The Al$_2$SiO$_5$ polymorphs in regional metamorphism

The Al$_2$SiO$_5$ polymorphs kyanite and sillimanite are found in regional metamorphic rocks. A rock formed at high pressure and low temperature may contain kyanite. A rock formed at high temperature or at high temperature and high pressure may contain sillimanite, which can be found in contact and regional metamorphism, both of which can involve high temperature. With increasing metamorphic grade, regional metamorphism follows a path from kyanite to sillimanite on the Al$_2$SiO$_5$ polymorph phase diagram.

Questions

1 Describe the rocks found in each of the Barrovian zones.
2 Explain why clay-rich parent rocks are the most useful in mapping metamorphic zones.
3 Explain the difference between a polymorph and a pseudomorph.

1   Below is a diagram of the rock cycle.

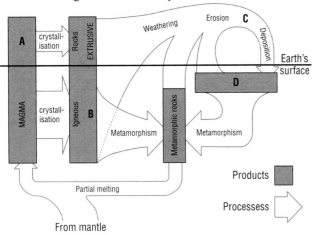

Figure 1

(a) (i)   Complete the table below using the diagram of the rock cycle.

Location	Process or product
A	
B	
C	
D	

[4]

(ii) Name two processes that occur after deposition to produce rock group **D**. [2]

(b) Explain how the crystal grain size of igneous rocks is related to the depth at which they crystallised. [2]

(c) Explain the difference between an era and a system. Give **one** example of each. [2]

Total 8

(OCR 2832 May 06)

2   Descriptions of three igneous rocks are given in the table below.

	Description
Rock A	• Flow banded • Light grey or red or brown colour • Very fine crystals <1 mm
Rock B	• Conchoidal fracture • Black colour • No crystals
Rock C	• Coarse crystal grain size • Greenish black crystals of augite and homblende • White crystals of plagioclase fedspar • White crystals of potash fedspar

(a) (i)   Identify the three rocks **A**, **B** and **C**. [3]

(ii) Describe with the aid of a sketch the term flow banding. [2]

(iii) Explain why igneous rock **B** has no crystals. [1]

(iv) Define the term conchoidal fracture. [1]

(b) Plagioclase feldspar, augite and hornblende are all part of Bowen's Reaction Series. They have been entered on the reaction series diagram below.

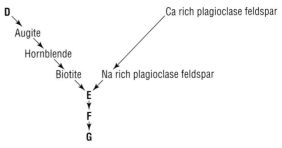

Figure 2

(i)   Name the minerals **D**, **E**, **F** and **G** from Bowen's Reaction Series. [4]

(ii) Explain the relationship of Bowen's Reaction Series to temperature. [2]

(iii) Name the minerals that form the discontinuous part of Bowen's Reaction Series. [1]

(OCR 2835 June 06)

(c) The table below shows the chemical composition by percentage of oxides of four igneous rocks **H**, **J**, **K** and **L**.

(i)   To which igneous rock groups do **H**, **J**, **K** and **L** belong? [4]

(ii) Describe the changes in the % of oxides of silicon and sodium compared to iron and magnesium across the four rock groups. [2]

Oxide %	A	B	C	D
SiO_2	46.0	73.0	60.0	43.5
Al_2O_3	15.0	13.0	17.0	4.0
Fe oxides	12.0	2.0	6.0	12.5
MgO	9.0	0.5	3.5	34.0
CaO	9.0	1.5	7.0	3.5
Na_2O	3.5	4.0	3.5	0.5
K_2O	1.5	4.0	1.5	0.3
others	4.0	2.0	1.5	1.7

Total 20

(OCR 2835 June 06)

3 **(a)** The table below shows the results of a student's research into the world's top 12 most deadly volcanic eruptions.

Rank	Volcano	Location	Year of eruption	Death	Major cause of death
1	Tambora	Indonesia	1815	92 000	Ash fall, starvation
2	Krakatau	Indonesia	1883	36 417	Ash fall, tsunami
3	Mount Pelée	Martinique	1902	29 025	Pyroclastic flows
4	Ruiz	Colombia	1985	25 000	Lahars
5	Unzan	Japan	1792	14 300	Volcano collapse, tsunami
6	Laki	Iceland	1783	9 350	Starvation
7	Kelut	Indonesia	1919	5 110	Lahars
8	Galunggung	Italy	1882	4 011	Lahars
9	Vesuvius	Italy	1631	3 500	Lava flows, lahars
10	Vesuvius	Indonesia	79	3 360	Ash falls, pyroclastic flows
11	Pandayan	Indonesia	1772	2 957	Pyroclastic flows
12	Lamington	Papua New Guinea	1951	2 942	Pyroclastic flows

(i) Explain why Indonesia has so many volcanic eruptions. [2]

(ii) Using the table calculate the percentage of eruptions that had **starvation** as a major cause of death. Show your working. [2]

(iii) Suggest reasons why the global summer of 1816 was very cold. [3]

Total 7

(OCR 2832 May 07)

4 The graphic log below shows a commonly found sequence of sedimentary rocks.

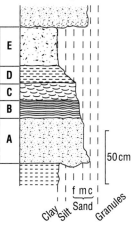

Figure 3

(a) **(i)** Using the graphic log, name and explain the formation of the sedimentary structure shown by the change in grain sizes in bed **A**. [3]

(ii) Flute casts are found at the base of bed **A**. Draw a labelled diagram of a flute cast. Explain how a flute cast is formed. [3]

(OCR 2835 June 06)

(b) The diagram below shows thin section drawings of two metamorphic rocks and their sedimentary parent rocks.

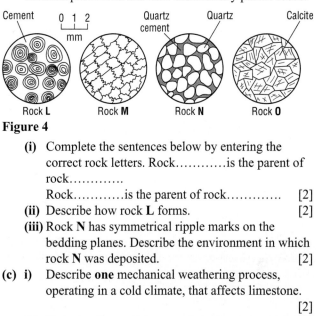

Figure 4

(i) Complete the sentences below by entering the correct rock letters. Rock............is the parent of rock.............
Rock............is the parent of rock............. [2]

(ii) Describe how rock **L** forms. [2]

(iii) Rock **N** has symmetrical ripple marks on the bedding planes. Describe the environment in which rock **N** was deposited. [2]

(c) **i)** Describe **one** mechanical weathering process, operating in a cold climate, that affects limestone. [2]

(ii) State the shape of the scree fragments. [1]

(iii) Describe **one** chemical weathering process that affects the limestone. [2]

Total 17

(OCR 2832 May 07)

5 **(a)** Describe how the following factors control metamorphism.
(i) temperature [2]
(ii) pressure [2]

(b) Regional metamorphic rocks form as a result of changes in both temperature and pressure.
(i) Name the rock type that is formed as a result of the regional metamorphism of pure limestone and pure sandstone. [2]

(ii) Explain why shales give rise to a wide variety of new metamorphic minerals when regionally metamorphosed. [2]

(iii) Define the following terms:
• index mineral [1]
• isograd [1]

(OCR 2835 June 06)

(c) Explain why rocks formed by contact metamorphism lack any foliation. [2]

Total 13

(OCR 2832 May 06)

6 Using diagrams explain the differences between sills and lava flows. [8]

(OCR 2832 May 06)

7 Describe with the aid of diagrams, the processes of compaction and cementation. [8]

(OCR 2832 May 07)

Practical tasks in geology assess skills in measurement, observation and recording of data. You will use geological maps, photographs and diagrams as well as laboratory or field data to complete the tasks.

The geological data you will be working with will be both **quantitative** (using numeric measurements and results) and **qualitative** (using descriptive observations). If you are studying a sedimentary rock then you will **measure** the grain size, the bed thickness and the dip, and **describe** from your observations the colour, grain shape, composition and any fossil content.

Whether your practical task is in the laboratory or in the field the same types of observations will be needed. Once you have enough data you will be able to evaluate by drawing conclusions from the data. This could be determining the environment of deposition of rocks and sediments or a sequence of events.

Scales

Using the scales on photographs or thin section drawings are essential for making correct measurements. Some scales use ×1, meaning that the size shown is the same as the actual size. A scale of ×0.5 means the feature shown is half size and ×3 means that the feature is three times larger.

Alternatively, a scale bar in mm, cm, m or km is used. An easy way to read a bar scale correctly is to mark the edge of a piece of paper to mark the length of the crystal or feature and then hold it against the bar scale. This is a method that saves the calculations!

Centre based task

Laboratory practical

You will need to carry out a practical task to show accurate measurements and observations. Many geological tasks in the laboratory are simulations because it is impossible to carry out experiments under the high pressures and temperatures and long time periods seen in nature.

The accuracy of an observation or measurement depends on the experimental or fieldwork techniques used, the skill of the person taking the measurements and the equipment used. Removing or minimising sources of error improves accuracy.

Decisions about the precision with which observations or measurements are made may take into account the nature of the investigation and an assessment of the sources of error. If observations or measurements are repeated, then the closeness of the repeated results is a way of judging reliability. The reliability of a set of observations or measurements depends on the number and accuracy of the individual observations or measurements.

Interpreting photographs

Photographs like those used throughout the book are very useful for observations and measurements and can be used to practice field sketches.

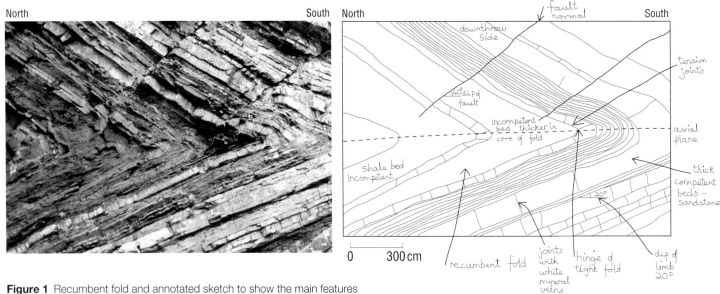

Figure 1 Recumbent fold and annotated sketch to show the main features

You may be given photographs showing:
- sedimentary structures such as ripples, cross bedding and graded bedding
- structures like dykes, xenoliths, folds, faults, joints and cleavage
- textures in rocks such as porphyritic, vesicular, schistosity, porphyroblasts, oolitic and clastic.

You may also be working with thin section drawings which are used for making measurements and for the interpretation and identification of rocks.

Photographs show too much detail so that your first step should be to make a sketch to highlight the main geological features (see Figure 1). Your sketch needs to be annotated with labels for all the key features and with suitable measurements. The measurements could be dips of beds or faults, grain size, crystal size or bed thickness. Use all the terms you can from the structural geology spreads in unit 1.

Evaluative task

The evaluative tasks provide data obtained either from a practical experiment in the laboratory or from field measurements. The data will be analysed using graphs or calculations. You may use line graphs, histograms, cumulative frequency curves or rose diagrams (circular graphs) to plot the data. These methods can be used to analyse sediments and sedimentary structures (see spreads 2.3.3 and 2.3.8 for details).

Whether the data has been collected in the field or in the laboratory there are sources of error that can cause the data to be inconsistent or to have anomalies. Field data are often inconsistent due partly to so much natural variation even in a small area. Measuring the dip of beds or faults is not exact because the reality is that they are irregular. Even with repeated measurements there can still be a range of readings when each person measures slightly differently. Dip and strike is measured using a clinometer and compass which can be combined as a compass clinometer.

Safety in the field or laboratory

You will need to consider safety issues in the laboratory as you would in any other scientific experiment. However risk assessments in the field are far more varied depending on the locality. Wherever there is a possibility of falling rocks in quarries or cliffs it is essential to wear a hard hat. If you are at a coastal exposure you should be aware of the times of the tides. Obeying the geological code of conduct is important. If you do use a hammer in the field than beware of possible dangers to others around you and damage to the environment. It is not possible to use a hammer at many localities, so check before you arrive.

Figure 2 A compass clinometer used for measuring angles and direction of dip

Flute casts as palaeocurrent indicators

The data on flute casts were collected from the bottom surfaces of a series of beds of greywacke. The orientation of each flute cast was measured using a compass. The current flows from the rounded end where the scouring action removes sediment creating a hollow on the bedding plane.

Orientation (degrees from north)	Number of cross bedding readings	Orientation (degrees from north)	Number of cross bedding readings
1°–30°	3	181°–210°	2
31°–60°	10	211°–240°	1
61°–90°	15	241°–270°	0
91°–120°	12	271°–300°	0
121°–150°	9	301°–330°	0
151°–180°	6	331°–360°	1

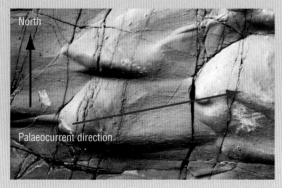

Figure 3 Flute casts and table of palaeocurrent direction data

Questions

1 Plot a rose diagram to show the flute cast orientation data. Use individual readings for each 30° segment.
2 Determine the main palaeocurrent direction and explain what could cause the pattern of palaeocurrents.
3 Describe the environment of deposition for the greywackes with flute casts and the interbedded black shales.
4 Explain with the aid of diagrams why the flute casts are found on the base of the greywacke beds.

Examiner tip

Porosity and permeability are key concepts throughout this Unit and you need to know the difference between them.

Key definitions

Groundwater is the water retained in the pore spaces of rocks below the water table.

Porosity is the volume of pore space.

Permeability is the rate at which a fluid flows through a rock.

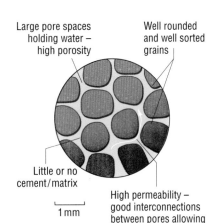

Large pore spaces holding water – high porosity

Well rounded and well sorted grains

Little or no cement/matrix

High permeability – good interconnections between pores allowing water flow

1 mm

Figure 1 Thin section diagram of desert sandstone with high porosity and permeability

Rock type	% porosity
Sandstone	15
Sand	35
Limestone	10
Clay	50
Shale	18
Granite	1
Basalt	1

Why is groundwater important?

Water is vital to all life on Earth and the supply of water is a fundamental issue at all scales: local, regional and global. The two main sources of useable fresh water are surface water and groundwater. Surface water is found in lakes, rivers and reservoirs. **Groundwater** is water held in the pore space of rocks beneath the ground.

Groundwater is the world's largest accessible store of fresh water and its significance cannot be underestimated, particularly in arid regions with little surface water. Today hydrogeologists are playing an increasingly important role in locating suitable groundwater resources.

Porosity and permeability of rocks

Porosity is the amount of pore space in a rock or sediment, usually expressed as a percentage of total rock volume. You can calculate porosity using the formula:

$$\% \text{ porosity} = \frac{\text{total volume of pore space}}{\text{total volume of rock/sediment}} \times 100$$

Permeability is the ability of a rock to transmit fluids such as water, oil or gas, and can be expressed as a rate of flow. You can calculate permeability using the formula:

$$\text{Permeability} = \frac{\text{distance water has travelled}}{\text{time taken}}$$

Factors affecting porosity

The most obvious factor affecting porosity is rock type. Crystalline igneous and metamorphic rocks have virtually zero porosity. The porosity of sedimentary rocks varies according to:
- The degree of sorting. A well sorted rock has a high porosity. A poorly sorted rock has a low porosity because the finer grains fill in the spaces between the coarser grains.
- The amount of diagenesis the rock has undergone. A loose unconsolidated rock has a much higher porosity than a rock that has undergone compaction and cementation.
- Grain shape. Rocks containing rounded grains have a higher porosity than rocks containing angular grains that fit together.
- The packing of the grains which is the way the grains fit together.

Grain size is not a factor in porosity. Coarse grained rocks tend to have large pore spaces but few of them. Fine grained rocks have small pore spaces but many of them.

Rocks may also develop secondary porosity through the presence of structures, such as joints and faults, which are particularly important in increasing the porosity of limestones. The porosity is only effective if the pore spaces are interconnected. Sandstones may typically have a porosity of 15% with most of the pores interconnecting. Although clay may have a porosity of 50%, its effective porosity is virtually zero.

Factors affecting permeability

A rock that has a high effective porosity with good interconnections between the pore spaces will also have a high permeability. Although grain size is not a factor in porosity, it is important in determining permeability. Coarse grained rocks have a higher permeability than fine grained rocks because there is less resistance to flow around coarse grains.

Secondary permeability results from the presence of fractures, such as joints and faults, and voids, such as caves produced by solution. The presence of these secondary structures is important in increasing the porosity of limestones, and also in increasing its permeability. Rocks, such as clay, mudstone and shale, with zero or very low permeability, are termed impermeable.

Groundwater and the water table

Most groundwater originates from rainwater that has infiltrated into soil and then percolated downwards through the pore space of rocks to reach the water table.

The **water table** is the level at which water sits within the ground. Rocks above the water table are unsaturated and have air and water in their pore space. Rocks below the water table are saturated and only contain water in their pore space. The shape of the water table generally follows the surface topography, but with less relief, and intersects the ground surface at lakes and most rivers. The position of the water table may change depending on the season and how much rainfall the area receives.

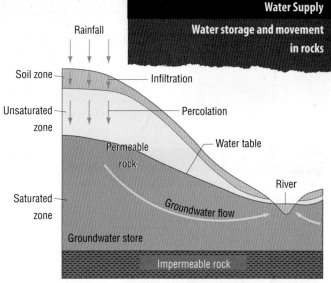

Figure 2 Cross-section of groundwater zones and the water table

Hydrostatic pressure and hydraulic gradient

Hydrostatic pressure results from the weight of the overlying column of water and increases with depth. The height of the overlying column of water is known as the hydrostatic head.

Pressure differences cause groundwater to flow. Water always flows down the **hydraulic gradient** from areas of high pressure to areas of low pressure. The rate at which the water flows is proportional to the drop in height of the water table. These concepts are critical for accurately predicting the movement of groundwater. You can calculate the hydraulic gradient using the formula:

Hydraulic gradient (quoted as a ratio) $= \dfrac{\text{difference in hydrostatic pressure or hydrostatic head}}{\text{distance between two points}}$

Key definitions

The **water table** is the surface separating unsaturated rock above from saturated rock below.

Hydrostatic pressure is the pressure at a point in a body of water due to the weight of the overlying column of water.

The **hydraulic gradient** is the difference in hydrostatic pressure between two points divided by the distance between them.

Worked example: calculating the hydraulic gradient

Figure 3 is a cross-section through part of the South Downs in Sussex. Calculate the hydraulic gradient of the water table between points A and B.

Hydraulic gradient $= \dfrac{\text{difference in hydrostatic pressure or hydrostatic head}}{\text{distance between two points}}$

$= \dfrac{130 - 100}{300} = \dfrac{30}{300} = 0.1 \text{ or } 1{:}10$

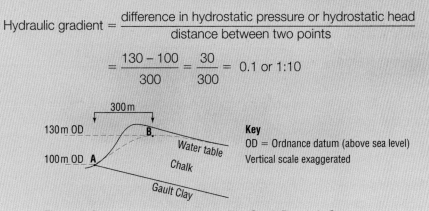

Key
OD = Ordnance datum (above sea level)
Vertical scale exaggerated

Figure 3 Cross-section through part of the South Downs in Sussex

Questions

1 Explain how compaction and cementation reduce the porosity and permeability of a rock.

2 Draw labelled thin section diagrams to compare the porosity and permeability of an oolitic limestone and a greywacke.

3 If a sandstone unit is 50 m thick and it takes 10 days for water to flow through it, calculate the permeability of the sandstone. Give your answer in mm per day.

Aquifers and groundwater storage

There is more water in the ground than in all the world's rivers and lakes combined. After the oceans, porous rocks contain the Earth's largest store of water. Groundwater is stored in aquifers, found predominantly within sedimentary rocks. **Aquifers** are bodies of rock with a high porosity so that large quantities of water can be stored within their pore spaces. They also have a high permeability so water can enter, flow through, and be extracted from the aquifer with ease.

Rocks that make suitable aquifers include poorly cemented sandstones, most limestones, fractured chalk and, in some cases, fractured volcanic rocks such as those in the Puy-de-Dome area of the Auvergne region of Central France. The principal aquifers of the British Isles are the Chalk, Permo-Triassic sandstones, Jurassic limestones and the Lower Greensand.

Aquifers with a **recharge zone** on the surface are replenished by rainwater and can provide a constant supply of water provided the rate recharge equals the rate of extraction.

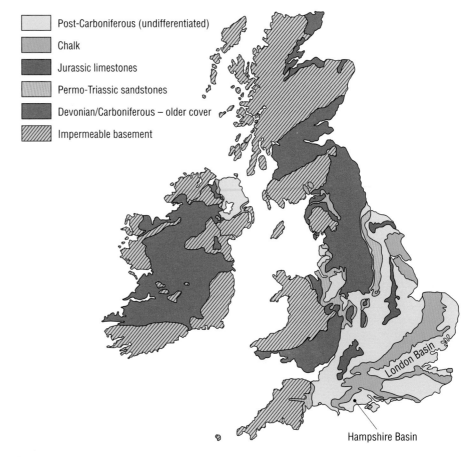

Post-Carboniferous (undifferentiated)

Chalk

Jurassic limestones

Permo-Triassic sandstones

Devonian/Carboniferous – older cover

Impermeable basement

London Basin

Hampshire Basin

Figure 1 Map showing the principal aquifers of the British Isles

Types of aquifers
There are two main types of aquifer, unconfined and confined:
- An unconfined aquifer is open to the atmosphere, under atmospheric pressure, and is recharged by rainwater from directly above. Water will need to be pumped to the surface from a well or borehole sunk into an unconfined aquifer.
- A confined aquifer is overlain by impermeable rocks and the groundwater held within it is under hydrostatic pressure. Groundwater can only be replenished in a confined aquifer if it has recharge zones that are open to the atmosphere.

A perched aquifer sits above the regional water table and is underlain by a lens of impermeable rock which prevents the water from percolating further downwards.

Aquifers can also be described as 'live' or 'fossil':

* A live aquifer is one that is currently being replenished by rainwater via a recharge zone on the surface.
* A fossil aquifer is no longer being replenished and represents a relic of a past wetter climate.

Fossil aquifers are non-renewable water resources and require careful management in order to sustain the area's water supply for as long as possible. Important examples of fossil aquifers include the Ogallala aquifer of central USA and those in the Nubian Sandstones underlying the Sahara Desert, North Africa. Isotopic dating of water from the Great Artesian Basin of eastern Australia has shown that some of it is nearly 2 million years old!

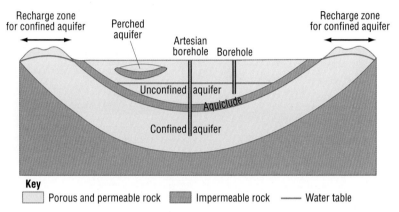

Key
☐ Porous and permeable rock ▨ Impermeable rock —— Water table

Figure 2 Cross-section showing the main components of aquifers for water supply

Artesian basins and artesian wells

Large, synclinal, confined aquifers are termed **artesian basins**, after Artois in France. If a borehole is sunk into an artesian basin the water may flow up to the surface. We call this an **artesian well**. The fountains installed in Trafalgar Square in 1843 initially flowed naturally under hydrostatic pressure as they are in the centre of the London Basin. Once the hydrostatic pressure falls the water has to be pumped to the surface.

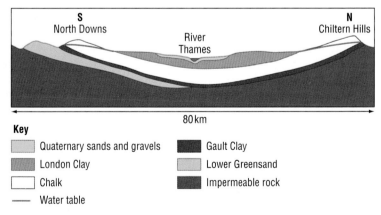

Key
☐ Quaternary sands and gravels   ■ Gault Clay
▨ London Clay   ☐ Lower Greensand
☐ Chalk   ■ Impermeable rock
—— Water table

Figure 3 Cross-section diagram of the London Basin

Questions

1 Describe the characteristics a rock would need to make it a good aquifer.
2 Draw labelled diagrams to explain the difference between an unconfined and a confined aquifer.
3 Make a copy of Figure 3. On your diagram, label and name the two main aquifers, the aquicludes and the recharge zones.

Case study

The London Basin is the best example of an artesian basin in the British Isles. The main aquifer is Cretaceous chalk, 180 to 245 m thick, sandwiched between the Gault Clay below and the London Clay above. The main recharge zones for the London Basin are the Chiltern Hills and the North Downs.

Groundwater was first abstracted from beneath London in the eighteenth century and made a significant contribution to the economic and industrial development of the city. Many businesses, including the Savoy Hotel and the Bank of England, had their own boreholes into the aquifer. At the peak of abstraction in the 1960s the water table under London had fallen by at least 50 m across an area of 200 km^2. This created problems of reduced water yield, poor water quality and surface subsidence.

Most of London's water supply now comes from surface water supplies, and this has led to a recovery of groundwater levels below the city to such an extent that the rising groundwater is now causing concern! Increased hydrostatic pressure within the chalk has caused saturation of the overlying London Clay. This is affecting the stability of foundations of some buildings and threatens flooding of tunnels, including the London Underground.

The Environment Agency currently has a network of 200 observation boreholes in London to monitor groundwater levels. Management of water levels is mainly done through control of water abstraction licences.

How to get groundwater from wells

Groundwater is **abstracted** by sinking a **borehole** and pumping the water to the surface. As water is pumped out of the ground from a **well**, the level of the water table falls around the well, leading to a **cone of depression**. We call the height difference between the water table and the level of water in the well the **draw down**. As water is pumped from the well, the reduction in hydrostatic pressure leads to a hydraulic gradient being set up and groundwater flows in towards the well.

Remember, if a borehole is sunk into an artesian basin the water will rise upwards under hydrostatic pressure to form an artesian well. The greatest pressure will be in the part of the aquifer with the highest hydrostatic head. This will save on pumping costs.

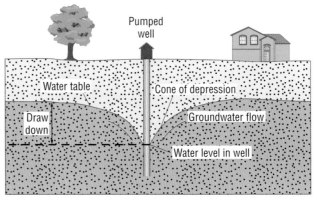

Figure 1 The effect of pumping water from a well

Problems caused by groundwater abstraction

The main problems are:

- Lowering of the water table. Shallow wells become dry and have to be sunk deeper. This is a particular problem if wells are situated too close together and their cones of depression overlap. This leads to a lowering of the whole water table.
- Subsidence at the surface resulting from the removal of water from the pore spaces of rocks. Rocks overlying the aquifer collapse downwards creating depressions at the surface which can be several metres in diameter. Subsidence results in compaction of the aquifer and a permanently reduced water storage capacity.
- Saltwater encroachment in coastal areas. Where aquifers occur at coastlines, the less dense fresh groundwater forms a lens floating on top of more dense sea water. Over-pumping disturbs the freshwater–saltwater interface and allows sea water to enter the aquifer. The groundwater becomes saline (brackish) and unfit for drinking. This has occurred at many locations around the coast of the British Isles.

Figure 2 A windmill pumping water from a well for agriculture

Threats to groundwater supply

The two main threats to our groundwater supplies are over-pumping and pollution:

- Over-pumping – if too much groundwater is extracted then there may not be enough left to provide a reliable public water supply.
- Pollution – groundwater is vulnerable to contamination from a variety of sources and once polluted is difficult to clean. Unconfined aquifers are more at risk from pollution than confined aquifers.

It is important that groundwater is tested to monitor its level and quality. The Environment Agency currently has 7300 groundwater level monitoring sites and 3500 groundwater quality monitoring sites in England and Wales.

Groundwater quality

As groundwater percolates downwards through the pore space of rocks, the rocks act as a natural filter removing impurities from the water. This natural filtration process not only removes chemical impurities, but can even remove bacteria and viruses. As a result groundwater does not always require treatment such as chlorination to make it fit for drinking. For this reason, many people may prefer to drink bottled groundwater or spring water rather than tap water.

Soluble minerals are dissolved from the rocks and taken into solution as the groundwater percolates downwards. These dissolved salts or ions can make the water taste good or bad and can be beneficial or harmful. Some people believe drinking water containing certain dissolved ions is good for their health. The ions present will depend on the rock types the water has passed through.

'Hard' groundwater contains dissolved calcium (Ca^{2+}) and magnesium (Mg^{2+}) ions. Hard water is harmless to drink but it leaves limescale in kettles and can be difficult to lather when you add soap.

Some groundwater contains naturally dissolved fluoride (F^-) ions. Fluoride in drinking water has been proved to reduce tooth decay, but too much fluoride (greater than 4 parts per million) has been linked to dental fluorosis, where teeth become discoloured and pitted, and more serious health problems, such as joint pain, liver and kidney disease.

Unfortunately, some places, including parts of India and Bangladesh, have naturally high levels of toxic arsenic in their groundwater, making it unfit for human consumption.

Typical mineral analysis	mg/l
Calcium	25.6
Magnesium	6.4
Sodium	6.4
Potassium	<1.0
Hydrogen carbonate	98.3
Sulfate	10.1
Nitrate	<2.5
Chloride	6.8
Fluoride	<0.1
Silicate	7.6
pH	7.4
Dry residue at 180°C	109.1

Figure 3 A label from a bottle of mineral water

Groundwater pollution

Groundwater is often under threat from pollution. This can be from a point source such as a factory which is relatively easy to pinpoint or from a more widespread, diffuse source which is much harder to track down and prevent. Sources of groundwater pollution include:

- nitrates, pesticides and microbes from agricultural run-off and sewage
- hydrocarbons and solvents from petrol stations and factories
- toxic fluids from landfill waste disposal sites
- acid mine drainage water containing toxic metals such as lead and cadmium from abandoned coal and metal mines.

Unfortunately, once groundwater in an aquifer does become polluted, the pollutants have a long residence time of thousands of years and it is virtually impossible to remove them.

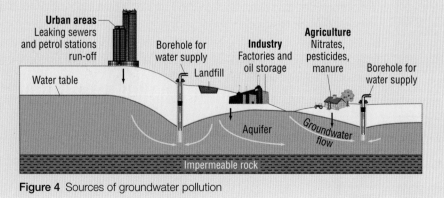

Figure 4 Sources of groundwater pollution

Questions

1 Draw a labelled cross-section diagram to show the effect of pumping water from a well.
2 Describe one problem caused by groundwater abstraction.
3 Give scientific reasons why some people prefer to drink bottled water rather than tap water.
4 Explain why unconfined aquifers are more at risk from pollution than confined aquifers.

What are springs?

Springs occur where the water table intersects the land surface and groundwater flows out onto the surface. This often occurs at the junction between permeable and impermeable rocks. Often a line of springs occurs along the boundary. We call this a spring line.

Water and life

A large spring can yield more than 1000 litres of water per second. Springs can be very important for water supply and for sustaining river flow. Springs are subject to variations in the height of the water table. As a result some may only flow intermittently, depending on the amount of rainfall and the season.

In deserts, oases of lush vegetation occur where aquifers intersect the land surface and water seeps to the surface. Such oases have been extremely important for the location of transport and trade routes in arid areas.

Types of springs

Lithological springs

Lithological springs are the result of changes in rock type. They occur where porous and permeable rock overlies impermeable rock. The water table will intersect the land surface at the junction between the two rock types. There will be a spring line along the base of the permeable rock.

Springs resulting from lithology also occur where impermeable igneous intrusions, such as dykes, cut through porous and permeable sedimentary rocks. Springs occur where the contact between the two rock types outcrops at the surface.

Springs at faults

Faults can produce springs if they have moved porous and permeable rock into contact with impermeable rock. A spring line will occur where the fault plane intersects the land surface.

Faults can result in the formation of pressurised springs if they intersect confined aquifers. Water under hydrostatic pressure from the confined aquifer will rise up the fault plane and flow out onto the surface.

Springs at unconformities

Unconformities can also result in the formation of springs. If porous and permeable rock lies unconformably on top of impermeable older rock, the water table will intersect the land surface at the junction between the two rock types. A spring line will occur where the plane of the unconformity intersects the land surface.

Lithological springs in a valley

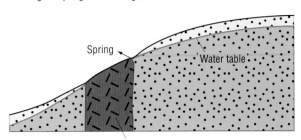

Lithological spring next to an igneous intrusion

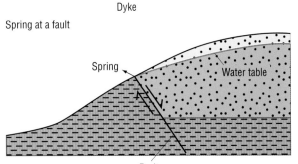

Spring at a fault

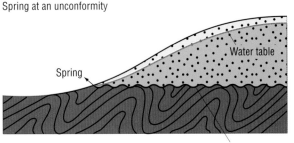

Spring at an unconformity

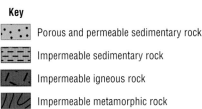

Key

:·:·:	Porous and permeable sedimentary rock
	Impermeable sedimentary rock
	Impermeable igneous rock
	Impermeable metamorphic rock

Figure 1 The location of springs

Case study

The city of Bath is famous for its thermal springs. The city was named Aquae Sulis ('the waters of Sulis') by the Romans and became a popular spa resort in the seventeenth and eighteenth centuries when 'taking the waters' became fashionable. The thermal spring waters were believed to be good for rheumatism, skin conditions, respiratory illnesses and digestive disorders.

At a temperature of 46°C, Bath has the hottest geothermal springs in the British Isles. Geochemical analysis shows the spring water is several thousand years old. It originated as rainwater that fell in the Mendip Hills and percolated downwards through a confined aquifer in Carboniferous limestone. The water was heated by the geothermal gradient as it reached depths of more than 2 km and was added to by older water from underlying Devonian sandstones. The water now rises up under hydrostatic pressure through fractures to emerge as thermal springs at Bath.

Tourism remains Bath's main industry and with signs that 'taking the waters' is making a comeback, a modern spa complex called the Thermea Bath Spa opened in the city in 2006.

Figure 2 A Bedouin woman with her goats drinking from spring water in the desert, Wadi Rum, Jordan

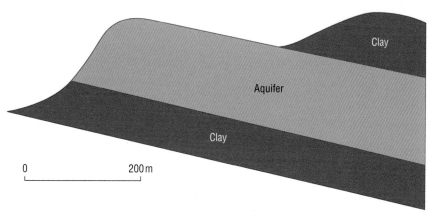

Figure 3 Cross-section through part of an aquifer

Questions

1 Copy Figure 3. On your diagram:
   (a) Draw a line to show the position of the water table.
   (b) Label the position of a spring.
   (c) Shade the area of the aquifer that is confined.
   (d) Explain why there will be a spring at the position you have chosen.

2 Explain why spring water is often suitable for drinking.

3 Describe the geological conditions leading to the formation of springs as a result of lithology, faults and unconformities. Diagrams are essential to illustrate your answer.

Water resources

Water resources in the British Isles

Britain has plenty of water overall and yet we have hosepipe bans and flooding, sometimes at the same time but in different parts of the country. There is no national grid for water supply and it is often organised locally.

Rainfall is much greater in the north and west compared to the south and east. So in the north and west (southwest England, Wales, Isle of Man, northern England, Ireland and Scotland) water supply is dominated by water abstraction from rivers and storage of water in surface reservoirs. The rocks in this area are older and impermeable with many igneous and metamorphic rocks. Less than 10% of the water supply comes from groundwater sources.

The southeast of England (the Home Counties, Kent, East Anglia and Lincolnshire) has the driest climate of the British Isles and the highest demand for water. Here water supply is dominated by groundwater abstraction and over 50% of the water supply comes from wells, boreholes and springs. The rocks are young, mainly porous and permeable sedimentary strata separated by impermeable clays.

Key definitions

A **dam** is a structure that holds back water.

A **reservoir** is a body of water behind a dam wall.

Hydroelectric power is releasing water stored behind a dam to turn a turbine to generate electricity.

Advantages and disadvantages of surface water supply

Advantages	Disadvantages
• Easy to abstract water from rivers, lakes or reservoirs by direct pumping • Water can be treated after use and put back into a river • Dams and reservoirs can be used for hydroelectric power generation • Reservoirs can be used for recreation and other purposes	• Water will need treatment • Seasonal, as the volume of water in rivers varies and water loss occurs through evaporation • Requires construction of expensive and environmentally damaging dams • Requires flooding of land for reservoirs • Reservoirs will eventually silt up • Construction of dams and reservoirs may trigger earthquakes • Requires sufficient rainfall and large river catchments – there is no backup in drought conditions

Advantages and disadvantages of groundwater supply

Advantages	Disadvantages
• Rocks act as a natural filter purifying the water • No loss of water through evaporation • No requirement for expensive and environmentally damaging dams • If water is from an artesian basin, the pumping costs will be low	• Requires sedimentary rocks and presence of aquifers • Problem of surface subsidence • Pollutants have a long residence time • Pumping costs as water has to be raised vertically • Groundwater is not always suitable for drinking due to the presence of dissolved salts making the water brackish

Sustainability of water resources

We are making increasingly greater demands on our water resources. Most of the water is used for agriculture. The need to ensure a reliable public water supply is a pressing issue, particularly in the light of our concerns about global warming and climate change.

Groundwater from live aquifers is a **renewable resource**. As part of the water cycle, groundwater is replenished by rainwater infiltrating into the soil and then percolating downwards through rocks to reach the water table.

Whether or not groundwater resources are **sustainable** is a different question. Groundwater supplies are only sustainable if the rate of extraction does not exceed the rate of replenishment. In addition, groundwater supplies are only sustainable if the natural system of filtration through rocks can clean the water fast enough and the water remains free from pollutants.

Fossil aquifers, such as the Ogallala aquifer of the central USA and the Great Artesian Basin of eastern Australia, are non-renewable water resources and ultimately unsustainable. Water extraction from parts of the Ogallala aquifer is more than a hundred times its recharge rate. Groundwater mining on this scale can not continue for much longer.

Key definitions

A **renewable resource** is one that is replenished by natural processes at a rate equal to or exceeding its rate of use.

A resource is **sustainable** if it is used in such a way that can continue into the future.

Recent initiatives in water resource management

As components of the water cycle, there is an intimate relationship between surface water and groundwater.

The natural replenishment of an aquifer can be supplemented by artificial recharge. Water may be pumped into the ground through boreholes or by using controlled flooding to spread water over a large area so that it can infiltrate the ground. The idea is to store surplus water in aquifers for future use. Parts of the London Basin are recharged with treated river water during the winter months. But at present artificial recharge is only used to a limited extent in the British Isles.

Of greater importance is the use of groundwater to maintain river flow during dry periods. Several major schemes in England, including the Shropshire Groundwater Scheme, have been designed to pump groundwater into rivers to ensure continuous public water supply during the summer months and to protect the river environment.

Case study

The Great Artesian Basin of eastern Australia provides the only reliable source of water for much of inland Australia. The basin is the largest and deepest artesian basin in the world. It underlies 23% of the continent and is estimated to contain 64 900 km^3 of groundwater.

At present, approximately two-thirds of the water extracted is wasted. Much of the waste results from evaporation of water from free flowing artesian boreholes. This waste can be easily prevented by capping the boreholes.

Concerns about drought and water shortages in Australia have reached such an extent that in January 2007 the Australian Government implemented its National Plan for Water Security. This is a $10 billion plan to address over-extraction of water in rural Australia. It will improve efficiency of water use and ensure sustainability into the future.

Case study

The River Severn provides water for many communities in the West Midlands. During the summer months the river level may be insufficient to meet demand.

The Shropshire Groundwater Scheme began in 1984 and is being developed in eight stages. It is designed to increase the River Severn's flow using groundwater and releases from the Llyn Clywedog and Llyn Vrynwy reservoirs in Wales.

The scheme has 64 pumping stations, each with 1 or 2 boreholes up to 220 m deep tapping the underlying Permo-Triassic sandstone aquifer. Groundwater is discharged into the river system through weirs and sand traps to ensure the water is suitably oxygenated and sediment free.

The scheme is licensed to abstract 330 million litres of groundwater per day. It is designed to operate for 5 to 15 weeks a year in 2 out of every 5 years. In the first 20 years of operation the scheme was used 6 times.

Questions

1 Describe the advantages and disadvantages of surface water supply from rivers and reservoirs.
2 Describe the advantages and disadvantages of water supply from groundwater.
3 Explain why groundwater supplies are more important in some areas than others.
4 Explain how water resources can be both renewable and sustainable if carefully developed and used.

Petroleum – 'black gold'

We depend on energy for heating, lighting and powering machinery. Over the last 200 years, we have steadily increased the amount of coal, oil, natural gas and uranium we take from the Earth to fuel our modern lifestyle. As coal, oil and natural gas are made from the remains of once living organisms they are collectively called fossil fuels.

Today we have a hydrocarbon-based society that is dominated by the burning and use of petroleum and its products. The word petroleum comes from Latin – *petra* = rock and *oleum* = oil. Petroleum includes natural gas (gas), crude oil (liquid) and asphalt (solid). In addition to its use as a fuel, petroleum forms the basis of the multi-million pound petrochemicals industry. Products include plastics, paints, synthetic fibres, synthetic rubber, pharmaceuticals and fertilisers.

How long will crude oil last?

Crude oil and natural gas are non-renewable resources. The price of crude oil is steadily rising and we now consume four barrels of oil for every new barrel discovered. Estimates suggest global oil production will peak at any time between now and 2030. As a result important questions are being asked:

- How long will supplies of this vital resource last?
- Can we find more?
- What impact is our dependence on petroleum having on the environment?

With over half of the geological profession employed in the petroleum industry, geologists have an important part to play in answering these questions.

Requirements for the formation and accumulation of oil and natural gas

Oil and natural gas originate in sedimentary basins. The main requirements to form economic accumulations are:

- a source rock
- maturation
- migration
- a reservoir rock
- a cap rock
- a trap.

Key definitions

A **source rock** is an organic-rich mudstone or shale containing abundant plankton that formed in low energy, anoxic, marine conditions.

The **maturation** process is where plankton is converted into petroleum by the effects of temperature and pressure during burial.

Migration describes the movement of petroleum from a source rock to a reservoir rock.

A **reservoir rock** is a highly porous and permeable rock capable of storing and yielding significant amounts of petroleum.

The **cap rock** is the impermeable rock above the reservoir rock preventing further upwards migration of petroleum.

A **trap** is a geological situation that concentrates petroleum in one place.

Examiner tip

A common misconception is that oil and natural gas rise upwards because they are less dense than rock. Instead it is because they are less dense than the water in the pore spaces.

Natural gas will form a horizontal layer above the oil, which in turn will form a horizontal layer above the water in the pore space, regardless of the dip of the beds.

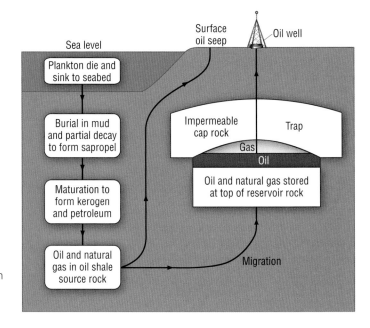

Figure 1 Geological requirements for the formation and accumulation of oil and natural gas

Environment of deposition of source rocks

Oil and natural gas are formed from the remains of microscopic marine organisms called plankton. These organisms float in the surface waters of the ocean and, after dying, sink down through the water column to accumulate on the seabed. The environment of deposition must be low energy so the tiny plankton can settle out of the water column. Conditions on the seabed need to be anoxic (lacking in oxygen) so the plankton will not decay or be scavenged and eaten by other organisms. Once on the seabed, anaerobic bacteria cause partial decay of the plankton to produce an organic mud called a sapropel.

Burial in fine grained sediment results in the formation of an organic-rich sedimentary rock called a **source rock**. Source rocks are black oil shales and mudstones. Their dark colour reflects their high organic carbon content and their fine grain size reflects the low-energy conditions of deposition.

Maturation of petroleum

As the source rock is buried it is subjected to compaction and, due to the geothermal gradient, an increase in temperature. Over time, the organic matter breaks down to form a mixture of organic compounds of carbon, hydrogen, oxygen, nitrogen and sulfur called kerogen and then petroleum. This process is called **maturation**. Petroleum forms between temperatures of 50 to 200°C – the 'oil window'. Below 50°C biogenic gas forms but, due to its shallow burial, is usually lost. Most oil forms between 50 to 100°C and natural gas, consisting mainly of methane, forms between 100 to 200°C. Above 200°C the hydrocarbons denature and are destroyed.

Migration from source rock to reservoir rock

Once formed the petroleum undergoes **migration** from the source rock to a reservoir rock. The main factors controlling migration are:

- Permeability of the rocks – there must be permeable rocks between the source rock and the reservoir rock.
- Pressure – oil and natural gas will migrate down the pressure gradient from high pressure to low pressure. This is usually up but can be down.
- Density differences – because oil and natural gas are less dense than the water in the pore spaces of rocks, they will percolate upwards until they encounter an impermeable layer or reach the surface.
- Viscosity of the oil – the higher the temperature, the lower the viscosity of the oil. The lower the viscosity of the oil, the more easily it will flow.

Reservoir rock

A **reservoir rock** must have a high porosity to be able to store significant amounts of oil and natural gas. It must also have a high permeability to allow the oil and natural gas to migrate into it and then be extracted from it. So the properties of a reservoir rock for oil and natural gas are the same as the properties of an aquifer for water. Suitable reservoir rocks include poorly cemented sandstones, most limestones and fractured chalk.

Cap rock

The reservoir rock must be overlain by an impermeable **cap rock**. The cap rock prevents further upwards migration of oil and natural gas. Without a cap rock, the oil and natural gas will continue to rise, eventually forming oil seeps and tar pits on the surface. Suitable cap rocks include fine grained sedimentary rocks such as clay, mudstone and shale and crystalline sedimentary rocks such as evaporites.

Trap

The final requirement for the accumulation of oil and natural gas is the presence of a **trap**. Traps are covered in spread 4.2.2.

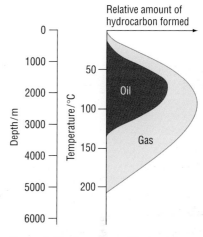

Figure 2 The formation of hydrocarbons during burial and maturation

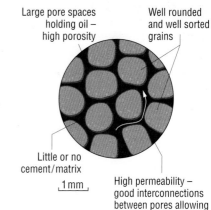

Figure 3 Thin section diagram of desert sandstone with oil in pore space

Questions

1 Describe the depositional environment of source rocks for oil and natural gas.
2 Explain how oil and natural gas form in a source rock.
3 Describe and explain two factors that control the migration of oil and natural gas.
4 Define the terms *reservoir rock* and *cap rock*.
5 Describe the properties of a good reservoir rock for oil.

What are traps?

Traps are where the geology allows oil and natural gas to be concentrated in one place, making them economic to extract.

Traps may be structural or stratigraphic in origin. Structural traps result from rock deformation and include anticlines, faults and salt domes. Stratigraphic traps result from the arrangement of the sedimentary rocks and include unconformities and those due to lithology (rock type).

All traps require the presence of a porous and permeable reservoir rock overlain by an impermeable cap rock. As you can see on the trap diagrams, gas always forms a horizontal layer above the oil, which in turn forms a horizontal layer above the water in the pore space of the reservoir rock.

Types of traps

Anticline traps

Anticline traps form when rocks are folded into arch shapes. Anticline traps were the first to be discovered and hold 80% of the world's known oil and natural gas reserves. Oil and natural gas will be concentrated in the top of the reservoir rock at the crest of the anticline provided it is overlain by a cap rock. The storage capacity of an anticline trap is determined by the size and shape of the fold. An open fold is likely to contain far more oil than a tight fold. The larger the fold the more oil it may store. Once an anticline trap is filled to capacity, oil and natural gas leak out laterally, at spill points, and migrate into adjacent rocks.

Fault traps

Fault traps form when movement along a fault plane results in a reservoir rock being moved adjacent to an impermeable rock. The impermeable rock on the opposite side of the fault prevents the oil and natural gas escaping laterally. The reservoir rock must also be overlain by a cap rock. Provided the strata are dipping, the oil and gas will migrate up dip and be trapped at the top of the reservoir rock adjacent to the fault. The fault itself must be sealed to prevent the oil and gas escaping up the fault.

Salt dome traps

Salt dome traps result from the presence of evaporites such as halite and gypsum. Evaporites have a lower density (2.3 g/cm³) than the surrounding rocks (2.5–2.7 g/cm³) and, much like magma, form diapirs that rise upwards towards the surface. These uplift and pierce the surrounding rocks to form salt domes. Salt domes are typically 1 to 10 km across and may extend as far down as 6 km. The overlying rocks are folded gently upwards into anticlines. Because evaporites are crystalline they are impermeable and form good cap rocks. Oil and natural gas may accumulate in dipping reservoir rocks adjacent to the salt dome or in anticline traps above the salt dome. Remember though, there must always be a suitable cap rock above.

Key

 Impermeable cap rock

Porous and permeable reservoir rock

Gas held in pore spaces

Oil held in pore spaces

Figure 1 Structural traps for oil and natural gas

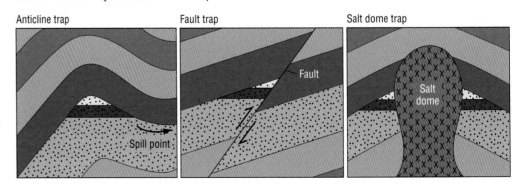

Unconformity traps

Unconformity traps form if reservoir rocks below an angular unconformity are overlain by cap rocks above the unconformity. Oil and natural gas will migrate up dip and be trapped just beneath the unconformity. The reservoir rock below the unconformity must have impermeable rocks on either side to concentrate economic amounts of oil and gas in one place.

Lithological traps

Lithological traps result from variations in rock type. Fossilised limestone reefs make good lithological traps if they are surrounded by impermeable rocks. Limestone reefs make ideal reservoirs because they have very high porosities and form in areas where there is abundant life to produce the organic matter needed for petroleum formation. Sandstones that formed as river channel, point bar or deltaic deposits often have a lens shape, making small but common traps. The river or delta clays around them make good cap rocks.

How can oil and natural gas be destroyed or lost from traps?

Oil and natural gas may be destroyed if the temperature increases above 200 °C due to:

- heat from an igneous intrusion or volcanic activity
- regional metamorphism where temperatures are high
- burial where the geothermal gradient results in temperatures higher than 200 °C.

Oil and natural gas may be lost from a trap by:

- erosion and removal of the overlying cap rock
- escaping upwards along an unsealed fault plane.

Unconformity trap

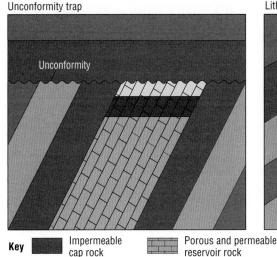

Lithological trap

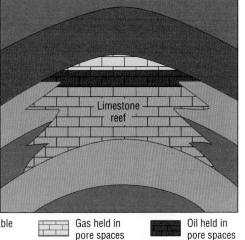

Key ▮ Impermeable cap rock · ▦ Porous and permeable reservoir rock · ▦ Gas held in pore spaces · ▮ Oil held in pore spaces

Figure 2 Stratigraphic traps for oil and natural gas

Questions

1 Define the term *trap*.
2 Describe, with the aid of labelled diagrams, different types of traps where oil and natural gas can accumulate.
3 Explain why locating a trap does not guarantee the discovery of economic quantities of oil and natural gas.

Finding oil and natural gas

Many geologists are employed in the search for 'black gold'. Initially, oil exploration was haphazard with very little understanding of the underlying geology. It relied on hit and miss 'wildcat' drilling around surface oil seeps with a less than 1 in 50 chance of striking oil.

Today oil and natural gas exploration is a very sophisticated, expensive, but still financially risky business. The high price of oil and gas ensures the potential rewards are great. Successful oil and gas exploration relies on interpretation of geological data from a variety of sources. In onshore oil and gas exploration, satellite imagery and geological mapping are used to identify areas suitable for closer inspection. This is not possible in offshore areas. Here successful oil exploration is dependent solely on the use of geophysical techniques and exploration drilling.

Geophysical exploration techniques

Seismic reflection surveys

Seismic surveys can be land-based or ship-based:

- Artificial seismic waves are generated by explosions or vibrations on land and by air guns in water. On land, vibrations can be generated by dropping a heavy 'thumper' mounted on a truck.
- The seismic waves travel into the Earth and are reflected at layer boundaries within sedimentary sequences.
- The reflected waves travel back up to the surface where they are detected by an array of receivers called geophones on land or hydrophones at sea. Their location is accurately pinpointed using Global Positioning Systems (GPS). Offshore seismic surveys are particularly efficient as a large number of hydrophones can be towed behind a ship. Also, a ship's path is not restricted like vibrotrucks are on land.
- The time taken for the reflected waves to arrive back at the receivers is called the travel time. This can be used to calculate the depth to the reflective layer. The data is used to plot a seismic profile. Seismic profiles show the subsurface layering and can be interpreted by geophysicists to identify potential traps.

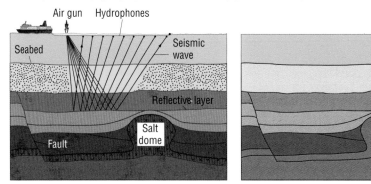

Seismic reflection survey

Interpreted seismic profile

Figure 1 A seismic reflection survey and the resultant seismic profile

Gravity surveys

Gravity surveys can be on land or airborne. They are useful for exploration for oil, natural gas and metals.

- An instrument, called a gravimeter, measures small variations in the Earth's gravitational field strength. The units of measurement are milligals (mGal). Gravimeters can be mounted in road vehicles, helicopters or planes, allowing rapid coverage of large areas. Survey points are located using GPS.

- The gravity data is corrected for the affects of latitude, altitude and topography leaving the variations resulting from the underlying rock types.
- Maps are plotted with lines joining points of equal gravitational field strength and anomalies can then be identified. A gravity anomaly is a departure from the normal value and may be positive or negative.
- A positive gravity anomaly results from an excess of mass. This may be due to the presence of an anticline or an uplifted block bounded by faults, which could be potential trap structures.
- A negative gravity anomaly results from a deficit of mass. This may be due to the presence of a low-density salt dome. In this case the exploration target would be around the edge of the salt dome at the zero milligal line.

Exploration drilling

When potential oil and natural gas traps have been located, exploration drilling is then carried out. Holes are drilled with cylindrical drill bits studded with diamonds. The rotating drill bit is cooled and lubricated by drilling mud containing the mineral barite to make it dense enough to reach the bottom of the hole. Millimetre-sized rock chips or a continuous core can be recovered from the hole. Recovering continuous rock core is very expensive so this is only done at critical depths.

Mud logging

Rock chips are brought up to the surface in the drilling mud. These are sieved from the mud, washed and examined under a microscope by geologists called mud loggers. Mud loggers identify the rock types and microfossils present at different depths down the hole. This allows them to build up a picture of the changing rock types down the hole and to correlate the geology between boreholes.

Down-hole logging

It is possible to mount geophysical instruments on a sonde. The sonde is passed down the drill hole on a cable called a wireline. The sonde then records data as it is slowly pulled up from the bottom of the hole.

Measurements made during down-hole logging include:
- Porosity: the higher the porosity, the higher the possible oil and natural gas content of a reservoir rock. It is also possible to interpret what fluids are present in the pore space – oil, gas or brine.
- Gamma ray spectroscopy: this counts the gamma rays emitted from rocks as a result of natural radioactive decay. Potential source rocks such as black oil shales and mudstones give a high gamma ray count. In comparison, sandstones and limestones produce a low count.
- Resistivity: this measures the resistance of the rock to the flow of electricity. Water is the main conductor present in rocks and gives a low resistance. The presence of hydrocarbons results in a very high resistance.

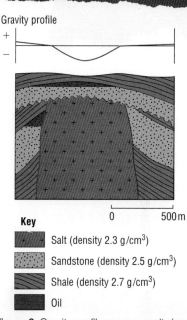

Gravity profile

Key

0   500 m

Salt (density 2.3 g/cm^3)

Sandstone (density 2.5 g/cm^3)

Shale (density 2.7 g/cm^3)

Oil

Figure 2 Gravity profile across a salt dome

Figure 3 A drill bit

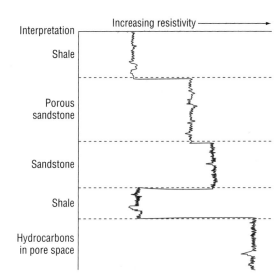

Increasing resistivity ⟶

Interpretation

Shale

Porous sandstone

Sandstone

Shale

Hydrocarbons in pore space

Figure 4 A down-hole electrical resistivity log

Questions

1 Describe how geophysical exploration techniques can be used to find oil and natural gas.
2 Explain the advantages and disadvantages of exploration drilling compared to a geophysical survey.

Reserves

As we have seen, oil and natural gas are extremely useful **natural resources**. Once exploration has established their presence, the amount present must be calculated. We call this the **reserves**.

Reserves can be proven, probable or possible. Proven reserves are those that we are certain are there. Probable reserves are those that we are reasonably certain are there. Possible reserves are ones that may become economic in the future if conditions are favourable. Reserves change: they can go up or down.

Oil and natural gas reserves can go up because:

- exploration discovers more
- technology improves so more can be extracted from existing reservoirs, from deeper water or from unconventional sources
- smaller oilfields become economic if prices rise.

Oil and natural gas reserves can go down because:

- they are being extracted from the earth
- calculations of reserves are incorrect
- smaller oilfields become uneconomic if prices fall.

Key definitions

A **natural resource** is any natural material that is useful and valuable.

Reserves are the amount of the resource that can be extracted at a profit using existing technology.

Case study

Royal Dutch Shell plc is one of the largest multinational oil companies in the world. In 2004, Shell faced a barrage of criticism when the company admitted it had overstated its proven oil reserves and was cutting them by 20%. Shell's share prices plummeted by 6% and the company was accused of recklessly violating accounting rules and guidelines. The crisis led to the dismissal of the Chief Executive Officer and a major shake-up within the company.

Shell is expected to pay out more than $700 million in fines to settle the reserves scandal. But the company still announced a gross profit of $26 billion in 2006, making it the most profitable British company ever.

Estimating reserves

The correct calculation of reserves is vital if oil companies are to make a profit and if supply is going to meet demand. Reserves calculations are made on the basis of incomplete geological data, volatile market prices and require the use of very sophisticated mathematical modelling. It is possible for genuine mistakes to be made, but companies may deliberately overestimate their reserves to boost their share prices!

Worked example: calculating reserves

The reserves of an oilfield are estimated to be 730 million barrels. If the rate of oil production is 200 000 barrels per day, calculate how many years the reserves will last.

$$730\,000\,000 \div (365 \times 200\,000) = 730\,000\,000 \div 73\,000\,000 = 10 \text{ years}$$

Primary recovery

To extract the oil and natural gas the reservoir rock is drilled into and a production well established. The well must be quickly capped off to prevent **blowouts** and oil spills. Directional drilling techniques are used so that a number of wells from one wellhead can tap the reservoir rock over a large area. In the case of Wytch Farm, in Dorset, extended reach wells go 10.7 km horizontally from the wellhead.

Initially the oil comes to the surface under natural pressure. The oil gushes to the surface due to:

- gases in the oil coming out of solution
- expansion of gas above the oil
- the hydrostatic pressure of the water in the pore space beneath the oil.

After the natural pressure dies away oil is pumped to the surface using submersible pumps or beam pumps called 'nodding donkeys'. Typically only 20 to 30% of the oil in the reservoir rock can be recovered by **primary recovery**.

Key definitions

A **blowout** occurs when oil gushes uncontrolled to the surface.

Primary recovery is where oil initially gushes to the surface under natural pressure and is then pumped out.

Secondary recovery is where water is injected below or natural gas injected above the oil to maintain the pressure.

The reservoir rock type will affect the percentage of oil recovery. The porosity and permeability of the rock are key factors, which will be determined by the grain size, roundness and sorting. The amount of matrix or cement will be factors, as will the presence of structures such as joints that affect permeability. Oil is thick and viscous with a high surface tension and sticks to the grains in the reservoir rock. At depth the rocks will be warmer so the oil will have a lower viscosity, but the rocks are likely to be more compacted so will have less pore space.

Figure 1 A nodding donkey pumping oil from a well, Kimmeridge Bay, Dorset

Secondary recovery

Secondary recovery techniques are used to extract more oil from reservoir rocks.
- Water flood drive – water is injected into the reservoir rock beneath the oil to maintain the pressure.
- Gas cap drive – natural gas, carbon dioxide or nitrogen gas are injected into the reservoir rock above the oil to maintain the pressure. Some gases also dissolve in the oil, lowering its viscosity.
- Thermal methods such as steam injection to increase the temperature and lower the viscosity of the oil.
- Detergents and other chemicals are used to reduce the surface tension of the oil to loosen it from the grains.
- Bacteriological methods – these are also being developed to digest and break down large hydrocarbon molecules to decrease their viscosity.

Even after secondary recovery, 20–30% of the oil remains unrecoverable. If technological innovations provide a way of extracting this oil, then reserves will increase.

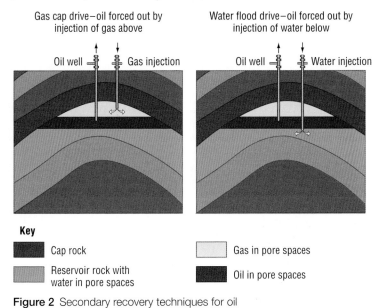

Gas cap drive – oil forced out by injection of gas above

Water flood drive – oil forced out by injection of water below

Oil well — Gas injection

Oil well — Water injection

Key
- Cap rock
- Reservoir rock with water in pore spaces
- Gas in pore spaces
- Oil in pore spaces

Figure 2 Secondary recovery techniques for oil

Questions

1 Describe how primary recovery of oil takes place.
2 Explain why the percentage recovery of oil from a reservoir rock may vary.
3 Describe the secondary recovery methods used to increase the percentage of oil recovery.
4 Explain why 20–30% of the oil remains unrecoverable after secondary recovery.

Figure 1 An oil flare

Environmental and safety problems of petroleum extraction

Oil and natural gas are released naturally into the environment from surface seeps. An oil spill is an unintentional release of hydrocarbons due to human activity. Spills may occur during extraction or transportation of oil. Such oil spills are both fire and environmental hazards.

Petroleum in any form is highly flammable and only the smallest spark is needed for devastating explosions and fires to occur. We only need to think of the dreadful oil fires that raged in Kuwait during the 1991 Gulf War or the 2005 Hertfordshire Oil Storage Terminal fire, to get an idea of their scale. The explosions that accompanied the Hertfordshire fire were reported as the largest in peacetime Europe. Offshore oil rigs and platforms are particularly at risk. In 1988, 167 people died in the Piper Alpha disaster when an oil platform in the North Sea exploded after a gas leak.

Although blowouts, where oil gushes uncontrollably to the surface, are rare these days they do still occur. Blowouts are extremely dangerous – they usually catch fire and burn ferociously. Specialist companies deal with blowouts and fight oil fires. Often the only way of extinguishing the fire is to drill a relief well to reduce the pressure at depth so the fire can then be put out with water.

Oil fires cause atmospheric pollution. Smoke from burnt crude oil contains a cocktail of dangerous chemicals including particulate matter (soot), sulfur dioxide, carbon monoxide, benzenes and dioxins.

Just as extraction of groundwater results in subsidence at the surface so does extraction of oil and natural gas. This causes environmental problems and can trigger small earthquakes.

Another environmental problem is the disposal of old oil rigs and platforms. One of the most popular disposal methods is to tow and sink them in deep water. When Shell proposed to do this with the Brent Spar oil rig in 1996 the negative publicity led to a rethink of this policy in Europe. But in America, some old oil rigs are being sunk and used as artificial reefs to provide habitats for coral and fish.

Environmental and safety problems of petroleum transportation

Oil and natural gas transportation is usually done by pipeline or seagoing tanker. We are probably most familiar with the environmental effects of oil spills from tankers, but spills from pipelines on land or on the seabed can be just as devastating. Oil spills at sea not only damage marine habitats and marine life, but also threaten coastal areas. The light fraction of oil floats and causes severe problems for seabirds. It can be contained using booms or be dispersed using detergents which make the oil sink to the seabed. The heavy fraction of oil is very difficult to clean up as it sinks to the bottom. Although not as obvious as oil on the surface, oil on the seabed is highly toxic and persists for a long time.

Pipelines are the most economical way of transporting oil and natural gas. They are made of steel or plastic, typically with a diameter of 30 to 120 cm. The oil and gas is kept flowing along the pipeline by a series of pumping stations. Pipelines are usually built above the ground, but may be buried in built-up, environmentally sensitive or potentially dangerous areas.

Figure 2 Oil spill clean up on a beach

Case study

The Trans-Alaska pipeline is probably the most famous oil pipeline. It is 1300 km long and was built to transport oil from Prudhoe Bay to the nearest ice-free port in Alaska.

Construction of the pipeline presented many challenges:
- It passes through a remote, mountainous and environmentally sensitive area.
- Much of the area is underlain by permafrost which becomes boggy and unstable if it melts.
- It passes over active faults that are prone to earthquakes.

Strategies used to stabilise the pipeline include:
- Building it on supports above ground.
- Using refrigeration plants to pump cold brine into pipes in the soil to prevent the permafrost melting.
- Building zigzags in the pipeline, rollers and shock absorbers in the supports to allow for movement during earthquakes.

The pipeline is surveyed several times a day by air and periodically pipeline inspection gauges ('pigs') are sent through it.

Has it been successful? Since the pipeline was built in 1977, 15 billion barrels of crude oil have been pumped along it. There have been a number of oil spills from the pipeline but it has survived several large earthquakes, including one of 7.2 magnitude on the Richter scale, in 2002.

Figure 3 Trans-Alaska oil pipeline on supports with rollers to allow movement

Underground storage facilities for natural gas

UK gas consumption is rising and to meet this demand we are now importing natural gas from abroad. Underground gas storage (UGS) facilities are being built to store the gas until it is needed at times of peak demand. Onshore facilities are more convenient than offshore ones, but may have to be sited in environmentally sensitive areas.

The two main options for storing gas underground are:
- Depleted oil and gas reservoirs. These are reservoirs from which all the recoverable oil and gas has been extracted. This leaves underground rocks capable of storing gas. The geology will already be well known and equipment left over from when the reservoir was in production can be re-used. To maintain the pressure 50% of the reservoir must be kept full of gas. This makes depleted oil and gas reservoirs attractive – because they were previously filled with hydrocarbons they still contain some gas and do not require injection of what will then become unrecoverable gas.
- Salt caverns. Evaporites are ideal rocks for the underground storage of gas because they are impermeable. Salt is a useful raw material for the chemicals industry and is extracted by underground mining or by solution mining. As the shape of old salt caverns is not ideal new cavities are usually created. This is done by dissolving the rock salt and pumping it out as brine. Natural gas can be replenished and withdrawn more quickly from salt caverns than from depleted hydrocarbon reservoirs.

There are currently operational depleted reservoir UGS facilities in the East Midlands and in Hampshire and there are salt cavern UGS facilities in Cheshire, East Yorkshire and Teesside. More are in the planning stages.

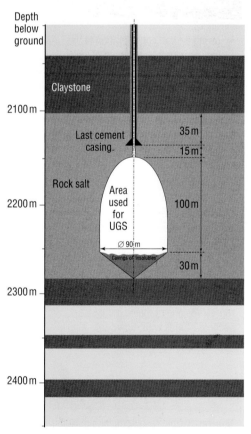

Figure 4 Proposed UGS facility to be excavated by solution of salt in Dorset

Questions

1 Describe the environmental problems which might result from offshore extraction of oil.
2 Describe one method of underground gas storage in rocks.

Oil and natural gas in and around the British Isles

The map shows the occurrence of oil and natural gas in and around the British Isles. Most occurs in offshore areas, particularly the North Sea. Offshore gas fields also occur in the Irish Sea. There are a number of small onshore oil and gas fields, the largest of which is Wytch Farm in Dorset.

Wytch Farm is Europe's largest onshore oilfield, comprising three oilfields that underlie Poole Harbour in Dorset. It was discovered in 1973 and has estimated reserves of 480 million barrels of oil making it one of the top 10 UK oilfields. The oilfield is operated by BP. It has a total of 103 wells and current production is 50 000 barrels per day. Oil is extracted from two main reservoir rocks – Jurassic Bridport Sandstone and Triassic Sherwood Sandstone. A source rock is Lower Jurassic Blue Lias clay.

What makes the oilfield unique is that it is located in an Area of Outstanding Natural Beauty. BP has adhered to a strict environmental protection policy including:

- giving careful consideration to the siting of operations, some of which are on Furzey Island in the centre of Poole Harbour
- landscaping and screening operations with trees
- regularly monitoring air and groundwater quality
- carrying out ecological surveys to assess any environmental impacts.

What is surprising is that most people visiting Poole Harbour have no idea that a large-scale commercial oil exploitation operation is going on right under their feet! The area is a haven for wildlife including rare species such as sand lizards, smooth snakes, warblers and red squirrels. So, to date, Wytch Farm represents one of the oil industry's success stories with regard to environmental sensitivity.

Key definitions

Non-renewable resources take millions of years to form and cannot be replenished on human timescales.

Unsustainable resources are those used in a way that cannot continue in the future.

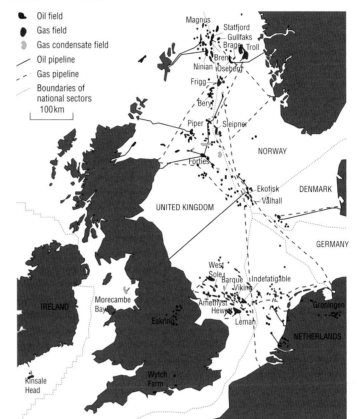

Figure 1 Oil and gas fields in and around the British Isles

Nearly all the oil and natural gas fields in and around the British Isles are in Mesozoic and Cenozoic age sedimentary basins. Older rocks are unlikely to contain hydrocarbons because they have been buried too deeply, have a low porosity due to greater compaction and may have been subjected to temperatures above 200 °C. In addition, the rocks will have suffered tectonic movements which may have resulted in any hydrocarbons escaping along faults.

North Sea oil and gas

North Sea oil was discovered in the early 1960s and the first production well came on line in 1971. Conditions in the North Sea make extraction a costly process and it was only when oil prices rose in the 1980s it became economic to exploit. In 1998, an offshore oil well in the North Sea cost between £5–15 million to put into production, depending on the depth of the water and the subsurface geology.

The North Sea is a shallow continental sea that was subjected to crustal extension during the Mesozoic when the Atlantic Ocean started to open. Faulting broke the area into a series of linear horsts and grabens that controlled sedimentation. The North Sea is separated into two sedimentary basins by an east–west trending ridge or 'high'.

- The Northern North Sea Basin has a variety of oil and natural gas fields. The main source rock for oil is the Jurassic age Kimmeridge Clay. Reservoir rocks are mainly marine sandstones and fractured chalk. Cap rocks are mainly clays with a great variety of traps.

- The hydrocarbon reservoirs in the Southern North Sea Basin do not contain any oil but only produce natural gas. This is because the source rock for this area is the Carboniferous Coal Measures. This source rock did not at any time contain the marine plankton needed for oil formation. Gas escaped from the coal as it formed and is mainly held in desert sandstone reservoir rocks. The cap rocks are often evaporites and the traps are mainly salt domes and their associated anticlines.

Sustainability of British oil and natural gas production

Oil and natural gas are **non-renewable** energy resources. They are fossil fuels that formed millions of years ago. Once they are burnt they are lost as gases into the atmosphere and cannot be recycled on a human timescale. As a result the use of fossil fuels is ultimately **unsustainable**.

Although estimates vary, at the end of 2005 proven reserves of British crude oil stood at 3.9 billion barrels and natural gas at 481 billion m^3. In 2005, total British production of oil was 760 million barrels and gas was 84 million m^3. As reserves fall, each year the production of both oil and gas is steadily declining. Great Britain has been a net importer of natural gas since 2004 and is expected to become a net importer of oil by 2010.

As we have seen in spread 4.2.5, new initiatives include the development of underground gas storage facilities to store imported gas. There is also the possibility of exploiting petroleum from unconventional sources.

Figure 2 A North Sea oil rig

Unconventional petroleum

Unconventional sources of petroleum include oil shales, tar sands and coal-bed methane. Historically the exploitation of petroleum from unconventional sources has been unpopular due to their higher production costs and greater environmental impacts. But as global reserves of oil and natural gas dwindle, more attention is being focused on them.

Oil shale is a general term for any fine grained sedimentary rock containing significant amounts of kerogen that did not undergo enough maturation to produce petroleum. Oil shale can be processed by steam injection underground to produce oil that can be pumped out. Alternatively oil shale can be mined and the kerogen converted into synthetic crude oil by chemical processing. Oil shale can also be burnt as a low-grade fuel in power stations.

The use of oil shales in the British Isles is not new. In the 1850s, oil was extracted from oil shales in the Midland Valley of Scotland. The oil was used in street lamps in Edinburgh and the spoil heaps left behind can still be seen on the outskirts of the city. The Kimmeridge Clay is the richest oil shale in the British Isles.

Large deposits of tar sands occur in Canada and in Venezuela. The Athabasca tar sands of northern Alberta cover an area of 141 000 km^2 of sparsely populated boreal forest and muskeg bogs. The reserves are estimated at 133 billion barrels and in 2005 annual production was 280 million barrels. Even allowing for projected increases in production, the reserves should last over 400 years! Not everyone is happy about this – environmentalists point to negative impacts already being seen on the Athabasca River and the increase in carbon dioxide and other greenhouse gas emissions. The Orinoco Oil Belt of Venezuela contains 90% of known global reserves of 'extra heavy' crude oil, which have a lower viscosity than tar sands. Despite opposition from some environmental groups, Orimulsion (an emulsion of water and Orinoco heavy oil) is burned in some British power stations.

Frozen gas hydrates present in ocean floor sediments and permafrost could also be a future energy resource. They produce large amounts of methane gas when melted.

Questions

1 Explain why oil and natural gas are non-renewable energy resources.
2 Explain why oil and gas are found in the northern basin of the North Sea.
3 Explain why only gas is found in the southern basin of the North Sea.
4 Describe the disadvantages of exploiting oil from oil shales.

Along with oil and natural gas, coal is a fossil fuel. Coal has been used as a fuel for more than 2000 years but it was not until the Scottish engineer James Watt patented his improved steam engine in 1769 that the industrial use of coal was fully developed. Coal powered the Industrial Revolution through the eighteenth and nineteenth centuries and was the mainstay of the British Empire.

Case study

The first half of the twentieth century saw the need for Britain to maintain coal supplies during both World Wars. Coal miners were exempt from being drafted into the armed forces.

Then, in the 1980s, there was a rapid decline in the coal mining industry in Britain. This was due to a number of political and economic factors:
- exploitation of 'cheap' North Sea oil and gas
- cheap foreign coal imports
- complex geology and thin seams of the British coalfields
- coal's reputation as a dirty fuel.

By 2000, the coal mining industry had almost disappeared in Britain.

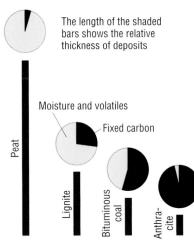

The length of the shaded bars shows the relative thickness of deposits

Moisture and volatiles

Fixed carbon

Peat

Lignite

Bituminous coal

Anthracite

Figure 1 Changes during coalification

Key definitions

A **coal seam** is a layer of coal, usually 1 to 2 m thick.

Coalification is the diagenetic process by which peat is turned into coal by the effects of heat and pressure during burial.

Rank describes the percentage of carbon in the coal.

The **coal series** is the sequence of increasing rank from peat to anthracite.

Climatic and environmental conditions for the formation of peat and coal

Peat and coal originate in deltaic sequences. The main requirements for formation are:
- land plants
- an anoxic environment
- rapid burial.

Peat and coal form from the remains of terrestrial vegetation. Land plants are only found from the Silurian Period (about 425 Ma) onwards and most coal formed during the Carboniferous Period. A hot and humid **climate** encourages rapid growth of trees, so most peat and coal forms in equatorial regions.

A swampy or boggy environment ensures conditions are anoxic (lacking in oxygen), which prevents decay of the plant matter. Anaerobic bacteria slowly change the plant matter into peat. To be preserved the peat must be rapidly buried in fine sediment.

Only deltaic **sedimentary environments** have sufficiently high rates of sedimentation and subsidence to build up the large thicknesses of peat required to form economic **coal seams**. So we associate coal formation with delta-top environments.

Coalification

As with any other sediment, peat undergoes diagenesis due to the effects of heat and pressure during burial. We call this process **coalification** and it is like the maturation process that forms oil and natural gas.

As peat undergoes thermal maturation and is compacted by the weight of the accumulating overburden, water and other volatiles are squeezed out. Oxygen is lost as carbon dioxide and water, and hydrogen is lost as methane. Nitrogen, hydrogen sulfide and other gases are also lost. Remember from spread 4.2.6 that the methane produced can migrate away and accumulate as economic quantities of natural gas. As water and volatiles are removed, the thickness of the coal deposit decreases and the carbon content increases. About 10 metres of peat is needed to form a 1 m thick coal seam.

The coal series of increasing rank

The **rank** of the coal increases with depth and temperature, producing the **coal series**:

peat → lignite → bituminous coal → anthracite

The rank is a measure of the maturity of the coal. As the rank of the coal increases, a number of physical and chemical changes occur. The most important change is the increase in carbon content. As the percentage of carbon increases, the calorific value or amount of heat energy released on burning increases. You can see the changes summarised in the table.

Increasing depth of burial, temperature and pressure ⟶			
Formation temperature (°C)	40–70	70–170	170–200
Rank of coal	Lignite	Bituminous coal	Anthracite
Appearance	Brown, dull, plant fragments visible	Black with dull and shiny layers	Black, shiny, glassy and iridescent
Typical % carbon (dry)	60	85	90
Calorific value on burning (kJ/g)	20	30	34
% volatiles	50	35	10
Density (g/cm³)	0.8	1.3	1.5
Reflectance	0.3	1.0	2.5
Increasing hardness ⟶			
Decreasing sulfur and other impurities, smoke and ash on burning ⟶			

Reserves and uses of coal

Coal is the most abundant of fossil fuels and the most widely distributed. Total proven world reserves of coal are 950 billion tonnes with 67% located in 4 countries: the USA, Russia, China and India. It is estimated that current reserves will last for 180 years but discovery of new deposits, improvements in technology and economic factors will change this. As oil and natural gas reserves decline, more coal is likely to be used to fill the energy gap.

Coal is primarily burned as a fuel. World coal consumption is about 5.3 billion tonnes per year, of which 75% is used for electricity generation. Bituminous coal is the main coal used, but some power stations use low ranking, highly polluting lignite. Some bituminous coal is used to make coke. It is made by baking bituminous coal at high temperatures without oxygen to drive off the volatiles. Coke is used in blast furnaces to produce iron and steel. In addition, coke and anthracite are burned as 'smokeless' fuels.

Methane can be recovered from coal, either directly from underground sources or by chemical and thermal gasification processes. Coal can also be converted to liquid fuels such as petrol and diesel but the process releases large amounts of carbon dioxide. By-products from coal processing are used to make plastics, synthetic fibres, dyes, soap and pharmaceuticals.

Figure 2 Piles of coal in an opencast mine

Questions

1 Describe the climatic and environmental conditions needed for the formation and preservation of thick deposits of peat.
2 Name and describe the process that converts peat into coal during burial.
3 Define the term *rank* and explain how it relates to the coal series.
4 Plot line graphs of the data from the table to show the changes in composition as rank increases.

	Peat	Lignite	Bituminous coal	Anthracite
Carbon	52%	66%	83%	93%
Hydrogen	6%	5%	6%	3%
Oxygen	31%	21%	9%	3%
Ash	11%	8%	2%	1%

5 Why is anthracite more valuable than lignite?

Coal has been mined for thousands of years. Initially coal was worked wherever it outcropped and the seam was followed into the ground parallel to the bed. These **adit** mines gradually developed into full underground mines. At one time there were hundreds of small coal mines in the British Isles.

Opencast coal mining

Opencast coal mining takes place from quarries or 'open pits' at the surface. All the rock above the coal seam has to be removed and the depth of this overburden will be critical to the economics of the mining operation. The sides of the open pit are dug at an angle and stepped to increase stability and prevent collapse. The flat parts of the steps are called benches. The angle of the sides will depend on:

* rock type – weak, incompetent rocks like clays will require shallower slope angles
* weathering – heavily weathered rock will be weaker and need shallower sides
* structures such as faults and joints weaken the rock and may need rock bolts, wire netting, shotcrete, rock drains or other ground improvement strategies.

The overburden is removed and piled up as **spoil heaps** near the edge of the open pit. Blasting is used to break the coal up and large machines called dragline excavators are used to extract it. A large bucket at the end of the dragline is dragged along the surface to scoop up the coal. The excavator can remove as much as 450 tonnes of coal in one pass. In Britain the thickest seams being worked are 2.5 m thick, while in the USA the thickest seams being worked are nearly 30 m thick. After mining is complete the land can be restored by backfilling the pit with the overburden.

Underground coal mining

Longwall mining is the main method of underground coal mining used in Britain today. A main **shaft** is dug from the surface and tunnels or roadways are driven out from the shaft. A ventilation shaft is also essential.

In longwall retreat mining, two horizontal roadways are driven out to the furthest point of the area of coal to be extracted. This allows the geological conditions to be assessed prior to mining. A coalface (the 'longwall') up to 400 m long is established between the two roadways. A rotating machine called a shearer moves to and fro along the coalface, cutting slices of coal. The coal falls onto a conveyer belt and is transported to the shaft and up to the surface.

The roof is held up by closely spaced, mobile hydraulic steel supports called chocks. Once a slice of coal is removed, the chocks are moved forward and the mined-out area is allowed to collapse. Mining takes place backwards, retreating towards the shaft. If the mined-out area does not collapse immediately a cavern can open up, which is dangerous as it puts immense pressure on the chocks. This system of deliberate collapse can cause subsidence on the surface.

Geological factors that can make underground coal mining difficult and uneconomic

The main problems are:

* Faults displacing the coal seam. Throws of as little as 1 or 2 m can disrupt production as the machinery has to be moved upwards or downwards. A coal seam on one side of the fault may give way to hard deltaic sandstones on the other, which can damage the shearer. In addition, faults are zones of permeability and weakness and may cause flooding or collapse of the roadway or shafts.
* Folds and steep dips. Longwall mining takes place horizontally and is not possible if the coal seams dip at an angle greater than about 5 degrees.

Figure 1 A dragline excavator

Key definitions

An **adit** is a horizontal tunnel dug into a hillside.

Opencast mining is mining from surface quarries.

Spoil heaps comprise waste rock piled up on the ground.

Longwall mining is a highly mechanised method of underground mining.

A **shaft** is a vertical opening to an underground mine.

Figure 2 A shearer for longwall coal mining

- Washouts resulting from river channel switching on the delta top. The peat is eroded away by the river, and river channel sands and gravels are deposited in its place. Not only does this mean the coal seam is lost, but there will be hard sandstones and conglomerates in its place.

- Seam splitting where one thick coal seam splits into several thinner, uneconomic seams. Seam splitting results from different rates of subsidence in different parts of the delta.

- Sandstones are hard and permeable so may allow flooding of the mine, especially if the water table is high. Rapid alternations of rock types with different hardness within the deltaic sequence also cause problems.

- Build up of methane gas. Methane is highly flammable and can cause dangerous underground explosions.

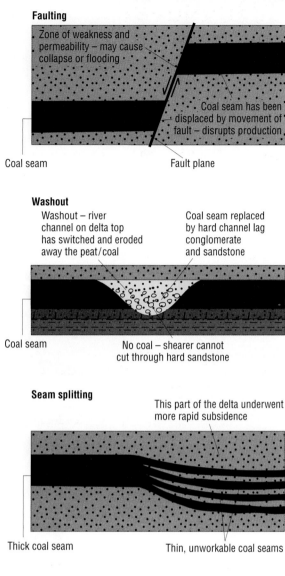

Figure 3 Geological problems that can make underground coal mining difficult

Economic and safety considerations of coal mining

Opencast coal mining is very efficient and high rates of production can be achieved. This is important as coal is a low-cost, bulk commodity. Coal can be economically extracted to depths of 100 m, or exceptionally 200 m if the stripping ratio of overburden to coal is less than 20 to 1.

Longwall underground coal mining is highly mechanised and in good geological conditions can achieve production rates comparable to opencast mining. This is vital if underground mines are going to remain profitable.

Opencast mining is cheaper than underground mining. The setup and working costs are lower and only a small workforce is required. Although the machinery is expensive, it is cheaper than the high-tech machinery needed for underground mining. Ventilation equipment is not required and thinner seams can be mined at a profit.

Opencast mining is also safer than underground mining. Despite improvements in safety, underground mining still remains a dangerous occupation. The main dangers are cave-ins and tunnel collapses, explosions cause by methane gas and flooding. Rescue of trapped mine workers is also difficult. The worst disaster in the British coal mining history was at Senghenydd in South Wales. In 1913, an explosion and subsequent fire killed 436 men and boys. Only 72 bodies were ever recovered.

Questions

1 Describe how coal is mined using opencast methods.
2 Name and describe one method of underground coal mining.
3 Describe the geological problems that can make underground coal mining difficult and uneconomic.
4 Research and identify the causes of some of the coal mining accidents that have happened worldwide.

Coal in the British Isles

Most of the coal in the British Isles is of Carboniferous age. At that time, Britain was part of Pangaea and located at the Equator so the climate was tropical, hot and humid. Coal formed in the topsets of **cyclothems** deposited by large deltas prograding from the north. The coal seams form between one tenth and one hundredth of the **Coal Measures** strata in the cyclothems. The map shows the occurrence of coal in the British Isles but not all of it constitutes reserves, as many of the seams are too thin or faulted to be economic to work.

Key definitions

A **cyclothem** is a repeated cycle of sedimentation.

Coal Measures is the name for the Carboniferous-age coal-bearing strata.

An **exposed coalfield** is where coal-bearing strata outcrops at the surface.

A **concealed coalfield** is where coal-bearing strata is below the surface, overlain by younger cover rocks.

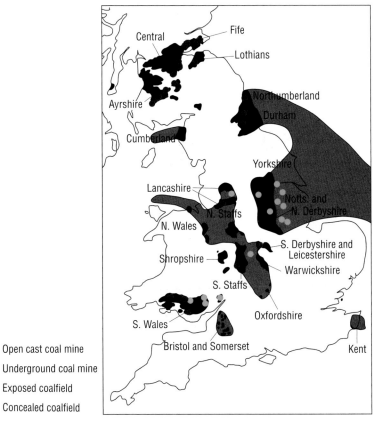

Key
- ● Open cast coal mine
- ● Underground coal mine
- ▮ Exposed coalfield
- ▮ Concealed coalfield

Figure 1 Location of coalfields and coal mining in the British Isles (September 2006)

Types of coalfield

Exposed coalfields were the first to be worked but as mining followed the seams underground **concealed coalfields** were then mined extensively. A few fields, such as the Kent coalfield, are totally concealed with no outcrop.

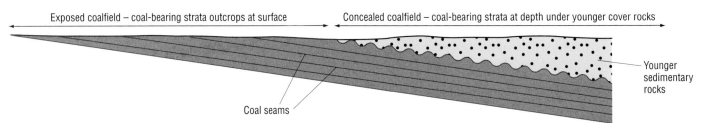

Exposed coalfield – coal-bearing strata outcrops at surface   Concealed coalfield – coal-bearing strata at depth under younger cover rocks

Younger sedimentary rocks

Coal seams

Figure 2 The difference between an exposed and a concealed coalfield

The South Wales coalfield

The Carboniferous Coal Measures of South Wales were deposited as deltaic sediments filling in an east-west trending sedimentary basin. South Wales was folded into a synclinal structure and deep burial in the centre of the syncline resulted in the formation of valuable anthracite. Strong deformation caused faulting and the complex geology has made the coalfield difficult to mine. So South Wales was the first coalfield to experience pit closures in the 1980s.

The Yorkshire coalfield

The Yorkshire coalfield is situated to the east of the Pennines. During the Carboniferous Period, deltaic sediments accumulated in a large sedimentary basin called the Pennine Basin. At the end of the Carboniferous, the rocks were folded into a large anticline producing the Pennines. The Coal Measures were eroded off the top of the anticline, leaving the Yorkshire and Lancashire coalfields on either side.

Environmental consequences of coal mining

Opencast coal mines cause short-term problems of noise, dust and visual pollution during the mining operation. Nearby rivers can also be polluted. Once the opencast operation is complete, by law, the area must be restored. This involves back filling the hole with overburden, covering it with top soil and seeding it with grass. The land is then returned to agricultural or other use. In parts of County Durham, the only remaining evidence of past opencast coal mining are fields bordered with wire fences rather than dry stone walls. However, original ecosystems are disturbed and restored areas may initially have a lower biodiversity.

The environmental legacy of underground coal mining can be long lived. Spoil heaps used to blot the landscape of British coal mining areas. As well as being unsightly, spoil heaps can be unstable and rainwater running off them will be contaminated. But today many spoil heaps have been reworked or removed. In a longwall underground mining operation, all that can be seen at the surface are the mine buildings with their winding gear.

Longwall mining can cause surface subsidence. As the mined-out area is allowed to collapse, a shallow subsidence bowl forms at the surface. Underground coal mining can also trigger small earthquakes. Another problem is the generation of acid mine drainage water. Once mines are no longer in use they fill up with water, which may flow out on to the surface. The water is highly acidic and laden with toxic metals that can pollute both groundwater and surface water.

Sustainability of British coal production

As with oil and natural gas, coal is a non-renewable energy resource so its use is ultimately unsustainable. But recent oil and gas price rises, coupled with advances in 'clean coal technology', have led to an increase in the price and demand for coal.

In the UK in 2005, total coal production was 20 million tonnes, while 44 million tonnes were imported. On 30 September 2006, there were 25 licensed opencast sites producing 10.4 million tonnes and 14 underground coal mines producing 9.6 million tonnes, employing a total of 5600 people.

In August 2007, it was announced that the Aberpergwn and Treforgan mines in South Wales are to reopen after being closed for 20 years. In addition, £50 million has been invested in the recently reopened Hatfield mine near Doncaster. This is good news for the British coal mining industry and suggests it does have a future.

Case study

Anthracite coal mining was the main economic activity of the once prosperous town of Centralia, Pennsylvania, USA. In 1962, an exposed coal seam caught fire when rubbish was being burnt at the local tip. Despite all attempts to put the fire out, it kept burning.

It was not until 17 years later, in 1979, the locals realised how serious the problem was. A petrol station owner found the temperature in an underground petrol storage tank was 77.8 °C. Elsewhere people discovered their cellar floors were hot to the touch and smoke was beginning to seep from the ground all over the town.

Aided by a $42 million relocation grant from the government, people started to move away. Most of the buildings were bulldozed to the ground and in 2002 the town's post code was withdrawn. The underground fire is still burning and estimates suggest there is enough coal left to fuel it for at least another 250 years!

Case study

Until the reopening of two pits in 2007, Tower Colliery was the last remaining underground coal mine in Wales. Coal mining began in the area in 1864, making it the oldest continuously worked underground coal mine in the British Isles.

In 1994, British Coal closed Tower Colliery on the grounds it was uneconomic to continue mining. Each of the 239 miners pledged their £8000 redundancy payouts and raised the two million pounds needed to buy the mine. The miners marched back to the pit on 2 January 1995 and production began again the next day. It has remained profitable ever since.

The reserves are now exhausted and the mine closed in 2008. New opencast mines have opened nearby.

Questions

1 Draw a labelled diagram to show the difference between an exposed and a concealed coalfield.

2 Describe the environmental problems that result from underground coal mining.

Where does geothermal heat come from?

The Earth's internal heat energy comes from two sources:

- release of stored gravitational energy from the formation of the Earth
- radioactive decay of heat producing elements such as uranium, thorium and potassium in the mantle and crust.

The increase in temperature with depth is known as the geothermal gradient. The average geothermal gradient is 25°C/km, varying from 10°C/km in continental shield areas to more than 70°C/km in volcanically active areas. Areas with the highest geothermal gradients tend to be at or near plate margins and this is where the prospects for geothermal energy are best.

Worked example: calculating the geothermal gradient

If the temperature in a borehole is 135°C at a depth of 4500 m, what is the geothermal gradient? Give your answer in °C/km. Assume the surface temperature is 0°C.

Convert metres into kilometres: 4500 ÷ 1000 = 4.5 km

Divide temperature in borehole by depth in kilometres: 135 ÷ 4.5 = 30°C/km.

Methods of geothermal energy extraction

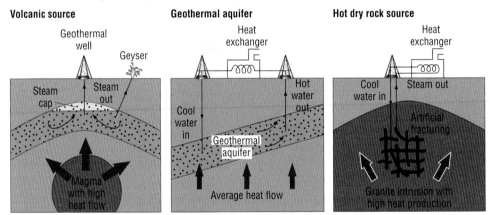

Figure 1 Methods of geothermal energy extraction

Volcanic sources

In volcanic areas, magma at temperatures of 700 to 1000°C heats the surrounding groundwater. The hot groundwater can be trapped in a similar way to oil and gas in porous and permeable rocks overlain by impermeable rocks. The pressure at depth usually prevents the water from boiling so it becomes superheated.

To exploit the geothermal energy, a borehole is drilled down into the rock. As superheated water rises up the borehole, the reduction in pressure causes it to 'flash' to steam. The steam may be used directly to drive turbines to generate electricity but usually heats water that is then used in the turbines. This reduces the problems of corrosive volcanic waters. The water is then pumped back into the ground after use to eliminate waste disposal problems and help extend the life of the well.

Geothermal energy from volcanic sources is used in Iceland, the USA, Japan, New Zealand, Italy and the Philippines. Iceland is the world leader and uses about 6000 GigaWatt hours of geothermal power a year. 87% of all homes in Iceland have their heating and hot water supplied by geothermal energy.

What is geothermal energy?

In our attempt to reduce our dependence on fossil fuels, attention has turned to renewable energy resources. **Geothermal energy** is one possibility. Geothermal energy is using heat energy that is the source for volcanic eruptions, geysers and hot springs. It is used to heat buildings, provide hot water and drive turbines to generate electricity.

Key definition

Geothermal energy is energy extracted from hot subsurface rocks or water.

Figure 2 Strokkur geyser erupting, Iceland

Geothermal aquifers

Hot water can be extracted from geothermal aquifers in deep sedimentary basins. If the geothermal gradient is 30°C/km, the groundwater will be above 60°C at depths of 2 to 3 km. Geothermal aquifers are interbedded with impermeable mudstones and shales, which have low thermal conductivities and act as insulators preventing heat loss.

Hot water is pumped to the surface, passed through a heat exchanger and used for space heating and hot water supply. The cooled waters are re-injected into the ground to maintain the water pressure in the geothermal aquifer.

Such schemes are currently operating around Paris and, until recently, in Southampton. The British Isles has a number of potential geothermal aquifers, the most promising of which are the Hampshire, East Yorkshire and Lincolnshire Basins.

Hot dry rock sources

Granite intrusions contain a higher concentration of radioactive heat producing elements than other rocks. The geothermal gradient in granites is about 40°C/km, giving temperatures of 200°C at depths of 5 km. But granites are dry rocks with low groundwater content.

In order to exploit this resource, paired boreholes are drilled into the granite. The granite is artificially fractured by injecting high pressure water or using explosives. Cold water is pumped down one borehole, heated by the hot rocks, and rises up the second borehole.

Suitable hot dry rocks in the British Isles include granites in southwest England, northern England and the Scottish Highlands. In 1977, a hot dry rock pilot project was run in Cornwall but was abandoned as uneconomic. In 2004, it was announced another project would go ahead on the site of a former cement works at Eastgate, County Durham. Hot dry rock sources are likely to become important in the future.

Advantages and disadvantages of geothermal energy

Advantages	Disadvantages
• If situated in the right location, geothermal energy can be very price competitive and reduces reliance on fossil fuels	• Production areas are geographically restricted – it requires suitable geology
• It does not produce carbon dioxide emissions	• There is the danger of volcanic eruptions or earthquakes in volcanically active areas
• It is sustainable as the water can be re-injected into the ground to extend the life of individual wells and solve the problem of disposing of saline groundwater	• Extraction of groundwater can cause surface subsidence and may trigger earthquakes
	• Each geothermal well is only viable for about 20–30 years
• Unlike other renewable energy resources it can work continually day and night and is not affected by changing weather conditions	• Groundwater is often saline and may contain toxic elements. The water is corrosive and salts may precipitate out and block pipes in the geothermal energy plant

Case study

In 2010 a geothermal power plant was proposed for the Eden Project in Cornwall.

Two boreholes will be used to circulate water through a hot artificial reservoir up to 5 km deep in the Cornish Granite. The rock at that depth is at about 180–190°C; water injected down the first borehole will be returned to the surface at around 185°C via the second borehole. The superheated water will be used to generate 3.5 MW of electricity, and will then be returned to the injection borehole. The electricity will be enough to supply Eden and around 5000 households. Before being returned to the injection borehole, the hot water will be used to heat the biomes at the Eden Project, as well as for other local projects such as polytunnels for vegetable and fruit production.

Figure 3 A geothermal energy plant in Iceland

Case study

Southampton created the UK's first geothermal energy scheme in 1986. Turned down for funding by the Department of Energy, the scheme was developed privately.

An 1800 m deep geothermal well was drilled into the Hampshire Basin, tapping into Triassic sandstones containing water at over 70°C. The highly saline water, under pressure, rose towards the surface and was then pumped up. The saline water was passed through a heat exchanger and heated clean water was then pumped through a network of underground pipes. The output was 2 MW of thermal energy.

The scheme heated a number of buildings in Southampton city centre. In 2001, Southampton won the prestigious Queen's Award for Sustainable Development. Sadly the scheme ceased to operate in 2003 when the submersible pump corroded and it was decided it was not economic to replace it. Other small schemes are still in operation elsewhere.

Questions

1 Describe how geothermal energy could be extracted from one area of the British Isles.
2 Describe the advantages and disadvantages of exploiting geothermal energy.
3 Calculate the temperature of groundwater at a depth of 500 m if the surface temperature is 10°C and the geothermal gradient is 65°C/km.

Key definitions

A **natural resource** is a useful and valuable natural material.

Mineral resources can be metallic and non-metallic or industrial minerals.

Reserves are the amount of the resource that can be extracted at a profit using existing technology.

An **ore deposit** is an accumulation of metal that may be economic to mine.

Average crustal abundance describes the amount of metal in average continental crust.

The **concentration factor** is the amount by which the metal is concentrated to make an ore deposit.

Why are metallic mineral resources important?

Metals are the foundation of our civilised world. The first metals used were gold and other metals found in their native state in the ground. Then around 3500 BC, humans learnt how to get copper and tin by heating their ores and the Bronze Age began. It was tin that drew the Romans to Britain, silver that lured the Spanish Conquistadores to South America and the 1848 gold rush that led settlers to California.

Imagine a world without metals. From cars to televisions, bridges to mobile phones, virtually every manufactured item you can think of contains metals. Our modern lifestyle relies on the use of metals and we are using up these non-renewable **resources** at an alarming rate. It is not just familiar metals like iron and copper which are being depleted. New technologies demand the use of other, often scarce, metals. For example, LCDs for flat screen TVs need indium. Estimates suggest global **reserves** of indium are only 6000 tonnes, which at current rates of extraction will last just 10 years.

Crustal abundance and concentration factors

Metals are scattered unevenly throughout the Earth's crust in amounts that are often too low to be economic to mine. In order to form an **ore deposit**, the metal must be concentrated above its **average crustal abundance** by geological processes such as igneous activity or weathering and erosion.

The **concentration factor** is the amount by which the metal has been concentrated above its average crustal abundance to form an ore deposit. You can calculate the concentration factor using the formula:

$$\text{Concentration factor} = \frac{\text{concentration of metal in ore (grade)}}{\text{average crustal abundance}}$$

Worked example: calculating the concentration factor

An ore deposit contains 3.5% copper and the average crustal abundance of copper is 0.007%. Calculate the concentration factor for copper.
Concentration factor = 3.5 ÷ 0.007 = 500.
So the copper has been concentrated 500 times above its average crustal abundance in the ore deposit.

Key definitions

Ore is the rock containing valuable metal(s) that is economic to mine.

An **ore mineral** is a mineral containing valuable metal(s).

A **gangue mineral** is a low-value waste mineral.

Ore deposits consist of rocks called **ores**. Ores are a mixture of valuable **ore minerals** and low-value **gangue minerals**. Quartz, calcite and pyrite ('fool's gold') are common gangue minerals. Look at the photographs of gold and pyrite – the differences really are very obvious! You can see a list of some common ore minerals and their properties in the table. Most ore minerals are compounds of either oxygen (oxides) or sulfur (sulfides).

Metal	Ore mineral	Formula	Colour	Form	Lustre	Hardness	Streak	Density (g/cm³)	Cleavage
Copper	Chalcopyrite	$CuFeS_2$	Brassy	Tetragonal	Metallic	3.5–4	Green-black	4.2	None
Gold	Gold	Au	Yellow	Cubic	Metallic	3	–	19.3	None
Iron	Magnetite	Fe_3O_4	Black	Cubic	Metallic	6	Black	5.2	Poor
Lead	Galena	PbS	Grey	Cubic	Metallic	2.5	Grey	7.5	3 at 90°
Tin	Cassiterite	SnO_2	Brown	Tetragonal	Adamantine	6–7	Brown	7.0	Poor
Zinc	Sphalerite	ZnS	Brown	Cubic	Adamantine	3.5–4	Brown	4.1	6 at 60°

Grade, cut-off grade and ore reserves

The **grade** is the amount of metal present in a mineral deposit. It is usually given as a percentage but may be quoted as grams per tonne for scarce metals. We call the minimum amount of metal that is economic to mine the **cut-off grade**. The cut-off grade for a metal is determined by a number of factors:

- The value of the metal – the more valuable the metal, the lower its cut-off grade.
- Demand – the higher the demand for the metal, the more valuable and lower its cut-off grade will be.
- The abundance of the metal – if they are useful, scarce metals will have a lower cut-off grade.
- The size of the ore deposit – large deposits will be economic to mine at lower cut-off grades than small deposits.
- Cost of mining and extraction – if it is costly to mine and extract a metal then the cut-off grade will be higher.

You can calculate the cut-off grade by rearranging the concentration factor formula:

Cut-off grade = average crustal abundance
× minimum concentration factor to be economic

The table shows the relationship between average crustal abundance, cut-off grade and minimum concentration factors for seven metals.

Metal	Average crustal abundance (%)	Cut-off grade (%)	Minimum concentration factor
Aluminium	8.1	35	4.32
Copper	0.007	0.4	57.14
Gold	0.0000004	0.001	2500
Iron	5.0	40	8
Lead	0.0015	4	2666.67
Tin	0.002	1	500
Zinc	0.007	4	571.43

You have probably realised there is a relationship between the cut-off grade and the reserves of a metal. If the cut-off grade goes up then the reserves will go down, because it will no longer be economic to mine lower grade deposits. If the cut-off grade goes down then the reserves will go up.

In the last hundred years, the cut-off grade for copper has reduced from 3% to 0.4%. This is because higher grade deposits have been worked out and technology has improved allowing profitable extraction of lower concentrations of copper.

Questions

1 Ore = ore minerals + gangue minerals. Define these terms.
2 Define the term concentration factor and explain how it is calculated.
3 The table shows data for three ore deposits. Copy and complete the table.

Metal in ore deposit	Average crustal abundance (%)	Grade (%)	Concentration factor
Aluminium	8.1	50	
Gold	0.0000004	0.02	
Tin	0.002		1000

4 Discuss the factors that determine the cut-off grade for a metal.
5 Explain why gold is more valuable than pyrite (fool's gold).

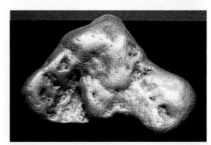

Figure 1 A gold nugget

Figure 2 Pyrite (fool's gold). Spot the difference!

Types of ore deposits

Each ore deposit is unique but we can group them by the geological processes that concentrated the metals within them. We divide ore deposits into three main groups:

- ores formed by hydrothermal processes
- ores formed by igneous processes within the Earth
- ores formed by sedimentary processes at the Earth's surface.

In the next four spreads, we look at the processes that formed each of these ore deposit types.

What are hydrothermal ore deposits?

Hydrothermal ore deposits are an important and varied group of ore deposits that form many of the world's richest ore deposits. Ores, including those of tin, tungsten, copper, lead, zinc, gold, silver, mercury and uranium, can all form by hydrothermal processes. All hydrothermal ore deposits have one thing in common – they formed from hot, aqueous (watery) fluids containing metals in solution.

There are three key requirements to form a **hydrothermal fluid**:

- a source of heat
- a source of water
- a source of metals.

This makes hydrothermal ore deposits complex as there are many possible sources for each of these components:

- The heat may come from magma in an intrusive or volcanic setting; it may come from metamorphism or simply from the increase in temperature with depth due to the geothermal gradient.
- The source of the water could be magma, groundwater, sea water or from chemical reactions during metamorphism.
- The metals could come from magma or be leached from any rock type as water passes through it.

We are going to look in detail at one example of a hydrothermal ore deposit – how veins of cassiterite, galena and sphalerite form in association with silicic igneous intrusions.

Hydrothermal veins of cassiterite, galena and sphalerite in association with igneous intrusions

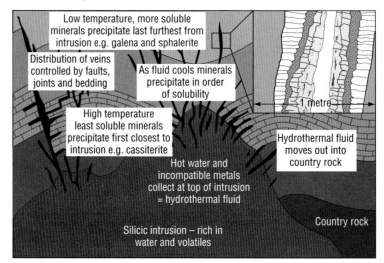

Figure 1 Cross-section diagram showing how hydrothermal veins form around igneous intrusions with insert showing a magnified view of a hydrothermal vein

Silicic intrusions such as granite batholiths are rich in water and other volatiles. Hydrothermal processes take place late in the cooling history of these intrusions during the final stages of crystallisation. Magma is the source of the heat, water and metals.

The sequence of formation of a hydrothermal **mineral vein** is:

- The outer part of the intrusion crystallises first, forming a solid shell. As the magma continues to cool and crystallise, water and 'incompatible' metals that do not fit into silicate minerals collect at the top of the intrusion to form a hydrothermal fluid. All the metals that were present in the magma are now concentrated in the hydrothermal fluid at the end of crystallisation.
- As the intrusion cools further the rock contracts and cooling joints form. The hydrothermal fluid moves out into the surrounding **country rock**, exploiting any weaknesses such as faults, joints and bedding planes. These then control the pattern of mineral veins. Groundwater may be drawn into the intrusion and a hydrothermal circulation system set up.
- As the hydrothermal fluid moves away from the intrusion it cools and may encounter chemically reactive country rocks such as limestone. This results in the **precipitation** of a mixture of ore and gangue minerals from the fluid.
- Veins are formed when minerals precipitate within fractures. Veins commonly show a symmetrical pattern with the first minerals crystallising at the edges and later formed minerals in the centre. Disseminated ore forms when ore minerals precipitate within the pore spaces of rocks.
- The ore minerals precipitate in order of temperature and solubility. This gives concentric zones of ore minerals around the intrusion.
- Cassiterite (tin ore) is the least soluble mineral and precipitates at the highest temperatures (above 400 °C) closest to or just inside the intrusion.
- Galena (lead ore) and sphalerite (zinc ore) are more soluble and precipitate at lower temperatures (below 250 °C) further away from the intrusion.

A good example of hydrothermal mineral zoning can be seen around the granites in southwest England.

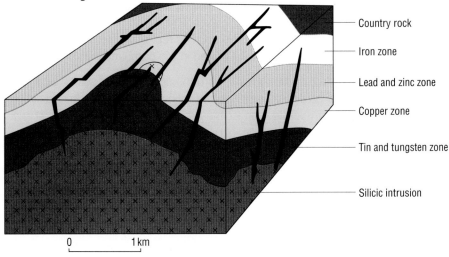

Country rock

Iron zone

Lead and zinc zone

Copper zone

Tin and tungsten zone

Silicic intrusion

0   1 km

Figure 2 Block diagram showing hydrothermal mineral veins around a granite in southwest England

Key definitions

A **mineral vein** is formed when minerals precipitate in a fracture.

Country rock is the older rock (often sedimentary) surrounding an igneous intrusion.

Precipitation occurs as solid minerals come out of solution.

Case study

Devon and Cornwall have a long history of mining dating back to the Bronze Age. A variety of metals including tin, tungsten, copper, lead and zinc have been mined from numerous 'lodes' – the local miners' term for veins of ore.

The hydrothermal veins originate from a large granite batholith intruded at the end of the Carboniferous. The country rocks are metamorphosed Devonian sandstones and shales, locally called the 'killas'.

Many of the hydrothermal veins formed along NNE-striking faults in the country rocks. Within the veins the metal ores are concentrically zoned around the granite outcrops – tin, then copper, then lead and zinc, and finally iron furthest out.

Mining in Devon and Cornwall peaked in the nineteenth century and then declined as the high grade ore was worked out and the price of copper and tin fell. South Crofty, the last working tin mine in Europe, closed in 1998.

Cornish tin mining has left an international legacy – Cornish miners took their expertise all over the world, as far afield as Australia and South America. Worldwide, 175 locations have known mining connections with Cornwall.

Questions

1. Describe how hydrothermal mineral veins form in association with igneous intrusions.
2. Explain the factors that affect the distribution of hydrothermal mineral veins in and around an igneous intrusion.
3. Research and write your own case study about another area where hydrothermal minerals occur.
4. 'Black smokers' at mid-ocean ridges form hydrothermal metal deposits. Research the type of metals and the processes that take place at black smokers.

Gravity settling of magnetite

Ore deposits formed by gravity settling are due to **magmatic differentiation** in mafic or ultramafic igneous intrusions. Gravity settling causes dense ore minerals to form a concentrated layer at the base of an intrusion. Gravity settling occurs early in the cooling history of the intrusion and depends on:

- metallic ore minerals, such as magnetite (Fe_3O_4), chromite ($FeCr_2O_4$) and ilmenite ($FeTiO_3$), that crystallise at high temperatures and are dense
- mafic or ultramafic magma that has a low viscosity
- slow rates of cooling and crystallisation, so that gravity settling has time to take place.

		Density (g/cm³)	Melting point (°C)
Augite	Silicate mineral	3.3	1150
Olivine	Silicate mineral	3.4	1450
Plagioclase	Silicate mineral	2.7	1100
Magnetite	Fe_3O_4	5.2	1600
Chromite	$FeCr_2O_4$	4.6	1500

Magnetite (iron ore) has a high melting point and is one of the first minerals to crystallise. As magnetite is dense and the magma is fluid, the magnetite crystals sink due to gravity. A **cumulate layer** of magnetite forms by **magmatic segregation** at the base of the magma chamber, just above the lower chilled margin.

Ore deposits formed by gravity settling can be very high grade as all the metals in the original magma are concentrated in the cumulate layer. The chilled margins have the same composition as the original magma. The rest of the intrusion is depleted in the metals as they are now concentrated in the cumulate layer.

Magmatic segregation can also result from the separation of sulfide and silicate liquids. Just as oil and water do not mix, neither do sulfide and silicate liquids – they are **immiscible**. Immiscible droplets of iron, copper, nickel and platinum sulfides form within mafic–ultramafic magmas as they cool. These droplets join together and, as they are denser than the silicate magma, sink to the floor of the intrusion to form a cumulate layer. Immiscible sulfide liquids can also be injected into fractures in the surrounding country rocks.

Residual deposits of bauxite

Residual deposits are an important group of sedimentary-related ores formed by surface processes. They are the only source of aluminium. Although aluminium is a common metal, making up 8.1% of the Earth's crust, it is not possible to extract aluminium directly from silicate minerals. The main ore of aluminium is bauxite – it is not a mineral but a mixture of hydrated aluminium oxides and hydroxides.

Chemical weathering is the concentration process for bauxite. Chemical weathering breaks down rocks so that soluble substances can be removed in solution. The insoluble **residue** left behind may be sufficiently rich in aluminium to form an economic ore deposit.

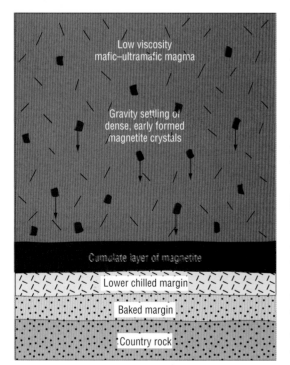

Figure 1 Cross-section showing how ore deposits form by gravity settling

Case study

The Bushveld Igneous Complex is an enormous 2.1 billion year old saucer-shaped mafic–ultramafic intrusion. It covers a surface area of 65 000 km², is 350 km wide and 7 km thick. It contains high grade ore deposits of magnetite, chromite and platinum sulfides.

The Complex has 5 zones of cumulate layering. It contains 29 separate chromite layers, each one up to 1 m thick. Reserves of chromite are estimated to be 3 billion tonnes with a grade of 43%.

One of the sulfide-rich layers, the Merensky Reef, contains 80% of the world's platinum reserves.

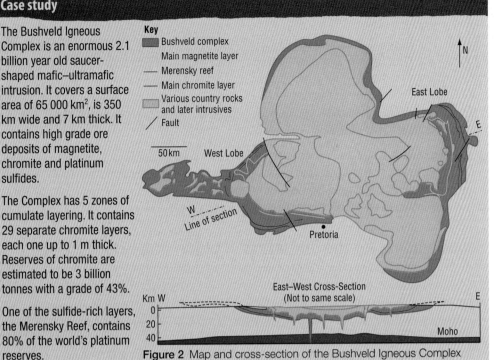

Key
- ■ Bushveld complex
- ■ Main magnetite layer
- — Merensky reef
- — Main chromite layer
- ■ Various country rocks and later intrusives
- ╱ Fault

East Lobe
E
West Lobe
50km
W
Line of section
Pretoria
N

East–West Cross-Section (Not to same scale)
Km W
0
20
40
Moho
E

Figure 2 Map and cross-section of the Bushveld Igneous Complex

The key requirements to form a bauxite deposit are:
- hot and humid tropical climate, causing intense chemical weathering
- aluminium-rich and iron-poor rock, such as granite or impure limestone
- groundwater with a pH between 4 and 10.

Aluminium, iron and silicon form some of the least soluble compounds. In **temperate climates**, the insoluble products of chemical weathering are soils containing hydrated iron oxides, clay minerals and quartz.

In hot, humid **tropical climates**, chemical weathering is more intense. High temperatures increase the rates of chemical reactions; water takes part in hydrolysis reactions and acts as a catalyst. Here clays are broken down into aluminium, iron oxides and silica. If the pH of the groundwater is between 4 and 10, even the silica is dissolved, leaving a soil called a **laterite** made of hydrated oxides of iron and aluminium. If the bedrock is poor in iron then only aluminium oxides are left.

So bauxite develops on iron-poor rocks, such as granite and impure limestone during extreme chemical weathering. The presence of joints in these rocks speeds up the rate of chemical weathering. Joints increase the permeability of the rock allowing water in and increase the surface area available for chemical reactions.

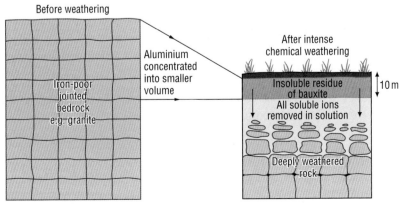

Before weathering

Iron-poor jointed bedrock e.g. granite

Aluminium concentrated into smaller volume

After intense chemical weathering
Insoluble residue of bauxite
All soluble ions removed in solution
10 m
Deeply weathered rock

Figure 3 Cross-section showing how residual ore deposits form

Case study

Bauxite mining is Jamaica's second largest industry. Despite the island's small size, it produces 8% of the world's bauxite but this comes at an environmental cost.

Jamaica's bauxite reserves are estimated to be 1.8 billion tonnes and annual production is 10 million tonnes. The bauxite is found very close to the surface and is mined by opencast methods from small, but numerous, deposits.

The bauxite mining companies claim they are trying to minimise the environmental effects of their activities but conservation groups disagree. The main problem is the disposal of fine-grained waste known as 'tailings'. Bauxite tailings are strongly alkaline and cause soil, surface and groundwater pollution.

Bauxite mining is now in direct conflict with Jamaica's tourism industry and a decision has to be made as to whether bauxite or tourism will be Jamaica's main foreign exchange earner.

Key definitions

A hot, humid **tropical climate** is hot (temperatures >21°C) and wet, with little variation throughout the year. Occurs near the Equator.

Laterite is a red tropical soil made of hydrated iron and aluminium oxides.

Questions

1 Describe the properties of magnetite that allow it to be concentrated by gravity settling.
2 Describe and explain how ore deposits of magnetite form in mafic to ultramafic igneous intrusions.
3 Describe and explain how residual deposits of bauxite form.
4 Explain the factors that control the rate of chemical weathering and formation of residual deposits.

What are placer deposits?

Probably the best known and often romanticised type of mineral exploitation is that of prospectors panning for gold. The prospectors fill their flat pans with river sediment and swirl it around with water in the hope of finding a gold nugget at the bottom of the pan. These prospectors are exploiting placer deposits. The word *placer* comes from Spanish and means 'reef' or sand bank.

Placer deposits are surface deposits formed by the sedimentary processes of weathering, erosion, transport and deposition. Dense, physically and chemically resistant minerals including cassiterite (tin ore), gold and diamonds can be concentrated by these processes into usually small, but high grade, ore deposits.

Requirements for the formation of placer deposits

The main requirements to form placer deposits are:
- pre-existing mineral veins exposed at the Earth's surface
- dense, physically and chemically resistant ore minerals
- erosion and transport processes that sort and separate the ore minerals from the gangue minerals
- suitable sites of deposition where the ore minerals will be concentrated.

How placer deposits form

Just like any rock, mineral veins exposed at the Earth's surface will be weathered. During weathering ore will be broken up by mechanical weathering or left as insoluble material by chemical weathering. The ore and gangue minerals will be separated into individual grains.

The weathered material is then transported. Most placer deposits are concentrated by the action of moving water in rivers and the sea. During transport the sediment is sorted by grain size, hardness and density. Less resistant minerals are worn away by the erosion processes of abrasion and attrition or dissolved by water.

Minerals found in placer deposits all have similar properties:
- Hard, with little or no cleavage, so they survive abrasion and attrition during transport. Gold is an exception. Gold is soft but because it is malleable it rolls into nuggets rather than being broken up.
- Chemically unreactive, so they are not dissolved and taken into solution.
- Dense, so they are deposited first when the current velocity slackens.

You can see the properties of some placer minerals in the table.

Mineral	Density (g/cm³)	Hardness	Cleavage	Solubility
Cassiterite	7.0	6–7	Poor	Insoluble
Diamond	3.5	10	4 perfect	Insoluble
Gold	19.3	3	None	Low

When the current velocity slows these minerals are preferentially deposited in one place, though mixed with unconsolidated sand and gravel.

Figure 1 A gold pan

Sites of deposition of placer minerals

Meander bends

When a river flows around a meander bend the current swings to the outside of the bend. The current velocity is fastest on the outside of the bend and slowest on the inside. This results in erosion on the outside of the bend and deposition on the inside to form a point bar. Placer deposits are found on the inside of meander bends.

Plunge pools

When a river flows from hard rock to less resistant rock, it erodes downwards producing a water fall. Turbulent water and boulders at the bottom of the waterfall scour out a deep hollow called a plunge pool. Dense placer minerals become trapped in the plunge pool.

Upstream of projections

Projections from the riverbed will trap dense placer minerals on the upstream side. This may be where a hard rock such as a dyke juts upwards and/or, on a small scale, on the upstream side of ripples.

Downstream of confluences

Where a fast flowing tributary joins a slower flowing river the current velocity will drop. This results in dense placer minerals being deposited to form a mid-channel sandbar.

On beaches

Rivers transport sediment into the sea. The sediment may move along the coast by longshore drift. Waves throw sediment up the beach and as the energy of the waves reduces on the backwash, dense placer minerals can be left behind forming beach placer deposits.

Meander bend (plan)

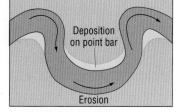

Plunge pool (cross-section)

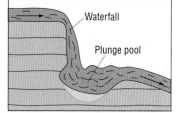

Projections in riverbed (cross-section)

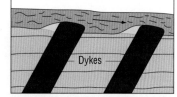

Confluence of tributary (plan)

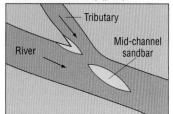

Beach (cross-section)

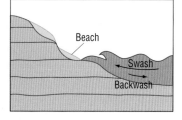

Key
- ▢ Placer deposit – deposition where velocity is reduced
- ⟶ Direction of flow

Figure 2 Sites of deposition of placer minerals

Case study

The Witswatersrand Goldfield in South Africa is a fossil placer deposit that accounts for 50% of the world's gold production. The Witswatersrand gold mines are up to 6 km deep – the deepest mines in the world.

The geological setting is a 400 km wide Precambrian sedimentary basin. Gold occurs in the matrix of quartz pebble conglomerates deposited in a large lake 2 billion years ago. The source of the gold is thought to be from weathered and eroded hydrothermal veins that outcropped in hills surrounding the lake.

The origin of the Witswatersrand gold deposits is of great interest to geologists as it provides good evidence that the sedimentary processes operating 2 billion years ago are similar to those still going on today.

Key definitions

Dredging is where material is scraped or sucked from the river or sea bed.

Hydraulic mining is the use of high-pressure water jets to dislodge material.

Advantages and disadvantages of placer mining

Recent placer deposits are loose, unconsolidated sands and gravels that are easily accessible and cheap to mine. Common mining methods include **dredging** or **hydraulic mining**. To some extent the ore minerals are already separated from the gangue minerals so less waste rock is produced. As a result it could be argued that placer mining has less environmental impact than underground mining.

The immediate environmental impacts of placer mining are very obvious – scars on the landscape; noise and dust during mining; and dredging and hydraulic mining stir up silt causing surface water pollution. In addition, because placer deposits tend to be small they are quickly exhausted.

Questions

1 Use labelled diagrams to explain how placer deposits can form at different locations along rivers.

2 Use the table of properties of common ore minerals in spread 4.3.1 to explain why cassiterite is found in placer deposits but galena is not.

3 Research where placer mining is taking place today and write a case study, which should include the minerals being mined and the environmental consequences.

Secondary enrichment and uranium ore deposits

Secondary enrichment of chalcopyrite in copper deposits

Secondary enrichment is not an ore forming process but an ore concentrating process. It is very important for increasing the grade of otherwise uneconomic copper deposits.

Chalcopyrite, a copper iron sulfide, is the main ore mineral of copper. Large, low grade ore deposits of chalcopyrite are formed by igneous processes. When rocks containing chalcopyrite are exposed at the Earth's surface they may undergo chemical weathering that can cause secondary enrichment.

Above the water table

Rainwater infiltrates into the exposed copper deposit and percolates downwards through the pore spaces. In the zone of oxidation above the water table, chemical reactions change insoluble copper sulfides such as chalcopyrite into soluble copper sulfates. The copper sulfates are dissolved, taken into solution and carried downwards by the groundwater.

A barren, **leached** zone is left near the surface covered by an insoluble iron oxide capping called a **gossan**. Although of no economic value, gossans are useful exploration targets as their presence suggests there may be ore deposits underneath.

Below the water table

The copper is carried downwards in solution to the water table. Just above the water table brightly coloured blue and green copper oxides and carbonates such as malachite and azurite are precipitated but these are usually of minor importance.

At the water table the conditions change from **oxidising** above to **reducing** below. Chemical reactions change the copper sulfates back into insoluble copper sulfides. This results in immediate reprecipitation of the insoluble 'secondary' copper sulfides just below the water table. All the copper that was spread out in the rock above the water table is now concentrated in a much smaller volume so the grade is higher. This high grade **enriched deposit** overlies the unweathered lower grade 'primary' copper ore at depth.

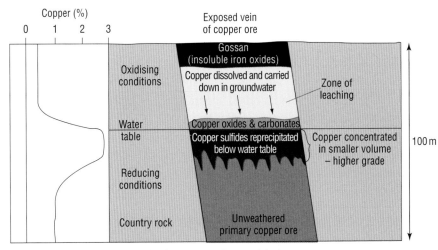

Figure 1 Cross-section showing how secondary enrichment occurs

Why is secondary enrichment important?

Mining companies often mine the area of secondary enrichment first to offset the capital costs of exploration and development. This is an important factor in the exploitation of a specific type of low grade, high tonnage hydrothermal copper deposit called a '**porphyry**' copper deposit. Bingham Canyon, Utah, USA, is a good example of a porphyry copper deposit that has undergone secondary enrichment.

Case study

The Bingham Canyon porphyry copper mine in Utah, USA is the largest man-made hole in the ground. The mine is owned by Rio Tinto plc and has been in production since 1906. The open pit is 4 km wide and 1.2 km deep – it takes half an hour to drive to the bottom and is visible to the naked eye from the space shuttle! The mine employs 1400 people and mineral processing, smelting and refining are carried out on site.

In its 100 years of operation, Bingham Canyon has been one of the world's most productive mines. To date, the mine has produced 15.4 million tonnes of copper, 652 tonnes of gold, 5386 tonnes of silver and 386 000 tonnes of molybdenum. The existing open pit will be exhausted by 2013, but underground mining will continue after that.

The ore deposit is associated with a 35 Ma igneous intrusion that intruded sandstones and limestones. Metallic ore minerals carried in solution by late stage hydrothermal fluids from the intrusion were precipitated in fractures in the surrounding country rocks.

More recently the upper parts of the ore deposit were exposed by erosion and underwent chemical weathering, resulting in formation of high grade secondary enrichment deposits. These were the first parts of the ore deposit to be mined. When the high grade enriched ore was worked out in 1980, only innovations in mineral processing technology allowed profitable extraction of the lower grade primary ore, which continues today.

Figure 2 An opencast porphyry copper mine

Uranium ore deposits in sandstone

Uranium is another useful metal found as a trace element in many igneous rocks. It is radioactive and is used as the energy source for nuclear power stations. In common with most metals, uranium can be concentrated in several different types of ore deposit. We are going to look at one example – how deposits of uranium ore form in sandstones.

As well as being radioactive, uranium is highly soluble. Uranium is easily dissolved and transported by water and then reprecipitated as a result of small changes in oxidation conditions. Due to its solubility in oxidising conditions, any uranium mineral exposed at the Earth's surface will undergo chemical weathering, be dissolved and taken into solution in surface and groundwater.

We know that groundwater flows through aquifers. Buried fossil river channels containing porous and permeable sandstones and conglomerates make good aquifers. When the groundwater meets a change in conditions from oxidising to reducing, uranium ore minerals are reprecipitated in the palaeo-channel sediments. Curved 'roll-type' uranium ore deposits form at the oxidation–reduction (redox) boundary. Often the redox boundary is at the water table.

In many sandstone-hosted uranium ore deposits there is a close association between the uranium ore and organic matter. It is highly likely that sulfur-reducing bacteria present in decaying vegetation are involved in the ore-forming process. There are examples of individual fossil logs that have been entirely replaced by uranium minerals, making small but high grade ore deposits! Uranium ore deposits of this type are found in the Colorado Plateau area of the western USA.

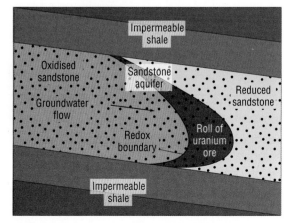

Figure 3 A roll-type uranium deposit in sandstone

Questions

1 The data in the table shows the changes in copper concentration with depth in an ore deposit.

Depth (metres)	Copper (%)
0	0.2
10	0.3
20	2.9
30	1.5
40	1.4

Plot a line graph of the data with depth downwards and copper concentration across. Draw a horizontal line on your graph to indicate the likely position of the water table. Label the zone of leaching, enriched ore and primary copper ore.

2 Draw a labelled diagram to explain how the grade of a copper ore deposit can be increased by the process of secondary enrichment.

3 Describe how uranium ore deposits can form in sandstones.

Metals' exploration is carried out by mining companies and government organisations to find economic ore deposits. It is an intensive, organised and expensive form of mineral prospecting. These days prospecting carried out by individuals is likely to be a leisure activity, but historically most of the famous ore deposits were found by prospectors with little equipment.

The main stages in a metals' exploration programme are:
- Area selection based on an understanding of models for ore deposit formation and knowledge of the regional geology.
- Regional reconnaissance exploration using a combination of broad geological mapping, remote sensing, regional geophysical and geochemical surveys to locate potential targets.
- Selection of a target followed up by detailed geological mapping, geophysical and geochemical surveys, trench digging and exploration drilling to identify the extent of any ore deposits found.
- Calculation of ore reserves using computer modelling. The size and grade of an ore deposit must be accurately determined to decide if it is economic to mine.

Geophysical exploration techniques for metals

Gravity surveys

In spread 4.2.3 we saw how gravity surveys can be used for oil and natural gas exploration. The principles for metallic mineral exploration are the same. Gravimeters mounted in planes, helicopters or land vehicles are used for regional surveys and hand-held instruments for detailed follow-up surveys in target areas.

Remember the gravity data is corrected, gravity anomaly maps plotted and then interpreted. A positive gravity anomaly could be due to:
- A high density mafic or ultramafic intrusion, which may contain ore deposits formed by gravity settling.
- The presence of dense, metallic ore minerals.

A negative gravity anomaly could be due to:
- A low density silicic intrusion, which may have hydrothermal mineral veins around it.

Magnetic surveys

Magnetic surveys can be airborne for regional surveys and land-based for detailed surveys. An instrument called a magnetometer measures small variations in the Earth's magnetic field strength. Survey points are located using GPS.

Two types of survey are possible:
- A transect survey where measurements are taken along a single line.
- A map survey where values are plotted on a map. Lines joining points of equal magnetic field strength are drawn on the map and anomalies identified.

Minerals rich in iron produce positive magnetic anomalies. This could be due to:
- A mafic or ultramafic intrusion, which may contain ore deposits formed by gravity settling.
- The presence of magnetite.

Electrical resistivity survey

In an electrical resistivity survey two electrodes are placed in the ground and an electric current passed between them. If the underlying rock is a good conductor it will have a low resistance. Metals are good conductors so rocks containing metallic ore minerals will have a lower resistance than other rocks. This method has been successfully used for gold exploration.

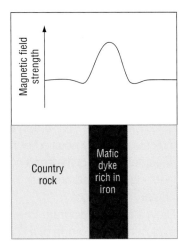

Figure 1 Cross-section showing a transect magnetic survey

Geochemical exploration techniques for metals

Geochemical exploration involves collecting samples and analysing them to find **geochemical anomalies**. Samples of rock, soil, stream sediment, drill core, water and even vegetation or atmospheric gases can be taken for analysis.

Geochemical exploration relies on the fact that metals in ore deposits will undergo **dispersion** by weathering, erosion and transport processes. So interpretation of geochemical data depends on a good understanding of how particular metals travel round the surface and near surface part of the rock cycle. This is determined by the stability of the metals and the climate and terrain of the area.

Stream sediment survey

Stream sediment surveys are used for regional exploration in temperate climates where there are rivers. Stream sediment samples are collected from riverbeds and analysed for the metals of interest. Interpretation is based on:

- Stream sediments downstream of the source will have anomalous metal values.
- Stream sediments upstream of the source will have normal metal values.
- The size of the anomaly decreases downstream due to dilution by surface water run off and sediment entering the river downstream.
- **Catastrophic dilution** occurs where tributaries meet.

The best sampling strategy is to sample each tributary immediately upstream of each confluence. The anomaly can be traced back upstream to its source area, which is then the target for more detailed exploration.

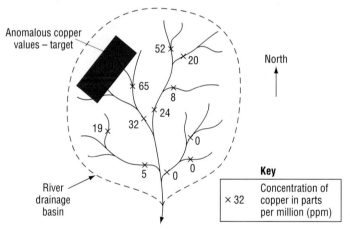

Figure 2 Map of a stream sediment survey

Soil survey

Soil surveys are used for local follow-up surveys in target areas where there is a lack of outcrop. Soil samples are usually taken using a systemic grid sampling strategy. Interpretation depends on:

- Soil samples on top and down slope of the source will have anomalous metal values.
- Soil samples up slope of the source will have normal metal values.

Questions

1. Describe how geophysical exploration techniques can be used to find metals.
2. Draw a cross-section diagram of a slope across an exposed lead-rich mineral vein. Label where there will be a soil geochemical anomaly for lead.
3. Explain why sampling each tributary immediately upstream of each confluence is the best sampling strategy to use for a stream sediment survey.

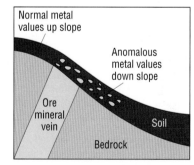

Figure 3 Cross-section showing how metals are dispersed in soils

Figure 1 Dump truck in an opencast mine

Environmental consequences of mining metals

Exploitation of metallic mineral deposits can have negative and long-lived impacts on the surrounding environment. In developed countries, like Britain, mineral exploitation is highly regulated and stringent legislation is in place to protect the environment. We have a legacy of old, abandoned mines that were not subjected to the same restrictions. In these cases it is rarely possible to establish who is responsible for paying for the cleanup and restoration.

Poorer developing countries are dependent on primary economic activities such as mining to generate foreign income. Often these countries do not have much in the way of environmental controls on their mining activities. Even large multinational mining companies may adopt different environmental policies towards mining in developed and developing countries.

Environmental problems of opencast metal mining

Surface metals' mines can be very large operations that can have a huge impact on the surrounding area. The main environmental problems of opencast metal mining are:

- Deforestation and removal of vegetation, resulting in loss of habitat for plants and animals.
- Noise and dust generated by mining machinery, blasting and large dump trucks used to transport ore.
- Visual pollution and landscape degradation, including holes left in the ground. Although many open pits are filled in and restored after mining, it is not possible to do this with very large quarries.
- Surface water pollution can result from all types of opencast mining but is especially severe if the mining method is dredging or hydraulic mining (see spread 4.3.4). These mining methods stir up silt that can have devastating consequences for aquatic ecosystems in rivers.

Case study

It was a unique and very visual pollution incident that caught the attention of the world's media. Wheal Jane was one of the last operating Cornish tin mines. It closed in 1991 and began to fill with water when the drainage pumps were switched off.

In January 1992, over 50 million litres of heavily contaminated acid mine drainage water burst from the disused mine and flowed into the Fal Estuary. The water had a pH of 3.1 and was laden with toxic metals including cadmium, arsenic, lead, zinc, copper and iron. Precipitation of iron hydroxides produced a bright orange ochreous plume that swept downstream and out to sea.

The impact was very visual and led to widespread public concerns about health and the impact on the environment and tourism. The National Rivers Authority (now the Environment Agency) immediately set up a temporary treatment system. Water was pumped from the mine, collected in the Clemows Valley tailings dam, and treated using lime to neutralise the acid and precipitate the dissolved metals. An experimental passive treatment system using limestone drains, reed beds and rock filters was also put into place.

The passive treatment experiment has since ended and all of the mine water is now treated by active chemical treatment. To date, treating the acid mine water discharge from Wheal Jane has cost in excess of £20 million!

Figure 2 The Wheal Jane pollution incident

Environmental problems of underground metal mining

Underground metals' mines are usually less visually intrusive than surface mines. Only small areas around the shaft are obviously disturbed but they may have serious environmental consequences. These include:

- Subsidence at the surface. Any mining method that removes material from underground leaving subsurface holes and cavities can cause subsidence. Subsidence can be predicted and planned for. The main problem is sudden collapse of unknown underground mine workings long after they have been abandoned.
- Creation of spoil heaps. These piles of waste rock may contain toxic metals and can be unstable. They must be carefully constructed and monitored.

- Pollution of both surface and groundwater by acid mine drainage water. Acid mine drainage water results from the presence of metal sulfide minerals such as chalcopyrite, galena and sphalerite. These sulfide minerals react with atmospheric oxygen to produce sulfur dioxide. The sulfur dioxide dissolves in water to form sulfuric acid. Not only does this increase the water's acidity, but toxic metals such as lead, arsenic and mercury are leached from the ores and taken into solution. As we saw in spread 4.1.3, pollution by acid mine drainage water is a major threat to surface and groundwater supplies.

Environmental problems of metallic mineral processing

Mining is only the first step in producing the many different metals we use. Mineral processing and extraction of metals from their ores also have serious and, in some cases, even worse environmental consequences. These include:

- Disposal of **tailings**. One of the first stages in mineral processing is crushing the ore to separate the ore minerals from the gangue minerals. Crushing produces fine-grained waste called tailings or slimes. Tailings not only contain toxic metals but also harmful chemicals used in the extraction process. Uranium tailings are a particular hazard because they are radioactive. In the past, the main options for disposing of tailings were storage in large surface ponds, or disposal in underground mine workings, rivers or the sea. There have been some well-publicised and unacceptable environmental disasters caused by the leakage of tailings into the surrounding area. Today mining companies in developed countries have to include the cost of safe storage and disposal of tailings in their initial feasibility studies.

- *In situ* or heap leaching to increase the grade of otherwise uneconomic ore deposits. This is particularly used in the extraction of copper, gold and uranium. *In situ* leaching involves drilling holes into the ore deposit and pumping in the leaching solution. Heap leaching involves piling broken ore onto an impermeable clay or plastic liner and spraying it with leaching solution. The solution percolates through the ore dissolving metals into solution. The **'pregnant' solution** is then collected for further processing. Leaching solutions are often acidic and in the case of gold extraction contain highly poisonous cyanide. Any accidental leakage would be highly polluting and damaging to the environment. Surface and groundwater pollution are the main concerns, along with dangers to wildlife, especially birds.

- **Smelting** of metal ores is a major source of atmospheric pollution. Smelters produce 8% of global emissions of sulfur dioxide, the main cause of acid rain. Dead zones occur around some smelters where soils are contaminated and vegetation has died leaving a barren, rocky wasteland. One of the most notorious examples is the nickel smelter at Sudbury, Ontario, Canada.

Key definitions

Tailings are the fine-grained waste produced during mineral processing.

In situ means 'in place', with no transport having occurred.

A **pregnant solution** is a metal-laden solution produced by in situ or heap leaching.

Smelting is the process by which an ore mineral is reduced to the metal by heating with a reducing agent such as carbon.

Figure 3 A smelter chimney

The future for metals' mining

Metallic minerals are a non-renewable resource and metals' mining is unsustainable on a global scale. The geological processes that concentrate metals into economic ore deposits are extremely slow and take millions of years. Dwindling ore reserves have not attracted the same publicity as those of oil and natural gas but we should be equally, if not more, concerned about them. There are no synthetic alternatives for metals and recycling is not always feasible due to technical difficulties and high energy requirements. In some cases demand for scarce metals for new technologies is outstripping their reserves to such an extent that it is not worth developing the technology any further.

It is very difficult to estimate global reserves of metals – both mining companies and governments are often reluctant to publish figures. But to give a few examples, 2007 statistics from the United Nations and the USGS suggest at current rates of extraction: global copper reserves will last 61 years; uranium 59 years; gold 45 years; and tin 40 years. Future generations will be faced with the prospect of having to exploit lower grade, less accessible ore deposits with ever increasing energy costs, unless we make a determined effort to find ways of conserving metallic mineral resources.

Questions

1 Compare the possible environmental effects of surface and underground mining of metallic mineral deposits.

2 Explain why metals' mining is an example of unsustainable resource exploitation on a global scale.

3 Research one example of pollution caused by a metals' mining or processing operation.

Use of building and construction materials

People have used building and construction materials for 12 000 years or more. The mighty pyramids of Egypt are made from blocks of rock weighing several tonnes each. Their construction was a major feat of engineering, which we still marvel at today. Building and construction materials are non-metallic rocks and minerals. They must have the right properties for the purpose they are to be used for.

Building and construction materials are relatively common, cheap, bulk commodities. In the past they were costly to transport so, where possible, local sources were used. This has greatly influenced British architecture – the granite buildings in Aberdeen, the limestone buildings in Bath and the sandstone buildings in Chester give local character.

Key definitions

Aggregate is the general name for unconsolidated construction materials of sand size and above.

Bitumen is a semi-solid hydrocarbon fraction of crude oil.

Types of building and construction materials

Building stone

Building stone or dimension stone is cut and dressed into blocks and used for buildings, kerb stones, floors and kitchen surfaces. Common building stones include limestone, sandstone, granite and marble. Slate is used for roofing tiles because its cleavage allows it to split into thin sheets. Building stone must be:

- competent with high load-bearing strength
- well jointed so blocks are easily extracted or soft enough to be sawn into blocks
- attractive in appearance
- occur in thick, uniform units with few structures or weakness to ensure a good-quality product
- impermeable and resistant to mechanical and chemical weathering.

Aggregate

Aggregate is used for many purposes. Each use requires aggregate with specific properties:

- Natural aggregate is sand and gravel mainly extracted from recent Quaternary river, glacio-fluvial and shallow marine deposits. Beds should be thick, without lateral or vertical variation, to give a consistent product. The sand and gravel must be clean with no impurities such as clay. Sand is used for mortar, concrete, ballast and as an abrasive. Pure quartz sand is used for glass-making. Gravel used to make concrete must contain rounded pebbles so they can slide over each other when it is poured.
- Crushed rock aggregate is mainly used for roadstone. Hard rocks crushed for aggregate include many igneous rocks, gneiss, limestone and greywacke, along with industrial waste such as furnace slag.

Roadstone

This is crushed aggregate that is mixed with **bitumen** and used to surface roads. Roads are constructed in layers with a base-course overlain by a top wearing-course. Aggregate used for roadstone must be:

- strong with a high impact and crushing strength to withstand the weight of traffic
- resistant to abrasion and mechanical weathering (e.g. freeze-thaw) so the surface does not break up
- impermeable and resistant to chemical corrosion (e.g. salting of roads in winter, chemical spills)
- skid resistant – each chipping must be made of more than one mineral with different hardness, so they wear down at different rates and do not polish
- and bond well to bitumen.

On balance, rocks such as basalt and dolerite are best. Granite is not a good choice because it suffers polishing. In reality, mainly local sources are used, so roadstones vary enormously.

Brick clay

Bricks are made from clay, mudstone or shale. Different compositions produce different coloured and types of bricks. The clay is moulded into the required shape and fired at high temperatures in a kiln. Thick beds with a constant composition are required. About 40% of British bricks are made from the Jurassic Oxford Clay. This has a high carbon content, which acts as an internal fuel when the bricks are fired, making the process more uniform and reducing energy costs.

Manufacture of cement and concrete

Cement is made from a mixture of crushed limestone or chalk mixed with some clay or shale. The limestone provides calcium carbonate and the clay provides silica and alumina. The mixture is roasted in a rotary kiln at about 1500 °C and 5% gypsum is added to prevent the cement setting too quickly. Concrete is made by mixing cement with sand and gravel or crushed rock.

Extraction of industrial rocks and minerals

The vast majority of industrial rocks and minerals are mined from opencast quarries. Mining of industrial rocks and minerals can cause similar environmental impacts to opencast metal mining (described in spread 4.3.7) but often on a larger scale.

Hard rock **quarries** use **drilling and blasting** to break the rock up. If the rock is well-jointed it may form ready-made blocks aiding extraction. Wire saws are used to cut softer rocks. Unconsolidated sands and gravels are mined from shallow open **pits** or excavated by **dredging**. There is usually insufficient overburden and waste rock to fill in old excavations. Open pits reaching below the water table flood when extraction and pumping cease.

Many exhausted opencast mines are simply left as holes in the ground. Other options include restoration (see spread 4.2.9), flooding and use for recreation or wildlife havens, or conversion to landfill waste disposal sites.

Two controversial strategies to satisfy our demand for these commodities are:
- The development of coastal 'super-quarries' in remote areas of Scotland and Ireland. Rock from super-quarries is cheaply transported by ship but they are often situated in areas of outstanding natural scenery. Some people view super-quarries as an example of the 'not in my back yard' (NIMBY) attitude to the environment.
- Offshore dredging for marine aggregates. This disrupts marine ecosystems, alters the shape of the sea floor, and changes the pattern of currents in ways that can increase rates of coastal erosion in certain places.

Key definitions

A **quarry** is an opencast mine for hard rocks.

Drilling and blasting is where shot holes are drilled into rock and filled with explosives that are detonated to break up the rock.

A **pit** is an opencast mine for poorly consolidated material such as sand, gravel, clay and coal.

Dredging is the method by which material is scraped or sucked from the river or seabed.

Figure 1 A stone quarry

Questions

1 Describe the geological materials used in the manufacture of cement, concrete and bricks.
2 Assess the suitability of **(a)** dolerite and **(b)** marble for roadstone aggregate.
3 Debate the arguments for and against the development of coastal super-quarries.

Why build dams and reservoirs?

Dams and **reservoirs** are built for a variety of reasons including water supply, **hydroelectric power**, flood protection, reclamation of wetlands or to improve navigation. The effects of building a dam can have far reaching consequences that may go beyond national borders and create issues for neighbouring countries.

Geological factors affecting the construction of dams and reservoirs

General conditions

- There must be a lack of seismic and volcanic activity in the area. Earthquakes may cause the dam to fail and in a volcanic eruption the reservoir may be filled with pyroclastics or lava.
- Valley sides need to be stable so mass movement is unlikely. If beds in the valley dip in towards the reservoir then landslips may occur, especially if competent, permeable rocks such as limestone are interbedded with incompetent, impermeable rocks such as clay.
- The river catchment needs to have sufficient rainfall and be underlain by impermeable rocks to promote surface runoff for collection in the reservoir. If the dam and reservoir is for drinking water, it is important that there are no exposed mineral veins containing toxic elements such as lead or arsenic that could get into the water supply. Ideally rivers should have a low sediment load so the reservoir does not silt up too quickly.

Foundations

The underlying rock should be:

- Strong and competent with a high load-bearing strength to support the combined weight of the dam and water. Ideally the rock should be a crystalline igneous or metamorphic rock or cemented sedimentary rock. Clay, mudstone and shale are weak, incompetent rocks with low load-bearing strength, so are generally unsuitable.

Figure 2 A concrete arch dam showing the curved wall and hydroelectric plant

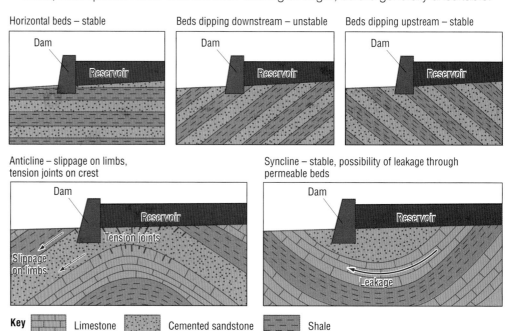

Figure 1 How structure and attitude affect dam and reservoir stability

- Impermeable to prevent leakage of water from the reservoir. Unfortunately, competent rocks often have joints, which may cause leakage problems. Although strong, limestone is usually permeable and may contain caves and solution cavities, so is best avoided.

The rock type also needs to be uniform. If the dam is sited on two rock types, differential subsidence may occur making the dam unstable. The depth of weathering is important as weathering weakens the rock and increases its permeability. Finally, the effects of previous human activity such as old underground mine workings should be considered as they could cause leakage or collapse.

Attitude of the strata
- Beds that are horizontal or dip upstream provide stable foundations.
- Beds dipping downstream are unstable. There is the potential for leakage and slippage along the bedding planes that may lead to collapse of the dam.

Geological structures
The presence of structures can cause problems:
- Faults are zones of permeability and weakness and may have different rock types on either side. The weight of the dam and water can reactivate old faults leading to an increase in seismic activity.
- Joints are zones of permeability that cause leakage. Joints are often more closely spaced than faults.
- Anticlines make unstable foundations because slippage can occur along bedding planes on the fold limbs. Tension joints on the crest of the anticline may allow leakage of water from the reservoir.
- Synclines are stable but water can bypass the dam through permeable beds.

Types of dams
We have seen from spread 4.4.1 that construction materials are bulky and costly to transport, so there needs to be a supply of suitable building materials near to the site of construction. There are two main types of dams:
- Embankment dams with a clay core held in place by piles of rock or earth. These are built in broad, shallow valleys. The weight of the dam is spread over a wide area so the foundations do not need to be very strong but they do require very large quantities of fill material.
- Masonry and concrete dams can be arch, buttress or gravity dams. They need a supply of cement and aggregate to make the concrete.

Ground improvement methods to prevent leakage from reservoirs
The site for construction of a dam and reservoir is rarely ideal and virtually all reservoirs leak to some extent. Ground improvement strategies used to prevent leakage from reservoirs include:
- **Grouting.** Holes are drilled into the rock and liquid cement pumped in. The cement fills pore spaces, joints and fissures, reducing permeability and increasing rock strength.
- **Clay** or **plastic lining.** Prior to filling, the reservoir is lined with an impermeable material such as clay or plastic to prevent leakage of water into the underlying rock. Clay is a good choice because if there is a local supply it will be cheap.
- **Cut off curtain.** This is an impermeable barrier, usually made of concrete, constructed as an extension below the dam. Cut off curtains are particularly effective at preventing leakage from dams situated on synclines. They also have a further benefit of strengthening the foundations and preventing slippage of beds dipping downstream.

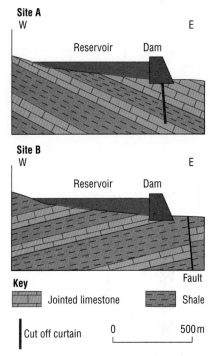

Figure 3 Two possible sites for dam and reservoir construction

Questions
1 Describe the geological factors that are important in the siting of dams and reservoirs for water supply.
2 Study Figure 3, showing two possible sites for the construction of a dam and reservoir:
   (a) for site A, describe the problems that could occur without a cut off curtain.
   (b) for site B, describe the problems that could affect the foundations of the dam.

Dams and reservoirs – environmental and social considerations

Environmental and social consequences of dam and reservoir construction

Dams and reservoirs are built with social considerations in mind. They have many benefits. They supply water for drinking or agriculture. The stored water can be used for hydroelectric power generation. Building dams and reservoirs have negative environmental consequences, which include:

- Flooding of land for the reservoir. This may result in the loss of agricultural land or villages being drowned and people having to relocate elsewhere. Valuable archaeological sites may be lost. Where forests are flooded, the decaying vegetation releases large quantities of carbon dioxide and methane, both potent greenhouse gases.
- Damage to aquatic ecosystems. This may be caused by changes in water depth, temperature and dissolved oxygen content downstream of dams. In addition, dams may prevent fish such as salmon swimming upstream to their breeding grounds. The dam may even cause ecological problems beyond the river mouth. After the Aswan Dam was built on the River Nile, the Mediterranean sardine fisheries collapsed due to a lack of nutrients being carried downstream.
- Silting of the reservoir. Over time the reservoir will gradually silt up as sediment is carried into it from upstream. Water released from dam spillways contains very little sediment as it is trapped in the reservoir.
- Risk of downstream flooding. Water engineers calculate how much water they need to release from reservoirs to ensure they do not overflow. Unexpected weather events such as more snow melt in the spring than usual or prolonged, heavy rainfall may mean there is not enough time to draw down the reservoir before it overflows.

Figure 1 Lake Nasser behind the Aswan Dam, from orbit

Case study

Widespread flooding affected much of the British Isles during the summer of 2007 – the wettest summer since records began. The floods affected thousands of businesses, tens of thousands of homes, with the estimated cost of damage being in excess of £2 billion.

At the end of June, cracks appeared in the Ulley dam, near Rotherham, leading to fears it might collapse. As a safety precaution, 700 people were evacuated from local villages and the M1 motorway was closed between junctions 32 and 36. The emergency services were drafted in to pump millions of gallons of water from the reservoir to ease the pressure on the damaged dam. Fortunately the dam held and disaster was averted.

The question now being asked is how safe is the Ulley dam and Britain's many other Victorian embankment dams that are now well over 100 years old?

Why do dams fail?

There are many reasons why dams fail but it is usually the result of a combination of factors including:

- poor choice of site
- poor design, construction or maintenance
- extreme weather conditions.

Sadly there are many examples of dam failures from around the world.

The St Francis dam collapse, California, 1928

The St Francis dam is just one of many dams that have been built on faults and later failed as a result. The 59 m high dam, built in the San Francisquito Canyon, was one of a number built to supply the rapidly expanding city of Los Angeles. Little notice was taken of the underlying geology, which consisted of sandstone and conglomerate in the west and mica schist in the east, separated by a 2 m wide fault zone.

During the construction phase several cracks appeared in the dam, some of which leaked as the reservoir filled. William Mulholland, the engineer responsible for the construction, dismissed them as minor and normal for a concrete dam of that size. On March 12, 1928, less than 12 hours after Mulholland had inspected the dam and declared it safe, it failed catastrophically. A wall of water, carrying huge pieces of the broken dam, rushed downstream destroying everything its path and claiming the lives of more then 600 people.

Afterwards, the point of failure of the dam was found to be at the faulted contact between the two rock types. The dam's failure is attributed to three main factors:
• unsuitable geology
• additional height being added to the dam that was not in the original design
• poor construction due to cost cutting.

The Vaiont dam disaster, Italy, 1963

From an engineering point of view, the deep, narrow Vaiont River valley in northern Italy seemed like an excellent site for a dam and reservoir. Unfortunately, the engineers ignored the geological warning signs:
• the weakness of the interbedded limestone and clay that dipped towards the reservoir on the south side of the valley
• the scar of an ancient landslide on the valley side above the reservoir
• a small landslide that occurred in 1960 while the reservoir was filling.

The concrete dam was completed in 1961 and, at 262 m high, was the world's second highest dam. In October 1963, there was a period of prolonged and heavy rainfall. Rainwater percolated through the permeable limestone and collected on top of a layer of impermeable clay. A slip plane developed between the limestone and clay and a huge mass of some 260 million m³ of limestone slid down the southern valley side into the reservoir. The dam withstood the force of the landslide but rock debris filled the reservoir, displacing the water over the top of the dam and creating a huge wave. The ensuing flood on the night of October 9, 1963, killed more than 2000 people. The Vaiont dam still stands today – a testament to good engineering and construction, but poor choice of site!

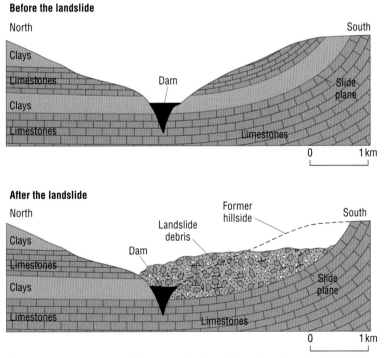

Figure 2 Cross-sections before and after the Vaiont dam disaster

Dams, reservoirs and seismic activity

There is a well known link between the building of dams and reservoirs and an increase in seismic activity. The weight of the dam and water in the reservoir may lead to earthquakes as the crust adjusts to the additional load. In addition, infiltrating water increases the pore fluid pressure in rocks so they become saturated and more liable to fail. Finally, water acts as a lubricant, making fault planes more likely to slip.

Questions

1 Describe some of the environmental and social consequences of dam and reservoir construction.

2 Explain how dam and reservoir construction can lead to an increase in seismic activity.

3 Choose one dam failure from around the world and research its causes and consequences.

Landslip and slumping hazards and road construction

Landslip and slumping hazards

Mass movements are slope processes ranging from very slow soil creep to virtually instantaneous rock falls. They include **landslips**, slides, **slumps**, flows and falls. Mass movements are the most underestimated class of natural hazard. They are usually much less spectacular than volcanic eruptions, earthquakes, fires and floods, but on an annual basis cause far more damage.

Natural factors that can cause landslips and slumping

Mass movement is seldom the result of one cause – usually a series of events lead to slope failure. The final trigger is often heavy rainfall, seismic activity or a volcanic eruption.

Rock type

- Strong, competent rocks are less likely to fail than weak, incompetent rocks. The rock type also influences the sort of failure. Strong, competent rocks tend to fail by slipping. Weak, incompetent rocks tend to slump.
- The porosity and permeability of the rock is also important as addition of water makes slope failure more likely.
- Geological structures such as bedding planes, joints and faults are planes of weakness in the rock. If present, the rock will often fail along them. The dip of bedding planes is also critical. If bedding planes dip in towards a valley, then blocks of rocks are likely to slide off them.
- Weathering weakens rock and produces loose fragments, increasing the risk of mass movement.

Slope angle

Slopes are stable if the forces resisting the downward movement of rock are greater than the forces driving the movement. Each rock type has a maximum stable slope angle. Clays are unstable at slope angles greater then 10 degrees, yet vertical walls of granite may be stable. In general, the steeper the gradient of slope in a particular material, the more likely it is to fail.

Water

Mass movements often happen after heavy rainfall or snow melt. Water adds weight to the rock and increases the pore fluid pressure acting as a lubricant, resulting in loss of friction and cohesion within the rock. Although clay is impermeable it will soak up large amounts of water, so becoming saturated, plastic and more liable to slumping. Some clay minerals swell up when wet, which reduces cohesion between grains.

Human factors that can increase the likelihood of landslips and slumps

- adding weight by building at the top of the slope
- removing material from the base of the slope for buildings or road cuttings
- leaking water mains and sewage pipes adding water
- removal of vegetation that intercepts water and binds the soil together
- creation of impermeable surfaces such as tarmac that increase surface run-off
- vibration from heavy traffic, machinery or blasting.

Road construction

Rocks underlying roads need to have a high load-bearing strength. The foundations must be stable with no faults, caves or underground mine workings. There must be good drainage so surface water can be controlled. There also needs to be a local supply of suitable aggregate for roadstone. To ensure the road stays at a suitable gradient, it may be necessary to make a road cutting or an embankment.

Road cuttings

Road cuttings through strong, competent rocks can have steep sides. If the rock is weak and incompetent, then very low-angle slopes are required, such as 6 to 8 degrees in clay. The dip of the beds is important. Horizontal beds and beds dipping away from the road cutting are stable. If the beds dip into the road cutting then rock falls, landslips and slumping are likely. If rocks are jointed, there is the possibility of loose blocks falling onto the road.

Embankments

Embankments are constructed where the road has to be built up over low lying areas. An embankment must be stable and strong enough to carry the load. A large amount of material will be required and the angle of slope of the embankment sides must be accurately calculated to guard against slope failure. Cut and fill techniques are often used where material is removed from a cutting and used to build an embankment.

Ground improvement strategies used to stabilise slopes and rocks

- **Slope modification**. The slope is reduced to a lower angle to increase its stability.
- **Retaining wall**. Usually constructed of concrete and used to support the sides of road cuttings.
- **Gabions**. Wire mesh boxes filled with rocks and placed as lateral toe support at the bottom of slopes to prevent failure by slumping.
- **Rock bolts**. Steel rods several metres long are drilled and cemented into rock faces. They pin loose blocks of rock to the sound rock behind and prevent rock falls. Rock bolts can only be used in competent rocks.
- **Rock drains**. Addition of water is a common cause of slope failure, so drains of broken rock can be constructed, especially in clay, to remove water and reduce the pore fluid pressure.
- **Wire netting**. This will fix surfaces in place and catch small rock falls.
- **Shotcrete**. Concrete is sprayed at high pressure onto rock surfaces. Shotcrete increases strength, reduces permeability, and protects the surface from weathering.
- **Vegetation**. Plants fix soil in place and reduce infiltration of water. It is one of the few effective stabilisation strategies for incompetent rocks such as clay.

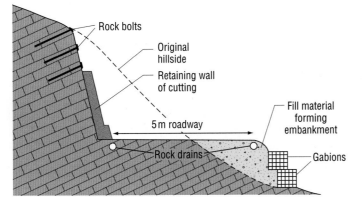

Figure 3 Ground improvement strategies used to stabilise cuttings and embankments.

Figure 1 Gabions along the side of a road

Figure 2 Rock bolts and wire netting

Case study

Shotcrete was invented in the early 1900s by Carl Akeley, an American taxidermist! He used it to fill his plaster models of animals. Later shotcrete was used to patch up weak parts of buildings and then for slope stabilisation.

Questions

1 Draw a labelled diagram to explain the problem that may occur if sedimentary beds dip into a road cutting.
2 Why is it difficult to stabilise rocks in a road cutting if they are deeply weathered?

209

The historic city of Istanbul in Turkey lies at the crossroads of Europe and Asia. The city is divided in half by the Bosporus Strait, one of the busiest shipping lanes in the world. At present two heavily congested road bridges connect the two halves of the city.

Construction of the Marmaray rail tunnel began in 2006. It will pass within 16 km of one of the world's most active faults, the North Anatolian Fault. In the past 70 years, there have been 7 earthquakes of magnitude 7 or higher on the Richter scale along the fault. The most recent one in 1999, struck the port of Izmit, 80 km east of Istanbul, killing over 18 000 people and causing more than $10 billion damage.

The tunnel has been designed to be earthquake-proof as an Istanbul earthquake is inevitable:

- It will be a submerged flexible tube sitting in a trench on the seabed.
- It will have flexible joints made from thick rubber rings reinforced by steel plates.
- There will be floodgates at both ends, which can be closed if the middle part of the tunnel floods.
- Foundations will extend 16 m below the seabed and mortar will be injected below that to prevent the problem of soil liquefaction.

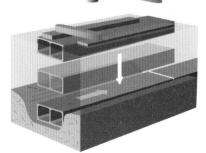

Sections of tunnel are floated into place and sunk into a pre-cut trench. Immersed tube tunnels can be engineered to withstand major earthquakes. For the Marmaray tunnel, 11 sections, each 135 metres long, will be lowered into position and joined with flexible rubber seals

Figure 1 The Marmaray rail tunnel, Istanbul

Tunnels – a brief history of use

Tunnels are used for many purposes – road, rail, water, sewage, power and communication. The Romans created the most extensive network of tunnels in the ancient world, mainly to carry water. In the seventeenth century, many tunnels were constructed for canals, which at the time were Britain's main transport system. With improvements in technology and the coming of trains in the nineteenth century, there was a tremendous expansion of tunnel building, including the Thames Tunnel finished in 1841 and the Severn Tunnel in 1886 – both are still in use. Today Britain is criss-crossed with many road and rail tunnels.

Geological factors affecting the construction of tunnels

As in all construction projects, ideally there needs to be a lack of seismic activity in the area. An earthquake could cause a tunnel to collapse. Many of the world's major cities lie on active fault lines and it has been necessary to dig tunnels in less than ideal places. Tunnels specially designed and engineered to withstand earthquakes are very expensive to construct.

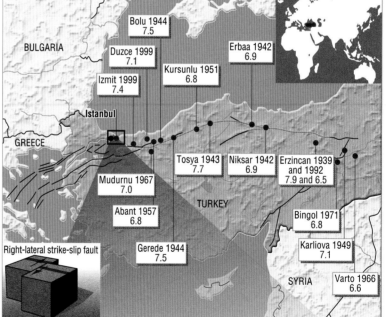

The history of quakes along the North Anatolian fault suggests Istanbul is due for a big one. Tunnelling through this earthquake zone demands a specialised design.

⌐ Fault lines

6.9 Earthquake magnitude

⌐ Path of earthquakes since 1942

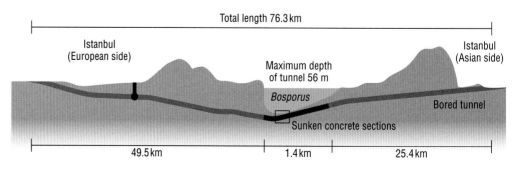

Rock type

Tunnelling may be through hard rock, soft rock or unconsolidated material. All require different approaches:

- Crystalline igneous and metamorphic 'hard rocks' are very strong and tunnels dug through them can sometimes be left unsupported. Usually the only method of tunnelling through hard rocks is drilling and blasting, which is slow and expensive. The amount of explosives used has to be carefully calculated, otherwise problems of **overbreak** or **underbreak** can occur. At depth in hard rock tunnels, the high confining pressure can cause dangerous rock bursts.
- Soft rocks are cheap and relatively easy to tunnel through but require lining with concrete or steel ribs. A specially designed tunnel boring machine can achieve tunnelling rates of 30 m a day in soft rocks. Sandstone, limestone and chalk are all fairly strong and can make ideal tunnelling materials.
- Weak rocks such as clay and shale and unconsolidated materials such as sands and gravels are very difficult to tunnel through. They are prone to collapse and leakage.

Lateral variation and changes in rocks types make tunnelling difficult, as the rocks may have different strengths. Weathering weakens rocks and variations in compaction and cementation also cause problems. Porous and permeable rocks allow water seepage into tunnels and the possibility of flooding.

Attitude of the strata

- Flat lying, competent, uniform strata are best for tunnelling.
- If the beds are dipping, then different rock types may be encountered along the length of the tunnel. Also slippage along dipping bedding planes may lead to rock falls into the tunnel.

Geological structures

The presence of structures can create some of the biggest challenges in tunnelling:

- Faults are zones of weakness as they may have breccias and fault gouge clay along them. They are zones of permeability that may allow the tunnel to flood. There may be different rock types on either side of the fault and, in the event of an earthquake, movement may cause the tunnel to collapse.
- Joints are also zones of weakness and permeability. They are often more closely spaced than faults and can be even more problematic. Loose blocks of rock between joints may fall out of the tunnel roof.
- Other linear structures, such as bedding planes in sedimentary rocks and foliation in metamorphic rocks, are also planes of weakness and may allow slippage or leakage of water along them.
- Folded rock sequences make tunnelling difficult due to changing angles of dip and slippage may occur on the fold limbs. However, if the fold is a gentle syncline it is possible to follow the dip of the fold and stay in one bed.

Groundwater

If the tunnel is below the water table then flooding may occur:

- Water may be free-flowing through unconsolidated sediments.
- Strong flows may occur along joints in limestone.
- Sandstones can develop high pore fluid pressures.
- Saturation of clays can lead to mobilisation and failure by slumping.

Ground improvement methods to prevent collapse and flooding of tunnels

Strategies to prevent tunnel collapse include:

- Lining with concrete segments or steel ribs.
- Use of rock bolts to secure loose blocks (see spread 4.4.4).

Strategies to prevent tunnel flooding include:

- Grouting the surrounding rocks (see spread 4.4.2).
- Using rock drains (see spread 4.4.4).

Key definitions

Overbreak is when too much rock is extracted.

Underbreak is when too little rock is extracted.

Case study

At 50.45 km long, the Channel Tunnel is the second longest rail tunnel in the world. It actually consists of three tunnels – two for trains, with a smaller service tunnel in between that acts as an emergency escape route.

It was technically possible to construct the tunnel well before it finally was. In 1881, engineers started digging trial tunnels from either side of the Channel, but progress came to a halt in 1883 due to British fears of an invasion from France.

It was not until 100 years later that geologists started to investigate the underlying geology, using geophysical surveys and boreholes. The structure was found to be a gentle syncline cut by a few faults. This allowed 85% of the tunnel to be dug in the Chalk Marl – chalk with mudstone mixed in. This proved to be an ideal tunnelling material – soft, but strong, with low permeability.

It took nearly 8 years for tunnel boring machines from France and England to cut their way through the Chalk Marl and meet in the middle. The total cost was over £10 billion – an 80% overspend!

Questions

1. Describe the likely problems that would be encountered during tunnelling through **(a)** granite, **(b)** limestone, and **(c)** sand and gravel.
2. Describe how the leakage of water into a tunnel could be stopped.

Coastal erosion and flooding

Coastlines are one of the most varied of all landforms. Erosion, transport and deposition processes are finely balanced and any disturbance to the coastal system will result in rapid changes until equilibrium is restored. Wave action is the dominant process in erosion and deposition. Sediment transport up and down beaches is caused by the **swash** and **backwash** of waves. If waves break at an oblique angle, **longshore drift** may transport sediment along the coast.

Case study

The 1953 North Sea storm surge was the worst natural disaster to strike northern Europe in the last 200 years. The surge was caused by an intense, rapidly moving, low pressure weather system that travelled southwards into the North Sea.

The funnel shape of the North Sea meant the water could not escape through the narrow Straits of Dover. Instead it piled onshore causing widespread flooding to eastern England and the Netherlands. Over 600 km² of land was flooded, resulting in the drowning of 307 people in England and over 1800 in the Netherlands.

Unfortunately, it could happen again, so the Thames Barrier was constructed to protect London. Completed in 1984, the barrier is 520 m wide, consists of 10 movable gates with 4 main openings between, each with a span of 61 m. Prior to 1990, the average number of closures was 2 a year, and since 1990 that has risen to 4 a year. In 2003, the Barrier was closed for 14 consecutive high tides the longest closure on record.

Figure 1 The Thames Barrier

Geological factors affecting coastal erosion

Rock type

The strength and hardness of rock influences the rate of erosion. Unconsolidated material offers the least resistance to wave attack and strong, competent rocks, such as granite, the most resistance. In Britain, areas composed of boulder clay deposited at the end of the last ice age are eroding the most rapidly.

Along rocky coastlines, the rock type determines the cliff profile. Strong, competent rocks form vertical cliffs dominated by marine erosion at the cliff foot. Weak, incompetent rocks form gently sloping cliffs, with marine erosion taking place at the cliff foot and weathering processes taking place on the cliff face.

Attitude of the strata

The steepest cliffs form where rocks are horizontal or dip away from the sea. The gentlest cliffs form where rocks dip in towards the sea. These tend to undergo landslips and slumping.

Where rocks of alternating resistance strike at an angle to the coastline, the more resistant rocks form headlands and the less resistant rocks form sheltered bays in between. Rocks of alternating resistance may also strike parallel to the coastline. If the sea breaks through a layer of resistant rock it will scour out the less resistant rock to form a bay with a narrow entrance, such as that found at Lulworth Cove in Dorset.

Case study

The Holderness coast of northeast Yorkshire is one of the most rapidly eroding in Britain. The coast is retreating by an average of 2 m a year, but individual events such as the 1953 storm surge can result in double that in just 24 hours. Since Roman times, the coast has moved 3 km inland and 50 villages mentioned in the Domesday Book of 1086 have disappeared.

The Holderness cliffs are composed of boulder clay. Pounding waves attack the base of the cliff and rainwater adds weight from above leading to failure by slumping. The fine grained clay is carried out to sea in suspension.

Difficult decisions need to be made as to how much more money should be spent on coastal defences in an area that is losing its battle with the sea.

Geological structures

Faults, joints and bedding planes are weaknesses in the rock that will be exploited by wave action. Selective erosion of headlands along these planes of weakness forms sea caves, blowholes, arches and stacks.

Strategies to reduce coastal erosion and flooding

Sea walls and banks

These have a dual function of protecting against both coastal erosion and flooding. Sea walls are built close to the high water mark and reflect wave energy. They are usually made of concrete and may be sloped, vertical or curved. Sea walls are effective in the short term but may be subjected to scouring, undercutting and increased erosion on the seaward side. Sea walls are expensive to build, costing up to £1000 per metre. Cheaper banks and mounds may be built, mainly to reduce the risk of flooding.

Figure 4 A groyne protecting a beach in southern England

Figure 2 Crumbling coastal defences

Figure 3 Landslip in chalk at the coast near Swanage, Dorset

Rock buttresses, revetments and rip rap

Rock buttresses and revetments are a relatively cheap way of protecting against coastal erosion. Large blocks of hard rocks such as granite are piled up in front of cliffs or sea walls to reduce wave action. The spaces between the blocks make them very effective at absorbing wave energy. Unfortunately, the rocks often need to be imported into the area so they tend to look unsightly and out of place.

Groynes

Wooden groynes are a familiar sight on many of our beaches and are one of the most effective methods of reducing sediment loss by longshore drift. Groynes usually extend out to sea at right-angles to the coast. Sediment builds up on the up-drift side of the groynes so the beach is retained. These days some groynes are made of large blocks of rock rather than wood.

Beach nourishment

Beach nourishment is one of the most popular 'soft engineering' strategies for coastal management. Imported sand is used to build up beaches. It is an expensive strategy and once begun needs regular maintenance to remain effective. To be successful, the texture of the imported sand must match that of the existing sand. When the sand is pumped onto the offshore part of the beach, it can bury plants and animals, block out light and disturb ecosystems.

Slope stabilisation

All the slope stabilisation methods described in spread 4.4.4 can be used to stabilise cliff faces and reduce the impact of weathering and erosion on coastal areas. However, high costs mean they are only used to protect built-up areas.

Questions

1 Draw labelled diagrams to show the sea cliff profiles resulting from **(a)** granite, **(b)** limestone dipping towards the sea, and **(c)** mudstone.

2 Research your own case study of one area affected by coastal erosion. Find out the geology and structure of the rocks, what protection methods are in place and how successful they have been.

Waste – a mounting problem

Getting rid of waste is a major problem for industrialised societies. We produce solid and liquid waste, some of which is hazardous. If waste disposal is not properly controlled, we run the risk of water pollution, soil contamination, air pollution and landscape degradation.

Our choices for waste disposal are:
- isolation by burying the waste
- incinerating, diluting or spreading out the waste
- recycling paper, glass, metals and some plastics.

In Britain, 85% of our waste is buried in **landfill** sites, amounting to a massive 111 million tonnes per year. People have the same attitude to landfill sites as they do to quarries. No one wants a landfill site on their doorstep, but we all produce waste and it has to go somewhere! Potential landfill sites include abandoned quarries and sand, gravel and brick pits, which are seen as ready-made holes in the ground. Unfortunately, the underlying geology means many of these sites are not ideal choices for waste disposal.

Figure 1 Waste disposal in landfill

Landfill waste disposal

The first solid waste landfill site was established in Britain in 1912. In a landfill site, each day's rubbish is compacted by heavy machinery and then covered with a layer of soil at least 15 cm thick to isolate it. When full, the landfill is sealed with a final layer of compacted soil 50 cm thick and the surface graded so that water runs off.

Environmental consequences of waste disposal in landfill

- In the short term, during the waste tipping operation, there are issues of noise, dust, smells, wind-blown litter and vermin infestations.
- Once complete, as biodegradable waste starts to decompose, the landfill undergoes settling and subsidence. Settlement is a major problem because it results in cracks and fissures opening up allowing rainwater to infiltrate into the waste.
- As rainwater percolates down through the waste, it dissolves soluble chemicals and collects microbial contaminants, producing a liquid we call **leachate**. The exact composition of the leachate will depend on the waste it has passed through, but it must be considered a threat to the environment unless proved otherwise. Landfill sites are point sources of pollution. Surrounding soils and groundwater in underlying aquifers are vulnerable to contamination by leachate, which forms a plume of pollution spreading out laterally in response to groundwater flow.
- Large volumes of methane gas are generated by the anaerobic microorganisms that thrive on the waste. Despite being highly flammable, there is little danger of explosions within the landfill because there is no oxygen present, but the gas must be vented off to prevent it building up to dangerous levels. Increasingly, the methane is being recovered and used as a viable fuel.

Key definition

Leachate is the fluid generated by water dissolving soluble chemicals from landfill waste.

Landfill waste disposal is where rubbish is buried in holes in the ground.

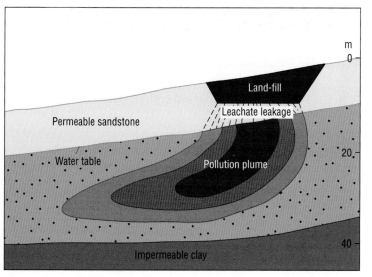

Figure 2 Plume of leachate pollution migrating laterally from a landfill site

Geological factors affecting landfill sites

Using a ready-made hole in the ground, such as an old quarry or brick pit, will reduce the cost of the landfill operation.

Rock type

Fine-grained, impermeable rocks such as clays are most suitable for landfill sites and it is best if they have thick, uniform, flat lying beds. Porous and permeable rocks such as limestone and sandstone allow flow of leachate. Limestone may be dissolved by acidic leachate leading to the formation of solution cavities, which will destabilise the site. Cementation acts as a barrier to leachate flow, but weathering can increase the permeability making leakage more likely. Crystalline igneous and metamorphic rocks may be suitable, but can be affected by jointing.

Geological structures and attitude of the strata

- Faults increase the permeability of rocks and provide escape routes for leachate.
- Joints in rocks such as limestone also allow downward leakage of leachate.
- Tilted or folded beds allow down-dip and lateral movement of leachate, which can migrate some distance away from the landfill site through permeable beds.
- Anticlines may have tension joints at their crests.

All of the above can lead to the escape of leachate and contamination of groundwater in nearby aquifers.

Groundwater

If the water table is high then there is less distance for the leachate to travel to reach underlying groundwater. The level of the water table may also vary in aquifers.

Ground improvement methods to prevent leakage of leachate

Strategies to prevent leachate escaping from landfill sites include:
- Grouting the surrounding rocks (see spread 4.4.2).
- Laying an impermeable clay or geomembrane (plastic) lining (see spread 4.4.2).
- Draining and collecting the leachate, which can then be treated or safely stored.

Examiner tip

Remember the definitions of porosity and permeability for the exam. Porosity is the volume of pore space and permeability is the rate at which a fluid flows through a rock.

We have seen they are key concepts throughout this unit as they control:
- how water is stored and flows through rocks.
- how oil and natural gas are stored and flow through rocks.
- the movement of hydrothermal fluids that form mineral deposits.
- the leakage of water into tunnels and mines.
- the leakage of water from reservoirs and landfill sites.

Questions

1 Debate the advantages and disadvantages of using abandoned limestone quarries for landfill waste disposal.
2 If leachate can move down through sandstone at a rate of 10 cm/day and the water table is at a depth of 5 m, calculate how many days it will take to reach the water table.
3 Research and write a short report describing the waste disposal options in your local area.

In 1994, Nirex, the British government's nuclear waste disposal body, identified an area near Sellafield in Cumbria to be used as a 'rock characterisation facility'. This was to be an underground laboratory to study the feasibility of developing it for nuclear waste disposal.

The scheme would have involved sinking two 5 m diameter shafts to a depth of 1020 m in the Borrowdale Volcanic Group rocks and then opening out caverns in which investigations could be carried out.

A public enquiry, held at the end of 1995, heard detailed evidence from both Nirex and many objectors, including Friends of the Earth, Greenpeace and the Irish Government. Members of the geological profession represented both sides – for and against. Eventually, the enquiry found in favour of the opposition and rejected the planning application. In 2006 the government decided to go ahead with geological disposal of nuclear waste.

Environmental geochemistry

As we become more concerned about the negative impacts our activities are having on the environment, new opportunities are opening up for geologists in the field of environmental monitoring. We have already seen the role geochemistry can play in metals' exploration, but it can also be used to identify and monitor the movement of both natural and man-made toxins in the environment. Environmental geochemistry involves the study of interactions between rocks, soils, water, organisms and the atmosphere and aims to provide a better understanding of how these components interact, particularly with regard to biogeochemical cycling.

Nuclear waste disposal

Nuclear waste presents a special problem because it remains radioactive for thousands or in some cases millions of years, depending on the half life of the isotopes present. The nuclear waste we produce today is a toxic legacy that will require very careful management well into the future.

Nuclear waste is classified as low level, intermediate level, high level or transuranic waste. Low level radioactive waste is usually disposed of in secure landfill sites. It is the high level and transuranic wastes that present us with the biggest problems. These categories of waste emit high levels of radiation, are often thermally hot, and have long half-lives. In the United Kingdom, high level waste is stored for at least 50 years, allowing it to 'cool' prior to solidification and disposal.

Safe disposal of high level radioactive waste must meet the following criteria:
- isolation for at least 250 000 years
- secure from accidental or deliberate entry
- safe from natural disasters such as floods, hurricanes and earthquakes
- no chance of leakage into the surrounding environment.

A number of possible nuclear waste disposal options have been proposed including:
- launching the waste into space in rockets
- burying it in sea floor sediments close to subduction zones
- placing it in secure containers on the ice sheets of Greenland or Antarctica
- burying it in an underground geological repository.

All of these options have their merits, but also have serious drawbacks. Burial in an underground geological repository is probably the least problematic of the choices.

An underground geological repository for nuclear waste would need to be:
- in a tectonically stable area
- within dry, impermeable rocks with a low water table
- free from the effects of potential natural hazards.

Evaporites have been suggested as a suitable rock type, as salt is dry and a good conductor of heat. Unfortunately, some hydrated evaporite minerals give out water when heated so pools of saline water could form. These would corrode storage containers and allow leakage of the radioactive waste.

At present the best option is storage in dry, competent rocks such as granite or volcanic rocks. Granite contains naturally high levels of radioactive elements making it less attractive. Probably the best choice would be burial in crystalline basement rocks below younger sedimentary cover rocks. This option has been suggested for disposal of nuclear waste from the Sellafield installation in Cumbria but has proved very unpopular amongst local people.

Radon gas pollution

One of the decay products of radioactive elements, such as uranium and thorium found naturally in rocks, is radon gas. Radon is also radioactive. Radon gas that seeps from rocks and soils can build up to dangerous levels in houses, posing a serious health risk. When radon is inhaled into the lungs, alpha particles bombard and damage cells causing an increased risk of cancer.

Geochemical surveys have been used to highlight which areas of the British Isles are naturally at high risk from radon pollution. These areas include the granites of southwest England, Scotland and Northern Ireland; phosphate rocks in Northamptonshire; black shales in Wales; and limestones in Derbyshire and Northern Ireland. Limestone is a particular problem because the leakage of radon is concentrated along fractures. House-to-house surveys are carried out in high risk areas and the problem can usually be eliminated by improved ventilation of affected buildings.

Heavy metal contamination of soils

Toxic, heavy metals such as lead, arsenic, cadmium and mercury can accumulate naturally in soils and as a result of human activities such as mining and smelting. There are a number of pathways by which heavy metal elements can enter the human body. They can be present in surface and groundwater supplies; they can be taken up by plants through their roots; or be present in the plants and soil ingested by grazing animals. If we then eat affected plants and animals, the heavy metals can enter our bodies. Heavy metals are dangerous because they bio-accumulate. This means their concentration in the body increases over time because they are not easily broken down or excreted.

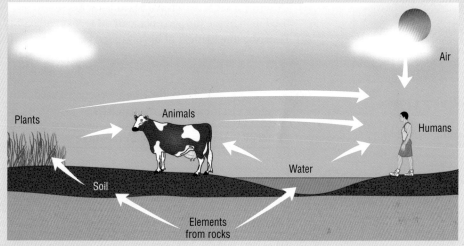

Figure 1 Biogeochemical pathways for the movement of elements

The British Geological Survey has been carrying out regional geochemical surveys both in the British Isles and abroad for over 40 years. The BGS aims to:

- identify areas of contaminated land
- improve our understanding of the links between geology and health
- study geochemical factors that affect habitats and biodiversity
- allow sustainable development of natural resources and management of waste disposal.

In the United Kingdom, data is gained from analysis of stream sediment samples taken every 1 to 2 km^2, supplemented by soil samples taken from urban areas. The stream sediment and soil samples are analysed for 48 elements and the data is used to compile a series of geochemical atlases.

Case study

Between 2004 and 2006, the Geological Survey of Northern Ireland completed the Tellus geochemical survey. Nearly 30 000 stream sediment, soil and water samples were collected and analysed for 60 elements and compounds. A complementary airborne geophysical survey was carried out using an aircraft flying at heights as low as 55 m!

The survey covered all of Northern Ireland and the results have been used to establish baseline geochemical signatures for rocks and to identify man-made disturbances. The data is being used by mineral exploration companies and environmental agencies.

So far, the results show naturally high levels of some heavy metals, including nickel and chromium, in certain places. Some streams have undesirably high levels of nitrates and phosphates due to over-application of fertilisers. Areas with naturally high levels of radioactivity have also been highlighted, allowing assessment of the risk from radon gas.

Figure 2 Aircraft carrying out geophysical survey during Tellus project

Figure 3 Stream sediment sampling during Tellus project

Questions

1 Suggest the advantages and disadvantages of each of the options suggested for nuclear waste disposal.

2 Describe the key requirements for a geological repository for nuclear waste.

1 The diagram below shows a cross-section through a hill.

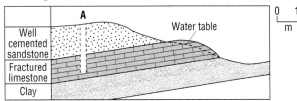

Figure 1

(a) (i) Describe the likely position of a spring on the cross-section. [1]

(ii) Explain why a spring is likely to form at this position. [2]

(b) The fractured limestone has a high porosity and permeability and is a good aquifer. Define the terms: *permeable* and *aquifer*. [2]

(c) (i) If a well was sunk at **A**, describe and explain what would happen to the groundwater within the limestone. [2]

(ii) What name is given to this type of well? [1]

(iii) State **one** problem that may occur if water is extracted from the well over a period of time. [1]

(d) Explain the difference between the terms *hydrostatic pressure* and *hydraulic gradient*. [2]

(e) (i) Give **one** advantage of surface water supply from rivers and reservoirs rather than supply from groundwater. [1]

(ii) Outline how groundwater can be used to maintain surface water supplies during dry periods. [2]

Total 14
(OCR 2833 May 2002)

2 (a) Describe the origin and formation of oil in a source rock. [3]

(b) Seismic reflection surveys are one method used to explore for oil and gas.

(i) Describe how a seismic survey is carried out. [2]

(ii) Explain how seismic surveys are used to identify potential oil and gas traps. [2]

(c) The cross-section below was drawn from the results of a seismic survey of an area where oil and gas are thought to be trapped.

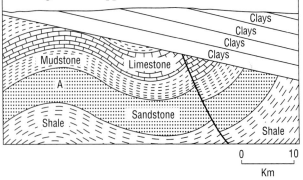

Figure 2

(i) One possible oil and gas trap has been located at **A** on the cross-section. Give **two** reasons why oil is likely to be trapped at this location. [2]

(ii) Name **two** other types of traps that can be seen on the cross-section. [2]

(d) Draw and label a thin section diagram to show the characteristics of a good reservoir rock for oil. [3]

(e) Data from **three** North Sea oilfields are shown in the table below.

	Auk Field	Brent Field	Fulmar Field
Percentage recovery	18%	33–56%	64%
Reservoir depth (m)	2361	2651 and 2865	3050
Reservoir rock	Permian carbonates and sandstones	Mid Jurassic sandstones	Upper Jurassic sandstones

(i) Describe **two** factors that affect the percentage recovery of oil from the oilfields. [2]

(ii) Explain why the percentage recovery varies within the Brent Field. [2]

(iii) Evaluate the data to suggest which of the oilfields is likely to have the best reservoir rock. [1]

(f) Describe a secondary recovery method that could be used to increase the percentage of oil recovery. [2]

(g) Describe **one** method of underground gas storage. [2]

Total 23
(OCR 5663 May 2000)

3 (a) The table below shows the energy resources used to generate electricity in the British Isles.

Energy resource	Percentage
Coal	30
Oil and gas	40
Nuclear	25
Renewable	5

(i) Calculate the total percentage of fossil fuels used as energy resources. [1]

(ii) Define the term *non-renewable energy resource*. [1]

(b) Coal is an important energy resource used in the British Isles.

(i) Complete the sequence below to show the coal series of increasing rank.

Peat → ..**A**.. → bituminous coal → ..**B**.. [2]

(ii) Define the term *rank*. [1]

(c) Draw a labelled diagram to show the difference between an exposed and a concealed coalfield. [2]

(d) Describe how coal is mined using the longwall retreat mining method. [3]

(e) Draw a labelled diagram to show how washouts can cause problems for underground coal mining. [2]

(f) Describe **one** advantage of opencast coal mining compared to underground mining. [1]

(g) Geothermal energy is a renewable energy resource.
  (i) Name **one** area in the British Isles where geothermal energy has the potential to be exploited. [1]
  (ii) Describe how geothermal energy would be exploited in the area you have named. [2]
  (iii) Give **one** disadvantage of exploiting geothermal energy. [1]

Total 17
(OCR 2833 May 2005)

4 **(a)** **(i)** Define the terms: *cut-off grade*; *reserves*. [2]
  (ii) Copper is now mined at a cut off grade of 0.4%, but the cut off grade was 1.5% 45 years ago. Why has the cut off grade decreased? [1]

(b) The diagram below is a cross-section through a mafic intrusion containing an iron ore deposit of magnetite.

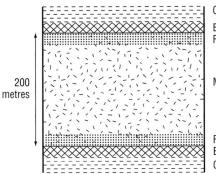

Country rock
Baked country rock
Fine grained mafic rock

200 metres

Medium grained mafic rock

Fine grained mafic rock
Baked country rock
Country rock

Figure 3

  (i) Describe the area on the diagram where the magnetite will be concentrated. [1]
  (ii) Describe and explain the process that caused the magnetite to be concentrated in this area. [3]
  (iii) Name and describe a suitable geophysical exploration technique that could be used to find this ore deposit. [2]

(c) Explain how residual deposits of bauxite (aluminium ore) are formed. [2]

(d) Explain how deposits of uranium ore are formed in sandstones. [2]

(e) Metal mining and processing operations have negative environmental consequences.
  (i) State **one** environmental problem caused by underground metal mining operations. [1]
  (ii) Describe how environmental geochemistry techniques can be used to recognise heavy metal contamination of soils. [2]

Total 16
(OCR 2833 May 2005)

5 **(a)** Match each of the geological materials, **1** to **5**, with the **most** likely product, **A** to **E**.

Geological materials	Products
1 Blocks of sandstone	**A** Brick
2 Clay	**B** Building stone
3 Crushed igneous rock	**C** Cement
4 Finely crushed limestone	**D** Concrete
5 Gravel	**E** Roadstone

[3]

(b) A possible dam and reservoir site, shown below, has been rejected because of the danger of landslips into the reservoir.

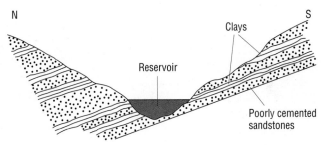

N   S
Clays
Reservoir
Poorly cemented sandstones

Figure 4

  (i) Give **two** reasons why the south side of the valley is likely to suffer landslips. [2]
  (ii) What effect could a landslip into the reservoir have? [1]

(c) Explain why heavy rainfall increases the risk of landslips and slumping. [2]

(d) Ground improvement methods can be used to stabilise rocks. Match the **most** suitable ground improvement method to each application.

Ground improvement method
1 cut off curtain
2 gabions
3 grouting
4 groynes
5 rock bolts

Application
A prevent loose blocks falling from a tunnel roof
B prevent leakage of water into a tunnel
C prevent slumping of a slope
D prevent sediment loss by long shore drift [4]

Total 12
(OCR 2833 May 2003)

6 Describe and explain the geological factors affecting the disposal of waste in landfill sites. [8]
(OCR 2833 June 2001)

What are fossils?

Fossils are the remains of living **organisms**. Most fossils are the hard parts of whole or fragmented organisms, such as the shells of a bivalve or the skeleton of a dinosaur. These are called **body fossils** as they represent the skeletal remains, or '**hard parts**' of the organism. The other main types of fossils are **trace fossils** including tracks, trails and burrows.

Factors that affect fossilisation

The type of fossilisation varies with the conditions during the life, death, transport and burial of an organism, plus changes in the sediments after burial. The important factors are listed below:

- **Original composition.** Many fossils are made of calcite or aragonite, which can be altered easily. Hard parts made of silica, such as radiolaria and some sponges, may be preserved unaltered.
- **Energy levels.** High energy produces lots of fragments; low energy produces more complete fossils.
- **Transport distance.** Fossils are fragmented during transport. This is due to abrasion or collisions causing breakage.
- **Rapidity of burial.** Faster burial means more chance of whole body fossils being preserved and less chance of scavengers eating them.
- **Amount of oxygen.** Accelerates breakdown of the organism due to bacterial decay and encourages scavengers.
- **Size of sediment.** Fine sediment preserves organisms better than coarse sediment. Only poor-quality fossils can be found in coarse sandstone or gravel, but fossils are found in a wide variety of sediments.
- **Diagenesis.** These are the changes within the sediments after burial. The composition and acidity of the percolating groundwater is important, as it may dissolve or replace the fossil with another mineral.

Types of preservation

Replacement

Replacement occurs when original material is dissolved atom by atom and substituted with another mineral. The most common type of replacement is the alteration of less stable aragonite to stable calcite. Equally, replacement could be with another mineral present in groundwater, such as hematite, an iron oxide sometimes found in sediments.

Aragonite and calcite are **polymorphs** of one another, with the formula $CaCO_3$. This means that the bonds are arranged in a slightly different way but the minerals have the same composition. Some shells such as bivalves, gastropods and corals are made from aragonite, which is less stable than calcite. Aragonite rearranges its chemical structure to form more stable calcite over time. Unaltered aragonite is only found in recent deposits.

Silicification

This occurs when percolating groundwater rich in silica dioxide (SiO_2) moves through the rock. The minerals dissolved in the groundwater crystallise out of solution and fill any pores or voids that may be present. If the fossil has been dissolved away by earlier groundwater movement, then the SiO_2 simply fills the void in the rock. However, if wood, shell or bone is still present, the pores may be filled by a mineral, increasing the density of the rock. Petrified wood is a common example.

Key definitions

An **organism** is something that was once alive. May be a single cell or multicellular (many cells).

A **body fossil** is the hard parts of an organism, such as the skeleton or shell.

Dissolution is the process whereby minerals that make up the fossils are dissolved away and removed in solution by groundwater.

Replacement is atom by atom substitution of one mineral for another.

A **mould** is the impression of the outside or inside of a fossil.

A **cast** is an infilled fossil void, usually with another mineral.

Figure 1 Photo showing examples of silicification – a fossil tree trunk, replaced by silica

Pyritisation

This is the replacement of original material by iron pyrite. It took place when the environment was devoid of oxygen (anaerobic) and the only live organisms were sulfur bacteria. The bacteria use sulfur in the environment to respire, which reduces the sulfur to bisulfide. The bisulfide then reacts with any iron in the environment to form iron pyrite. This then replaces the fossil material. Pyritisation commonly occurs in deep sea environments with an anoxic sea bed, or in shallow swamps.

Carbonisation

The process occurs during burial as the overlying mass of rocks increases the pressure and temperature. This allows volatiles or gases within the organic material to be driven off. This reduces the amount of oxygen, methane, carbon dioxide and water and increases the carbon content overall, preserving plants or animals such as graptolites as a thin film of carbon within shale or mudstone.

Mould and cast formation

Moulds are formed when fossils are dissolved out of the rock they are in. These are usually made of $CaCO_3$. This leaves a void or hole in the rock. Breaking this rock open will reveal an **external mould** of the fossil. If the fossil was filled with sediment before complete burial, the sediment may reveal an **internal mould** showing internal structures along with any impressions of soft tissues within.

A **cast** is formed when the void is infilled with another mineral, such as iron pyrite or silica. These can be seen as counterparts to external moulds when breaking the rock open. Equally, casts can be made in the laboratory by infilling moulds with latex or modelling clay.

Figure 2 Pyritisation – of an ammonite

Figure 3 Carbonisation – ferns

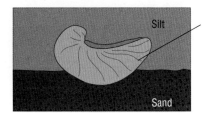

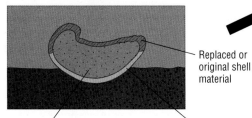

Figure 4 Diagram to show fossil mould and cast formation

Silt

The fossil is encased in sediment on the sea floor

Sand

Rock splits along a line of weakness

Internal mould

External mould

Replaced or original shell material

Sediment infill, which occurred at the time of burial

Voids where the shell has been dissolved away

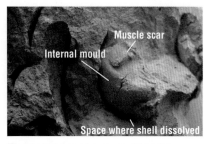

Figure 5 Internal and mould cast in Jurassic Portland limestone. The space is where the original shell has been dissolved away

Muscle scar

Internal mould

Space where shell dissolved

Questions

1 Explain how silicification, pyritisation and carbonisation differ.
2 What is the difference between moulds and casts?
3 Explain how transport distance, size of sediment and diagenesis can affect the quality of preservation.

Key definitions

Low-energy refers to the velocity of the water during deposition moving slowly or not at all. Examples of a low energy environment are a swamp, deep sea, a lake or a pond.

Anaerobic means without oxygen. This term is used to describe conditions within a sediment.

Anoxic means water without oxygen. Standard decomposing bacteria cannot live without oxygen, nor can scavengers.

What is exceptional preservation?

Exceptional preservation means that the fossils have very fine detail or the remains of **soft** tissues are preserved. 'Soft tissue' may be the whole animal, such as a worm or jellyfish, or may be only part of the animal, such as muscle or gills, preserved along with other hard parts. It is usually only the hard parts that are preserved as fossils, so exceptional preservation is very rare. Terrestrial animals have comparatively little chance of preservation unless they are washed into lakes, as the land surface is largely an area of erosion.

Ideal conditions for exceptional preservation to take place

For the few organisms that are fossilised, there is a sequence of stages that normally occur in the transition from dead body to fossil:

- rapid burial in a protective medium such as soft, fine clay, to protect hard parts from the destructive action of scavengers and the weather
- burial in **low-energy** conditions for the best chance of fossilisation
- lack of oxygen – **anaerobic** conditions reduce decay
- pH – decay is slowed down in conditions of high acidity – as in peat swamps.

Modification of the hard tissues by early diagenesis can destroy detail. This could be compaction or replacement of the original shell. Even after the fossil has formed, physical processes cause disarticulation of shells or abrasion. Chemical processes mean that hard parts composed of calcium carbonate are liable to be dissolved by weakly acidic groundwaters.

Summary of exceptional preservation

Conditions that must occur	Reasons
Quick burial in sediment, before or shortly after death	No time for breakage, scavenging or decay of material
Fine grained sediment	Fine particles preserve detail
Anaerobic conditions	No bacterial action, therefore no decay of soft tissue
No scavenging animals	Not fragmented, damaged or eaten
Original material replaced early in diagenesis	Less detail is lost as there is less alteration of the original material

The incomplete fossil record

The fossil record is biased, especially in the types of organisms preserved. When an organism dies, bacteria act to decompose the soft parts. The only parts that usually survive are skeletal structures, if present, especially if they are mineralised skeletons ('hard parts') impregnated with crystals of calcium carbonate (calcite or aragonite), calcium phosphate or silica. Animals with mineralised skeletons include corals, brachiopods, molluscs, echinoderms and many chordates. It is no wonder that the fossil record is biased towards these groups, whilst those lacking a mineralised skeleton, such as worms, jellyfish and insects, are poorly represented.

Case study

Exceptionally preserved fossils can be found in the British Isles. One such example is *Charnia*, the remains of a soft bodied, primitive animal similar to a coral. The remains were alive around 575 Ma ago and are found in Charnwood Forest, Leicestershire. They are amongst the oldest fossils known in the world. They belong to a suite of fossils known as the Ediacaran fauna.

Methods of exceptional preservation

Amber

Amber is tree resin that has hardened and been preserved. Resin flowed from wounds or cracks in tree bark and accumulated on the branches and trunks. When the resin was warmed in the sun, it flowed down the trunk. Animals became trapped in the resin, and were buried in later flows. The amber then became much harder by a series of chemical reactions. The animal and plants found within the amber tells us what inhabited ancient forests.

Amber is formed from the resin of the extinct pine tree, *Pinus succinifera.* These formed 'amber forests' in Scandinavia during the Eocene and Oligocene. Baltic amber is very famous and is used for jewellery and is sometimes called 'the gold of the north'. Small animals such as spiders and flies are common in amber.

Tar

Tar pits formed when hydrocarbons that had migrated upwards formed pools of asphalt. Water accumulated on top of the tar, forming a water hole which enticed animals. Animals that became trapped attracted others and they too became trapped. The most famous tar pit is at Rancho La Brea, California and this has yielded over 660 species of organisms, including single-celled organisms, pollen, seeds, insects, spiders, fish, frogs, salamanders, snakes, turtles, birds and mammals trapped and preserved within it. Sabre toothed cats, *Smilodon*, and woolly mammoths are amongst its victims.

The Burgess Shale

The Burgess Shale was discovered in the Canadian Rocky Mountains in 1909 by Charles Walcott, a famous geologist. The fossils are of Cambrian age and offer a snapshot into the evolution of life on Earth. The animals found in this deposit are all extinct. Some show similarities to animals that are alive today and may be distant relatives.

There are many fossil Arthropods, such as trilobites and lace crabs. The limbs, antennae, gills, gut and other soft tissues are replaced by a type of clay mineral.

Other strange species included velvet worms, which were soft bodied and some segmented worms with bristles. The existence of many of these animals would never have been known if the Burgess Shale had not been discovered.

Figure 1 Wasps in amber

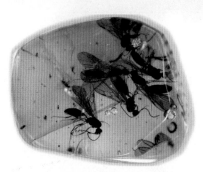

Figure 2 Burgess shale trilobite fossil

Figure 3 Archaeopteryx specimen

How science works

The Burgess Shale is globally important. However, there is an even older deposit of Lower Cambrian age in China, known as the **Changjiang Formation**. This formation provides an even earlier window on the evolution of life, showing some species that are not found in the Burgess Shale. This deposit really does represent the '**Cambrian Explosion**' and the dawn of more complex life.

Evolution of life throughout the Lower Palaeozoic can be traced in other rare deposits. One is the **Soom Shale** found in South Africa, which is of Ordovician age. More recently there has been the discovery of a deposit in England, called the **Herefordshire Lagerstätten**. Using modern techniques palaeontologists have produced three dimensional images of animals that lived during the Silurian. This English deposit is the first known occurrence of exceptional preservation from the Silurian, there may still be others to be discovered.

The Solenhofen Limestone, Germany

This Jurassic limestone contains a 'bird-like' animal called *Archaeopteryx*. Unlike all living birds, this animal had a full set of teeth, claws on its wings, a flat sternum (breast bone) and a long, bony tail. However, its feathers, wings, furcula (wishbone) and reduced fingers are all characteristics of modern birds.

Questions

1 Explain how methods of exceptional preservation allow soft tissues to be preserved.
2 List the environmental conditions that must occur for preservation to be exceptional.
3 Research the varied fossils of the Burgess Shale. How can fossils in the Burgess Shale help us understand evolution of life on our planet?

Trace fossils and interpreting palaeo-environment

What is a trace fossil?

Trace fossils provide glimpses of the nature and behaviour of ancient organisms in the geological record. Trace fossils are extremely important as they can help us interpret the palaeo-environment.

This type of fossil has an exceptionally long fossil record, and some of the evidence of the earliest multicellular animals is derived from trace fossils.

Trace fossils preserve the **activity** of an organism, not the organism itself. These traces can be regarded as fossil **behaviour** or evidence of the lives of the organisms that made them. These include **tracks**, **trails**, burrows, borings and excrement (coprolites).

Trace fossils are not necessarily formed by the same organism, even though they may look identical. For example, a burrow could have been inhabited by a bivalve, a crustacean or a worm, which have not been preserved. One animal may also produce many different types of trace fossil, such as walking tracks, trails or **resting traces**.

How to make a trace fossil

An organism walks across soft, fine sediment and leaves the imprint of its feet. There is then a very small chance that the footprints will be filled in by sediment before they are destroyed by water currents or wind. If they are infilled, the trace fossil may be seen on the base of the infilling sediment, so may stand out.

Skolithos X 0.5
Vertical burrow

Diplocraterion X 0.5
U-shaped burrow

Thallasinoides X 0.2
Branching burrow

Rusophycus X 1
Trilobite resting trace

Cruziana X 1
Trilobite walking tracks

Figure 1 Trace fossil morphology

Types of trace fossils

Most trace fossils are found in low-energy environments because higher-energy conditions would immediately destroy the traces left. The sediments found in such conditions are generally fine grained, such as mud, clay or silt. **Terrestrial** trace fossils are much rarer than those found in marine conditions, because they may be weathered or eroded before they can be preserved.

A comparison of the main types of trace fossils is given in the table.

	Description	Conditions	Example
Tracks	Found on the surface of bedding planes, formed as an animal walked across its surface	Soft or muddy fine grained sediments. Terrestrial or marine	Walking traces of arthropods, dinosaurs or humans. Usually the imprints of legs or feet
Trails	Traces made by whole or parts of animals, at rest or travelling along the surface of sediment	Soft or muddy fine grained sediments. Terrestrial or marine	Resting traces showing gill or leg structures. A trilobite dragging its tail along behind it. Starfish impression
Burrows	Vertical, U-shaped, stacked or branching burrows. May be for dwelling, locomotion, protection or feeding	Substrate must be soft sand or mud for organism to burrow. Burrowing can mix layers of sediment by bioturbation	U-shaped *Diplocraterion*, vertical *Skolithos* or branching *Thallasinoides*
Borings	Structures formed in rock or wood	Evidence of a hard substrate	Burrowing bivalves such as *Teredo*
Excrement	Faecal pellets (<10 mm) and coprolites (>10 mm). Evidence of large animals in the environment	They need to be covered quickly, before they break up in currents or bacterial action breaks them down	Dinosaur dung. Can be rich in phosphate
Root structures	Woody-looking impressions in rocks or preserved as lignite	Shallow marine, deltaic or terrestrial conditions	Root often branching from trees or other plants

Figure 3 a Large U-shaped burrow into limestone infilled with clay and **b** Burrows both vertical and horizontal with sediment mixed by bioturbation

Case study

A track of a dinosaur gives us information about the animal that made it:
- Shape of the soft parts – these are left as impressions in very fine sediment. The familiar three toes can often be seen, along with impressions of claws.
- Patterns of scales on the skin – only rarely preserved in very fine sediment.
- Weight – can also be estimated by looking at the size and length of the feet.
- Running or walking speed – this can be calculated by estimating the height of the animal based on its foot length. Generally steps further apart mean that the animal was moving fast.

Walking

Running

Figure 2 Dinosaur tracks and photographs showing dinosaur footprints

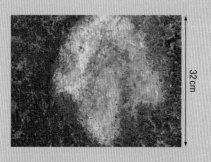

32 cm

Questions

1 Define the term *trace fossil*.
2 Explain why some trace fossils may give us information about the type of substrate in which the organism lived.
3 Explain why trace fossils on land are rarer than those found in marine conditions.

Modes of life

Organisms have evolved to live in all environments. They live in various parts of the water column, on or in the sediment. They may hunt, scavenge or filter feed. They may swim, float, crawl or remain fixed in one position. The flow diagram shows the technical terms used to describe different modes of life.

Figure 1 Flow diagram – terminology of different modes of life

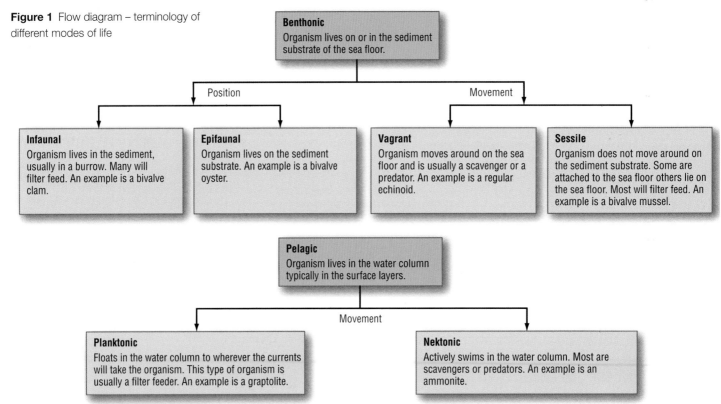

Benthonic
Organism lives on or in the sediment substrate of the sea floor.

Position

Movement

Infaunal
Organism lives in the sediment, usually in a burrow. Many will filter feed. An example is a bivalve clam.

Epifaunal
Organism lives on the sediment substrate. An example is a bivalve oyster.

Vagrant
Organism moves around on the sea floor and is usually a scavenger or a predator. An example is a regular echinoid.

Sessile
Organism does not move around on the sediment substrate. Some are attached to the sea floor others lie on the sea floor. Most will filter feed. An example is a bivalve mussel.

Pelagic
Organism lives in the water column typically in the surface layers.

Movement

Planktonic
Floats in the water column to wherever the currents will take the organism. This type of organism is usually a filter feeder. An example is a graptolite.

Nektonic
Actively swims in the water column. Most are scavengers or predators. An example is an ammonite.

Problems occur when we do not really know the mode of life of a fossil group. This is certainly true for the extinct trilobites, graptolites, some ammonoids and dinosaurs. For some groups, we can only infer the mode of life, by comparing them with modern-day equivalents. For example, belemnites are similar to modern-day squid, and so we infer the same mode of life.

We make many assumptions doing such comparisons, which may or may not be correct. Research sometimes sheds new light on old ideas, which may lead to old ideas being rejected. New hypotheses are then formulated to replace old ones.

Assemblages

It is rather unusual to only find one type of fossil in a rock. If conditions for life were good, then many different types may be found together. This is called an **assemblage**. The fossils found in assemblages can give clues to the palaeo-environment that existed at the time.

Life and death assemblages

When organisms die their shells are usually transported, partly broken and deposited as masses of mixed shells. When such an accumulation is preserved it is called a **death assemblage** because the fossils are not in their living positions. It can be recognised by:

- broken, fragmented or abraded shells
- sorting of shells by size
- alignment of shells by currents
- mixture of organisms that could not have lived together in the same environment, such as calm water and high-energy bivalves.

Fossils found in their living positions form a **life assemblage**. This is where organisms are preserved, fossilised in their life position such as a reef community or as burrowing organisms preserved in their burrows. The fossils will not have been transported and they will be complete and in the position in which they lived. Life assemblages are rare compared to death assemblages.

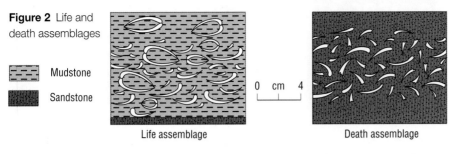

Figure 2 Life and death assemblages

Mudstone

Sandstone

0　cm　4

Life assemblage

Death assemblage

Derived fossils

This is where organisms, which were originally preserved in an old sedimentary layer, are then eroded and transported and deposited in a younger layer. For example, a Jurassic ammonite found in Quaternary sediments must be derived. **Derived fossils** are often rounded or broken because they have been transported.

Assemblages and palaeo-environments

As a rule, **thick**-shelled organisms were robust enough to withstand **higher energy** conditions than thin-shelled organisms. This could then be backed up by other evidence, such as pockets of broken shells concentrated in layers and the type of sediment itself. Times of low energy may result in finer grained sediments, such as micritic mud, whilst times of higher energy may result in layers of silt and sand. The table below shows some possible assemblages and an interpretation for each assemblage.

Environment	Possible assemblage	Description
High-energy continental shelf	Thick-shelled brachiopods and bivalves. Fragments of trilobites or other broken fossils such as corals. Microfossils	Fragmentation suggests high energy. This is supported by the thick-shelled fauna
High-energy shallow marine	Thin-shelled burrowing bivalves. Thick-shelled bivalves or those which show methods to attach to the substrate. Broken fossil remains. Microfossils	Fragmentation suggests high energy. Burrowers do not need thick shells, but this suggests soft sediment. May be in the littoral zone or shallow marine
Low-energy shallow marine	Brachiopods or epifaunal bivalves with wide shells, mostly articulated. These do not show any method of attachment. Irregular echinoids. Burrowing bivalves. Microfossils	Wide shells suggest the need to spread the weight on a soft substrate. Burrowers also suggest a soft substrate
Low-energy deep marine	Complete specimens of graptolites or cephalopods. May have many microfossils	No bottom dwellers. This could mean that the conditions were anoxic. Complete specimens suggest low energy as they have not been broken up
Low-energy deltaic/ terrestrial	Plant stems, leaves and spores. Insects and gastropods	Presence of plant material may mean terrestrial or deltaic conditions. It certainly signifies a close proximity to land

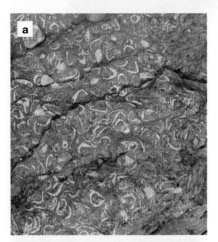

Figure 3 Fossil assemblages in **a** Jurassic limestone and **b** Cretaceous clay

Key definitions

Anoxic describes water which lacks oxygen (anaerobic).

Articulated describes organisms found whole or connected as in life.

Derived fossils are fossils found in one rock, weathered out and re-deposited in another rock. Different fossils may give conflicting dates.

Disarticulated describes organisms found as fragments, such as separate shells or parts of trilobites.

A fossil life assemblage is a collection of organisms found within sediments in the same position as they would have been when they were alive. An example would be a bivalve in a burrow.

A fossil death assemblage is a collection of organisms found in a different place and position than they occupied in life. An example would be disarticulated shells.

The littoral zone is the high-energy area between high and low tide.

Questions

1 Explain why it is useful to know the rock type when looking at fossil assemblages.
2 Distinguish between life and death assemblages.
3 Write definitions for the following terms: nektonic, planktonic, pelagic, benthonic, infaunal and epifaunal.

Classification

Trilobites are the earliest known organisms, which belong to the phylum **Arthropoda**, a phylum which includes familiar creatures such as lobsters, crabs, insects and spiders. It also includes some extinct forms such as eurypterids (sea scorpions) and, of course, the Class **Trilobita**. Trilobites are so-called because their skeleton is divided parallel to their long axis (longitudinally) into three (tri) lobes (lobite). They are also divided into three sections along the axis – cephalon (head), thorax and pygidium (tail). Trilobites evolved in the Cambrian and became extinct at the end of the Permian period.

The arthropod skeleton

The most distinctive characteristic is that arthropods have a hard **exoskeleton** (outside skeleton), made of a tough substance called **chitin**. The skeleton itself acts as anchorage for muscles, which are inside the animal. The exoskeleton acts like a suit of armour, where plates move separately with the movement of the animal.

Arthropods have jointed legs and antennae, known as **appendages**. The appendages in trilobites were present on many of the body segments and were used for moving and feeding. Each **pleuron** had a pair of jointed legs, which were probably used for walking or swimming. These also had **gills** attached for respiration (see diagram showing position of legs and gills). The cephalon had antennae attached in addition to three or more pairs of **head legs**, which had a feeding and sensory role. The position of these can be seen in red on the diagram showing trilobite morphology. The appendages are only preserved in very rare circumstances, such as in the Burgess Shale.

Morphology
Cephalon

The cephalon is made up of several structures, including the eyes, facial sutures, free cheeks, fixed cheeks and glabella. The eyes were **compound** eyes, similar to modern-day arthropods. They consisted of many small lenses made of calcite and allowed wide-angled vision. Spines may be attached to the glabella at the genal angle. These spines and those elsewhere on the trilobite were probably for defence from predators or to spread the animal's mass, by providing a large surface area.

Thorax

The thorax is made up of thoracic segments, each possessing a pair of appendages and gills in life. Each thoracic segment consists of two pleurae and a segment from the axis. Each pleuron may also have spines extending from them, depending on the mode of life. This part of the skeleton is made of many individual plates articulated together, making the thorax very flexible. Some trilobites were so flexible that they could curl up into a ball, or **enroll**, rather like a hedgehog. The ability to enroll was probably a defensive mechanism.

Pygidium

The pygidium or tail is composed of several segments **fused** together. Study the diagram showing trilobite morphology and read more about the function of each of its parts.

Figure 1 Photo of trilobites (×1) in siltstone

Key definitions

The exoskeleton:
- Provides protection and support;
- Provides attachment for muscles;
- Made up of three layers. A waxy outer layer and two further layers of chitin and protein. The middle layer may be impregnated with calcium carbonate for increased strength;
- May have had sensory hairs emerging from the exoskeleton to detect chemicals or changes in the environment.

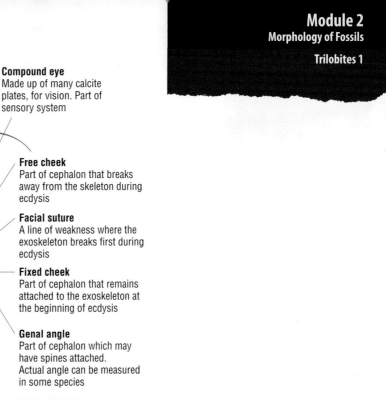

Key
Cephalon
Thorax
Pygidium

Glabella
Part of cephalon which is formed by the presence of the stomach, which is inside the head. Its shape may indicate diet

Compound eye
Made up of many calcite plates, for vision. Part of sensory system

Antenna
To detect environment. Part of sensory system

Appendages – headlegs
To detect environment and feeding

Appendages – walking or swimming legs
For locomotion and gill attachment

Free cheek
Part of cephalon that breaks away from the skeleton during ecdysis

Facial suture
A line of weakness where the exoskeleton breaks first during ecdysis

Fixed cheek
Part of cephalon that remains attached to the exoskeleton at the beginning of ecdysis

Genal angle
Part of cephalon which may have spines attached. Actual angle can be measured in some species

Thoracic segment
One thoracic segment, made up of three articulating plates

Pleuron
Segment adjoining the axis

Pygidium
Fused tail piece which may have spines. This may stabilise the animal

Axis
Central lobe running down the length of the trilobite exoskeleton

Figure 2 Trilobite morphology

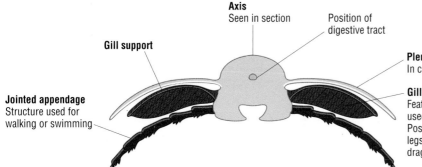

Axis
Seen in section

Position of digestive tract

Gill support

Pleuron
In cross-section

Gill
Feathery structure used for gas exchange. Positioned above the legs, so that it did not drag on the sea floor

Jointed appendage
Structure used for walking or swimming

Figure 3 Cross section of one thoracic segment showing position of legs and gills

Ecdysis

Modern-day arthropods such as crabs give us the key to understanding how the trilobites lived. We can infer that the exoskeleton could not grow, but at various times during a trilobite's life would be shed, a process called **ecdysis** or moulting. The exoskeleton fractured along lines of weaknesses, such as the **facial sutures** (see diagram showing trilobite morphology). This separated the fixed cheek from the free cheek along the visual surface of the eye. The animal was then able to free itself, perhaps by wriggling. After moulting there would have been a period of rapid growth, before the new exoskeleton was completely formed. Ecdysis left the animal vulnerable to predators as the skeleton was temporarily flexible to allow stretching to accommodate a larger animal.

Questions

1 Explain why the trilobites are considered to be arthropods.
2 Give two examples of modern-day arthropods.
3 Give the function of the following morphological features: facial suture, pleuron, glabella and pygidium.

Trilobites lived in the oceans of the Cambrian and Ordovician periods, beginning around 540 million years ago, with a diminishing number of families existing until the Permian extinction. The morphological diversity actually peaked in the Ordovician. To have survived for nearly 300 million years is a testimony to the successful design and adaptability of trilobites. They were probably the first organisms on Earth to have good vision with an advanced design of eyes.

Adaptive radiation

Trilobites evolved to be a variety of different shapes and sizes, probably as a response to the environment they lived in and the selection pressures in that environment. We are going to look at four very different types of trilobite and consider their adaptations and relate these to different modes of life. The four genera we are going to use as examples are: *Calymene*, *Agnostus*, *Deiphon* and *Trinucleus*. The ideas on mode of life are transferable to other species of trilobite.

Throughout this section refer both to the diagram of trilobite **morphology** in spread 5.2.1 and the diagram showing the different morphological types of trilobite.

Benthonic (e.g. *Calymene*)

These are generally large trilobites, which show little streamlining and have complex compound eyes. They generally had a lot of pleura, which meant they had the ability to enroll for protection. We can infer their mode of life as **benthonic**, bottom dwelling, **epifaunal**, animals living on the **substrate**. As bottom dwellers, they crawled on the sea floor looking for food as active hunters on smaller invertebrates or as scavengers. As well as giving them a good depth and field of vision, the eyes would have been sensitive to movement. This would have helped them detect food and predators, an advantage over other bottom dwellers in the same environment.

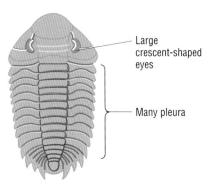

Large crescent-shaped eyes

Many pleura

Figure 1 Calymene ×0.5

Figure 2 Enrolled trilobite

Morphological feature	Probable function or reason
Many pleura	Supports many pairs of legs for walking (one pair per pleuron)
	Supports many pairs of gills for respiration
	Thorax is flexible and these trilobites had the ability to enroll for protection. When rolled up, the vulnerable soft underside and mouth were hidden
Crescent-shaped compound eyes, set high on the cheeks	Ability to see forwards, sideways and backwards (360-degree vision). No need to see underneath the animal as it lived on the sea floor
	Complex eyes may mean that the animal was an active hunter or scavenger
Large and not streamlined	No need to be small, light or streamlined, as animal did not swim or float but walked on the sea floor. Trace fossils of trilobite tracks – walking, resting and foraging for food show movements on the sea floor

Planktonic (e.g. *Agnostus*)

These are small and probably light trilobites, which were blind as they lacked eyes. They generally had few pleura, and therefore few legs or gills. They are widespread geographically, found in sediments such as shales formed in low-energy deep waters. This suggests that they had a **planktonic** lifestyle. It is possible that the lack of eyes means a benthonic lifestyle in deep, cold water on the ocean floor in minimal or no light, where they would have fed on detritus. More data is needed to decide between these two theories and perhaps they lived in different ways depending on age or species.

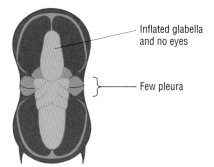

Inflated glabella and no eyes

Few pleura

Figure 3 Agnostus ×3

Morphological feature	Probable function or reason
No eyes or very small eyes	Blind or nearly blind, which may mean that the animal did not hunt and its food source was filtered from the sea water or from organic rich sediment
Inflated or large glabella and large pygidium	May be filled with fat or gas, which has been interpreted as a possible floatation device for buoyancy in water column
Very small size, some just 2 mm long and most <10 mm	Small to possibly stay afloat in water column
Few pleura	Few legs, which may be used as paddles or to steer animal Limited flexibility and movement restricted

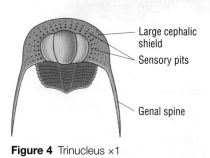

Figure 4 Trinucleus ×1

Nektonic (e.g. *Deiphon*)

These are small trilobites, which show some streamlining and have complex compound eyes on stalks. An inferred mode of life is pelagic, living in the water column and **nektonic**, actively swimming, possibly as active hunters.

Morphological feature	Probable function or reason
Eyes on stalks	Ability to see forwards, sideways, backwards and unusually underneath the animal. This means that it could also look down Complex eyes may mean that the animal was an active hunter or scavenger
Inflated or large glabella	May be filled with fat or gas, which has been interpreted as a possible floatation device for buoyancy in water column
Very small size	Small to stay afloat in water column
Numerous separated pleura, with spines	Had many legs for swimming The spines and separated pleura increased surface area to aid buoyancy

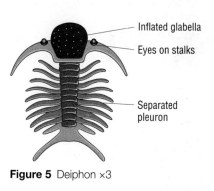

Figure 5 Deiphon ×3

Burrowing (e.g. *Trinucleus*)

These trilobites lack eyes and have a shovel-shaped modified cephalon with pits running along its margins. The inferred mode of life is benthonic, living on the substrate as epifaunal organisms or **infaunal**. They may have dug shallow burrows for protection or probably to feed on the organic-rich sediment. Eyes would have been useless at the estimated 200 m depth where these trilobites lived, where light does not penetrate.

Morphological feature	Probable function or reason
No eyes (blind)	Lack of eyes means that the animal was unlikely to hunt and its food source was probably available in the environment as organic-rich sediment
Wide cephalic fringe (large cephalon)	Maybe used to spread its mass on soft substrate or as a digging tool to produce shallow burrows
Extended genal spines	To spread its mass on soft substrate As a defence against predators
Pitted cephalic fringe	Pits may have housed sensory hairs in life These may have been able to detect the movement of prey and water currents on the sea floor, chemicals or temperature

Questions

1 Explain why some trilobites evolved wide cephalic fringes.
2 List two adaptations of a benthonic trilobite.
3 List the differences between the adaptations of a pelagic and a nektonic trilobite.
4 Research a range of other trilobites looking for variations in size, in number of thoracic segments, in defensive spines and in the size and shape of eyes.

Corals belong to the phylum **Cnidaria**, which includes sea anemones and jellyfish. Although simple marine organisms, their bodies consist of two layers, an outer ectoderm and an inner endoderm, **stinging** cells called **nematoblasts**. Corals themselves belong to the class **Anthozoa** and have a calcium carbonate skeleton, which is of immense importance in the geological record. Early corals evolved in the Cambrian and modern corals are alive today.

Figure 1 Coral polyps (×1)

Coral morphology

The modern-day coral **polyp** is a soft bodied organism that secretes a calcium carbonate skeleton. The **corallum** is the whole skeleton of a solitary or colonial coral. There are two main types of coral, **solitary** and **compound**:

- Solitary corals have only one polyp, which secretes a single skeleton.
- Compound corals have many polyps living together in a communal fashion, with many skeletons or **corallites** fused together. Colonial forms have skeletons which may also branch.

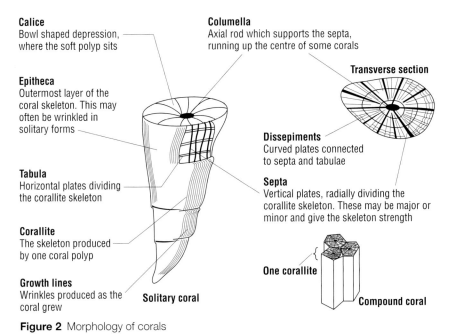

Figure 2 Morphology of corals

Rugose, tabulate and scleractinian corals – what is the difference?

There are three main orders that are important in the fossil record: **Rugosa**, **Tabulata** and **Scleractinia**. At first glance they look similar, but there are differences between these three types, which are illustrated in the diagram and highlighted in the table of comparison below.

Rugose corals

These extinct corals are either solitary or colonial. The **epitheca**, or outer layer, is often wrinkled in solitary forms and they may be 'horn shaped'. The corallites are usually large with no mural pores or connections between the corallites. They show one plane of symmetry, known as **bilateral** symmetry. This symmetry is picked out by the distinct septa, the plates that run vertically in the skeleton. When the corals started to grow, there were initially six primary septa. New septa were only added in four of the resulting spaces (see diagram showing septa). This complex arrangement of the septa is diagnostic of rugose corals. They always have a columella and may have dissepiments between the septa, but these were not always present.

Tabulate corals

These extinct corals are always colonial with well developed tabulae. The corallites are usually small and mural pores may be present in some species. They show **radial** symmetry, but the development of septa is either poor or absent. They may have dissepiments, but they were not always present and they do not have a columella.

Scleractinian corals

These corals are either solitary or colonial and they form reefs today. The corallites are usually small with no mural pores between the colonial forms. They show radial symmetry, known as **hexagonal** symmetry. This symmetry is picked out by the distinct septa in the skeleton, which shows six primary septa and evenly developed secondary septa between them. They may have dissepiments and they always have tabulae.

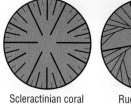

Scleractinian coral   Rugose coral

Figure 3 Septal growth in rugose and scleractinian corals

	Type of coral		
	Rugose	**Tabulate**	**Scleractinian**
Geological range	Ordovician to Permian (extinct)	Cambrian to Permian (extinct)	Triassic to Recent (extant)
Tabulae	Always present	Present and well developed	Always present
Corallites	Large	Many small	Many small
Dissepiments	Sometimes present	None or sometimes reduced	Always present
Symmetry	Bilateral	Radial	Radial
Columella	Always present	Not present	May be present
Septa	Major septa at 6 points, with 4 sets of minor septa	Sometimes present but reduced or poor	Major septa at 6 points radially
Colonial/solitary	Colonial or solitary	Always colonial	Colonial or solitary
Mural pores	None	Mural pores may be present	None
Example	*Lithostrotian* sp.	*Halysites* sp.	*Thecosmilia* sp.

Key definitions

Mural pores are connections between adjacent corallites, perhaps for communication.

Bilateral symmetry is where something has one plane of symmetry with two identical halves.

Radial symmetry is where many planes of symmetry can be seen.

Extant describes a species that still exists today.

Colonial
Many corallites together

Tabulae
Well developed

Mural pores
May be present

Transverse section
Tabulate coral (×1)

Longitudinal section
Tabulate coral (×1)

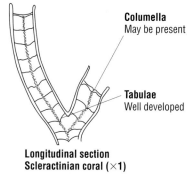

Columella
May be present

Tabulae
Well developed

Longitudinal section
Scleractinian coral (×1)

Dissepiments
May be present

Septa
Well developed, showing six fold radial symmetry

Transverse section
Scleractinian coral (×1)

Figure 4 Tabulate and scleractinian corals

Questions

1 List the main morphological features of a coral.
2 Give one characteristic of rugose, tabulate and scleractinian corals that may be used to tell each order apart.
3 Use the Internet to find photos showing the main different types of coral. Label any features that you recognise.

How do modern corals live?

The present is the key to the past. We often work out how extinct animals lived by looking at their modern-day counterparts. Looking at corals today, we find some species have a type of algae living inside them. These algae, a dinoflagellate, are called **zooxanthellae**. There is a **symbiotic relationship** between the algae and the coral. The zooxanthellae can photosynthesise as they contain many chloroplasts inside their cells. They take the carbon dioxide, phosphates and nitrates produced as waste from the coral and use them to produce oxygen, water, amino acids and sugars. The coral uses the waste from the zooxanthellae, as they in turn use the coral waste. These organisms cannot survive without each other and the success of coral reefs is dependent upon this relationship.

Soft tissue

The soft tissue is not preserved, but we assume that fossil corals had similar soft tissue to modern-day corals. Soft bodied **polyps** sit on top of the hard secreted skeleton, or **calice**. The polyp itself has tentacles, which it extends for feeding purposes, usually at night. Food particles in the water or zooplankton are extracted, sometimes paralysed with the aid of the stinging cells, or they may become trapped in mucus, which is secreted from the polyp. Whatever the method, food is passed to the mouth and into a primitive gut for digestion. Undigested material and waste is removed through the mouth, as they do not have an anus. This sort of feeding is in addition to the nutrients supplied by the zooxanthellae.

Conditions needed for good coral growth

Some corals can be found in all seas and oceans. These are usually solitary corals, which can survive in temperate or tropical waters. Reef building corals require more specific conditions to be able to grow and survive. For this reason, they only occupy a zone between 30 degrees north and 30 degrees south of the Equator, and are considered to be tropical. They need:

- to be at or just below sea level. Water depth is important as light is filtered out at depth. Few reef building corals are found below 30 m;
- clear waters, as they need sunlight so the algae that live within them can photosynthesise;
- water needs to be free from particles of mud or sediment that may clog the polyps. This means that they tend to be offshore and far from rivers or other sources of sediment;
- high-energy levels or wave action, as this incorporates more oxygen into the water and circulates the correct level of nutrients by upwelling;
- fully marine, with a salinity of 30–40 parts per thousand;
- temperature between 23 and 27 °C.

Global distribution (modern-day reefs)

Most coral reefs are found between 30 degrees north and 30 degrees south of the Equator. They are found generally on continental shelves, close to land or as coral islands or atolls in the oceans. Good examples of modern coral reefs are: the Great Barrier Reef, Australia; many of the islands in the Caribbean, such as the Bahamas; and the Maldives in the Indian Ocean. We assume that the distribution of fossil reefs was controlled by the same factors as modern-day reefs.

Figure 1 Photos showing modern-day corals (×1)

Key definitions

Zooxanthellae is a type of algae (dinoflagellate) that lives inside modern-day coral cells.

Symbiotic relationship describes two organisms living together for mutual benefit, neither of which can successfully live without the other.

Coral bleaching is where a small increase in temperature or pollution causes the polyps to die, killing the reef.

Modern-day coral problems

It has been found that modern-day corals are very sensitive to environmental change. Very small changes in temperature can cause **coral bleaching** to occur. There are, of course, many modern-day threats to coral reefs, such as global changes (El Nino and La Nina), overfishing, dredging and pollution.

How are modern reefs formed?

There are several types of modern reefs:

- Fringing reefs meet the land and some parts may be above sea level at low tide.
- Barrier reefs are further out to sea, with a lagoon separating the land from the reef.
- Atolls or coral islands are ring-shaped reefs found far offshore. The formation of atolls is due to hot spot activity as the volcanoes create an area of shallow sea. The weight of the volcano means that the crust gradually sinks and the Moho sags below the shield volcano.

The coral growth needs to be fast enough to keep pace with the subsidence. Modern-day reefs grow at between 1 and 10 cm per year. The thickness of the reef will increase over time, as it grows up and forms a massive unbedded reef limestone.

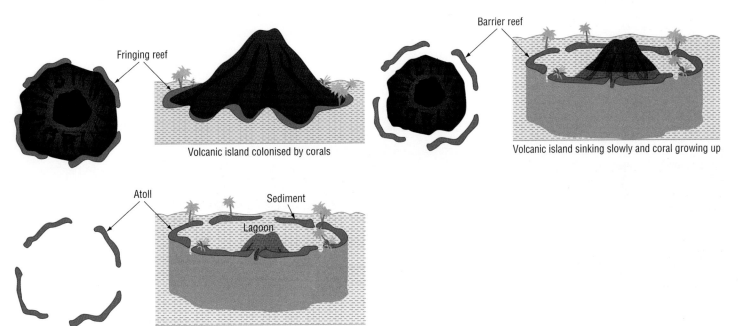

Fringing reef

Volcanic island colonised by corals

Barrier reef

Volcanic island sinking slowly and coral growing up

Atoll

Sediment

Lagoon

Volcanic island sinking below sea level and sediment forming from broken coral fragments

Figure 2 Formation of coral reefs (height exaggerated)

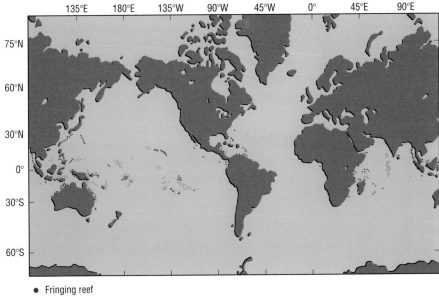

- Fringing reef
- Barrier reef
- Atolls

Figure 3 Map showing modern-day distribution of reefs in the tropical regions where there is shallow water. They are most common on the windward side of landmasses, such as the Great Barrier Reef on the east coast of Australia

Questions

1 Describe the environmental conditions needed for good coral growth.
2 Describe and explain the symbiotic relationship between modern corals and zooxanthellae.
3 Research and find the global position of fossil reef systems (Carboniferous, Devonian and Silurian).

What are brachiopods?

These are benthonic, sessile, marine organisms enclosed between two unequal-sized valves. They may be attached to the substrate, free lying or more rarely, burrowers. They evolved during the Cambrian Period, becoming widespread and dominant in the fossil record, especially during the Palaeozoic Era. They are still alive today, but are greatly reduced in numbers. Brachiopods were almost wiped out at the Permian–Triassic extinction event and there were also major losses at the Triassic–Jurassic boundary.

Classification

Brachiopods belong to the phylum **Brachiopoda** and are considered a minor phylum today.

Most brachiopods possess **teeth** and **sockets**, have shells made of calcium carbonate and have a mineralised **lophophore support structure** inside their shells. These are numerous in the fossil record and are an important part of fossil assemblages from many different environments.

Some brachiopods do not possess teeth and sockets and do not have diductor muscles. Most construct their shells from **chitin** and **calcium phosphate**, rather than calcium carbonate. They are smooth and small, with an oval or circular outline. As they have never existed in large numbers, they are geologically unimportant, and the species have remained relatively unchanged since the Cambrian Period. *Lingula*, a burrower, is an example of an inarticulate brachiopod.

Brachiopod morphology

Each valve shows **bilateral** symmetry, meaning that the whole organism is not symmetrical along the hinge line, just centrally bisecting the valves down a median plane. The valves themselves are of uneven sizes. Modern-day brachiopod shell sizes range from less than 5 mm to just over 8 cm, and a few gigantic forms have been found measuring 38.5 cm in width.

The **pedicle valve** has the pedicle foramen through which a fleshy stalk, the **pedicle**, protrudes. The pedicle attaches the brachiopod to the sea floor. It is made of muscle and so has the ability to align the brachiopod into the current. Some brachiopods did not have a pedicle and must have rested freely on, or just within the substrate. The **brachial valve** contains supports for the lophophore.

How do modern brachiopods live?

Studies of modern-day brachiopods show us the soft tissues and the other internal structures of the animal (Figure 1). We can then compare structures from the fossil record and infer the mode of life of fossil forms.

Shell secretion

The shell is secreted by the soft tissue of the mantle inside of the shell. This is similar to bivalves, but this similarity has arisen by independent paths of evolution, as the bivalves and brachiopods evolved from completely different soft-bodied ancestors.

Case study

Lingula has changed little since the Cambrian period. Modern *Lingula* lives successfully in brackish or shallow intertidal conditions. It is thought that fossil forms may have inhabited other environments too. The pedicle (a muscle) extends deep into the burrow acting like a foot. When disturbed, the pedicle contracts and the brachiopod sinks low into the burrow for protection.

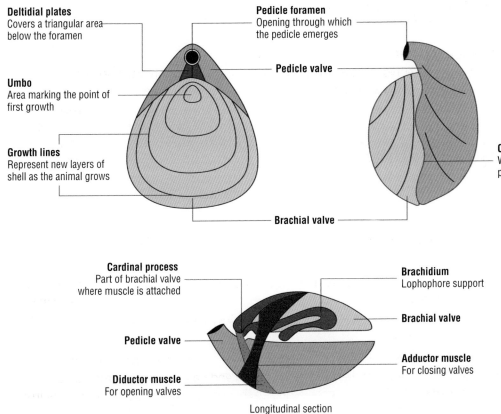

Deltidial plates
Covers a triangular area below the foramen

Pedicle foramen
Opening through which the pedicle emerges

Pedicle valve

Umbo
Area marking the point of first growth

Growth lines
Represent new layers of shell as the animal grows

Commisure
Where brachial and pedicle valves meet

Brachial valve

Cardinal process
Part of brachial valve where muscle is attached

Brachidium
Lophophore support

Brachial valve

Pedicle valve

Adductor muscle
For closing valves

Diductor muscle
For opening valves

Longitudinal section

Figure 1 Morphology of brachiopods

Feeding

All members of this phylum are filter feeders. They feed with the aid of a **lophophore**. The lophophore takes up about two-thirds of the space inside the shell, with the body of the animal occupying the remaining third. The lophophore is fluid-filled, covered on the outside by a large number of sticky filaments lined with **cilia**. The beating of the cilia generates currents, which bring in fresh water and removes waste water. The filaments act as a net for trapping food particles, which are then passed down a groove to the mouth. They feed on microscopic organisms and particles of organic matter.

Filter feeders make special efforts to separate water already filtered from fresh supplies. This is especially important for free-lying brachiopods, which may be closer to the sediment on the sea floor. One way of separating currents is a fold in the edge of the shell, which divides the inhalant and exhalent currents.

Opening and closing valves

To be able to feed the brachiopod has to open its valves to let in fresh water. It opens its valves by contracting the diductor muscles. These are attached to the cardinal process on the brachial valve and to the central part of the pedicle valve. The valves open, articulating on the teeth and sockets. To close the valves, the adductor muscles contract. The adductor muscles are attached to the central parts of both the pedicle and brachial valves. Where the muscles are attached, they leave a **muscle scar**. The muscle scars of fossil specimens are only occasionally seen, as brachiopods are usually found with both the shells joined together (articulated).

How science works

The modern terebratulid *Neothyris* is found living around the shores of New Zealand. The numbers are threatened here due to 'aquaculture', or farming in the sea.

The increase in sedimentation and changes in the water quality due to farming mussels and salmon alter the reproductive rate of the brachiopods. Trawling the seabed also destroys the habitat in which they live.

Such environmental sensitivity may have contributed to the decline of brachiopods throughout geological history.

Questions

1 Explain how the valves of the brachiopod can be opened and closed.
2 Describe how modern-day brachiopods feed.
3 Sketch a diagram, from memory, showing the external morphology of a brachiopod. Label as many features as possible.

Adaptive radiation

Brachiopods evolved into a variety of different shapes and sizes, probably as a response to the environment in which they lived and the selection pressures in that environment. Specific adaptations have been linked to three main environments: turbulent water, quiet water and a soft, muddy substrate.

Adaptations linked to turbulent water

Adaptation	Possible reason for adaptation
A large pedicle opening	To support a large pedicle for secure attachment to the substrate
Strongly ribbed valves	To strengthen shell against wave action
A folded or zigzagged margin	To reduce the amount and size of sediment moving into the shells when the valves are open
A thick and heavy shell	To provide extra stability on the substrate and prevent rolling in the current

Adaptations linked to quiet water

Adaptation	Possible reason for adaptation
May have a median fold or sulcus	To separate currents of water entering and leaving the animal. Prevents mixing of fresh water and waste
May have extension of the valves to form 'wings'	To provide a large surface area to prevent sinking into the sediment (quiet waters are often muddy environments)
Smooth or weakly ribbed valves	No need to be robust in quiet conditions.
No pedicle opening	Pedicle not needed for attachment

Adaptations linked to a soft, muddy substrate

Adaptation	Possible reason for adaptation
Valves flat with a large resting area	To provide a large surface area to prevent sinking into the sediment
One margin of the shell may be turned upwards, away from the sediment	To ensure that some part of the shell remains out of the sediment for feeding

Types of brachiopods

Brachiopods are classified on the external morphology of their shells, as the internal mineralisation is often difficult to see. Some of the common forms are described below and their mode of life is inferred.

Rhynchonellids – Ordovician to Recent (extant)

During the Mesozoic, these brachiopods are the most abundant. The hinge line is short and curved – **astrophic**. The shells are strongly ribbed so that they were able to cope with high-energy conditions. A small pedicle foramen is present, showing that they were attached to the sea floor. The **commisure**, the line between the two valves, is zigzagged so that the edge of the shell stops larger particles getting in. The strong **fold and sulcus** is also clearly developed in species of *Rhynchonella*, which were common in the Jurassic.

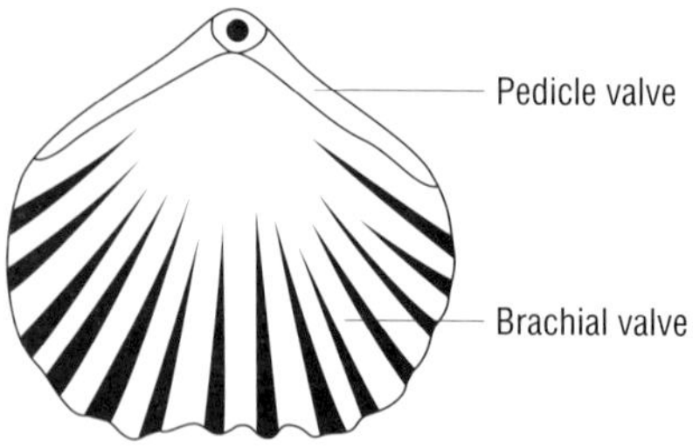

Rhynchonellid (x1)

Pedicle valve

Brachial valve

Figure 1 Rhynchonellid brachiopod showing strong ribbing

Spiriferids – Ordovician to Jurassic (extinct)

Spiriferids are easy to identify. They have a long straight (**strophic**) hinge line, which is so wide that they look winged. They often have a fold and sulcus in the middle of each valve. The feature that gives the spiriferids their name ('spiral-bearers') is the internal support for the lophophore. This lophophore support system is a spiral shape, called spirella. Spirifer was common in the Carboniferous. They were not attached but lay on the sea floor with the folded edge of the shell clear of the sediment for respiration and feeding.

Productids – Devonian to Permian (extinct)

The most characteristic Carboniferous brachiopods are the productids. The genus *Productus* itself was very abundant, with a wide geographical range, and some species are large, over 60 mm across. The shell is semicircular and thick, with a straight hinge line. The pedicle valve is usually large and strongly convex, helping the organism to stay in place on the sea floor, whilst the brachial valve is flat and lid-like or concave. Both valves have radiating ribs, with hollow tubular spines, often of great length. There is no opening for the pedicle so it is probable that the *Productus* used the long fragile spines on the pedicle valve to anchor themselves firmly in the mud or ooze of the sea floor.

Terebratulids – Devonian to Recent (extant)

Terebratulids are the most abundant brachiopods today but were also common in the Jurassic and Cretaceous. The hinge line is astrophic, being short and curved. They have a circular pedicle foramen where the foramen protruded from the valve for attachment to the sea floor. The smooth valves are ovoid, giving a streamlined shell shape. Many are found in oolites and sandstones, so we know they could live in high-energy environments.

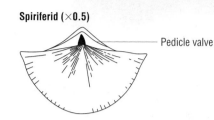

Spiriferid (×0.5)

Pedicle valve

Figure 2 Spiriferid brachiopod showing a long straight (strophic) hinge line or wings

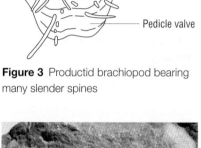

Productid

Spine

Pedicle valve

Figure 3 Productid brachiopod bearing many slender spines

Figure 4 Long hinged *Productus*

Pedicle foramen

Pedicle valve

Brachial valve

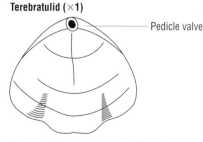

Terebratulid (×1)

Pedicle valve

Figure 5 Terebratulid brachiopod showing a curved (astrophic) hinge line and smooth valves

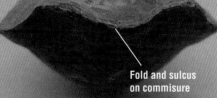

Fold and sulcus on commisure

Figure 6 *Terebratula*, showing three different views

Questions

1 Describe the morphological features that suggest a brachiopod lived in a turbulent sea.

2 Research the types of brachiopods that are alive today. What is their global distribution?

3 Describe and draw a diagram to show how brachiopods were attached to the sea floor.

Classification

Echinoids belong to the phylum **Echinodermata**, which includes crinoids, sea cucumbers and starfish. Organisms belonging to this phylum have **five-fold symmetry**, an obvious characteristic seen in starfish, which usually show five radiating legs. They also have soft tissue called **tube feet** in life.

Echinoids are also called sea urchins and belong to the class **Echinoidea**. There are two main types: **regular** echinoids showing five-fold radial symmetry and **irregular** echinoids showing **bilateral symmetry**. Irregular echinoids have evolved from regular echinoids.

Morphology – regular echinoids

The skeleton

This is called the **test**, and is in the shape of a hemisphere. It consists of many interlocking plates made of calcite, which define areas called **ambulacra** and **interambulacra**. There are ten of these areas in total, five ambulacra and five interambulacra, which alternately radiate from the top of the animal. This arrangement of plates gives the animal its five-fold symmetry. The ambulacra are narrower, consisting of two rows of plates, which are perforated by **pore pairs**. In life these would have **tube feet** protruding from them. The interambulacra are wider, again consisting of two rows of plates and may have tubercles on their surface. Tubercles have spines attached in life and there is a covering of soft tissue or skin over the outside of the test.

Key definitions

Five-fold symmetry means there are five planes of symmetry on the test, each giving a mirror image. These form a radial pattern.

Bilateral symmetry means there is only one plane of symmetry on the test.

Test is the name given to the skeleton of the echinoid, made of small plates of calcite.

Tube feet are the soft tissue, which extend out of the test through pairs of pores.

The **water vascular system** is the hydraulic system that allows the animal to extend its tube feet by forcing water into its tissues. The amount of water is controlled by the madreporite.

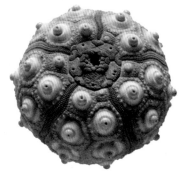

Figure 1 Regular echinoid

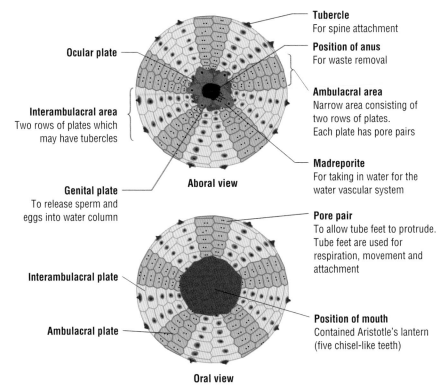

Figure 2 Regular echinoid morphology

The apical system

This is in the centre of the upper or aboral surface. The apical system or disc consists of ten plates arranged in two rings around a central anus. There are five **genital plates**; the largest of these is the **madreporite**, which is perforated by many tiny pores allowing water to enter the animal's **water vascular system**. In between these larger plates are smaller **ocular plates**. The anus itself is surrounded by a membrane, called the **periproct**. The anus and apical system is on the aboral surface allowing the waste, eggs and sperm to be taken away more easily by the currents.

The mouth

The mouth is in the centre of the lower or oral surface. The mouth itself is surrounded by a membrane, the peristome. The edges of the test are turned inwards, to produce a lip, called the **perignathic girdle**. This allows the feeding apparatus to be attached and supported inside the test. There are five jaws, each with a sharp single tooth supported inside the mouth, called **Aristotle's lantern**. These teeth can scrape algae or other food from the substrate and pass it inside the animal towards the gut. The mouth is on the underside to aid easy feeding.

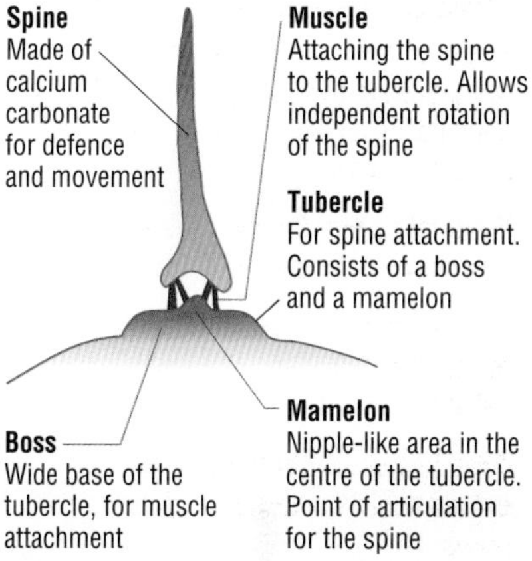

Tube feet

Tube feet have three main functions: attachment, movement and are also used as an exchange surface for respiration. They extend through the test, passing through the pore pairs and are part of the water vascular system. The exchange of oxygen and carbon dioxide takes place directly through their membranes. Water enters the animal through the madreporite and is eventually passed into the tube feet. Tube feet are also used to attach the animal to rocks, acting as suckers to secure them in place and helping the animal to move along the sea floor.

Spine
Made of calcium carbonate for defence and movement

Muscle
Attaching the spine to the tubercle. Allows independent rotation of the spine

Tubercle
For spine attachment. Consists of a boss and a mamelon

Boss
Wide base of the tubercle, for muscle attachment

Mamelon
Nipple-like area in the centre of the tubercle. Point of articulation for the spine

Figure 3 Echinoid spines and spine attachment

Spine attachment

Spines are attached to the test where the tubercles protrude on the interambulacral plates. The tubercles consist of two parts: the boss, a wide base, and the mamelon, a nipple-like structure in the centre of a boss. Muscle attaches the spine to the boss, and as muscle, it can contract and cause the spine to move in a coordinated manner. This means that the echinoid can rotate the spines and use them for walking. These spines are also used for defence against predators. After death the soft tissue (muscle) decays and the spines become disarticulated from the rest of the body.

Mode of life

Regular echinoids live on rocky shores, a high-energy environment, which is reflected by their robust test and spines. They feed by grazing on algae that live on the rocks or by scavenging for other food particles. The jaws scrape off the food and pass it to the gut. They move along the shore in any direction, clinging to rocks using tube feet and rotating their spines, essentially walking along the surface. The size of the tubercles reflects the size of the spines that can be attached. Larger tubercles can support large spines, which may be of a large mass. Spines also help defend the animal from predators.

Figure 4 Photo showing echinoid spines (×0.5)

Questions

1 Describe three functions of tube feet.
2 What are the features of animals that belong to the phylum Echinodermata?
3 Describe how regular echinoids lived.

Morphology – irregular echinoids

Irregular echinoids are characterised by having the anus outside of the apical system. The anus has moved towards the edge of the test, or towards the posterior. This means irregular echinoids are **heart**-shaped and have bilateral symmetry. These adaptations are to allow the irregular echinoid to live in a burrow. Examples include the Cretaceous form, *Micraster* and the modern-day sand dollar.

Mouth and adjacent areas

The mouth is still on the underside of the test, but often it has moved away from the centre. The mouth lacks jaws and the perignathic girdle found in regular echinoids. Instead the animal takes in particles from sea water and filters these. There is a large lip called the **labrum**, projecting on the lower side of the mouth. The labrum is used to direct the currents and prevent unwanted sediments getting into the mouth. Behind the labrum there is a modified set of interambulacral plates, forming the **plastron**. The plastron has small tubercles for attachment of spines. These small spines are used to help dig a burrow or for movement within it.

Petaloid ambulacra

The ambulacra do not extend all the way down from the top to the mouth, but form a flower-shaped structure called the **petaloid ambulacra**. These have many small pore pairs for tube feet on the top of the echinoid. The petaloid ambulacra at the anterior of the animal are larger than the others, and form the anterior groove. This is lined by **cilia**, which beat to generate currents to pass food particles to the mouth, and is called the fasciole. Very long tube feet extend from the anterior ambulacra, which are used to help dig the burrow and keep it stable.

Sub-anal fasciole

There is another modified area close to the anus, which has many beating cilia to take waste particles and direct them into the sanitary tube. The tube feet on the two posterior ambulacra are modified to keep the burrow clean and maintain the sanitary tube.

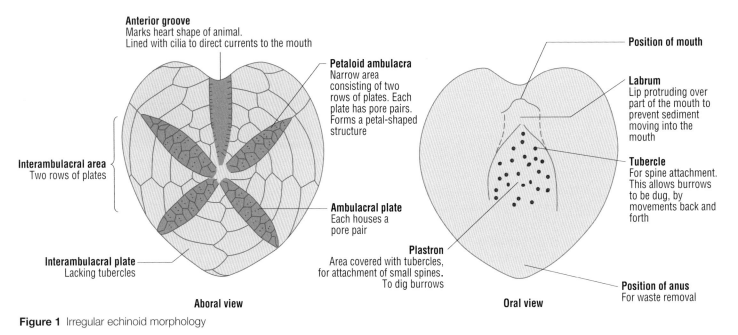

Anterior groove
Marks heart shape of animal.
Lined with cilia to direct currents to the mouth

Petaloid ambulacra
Narrow area consisting of two rows of plates. Each plate has pore pairs. Forms a petal-shaped structure

Interambulacral area
Two rows of plates

Interambulacral plate
Lacking tubercles

Ambulacral plate
Each houses a pore pair

Plastron
Area covered with tubercles, for attachment of small spines. To dig burrows

Aboral view

Position of mouth

Labrum
Lip protruding over part of the mouth to prevent sediment moving into the mouth

Tubercle
For spine attachment. This allows burrows to be dug, by movements back and forth

Position of anus
For waste removal

Oral view

Figure 1 Irregular echinoid morphology

Mode of life

Irregular echinoids usually live in soft sediment and in a low-energy environment (infaunal). They do not have jaws and have a reduced sized mouth area (peristome) because they filter feed. Instead they dig burrows, using the spines on the plastron. Irregular echinoids are often wedge-shaped so that they can move easily through the sediment. The cilia in the anterior groove beat to generate currents, which are directed to the mouth, where particles are removed. Cilia in the sub-anal fasciole also generate currents to remove waste and direct it into the anal tube. The echinoid respires by extending its tube feet from the petaloid ambulacra, up and out of the burrow, so that exchange of gases can occur. As irregular echinoids evolved, the petaloid ambulacra became longer, for more efficient gas exchange.

Differences between regular and irregular echinoids

A table of comparison is given below.

	Regular echinoid	Irregular echinoid
Mode of life	Benthonic, epifaunal Vagrant on the seabed High energy	Benthonic, infaunal Lives in burrows Low energy
Feeding	Uses jaws, called Aristotle's lantern to graze on seabed. Commonly eats algae which grow on rocks	Particle feeds. Extracts microorganisms from sea water
Symmetry	Five-fold radial (5 planes of symmetry)	Bilateral (1 plane of symmetry)
Ambulacra	Run from the centre of the aboral surface to the oral surface	Run from the centre of the aboral surface but terminate forming petaloid ambulacra
Interambulacra	Run from the centre of the aboral surface to the oral surface	Modified over test surface. Fused together over oral surface. Maybe modified, for example, one forms the plastron
Function of tube feet	Respiration, attachment and movement	Respiration, digging and maintaining the burrow and anal tube
Fascioles	Absent	Two present, one to direct water to the mouth and one to direct waste away from the echinoid

Case study

Micraster was an infaunal echinoid living in a burrow below the sediment surface. The test is clearly bilateral and there is a deep anterior groove to take water containing organic particles to the mouth. The tube feet keep a supply of nutrient-laden water moving into the burrow. The anus has a waste tube behind it.

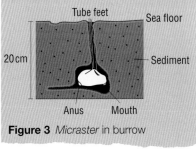

Figure 3 *Micraster* in burrow

Case study

Sand dollars are alive today but there are similar fossils, *Clypeaster*, found in Jurassic rocks. The test is covered with short, movable, fur-like spines that aid in movement through sand while feeding. The aboral surface has five petalloid ambulacra. The petalloid ambulacra also contain tube feet that are used for respiration. The sand dollar can bury itself by pushing through the substrate at a slight angle. When excavated, they can rebury themselves in 6–12 minutes.

They feed upon the organic material, including diatoms, found in the coarse biogenic sands in which they are buried.

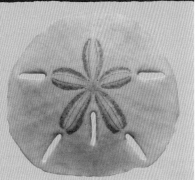

Figure 2 Sand dollar, an irregular echinoid

Questions

1 Describe the differences in morphology between regular and irregular echinoids.

2 Explain the reasons why the anus and mouth migrate in irregular echinoids?

3 What other features may have changed in an irregular echinoid as it evolved over time?

Classification

Bivalves are geologically very widespread, having evolved to live in most aquatic environments. They evolved in the Cambrian and are alive today (extant). They belong to the phylum **Mollusca**, which includes familiar creatures such as cuttlefish, squid and snails. Bivalves themselves belong to the class **Bivalvia** and may live in marine or fresh water. Common modern-day bivalves are cockles, clams, scallops, razor shells and mussels.

Morphology

The most distinctive characteristic of bivalves is that they have two calcareous valves, which are usually of equal size (**equivalve**). Most bivalves have a plane of symmetry running along the hinge line. A few have valves of unequal sizes (**inequivalve**).

Valves may be either **left** or **right**, depending on the direction in which the umbone is pointing. If you hold the shell with the umbone pointing away from you, then the valve on the left is the left valve and the one on the right is the right valve. The **umbone** sits directly above the **hinge line**, where the valves are joined together. The hinge itself consists of protruding teeth and sunken pit-like sockets. These articulate against one another when the valves open and close, keeping the structure stable. On the outside of the shell, where the valves are joined, is the hinge plate. A ligament covers this area in life, either internally or externally, but it decays on death.

Some bivalves have valves that close completely; others have a gape or opening where soft body parts such as a foot or **siphon** may extend. Gapes tend to be features belonging to burrowing bivalves. The outside of the valves may show growth lines or ornament.

Internal morphology

The shell itself is secreted by the **mantle**, part of the soft tissue inside the bivalve. The position of the soft tissue is marked by the **pallial line** on the inside of the shell. There may be a pallial **sinus** or bend in the pallial line. This is present when the animal had siphons, which it extended out of the shell. Pallial lines and sinuses are evident in fossil and modern bivalves. Other indications of the soft tissue are the muscle scars. These are where strong **muscles** attached to the shell, enabling it to be closed. The gills are not preserved in fossil bivalves (Figure 1).

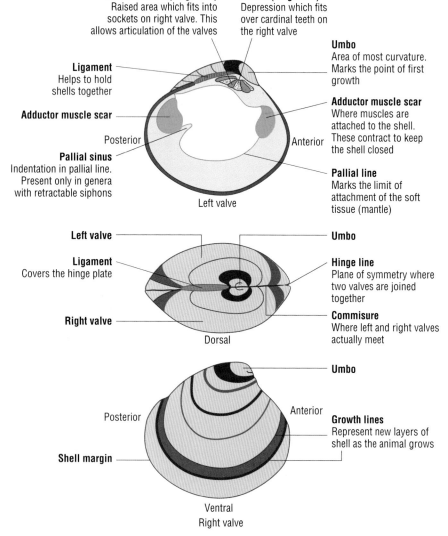

Cardinal teeth (hinge line)
Raised area which fits into sockets on right valve. This allows articulation of the valves

Socket (hinge line)
Depression which fits over cardinal teeth on the right valve

Umbo
Area of most curvature. Marks the point of first growth

Ligament
Helps to hold shells together

Adductor muscle scar
Where muscles are attached to the shell. These contract to keep the shell closed

Adductor muscle scar

Posterior

Anterior

Pallial sinus
Indentation in pallial line. Present only in genera with retractable siphons

Pallial line
Marks the limit of attachment of the soft tissue (mantle)

Left valve

Left valve

Umbo

Ligament
Covers the hinge plate

Hinge line
Plane of symmetry where two valves are joined together

Right valve

Commisure
Where left and right valves actually meet

Dorsal

Umbo

Posterior

Anterior

Growth lines
Represent new layers of shell as the animal grows

Shell margin

Ventral
Right valve

Figure 1 Bivalve morphology

How to tell the difference between bivalves and brachiopods

Morphological Features	Bivalves	Brachiopods
Shell shape and symmetry	Bilaterally symmetrical about a plane passing between the two valves Each valve is asymmetrical about a line from the umbo to the ventral margin Two identical valves – left and right	Always bilaterally symmetrical about a plane from the umbo to the anterior margin Each valve is symmetrical about a line from the umbo to the anterior margin Two different size valves – larger pedicle valve and smaller brachial valve
Composition of shell	Calcareous and partly organic in 3 layers	Calcareous
Shell size	A few mm to 1 m (giant clam)	Generally 2–10 cm
Opening and closing mechanisms	A pair of adductor muscles contract to keep the valves closed When muscles are relaxed the external ligament pulls the valves open. They leave a pair of muscle scars at the anterior and posterior Some bivalves have only one central muscle – monomyarian	Adductor – muscles contract to close the valves. They leave a pair of muscle scars in the pedicle valve and two pairs in the brachial valve Diductor – muscles contract to open the valves. Two pairs run from the floor of the pedicle valve to the cardinal process in the brachial valve
Umbos	First formed part of the shell lies in front of the ligament on both valves	First formed part of the shell top portion of both valves
Growth lines	Concentric markings parallel to the edge of the shell	Concentric markings parallel to the edge of the shell
Ribs	Radial markings forming from fine lines to coarse ribs and grooves	Radiating lines from the umbo of the shell
Foot	Found at the posterior end used for movement and digging	None
Pedicle	None	Pedicle for attachment to rocks
Orientation of valves	Right and left valves hinged on the dorsal surface of the body by the ligament. Separate along the other margins, distinguished as anterior, ventral, posterior	Ventral side of body is known as the pedicle valve. Dorsal side is brachial valve. Pedicle valve is larger projecting at the posterior end beyond the brachial valve. The opposite margin is the anterior
Pallial line and sinus	Clearly seen around the margin of the shell	None
Respiration and feeding	Gills	Lophophore attached by brachial supports
Teeth and socket	Dentition – collective term for teeth and sockets all along the hinge plate. Cardinal teeth under umbo and lateral teeth beyond umbo or many similar teeth and sockets all along the hinge plate	Two teeth within the hinge apparatus of the pedicle valve. Socket – this is where the teeth fit into two sockets in the brachial valve

Questions

1 Describe how modern-day bivalves feed.
2 Give two examples of modern-day bivalves.
3 Explain the difference in symmetry between equivalve bivalves and brachiopods. Use labelled diagrams.

Figure 1 Photo of *Mytilus* attached to rocks in the littoral zone (×0.5)

Byssally attached

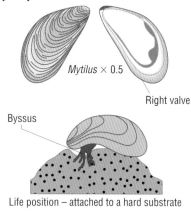

Mytilus × 0.5

Right valve

Byssus

Life position – attached to a hard substrate

Figure 2 Morphology of *Mytilus* – a byssally attached bivalve

How do modern bivalves live?

Studies of modern bivalves show us the soft tissues and internal structures of the animals. Bivalves have evolved to exploit most ecological niches:

- can be benthonic vagrant forms
- fixed to the substrate with cement or by using a byssus
- be freelying
- shallow or deep burrowers.

Some are found in high-energy shallow seas, others in calm waters of the continental shelf. There are forms that can live in fresh water and brackish water, as well as the sea. One form of clam has been found living close to the smokers of hot sulfide-rich water at mid-ocean ridges, at great depths where the pressure is high and there is no light.

Feeding

They feed by using **siphons**, which extend either to the edge of the shell or some way out of the shell. There are **inhalant** and an **exhalent** siphons. The inhalant siphon brings in fresh water and the exhalant siphon removes waste water. This is an example of evolution, so that fresh and used water do not mix. Particles are removed from the water by the gills, therefore they are filter feeders. Burrowing bivalves have long siphons to reach the top of their burrow.

Opening and closing valves

To be able to feed, the bivalve has to open and close its valves to let in fresh water. Adductor muscles contract to keep the shell closed in life, which is why shellfish such as mussels open on cooking and disarticulate on death. Where the muscles are attached, they leave a **muscle scar**. The muscle scars of fossil specimens can be seen in disarticulated specimens. The valves are opened by a ligament.

Moving

Some bivalves are vagrant and can move around using a muscular foot. Many bivalves are burrowers, and the foot is used to burrow into the sediment. Some bivalves are sessile and do not move on or in the seabed.

How epifaunal bivalves have adapted to their environment

Bivalves evolved into a variety of different shapes and sizes. We are going to look at three different types of epifaunal bivalves and consider their adaptations and relate them to different modes of life. The three genera we are going to use as examples are *Mytilus*, *Ostrea* and *Gryphaea*. The adaptations are to prevent the organism from being washed away by high-energy tides and currents and to exploit different substrates.

Mytilus type – byssally attached

A **byssus** is a thread-like structure that attaches the bivalve to the substrate, usually a rock. Some juvenile bivalves may use a primitive byssus for stability. Only a few bivalves continue to use them into adulthood. An example today is *Mytilus*, or the common mussel. Mussels are moved around by the currents when the tide is in, so that they can filter feed.

Morphological feature	Probable function or reason
Byssus	Attachment to a hard substrate (rock), or another shell by the strong and flexible byssus. This allows it to live in very high-energy conditions in the littoral zone
Shell covered in a layer of periostracum	To protect itself from acidic rainwater or river water
Strong shell	To prevent breakage of the shell when collisions occur in high-energy littoral environment
Streamlined and unornamented shells	No sharp edges to cause damage to itself or others in the colony and for protection against strong currents
Large adductor muscles	To hold the valves tightly together to stop the shell drying out at low tide

Ostrea type – cemented

Ostrea are a type of oyster. Modern-day oyster larvae attach to the sea floor when they find a suitable substrate, by secreting **cement** from the mantle. They always become attached by their left valves. Oysters often take on the shape of their substrate. Any irregularities in the left valve are reflected in the right. The left valve is generally larger than the right valve. They have a single large adductor muscle.

Morphological feature	Probable function or reason
Cement	Attachment to a hard substrate (rock)
Strong, thick shell	To withstand high-energy currents
Strong adductor muscle	To be able to keep heavy shells closed in high-energy conditions and be able to open them to filter feed
Right and left valves of different sizes. Uneven shells with irregularities	The larger left valve is cemented to the rock and the smaller right valve is like a lid. It enables the valves to close exactly when not feeding. The shell irregularities are often the same shape as the substrate

Gryphaea type – free lying

Gryphaea are a type of extinct oyster, so we assume that they had a similar life cycle to modern-day oysters. They were not attached to the substrate, but simply **rested** on a **convex left valve**. As a result, the left valve was much larger than the right. This gave a 'snowshoe effect' to the **resting area** of the bivalve, preventing it from sinking into the sediment. These are often found in mudstones and calcareous mudstones, which would have been soft mud when the animals were alive.

Morphological feature	Probable function or reason
Large curved and rounded left valve	Large resting area, which means that there is a large surface area of the bivalve in contact with the substrate. This prevents the bivalve sinking in soft mud. It is not attached but uses the weight of the valve to keep it in place
Small right valve – lid-like	Ensures that the centre of gravity is low for stability, to stop the bivalve being turned over in the currents
Strong, thick shell with lots of growth lines	To withstand high-energy currents. Curved shape helps keep the feeding edge of the shell above the sediment

Cemented

Ostrea × 0.5

Right valve

Life position – attached to a hard substrate

Figure 3 Morphology of *Ostrea* – a cemented bivalve

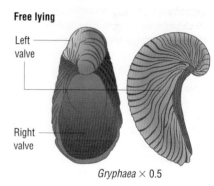

Free lying

Left valve

Right valve

Gryphaea × 0.5

Right valve

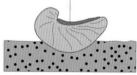

Life position – resting on a soft substrate

Figure 4 Morphology of *Gryphaea* – a free-lying bivalve

Key definitions

The **snowshoe effect** describes the rounded large resting area, which means that the bivalve does not sink into the sediment.

A **soft substrate** is a fine sediment, such as mud or clay.

Questions

1 Explain how the smooth, elongate shape of a mussel is adapted to live in a high-energy environment.
2 How do strong growth lines contribute to shell strength?
3 Explain why free lying and cemented bivalves have different sized valves.

Adaptations of infaunal and nektonic bivalves

How infaunal bivalves have adapted to their environment

Burrowing bivalves have developed shell types and strategies to enable them to live in shallow, medium and deep burrows. They generally have elongated valves; the longer the valves the deeper the ability to burrow. They need substantial **siphons** to be able to extend them out of the burrow. If the burrow is deep, then the siphons are long and the pallial sinus is large. We are going to look at two different types of modern burrowing bivalve and consider their adaptations and relate them to different modes of life. The two species we are going to use as examples are *Cytherea* and *Solen*. The same ideas can be applied to fossil and extinct forms of bivalves.

Throughout this section, refer both to the diagram of bivalve morphology in spread 5.2.9a and the diagram of the different morphological types of infaunal bivalve.

Shallow burrowers

Cytherea is a type of clam that is benthonic and commonly lives in a sandy substrate. It has a shallow pallial sinus, which indicates short siphons. The shell is rounded and the valves close completely, indicating that it is a shallow burrower.

Morphological feature	Probable function or reason
Ribs or strong growth lines	To help grip the sediment when burrowing. Some do not have this feature
Small pallial sinus and no gape between the shells	Indicates short siphons, which are completely retractable
An unornamented and streamlined shell with growth lines	To enable it to move easily through the sediment to form a burrow. Some do not have this feature
Large adductor muscle scars	For attachment of large muscles needed to open and close the valves in a burrow. The burrow may be in a high-energy environment, perhaps the littoral zone
Ability to completely close valves	This gives protection from predators and from desiccation, so they can live in the littoral zone

Deep burrowers

Solen is a type of razor shell that commonly lives in a sandy substrate. It has a very deep pallial sinus, which indicates very long siphons. The shell is extremely elongate and the valves do not close completely, giving it a permanent gape both to the **anterior** and the **posterior**. The shell is smooth.

Morphological feature	Probable function or reason
Large pallial sinus	Indicates long siphons
Unornamented and streamlined, very elongate shell	To enable it to move easily up and down through the sediment in a burrow. When the tide is in, it moves up to feed and down again when the tide goes out
Small adductor muscle scars	There is no need to open and close the valves in the burrow. The burrows may be in a high-energy environment, perhaps the littoral zone
Anterior and posterior gapes	The gapes indicate that the siphons and foot cannot be retracted into the burrow. The strong muscular foot moves the bivalve up and down and the siphons are for feeding and respiration

Case study

The burrowing cycle:
1. The bivalve extends the muscular foot down into the sediment (sand or mud) and inflates the end of the foot.
2. The adductor muscles contract, closing the shell and forcing blood into the foot, causing it to inflate further. Water is also forced out of the shell at this stage.
3. The foot anchors the bivalve in place and the bivalve pulls itself down through the sediment.
4. The adductor muscles relax and the foot can be retracted. The bivalve then sinks down into the sediment.
5. This may then be repeated to burrow deeper.

Key definitions

The **anterior** part of a bivalve is where the siphons extend out of the shell.

Infaunal means living in the sediment, usually in a burrow.

The **littoral zone** is an area between high and low tide. This is a very high-energy environment.

Nektonic means actively swims in the water column.

Monomyarian bivalves have a single powerful adductor muscle.

The **posterior** part of a bivalve is where the foot extends out of the shell.

Retractable means that siphons can be withdrawn completely inside the shell when the bivalve is not filter feeding.

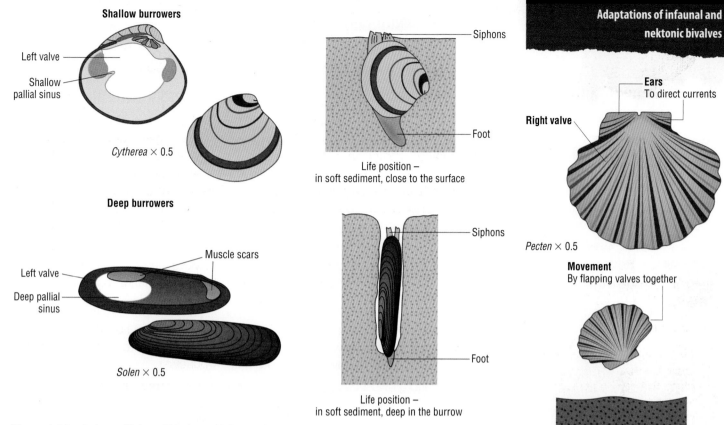

Figure 1 Morphology of infaunal bivalves

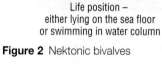

Figure 2 Nektonic bivalves

How nektonic bivalves have adapted to their environment

These swimming bivalves have a single powerful adductor muscle (**monomyarian**) to close the valves to expel water and move the bivalve. The internal ligament acts in opposition and opens the valves. The valves are flattened on one side and rounded on the other, rather like an aeroplane wing. This makes swimming more efficient. The valves themselves are thin, but corrugated with ribs. They have 'ears' or extensions around the umbone to direct water currents. The species we are going to look at is *Pecten,* or scallop. *Pecten* does not swim in the water column all of the time, rather as a response to escape from predators in short bursts. The same morphological ideas can be applied to fossil and extinct forms of bivalves.

Morphological feature	Probable function or reason
Ribbed, corrugated thin valves	Corrugated valves give strength without the weight of a thick shell, rather like cardboard. So the shell can be thin but strong
One flattened valve and one curved	Gives a hydrofoil effect to allow movement through the water when swimming. Keeps the animal free of the sediment when resting on the sea floor
Monomyarian adductor muscle	One large, central, strong muscle needed to repeatedly contract to close the valves. An internal ligament opens the valves
Have 'ears' extending the hinge line to give a long straight line	These direct the water currents away from the shell. The movement of the bivalve points towards the umbone. The hinge line improves stability
Numerous tiny eyes in the edge of the mantle among the sensory tentacles	Eyes are able to sense shadows or movement so if a predator such as a starfish casts a shadow the scallop will close the shell or swim away

Questions

1 List the features of a deep burrowing fossil bivalve.
2 Explain how nektonic bivalves swim.
3 Describe the type of muscles that you would find in the following types of bivalve: burrower, free lying, cemented and nektonic.

Classification

Gastropods belong to the phylum **Mollusca**, class **Gastropoda**. They are now the most abundant group of molluscs and show adaptations to live in a wide range of environments. Although most are shallow marine animals, they have adapted to fresh water and are found on land (although they do not like it too dry). Modern examples include whelks, snails and slugs.

How would you recognise a gastropod?

This is easy as the animal is still in existence and it is recognised by its soft parts. This gives us a problem when considering fossil examples, as the soft tissue is usually not preserved.

How do modern gastropods live?

The gastropod has a recognisable **head** with tentacles for sensing its surroundings. This marks the anterior for the animal. It crawls along on a muscular **foot** with the rest of its soft parts tucked up inside the shell. To manage this, its guts have had to twist through 180 degrees, which is the biological distinguishing characteristic of a gastropod. When threatened, the whole body can be withdrawn into the shell.

As the gastropod grows it does so by laying down calcium carbonate (mostly aragonite) on the lips of the aperture. The outer lip grows faster than the inner to achieve coiling as well as increase in size. Each complete coil is called a **whorl**. The soft body occupies the last whorl, which can therefore be termed the **body chamber.** The rest coils up to the apex to make up the **spire**.

Types of coiling

Most of the coiling is right-handed or **dextral**, which ends up with a view of the open end, or aperture on the right. Coiling to the left is known as **sinistral**. The shell itself is usually a single conical tube, coiled in a spiral (helical). A good way to distinguish a gastropod from a cephalopod, is that there are no chambers within the shell. The internal morphology can be seen when the fossil has been broken, eroded or cut. Not all gastropods show **helical** coiling, as some, notably freshwater species, are coiled in a plane (**planispiral**) and some strange cephalopods show helical coiling.

Key definitions

The **apex** is the point at which growth and coiling begins.

The **body chamber** is the last whorl in which the soft parts are housed.

Dextral describes the coiling of the shell to the right.

Helical means coiled to form a spire.

Planispiral means coiled in a single plane, a flat spiral, rather than the normal helical spire.

Siphon means that the mantle is extended as a tube, which allows clean water to be directed onto the gills.

Sinistral describes the coiling of the shell to the left.

The **spire** includes all the whorls, except the last whorl.

A **whorl** is one complete coil of the shell.

Examiner tip

In order to display the important features of the shell, they are drawn with the spire pointing upwards and the interesting parts of the aperture facing you. When you are interpreting diagrams to compare modes of life, it helps to remember how that shell would be orientated when it was alive.

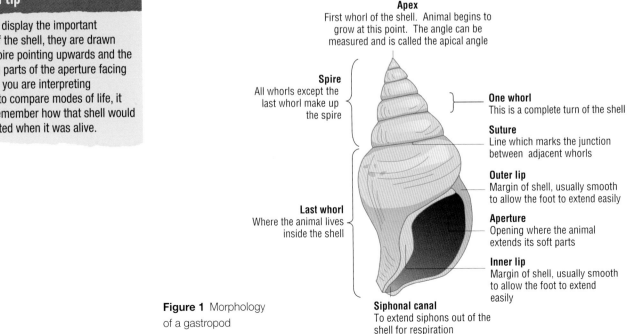

Apex
First whorl of the shell. Animal begins to grow at this point. The angle can be measured and is called the apical angle

Spire
All whorls except the last whorl make up the spire

One whorl
This is a complete turn of the shell

Suture
Line which marks the junction between adjacent whorls

Outer lip
Margin of shell, usually smooth to allow the foot to extend easily

Last whorl
Where the animal lives inside the shell

Aperture
Opening where the animal extends its soft parts

Inner lip
Margin of shell, usually smooth to allow the foot to extend easily

Siphonal canal
To extend siphons out of the shell for respiration

Figure 1 Morphology of a gastropod

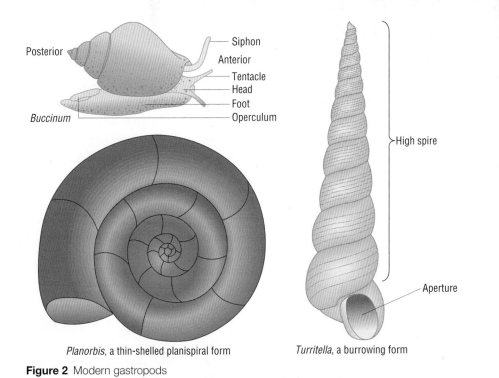

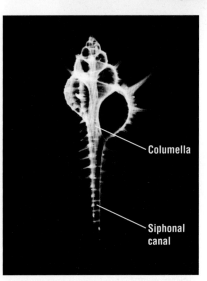

Figure 3 Cross-section of a Gastropod showing the columella and a long siphonal canal

Figure 2 Modern gastropods

Planorbis, a thin-shelled planispiral form

Turritella, a burrowing form

Mode of life

The shape and construction of the shell is a good indication of the mode of life. Forms with a large siphonal canal have this to separate inhalent and exhalent currents. Thin delicate shells, as seen in freshwater species, are an indication of low energy; conversely a thick, ribbed or ornamented shell indicates high energy.

Turritella does not increase much in size with each coil, so ends up as a tapered shell with a small apical angle. This allows it to live in high energy conditions, burrowing into the sediment with the aperture upwards. The long spire helps to anchor it in place. *Turritella* is a filter feeder.

Buccinum, or the common whelk, has a short siphon that extends upwards and forwards. Through this siphon the animal can take in clean water for respiration as it ploughs through the muddy sea floor. *Buccinum* is an example of a carnivorous gastropod using their rasp-like tongue on the soft tissue of its prey, either alive or dead. Many marine forms take a more aggressive stance. One species, *Natica*, uses acid to soften the shell of its prey, drills a hole and then scoops out the soft body of the animal to feed.

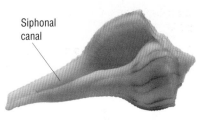

Figure 4 Gastropod with a long siphonal canal showing sinistral coiling

Questions

1 Describe the features that would distinguish a gastropod living in a deep water environment from a shallow water dweller.
2 How can you distinguish between a cephalopod and a gastropod?
3 List two ways in which terrestrial snails have evolved to live out of the water.

Belemnites

Belemnites belong to the phylum **Mollusca** and the class **Cephalopoda** and were abundant during the Jurassic and Cretaceous. These extinct forms are interesting as their shell was enclosed by soft body parts. This is unlike the nautiloids and ammonoids, which had external shells. They are closely related to squid and cuttlefish, which allow us to infer that each had a head and tentacles. They are classed as cephalopods as they have chambered shells, linked by a siphuncle.

Belemnite morphology

The only part normally preserved is the solid **guard**, a bullet-shaped calcite mass. It has a conical cavity in the anterior in which the more fragile, chambered **phragmocone** might be found fossilised. The chambers of the phragmocone represent the growth stages of the animal, with the last body chamber open. These chambers were used for buoyancy and could be adjusted using a **siphuncle**. The guard is a counterweight necessary to balance the head and tentacles. Occasionally the **pro-ostracum** is preserved; this is an extension to the guard, which may have had a protective function, perhaps protecting the tentacles.

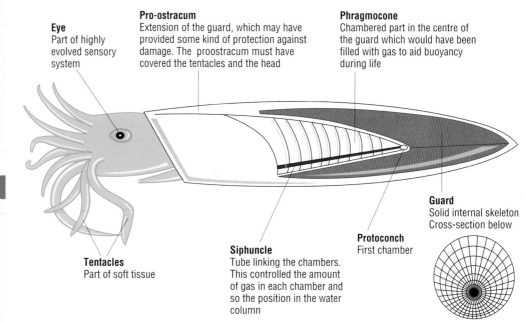

Eye
Part of highly evolved sensory system

Pro-ostracum
Extension of the guard, which may have provided some kind of protection against damage. The proostracum must have covered the tentacles and the head

Phragmocone
Chambered part in the centre of the guard which would have been filled with gas to aid buoyancy during life

Tentacles
Part of soft tissue

Siphuncle
Tube linking the chambers. This controlled the amount of gas in each chamber and so the position in the water column

Protoconch
First chamber

Guard
Solid internal skeleton Cross-section below

Figure 1 Belemnite morphology

Mode of life

It is assumed that the belemnites swam in the same fashion as squid, and were nektonic animals. As with modern analogues, they could have swim both vertically and horizontally. This vertical movement was probably controlled by gas in the chambers, whilst the horizontal movement was largely controlled by the tentacles and jet propulsion. When they died they would have fallen through the water column and due to their streamlined shape, could have been aligned by any currents. The alignment of the bullet-shaped guards by currents can give excellent **palaeocurrent** information as a death assemblage (Figure 2).

Crinoids

Crinoids belong to the phylum **Echinodermata** and the class **Crinoidea**. They have calcareous plates, which show the same five-fold symmetry displayed by other echinoderms, such as the echinoids, but usually have a completely different mode of life.

Figure 2 Modern-day cephalopods

Crinoid morphology

There are four main parts to the crinoid: the holdfast, stem, calyx and brachia. The **calyx** contains most of the soft parts of the animal. This is supported on a stem made of plates called **ossicles**. The calyx has arms or **brachia**, which gather food particles and pass it to the mouth in the upper surface of the calyx. All of these parts are made of calcareous plates, maybe with a thin organic covering to hold them together but the brachia and the stem are both flexible. The stem that holds the organism above the sea floor is made of ossicles, which are discs with a central hole. A 'string' of living material passes through the centre of the ossicles, drawing them together rather like a necklace. The stem is both strong and flexible. Brachial plates are similar but may have a V-groove on the upper surface along which the food particles are moved by cilia.

When the animal dies, the organic matter holding the crinoid together will decay and the skeleton falls apart. The degree to which it is disarticulated can indicate the energy of the environment before burial. The brachia are more easily disarticulated than the stem.

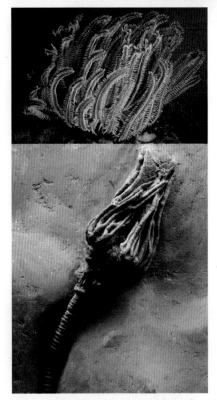

Figure 4 Modern-day sea lily (top) and fossil crinoid (bottom)

Brachia
Delicate structures which waft in the currents collecting particles of food, using cilia

Calyx
Main part of crinoid which houses the soft tissues. Consists of infrabasal, basal and radial plates showing five–fold symmetry

Anal tube
Structure protruding from the centre of the calyx. This gets rid of the waste material without it mixing with fresh water

Stem
Composed of calcite plates, with the centres linked together with soft tissue

Ossicle
Calcite plate making up part of the stem

Position of soft tissue

Holdfast
For attachment to the substrate, sometimes called 'roots'

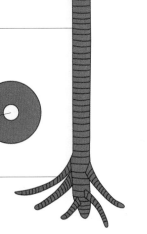

Figure 3 Crinoid morphology

Mode of life

Crinoids today are either **sessile** (stemmed forms, the sea lilies attached to the seabed) or **nektonic** (free swimming, feather stars). Studies have shown that fossil crinoids were mostly of the stemmed attached type. They are not good for interpretation of the environment as they are presently found at almost all water depths. Present-day crinoids do not seem to match the environments shown by the fossil record, being mostly associated with shallow marine reefs. They first appeared in the Ordovician and are still alive today. They are important in the fossil record because they are abundant in the Upper Palaeozoic, where the bioclastic limestone can be largely composed of fragmented crinoids.

Questions

1 Using the data provided in the table, plot a rose diagram. Put the values into 30-degree classes for plotting. What direction was the palaeocurrent flowing? Why are most belemnite guards facing a particular direction?

Orientation (degree)	Orientation (degree)
052	038
073	059
067	061
245	072
252	055
063	067
236	245

2 What features do echinoids and crinoids have in common?

3 Compare the morphologies and modes of life of an ammonite and a belemnite.

What are microfossils?

There is no difference between microfossils and macrofossils, other than size. If you need a microscope to see it properly, it is a microfossil.

Microfossils can be used to correlate rocks. They can be found in the chippings produced when drilling boreholes and these contain thousands of undamaged microfossils. Some rocks such as chalk or chert are composed almost entirely of microfossil remains. Their preservation in ocean floor sediments makes them ideal for investigating evolutionary theory.

Different microfossil groups

The focus here is on the microfauna: **ostracods**, **foraminifera**, **conodonts** and **radiolarian**. Discussions also include microflora: **spores** and **pollen**.

Ostracods

These are complex crustaceans, related to trilobites and crabs. They have two valves, a hinge with teeth and sockets and adductor muscles to close them, which is similar to bivalves. They are usually less than 2 mm in length. The shell or **carapace** is made of chitin or calcium carbonate.

Ostracods range from the Cambrian to the present day, although the earliest groups are now extinct. They have a long stratigraphic range and mainly a benthonic mode of life, which limits their use in dating rocks. They are superb palaeo-environmental indicators, having different forms in waters of the entire range of salinity.

Foraminifera

These are mostly simple single-celled creatures with a protective shell or **test**. They range in size from 1 μm to around 110 mm. Early forms had tests of particles glued together for protection, while more advanced forms secrete an amazing diversity of shells. Modern foraminifera capture their food using thread-like structures, which extend through holes in the test. Most forms are benthonic (sessile or vagrant) but a few such as *Globigerina* are planktonic.

They range from early Cambrian to the present day, although the planktonic forms were not common until the Mesozoic. This group have proved to be an excellent stratigraphic tool used extensively in the oil industry. Research has enabled detailed ranges to be determined for many different species. This also provides evidence of how evolutionary change occurs.

Conodonts

These microfossils range from 200 μm to 5 mm and are the teeth of a soft-bodied creature. These are composed of calcium phosphate, apatite, occur in pairs and are known as conodont **elements**. The earliest conodonts are found in Precambrian rocks and died out in the Permo-Triassic extinction event.

a

b

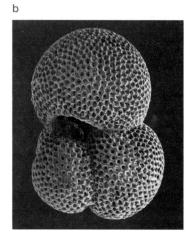

c

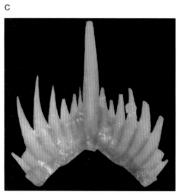

Figure 1 Examples of microfossils
a Ostracod
b Foraminifera
c Conodont

How science works

Conodonts are thought to be from the mouthparts of an animal similar to a hagfish, although there have been many proposed organisms. The origin of these fossils is a question which is not completely answered, even though associated soft tissues have been discovered in certain parts of the world. They are extremely useful stratigraphic tools, as few other microfossils are found in such large numbers in the Palaeozoic.

Radiolaria

These are marine, planktonic animals, which range from 30 μm to 2 mm. They are composed of silica and occupied niches near the surface to hundreds of metres depth. They are remarkable in that they have a rich diversity of delicate silica skeletons, thus are preserved at depths below the **CCD** and are easy to recover. Although they have been around since the late Precambrian, they are excellent stratigraphic and palaeo-environmental tools.

Spores and pollen

Terrestrial vascular plant spores and pollen are designed to be tough, as they are composed of sporopollenin. Spores are produced by plants such as mosses and ferns, and pollen is the product of seed bearing plants. They are between 10 and 200 microns in diameter.

The earliest preserved terrestrial plants are from the Late Silurian, but spores were found earlier in the Ordovician. The earliest plants producing pollen were from the Late Devonian, and these diversified in the Cretaceous, to make life miserable for hay fever sufferers today. Both spores and pollen were produced on plants that either lived on land or in a marginal shallow water environment. However, these can be easily washed out to sea and found in sediments of a different environment.

Evolution

Biological evolution is the process by which the inherited characteristics of a population are passed on from parent to offspring. The English naturalist **Charles Darwin** is the best-known contributor to several theories of how this has resulted in the species we know today. His work was mostly based on living species and could be summarised as a gradual change resulting from natural selection. **Alfred Wallace** should also be famous, as he jointly proposed the theory with Darwin.

They reasoned that some of the random variations resulting from cross-breeding and mutations are advantageous. The individuals who were more able to adapt would be more likely to pass these characteristics to their offspring and so the changes would spread in the population. The phrase 'survival of the fittest' described the mechanism well. Eventually there would be so many small changes that a new species would have to be acknowledged. A species is an organism that can interbreed to produce fertile offspring. The technical description for this view of evolution is **phyletic gradualism**.

Evidence from the fossil record has been sought to prove this theory. This is not as easy as it first appears. Preservation as a fossil is a rare circumstance, and the geological record itself is full of gaps. Also, the fossils that are found may not show important changes, such as in the soft tissues.

a

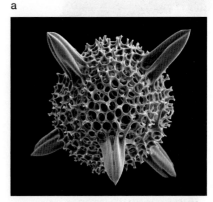

b

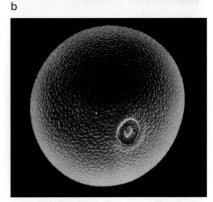

Figure 2 Examples of microfossils
a Radiolaria
b Pollen **grain**

Key definitions – evolution

Evolution is change in the genetic material of a population of organisms through successive generations. It is a gradual process in which something changes into a different and usually more complex or better form.

Theories of evolution

There are several theories, summarised here:

- **Gradualism** is the process of gradual evolutionary change over time, as understood by the Darwin–Wallace theory. This involves 'creation' of new characteristics or genes due to cross-breeding and mutations.
- **Genetic drift** is especially apparent when there are few selective pressures on the population; the random sampling of parent genetic material in the offspring can eventually lead to the elimination of some characteristics or genes.
- **Gene flow** involves the exchange of genes between populations by migration or pollination.
- **Punctuated equilibrium** reinterprets fossil evidence. It says that for long periods very little change occurs in the population as it expands. At the limits of its environment, the population is forced to adapt and a new species, which is more successful than its parent stock, takes over in a short time. There is no need to hypothesise that the intermediate stages in gradual evolution have been lost – the 'missing links' were never there.

Questions

1 Which of the microfossils would be the most difficult to separate from a fragment of limestone?
2 Why are microfossils such an important stratigraphic tool in the oil industry?
3 Why can microfossils provide better evidence for evolutionary mechanisms than macrofossils?

Graptolites belong to the phylum **Hemichordata**, class **Graptolithinia** (graptolites) and to the order **Graptoloidea** (graptoloids). Hemichordates include modern examples, such as worm-like marine animals called pterobranchs. These have a primitive notochord, and are therefore a possible ancestor of chordates. As graptolites are all extinct it is very difficult to be sure of their biological affinities and how they lived.

Graptolites include the order Dendroidea, a multi-stiped ancestral version of the graptoloids, different enough to be given their own order. The name graptolite comes from Greek *graptos*, meaning 'written', and *lithos*, meaning 'rock', and many look like ancient hieroglyphs on rock surfaces. This is partly because the fossils are often found as two-dimensional, flattened specimens. Rare three-dimensional specimens have allowed researchers to reconstruct the skeleton, showing that it was a colonial organism.

Graptoloid morphology

These were colonial organisms whose individuals laid down a **scleroprotein** skeleton in an orderly fashion. Based on similarities to modern hemichordates, it is thought that zooids lived in and built up tubes called thecae. The first zooid secreted a tube, called the **sicula**, which often had a long tapering point. **Thecae** were stacked vertically on top of each other and on top of the sicula. This may have been due to asexual budding from the first zooid. The thecae overlap and make up the **stipes**. True graptolites had varying numbers of stipes making up their entire skeleton, the **rhabdosome.**

> ### Key definition
>
> **Sicula** is a conical structure in which the first member of the colony lives.
>
> **Theca** is a tube built onto the sicula, in which later members of the colony live.
>
> **Stipe** is the stack of thecae built up to form a colony.

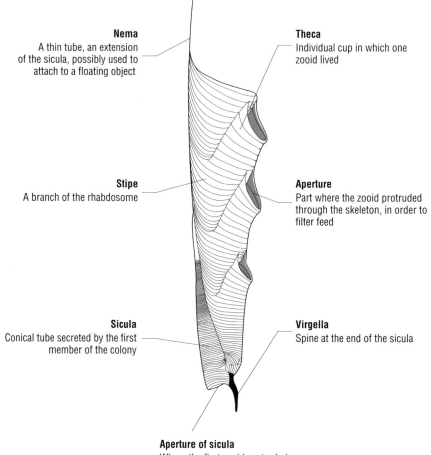

Nema
A thin tube, an extension of the sicula, possibly used to attach to a floating object

Theca
Individual cup in which one zooid lived

Stipe
A branch of the rhabdosome

Aperture
Part where the zooid protruded through the skeleton, in order to filter feed

Sicula
Conical tube secreted by the first member of the colony

Virgella
Spine at the end of the sicula

Aperture of sicula
Where the first zooid protruded through the skeleton

Figure 1 Graptoloid morphology based on the example of *Monograptus* – a single-stiped form

Graptolite mode of life

Planktonic

The ancestral dendroids were attached to the sea floor (sessile, benthonic) but the graptoloids lived within the water column and were probably pelagic. The aperture of the **sicula** faced downwards and the whole colony is presumed to have floated or been attached to some floating object by means of the **nema**. Some species appear to have been arranged around the outline of what could have been a flotation aid, which may have been a gas filled membrane. Models of graptoloids often spiral as they sink and although this would make them more efficient filter feeders, it is not clear how they rose again. Most appear to conform to this planktonic mode of life, though some may have been active swimmers.

The similarity with pterobranchs

The close similarity with the rare present-day pterobranchs and the structure of the **rhabdosome** leads us to believe that the graptoloids were filter feeders. Modern-day pterobranchs attach themselves to the sea floor to a depth of up to 600 m. The colonies are small, in the order of 2 to 3 cm. Each zooid lives in its own tube or depression, which varies from species to species. The zooids in pterobranchs emerge from the tubes they have made from collagen to trap food particles from the water. They filter the water with the help of cilia and tentacles. The presence of cilia shows us that the pterobranchs may be closely related to the echinoderms.

How science works

Some researchers believe that the few bottom dwelling pterobranchs are direct descendants of the graptolites of the Palaeozoic and others think that they are indeed graptolites. Further research will help to decide this conundrum. The real problem is how to work out the mode of life of an extinct group from very little evidence.

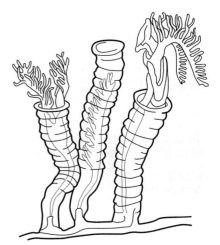

Figure 2 A modern-day pterobranch

Preservation and importance as a zone fossil

The graptoloids appeared in the early Ordovician and rapidly became the dominant marine fauna. This success continued into the middle Silurian at which point they began to decline, and they were extinct by the early Devonian. Their rapid evolution, abundance and planktonic mode of life made them ideal zone fossils. They are used to zone much of the Ordovician and Silurian.

Their protein-based composition meant that they did not dissolve when they fell into deep waters. They are delicate and were liable to scavenging and decay in shallow oxygenated waters, so are collected in vast quantities in the anoxic mud of the sea floor. We assume that they occupied many environmental niches, but are preserved best in low-energy conditions. They became extinct when fish evolved, but we have no way of knowing if the two occurrences are connected.

Examiner tip

After death, graptoloids sank and were preserved in deep water, low oxygen, low-energy muds (as a death assemblage).

Most of them probably *lived* in the oxygenated upper waters. There is a possible confusion between their mode of life and the rocks (facies) they are found in.

Sometimes currents on the sea floor aligned the graptolites and so palaeocurrent directions can be determined.

Questions

1 How does the sicula differ in shape from the later thecae in the rhabdosome?
2 What is the evidence that graptoloids were filter feeders?
3 Why are graptolites considered to be good zone fossils?

Although their stratigraphic range is limited essentially to the Ordovician and Silurian periods, the graptoloids underwent complex and rapid evolutionary changes. These changes can be simplified by breaking them down into four trends. Be aware that there are exceptions to all of these!

Changes in the number of stipes

Early graptoloids had up to eight stipes, but later in the Ordovician the two-stiped forms were more common. In the Silurian, single-stiped *Monograptus* is a common fossil. The trend is from many stipes in the Ordovician, to only one in the Silurian.

Changes in the attitude of the stipes

The attitude of the stipes is compared to the sicula, which always has the aperture pointing downwards and the nema pointing upwards. Subsequent theca forming stipes may grow downwards (**pendent**), outwards (**horizontal**) or upwards (**scandent**).

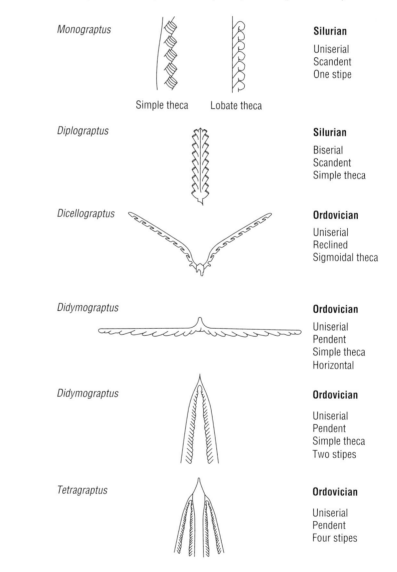

Figure 1 Changes in graptolite morphology over time

> **Examiner tip**
>
> Although you do not *have* to recall generic names of graptoloids, it may be quicker and easier to quote a few names rather than describe them.
>
> Some are easy to remember, such as:
> - *Tetragraptus* had four stipes.
> - *Monograptus* had one stipe.

> **Examiner tip**
>
> Stipe attitude – be careful when drawing examples. In pendent forms the thecae face inwards and for scandent forms the thecae face outwards. Otherwise you could be drawing a pendent form when you meant a scandent.

Figure 2 Silurian graptolite *Monograptus*

Figure 3 Biseral graptolite showing a nema

There is a very rough trend from pendent to scandent with time. Early graptoloids were **pendent** or **horizontal** (although **scandent biserial** forms were around at the same time). Scandent carried on but pendent and horizontal were replaced by **reclined** forms. The latest Silurian forms were almost all scandent, including *Monograptus*, which can be difficult to orientate in some diagrams.

Changes in the shape of the thecae

Over time, the thecae evolved from simple tubes to more elaborate shapes. This evolutionary trend must have ensured more efficient filter feeding, reducing the competition between zooids for suspended nutrients.

Many early forms had simple thecae with uncomplicated apertures, which were arranged along the stipe close together or with only a slight overlap. Although simple forms persisted, elaborate thecae were found later in the Ordovician and in the Silurian. Many of these had hooked or curved ends or were more widely separated along the stipe, called isolate. The detail seen on well preserved three-dimensional specimens has greatly improved our knowledge of their morphology.

Changes in the arrangement of thecae on the stipe

If the thecae are arranged on one side of the stipe, the graptoloid is **uniserial**. If it has thecae on both sides, it is **biserial**. Some species show an intermediate stage in which two uniserial stipes are half-zipped together to give a biserial lower half.

The general trend is that early forms were uniserial. with some becoming biserial in the Late Ordovician. The Silurian forms were uniserial. Trends which revert are more difficult to explain in terms of evolutionary advantages.

There are many examples of uniserial and biserial graptoloids. Be aware that they are not simply a progression with one group being replaced by the next. Some groups, such as the diplograptids, coexisted with all the other examples shown.

General trends

None of these evolutionary trends is cut and dried – just like life. Characteristics of different species often overlapped with others or appeared out of order. However, those general tendencies to fewer stipes, scandent attitude and complex thecae are a good working guide.

Figure 2 Ordovician graptolite *Didymograptus*

Questions

1 Describe the features of a typical graptolite found in rocks of Ordovician age.
2 Why might a horizontal or reclined form be a more efficient filter feeder than a pendent form?

259

Classification

Nautiloids and ammonoids are sub-classes of the class **Cephalopoda**. Cephalopods (along with gastropods and bivalves) belong to the phylum **Mollusca**. Modern cephalopods are marine dwellers and tend to be predators such as squid, cuttlefish and the octopus. One living cephalopod, *Nautilus* has an external shell, a survivor from the days when cephalopods were extremely successful in the late Palaeozoic and Mesozoic seas. Cephalopods were so varied that they are useful zone fossils for the Mesozoic, *Nautilus* provides valuable information on how fossil cephalopods functioned and their modes of life.

Nautilus, morphology and mode of life

Modern-day *Nautilus* lives in a coiled conical shell, which originates at a **protoconch**. As the organism grows in the final **body chamber**, it seals off older chambers with a wall called a **septum** (plural septa). These are then empty chambers, which are joined by a narrow tube called a **siphuncle**. The siphuncle extends all the way back to the original chamber. The siphuncle can be used to adjust the proportion of gas and liquids within the chambers, which helps control the position of the animal in the water column. This works rather like a submarine's ballast tanks.

Figure 2 Nautilus shell external and internal cross-section showing septal necks

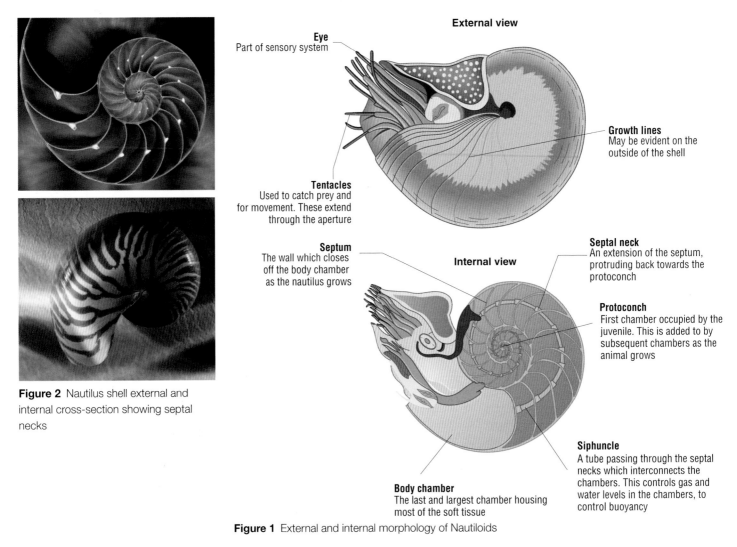

External view

Eye
Part of sensory system

Growth lines
May be evident on the outside of the shell

Tentacles
Used to catch prey and for movement. These extend through the aperture

Septum
The wall which closes off the body chamber as the nautilus grows

Internal view

Septal neck
An extension of the septum, protruding back towards the protoconch

Protoconch
First chamber occupied by the juvenile. This is added to by subsequent chambers as the animal grows

Body chamber
The last and largest chamber housing most of the soft tissue

Siphuncle
A tube passing through the septal necks which interconnects the chambers. This controls gas and water levels in the chambers, to control buoyancy

Figure 1 External and internal morphology of Nautiloids

Forms of coiling
- **Involute** means that the inner coils are almost hidden by the last one. This is the type of coiling shown by *Nautilus*. Involute coiling produces a narrow umbilicus.
- **Evolute** means that all the earlier coils can be seen, and shows off the earlier coils and a wide umbilicus. This sort of coiling is common in ammonoids).
- **Planispiral** means that the shell is coiled in a single plane.

Ammonoid morphology

In contrast to the nautiloids, the coiling can be **evolute** and there may be ornament such as **ribs** on the exterior of the shell. Some also have a **keel**, which stuck out from the outer margin and probably provided stability when the cephalopod was in motion. Some forms have a slot in the outer (ventral) margin called a **sulcus**, which presumably had the same effect.

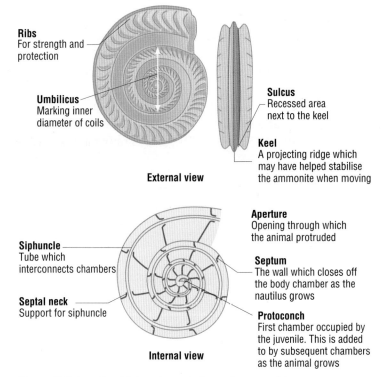

Ribs
For strength and protection

Umbilicus
Marking inner diameter of coils

Sulcus
Recessed area next to the keel

Keel
A projecting ridge which may have helped stabilise the ammonite when moving

External view

Siphuncle
Tube which interconnects chambers

Septal neck
Support for siphuncle

Aperture
Opening through which the animal protruded

Septum
The wall which closes off the body chamber as the nautilus grows

Protoconch
First chamber occupied by the juvenile. This is added to by subsequent chambers as the animal grows

Internal view

Figure 3 External and internal morphology of ammonoids

Ammonoid modes of life

Nektonic – lateral movement
The tentacles are used in a gentle swimming motion in some living species; those same tentacles could have been used to pull the creature along the sea floor. The more interesting method of locomotion is the jet propulsion used to propel the cephalopod backwards. In times of danger the water, which is circulated through the mantle for respiration, can be forcibly expelled through a tube beneath the tentacles called the funnel. The funnel can be aimed to give some choice of direction (but always backwards).

Nektonic – vertical movement
The empty chambers all have a mixture of gas and liquid. The gas is nitrogen rich. The relative volumes of liquid and gas can be adjusted using the siphuncle: more gas gives more buoyancy and the cephalopod rises in the water column, more liquid and it sinks. *Nautilus* moves up from 400 to 70 m at night to feed, a change in pressure of nearly 40 atmospheres.

Hunter killer
Evidence points to cephalopods being predatory, hunting their prey. This does not mean that they were very fast moving; the jet propulsion could just be for emergency escape purposes.

Key definitions

The **body chamber** is where the animal lived.

The **protoconch** is the initial, embryonic shell in the centre of the coiled animal. New chambers are added onto this as the animal grows.

Septal necks are where the septa are pierced to allow a tube of soft tissue through. Septal necks extend to support this tissue.

The **septum** is the wall of the chamber. This is the back wall when it is part of the body chamber.

A **siphuncle** forms a continuous, delicate tube. That tube connects all chambers.

A **suture** is the line along which the septum and the shell fuse.

The **umbilicus** is the diameter of the depression between the inside margins of the last coil.

Questions
1 Explain how ammonoids were able to move both vertically and horizontally in the water column.
2 Draw diagrams to illustrate the differences between involute and evolute.

Nautiloids are the earliest cephalopods, first appearing in the Upper Cambrian. Many of the early nautiloids were not coiled but straight, and were known as orthocone nautiloids. They were prolific in the Palaeozoic but only the coiled forms survived into the Mesozoic.

By the Devonian, the ammonoids were clearly distinct from the nautiloids. They remained relatively unchanged until the Triassic, when they began to diversify. Some of these were extinct by the end of the Permian in the major extinction event. One surviving single family went on to populate the Jurassic seas with rapid evolution. After the Jurassic, they declined throughout the Cretaceous, producing some unusual forms as they did so (the **heteromorphs**) and were finally wiped out by the K–T extinction event.

Surprisingly, the nautiloids managed to live through the extinction, but numbers dwindled to the present day. The belemnites probably evolved from the straight-shelled nautiloids during the Upper Carboniferous. Their closest living relatives are squid.

Changes in suture lines

The suture line marks where the wall of the chamber, the septum, fuses with the inside of the shell.

The most accepted explanation for changes in the suture types are linked with strength and the ability to exploit different environments. The septum probably had to withstand high pressures and the early forms were simply domed to strengthen them. Later forms had crenulations along the length, rather like corrugated iron, giving more strength. The strength of the join with the shell is also enhanced by an increase in its length. A stronger shell structure allows a greater range of depths for hunting but it needed to be light to allow for better acceleration. A more convoluted septum might also provide a more secure anchorage for the soft tissue. Whatever the advantages for the organism, the complexity of the sutures alone is enough for us to classify important groups of cephalopods.

To describe the degree of complexity of the suture lines, there need to be a few common rules. Orientation on a coiled tube is tricky. The suture line is drawn with the outside of the shell (**venter**) on the left and the inside (**umbilicus**) on the right. An upwards arrow points towards the **aperture**.

The earliest cephalopods had very simple suture lines; the nautiloids range from a straight line to a few gentle curves. These are named after a common group of Lower Palaeozoic straight-shelled nautiloids, *Orthoceras*. The term **orthoceratitic** means that the sutures are very simple. Modern-day *Nautilus* only shows curved sutures.

The ammonoid sutures were very complex. The Palaeozoic forms are called **goniatites** after the angular shape of their suture lines. Both saddles and lobes are smooth. Most goniatites perished in the Permo-Triassic extinction and those who survived were outnumbered by a group with more complex sutures, the **ceratites**.

Ceratites developed frilly or more complex lobes, whilst their saddles remained simple. Their numbers dwindled into the Permian and the Lower Triassic. The sutures are appropriately described as **ceratitic**.

In the Upper Triassic, the true ammonites became dominant. They have frilly or complex folds on both lobes and saddles. The sutures are very complex and are described as **ammonitic** sutures.

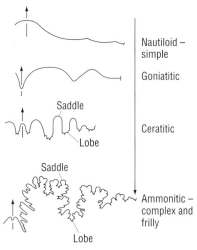

Figure 1 A comparison of nautiloid, goniatitic, ceratitic and ammonitic sutures

Figure 2 Detail of ammonitic suture on a Jurassic ammonite

Changes in internal structures

Compare the internal structure of the ammonite; the later septal necks in ammonites face towards the aperture. The earlier chambers inhabited by the ammonite often have the septal necks pointing backwards. The development of the ammonite appears to mirror its evolution. Nautiloids have their septal necks facing towards the protoconch.

The other obvious difference in the internal structure is that the nautiloid siphuncle passes through the centres of the septal walls. Compare with the ammonoid, which has the siphuncle positioned closer to the venter. It is assumed that this improved the ability of the animal to adjust its buoyancy.

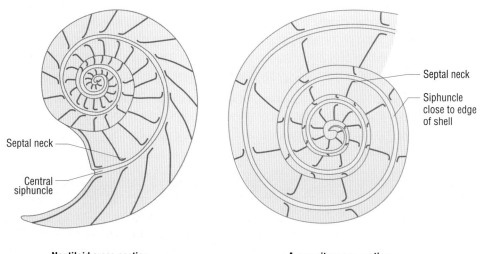

Nautiloid cross-section   **Ammonite cross-section**

Septal neck

Siphuncle close to edge of shell

Septal neck

Central siphuncle

Figure 3 Comparing the internal structures of ammonoids and nautiloids

Changes in external structure

The nautiloids were smooth shelled and so were most of the goniatites. Ammonites show a variety of ornament, which may reflect the increasing danger they faced from predators. Some are streamlined as if to escape and some are heavily armoured with ribs and tubercles, probably for protection. Modern-day *Nautilus* has excellent camouflage and is almost invisible in the water. Some fossil cephalopods also preserve colouration, assumed to be for protection.

The heteromorphs

Many Cretaceous fossils show bite marks caused by reptiles and crabs. This pressure may have been a factor in the evolution of the extreme forms seen in the heteromorphs. Many exhibit loose coiling in more than one plane. These strange forms are often referred to as the uncoiled ammonites. They may be evolutionary extremes or, more likely, adaptations to exploit different environmental niches. Some may have floated close to the surface, while others are thought to have crawled along the seabed using their tentacles.

Figure 4 Photo of an uncoiled heteromorph ammonite

Questions

1 How do nautiloids and ammonoids differ internally?
2 How could you distinguish a Palaeozoic ammonoid from a Mesozoic specimen?
3 Describe the evidence to suggest that cephalopods went from straight to coiled and back to uncoiled forms as they evolved.

Amphibians were the first land-dwelling creatures with four legs, known as **tetrapods**. They evolved from **lobe-finned fish** in the late Devonian to early Carboniferous. They then ventured forth into **terrestrial** environments, where they would later evolve into reptiles, birds and mammals.

Key definitions

An **amphibian** is a creature with two life styles, one in water, the other on land.

Lobe-finned fish are fish that possessed both lungs and gills and had four fleshy fins supported by bones in a similar structure to a hand, e.g. lungfish.

A **swim bladder** is a sack-like structure, which can be filled with gas or fluid, to control buoyancy in fish.

A **tetrapod** is a creature with four limbs.

Terrestrial describes anything relating to land.

What are lobe-finned fish?

Lobe-finned fish are **lungfish**. These fish had the ability to breathe both in and out of water. They had robust fleshy fins with an arrangement of central bones inside, similar to the structure of bones in a hand, which would have allowed for more mobility and support (especially on land). The only disadvantage of this design was that there was no strengthening girdle connecting the bones at the extremities to the rest of the skeleton. This gave an area of weakness. These fins would later evolve into the limbs needed for life on land.

Lobe-finned fish also had functional lungs, which were modified **swim bladders**. This allowed them to breathe out of water, a great advantage to start the transition to life on land. They could move from one water source to another and exploit life on land, with the absence of predators.

But how do we know this about the lobe-finned fish? There are many fossil remains of these creatures found in Devonian strata, and some even earlier that show the skeletal structure. There are also live specimens that can be found on Earth today.

Another piece of evidence is that **coelacanths** were thought to be extinct. They are known as 'living fossils'. These have morphological features that have remained virtually unchanged for millions of years. Coelacanths are marine fish that do not have lungs, which suggests that lungfish are more closely related to the first amphibians.

Case study

Once thought to be extinct, the **coelacanth** was rediscovered in 1938 off the Comoros Islands, living between 150 and 300 m down. Before then it was believed to have disappeared more than 65 million years ago.

Coelacanths were roaming the oceans when their close relatives became the first vertebrates to venture onto land. They shared the oceans with trilobites and primitive molluscs, in forms very similar to the modern coelacanth.

The limb-like ventral and pectoral fins make it possibly the first fish to crawl out of the sea. That could make them the closest living relative to the ancestor of all amphibians, reptiles, birds and mammals. However, this could be the lungfish, so debate still rages. The coelacanth group reached its peak around 200 million years ago and have been gradually declining since the Triassic.

Figure 1 Photos showing **a** lungfish and **b** coelacanth

Similarities between the lobe-finned fish and the early amphibians

- The four fins of the lobe-finned fish and the four limbs of the early amphibian's skeletal structures were very similar.
- Their limbs were in the same position on their bodies.
- They both lacked claws or nails.
- The skull morphology, the jaw bone and teeth of the lobe-finned fish and amphibians were very much alike.
- The amphibian's skull became more slender, with the temporal and opercular bones becoming smaller in size, and the jaw bones becoming more fused together.
- The teeth of both the lobe-finned fish and amphibians were complex.
- Early amphibians still had a tail fin, suggesting it still spent a great deal of time in the water. Its body shape and presumably its movement still resemble that of the lobe-finned fish.
- Also, the early amphibians still had traces of small bony scales on the skin, a trait of fishes.

Adaptation to life on land

As well as having similar characteristics to that of lobe-finned fish, the newly evolved amphibians also had some other features entirely unique, which allowed them to adapt to life on land. These included:

- The development of a girdle connecting the limb bones to the skeleton for better movement on land.
- A more robust skeleton strengthening the vertebral column and rib bones, for support on land.
- Eyelids formed to help keep eyes moist, as it was no longer always submerged in water.
- The development of a double-loop circulatory system with a three-chambered heart to pump mixed blood before and after it had been to the lungs. This allowed a more efficient gas exchange to take place, so it could provide its more active cells with the oxygen and to remove waste products more efficiently.
- A tongue formed within its mouth, which could be used to catch prey, as well as having a sensory role.
- Ears adapted so it could detect sound waves through the thin medium of air, allowing it to listen to its surroundings for prey or predators.

However, even with new adaptations to terrestrial life, the early amphibians still had to remain close to a water source. They still used their skin for gas exchange, so they had to keep it moist to allow the transfer of oxygen and carbon dioxide. They also had to lay their eggs in water, because without it their eggs would dry out, as they were only protected by a layer of jelly and not a shell. The young would hatch into aquatic larvae with gills, and then undergo metamorphosis to develop into a terrestrial adult able to walk on land. It was not until the development of the amniotic egg that evolution proceeded to give rise to such creatures as the dinosaurs, birds and mammals.

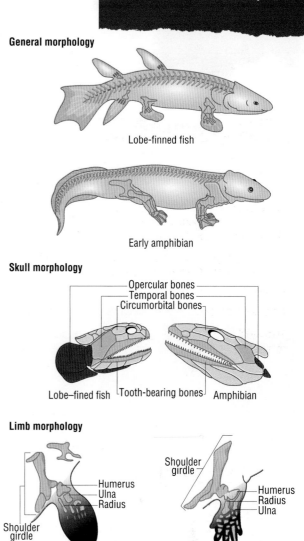

Figure 2 Diagrams showing **a** general morphology **b** skull morphology, and **c** limb morphology of lobe-finned fish and early amphibians

Case study

At first they thought the fossil was just a fragment of a lungfish snout – interesting, but not earth-shaking. In 2002, geologists went to Ellesmere Island, high in the Canadian Arctic, in search of the fish that first dragged itself out of water nearly 400 million years ago, the evolutionary forebear to all land vertebrates.

That unassuming fragment of bone helped geologists of the University of Chicago to one of the most important fossil finds of the decade: several specimens of an almost perfect intermediate between fish and land vertebrates – tetrapods. All are so beautifully preserved that the researchers could see almost every detail of their skeleton. The new creature was named *Tiktaalik* – from the Inuit name for a large, shallow-water fish.

Several fossil fish with amphibian-like features have been found. The fish's fins became the amphibian's rudimentary legs. The head, bound rigidly to the body by bony plates, turned into a mobile neck.

The first amphibians lived at the time that the first major terrestrial ecosystems were establishing themselves. Full-grown forests with roots a metre deep were developing, where formerly just mosses and other tiny, shallow-rooted plants grew.

Precis from Issue 2568 of *New Scientist*, September 9, 2006, pp. 35–39.

Questions

1 What is a lobe-finned fish?
2 What are the similarities between lungfish (lobe-finned fish) and the early amphibians?
3 Describe and explain three adaptations of an early amphibian for life on land.

The classification of **dinosaurs** relies entirely on the shape of the bones. Other sources of knowledge include fossil faeces (coprolites), trackways, gastroliths and feathers. Relationships can be determined by looking at common characteristics of dinosaurs, and the main differences are evident in the bones of the hip. By looking at these shared characteristics, we define two main classes of dinosaurs, **Saurischia,** meaning 'reptile hipped' and **Ornithischia,** meaning 'bird hipped'.

How science works

Sir Richard Owen (1842) was the first person to recognise that all dinosaurs belonged to one distinct group. He also decided to use the term 'Dinosauria', which means 'terrible lizard'.

Figure 1 Nest of dinosaur eggs

The amniotic egg

Dinosaurs are believed to have laid **amniotic eggs**. These eggs are one of the most significant features in reptile evolution, as it allowed for life on land without the need for a water source in which to reproduce. Instead the egg provided the aquatic environment needed for the development of the embryo within the egg itself.

The first advantage for life on land was the development of a hard outer shell, which provided protection whilst remaining porous. This allowed the diffusion of oxygen into the egg and carbon dioxide out, allowing respiration to take place. The yolk sac provided the embryo with food and the albumin supplied water and nutrients, eliminating the need for a larval stage. Instead the embryo would develop directly into a miniature version of the adult.

Evolution of dinosaurs

Dinosaurs began to evolve after the Permo-Triassic extinction wiped out much of life on Earth, perhaps filling newly vacant ecological niches. They evolved into two separate classes, Saurischia and Ornithischia. The Saurischia were divided into two: Therapoda, including birds and the well-known dinosaur, *Tyrannosaurus*; and Sauropoda, including *Diplodocus*. Ornithischia includes the *Iguanodon*.

Key definitions

Amniotic eggs are types of eggs produced by birds and reptiles, with shells.

Archosaurs are a group of reptiles dominating the Triassic. These were the ancestors of dinosaurs, birds and crocodiles.

A **dinosaur** is a Mesozoic reptile with an upright walking position or gait.

Gastroliths are stones swallowed by animals to stay in the stomach and grind the food that they eat. This is usually alongside a gizzard, which is a lining inside the stomach to protect it from damage.

Ornithischia is one of the main divisions in dinosaur classification, in which two bones in the hip point backwards. This is the same as in birds, so they are known as 'bird hipped'.

Phylogeny is the origin and evolution of a species.

Pubis is the pubic bone.

Saurischia is one of the main divisions in dinosaur classification, in which one of the bones in the hip points forward. This is known as 'reptile hipped'.

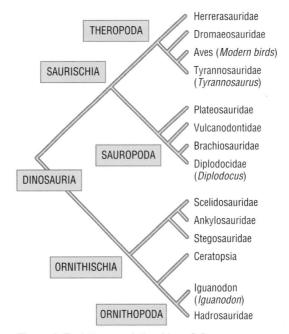

Figure 2 Evolutionary relationships of dinosaurs

Dinosaurs evolved from their immediate ancestors, known as **Archosaurs**, in the Triassic. At this point the continents were joined together to form the supercontinent of Pangaea. This meant that much of the interior was dry and hot. The Archosaurs are believed to have thrived in this environment.

How they actually evolved into dinosaurs is a matter of debate, but by the late Triassic there were several Therapod dinosaurs. The dinosaurs then rapidly diversified into several different types, all carnivorous.

During the Jurassic, the supercontinent began to break up, with many land bridges remaining between the fragmented landmasses.

The Jurassic climate was milder than the Triassic, allowing larger dinosaurs to evolve. Many large Sauropods evolved, such as *Diplodocus*, which ate a vegetarian diet. Ornithischian herbivores were evolving at the same time, such as *Stegosaurus*. *Iguanodon*, another Ornithischian dinosaur, evolved a horny beak with which to graze on low vegetation – but not grass, which did not exist at that time.

During the Cretaceous, there had been further movement of the continents and many land bridges had disappeared. The climate was cooler than both the Triassic and the Jurassic. This geographical isolation meant that there was increased evolution along separate lines. The Saurischian dinosaurs were becoming rare, but there was an increase in Ornithischian dinosaurs, usually of smaller size. This change from large to small may be a result of environmental stresses, change in diet as flowering plants evolved or a response to climate change.

Towards the end of the Cretaceous, the largest Therapod dinosaur evolved, *Tyrannosaurus*. The duck-billed dinosaurs and well-known horned dinosaurs such as *Triceratops* also evolved at this time. Horn development probably served as a defensive weapon.

Characteristics of Saurischian dinosaurs

This group includes the well-known carnivore *Velociraptor*, popularised by the film *Jurassic Park* and the herbivore *Diplodocus*. See Figure 3 showing hip arrangements in Saurischia and Ornithischia.

Features include:

- The primitive arrangement of the hip bones is similar to reptiles, in which the pubis points forward.
- They have long, S-shaped flexible necks, allowing rapid and precise movement.
- Hands consisted of only three digits (fingers). The digits were asymmetrical with the first digit similar to a thumb, allowing the hand to grasp and with the second digit being the longest of the three.

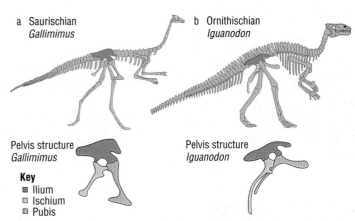

Key
- Ilium
- Ischium
- Pubis

Figure 3 Arrangement of hip bones in **a** Saurischia and **b** Ornithischia

Characteristics of Ornithischian dinosaurs

- The arrangement of the hip bones is similar to birds, in which the pubis points backwards.
- The front teeth are small or absent, replaced at the front with a horny beak which later became broader, giving them the name 'duck-billed dinosaurs'.
- Many Ornithischian dinosaurs were armoured with bony plates, such as the *Stegosaurus*. These were thought to be a defence mechanism against predators, but could have also acted as heat-exchangers. The fossilised plates have tiny grooves, which may have housed blood vessels allowing heat to be given off or taken in.

Figure 4 *Hypsilophodon*, Ornithischian dinosaur from the Isle of Wight

Questions

1 Why were amniotic eggs so important in dinosaur evolution?
2 Describe the differences between Ornithischian and Saurischian dinosaurs.
3 Research the distribution of dinosaur remains in the UK. Where would you have the best chance of finding dinosaur fossils?

Diplodocus (Saurischia, Sauropoda)

Diplodocus was a **Sauropod** herbivore common in the Jurassic and the Cretaceous. It had a long slender skull, which was small compared to the rest of its body. It also had an extremely long neck, which it carried parallel to the ground. This allowed it to reach vegetation in forests where most other Sauropods could not venture due to their large size. Its long neck could have also helped it to search for foliage in wetlands. Peg-like teeth are only found to the front of the jaw and unlike many other herbivores' teeth, are not differentiated into grinding and tearing teeth, suggesting that it bit off vegetation and swallowed it whole. This would have made digesting plant material difficult, so it is believed that bacterial action and swallowed stones (**gastroliths**) aided the digestion of its food. Its body was long but lightly built. The spine had extra bones underneath it, these bony protrusions running both forwards and backwards (anvil-shaped), providing support and extra mobility of the neck and tail. Its tail was long and whip-like, which could have been used for defence.

Figure 1 Diplodocus

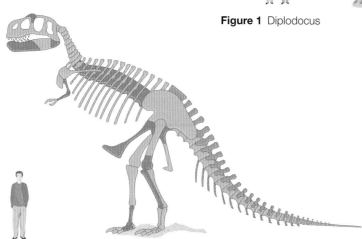

Figure 2 Tyrannosaurus

Tyrannosaurus (Saurischia, Therapoda)

The largest of all terrestrial predators, the *Tyrannosaurus*, was a **Therapod** carnivore and walked the Earth in the late Cretaceous. Was the *Tyrannosaurus* a predator or a scavenger? There are many arguments against them being predators; for example, they had small eyes while large eyes are more suitable to spot prey. It had small arms, not suitable for grasping onto prey. The back legs on which it walked were huge, indicating slow movement, which once again is not ideal in a predator. What these large legs did prove was that it was capable of walking large distances, an adaptation of a scavenger. As well as this, the *Tyrannosaurus* had large **olfactory lobes**, another adaptation to scavenging.

However, there are arguments against scavenging. Many predators today are happy to scavenge meat if it is readily available, but most prefer it fresh. Also, many predators are successful hunters without having to use their forelimbs. Whether or not the *Tyrannosaurus* was a slow animal is difficult to determine as few traces can be identified as made by *Tyrannosaurus*. It could have been a predator, a scavenger or both. It was a meat eater as its teeth were relatively large, curved and jagged, making them ideal for tearing flesh from the carcass.

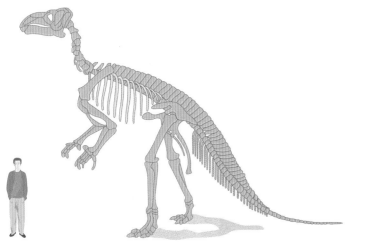

Figure 3 Iguanodon

Iguanodon (Ornithischia, Ornithopoda)

Iguanodon appeared in the late Jurassic and was in the class known as **Ornithopoda**. It was a large, heavily built creature with heavy shoulders and forelimbs. Its skull was large with a horse-like snout ending in a horny toothless beak, which was used to crop vegetation. It could then mince its food with a long series of leaf-shaped cheek teeth (resembling the teeth of living iguanas), due to a hinged upper jaw which was able to flex from side to side. This meant that the upper teeth could grind down on the lower as it bit down hard on vegetation. Its hands had three digits (fingers), which ended in hooves and had a large, conical thumb spike, thought to be a weapon or used to obtain food. The most outstanding feature of the *Iguanodon* was its ability to be **quadrupedal**, in which it used its tail as a counter balance, and **bipedal** to run or to rear up and swing its spike-like thumb in defence.

Evolution of birds

There are several theories to explain the evolution of birds, all based on flimsy evidence. The most accepted of these it that birds are thought to have evolved from Therapod dinosaurs in the Jurassic. Therapod dinosaurs are thought to be the closest relatives of birds and the first birds had many skeletal similarities to **coelurosaurs**. For example:

- Hollow thin-walled bones, to make the bones lighter
- S-shaped curved neck
- Elongated arms and forelimbs, and clawed hands
- The pubis shifted from an anterior (forward position) to a posterior (backward position)
- Large orbits (eye sockets in the skull)
- Hinged ankles (reduces rotation of the ankle).

Archaeopteryx

Archaeopteryx is the first known bird-like fossil. It is believed to be intermediate between birds and reptiles. This was a semi-arboreal animal (a creature that lived in trees) capable of gliding and sustaining flight, although some believe it had poor flight and simply glided (Figure 4b). These are groups that show characteristics of dinosaurs and birds, known as 'dinobirds'.

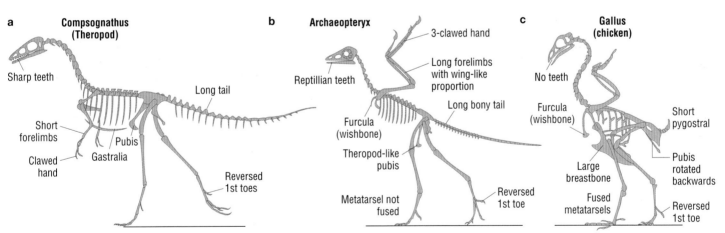

Figure 4 Comparison of skeletons: **a** Therapod; **b** *Archaeopteryx*; **c** modern bird

Reptilian/dinosaur-like features (*Compsoynathus*)
- Long, bony lizard-like tail
- Three digits (fingers) on the wings, each digit had a claw
- Snout with developed reptilian teeth
- Reptilian skull and brain
- The **sternum** was not bony or keeled
- Gastralia ('belly ribs') were present
- S-shaped curved neck

Bird-like features (*Archaeopteryx*)
- Wings for flight
- Feathers
- Hollow bones
- Legs directly underneath the body
- A **furcula** was present
- Reversed big toe

Questions

1 In what ways are birds, *Archaeopteryx* and Therapods similar?
2 Compare how *Diplodocus* and *Tyrannosaurus* are adapted to different modes of life.
3 Explain how the *Iguanodon* is adapted to its mode of life on land.

Mass extinctions through geological time

What is a mass extinction?

A mass extinction is when there is a massive decrease in the **number** of different species, over a relatively **short** period of time, perhaps spanning several thousand or a few million years. For any one species, **extinction** is catastrophic. The normal process of extinctions occurs continually, generating a regular change of all the species living on Earth, called background extinction. Sometimes, however, extinction rates rise suddenly for a relatively short time – as a mass extinction event.

The most famous of the mass extinctions is the Cretaceous – Tertiary mass extinction (K–T) – because it is when the dinosaurs became extinct. This was the most recent large-scale mass extinction and has been well documented. Mass extinction events are not rare and some environmentalists and biologists believe that we are in the middle of another major mass extinction event, fuelled by man's effect on the environment.

Mass extinctions through time

Mass extinction events have occurred throughout geological time, with remarkable frequency. There have been **five** major mass extinctions and many more minor ones. The 'big five' are:

- the Ordovician–Silurian boundary
- an event towards the end of the Devonian
- the Permian–Triassic boundary
- the Triassic–Jurassic boundary
- and the Cretaceous–Tertiary boundary.

Each of these extinctions affected well-established genera. Some losses affected one main type of habitat such as shallow marine dwellers, whilst others had more widespread, global implications.

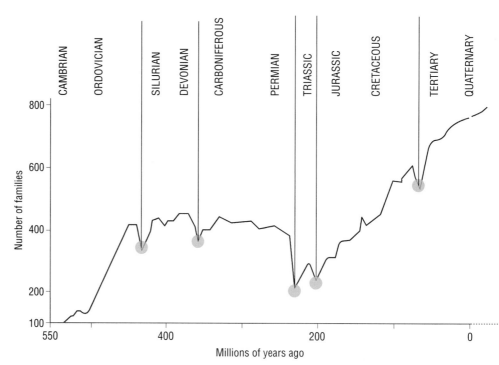

Figure 1 Graph showing mass extinction events over geological time

Extinction event	Time	Organisms most affected	% extinct of groups alive at the time
Ordovician-Silurian	443 Ma	Plankton and bottom dwellers, particularly brachiopods and trilobites. 100 families extinct – more than half of the bryozoan and brachiopod species extinct	27% of all families 57% of all genera
Late Devonian	375 Ma	Shallow marine ecosystems, especially corals, brachiopods and trilobites	19% of all families 50% of all genera
Permo-Triassic	251 Ma	Marine organisms, 95% of all marine species – most brachiopods, corals, ammonoids, echinoids and trilobites. Land reptiles – 50% of all animal families and many trees die out	57% of all families 83% of all genera
Triassic-Jurassic	200 Ma	Sea and land animals (amphibians and reptiles). Many ammonoids. 35% of all animal families die out. Most early dinosaur families became extinct	23% of all families 48% of all genera
Cretaceous-Tertiary	65 Ma	Bivalves, belemnites, dinosaurs, ammonites, pterosaurs, plesiosaurs, mososaurs, many families of fish, bivalves, echinoids and many others	17% of all families 50% of all genera

Case study

Recognising a mass extinction can be tricky. Look for the following features:
- different organisms above and below a boundary
- possible unconformity
- possible clay layer (ash) which may contain iridium.

Mass extinctions allow other groups and species to diversify and evolve. Without the extinction of the dinosaurs, mammals may not have become the most dominant organism.

Mass extinctions kill off many **species**, but the empty niches left behind may allow other **genera** to adapt into new ecological niches, allowing life to diversify. Mass extinctions are usually followed by a rapid increase in the number of new species, fuelling adaptive radiation.

The mass extinction hypothesis

Mass extinctions have attracted a lot of interest over the years. In line with other scientific ideas, there are many **hypotheses** to explain mass extinctions. Nothing is universally accepted about the cause of mass extinctions. It is important to remember that these ideas are refined over time; some ideas are rejected and others have their evidence strengthened. It may be that some, all or none of these ideas may be the real reason behind these events. The evidence is for you to consider. Remember what 'hypothesis' means; it is to be tested and accepted, refined or rejected. There is no right answer, just the balance of probability.

Extinction is the process in which groups of organisms (species) die out. If the birth rate is less than the death rate over time, extinction results. Extinction is a natural result of evolution. Species go extinct when they are unable to adapt to changes in the environment or compete effectively with other organisms. Well over 99% of the species that have ever lived have become extinct.

It is almost impossible to assess the real nature of a mass extinction, as the fossil record shows such a small and biased number of organisms preserved. How quickly a mass extinction occurs is a matter of debate. Do organisms die out gradually or catastrophically? Mass extinctions are not usually single, instantaneous events. Most seem to take place gradually, over at least 100 000 years of environmental deterioration. It is possible that events moved more quickly than this, but we have no means of measuring if they did. Unfortunately, the fossil record is not good enough to tell us the answers.

Questions

1 Explain what is meant by the word 'extinction'.
2 Describe the patterns of extinction over geological time.
3 What does the word hypothesis mean? Why are hypotheses refined or rejected in science?

Permo-Triassic mass extinction

What do we know?

This was a massive extinction event, the biggest in geologic history, which occurred around **251 million years ago**, marking the end of the Palaeozoic Era. The event itself was not abrupt, there being a gradual decline in species over several million years. Around 95% of all marine invertebrates became extinct, including trilobites, tabulate corals, rugose corals and many brachiopods. Other groups, such as foraminifera and cephalopods, were greatly depleted. Extinctions also happened on land, with a huge number of plant species, 77% of tetrapods, large amphibians and some insects becoming extinct, indicating that this was a truly global event.

Hypotheses to explain the Permo-Triassic mass extinction

Supercontinent formation – at the end of the Permian, **Pangaea** was formed when all the world's continents collided together. This formed one large landmass, called a supercontinent. The evidence to support this landmass comes from plate reconstructions and the stratigraphic record. This presence of one large landmass had several effects:

- There were fewer continental shelves so there was a lack of habitat for shallow marine dwellers. This is backed up with evidence that shows a massive decline in shallow marine species.
- Presence of a single continent caused rapid fluctuations in climate, and unstable weather patterns.
- A single continent reduced the input into the oceans from rivers and estuaries. This would have significantly decreased the amount of nutrients available for shallow marine life and may have altered the salinity of the oceans.
- Widespread glaciations occurred in the southern hemisphere (Australia, South Africa, South America and Antarctica). This caused the sea level to fall (regression), reducing shallow shelf environments.

Major volcanic activity (Siberian Traps) – this is believed to be the largest volcanic eruption in Earth history. It is probably not a coincidence that they correspond with the largest extinction event in geological history. The volcanic rocks are largely flood basalts, thought to be from a very large mantle plume intersecting the surface. Today the volcanic rocks cover an area greater than the size of Europe, about two million km^2. The eruptions were thought to last for around one million years. This volcanic activity had several effects:

- The emission of poisonous gasses would kill many plants and animals in close proximity.
- The gases and ash particles emitted during the eruption could have initially lowered the global temperatures by blocking the heat from the sun. As this was on such a large scale, the global change in temperature could have been significant, causing global glaciations and a fall in sea level. This cooling event could have lasted from hundreds to thousands of years.
- The emission of greenhouse gases such as CO_2 and SO_2 could have caused an increase in global temperatures, after the cooling period had ceased. This effect is believed to have lasted for thousands to millions of years.

Methane hydrates (methane ice) – this is a solid form of methane, believed to have formed within the sediments, which remains solid and stable up to around 18 °C. The global increase in temperature at the end of the Permian is also thought to have triggered these methane hydrates in the seabed to become mobile and gaseous, causing them to be released. This could have disrupted life in the seas and increased the greenhouse gases in the atmosphere.

Key definitions

Pangaea is the name given to the supercontinent which formed at the end of the Permian Period.

Traps are large scale volcanism resulting in the formation of dark-coloured igneous rocks (basic).

Figure 1 Reconstruction of Pangaea

Cretaceous–Tertiary (K–T) mass extinction

What do we know?

This is a large extinction event and 75% of species became extinct around 65 million years ago. This marks the end of the Mesozoic Era. Once again, the event was gradual, showing a decline in species over several million years, leading finally to an abrupt extinction event. Marine casualties included large reptiles (ichthyosaurs), brachiopods, ammonites, coccoliths, foraminifera, belemnites, fish and some bivalves. Losses on land included dinosaurs, pterosaurs and plants. However, some groups were relatively unaffected by this extinction event. Animals such as crocodiles, turtles, lizards, mammals and birds all made it through without many casualties. The extinction of the dinosaurs did leave a large ecological niche, which mammals largely filled.

Hypotheses to explain the Cretaceous–Tertiary mass extinction

Impact of an asteroid or meteorite – this remains a popular theory and there is a lot of evidence to suggest that a large object did hit the Earth 65 million years ago:

- A layer of **iridium** can be found concentrated in clays at the boundary. Most iridium comes from space.
- **Shocked grains of quartz** are found at the boundary as a thin layer within the sediments.
- The presence of **tektites**, usually found near impact craters. Tektites have a very low water content suggesting they may not have formed on Earth, or they formed as the rock had melted very quickly on impact at the surface and were then thrown into the air.
- There is large-scale sedimentary evidence in Texas that there was a huge **tsunami** at this time.
- A large meteorite crater can be found on the Yucatan Peninsula in Mexico, at Chicxulub. The crater is shown by gravity variations across the region, and shows a circular depression about 180 km in diameter. Although there are other contenders, it is the most likely impact site for the meteorite.

Key definitions

Iridium is a transition element, rare on Earth, but found in meteorites. Luis Alvarez (1980) first proposed this as evidence that a giant object hit the Earth.

Shocked quartz is grains of quartz that has characteristics showing it to have been deformed under high pressure. It was first discovered at nuclear testing sites, and linked with meteorite impacts.

Tektites are spheres or irregular shaped lumps of solidified molten rock, a few centimetres in diameter, black or green in colour, which are thought to have formed as a result of extremely high pressures and temperatures.

A **tetrapod** is a four-limbed vertebrate.

A **tsunami** is a massive wave formed either due to an underwater earthquake or a meteorite impact.

Figure 2 Photos to show **a** shocked quartz grains and **b** tektites

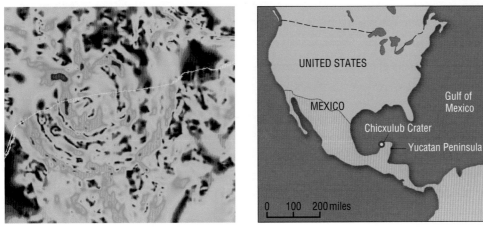

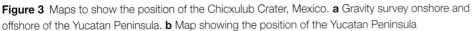

Figure 3 Maps to show the position of the Chicxulub Crater, Mexico. **a** Gravity survey onshore and offshore of the Yucatan Peninsula. **b** Map showing the position of the Yucatan Peninsula

Major volcanic activity (Deccan Traps) – there was another enormous series of eruptions in India, covering an area of roughly $500\,000$ km^2. The eruptions took place over about 30 000 years. The effect of this volcanism was probably the same as with the Siberian Traps (see above).

Questions

1 What organisms were affected by the Cretaceous–Tertiary and the Permo-Triassic extinctions?

2 Explain how volcanism can contribute to extinction.

3 A meteorite could have caused the Cretaceous–Tertiary extinction. What is the evidence for this?

Geologists have a different timescale than most people. A short time in geological terms can be measured in millions of years! We talk about 'recent' for sediments or fossils formed in the last million years. Comprehending geological time is a stretch of the imagination. The term 'deep time' is used to describe the vast expanse of time in the geologically ancient past.

Putting actual dates in millions of years to the geological timescale is done by radiometric dating. Geologists have calculated the age of Earth at 4.6 billion years. But for humans whose life span rarely reaches more than 100 years, how can we be so sure of that ancient date?

Establishing an absolute timescale

An absolute timescale uses measured ages to correlate rock units around the world. This became possible for geologists following the understanding of radioactivity in the early part of the 1900s. The well-established relative age of rocks based on stratigraphy and fossil assemblages was gradually 'fixed' as radiometric ages were added.

Naturally occurring radioactive isotopes in rocks are unstable and break down (decay) at a statistically constant rate. This rate of decay can be measured and expressed as the **half-life** of the isotope – the time taken for half of the unstable parent atoms to break down to stable daughter atoms.

If the relative amounts of parent to daughter atoms in a rock sample can be measured, then we know how many half-lives have passed since the parent was created. For example, if the ratio of parent to daughter is 25:75, then two half-lives have passed since the radioactive atom was created. The relative amount of parent and daughter atoms is measured using a mass spectrometer. New techniques for radiometric dating are being developed using laser ablation or electron microprobes, which allow dates to be obtained without destroying the rock sample.

Scarcity of radioactive minerals

Radioactive isotopes are only found in small quantities in some rock-forming minerals. As a result, only a few rocks can be dated radiometrically. Putting actual ages to the geological timescale is therefore very difficult, unless there are igneous intrusions or volcanics mixed in with the sedimentary rocks. Dating sedimentary rocks on their own dates when the fragments were formed – not the rock.

To obtain enough material for an accurate analysis is difficult. It may involve crushing the rock and picking out the required minerals such as zircon or muscovite from the granite.

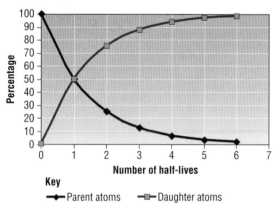

Figure 1 Relative amounts of parent and daughter atoms with increasing half-lives

Key
—◆— Parent atoms —■— Daughter atoms

Case study

Most of the lunar rocks are extremely old compared to rocks found on Earth. They range in age from about 3160 Ma to about 4500 Ma. The youngest basaltic eruptions are believed to have occurred about 1200 Ma. In contrast, the oldest ages of rocks from the Earth are about 3800 Ma with rocks still forming today.

Examiner tip

^{14}C is not used by geologists because the half-life is too short (around 5730 years).

Parent isotope	Daughter isotope	Found in	Half-life (Ma)	Use
^{238}U	^{206}Pb	Zircon, uraninite	4500	Can be used to date igneous rocks from 10 to 4600 million years
^{235}U	^{207}Pb		710	
^{40}K	^{40}Ar	Muscovite, biotite, hornblende, glauconite (found in sedimentary rocks)	1260	Can be used to date igneous (often volcanic rocks), metamorphic and a few sedimentary rocks from 100 000 to 4600 million years
^{87}Rb	^{87}Sr	Muscovite, biotite, potassium feldspar	50 000	Can be used to date igneous and metamorphic rocks from years 10 to 4600 million years

Dates are generally given with a margin of error, such as ±15 million years, because there are difficulties in obtaining accurate dates. It could be due to equipment, contaminated samples or differences between individual minerals and whole rock dates.

Problems with dating sedimentary rocks

Obtaining accurate dates for sedimentary rocks is very difficult because weathering and erosion tend to break the closed system that is essential for a reliable date. Problems are due to loss of gases where weathering has allowed the argon to escape, resulting in a date that is younger than it should be. Especially in sedimentary rocks, where glauconite is the only mineral with ^{40}K, initial amounts of the isotope can be difficult to determine.

Sedimentary rocks are made up of fragments of older rocks. The clasts could have a range of ages all older than the rock being dated. Radiometric dates can therefore be very misleading, giving much older dates.

Problems with dating metamorphic rocks

Metamorphic rocks also cause problems. Different minerals become **closed systems** at different temperatures. Parent or daughter atoms can be lost or gained during heating events. $^{40}K^{40}Ar$ has closure temperatures between 150 and 550 °C, depending on the mineral used. During a series of metamorphic events the radiometric clock will have been reset in some minerals and not in others – a variety of conflicting dates is possible. However, these can be very useful, even telling us the dates for the start and end of a metamorphic event.

Problems with dating igneous rocks

There are even problems associated with dating igneous rocks, as large-scale intrusions may take tens of millions of years to cool – different parts reach the closure temperature at different times. The most reliable igneous rock dates are therefore minor intrusions and extrusions that cool rapidly.

Potassium-argon dating

Potassium-Argon (K-Ar) dating is the most widely used method of radiometric dating. Potassium is a component in many common minerals and can be used to determine the ages of igneous, metamorphic and a few sedimentary rocks.

The radioactive isotope ^{40}K decays to ^{40}Ar and ^{40}Ca with a half-life of 1.26×10^9 years. ^{40}K decays to produce two isotopes. $^{40}Calcium$ is the beta particle formed but this cannot be used for dating as it is indistinguishable from the calcium commonly occurring in many rocks. Fortunately, 11% decays to form the stable alpha particle ^{40}Ar. This is a gas, which is not formed in any other way, but has the disadvantage that it can easily escape from the mineral lattice, especially when heated. Loss of this daughter product leads to an underestimate of the rock age.

In order to determine the ^{40}Ar content of a rock, it must be melted and the isotopic composition of the released gas measured via mass spectrometry. It is also necessary to separately measure the amount of ^{40}K in the sample. This can be measured using flame photometry or atomic absorption spectroscopy. The ratio between the ^{40}Ar and the ^{40}K is related to the time elapsed since the rock was cool enough to trap the Ar.

This method dates the time of crystallisation of the mineral that is being dated so is best used with rocks that contain minerals that crystallised over a short time period. This method should also be applied only to minerals that remained in a closed system with no loss or gain of the parent or daughter isotope.

Rubidium-strontium dating

Rubidium has several isotopes, ^{87}Rb being the most useful one. Because it has such a long half-life, there is some uncertainty attached to it (quoted as between 47 000 and 50 000 Ma). It decays to form $^{87}Strontium$ as the daughter isotope. This is a solid and therefore unlikely to be lost from the rock. Rb-Sr dating is thus more useful for metamorphic rocks than K-Ar.

Figure 2 Muscovite mica crystal that could be used for radiometric dating

10 cm

Examiner tip

The half-life of ^{40}K is stated as 10 times the correct value in some well regarded text books – beware! The correct value is 1260 million years.

Part of the problem is that the American billion and the UK billion differ.

One English billion = $1\,000\,000\,000\,000 = 10^{12}$

One American billion = $1\,000\,000\,000 = 10^{9}$

Questions

1 Why is Rb-Sr more suitable as a method of measuring the age of metamorphic rocks?

2 What ratio of ^{40}K to ^{40}Ar would be found in a minor intrusion that had cooled 3780 Ma?

3 Give examples of problems in obtaining accurate radiometric dates from sedimentary, metamorphic and igneous rocks.

4 Draw a half-life curve for $^{87}Rb^{87}Sr$, taking the half life as 50 000 million years.

Stratigraphic methods

Stratigraphy is the study of strata or layers of rock. Relative dating is a way of determining whether one layer of rock is older than another. There are five main types of relative dating, sometimes called 'laws':

- original horizontality
- principle of superposition
- way-up criteria
- included fragments
- cross-cutting relationships.

Original horizontality

Most sedimentary rocks are originally deposited in shallow seas. For example, clasts carried down by rivers are deposited as beds, with breaks in deposition showing up as bedding planes. These beds are commonly laid down horizontally or very close to horizontal. It is therefore assumed that if layers of rock are tilted, then they have moved from this original horizontal position.

The principle of superposition

This principle states that the rocks at the bottom of a sequence are always the oldest and younger rocks were laid down on top of older ones. For example, rocks at the bottom of cliffs are older than those at the top. This assumes that the rocks have not been turned upside down.

Way-up criteria

These structures can only form one way up and so if these are present we can tell if the rocks have been turned upside down. These are illustrated in spread 2.3.7 and include:

- Desiccation cracks, which dry up with the cracks pointing to the oldest rocks.
- Graded bedding, where the large particles sink to the bottom first, followed by finer sediment.
- Rootlets always grow down into soil.
- Cross bedding, these can only be truncated on the upper surface.
- Fossils can sometimes be found in life position and so indicate the way they lived.

Included fragments

Fragments eroded from an older rock can be found within younger rock. The fragments have to be older than the rocks that they are found in:

- Xenoliths found in igneous rocks have to be older, as they are fragments of country rock that fell into the magma due to stoping.
- Derived fossils are also older than the sediments they are found within. They have been eroded from older beds and redeposited in younger beds.
- Pebbles in a conglomerate are older rocks eroded and then redeposited.

Figure 1 Superposition in horizontal beds

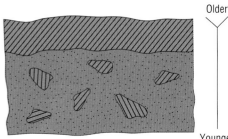

Figure 2 Included fragments and relative ages

Cross-cutting relationships

Features which cut through rocks must be younger than the rocks they cut. An example could be a dyke, which cuts through sediments. The sediments had to be there first for the dyke to be able to intrude into them. Similarly structures such as faults that cross-cut strata are, by definition, younger than the beds they cut.

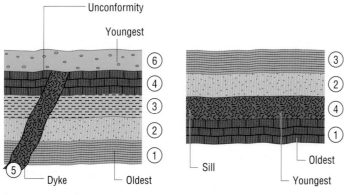

Figure 3 Intrusions cross-cutting strata

Unconformities

Unconformities represent a break in deposition and erosion of the succession. They are a gap in the geological record in which there may be time to fold and erode the older rocks before new sediments are deposited above the unconformity. There is often a dip in the oldest beds, meaning that rocks of various ages are in contact with the young beds above. When there is no change in dip across the unconformity, it may be recognised by erosion, rootlets or missing parts of the fossil record.

Fossils and relative dating

For fossils to be a reliable tool in establishing relative ages, it is important that they evolved rapidly, showing obvious preserved changes. Ideally they should be widespread, numerous and in a variety of rock types or environments to allow us a chance of finding them.

The process of identifying fossil species allowed us to divide up the geological record into divisions, based on their fossil content. Unknown rocks were placed in their correct order by identifying their fossil species. Clearly this is more difficult in depositional environments where little evidence of life is preserved, such as deserts. It was also difficult before the evolution of life with preservable hard parts, in the Precambrian.

Drilling boreholes brings up chippings from all depths of the well. The samples can be analysed for their microfossil assemblage and a relative age established. It is important therefore to search for the oldest microfossils in any borehole sample.

Summary – the geological timescale

The recognition of fossils in rock strata and use of these 'laws' of stratigraphy has allowed rocks around the world to be classified by their relative ages. They have been put into the appropriate era, period or epoch. These divisions of the geological timescale were later given absolute ages by radiometric dating. The timescale is therefore a mix of evidence using zone fossils, fossil assemblages and radiometric dates where possible.

Questions

1. Describe the five types of relative dating. Draw diagrams to illustrate one example of each.
2. Draw a cross-section incorporating sills, dykes, faults, folds and unconformities. Challenge a friend to establish the geological history.

Relative and absolute dating can be used to work out the geological history – the sequence of events – from a map or cross-section. It is no harder than the principles of superposition, cross-cutting features and included fragments, but it is all integrated together.

Identifying structures on Figure 1

Folding type

The dip arrows on the map and the repeated outcrop of the mudstone and sandstone beds show that the map area is an anticlinal fold. In anticlines, the oldest beds are in the axial, central part of the fold. This knowledge allows you to draw a simple section.

Folding of the beds is along a nearly N–S axis, with the axial plane trace lying near the centre of the clay bed between the dip arrows. The dip of the limbs is different with the western limb at 31 degrees while the eastern limb dips west at 24 degrees – making this an asymmetrical fold. The western limb has a narrow outcrop so the dip is steeper than the east limb with a wider outcrop.

Which fault came first?

Faults can also cross-cut each other and can therefore be used to determine the order of events. In this case, F2 is the oldest followed by F1, which has not been affected by F2. The final phase of faulting F3 cuts and displaces both F2 and F1, as well as the dyke and fold.

Igneous intrusions

Dolerite 2 is a transgressive sill as it is mainly concordant to the beds but does cross from the clay bed to the sandstone. It is younger than the beds into which it is intruded and older than all the faults as both F2 and F3 cut the sill. A sill can be recognised by the way the igneous rock follows the beds.

The dyke of dolerite 1 is discordant – cutting across all the beds and structures with a straight line outcrop. It is younger than the beds, fold and F1 and F2, but older than F3 which has displaced it.

Since all these events took place, the area was eroded to give a flat landscape and expose the older beds.

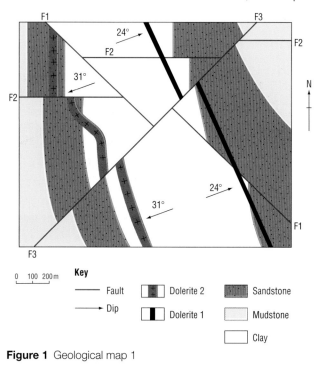

Key

0 100 200 m

— Fault
→ Dip

Dolerite 2
Dolerite 1

Sandstone
Mudstone
Clay

Figure 1 Geological map 1

Identifying structures on Figure 2

- In this case you need to start by working out the order in which the beds were deposited. The youngest beds are always in the centre of the syncline so the oldest beds are the mudstone, then the sandstone, followed by the shale.
- The folding is a symmetrical syncline with the limbs dipping at 45 degrees and the axial plane trace is NE–SW.
- Two faults trending NW–SE cut across the fold. There is no horizontal displacement because the axial plane trace of the fold is not displaced. The vertical movement can be determined by looking at the outcrop pattern of the fold. The shale in the centre of the fold has a narrower outcrop on the upthrow side of a syncline so the west side has been downthrown.

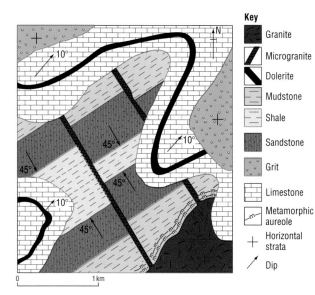

Key

Granite
Microgranite
Dolerite
Mudstone
Shale
Sandstone
Grit
Limestone
Metamorphic aureole
Horizontal strata
Dip

Figure 2 Geological map 2

Igneous intrusions

The granite batholith intruded into the sediments and formed a metamorphic aureole affecting the mudstone. This would be metamorphosed by contact metamorphism into a spotted rock, and very close to the granite a hornfels. The microgranite dykes formed at the same time as the granite. Some of the magma was able to take advantage of the planes of weakness along the fault lines that cut the folded beds. The magma cooled more rapidly in the minor intrusion so that the crystal size is medium instead of coarse for the granite.

Unconformities

An angular unconformity is recognised by:

- beds and structures being cut off by the younger unconformable beds
- difference in the angle of dip between the older and younger beds.

There must have been a period of erosion after the folding, faulting and intrusion of the batholith and then the limestone was laid down unconformably. This is lying on top of the older beds. The limestone has been intruded by a concordant sill and tilted NE 10 degrees.

Another period of erosion was followed by the grit being laid down unconformably as it cross-cuts the sill. It is still horizontal.

Relative and absolute dates used with maps and cross-sections

We can add palaeontological knowledge to improve our understanding of the relative ages to the cross-cutting relationships formed by faults, intrusions, folding and unconformities. See if you can write a detailed geological history for the cross-section without looking at the answer below:

- The cross-section shows that the oldest bed is the lowest, which is the conglomerate with shale above.
- These beds are older than 170 Ma as the dyke cross-cuts them.
- The dyke has baked the rocks on either side, causing a narrow zone of metamorphism.
- A period of tilting and erosion took place.
- Then limestone was laid down unconformably. It contains ammonites, which allow it to be zoned. It formed between 170 and 38 Ma.
- A lava flow cross-cuts the limestone, which suggests that there was a period of erosion before the volcanic activity. It is likely to be a lava flow and not a sill, as there is only one baked margin below which formed a thin layer of marble.
- The sand and gravel contains rounded ammonites, which are likely to be derived by erosion from the limestone below. The sand and gravel is younger than 38 Ma.

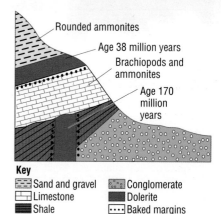

Figure 3 A cross-section with data on fossils and radiometric ages of the igneous rocks

Key labels: Rounded ammonites; Age 38 million years; Brachiopods and ammonites; Age 170 million years

Key
- Sand and gravel
- Limestone
- Shale
- Conglomerate
- Dolerite
- Baked margins

Case study

In addition to simplified geological maps, you may be asked to interpret photos of outcrops. In order for this to be possible under exam conditions, these are mostly straightforward vertical sections showing structures (faults, folds and angular unconformities). Bed thicknesses, joint, dips and fault displacements can be labelled. You will be asked to draw a simplified sketch of the photo to describe the geological history and allow labelling of your interpretation.

Figure 4 The older beds are Devonian sandstones with Triassic conglomerates above

Questions

1 Write a geological history for Figure 1.
2 Write a geological history for Figure 2 and include the following information to add a timescale. The shale contains graptolites with a single uniserial stipe. The limestone contains the long-hinged brachiopod *Productus* and goniatites. The grit is red in colour with cross bedding and channels and imbricate structures and contains no fossils.
3 Sketch and label the photo (Figure 4) adding measurements and describe the events that have formed these rocks and structures.

The geological or stratigraphic column included in this text is the result of major scientific efforts, which continue today to refine the detail.

In 1650, Archbishop Ussher concluded that the Earth had been formed on the night of October 23rd, 4004 BC. To disagree with his biblical study was to attract considerable disapproval, yet it seemed obvious to some observational Earth scientists that the planet must be a great deal older.

The age of the Earth by the salt content of the oceans

How could the age of the Earth be calculated? Joly used a very clever method in 1899. This Irish geologist assumed that the oceans had started as fresh water and that salt had been steadily added by rivers. To find the age of the oceans, all he needed to do was divide the amount of salt in the oceans by how much is added per year!

You can see that there is plenty of scope for mistakes here. Finding the salt contents of all rivers and their annual discharges would be a hard task, even with global resources today. Joly estimated that there were 160 million tonnes of sodium added to the oceans each year. The oceans have a remarkably constant salt content of about 0.35 % so after a quick estimate of the oceans' volume he arrived at an age of 90 Ma.

This, as you know, is far too small but is a vast improvement on the 6000 year age. If Joly had taken into account the salts taken out of the seas (e.g. as evaporites) and the changes in the amount of salt carried from the land over geological time, he would have arrived at an age closer to 2500 Ma. Still too low, but not a bad effort.

The age of the Earth by rates of cooling

If you had carelessly forgotten making several cups of coffee whilst reading a fascinating geology textbook, you might be able to tell which was the oldest by how cold each had become. The scientist in you *might* measure the temperatures and the rate at which temperatures dropped – not at a fixed rate but one that dropped more slowly as coffee approached room temperature.

In 1862, Lord Kelvin set out to estimate the age of the Earth using the same principles. He was a world-class physicist and used the best experimental data available to him. The amount of heat flowing out of the Earth depends on the conductivity and the **geothermal gradient**. He obtained that gradient from measurements of the increase of temperature with depth in mines (25–30 °C per kilometre). Conductivity is measurable using machined rock samples in the laboratory.

Kelvin assumed (correctly) that the Earth had started off as a molten body. His result of between 20 and 40 Ma did not satisfy many geologists, who saw field evidence that rocks had formed over much longer time spans. What Kelvin could not know was that the Earth was being continually heated by radioactive decay – it appeared to have been cooling for only a short period.

Case study

Accumulation rates of sediments	
Sediment	**Range of rates (mm/year)**
Calcareous ooze	0.01 to 0.1
Reef limestones	1 to 300
Mudstones	0.001 to 1
Sandstones	1 to 10 000
Conglomerates	50 to 50 000

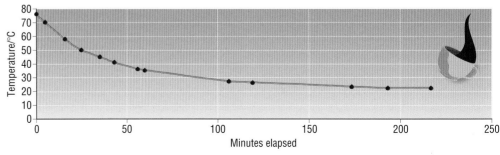

Figure 1 Cooling coffee with time

Rates of sedimentation and the age of the Earth

If you knew how long it took for a metre thickness of sediment to be deposited, and how many metres of sediment had been deposited altogether, then you could do a calculation to put a lower limit on the age of the Earth.

As soon as you try this you run into problems. There are lots of variables in geology. Coarse sediment in a delta or alluvial fan accumulates rapidly, and a single flash flood in a wadi can deposit a metre or more of poorly sorted sediment. At the other end of the scale, fine sediments such as those of the ocean floor accumulate extremely slowly.

Another obvious difficulty is that different thicknesses of sedimentary rock are to be found in different parts of the world, depending on geography as well as geology. The principle of **Uniformitarianism** tells us to expect just that. At the extremes you can immediately think of parts of the world that are suffering erosion rather than deposition. These are the unconformities of the future.

Sediment needs compaction to form sedimentary rock. A thick deposit of wet sediment will be much reduced by the time it is lithified. At depths greater than 10 km, the pressures and temperatures are high enough to form metamorphic rocks, so how are we going to find out what thickness of sedimentary rocks they represent. It is another tough question and contributed to the spread of answers that came from the geologists using thickness of sedimentary rocks to find the age of the Earth. These varied from 3 to 1600 Ma, depending on the rate of deposition used.

Figure 2 The thick layers of greywacke probably formed from turbidity currents in a few days. The thin layers of black shale took thousands or even millions of years to form from suspended clay particles

The geological column

The simplified version illustrated shows the Phanerozoic eon subdivided into three eras. These mark drastic changes in the fossil content of the rocks as the mass extinctions of the Permian–Triassic and Cretaceous–Tertiary boundaries took their effects. Up to 95% of species were wiped out and a sudden evolutionary radiation of new species occurred to occupy the vacant environmental niches.

Each era is divided into a number of **periods** on the basis of important changes in fossil species that are recognised worldwide. For example, the appearance and extinction of the graptoloids occurred principally between the beginning of the Ordovician and the end of the Silurian. Fossil evidence has been used to further subdivide the periods into **epochs** and then even smaller divisions. The useful zone fossil ammonites and graptolites changed so rapidly that some divisions are as short as 80 000 years.

The actual length of the periods could not be known until radiometric dates were added to the palaeontological knowledge. Sediments may be covered by lava or ash containing radioactive minerals, which give an absolute age limit to the rocks beneath. With the help of dates from igneous rocks from all over the world and the use of cross-cutting relationships, the boundaries of the divisions of the geological column have been approximated then refined as more data became available. You will notice differences in ages given in older textbooks. This book follows the timescale established by the International Commission on Stratigraphy in 2006.

Questions

1 Outline how the age of the Earth was estimated using the salt content of the oceans.
2 Explain why Kelvin's calculation of the age of the Earth was such an underestimate.
3 Rocks of the Cretaceous system in the United Kingdom have a total thickness of 1600 m. If the Cretaceous period lasted around 70 Ma, what is the rate of accumulation of these rocks in mm/year? How does this compare with the range of rates quoted in the table?

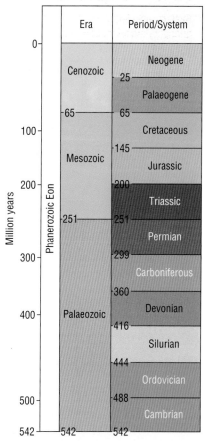

Figure 3 Simplified version of the geological column. Ages of boundaries are given to the nearest Ma. The traditional divisions of Tertiary and Quaternary have been promoted to sub-eras. The Q-T boundary occurred some 2.6 Ma before present

Correlation is the process of matching beds in geographically different areas, often for economic purposes such as coal or oil exploration. Most correlation work is done using borehole data. The closer the boreholes are, the greater the certainty of the data. With increased distance between boreholes there is more chance of a fault or lateral variation, which makes correlation difficult.

Biostratigraphic correlation

If two widely separated rock units contain a sequence of identical zone fossils, then the rocks have the same relative age. Using graptolites, ammonites and some microfossils, rocks can be correlated worldwide.

Methods of biostratigraphic correlation

1 **First or last appearance** (extinction) of zone fossils, but when fossil groups first appear they can be difficult to find at the first point, as they may be very rare initially. The same applies towards the end of a fossil's range. The correlation on the top diagram has been done using first and last appearances for each of the fossil zones.

2 The **range** of a zone fossil can be very helpful when used with other fossils. Some fossils, such as B shown on the bottom diagram, have a short time range, others such as A have a longer time range, but where two or more fossil ranges overlap, for example, C and D, a particular biozone can be precisely determined. Zones are often named after an index fossil. The shorter the time range, the better the zone fossil.

3 A **fossil assemblage** is when a number of different fossils are found in one bed. On the diagram, bed 3 can be defined by having assemblages of fossils A C D E.

Problems of biostratigraphic correlation

- Many fossils, especially benthonic invertebrates, are restricted to particular environments, for example, lime-mud sea floor, reef and sandy sea floor, so are found in just a few rock types.
- Some kinds of fossils are very long-ranged. Their rates of evolutionary change were very slow, so are no use for establishing biozones.
- Good zone fossils such as the graptolites are delicate and are only preserved in quiet environments, being destroyed by more turbulent conditions.
- Derived fossils confuse the true sequence of beds. They will give an age far older than the rock they have ended up in after erosion and redeposition.
- Not all sedimentary rocks contain fossils. In particular, rocks laid down in glacial, fluvial and desert environments on land are unlikely to have any fossils.

Lithostratigraphic correlation

This is based on recognising rock types or, more usually, a sequence or succession of rock types. If you are very lucky, the succession may have a marker horizon – a bed so easily distinguished that you instantly know where you are in the sequence. These are always unusual, such as an oxidised red bed in a sequence of dark rocks.

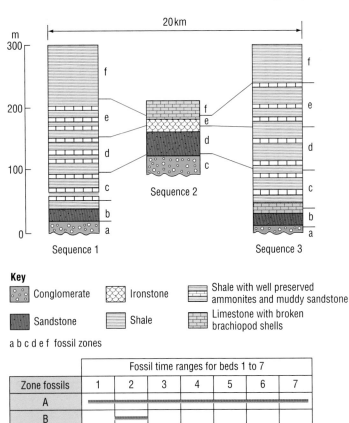

Key

- ▢ Conglomerate
- ▨ Ironstone
- ▤ Shale with well preserved ammonites and muddy sandstone
- ▨ Sandstone
- ▤ Shale
- ▦ Limestone with broken brachiopod shells

a b c d e f fossil zones

Fossil time ranges for beds 1 to 7							
Zone fossils	1	2	3	4	5	6	7
A							
B							
C							
D							
E							

Figure 1 Biostratigraphic correlation methods using first and last appearances of fossils in boreholes and fossil ranges and assemblages

Methods of lithostratigraphic correlation

1 You could correlate using a sequence of beds. If you used the sequences in the diagram above for biostratigraphic correlation, then you would correlate the sandstones overlying conglomerate for all three boreholes. But you know from the fossil zones that this would be wrong. Without fossil evidence, lithostratigraphic correlation is very difficult.

2 Looking at the thicknesses of beds is a bit like recognising a barcode; it does not matter if the whole thing is large or small, it is the sequence of thin and thick bars that gives you the information. Such a correlation might work for identifying where you are in a coalfield. This has immense economic importance – is it worth drilling further to find a good thick seam such as was worked in a neighbouring field?

3 The composition of beds may be distinctive with a rare mineral present in a bed. The Cretaceous–Tertiary boundary rocks are correlated on the presence of iridium.

Problems of lithostratigraphic correlation

1 **Lateral variation** – where sediments change type horizontally:

- Sedimentary deposits change in thickness laterally, for example, closer to the source of the sediment beds may be thicker, further away they may be thinner. This is clear for turbidite sequences formed in deep sea areas.
- In a fluvial environment, point bar sands are being deposited at the same time as flood plain clays. In a shallow sea environment, there will be sandstones being laid down close to the beach, while at the same time clays are being deposited offshore in the low-energy environments.
- Similarly deltaic sediments have different sediments forming in the delta top, front and offshore areas at the same time.

2 **Diachronous beds** – where one sediment type is laid down at different times. The result of different sediments being laid down at the same time is diachronous beds which cut 'across time'. A good example is where a delta is building out into the sea (see spread 2.3.13). Over the years, a continuous layer of sands is left behind. These sands get younger from land to sea – they are definitely *not* the same age. The same is true for the other rock types in a delta cycle.

Chronostratigraphic correlation

This is matching events which may be possible over large areas. Sometimes worldwide changes in sea level result in unconformities over large areas, which can then be correlated.

Using tuffs from a volcanic eruption

A tuff is the rock resulting from pyroclastic deposition. When a violent eruption occurs, ash is blasted tens of kilometres into the atmosphere and is laid down over enormous areas at exactly the same time – geologically instantaneously.

The tuff that forms from the ash is the best of all rocks to use for correlation because:

- You can carry out a chemical analysis to determine an exact composition match.
- It is laid down over large areas of land and sea very rapidly.
- It can be used to obtain a radiometric date, such as K-Ar.
- Can be used for both relative and absolute dating.

Using varves from glacial lakes

In the summer, glacial ice melts faster and the increased flows carry down silts into the lake to make a thin pale layer. During the winter, there is no meltwater and the lake itself may freeze over. The result is very low-energy deposition of clay particles and organic matter that grows under the ice to produce a thin dark layer. One year is recorded as a pair of layers on the lake bed. This means that you can count layers to find out how many years are represented in the sequence. The correlation is provided by thicker layers resulting from hotter summers, the pattern of thick and thin bands being the same for all lakes in the same area.

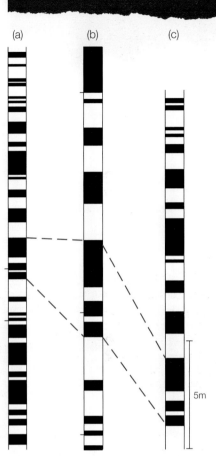

(a) (b) (c)

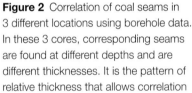

5m

Figure 2 Correlation of coal seams in 3 different locations using borehole data. In these 3 cores, corresponding seams are found at different depths and are different thicknesses. It is the pattern of relative thickness that allows correlation

Questions

1 Look at the borehole sequences of coal seams for lithostratigraphic correlation. Which borehole has the oldest rocks?

2 Why might a biostratigraphic correlation be better using graptolite species rather than trilobites?

3 When does a lithostratigraphic correlation most likely disagree with the fossil and chronostratigraphic evidence?

We already know that the eras and periods of the Phanerozoic timescale were defined by the extinction and first appearance of important fossil groups. Now is the time to see how the fossil groups we know fit into that story.

Corals

The widespread corals are a useful stratigraphic tool, if you can recognise which group the fossil belongs to. Rugosa and Tabulata are both extinct – they did not survive the Permian. Rugose corals peaked in the Lower Carboniferous, while tabulate corals were abundant in the Silurian and Devonian. Scleractinian corals did not appear until the Triassic and are still common today. Corals are excellent environmental indicators.

Brachiopods

Brachiopods flourished in the Lower Palaeozoic, dominating Ordovician fauna. Most long-hinged families of brachiopods died out in the P–T extinction, though a few continue to the present day. Most of the Mesozoic to Recent forms are short-hinged. So long-hinged are Palaeozoic and short-hinged are Mesozoic or younger – *but* there are exceptions! Note that the bivalves which occupy many of the same ecological niches rapidly increased in numbers when the brachiopods declined. Is it a coincidence?

Ammonoids

The ammonoids are very useful in zoning the Upper Palaeozoic and Mesozoic eras. The Palaeozoic goniatites (Devonian to Permian) had simple angular sutures. In the Permian, ceratites took over; they had a more complex suture with frills on the lobes. In the Middle Triassic, true ammonites became dominant with their very complex frilly sutures. The ammonites are used as zone fossils to correlate marine rocks of the Devonian and Carboniferous, as well as the Jurassic and quite a bit of the Cretaceous. They did not survive the mass extinction at the K–T boundary.

Trilobites

Trilobites appeared in considerable variety and numbers in the Early Cambrian. These organisms dominated the seas during the Lower Palaeozoic and were the most advanced organisms on Earth. They reached a maximum in the Middle Ordovician and then went into decline to become rare in the Carboniferous and extinct in the Permian.

Graptolites

True graptolites are first seen in the Early Ordovician, quickly becoming a dominant part of the marine fauna. They were abundant until the Middle Silurian when they went into decline to become extinct in the Early Devonian. They are another extinct Palaeozoic fossil group and a very important group of zone fossils.

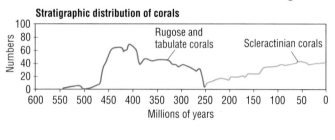

Stratigraphic distribution of corals

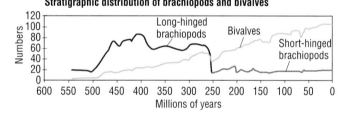

Stratigraphic distribution of brachiopods and bivalves

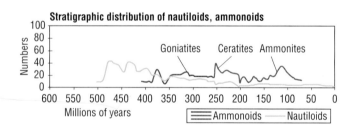

Stratigraphic distribution of nautiloids, ammonoids

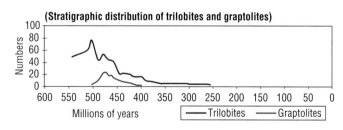

(Stratigraphic distribution of trilobites and graptolites)

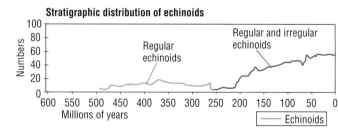

Stratigraphic distribution of echinoids

Figure 1 Stratigraphic ranges and relative abundance of fossil groups

Echinoids

Echinoids are used in a straightforward way to distinguish between the Palaeozoic era and younger rocks. Regular echinoids first appear in the early Cambrian but are rare until the Carboniferous. Irregular echinoids are not seen until the Lower Jurassic and did well in that period and the Cretaceous. They are both still in existence.

What makes a good zone fossil?

Now that you understand what is needed to define a time in geological history, you could make a wish list for the type of fossil that would be the most useful. The ideal zone fossils:

- evolve rapidly so that each species only has a short stratigraphic range, so that they define a very precise part of the geological column. A fossil such as the cephalopod, *Nautilus* would be useless as it has not changed in the last 400 Ma;
- are abundant (that is common when it was alive *and* easily preserved as a fossil), if it is to be found by geologists in the rocks they are trying to correlate;
- are easily identified remains. The differences between species must be obvious;
- are found in lots of different rock types so they are free floating or free swimming in all waters. If it is restricted to one environment of deposition it may only be found in one facies. This would restrict its use as a zone fossil;
- have a wide geographical distribution, preferably worldwide regardless of climate;
- have strong, hard shells or skeletons to enable them to be commonly preserved.

To hit all of these criteria would be remarkable – in fact all but a few of the tens of thousands of fossil species are not suitable as zone fossils. Often the mode of life of the organism is the deciding factor. Two of the best examples of zone fossils are the ammonites and the graptolites. What do they have in common? Almost nothing except that they were both **pelagic**; ammonites swam (**nektonic**) and graptolites floated (**planktonic**). This meant that they were widely distributed across the oceans and when they died fell into a variety of marine environments.

Stratigraphic ranges – the detail

The range of fossil groups is often marked onto geological column diagrams as a vertical line. More information about the diversity of genera can be seen if the line is made into a 'kite' diagram – the thickest part of the line representing the maximum diversity.

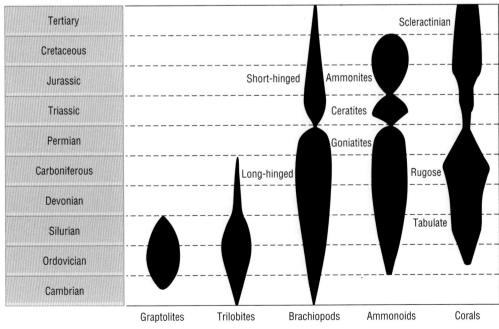

Figure 2 Diversity and range of fossil groups. The wider the bar, the more organisms existed

Graptolites as zone fossils

Graptolites evolved rapidly, they have clearly different morphologies and are used to establish zones in the Ordovician and Silurian as short as 4 Ma. This is excellent accuracy considering how long ago they were fossilised. Their scleroprotein skeleton means that they are preserved in deep water, anoxic environments where calcareous fossils would have dissolved due to the acid water. However, such a skeleton means that they are too delicate to ensure preservation in shallow oxidising marine environments.

Ammonites as zone fossils

Ammonites roamed the oceans ensuring wide distribution. Their strong calcareous exoskeletons provided an excellent prospect for preservation. They evolved rapidly and were numerous, so they tick most of the boxes for good zone fossils! They are rare in high-energy seas as they would probably be destroyed.

Microfossils as zone fossils

Microfossils are found in very large numbers. Their size means that although tricky to work with, they are preserved in the small chippings returned by drilling muds from boreholes. They are mostly calcareous but some forms, such as Radiolaria, have silica skeletons, which will survive below the Carbonate Compensation Depth or can be extracted undamaged from limestone by dissolving it in HCl. From an economic geology viewpoint, they are by far the most useful for correlating boreholes.

Questions

1 Look at the graphs showing the numbers of fossils in groups over time. Describe the effect of the mass extinctions at the Permian–Triassic and Cretaceous–Tertiary boundaries.

2 Research the use of microfossils by oil companies. Identify the microfossil groups most often used as zone fossils.

In recent years there has been an increasing level of debate between scientists and politicians around the world over mankind's influence on global climate. Opinions vary on exactly what changes have occurred and what the future will bring, but the majority of scientists believe that the effects we are seeing are too rapid and extreme to be caused by natural climate change.

What is climate?

When you think of different places around the world it is easy to see that there are differences in the types of weather they experience. Some places are colder and have regular snowfall, while others are so hot that rain hasn't fallen in centuries or longer.

The **weather** that a place experiences can be caused by many factors. These could be as simple as being closer to the poles and receiving less of the sun's heat, or more complex like the benefits felt in the UK due to the consistent flow of warm air from the Gulf Stream. The combination of all these factors over a number of decades gives every place on Earth its own average temperature, precipitation and amount of sunshine. This is the **climate**.

Icehouse and greenhouse

The term 'greenhouse' has been used all over the world for many years now, but for scientists it has a particular meaning. When we look at the Earth on a geological timescale we can see periods where the planet has been hotter than average and periods where it has been colder. We refer to the warm periods as Greenhouse Earth and the cold as Icehouse Earth.

We currently live in an icehouse where large continental ice sheets exist at both poles. The onset of this icehouse began in Antarctica 34 million years ago and in the Arctic about 2 million years ago. At least three times during Earth's history, the planet has been in a 'deep freeze', when ice sheets extended from the poles to the tropics.

Icehouse

Icehouse events are characterised by lower temperatures, ice caps and glaciers. The ice sheets from the last period of glaciation, called the 'ice age', are still present in Antarctica and Greenland. The huge increase in ice coverage then increases the drop in global temperatures by reflecting more of the Sun's radiation back into space.

Greenhouse

Greenhouse events are characterised by a lack of ice coverage and an overall increase in global temperatures. They can be caused by an increase in the amount of solar radiation reaching the Earth or a change in the concentration of gases in the atmosphere.

Extinction events

The extinction of species can be influenced by climate change. Most organisms thrive in a relatively limited range of conditions, and if the conditions in an area change then the species living there will alter. If the changes happen on a global scale then whole species or groups of species can be wiped out. An example of this is the mass extinction at the Permian–Triassic boundary where 96% of marine life and 70% of terrestrial life became extinct. This followed a major glaciation that affected Antarctica, Africa and South America when they were all joined as Gondwanaland. It was similar to the current icehouse, with continental ice sheets in the southern hemisphere and low atmospheric carbon dioxide concentrations.

Key definitions

Weather is the state of the atmosphere at a given time and place, with respect to variables such as temperature, moisture, wind velocity and barometric pressure.

Climate is the long-term weather pattern of an area, including temperature, precipitation and wind. Climate is how weather acts over many years.

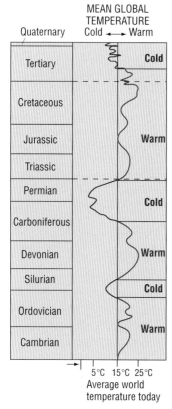

Figure 1 Mean global temperatures throughout geological time

Gathering evidence

The consequences of climate change are not limited to increases and decreases in global temperature, but temperature is always a crucial factor, so finding palaeotemperatures is the focus of many climate researchers' time.

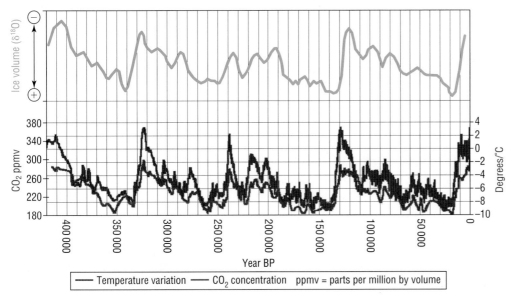

Figure 2 Oxygen isotope (the values are expressed as delta ^{18}O, which is the difference in the ratio compared to the world standard) compared to CO_2 and temperature measured in ice cores based on data from the Vostok station in Antarctica

Oxygen isotopes and temperature change

Water may not appear to change in any obvious way, but the atoms of oxygen within it can vary. Oxygen has three stable isotopes, ^{16}O, ^{17}O and ^{18}O. The majority (~99.76%) of the world's oxygen is ^{16}O, but a noticeable percentage (~0.20%) is ^{18}O.

The difference between these two isotopes is that the lighter ^{16}O is removed more easily by evaporation, so when water evaporates from the ocean it tends to leave more ^{18}O behind, altering the ratio of the two isotopes.

Under normal circumstances the ^{16}O in the evaporated water is returned to the ocean after falling as rain or snow and draining or melting through the river system. In periods of glaciation the light oxygen is trapped in the ice caps and glaciers. As temperatures drop globally the ratio of ^{18}O to ^{16}O changes. More ^{18}O is present in colder temperatures than in warmer temperatures, so if carbonate is formed at 20 °C, it will contain a higher proportion of ^{16}O than if it formed at 10 °C.

Once the ice caps have melted and the ^{18}O to ^{16}O ratio has returned to normal, the only evidence of the change remains in the shells of organisms living in the sea. The oxygen in the calcium carbonate shells of bivalves, belemnites and microfossils like foraminifera comes from the sea water and carbon dioxide.

Carbon isotopes and temperature change

Isotopes of carbon have been used in a similar fashion. The common ^{12}C accounts for the majority (~98.9%) of the carbon in the global cycle, but there is a small amount of the heavy isotope ^{13}C (~1.1%).

The temperature-dependent process using carbon isotope ratios is similar to that of oxygen, so that delta ^{13}C values from pelagic and benthic fossils can be correlated with climate change. Plants preferentially take up ^{12}C. Thus, during glacials, when the terrestrial biomass was greatly reduced, the ocean was relatively depleted in ^{13}C. Carbon isotopes are more useful than oxygen isotopes for stratigraphic purposes in the remote past up to 10 million years ago because they are more resistant to diagenetic change.

Questions

1. How would you describe temperatures today compared to temperatures 100 000 years ago? How would you describe temperatures today compared to temperatures 20 000 years ago?
2. Explain why changes in temperature can cause extinctions. What are the implications for animal life today?
3. Isotope chemistry is becoming very important for identifying changes through time. Research other uses or isotopes that can be used to give us data about ancient environmental conditions.

What causes climate change?

The amount of heat energy from solar radiation arriving at the surface of the Earth varies according to where on the planet you are. Because of the tilt of the Earth's axis, a smaller surface area at the Equator will receive the same amount of radiation as a larger area nearer one of the poles. In the high latitudes more energy is radiated back into space than is absorbed, while the opposite is true in low latitudes. This heat energy is presently distributed by wind systems caused by convection and ocean currents, such as the Gulf Stream.

Runaway effects

This equilibrium is delicately balanced so that small changes could easily cause positive feedback – a runaway effect.

- Increased snowfall in a cooler period would reflect more radiation back into space due to the high albedo – so then the temperature would drop even further. This results in increased snow and ice forming and so even more reflection, which could lead to the entire planet being iced over – the 'Snowball Earth'.
- A small increase in temperature allows the oceans to release more CO_2 than they absorb (solubility drops as temperature rises). More CO_2 traps more infrared radiation, raising the temperature of the atmosphere and oceans and releasing yet more CO_2. This could be the beginning of a greenhouse world.

Predicting the changes

Research has been conducted over the past few decades to try and predict future changes in climate by finding evidence of climate change in the past. By analysing geological data, climate scientists like Sir Nicholas Shackleton were able to find patterns that suggested global temperature rose and fell in a predictable pattern caused by natural variations.

Milankovich cycles

The cycles are caused by changes in the amount of radiation reaching the Earth from the Sun over time. This is not because the Sun changes its output of energy, as that has remained relatively constant, but because the Earth's orbit around the Sun varies in three predictable cycles.

- **Eccentricity:** the Earth's orbit changes shape to become more elliptical over a period of 100 000 years. At present the eccentricity is almost at a minimum with a difference of around 6% in received radiation between January and July. At maximum eccentricity this difference increases to between 20% and 30%, which has a massive effect on climate.
- **Obliquity:** the tilt of the Earth's axis, which is responsible for our changing seasons, changes up to 3° with a cycle of 41 000 years. A smaller tilt promotes the growth of ice sheets as warmer winters result in more moisture and snowfall.
- **Precession:** eccentricity and obliquity together cause this further cycle where the inclination of the Earth's axis changes in relation to where it is on the orbit. This cycle operates in periods of 19 000 and 23 000 years. At the moment we are closest to the Sun so northern winters are slightly warmer than 11 000 years ago when the planet was farthest from the Sun. Slow changes in the direction of the axis of the Earth as it orbits results in greater seasonal contrasts.

Surface	Albedo/reflectivity (%)
Fresh snow	80–95
Ice	20–40
Desert sands	35–45
Forest	15–20
Water (solar elevation 30°)	6
Water (solar elevation 60°)	3

Table showing reflectivity (albedo effect) of different surfaces

Key definitions

Albedo effect is the extent in which an object or medium reflects light. For example snow will reflect a high percentage of light energy.

Aphelion is the point in a planet's orbit when it is furthest from the Sun. Usually an elliptical orbit.

Perihelion is the point in a planet's orbit when it is closest to the Sun. Usually a circular orbit.

Ka is thousands of years.

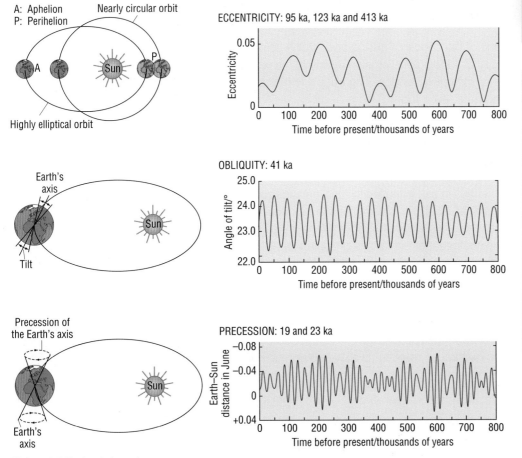

Figure 1 Milankovitch cycles

How science works

The position of the continents has major effects on global climate.

The present distribution of continents encourages the ocean currents to redistribute heat energy around the globe. If the continents were over the poles, it would encourage accumulations of snow and ice, which reflect radiation, so reducing the temperature. There would be a greater contrast in temperature between the poles and the Equator.

Evidence for Milankovitch cycles

The work to identify the link between Milankovitch cycles and glaciations was carried out by painstaking analysis of data from oxygen isotopes (see spread 5.5.1) covering the recent geological past. Once this work was carried out, many geologists started to look for evidence of these cycles elsewhere in the stratigraphic record.

The Blue Lias and Kimmeridge Clay

For many years geologists studying the Blue Lias rocks of the Lower Jurassic in Lyme Regis, Dorset noticed the way the layers of rocks changed from clay to limestone and back again. The pattern of beds created seemed so regular that it must have an explanation.

Analysis of these rocks has shown that the change in environment from a clay-rich sea to a limestone-producing sea happened on a roughly 41 000-year cycle. This correlates with the obliquity of orbit predicted by Milankovitch cycles.

Attempts to identify a 100 000-year cycle have been met with scepticism from some experts, but work carried out on clay found at Kimmeridge Bay in Dorset on Upper Jurassic rocks has identified regular Milankovitch cyclicity.

Key definition

Milankovich cycles are cyclical changes in the rotation and orbit of the Earth, correlating with climatic effects.

Figure 2 Clay and limestone layers in the Lias of Somerset

Questions

1 Draw a summary table to show the differences between eccentricity, obliquity and precession.
2 Research how Milankovich cycles were identified from deep-sea drilling cores.

One of the concerns arising from global climate change is that sea-level rise will lead to coastal flooding and erosion. Many of the world's major cities are close to present sea level, including London. The trouble is that changes in sea level are remarkably difficult to measure, even today. This is because sea level varies with tides, atmospheric pressure or wind, temperature and salinity variations, and also because the land may be rising or falling.

Where is sea level?

Sea level varies globally in a range of ± 2 m and can vary locally e.g. sea level is about 20 cm higher on the Pacific side of the Panama Canal than the Atlantic.

In the UK, mean sea level is measured at Newlyn in Cornwall and Liverpool, using tide gauges to give Ordnance Datum for the 0 m height on UK maps.

Sea level today is very near the lowest level ever. The lowest was in the Triassic, about 250 million years ago. For this reason, sea level today is more likely to rise than fall.

Small changes in climate can have noticeable effects during human lifetimes. During the last ice age about 20 000 years ago the world's sea level was about 130 m lower than today.

Isostatic and eustatic sea-level changes

Changes in sea level due to local subsidence or uplift are referred to as **isostatic**. For example, Scotland is rising as it is rebounding now that it is free of several kilometres of ice which has weighed it down since it was deposited during the last ice age. In contrast, the southeast of England is dropping by almost a millimetre each year. This is bad news when combined with the worldwide rising sea levels.

Changes in sea level due to changes in the volume of water in the oceans are called **eustatic**. This can be caused by the melting of the polar ice caps releasing more water into the oceans. When the ice advances and more water is held in the ice caps then sea level falls. Eustatic change is also caused by a rapid rate of sea floor spreading, causing the mid-ocean ridge to swell with magma. This causes sea level to rise.

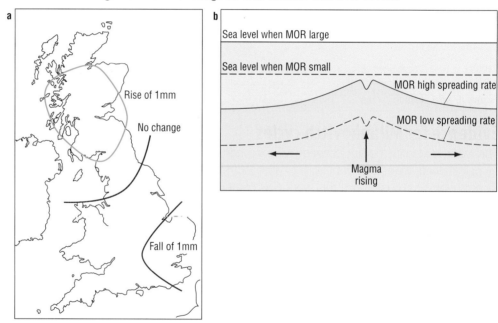

Figure 1 a Isostatic change in the British Isles after the ice melted and the weight of ice on Scotland was removed. **b Eustatic change** where the high spreading rate causes the mid-ocean ridge to expand

Measuring past sea levels

There are three main ways that geology is used to interpret ancient sea levels:

- Using seismic evidence to find unconformities where transgressing seas have resulted in the sea laying down younger beds that cover the older strata as the seas deepen. When the sea retreats regressions can also be identified as unconformities.
- Using exposed geology to estimate the areas of flooded continents through time. The effects of sea-level change are seen on the continental shelf and upper part of the continental slope. When sea level falls there will be raised beaches and cliff lines. When sea level rises then forests will be submerged and marine organisms can be found in the younger sediments.
- Using oxygen isotope ratios to assess the past temperatures and therefore the amount of ice.

Key definitions

Isostatic sea-level changes are due to uplift or subsidence of the continental crust. Crust often sinks when loaded with ice or sediment, rising again when such loads are removed. These are only seen in the affected region.

Eustatic sea-level changes are due to changes in the volume of the ocean basins or volume of water in them. These changes are seen worldwide.

Isostatic rebound is the rising up of land masses that were once depressed by ice. This is evident in Scotland today where raised beaches can be seen.

Vail's sea-level curves

The seismic interpretation of sea-level curves was pioneered by a team at Exxon, the oil company led by Peter R Vail, and later revised by Haq. Oil companies need to understand sea-level changes for successful oil exploration. Graphs produced using this technique are known as the Vail sea-level curves.

From the Triassic to the present, these sea-level curves identified more than 100 global sea-level changes. When looked at over millions of years the combination of all the data on sea-level changes shows patterns at many levels. If the graph is smoothed a little it shows a pattern over tens of millions of years of frequent transgressive and regressive events, known as second-order cycles. If the graph is smoothed further it shows a broad cycle lasting hundreds of millions of years as first-order cycles, which coincide with times of major continental plate break-up.

The high sea level that existed in the Cretaceous occurred at the same time as the opening of the Atlantic Ocean when the rate of sea floor spreading was high. Sea-level oscillations have continued with a rough periodicity of 100 000 years linked, to astronomical cycles, superimposed on a gradual rise.

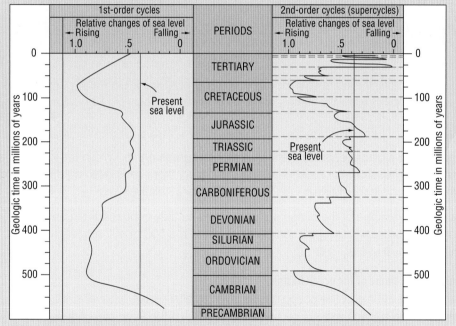

Figure 2 Changes in sea level through geological time (after Vail *et al.* 1977)

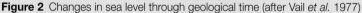

Geological evidence for sea-level changes in the Pleistocene

Three different approaches were used in the investigation of Pleistocene glaciations:

- Studies of deep-sea microfossil assemblages from Atlantic cores of deep-sea sediments with palaeomagnetic dating shows that about 30 glacial events occurred during the Pleistocene.
- Measurement of the ratio of ^{18}O to ^{16}O in the skeletons of benthonic foraminifera. These changes cannot be due to temperature variations because the deep ocean basin temperature is constant, between 0 °C and 2 °C. The ^{18}O to ^{16}O ratios in shells show the volume of ice temporarily removed from the system. Comparing the isotopic composition of foraminifera at the height of the last glaciation when sea level was at its lowest, with isotope ratios in modern forms, when sea level is higher allows us to calibrate past records of ^{18}O to ^{16}O ratios to interpret sea-level changes.
- Study of uplifted coral reef terraces on tropical islands shows that sea level was higher in the past.

Questions

1. Divide the following items of evidence of sea-level change into those that show ancient higher sea level and those that indicate lower sea levels:
   - *submarine forest*
   - *raised beach*
   - *marine shale with younger fluvial sands above*
   - *coral reef terraces*
   - *marine rocks overlying terrestrial rocks*
   - *raised cliff line*

2. There was a major marine transgression in the Cretaceous when the Chalk Seas covered much of the British Isles. Describe the type of sea-level change and the probable cause.

3. Explain why the Vail sea-level curve shows such big variations in sea level at the end of the Tertiary and in the Quaternary.

Mechanisms of sea-level change

The effects of a sea-level change on life depend on how fast the changes occur and the distribution and height of the continents. To change global sea level, which is a eustatic change, either:

- the volume of water in the oceans has to change; or
- the volume of the ocean basins is altered.

Changing the volume of water in the oceans

The change in the volume of water is closely linked with climate changes and involves locking up water on land, as ice and snow results in a fall in sea level.

Melting and freezing ice and sea-level changes

At the time of the maximum glaciation of about 12 000 years ago, people were probably living on the floor of what is now the English Channel and the North Sea, where submerged prehistoric sites have been found. The rising sea level gradually separated Britain from the rest of Europe and formed submerged forests around the coast of England and Wales.

As an example, the interglacial melting of all the Greenland ice cap would provide a sea-level rise of 7 m, while the melting of the ice of Antarctica could provide a 75 m rise.

Key definitions

Regression is when the sea level falls or the land rises resulting in shallow sea areas becoming land.

Transgression is where the sea level rises and floods the land resulting in large areas of shallow seas.

When there is a glacial episode there is a marine **regression** and when the ice melts a marine **transgression**. For most of the Earth's history there have been no polar ice caps so this mechanism for changing the volume of water is relatively rare.

Changing the volume of the ocean surface waters as they contract or expand has a much smaller effect. Raising the temperature of the top 500 m of the oceans by 1 °C gives a sea-level rise of 10 cm.

Changing the volume of the ocean basins

Changing the volume of the ocean basins involves altering the relative levels of the continents and ocean basins. One simple idea is that if there are lots of new ocean ridges, they will occupy a lot of volume and water will be displaced onto the continents. Calculations of the volume of the ridges in the past fit well with the Vail sea-level curve. Long-term high sea levels correspond with times of high plate velocities when lots of new material is being formed by sea-floor spreading at the mid-ocean ridges. In turn this results in increased rates of subduction causing subsidence and flooding of continental margins.

Variations in the rate of mantle convection and the consequent plate tectonic outcomes are causes of long-term cycles in sea level.

Slightly shorter term are the effects of mountain building. Major orogenies cause a thickening of the continental crust by folding and thrusting. Over time, those elevated mountain areas are eroded and the sediment infills the basins, steadily raising sea level again.

The opposite plate tectonic action of breaking up continental plates by continents splitting at new mid-ocean ridges and then sea-floor spreading results in a thinning of the crust (extension). The continents sink isostatically and there is an increased addition of sediment to the ocean basins, both resulting in the sea level rising.

The Cretaceous marine transgression

The breakup of Gondwanaland and then Laurasia in the Jurassic greatly increased the length of the mid-ocean ridge system. During the Cretaceous these mid-ocean ridges were very active, with high rates of sea-floor spreading and a worldwide rise in sea level. About 40% of the continents were flooded and nearly all of the British Isles was covered by the Chalk Sea. It is estimated that sea level was 200–250 m higher than it is today.

Sea level, climate change and mass extinctions

Just as ice and snow reflect incoming solar radiation, water has the property of efficiently absorbing it. Thus, when larger areas are covered by sea water, the mean temperatures should increase. There are some striking correlations between the mass extinctions and changes in sea level. There is ongoing debate as to the reasons for them.

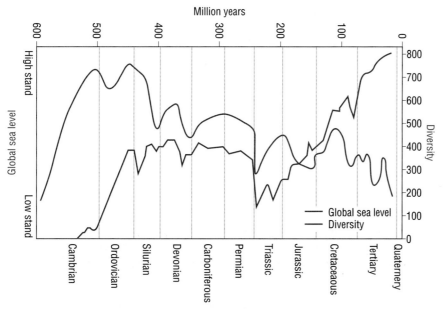

Figure 1 The five major mass extinctions of the Phanerozoic compared with the sea-level changes

Mass extinction and sea level falling

It has long been believed that a larger area of shallow, warm seas with lots of nutrients are good for marine life, so species diversity should be high after transgressions. Conversely, the deep waters that result from regressions are not ideal for most species, so regressions ought to see lower diversity. Mass extinctions can be caused by the reduction in shallow sea habitat as a result of regression. It is also accepted that it is the rapidity of the temperature change or rapid fluctuations in sea level that would be most damaging to marine species.

The major changes in sea level and the mass extinction events show a remarkable agreement. This does not necessarily mean one caused the other. It could be that both were caused by variations in some other factor – the easy choice would be climate change.

Mass extinction and sea level rising

One link between transgression and mass extinction is thought to be the increase in the area of shallow waters, which seems to have triggered blooms of marine plankton. Bacterial decomposition of the plankton resulted in high biological oxygen demand and therefore anoxic conditions and mass extinction. We can recognise anoxic events by formation of black shales rich in organic material.

The Permian–Triassic extinction

There is mounting evidence that the world's oceans became anoxic in the Late Permian. This is seen at high and low latitudes and at a range of shelf depths extending into very shallow water. A rise in sea level caused the deeper, more poorly oxygenated waters to extend into the shallow sea areas. Suffocation would provide an excellent means of killing many of the species around at the time.

The end Cretaceous K–T extinction

There was a major fall in sea level at the end of the Chalk deposition which was probably rapid in terms of geological time – about 100 000 years. Sea level fell by 70–100 m and would have changed the marine habitats, perhaps causing the extinction of the ammonites and foraminifera in the sea. The impact of a large asteroid and extensive volcanic activity in the Deccan traps of India would then have added other reasons for extinction, especially on land.

Questions

1 If sea levels rose by 110 m during the Jurassic, what is the overall rate of sea-level rise in mm per year? How does this compare to the 2007 eustatic rise of 3 mm? Suggest an explanation for the difference.

2 What causes sea-level changes with a cycle of around 300 Ma, and what causes much shorter-term changes? What are the relative sizes of these two effects?

3 How might transgressions be linked to mass extinctions?

In the Cambrian, southern Britain was some 60°S of the equator, and due to plate tectonics it is now 51°N of the equator. There is evidence for this northward drift in the geological record of the rocks and fossils in the British Isles.

Fossil evidence for changing climate

Today the British Isles are in a temperate climatic belt with a varied fauna and flora on land and in the surrounding shallow seas. However, recent climate is not a good guide as we are still in the Quaternary Glaciation though currently in an interglacial period. Before the last glacial period, elephants, bison, hippopotamuses, cave lions and hyenas roamed southern Britain. Therefore the climate was subtropical. Their habitats were deciduous woodlands of oak, elm, hazel, lime, birch and alder. When the ice returned during the most recent glacial period about 10 000 years ago, an ice sheet covered most of Britain except the south, so it was too cold for these animals and their habitats. We use knowledge of modern plants and animals to identify ancient climates. The oxygen isotopes found in bivalve and foraminifera shells are used to find the water temperature which can help identify palaeolatitude.

Corals

Modern reef corals live in a narrow range of water depths and temperatures. They only thrive and build reefs where they can successfully exploit their symbiosis with algae. This means they are restricted to the warm tropics mostly within 30°N and 30°S of the Equator. We can assume that fossil reef building corals required the same tropical conditions. Fossil coral reefs are found in Silurian and Lower Carboniferous rocks, so must have formed when the British Isles was in tropical regions.

Plants

Plants are excellent indicators of climate and, therefore, palaeolatitude:
- Tree rings from Ireland and England span a period of 7000 years. When the tree rings were narrowest it suggests the driest period experienced by the trees, approximately 5200 years ago.
- The presence of tree rings means there were variations in growth rate due to a seasonal climate. The lack of tree rings in Carboniferous plant fossils indicates a non-seasonal equatorial climate.
- Upper Carboniferous plants grew to heights of 40 m. The productivity and exceptional height of some species indicates they grew in a hot, humid equatorial climate and latitude.
- Leaf shape can be linked to temperature and palaeolatitude. In modern vegetation the ratio of toothed to smooth margined leaves changes with mean annual temperature. Plants in warm areas have smooth leaf edges.
- Leaf size is related strongly to temperature, humidity/water availability and light levels. Large leaves occur in humid conditions, and size decreases with decreasing temperature or precipitation.

Pollen grains can survive in sediments for millions of years and may be transported into marine sediments. They are very distinctive under the microscope and pine and birch pollen will indicate cool conditions compared to oak and beech.

Lithological evidence

Rock types can be linked to latitudes in the same way that plants can.

Coal

In order to produce peat in sufficient thicknesses to be compressed into economic coal seams, there has to be a highly productive ecosystem. Rapid plant growth requires high rainfall and high temperatures such as in the tropical rainforests found in equatorial regions.

Figure 1 Colonial reef building corals in the tropics

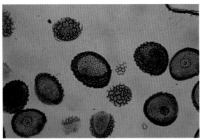

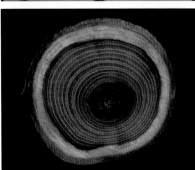

Figure 2 Pollen grains under the microscope and tree rings showing variation in thickness

Desert sandstone

Sands exposed to the air develop a red colour as the iron hydroxide oxidise to haematite. Desert sands are fine grained, very well sorted, with well rounded grains consisting mostly of quartz. They are transported by wind to produce spectacular dunes. Dune-forming desert latitudes are generally around 20–30° south or north of the Equator.

Evaporites

Evaporites form where rainfall is low and evaporation is rapid in the hot deserts. Evaporites today are found at latitudes of about 20–30° south and north, so the same is likely for ancient deposits.

Tillites

Tillites are ancient boulder clay deposits so are glacial deposits, which are most commonly formed at high latitudes of 60° north or south. However, there are glacial deposits in low latitudes as small areas of high-altitude glaciers as well as regional ice fields formed when almost the entire planet was ice-bound, a 'Snowball Earth'.

Reef limestone

Today, reef limestone is built mainly of colonial corals which are restricted to latitudes of less than 30°, so all reef structures are diagnostic of this latitude.

Figure 3 Desert sandstone forming sand dunes in the desert

The northward drift of the British Isles

We can use all the evidence provided by the rocks and fossils to identify the palaeolatitude for the British Isles throughout the geological record.

- Tillites are found in Precambrian rocks in the west of Scotland, suggesting a glaciation – perhaps a 'Snowball Earth'.
- The colonial corals in the reefs of the Silurian Wenlock Limestone suggests shallow tropical seas.
- Reef limestones of the Lower Carboniferous in the Pennines again suggest tropical seas.
- The coal measures of the Carboniferous formed in equatorial rainforests growing on a huge delta extending from Scotland to Kent.
- The Permian and Triassic rocks include the red desert sandstones and evaporites of the Cheshire Basin which formed within 30°N of the Equator.
- Some colonial corals in the Jurassic mean tropical seas north of the Equator.
- The Chalk Seas of the Cretaceous represent temperate conditions as the British Isles move northwards into cooler climates.

Period	Diagnostic rock types	Approximate palaeolatitude
Quaternary	Glacial deposits	55°N
Tertiary	Palms and tropical plants	40°N
Cretaceous	Chalk	35°N
Jurassic	Rare colonial corals	30°N
Triassic	Desert sandstones	31°N
Permian	Desert sandstones/ evaporites	12°N
Carboniferous	Reef limestones, coals	0
Devonian	Desert sandstones	20°S
Silurian	Reef limestones	30°S

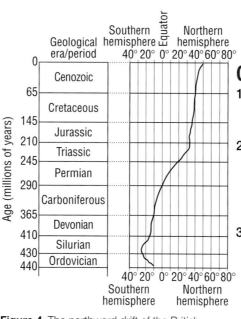

Figure 4 The northward drift of the British Isles

Questions

1 Why are colonial reef building corals restricted to the photic zone?

2 Name a sedimentary structure that could be used to indicate palaeowind direction in the Permian and one that would indicate arid conditions.

3 An analysis of lake sediments shows a shift from birch pollen to beech pollen over a geological time span. Would palaeomagnetic measurements for the same period reveal a northward or southward shift?

1 (a) (i) Descriptions are given below for different types of fossil preservation. Match the terms (**1–5**) to the descriptions **A–E**.

Description	Term
A Heat changes plant matter into carbon films by loss of volatiles during burial	**1** Replacement
B Porous shells are replaced by SiO_2 from solution	**2** Carbonisation
C Original shell is changed forming new crystals	**3** Silicification
D Impressions of soft or hard parts, usually when original minerals have dissolved away	**1** Recrystallisation
E Minerals deposited in pore spaces of shells, commonly $CaCO_3$ or iron minerals	**5** Moulds

[4]

(ii) Replacement by iron pyrites is called pyritisation. What environmental conditions are needed for this to occur? [2]

(iii) Aragonite often forms the shells of organisms. Explain why aragonite does not occur in fossils older than the Cainozoic. [2]

(b) The likelihood of a fossil being preserved in any environment is called the preservation potential. Explain how fine grained sediment, high-energy conditions and early diagenesis will affect the preservation potential of an organism. [6]

(c) Describe the exceptional preservation of organisms in amber and tar. [4]

(OCR June 2006)
Total 18

2 (a) Fossil **G** shows a dorsal and ventral view of a benthonic trilobite.

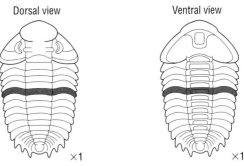

Figure 1

(i) Label the following morphological features on the appropriate diagram.
  - genal angle
  - glabella
  - mouth
  - pleuron [4]

(b) The diagram below shows a cross-section through the thoracic segment shaded on fossil **G**.

Figure 2

(i) Draw and label the position of the gills and legs on the above diagram. [2]

(ii) Give **two** pieces of evidence to support the hypothesis that fossil **G** is an arthropod. [2]

(c) Describe and explain the changes in morphology that trilobites developed to enable them to adopt the following modes of life: nektonic, infaunal and planktonic. [6]

(d) Fossils **J** and **K** are trace fossils formed by trilobites.

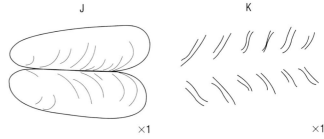

Figure 3

(i) Explain how trilobites formed these trace fossils. [2]

(ii) What evidence do these trace fossils give us about the conditions on the sea floor at the time of their formation? [2]

(OCR June 2006)
Total 18

3 **(a)** Fossil **A** is an echinoid. The diagrams below show two different views of fossil **A**.

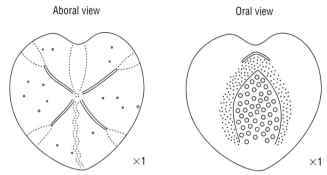

Aboral view   Oral view

×1   ×1

Figure 4

   (i) Name the group of echinoids to which fossil **A** belongs. [1]

   (ii) Describe, using technical terms, the type of symmetry shown by fossil **A**. [1]

   (iii) On the appropriate diagram, label the following morphological features.
     anterior groove   plastron   position of the mouth
     [3]

(b) The diagram below shows a close-up view of part of fossil **A**.

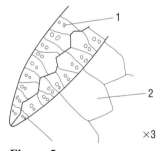

×3

Figure 5

   (i) Identify the morphological features **1** and **2**. [2]

   (ii) Explain the function of morphological feature **1**. [2]

(c) **(i)** Describe how regular echinoids feed. [2]

   (ii) Describe how irregular echinoids feed. [2]

   (iii) Explain the function of the fasciole and plastron, features found in some echinoids. [4]

(OCR January 2006)
Total 17

4 **(a)** Here is a list of six common geological terms.

   1 biostratigraphy   **2 Cainozoic**   **3 era**
   4 Mesozoic   **5 Palaeozoic**   **6 period**

Select the most suitable term to match each description.

Description
A Began 65 Ma ago, until the present day
B Began around 590 Ma ago
C Palaeozoic is an example
D Dating of rocks using fossil remains
E Time unit defined by specific rock and fossil types

[5]

(b) Explain how the relative ages of rocks can be determined using the following methods. Use diagrams to illustrate your answers.

   (i) Way up structures. [2]

   (ii) Cross cutting relationships. [2]

   (iii) Included fragments. [2]

(c) **(i)** Name **one** method of radiometric dating of rocks. [1]

   (ii) Explain how absolute dates can be determined using radiometric methods. [3]

   (iii) Explain why sedimentary rocks are difficult to date using radiometric methods. [2]

   (iv) Explain why metamorphism causes problems with radiometric dating. [2]

(OCR January 2006)
Total 19

5 **(a)** **(i)** Describe and explain how plate tectonics and the position of the continents can affect the global temperature. [4]

   (ii) Changes in global temperatures can also be explained by Milankovitch cycles. Describe a Milankovitch cycle. [2]

   (iii) One factor that controls Milankovitch cycles is thought to be eccentricity. Describe and explain how eccentricity can affect climate. [4]

Total 10

6 Describe the morphological changes that occurred in ammonoids as a result of evolution throughout the Palaeozoic and Mesozoic. [12]

(OCR June 2005)

7 Describe and explain the morphological changes and evolution of graptolites in the Lower Palaeozoic. [11]

(OCR January 2005)

Practical tasks in geology will assess skills in measurement, observation and recording of data in the same way as Unit 3 for AS. You will again use geological maps, photographs and diagrams as well as laboratory or field data to complete the tasks.

Geological maps and graphic logs can be used in the centre based tasks, the field or the evaluative task. Economic geology can provide good sources of data for analysis. A suitable site for extraction of oils or metals can be identified from geophysical or geochemical field data. Photographs and data on building stone or roadstone can be used to identify a suitable material for the purpose.

Interpreting maps for the centre based task

Geological maps show a range of beds which may have been folded, faulted, intruded and/or eroded. You may be asked to describe the sequence of events that took place. Spread 1.4.8 explains how to analyse a map.

Using cross-cutting relationships to determine the youngest and oldest events is the key to working out the order of events and therefore the geological history of the map. Where a feature such as a dyke or fault cuts through or displaces beds it must be the younger. Using the rules of folded beds from Unit 1 structural geology means that

- the youngest beds will always be found in the centre of a syncline
- the oldest beds will always be found in the centre of an anticline.

An unconformity will form on older, eroded beds that are usually at a different angle to the younger unconformable beds.

Always start your geological history with the oldest event and describe the order of deposition of the beds and each event in turn. Plenty of detail to describe the type of structure or intrusion is needed rather than a list. Don't forget erosion – it does not form a feature but must be present before an angular unconformity.

Evaluative task

The evaluative task will test the ability to analyse and evaluate geological data from either the laboratory or the field. The data will rely on both the AS units and the A level units so will include using rocks, minerals and fossils.

Drawing and evaluating graphic logs

A graphic log is a graphical method of recording observations and measurement of a sequence of sedimentary rocks often in a cliff or quarry face. When measuring for a log, start at the base of the outcrop and, where possible, record the following information for each bed:

- Composition of both grains and cement or matrix.
- Grain size, sorting and shape with colour, and the degree of cementation or weathering.
- Identification of the sedimentary rock.
- Thickness of beds in cm and describe any lateral variation.
- Nature of bedding planes as uneven, erosional or gradational where one bed gradually changes to another.
- Record any sedimentary structures presentation and measurements of them.
- Any fossils should be identified and variations in size, abundance, distribution and orientation recorded.

The grain size controls the graph. The bottom scale is used to draw a bed to extend out to the correct grain size. So a conglomerate will extend to the right further than a fine sandstone.

Symbols on graphic log

Using standard symbols is a real help when drawing a log, making it simple for others to interpret. Dots are used for sand and sandstone – large for coarse sand and small for fine sand. Open circles are used for pebbles. Dashes are used for clay or mudstone – dash dots for siltstone and continuous lines for shales. A brick effect is used for limestones.

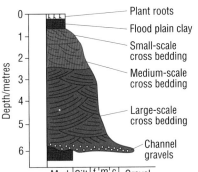

Figure 1 Graphic log of a fluvial sequence

Drawing a graphic log and using it to interpret palaeoenvironments

1 Complete a graphic log for the beds A (oldest) to G (youngest) described below. Take the complete height of the section and choose an appropriate scale to represent this cliff section.
2 Plot each bed on a graphic log blank, starting with the oldest at the bottom of the page.
3 Show each bed at the correct grain size and with the correct symbol. The cross bedding symbol of curved lines is drawn on top of the sandstone symbol.
4 Where the base of a bed is eroded show it as an uneven line on your log.
5 Add descriptive details of the beds in the right hand column – colour, composition, sedimentary structures, bedding details and fossil content.
6 A bed may change from bottom to top, so use a combination of symbols from the edge of the bed up to show a change from one grain size to another.
7 Interpret all the evidence to describe the changing environments in which beds A to G formed.

Bed A is a purple siltstone with thin beds (laminations), contains muscovite mica and is 12 cm thick.
Bed B is 52 cm thick and is a red, medium sandstone, well sorted with large scale cross bedding.
Bed C is cross cutting and uneven at the base and is a conglomerate with pebbles up to 27 mm across. The matrix is a red silt and the bed is 18 cm thick.
Bed D is a pebbly sandstone with all the pebbles at the base and grading up into a brown, coarse sandstone 32 cm.
Bed E is a fine sandstone, yellow–white in colour, 28 cm thick.
Bed F is a mud, light grey in colour with black, carbonaceous roots 42 cm thick.
Bed G is a medium sandstone nearly white in colour with small brachiopods. It is 15 cm thick.

Anomalous data

When individual readings fall outside the main set of the data these results are anomalous (not typical, or different from expected). There are various possible reasons for these anomalous points and explaining them is a key part of evaluating results. Anomalies could be due to:

- experimental error so that the points are wrong
- errors in measuring
- natural variation where measurements vary, e.g. on fossils as there are always some organisms outside of the normal range.

Evaluating fossil data

In some areas large numbers of fossils can be found and either collected or measured in the field. Data can then be used to analyse the nature of the assemblages by observing the orientation of fossils, whether they are whole, broken or disarticulated, and the sizes of the fossils. Where there are many fragmented fossils it is likely to be a death assemblage where fossils have been transported and then deposited. The graphs in Figure 2 show two populations of fossils that can be analysed.

Geoconservation

The aim of geoconservation is to promote the conservation of our Earth heritage and to ensure that we pass it on in good order to future generations for investigation, education and enjoyment. It encourages care and conservation of Earth heritage sites and the rocks, minerals and fossils found. Collecting should always be responsible so that exposures are not damaged. Where fossils are relatively common, or the sites are coastal cliffs that are being eroded or quarries that are being actively worked, then collecting is not a problem as long as you have permission. Collecting fossils that might otherwise be destroyed can be beneficial to science, provided that they are properly documented and made available for study. Responsible fossil collecting can be a valuable activity and safeguards our fossil heritage.

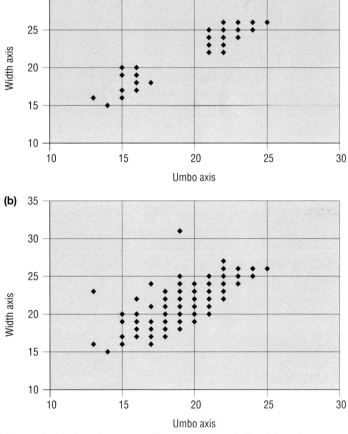

Figure 2 Graph **a** shows two different species of a brachiopod. Graph **b** shows a single species with individuals of all growth stages from small young brachiopods to larger, older ones. Two of the fossils measured are anomalous

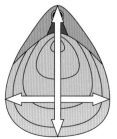

Figure 3 Brachiopod fossil showing where measurements were taken

Examination answers

Unit 1

1 (a) (i) Moho – line below either sort of crust
continental crust – dotted area
oceanic crust black area [3]

(ii)

	age of the oldest rocks	average composition	average thickness (km)	density g/cm³
oceanic	180 Ma Jurassic	mafic/basalt	7 km ±3 km	2.9
continental	3900 Ma Precambrian	felsic/ intermediate/ granite	35 km ±5 km	2.7

[4]

(b) stony meteorites match the mantle;
metallic meteorites match the core;
iron nickel has the right density for the core;
the outer core has convection of the iron which
creates the Earth's magnetic field [3]

(c) (i) geothermal gradient [1]

(ii) it is partially melted (5%) [1]

(iii) peridotite [1]

(d) (i) Venus Mercury Mars [2]

(ii) formed at same time from nebular cloud of matter
formed of same density material coalesced from
cloud;
density calculations mean they are all similar;
close to the 5.5 g/cm³ of the Earth [3]

Total 18

2 (a) (i) mantle – white layer;
outer core – light grey layer;
L wave on surface (to max 90 epicentral angle)
P wave as curve in mantle/straight through core
or curved in core [4]

(ii) **C** P, S and L waves all present;
large amplitude of stronger waves of greater
energy;
D no S waves or L waves/only P waves;
smaller amplitude as weaker waves of low energy
later arrivals [4]

(iii) P and S wave shadow zone [1]

(iv) P waves are refracted and S waves are stopped
by the liquid (outer) core [2]

(b) (i) MOR or axial rift valley where magma is rising or
divergent plate margin along transform faults;
conservative plate margin along the fault line;
convergent plate margin in the subduction zone
or Benioff zone where friction between plates
occurs [2]

(ii) craton or shield area/ocean basin or abyssal
plain/in the middle of plate [1]

(c) rubber foundations/flexible joints/X frame struts/
flexible structures/weights at top of the building to
counterbalance sway to resist vibration
very strong structures/deeper foundations/reinforced
concrete/shatter proof glass/strict building codes to
reduce destruction/not building on weak or
unconsolidated or made ground or reclaimed land [2]

Total 16

3 (a) (i) (point) where earthquake energy is released/point
of origin of earthquake/directly below epicentre [1]

(ii) record/reading of an earthquake/waves recorded
by seismograph/print out from seismograph [1]

(b) (i) using Mercalli scale/questionnaires of effects/
eyewitness account/mapping effects/description
of damage caused/effects at epicentre of relative
damage [1]

(ii) amplitude of earthquake waves on seismogram/
using Richter scale/energy released [1]

(iii) A on solid rock;
B on unconsolidated ground/soft sediment
depends on type of ground [2]

(c) area of general activity but no earthquakes recently
on one section;
plotting of earthquakes;
periodicity of earthquakes predict one where none
recently [2]

Total 8

4 (a)

Tectonic feature	Description
G	5
H	4
J	2
K	1

[4]

(b) (i) divergent [1]

(ii) in the rift zone with movement away from the rift
zone [2]

(iii) transform fault displaced 60 km [2]

(c) (i) 3.33 cm/yr [1]

(ii) Axis through central normal polarity region. The
magnetic polarity stripes are symmetrical about
this line. [2]

(iii) spreading occurs at different rates/along different
ridge segments/effects of small faults/effects of
transform faults/variations in rates of volcanic
activity [2]

(d) Trench at junction of plate, Benioff zone as zone inclined at 45° along top of subducting oceanic plate, volcanoes above rising magma in continental plate, batholiths deep in continental crust near rising magma, fold mountains on continental plate and the direction of movement towards each other. [6]

Total 20

5 (a) (i) reverse fault formed by compressive forces [2]
    (ii) 70° angle of dip [1]
(b) (i) fault breccia
       fragments of rock broken by movement of faults [2]
    (ii) slickensides;
       scratches form parallel to the direction of movement of faults/due to irregular fault surfaces moving against each other [2]
(c) (i) overfold – overturned limb;
       cleavage planes parallel to axial plane;
       cleavage planes in clay beds [3]
    (ii) recumbent fold with axial plane at a low angle cut by a thrust at a low angle displacing the limbs. [2]

Total 12

6 Tectonic joints Labelled accurate diagram to show tension joints due to extension/extension around a fold hinge with cross-joints (90°) to fold axis or shear at (45°) to fold axis.
Occur in competent rocks e.g. limestone or sandstone. [2]
Cooling joints Labelled accurate diagram showing hexagons/polygons in columns.
Caused by contraction inwards of magma or lava or intrusion as it cools so they form at 90° to the cooling surface. [2]
Angular unconformity Accurate diagram showing beds above and below the unconformity dipping at different angles.
Unconformity represents a time gap between older and younger beds with uplift, folding and erosion before deposition of the younger beds. [2]
Slaty cleavage Labelled accurate diagram to show thin cleavage planes parallel to the axial plane of a fold and only in incompetent clays. [2]

Total 8

7 Fit along coastlines of continent at the edge of continental shelf or at 1000 m contour on continental slope. Few overlaps due to younger rock deposited and few gaps due to erosion.
Matching rock types with examples of specific sequences such as lake clays and evaporites.
Rocks laid down under specific climatic conditions at specific latitudes e.g. corals in tropics/evaporites in tropics/coal equatorial.
Same ages of rocks on different continents.
Same trend of rocks or orogenic belts on different continents.
Structures such as fold mountains, faults and cratons split across continents.
Fossils that could not have crossed an ocean the same on both continents e.g. *Mesosaurus* or *Glossopteris.*
Striations and erratics left by ice sheets now near Equator but must have formed near the poles.
Palaeomagnetism shows that polar wandering curves match for continents now separate so ancient latitudes can be measured from palaeomagnetism.
Iron particles in igneous rock aligned north now pointing in different direction so continents have moved.
2 marks for each piece of evidence and 2 for detail.
Maximum 2 for each piece of evidence.

Total 8

Unit 2

1 (a) (i) A = lava or pyroclastics
       B = intrusive
       C = transport
       D = sedimentary [4]
    (ii) any two from lithification, burial, diagenesis, compaction, dissolution, cementation, recrystallisation [2]
(b) rocks are poor conductors of heat, cooling is slower at depth and slower cooling produces coarse crystal grain size [2]
(c) An era is a major period of time, e.g. Palaeozoic or Mesozoic while a system is rocks laid down in a short period/a subdivision of an era, e.g. Jurassic or Silurian [4]

Total 12

2 (a) (i) A = rhyolite; B = obsidian; C = diorite [3]
    (ii) bands contorted with dark and light bands due to minerals being aligned or banding [2]
    (iii) no time for crystals to form [1]
    (iv) a series of parallel semi-circular lines along which the rock has broken [1]

(b) (i) D = olivine; E = orthoclase/potash/K feldspar; F = muscovite mica; G = quartz [4]

(ii) olivine and Ca rich plagioclase are high temperature >1600° quartz/G is lower temperature 800° [2]

(iii) left part of diagram minerals D to biotite [1]

(c) (i) H = mafic; J = silicic; K = intermediate; L = ultramafic [4]

(ii) % of silicon and sodium increase from ultramafic to silicic.
% of magnesium and iron decrease from ultramafic to silicic. [2]

Total 20

3 (a) (i) island arc or convergent plate boundary where there is subduction;
partial melting means formation of magma as the melting point is lowered by release of water and heat is produced by friction [2]

(ii) $2 \div 12 \times 100/100 \div 12 \times 2 = 16.66\%/16.6\%/16.7\%$ [2]

(iii) There was a major eruption in 1815 and the global extent of the cooling depends on the force of the eruption; ash and volcanic gases in the atmosphere are thought to be responsible for global cooling as they absorb or reflect solar radiation.
The location of the volcano with respect to the Earth's global atmospheric circulation patterns is key. [3]

Total 7

4 (a) (i) graded bedding; forms from a turbidite due to rapidly decreasing energy so heavier particles are deposited first [3]

(ii) River- or seabed has turbulent water which erodes beds in an asymmetric cross-section giving a heel shaped plan view then sediment infills the eroded hollow. [3]

(b) (i) L is the parent of O; N is the parent of M [2]

(ii) rolling of a pellet or oolith or rock/shell fragment or sand grain;
in carbonate mud which forms concentric layers of $CaCO_3$;
deposited from sea water saturated in calcium carbonate where there are high rates of evaporation causing $CaCO_3$ to be precipitated tidal/wave action under high/medium energy conditions rolls the particles [2]

(iii) under water/bi-directional currents;
inter tidal/sea floor/large lake/affected by wave action [2]

(c) (i) water freezes in joints/bedding planes
water expands (9%) on freezing/exerts pressure which forces rock apart [2]

(ii) angular [1]

(iii) rainwater containing dissolved CO_2 becomes carbonic acid
acid water reacts with carbonates/limestone forms soluble hydrogen carbonates/
$CaCO_3 + H^+ + HCO_3^- \rightarrow Ca^+ + 2HCO_3^-$ [2]

Total 17

5 (a) (i) higher the temperature the greater the degree of change/lower temperature minerals replaced by those stable at higher temperature, or reverse argument/minerals plastic allows diffusion of ions. [2]

(ii) pore pressure/load pressure/compressive stress [2]

(b) (i) marble
quartzite [2]

(ii) shales are polymineralic/clay minerals contain a wide variety of elements/fine grain size increase rate of reaction [2]

(iii) zone = sequence of metamorphic rocks characterised by the appearance of a characteristic index mineral/area showing same grade of metamorphism
index mineral = mineral used to define a zone.
Isograd = line joining points of equal metamorphic grade/boundary between metamorphic zones [3]

(c) contact metamorphism due to heat only; foliation requires pressure [2]

Total 13

6 *Differences*

1 baked zone above and below sill but only below lava flow;

2 sills may include xenoliths of overlying rock but lava flows only include underlying rock;

3 sills have two chilled margins but lava flows have one;

4 lava flows have vesicles or amygdales at the top but sills do not;

5 phenocrysts have random orientation in sills but show preferred alignment in lava flows;

6 lava flows may have pillow shapes but sills do not;

7 sills have medium sized crystals in the middle but lava flows have fine crystals only;

8 lava flows have reddened/weathered top. [3]

Explanations

1 sill intruded between country rocks but lava extruded onto surface;
2 there are no rocks overlying lava flows when they are formed;
3 sills are cooled by contact with the country rocks at top and base;
4 pressures are lower at the surface than at depth allowing gas bubbles to rise to the top of lava flows;
5 movement of the lava causes any large elongate crystals to line up in the direction of flow;
6 eruption under water;
7 sills cool more slowly than lava flows; lavas are weathered/oxidised at the surface;   [3]
8 Diagrams which illustrate the differences   [2]

Total 8

7 compaction due to mass of overlying sediment/ hydrostatic pressure/load pressure/compression;
fluids squeezed from pore spaces/porosity reduced/no pore spaces;
grain contact solution eliminates porosity;
close packing of grains/volume reduction/density increase;
primarily affects clays;
cementation due to fluids passing through pore spaces/ minerals carried in solution;
minerals precipitate in pore spaces/named minerals/ crystallise out/deposited in pore spaces porosity reduced further/reduced permeability;
pressure welding/pressure solution; primarily affects quartz/sand grains;
compaction and cementation are diagenetic processes/ both affect sediments/lead to lithification of sediments;
diagrams for both compaction and cementation

Total 8

Unit 4

1 (a) (i) spring where the upper or lower boundary of the fractured limestone intersects the surface   [1]
      (ii) springs form at the boundary between permeable and impermeable rocks; springs form where the water table intersects the land surface; springs form where groundwater flows out onto the land surface; groundwater is prevented from moving downwards through the impermeable clay   [2]
   (b) permeable – water can flow through the rock
      aquifer – porous and permeable rock capable of storing and yielding groundwater   [2]

   (c) (i) water will rise up the borehole/water will flow out onto the surface;
      water is under high hydrostatic pressure/water is confined/pressure is released   [2]
      (ii) artesian   [1]
      (iii) level of water table falls/cone of depression forms/hydrostatic pressure drops so water no longer flows up/subsidence at surface/salt water encroachment (if near coast)   [1]
   (d) hydrostatic pressure – water pressure at a point in a body of water/pressure caused by the weight of overlying column of water/hydraulic head;
      hydraulic gradient – difference in hydrostatic pressure/hydraulic head between two points divided by the distance between them/slope down which the water moves/slope of the water table   [2]
   (e) (i) readily accessible/easy to extract by direct pumping/dam and reservoir can be used for other purposes, e.g. recreation, HEP generation   [1]
      (ii) surplus water is stored in aquifers until needed; groundwater is pumped from boreholes and discharged into rivers; the water is passed through sand traps to remove sediment; the water is passed through weirs to ensure it contains oxygen   [2]

Total 14

2 (a) requires abundant marine plankton; low energy conditions/rapid burial in fine grained sediment; low oxygen/anoxic conditions on sea floor; role of (anaerobic) bacteria causing partial decay; temperatures of 50 to 200 °C for the plankton to be converted to petroleum; pressure/compression causing conversion of plankton to oil; formation of kerogen/sapropel; the petroleum takes time to mature   [3]
   (b) (i) air gun/explosion is used to generate seismic waves; seismic waves are reflected back to the surface; reflected seismic waves are detected by geophones/hydrophones; travel time of returning seismic waves is recorded   [2]
      (ii) a seismic profile is plotted;
      depth to reflective beds/layers can be calculated;
      the subsurface layering is shown;
      geological structures that may be traps can be identified   [2]
   (c) (i) anticline forms a trap; sandstone is a suitable reservoir rock as porous and permeable; mudstone is a suitable cap rock as impermeable   [2]

(ii) fault trap;
unconformity trap [2]

(d) well rounded, well sorted grains;
large pore spaces between grains holding oil;
high permeability/good interconnections between
pores; little or no cement/matrix; grain size
0.5–2 mm [3]

(e) (i) rock type – effective porosity/permeability of
rock/grain size/roundness/sorting of grains/
amount of matrix; presence of structures/joints/
fractures;
degree of cementation/compaction/lithification
viscosity of oil/temperature of oil/depth of oil
pressure oil is under/volume of gas in solution [2]

(ii) porosity/permeability of sandstone varies
amount of cementation/matrix varies;
depth varies – affects pressure/temperature/
viscosity [2]

(iii) Fulmar field – highest percentage recovery [1]

(f) water flood drive – water is pumped into rock below
oil to maintain pressure;
gas cap drive – gas is injected into rock above oil to
maintain pressure;
thermal methods – use of steam injection to increase
temperature/lower viscosity;
use of detergents/chemicals/surfactants/bacteria/to
reduce surface tension and lower viscosity [2]

(g) gas is stored underground for use at times of peak
demand; a cushion of gas must be kept in reservoir
either
use of depleted oil and gas reservoirs; geology is
already known and pumping equipment is in place
or
use of salt caverns; evaporites are impermeable;
cavities are created by dissolving the rock salt and
pumping it out as brine [2]
Total 23

3 (a) (i) 70% [1]

(ii) take millions of years to form/can only be used
once/can't be renewed within human lifespan/a
finite resource [1]

(b) (i) A = lignite and B = anthracite [2]

(ii) the percentage of carbon in the coal/the maturity
of the coal [1]

(c) suitable diagram(s) to distinguish the two types
exposed – coal bearing strata outcrops at surface
concealed – coal bearing strata under younger cover [2]

(d) (two) roadways/tunnels are driven out from the shaft;
a long/long wall coalface is established; the coal is
cut with a mechanical cutter/shearer; coal falls onto a
conveyor belt; the roof is supported by mobile
hydraulic chocks/supports; the mined area is allowed
to collapse; mining takes places backwards/retreating
towards shaft [3]

(e) suitable diagram with labels: river channel sediments/
wash out shown cutting into coal seam/washout
formed by channel switching on delta top/no coal
present/shearer cannot cut through hard sandstone [2]

(f) opencast mining is cheaper because it is more
efficient/requires less manpower/has lower setup
costs/requires less high tech equipment/has no
requirement for pumping/ventilation/thinner seams
can be mined profitably;
opencast mining is safer because there are no
dangers of collapse/flooding/(methane) gas build
up [1]

(g) (i) geothermal aquifers – Southampton, Hampshire
Basin, East Yorkshire, Lincolnshire
hot dry rocks – granites in southwest England,
northern England, Scottish Highlands [1]

(ii) *either*
geothermal aquifer – sedimentary basins with
higher than normal geothermal gradient/aquifers
interbedded with impermeable mudstones/shales
that act as insulators/hot water is pumped up and
passed through heat exchanger/cooled waters
are re-injected into the ground to maintain water
pressure in aquifer
or
hot dry rock – granites have a higher content of
heat producing radioactive elements than other
rocks/rock is artificially fractured/paired boreholes
are drilled into granite – cold water is pumped
down and hot water is pumped up [2]

(iii) production areas are geographically restricted/
possibility of dangerous volcanic eruptions/may
cause subsidence or trigger earthquakes/pipes
corrode or become blocked by precipitated
salts / each well is only viable for a few years [1]
Total 17

4 (a) (i) cut-off grade – the minimum grade that is
economic to mine
reserves – the amount of the resource that
can be extracted at a profit using existing
technology. [2]

(ii) higher grade deposits are worked out improvements in mining/mineral processing have allowed profitable extraction of lower copper concentrations [1]

(b) (i) horizontal layer at the base of intrusion immediately above lower chilled margin [1]

(ii) magnetite is dense/heavy/high temperature/ crystallises early; mafic magma is fluid/has a low viscosity; magnetite undergoes gravity settling/ magmatic segregation/differentiation; magnetite forms a cumulate layer at the base of the intrusion [3]

(iii) magnetic survey – proton magnetometer used/ detects variations in Earth's magnetic field/lines joining points of equal magnetic field strength are plotted on map/magnetite gives positive anomaly

or

gravity survey – gravimeter used/lines joining points of equal gravitational field strength are plotted on map/magnetite gives positive anomaly/ magnetite has higher density than surrounding rocks

or

electrical resistivity – two probes/electrodes are put in ground/electric current is passed between them/magnetite has a lower resistance/higher conductivity than surrounding rocks [2]

(c) (extreme) chemical weathering/hydrolysis requires hot and humid/tropical/equatorial climate soluble elements/ions/minerals removed in solution leaves insoluble residue of aluminium (oxides and hydroxides) [2]

(d) Soluble uranium minerals are dissolved in surface or groundwater; sandstones have a high porosity/ permeability/groundwater flows through them; where the conditions change from oxidising to reducing uranium minerals are precipitated; uranium is often associated with organic matter/wood; sulfur-reducing bacteria may play a role in ore formation [2]

(e) (i) subsidence at the surface/creation of spoil heaps/acid mine drainage water [1]

(ii) soil or stream sediment samples are collected; samples are analysed for heavy metals such as lead, arsenic, cadmium, mercury; results are plotted on maps and areas with higher concentrations than normal are identified [2]

Total 16

5 (a) 1 blocks of sandstone = B building stone
2 clay = A brick
3 crushed igneous rock = E roadstone
4 finely crushed limestone = C cement
5 gravel = D concrete
4/5 = 3 marks, 2/3 = 2 marks, 1 = 1 mark [3]

(b) (i) beds dip in towards reservoir on this side; interbedded competent sandstone and incompetent clay; permeable sandstone on top of impermeable clay; sandstone is poorly cemented/ weak; clay is plastic/low friction/weak; rainwater will percolate down through sandstone (to clay); slip plane will develop between sandstone and clay/along bedding planes [2]

(ii) flooding down valley/creates large wave/collapse of dam/infilling of reservoir [1]

(c) water adds weight; water acts as a lubricant/causes loss of friction/loss of cohesion; water increases the pore fluid pressure/rocks become saturated/ waterlogged/absorb water; presence of water causes swelling (of clay minerals) – reduces strength [2]

(d) 5A; 3B; 2C; 4D [4]

Total 12

6 rock type – fine-grained impermeable rock is best, e.g. clay; porous and permeable rocks, e.g. sandstone, limestone, are undesirable; limestone may contain caves/ cavities/be dissolved by acidic leachate; well cemented rock is best; weathering can increase permeability making leakage more likely; crystalline igneous and metamorphic rocks may be suitable [4 max]

structures – faults increase permeability/provide escape routes for leachate; joints increase permeability/allow escape routes for leachate; tilted/dipping/folded beds allow down dip/lateral movement of leachate; anticlines may have tension joints at their crests [4 max]

other considerations – requires low water table; level of water table may vary in aquifers; ready-made hole in ground such as old quarry or brick pit will reduce costs; ground improvement strategies may be employed – grouting/impermeable lining/drainage and collection of leachate [4 max]

Total 8

Unit 5

1 (a) (i)

Term	Description
replacement	E
carbonisation	A
silicification	B
recrystallisation	C
moulds	D

[4]

(ii) anaerobic sea floor; sulfur fixing bacteria living on bottom; low energy; iron pyrites forms on seabed [2]

(iii) aragonite unstable or polymorphs change; alters to more stable calcite; all older than Caenozoic – aragonite altered to calcite; recrystallisation occurs [2]

(b) (i) *Fine grained sediment*

preserves finer detail or clay minerals delicate; less damage due to grain impact of larger sediments; usually quieter conditions or fewer currents to break up fossils [2]

High energy conditions

breaks up fossils on death or less whole or undamaged specimens; fragments moved in currents and eroded; usually fragment size is larger or less detail preserved [2]

Early diagenesis

alteration early means less loss of features; direct replacement of minerals yields high amount of detail; original material may be preserved [2]

(c) *Amber*

resin flows down tree trapping organisms; preserves chitin or exoskeleton not soft tissue; hardens or recrystallises to form stable amber [2]

Tar

animals attracted to tar as it looks like a waterhole and they fall in; attracts other animals; anaerobic or little decay or antiseptic properties [2]

Total 18

2 (a) (i) genal angle – on either specimens at edge of cephalon;

glabella – between eyes of dorsal view;

mouth – indicated at anterior end of ventral view;

pleuron – shaded or indicated on dorsal view [4]

(b) (i) feathery gills are positioned above the jointed legs [2]

(ii) jointed appendages or legs;

exoskeleton or composed of chitin;

complex limbs or evidence of articulation;

ecdysis or moulting [2]

(c) *Nektonic*

separated pleura to allow greater surface area to float or for greater flexibility to swim; inflated glabella as a floatation device to remain in water column; spines present for protection [2]

Infaunal

no eyes or blind as eyes not needed either nocturnal or live in burrow or deep water; pitted cephalon or sensory hairs present to allow animal to make sense of environment or detect currents; large shovel shaped cephalon for burrowing into sediment or to increase surface area on soft sediment to prevent sinking [2]

Planktonic

small body so it was small for floating in water column and no need for flexibility; inflated glabella and or pygidium or fat or gas filled or separated pleura for buoyancy in water column [2]

(d) (i) *Fossil J*

resting trace/trilobite stationary/marks from exoskeleton/gills or legs [1]

Fossil K

walking traces/(double imprint) may be legs and gills touching sediment [1]

(ii) fit for life and aerobic/soft substrate to leave marks/lack of currents/low energy/sediment movement destroy traces/organic material available for food [2]

Total 18

3 (a) (i) irregular/*Micraster* [1]

(ii) bilateral symmetry [1]

(iii) anterior groove – dip or shallow part of anterior margin;

plastron – posterior of the labrum (anywhere in large dotted area);

mouth – anterior of labrum (between groove and labrum) [3]

(b) (i) 1 = paired pores;

2 = interambulacral plate [2]

(ii) allows protrusion of tube feet through the skeleton; for respiration; attachment; locomotion or movement [2]

(c) (i) Aristotle's lantern; 5 parts to jaw structure; actively scavenged [2]

(ii) no jaws; mouth moved to anterior/developed lip or labrum; current moves down anterior groove; allows easier access for particle feeding/filter feeding/lived in burrow [2]

(iii) *Fasciole*
cilia line fasciole; cilia beat to create currents; remove waste from echinoid and put waste in sanitary tube [2]
Plastron
specialised spines or digging spines; designed to move backwards and forwards; used to dig burrow [2]

Total 17

4 (a) A2; B5; C3; D1; E6 [5]

(b) (i) labelled diagram of suitable structure (e.g. cross bedding, graded bedding, sole structures, pillow lavas, unconformities)
explanation of oldest and youngest structures, with reasons [2]

(ii) labelled diagram of geological feature (e.g. dyke); oldest features cut by younger ones [2]

(iii) diagram of included fragments (e.g. conglomerate); fragments included must be older than the surrounding rock [2]

(c) (i) Potassium–Argon/Uranium–Lead/Rubidium–Strontium [1]

(ii) half-lives example; parent atoms decay or emit particles; products as daughter isotopes measured (ratios); parent isotope measured; produce a suitable labelled diagram or graph; explanation of how time is calculated [3]

(iii) loss of daughter elements or loss of gas; weathering or erosion; sedimentary particles of many ages as you date particles not the rock itself; diagenetic minerals in sediments rare (e.g. glauconite) [2]

(iv) loss of daughter elements or loss of gas; resetting of geological clock; introduction of foreign material into system; discordant dates of whole versus mineral dating; metamorphism or igneous activity or fluid activity [2]

Total 19

5 (a) (i) plate tectonics mean supercontinents can form periodically; Pangaea is an example; this happens about every 300 million years; supercontintents disrupt oceanic circulation (eg North Atlantic Drift); surface heat is not distributed across the globe; colder poles and warmer tropics result/ greater extremes in temperatures [4]

(ii) changes in the physical movement of the Earth; alters the amount of solar radiation hitting the Earth; results in climate change [2]

(iii) this is the change in the shape of the orbit around the Sun; this goes from circular (no ellipse), to elliptical; varies between 0 and 5% on a cycle of about 100 000 years; this alters the distance of the Earth from the Sun changing the short wave radiation that reaches the surface; this varies the amount of radiation received during different seasons [4]

Total 10

6 Ammonoids evolved in Lower Devonian; evolved from Nautiloids/Orthocone nautiloids; angular sutures; little ornament/growth lines only e.g. *Goniatites* sp; suitable diagram with labels; ceratites in Triassic; extinct at end of Triassic; smooth saddles and toothed lobes; suitable diagram with labels; ammonites in Jurassic and Cretaceous; extinct at end of Cretaceous; frilly saddles and lobes/complex sutures; move from involute to evolute forms; large number of species – showing adaptive radiation; gradual uncoiling at end of Cretaceous e.g. *Hamites*; some completely uncoiled; exploitation of different habitat, e.g. bottom dwelling rather than water column; change in position of siphuncle/eccentric siphuncle; increase in diversity of ornament; increase in types of coiling; suitable diagram with labels; gradual folding of septa makes animals stronger; enables animal to support higher pressure of water; possible exploitation of deeper habitats/different habitats

Total 12

7 Diagram of pendent/two-stiped form; biserial form; scandent form; uniserial form; multi-stiped form; early forms from Ordovician; numerous branches or 4 stipes/ Generic names stated – *Tetragraptus*; early forms uniserial; reduced number of stipes later in Ordovician/ e.g. *Didymograptus*; early forms pendent; may be reclined or horizontal; later forms scandent; single-stiped forms with thecae back to back/biserial; mixed forms like/ *Dicellograptus*/scandent forms; single row of thecae/ uniserial form/*Monograptus*; Silurian age uniserial forms; early thecae all simple; later thecae sigmoidal/hooked/ elaborate; complex forms show curving or spirals; changes in number of stipes due to change from benthonic to pelagic; reduction in stipes reduces weight to allow floating; buoyancy devices allow free floating; complex thecae provide better protection for zooids

Total 11

Spread answers

1.1.1

1 The NASA website is the best single source of information. Useful search terms being NASA, space, missions (www.science.hq.nasa.gov/missions).
2 Volume of Olympus Mons is 2545714 cubic kilometres so it is 98 times larger than Mauna Loa.
3 Since Mercury is the closest planet to the Sun, the temperature on the surface of Mercury is very high. At night the surface temperature is as low as (–183°C) and in the day the surface temperature rises to about 427°C). These changes in temperature are due to its rotation and lack of atmosphere.

1.1.2

1 Meteorites are of two main types – stony and metallic. As they formed at the same time from the same materials as the Earth they should have the same composition. Stony meteorites match the mantle and metallic the core.
2 No weathering, erosion on the Moon as no atmosphere or water. Craters on Earth are also destroyed by plate tectonics.
3 Huge shield volcanoes and extensive lava flows on both Venus and Mars are much larger than on Earth. Volcanic activity may still be occurring on Venus and some domes suggest viscous magma. Very active volcanoes on Io, a moon of Jupiter, are erupting liquid sulfur dioxide or gaseous salt.

1.1.3

1 Scale drawing similar to Figure 1. The oceanic crust is the thickness of a pencil line.
2 The crust is the area above the Moho average 35 km thick while the lithosphere is crust and part of the upper mantle so up to 150 km thick.
3 A solid rock can flow very slowly as a rheid if there is a small amount of partial melting and convection currents help it to flow as hotter material rises.
4 The continental crust is thickest under the Himalayas and specifically under Everest.

1.1.4

1 Boreholes on the ocean floor have to be drilled from a drill ship and it is much more difficult to join the lengths of steel for drilling. In 2007 a deep sea drill ship started drilling off Japan and will try to drill to 3500 m below the ocean floor (Integrated Ocean Drilling Program (IODP)). The Kola deep drilling project in Russia ended in 1994.
2 Samples of upper mantle peridotite can be seen in ophiolites and as xenoliths in kimberlites.

3 Graph to show depth on y-axis from 0 to 50 km and temperature from 0 to 1200°C with points plotted where the average is 30°C/km.

1.1.5

1 Seismic waves are constantly refracted as they travel through the Earth and the incompressibility increases with depth so that the path is curved.
2 A discontinuity is a boundary between the layers in the Earth.
3 The Gutenberg Discontinuity separates the solid mantle made of silicates from the liquid outer core made of iron nickel.
4 The P wave shadow zone is restricted to 103° to 142° while the S wave shadow zone is much larger from 103° to 103°.

1.1.6

1 Palaeolatitude helps to determine the position of continents over time and is used to date continental drift.
2 Longitude lines run from pole to pole and there is no difference in magnetism.
3 Palaemagnetism is ancient magnetism preserved in the rocks.
4 Iron particles in a magma rotate and align parallel to the Earth's magnetic field at the time. Once the rock is solid the iron particles are fixed in position.

1.2.1

1

P waves	fastest	arrive first	compressional	body wave	
S waves	slower	arrive second	transverse	body wave	will not pass through liquid
L waves	slow	arrive last	horizontal	surface wave	

2 Incompressibility increases with depth.
3 Refraction at the Gutenberg Discontinuity is due to the change in state from solid mantle to liquid outer core.
4 S waves will not pass through it.
5 Curved paths are due to gradual increase in incompressibility and density with increasing depth.

1.2.2

1 $30 \times 30 \times 30 = 27\,000$.
2 Use the USGS website www.earthquake.usgs.gov
3 Sandstone when cemented is hard and will vibrate but the intensity will not be high for the distance away from the epicentre. The unconsolidated sand will be full of water and is likely to have a high earthquake intensity and may undergo liquefaction.

4 Intensity is a measure of the damage caused while magnitude is a measure of the amount of energy released.

1.2.3

1 2000 km

2 rock, stress, plate, strain, energy, stored, deformation, fracture, movement, fault, released, earthquake. (There are lots of alternative answers for this brief summary.)

3 Isoseismal lines are useful when looking at local effects which vary depending on rock type but you do not have the data until many weeks after an earthquake to identify where the epicentre is located. Seismographs give a quick answer using the method shown in Figure 3b.

1.2.4

1 Use websites to research large destructive earthquakes such as Turkey in 1998, Armenia in 1988, Pakistan 2005, Mexico City 1985, Kobe Japan 1995.

2 A tsunami from an earthquake in Alaska would take 14 hours to reach northern Australia.

3 All effects are minor, generally fallen chimneys and brickwork, from magnitude 5.5.

1.2.5

1 Using the methods listed in the text as search words identify graphs and diagrams where the method has been used.

2 Arguments for issuing warnings are saving lives. The arguments against include the inaccuracy, possible mass panic and traffic chaos, property values and businesses affected adversely, geologists getting sued!

3 Triangular shape wider at base than top for better stability, systems at roof level using counterbalances.

1.3.1

1 Coastline is constantly moving as sea level changes so is not the geological edge of the continents.

2 Palaeomagnetism was not known in Wegener's day.

3 Britain has rocks that could only form in hot tropical latitudes e.g. coal and red desert sandstones. Fossils such as corals also indicate warmer climates.

1.3.2

1 Rocks get older, sediment gets thicker, sea floor is lower and flatter, heat flow is lower, gravity is lower.

2 Convection cells in the mantle carry the rigid lithosphere and the continents across the partially melted asthenosphere.

3 Internet sites are plentiful.

1.3.3

1 Pacific 3.4 cm/yr and Atlantic 1.2 cm/yr. Indian Ocean is spreading fastest.

2 Graph with line showing irregular points and line of best fit.

3 2 cm/yr.

1.3.4

2 Rift valleys are tensional features that form as plates move apart and have normal faults at the sides. Trenches are above the top of a subduction zone where the oceanic plate is moving down and faults are thrusts formed under compression.

3 Mid-ocean ridges are formed from basalt lavas erupted due to rising magma at a divergent plate margin. Fold mountains are formed from deformed sediments, volcanic rocks and igneous intrusions at convergent plate margins.

4 Sea level changes as the ice melts or forms at the poles. Earth movements move the land up or down.

1.3.5

1 There is no subduction occurring – all activity is shallow.

2 The mantle is hot and plastic at that depth so the rock does not fracture.

3 Deep earthquakes are restricted to subduction zones while shallow earthquakes are found at all types of plate boundary.

1.3.6

1 Continental and oceanic lithosphere plates moving on the asthenosphere, diverging at MORs and subducting or colliding at convergent plate margins.

2 Continental drift is just the evidence for the movement of continents with nothing about the oceans. Plate tectonics is what is happening at plate margins and is modern activity as well as evidence in old rocks.

3 Volcanoes, trenches, rift valleys, high heat flow, fold mountains and gravity anomalies.

4 Plate boundaries can be seen on land as active fault lines where earthquakes occur. The San Andreas Fault is a good example or walk across an MOR in Iceland.

1.3.7

1 Look for areas of many, small, shallow-focus earthquakes, basalt lava from fissure volcanic activity and high heat flow, a largely submarine mountain chain forming the MOR, black smokers and transform faults cutting the MOR.

2 Important source of valuable metal ores.

3 Cross-section to show sediments, basalt pillow lava, dolerite dykes, gabbro and peridotite.

4 Cross-section to show MOR, axial rift, heat flow, volcanic activity, rising magma, age of ocean crust symmetrical and older away from MOR, sediment symmetrical, thicker and older away from MOR and magnetic anomalies.

1.3.8

1 Divergent is where two plates are moving apart and mafic magma rises up. Convergent is where two plates move towards each other and collide forming fold mountains and if oceanic continental subduction takes place.

2 There is no subduction so no melting plate or rising magma to form the volcanoes.

3 Intermediate magma has a lower viscosity than silicic magma. The difference in viscosity means that the thick, sticky, silicic magma will not mix.

4 The oceanic plate always subducts as it is more dense than a continental plate.

1.3.9

1 A divergent plate margin is where two plates are moving apart and magma rises up at an MOR while at a conservative plate margin the plates slide past each other with no volcanic activity.

2 A subduction zone is where an oceanic plate descends. The Benioff zone is the line of earthquakes that occur on the top edge of the descending plate.

3 It forms the boundary between the American and Pacific plates rather than just a fault within a continent.

4 9 million years.

1.3.10

1 Either whole mantle convects as one large cell or there are two sets of cells. The top cells are lithosphere, asthenosphere and upper mantle down to 700 km and the bottom cells are in the lower mantle down to the outer core boundary.

2 No convection probably means no plate tectonics so no earthquakes or volcanoes but no new water or volcanic gases entering the atmosphere.

3 Ridge push is caused by the magma at an MOR pushing the plates apart through the dolerite dykes. Slab pull is the subducting plate dragging the lithosphere plate behind it as gravity pulls it down.

1.3.11

1 A hot spot is where a mantle plume reaches the surface. The mantle plume is magma rising through the mantle perhaps from the core–mantle boundary.

2 The plate movement is towards the northwest and the older islands used to be above the mantle plume but have been carried away.

3 Distance is 160 km and the age difference is 1.8 Ma so the rate of sea floor spreading is 8.9 cm/yr.

1.4.1

1 5° to the right.

2 forces come from top left and bottom right.

3 A rock with a low elastic limit and large plastic deformation will be incompetent.

1.4.2

1 Similar diagrams to Figure 1.

2 Joints are fractures so will develop in brittle rocks. Incompetent rocks are plastic so do not fracture.

3 Internet research.

1.4.3

1 Figure 2 Downthrow side is on the right/east, dip is 60° and the throw 1 m. Figure 4 the dip is 20°

2 A fault displaces the beds while a joint does not.

3 Labels of downthrow, fault plane, throw, angle of dip, footwall, hanging wall on both diagrams.

1.4.4

1 Faults produced by tension. Draw and label normal faults, fault zone, beds, bedding planes, fault plane, throw, angle of dip, footwall, hanging wall and joints. Measure throws and dip of faults and beds.

2 Many small earthquakes on transform faults as lava is erupted for sea floor spreading regularly. Movement occurs in segments of MOR depending on the amount of new material being formed.

3 Great Glen is a strike-slip fault within a plate. It shows more than one period of movement with dextral movement in the Tertiary after the sinistral Caledonian movement. The San Andreas is also a strike-slip fault but is at a plate margin between the North American and Pacific plates so is called a conservative margin. The relative movement is dextral as a result of the Pacific plate moving faster than the North American plate though both move to the northwest.

1.4.5

1 A symmetrical anticline has both limbs dipping at the same angle and is an upfold with the oldest beds in the centre. An asymmetrical syncline has one limb at a steeper angle than the other and is a downfold with youngest rocks in the centre.

2 Symmetrical anticline to be drawn and labels to include limbs dipping at 20°, axial plane vertical with tension joints at the crest of the open fold.

3 Asymmetrical anticline with north limb dipping at 70° and south limb at 40°. It is just a closed fold with an inter-limb angle of 70°. The axial plane is inclined to the north. There are tension joints many infilled with white mineral veins at the crest in the competent beds.

1.4.6

1 Cross-sections show a syncline for a basin and an anticline for a dome.

2 Characteristics are inverted limb, closed or tight folds and steep angles of dip for overfolds and low for recumbent folds.

3 Left is a fold with a vertical limb still an asymmetrical anticline. Right is asymmetrical syncline.

1.4.7

1 Drawing to show cleavage planes parallel to the axial plane of the fold and only in incompetent beds.

2 Sandstone grains of quartz are rounded so can not be aligned at 90° to the pressure in order to form cleavage.

3 Compression structures are: all folds, reverse faults and thrusts, cleavage. Tensional structures are normal faults, horst and graben, joints.

1.4.8

1 Diagram like the second diagram in Figure 2 but with arrows reversed and oldest/youngest beds reversed.

2 Same diagram on page 52 on the left.

3 Student's own work.

4 Beds laid down, folded into anticline and then faulted. The displacement shows that bed thickness changes so rocks were hot and plastic and faulting probably happened at the same time as the folding. Tension joints have been infilled with a white mineral. Downthrow side is on the right.

2.1.1

1 Repeated sequence of processes that link all three major rock groups.

2 Sediments are buried and grains move into closer contact due to pressure of sediment above. They become compacted. Fluids containing ions in solution circulate through pore spaces. Minerals crystallise in the pore spaces cementing the grains forming sedimentary rock.

3 Metamorphic rocks are formed by recrystallisation of existing rocks in the solid state. Igneous rocks are formed by the crystallisation of minerals from magma or lava, both of which are liquid.

2.1.2

1 A rock contains a mixture of minerals. A mineral has a definite chemical composition but a rock does not.

2 Calcite reacts strongly with dilute HCl. Calcite is lower hardness (3) than quartz (7).

3 The minerals are hornblende (elongate crystals with six sides, there are two cleavage directions at 120°), augite (roughly equidimensional crystals with eight sides, there are two cleavage directions at 90°), olivine (poorly shaped crystals that are olive green and have conchoidal fracture) and garnet (no cleavage, hardness 7–7.5, often but not always, red in colour).

2.1.3

1 Metamorphic.

2 Sedimentary.

3 Igneous – augite and olivine (hornblende also occurs in metamorphic rocks); metamorphic = garnet.

2.1.4

1 Relative dating uses comparisons (older than/younger than). Absolute dating uses ages in years.

2 Carboniferous.

3 Explanations should refer to the law of cross-cutting relationships for igneous rocks; superposition, floral and faunal succession and included fragments for sedimentary rocks.

2.2.1

1 (a) Both mafic/dark colour. Basalt is fine grained/extrusive. Dolerite is medium grained/intrusive.

(b) Both are fine grained/extrusive. Rhyolite is silicic/contains >63% silica/light colour. Andesite is intermediate /63 – 52% silica/grey colour. (c) Both coarse grained/intrusive. Granite is silicic/contains >63% silica/light colour/has abundant K feldspar/quartz. Gabbro is mafic/contains 52 – 45% silica/dark colour/has abundant plagioclase/mafic minerals.

2 Light cannot pass through the rock, as reflected by microcrystals. Crystallites (<.005 mm) of iron oxide within the glass make it black in colour.

3 Main distinguishing characteristics are colour, whether or not quartz is a prominent mineral and the type of feldspars.

2.2.2

1 Hypabyssal rocks have crystals that are 1–5 mm in size. Individual crystals can be seen but are difficult to identify. Plutonic rocks have crystals that are greater than 5 mm. They can be seen and identified in hand specimens.

2 To ensure your results are comparable, always measure the long axis of each crystal.

3 The world's largest crystal was found within a pegmatite (a very coarse grained igneous rock). It was over 10 m long.

2.2.3

1 Hypabyssal rocks result from slow cooling below the surface. Plutonic rocks result from very slow cooling deep below the surface.

2 Glassy texture only forms when magma cools very rapidly so that the rock has no crystals.

3 Porphyritic texture forms where a rock has two stages of cooling. The large crystals are feldspar phenocrysts formed first by cooling slowly. The magma contains the elements necessary for the growth of feldspar. Amygdaloidal texture is where vesicles are later infilled by minerals (commonly calcite or quartz) deposited from groundwater.

2.2.4

1 (a) potassium feldspar (b) plagioclase feldspar (c) olivine.

2 Granite.

3 Gabbro is coarse grained, basalt is fine grained; orthoclase feldspar is most abundant in granite, plagioclase feldspar is most abundant in granodiorite.

2.2.5

1 Ca-rich plagioclase feldspar is abundant

2 Vesicles are infilled by secondary minerals to produce amygdaloidal texture.

3 Basalt is fine grained, dolerite is medium grained; plagioclase feldspar is prominent in gabbro but peridotite is largely composed of olivine.

4 'Black granite' worktops are often basalt.

2.2.6

1 Diagrams should look like simplified versions of Figure 1 and the top diagram in Figure 2.

2 Rhyolite is paler in colour and may contain flow banding, but andesite does not.

3 What is now North Wales was located at a convergent plate margin at the time.

2.2.7

1 Olivine forms at high temperatures and is found in ultramafic rocks. Quartz forms at lower temperatures and is found in silicic rocks.

2 Augite.

3 The high temperature minerals. They are formed at high temperatures and pressures within the Earth and are unstable at the low temperatures and pressures at the Earth's surface.

2.2.8

1 They crystallise early at high temperatures; they are high density.

2 Magma at the base of the chamber is at a higher temperature (nearer to the source) than the magma near the top (nearer to the Earth's surface which is cooler). Magma at the base is thermally expanded which lowers density and it rises. Magma nearer the top is cooled, contracts, becomes denser and sinks.

3 About 54%.

2.2.9

1 Sills are concordant. They follow the bedding planes/have the same trend/strike. (Transgressive sills cross them where they step from one bedding plane to another.) Dykes are discordant. They cut across the beds in the surrounding country rock/have a different trend/strike.

2 Average width of dykes on Mull is $763 \text{ m} \div 375 = 2.03 \text{ m}$; average width of dykes on Arran is $1800 \text{ m} \div 525 = 3.4 \text{ m}$. Crustal extension in Mull is $7.63 \times 10^2 \text{ m} \div 2 \times 10^4 \text{ m} \times 100 = 3.8\%$; in Arran it is $1.8 \times 10^3 \text{ m} \div 2.5 \times 10^4 \text{ m} \times 100 = 7.2\%$.

3 Magmatic differentiation can produce granitic rocks from basic magmas.

2.2.10

1 Sills have two baked margins, lava flows only have one below. Sills may contain xenoliths from rocks above as well as below, lava flows only contain xenoliths from the rock below. Sills very rarely contain vesicles, lava flows commonly have vesicular or amygdaloidal upper surfaces. Sills have a regular upper surface, lava flows have a rubbly or weathered/reddened upper surface.

2 Both are areas around an igneous intrusion where the country rocks have been changed by heat. Baked margins are associated with minor intrusions and are a few cm to a few m wide. Metamorphic aureoles cover a much wider area (hundreds of m to several km) around a major intrusion, usually a batholith.

3 Basalt is fine grained and often has vesicular or amygdaloidal texture. It sometimes has hexagonal jointing. All these are consistent with an origin as an extrusive rock. Gabbro is coarse grained indicating that it cooled slowly at depth as a plutonic rock. Rhyolite is fine grained and contains flow banding, indicating an origin as an extrusive rock. Granite is coarse grained indicating that it cooled slowly at depth as a plutonic rock.

4 The account could describe the extent and thickness of the Whin Sill and explain that it is transgressive. The Tertiary lavas could be linked to their plate tectonic setting. Outcrop patterns and textures could be included.

2.2.11

1 They are all fine grained.

2 The difference is due to viscosity. A thin cooling skin on a low viscosity flow remains plastic and becomes folded into ropy forms as the lava beneath continue to move (pahoehoe). With more viscous flows the chilled surface becomes thicker before the slower movement of the lava beneath breaks it into large angular blocks (aa).

3 Silicic magma has high viscosity. This prevent gases from escaping as it rises. The top of the magma becomes filled with gas and becomes pumice. Sometimes the expanding pumice is thrown into the air as gases escape violently. The nuée ardente cloud that results is dangerous because it is very hot, contains large blocks of rock and toxic volcanic gases that move at high velocity.

2.2.12

1 The cross-section should show the vent and crater. There are alternating layers of lava flows and pyroclastics. The coarser pyroclastics are nearer to the crater and the finer ones further away.

2 Viscosity increase with silica content, so that mafic lavas are the least viscous and silicic lavas the most viscous with intermediate between the two.

3 Pinatubo and Mt St Helens are already described but there is more detail available. Mt Ruapehu in New Zealand is worth researching.

2.2.13

1 The map should show the main ocean ridges in addition to the named locations in the task.

2 Pillow lavas tend to be oval in cross-section. The lower surface of pillows sags down into the space between the pillows beneath it. This forms a downward pointing extension of the pillow if it is the right way up.

3 Research should include hazards to people and property.

2.2.14

1 Mafic magma is low viscosity. Gases can escape easily. Silicic magmas have high viscosity. Gases build up within the magma until they escape in violent explosions.

2 A crater is smaller in diameter (up to 1 km) than a caldera (>1 km). It is the site of eruption of lava, gases and

pyroclasts. A caldera forms when the level of magma in the magma chamber drops, after violent eruptions. This leaves voids beneath the volcano into which the top collapses.

3 Shield volcanoes form at divergent plate boundaries because these are sites where mafic magma originating in the mantle is able to reach the surface. Strato-volcanoes form at convergent plate boundaries due to the higher viscosity magma, produced by differentiation and assimilation of continental rocks. Alternating explosive and effusive eruptions lead to the formation of strato-volcanoes.

4 Volcanoes at convergent plate boundaries would be a good place to concentrate the research.

2.2.16

1 Sulfur dioxide molecules remain in the upper atmosphere for years. They absorb solar radiation and reflect it back into space.

2 Geothermal energy is the main benefit in these locations.

3 Advantages: geothermal energy; fertile soils; tuff used as building material/can be used in cement manufacture; Disadvantages: hazards to life and property from lava flows, pyroclastic flows, blast, toxic gases.

2.3.1

1 Carbon dioxide gas in the atmosphere reacts with rainwater and pore water in the soil to form carbonic acid. This reacts with minerals causing some ions to go into solution.

$$CaCO_3 + H_2CO_3 \rightarrow Ca^{2+} + 2\ HCO_3^-$$

calcite + carbonic acid = calcium hydrogen carbonate ions in solution.

2 The minerals in rocks are stable in conditions that exist at the depth where they formed. Minerals that form first in Bowen's Reaction series are the ones formed at greater depths. They are the least stable in conditions at the Earth's surface and are the most easily weathered.

3 Weathering is affected by temperature and availability of water. Both of these factors are controlled by climate.

2.3.2

1 Difference: weathering occurs *in situ* but erosion implies transport. Similarity: both involve the breakdown of rocks.

2 The longer they have been in transport the more they will have been affected by attrition.

3 (a) (b) Sand requires least energy. Boulders, cobbles and pebbles over about 30 mm diameter are deposited.

4 At very high velocities the finest and the coarsest grain sizes are eroded. No deposition takes place.

2.3.3

1 These can be drawn as histograms (Figure 3) or cumulative frequency curves (Figure 4). The dune sand is well sorted. The river and beach sands are moderately sorted. The glacial till is poorly sorted.

2 Wind and ice vary in terms of energy and viscosity. Ice transported grains tend to be in contact with one another or with the rocks beneath. This gives pebbles polished or scratched (striated) surfaces. Abrasion produces fine grained fragments. Melting leaves poorly sorted deposits. Wind only has the energy to transport fine to medium sand size grains and so deposits are better sorted. Its lower viscosity leads to frequent collisions between grains allowing attrition to increase roundness and reduce grain size further. It also gives grain surfaces a frosted appearance.

3 Dune: $0.8 \div 2 = 0.4$
Beach: $1.0 \div 2 = 0.5$
River: $1.7 \div 2 = 0.85$

4 Qualitative methods can be used in the field/without laboratory equipment. Quantitative methods facilitate statistical analysis and estimation of error.

2.3.4

1 They are classified by grain size. < 0.0625 mm – mudstone, shale, clay, siltstone; 2–0.0625 mm sandstones; >2 mm – conglomerates and breccias. Grain shape is used to distinguish between conglomerate, which has rounded clasts and breccia.

2 They contain fossils or fragments of fossils.

3 Figure 2a by traction in a very high energy river; b by traction in a high energy river; c by saltation in a river with varying energy.

2.3.5

1 Poorly sorted coarse grain size with angular fragments.

2 Similarity: both are composed of sand sized grains. Difference: Arkose contains at least 25% K feldspar, greywacke mainly consists of rock fragments.

3 Desert sandstone is red in colour because it forms in oxidising conditions and iron oxide covers the quartz grains. It is well sorted because the grains are wind transported. They are well rounded due to attrition which occurs during wind transport. Collisions between grains give the surfaces a frosted appearance.

2.3.6

1 Diagram should be labelled and have a scale bar. Coccoliths should be <0.002 mm diameter.

2 They are biologically not mechanically formed.

3 Deposited in shallow marine conditions, above wave base, where energy levels were occasionally high due to storm waves.

2.3.7

1 The diagram should be labelled and have a suitable scale. Since it is inverted the cross bedding would appear convex upwards and flatten out towards the top.

2 From right to left.

3 The wind blown sand grains would be well rounded.

4 The graded bed should have the larger grains at the base. This is the surface nearest to the core of the fold. It appears upside down on the inverted limb.

2.3.8

1 The cracks are wider at the top because evaporation of water from the mud is greatest near the surface, which receives most solar heat energy.

2 Flute casts and cross bedding.

3 They show which is the right way up. Sedimentary rocks are deposited so that younger rocks are above older rocks.

2.3.9

1 Mud and clay are much more affected by compaction than sandstones.

2 Layers of sediment accumulate, one on top of another, their mass produces load pressure. This acts vertically and affects the sediments below causing compaction to take place. Grains become more closely packed together and this reduces the porosity of the sediment. Groundwater containing silica in solution, from pressure solution of quartz, flows through the pore spaces and where conditions are right quartz is precipitated forming a cement which binds grains together to form orthoquartzite.

3 Plant remains fall into swamps and the process of decay uses up the available oxygen. Anaerobic bacteria change the plant material into peat. If peat is buried beneath other sediments it is subjected to increased pressure and temperature which expels water and volatiles (e.g. CH_4 and CO_2). This reduces volume and increases the proportion of carbon it contains.

2.3.10

1 When ice melts it deposits material of all sizes in the same place. This forms boulder clay.

2 The striated surfaces are produced when rock fragments in the base of moving ice scratch the rock over which they pass. Till is deposited from melting ice sheets.

The cross bedded gravels and sands are deposited from outwash streams coming from melting ice. The gravels are deposited nearer to the ice sheet than the sands. Most of the finer mud and silt is carried further away, often to lakes, where it is deposited as varves.

3 Cracks in the ground fill with meltwater in the spring. In winter the water freezes and expands, widening the crack. Each winter the crack is widened, forming an ice wedge. The enlarged crack is filled with sediment that has been washed in, forming an ice wedge cast.

4 There should be examples of till, fluvio-glacial sands and gravels, varves and erratics.

2.3.11

1 Clay deposited in low energy conditions on the floodplain. Gravels are high energy channel lag deposits. Upward fining cross bedded sands represent point bar deposits with energy levels decreasing with time. Cross bedded silts and clays deposited in low energy flow. Clay represents low energy floodplain, only covered with water when the river floods. Plant roots indicate non fluvial or marshy conditions. The sequence is formed by the migration of a meandering channel and represents changing environments in one place through time.

2 Breccias contain angular clasts, but in conglomerates they are sub rounded. Both are poorly sorted arkoses contain angular to sub-rounded clasts. They are moderately well sorted.

3 Diagrams should show lateral migration of a meander bend and label erosion/bank undercutting on the outer part of the bend and deposition/point bars on the inside.

4 This should include conglomerates, sandstones and siltstones.

2.3.12

1 It is more soluble than calcite or gypsum which are deposited earlier and appear nearer to the shore of the playa lake.

2 Salt crystals form when the lake dries up. When in contact with water the salt dissolves. The cubic mould left is infilled by sediment or a secondary mineral. The shape of the original salt crystal is preserved.

3 Clay sized grains deposited as a playa lake dries up. Evaporites precipitate as water evaporates. Flash flood transports coarser material from nearby mountains. Winds transport fine grained sand which is deposited to form sand dunes. Silt and fine sand deposited in moving water producing ripple marks. Playa lake sediments deposited in low energy conditions with precipitation of evaporites as the lake dries up.

4 This should include desert sandstones with large-scale cross bedding, fine grained sandstones with small-scale cross bedding, mudstones with ripple marks and evaporites, particularly halite and gypsum.

2.3.13

1 Equatorial.

2 Coal formed in swamps. Subsidence and emergence of the land resulted in marine transgressions and regressions so that swamp conditions were sometimes present and sometimes not. Changing sea levels/isostatic readjustment/delta switching are possible explanations.

3 River water spreads out and loses energy. It is the decrease in energy that causes deposition of sediments with the coarsest grains first. There must be little wave or tidal action to allow the sediment to build up at the mouth of the river.

4 This should include the Millstone Grit deltas, shale, siltstone, sandstone and coal as part of cyclothems.

2.3.14

1 Beach conglomerates form in high energy conditions where shells are broken by the large fragments being transported.

2 Both may contain cross bedding. Glauconite is found in some sandstones formed in shallow seas, not in rivers. Shallow marine sands tend to be finer grained than river sands.

3 Transport in shallow seas may be by longshore drift or by rip currents. These currents are uni-directional and asymmetrical ripple marks may form. Tides are bi-directional and may produce symmetrical ripple marks.

4 This should include glauconitic sands.

2.3.15

1 They form in shallow seas where tiny grains of sand, shell fragments or pellets are rolled in carbonate mud by tidal currents and wave action. Around this nucleus concentric layers of calcium carbonate, in the form of aragonite, are precipitated from the sea water.

2 Corals provide the main framework of a reef, but other organisms also live on and around reefs.

3 This should include reef, bioclastic, oolitic and fossiliferous limestones including crinoidal.

2.3.16

1 Halite is more soluble than gypsum. The degree of evaporation may not have been sufficient for it to be precipitated.

2 Ripple marks and desiccation cracks should be described.

3 When salt is deeply buried/under high pressure it behaves plastically. Because it is less dense than surrounding rocks it rises to form salt domes.

4 This should include plate tectonic events that led to a fall in sea level in the Mediterranean due to the closing of the Straits of Gibraltar. Sediments in buried gorges of rivers, sabkha sequences and evaporites associated with barred basins are significant evidence.

2.3.17

1 Submarine canyons.

2 Coarse grains are deposited in high energy and finer grains from low energy conditions. The size of the grains is related to energy so the rocks shown in the graphic log sequence show high energy at the base and lower energy towards the top.

3 CO_2 content and water temperature vary, as does the rate of supply of $CaCO_3$. This means that the degree of saturation and therefore the CCD varies from place to place in the oceans and has throughout geological time.

4 This should include shales with graptolite fossils, siltstones, greywackes and turbidite sequences.

2.4.1

1 Contact metamorphism: temperatures are generally high but pressure is low.
Burial metamorphism: medium to high pressure and relatively low temperature.
Regional metamorphism: low to high temperature and low to high pressure.

2 Destruction of fossils, beds and sedimentary structures, hardening of the rock, a change in colour, alignment of minerals and the growth of new metamorphic minerals.

3 Reactions that depend on pressure only are less common than temperature dependent reactions.

2.4.2

1 Gneiss.

2 Diagrams should have a scale. Labels could show (slate/schist): fine grained/medium grained; slaty cleavage with relict bedding/schistosity without relict structures; garnet porphyroblasts in schist only.

3 Diagrams should have a scale. Labels could show that both contain flat/tabular minerals and show schistosity but gneiss also has a granoblastic layer which is lighter in colour.

2.4.3

1 Impurities in the parent limestone give some marble a range of coloured streaks.

2 Because these rocks do not contain platy minerals like mica they do not show foliation.

3 Quartzite is composed of interlocking quartz crystals. There is no cement between the grains. There are no sedimentary structures or fossils.

2.4.4

1 Any two of marble, quartzite, hornfels and spotted rock.

2 Diagrams should have a scale and be labelled.

3 Bedding is produced by sedimentary processes which result in horizontal layers. Slaty cleavage is usually parallel to the axial planes of folds. Slaty cleavage may be at any angle to bedding.

2.4.5

1 Metamorphic aureole.

2 Up to 2.4 km from 10 km intrusion; up to 1.3 km from 5 km intrusion; up to 0.5 km from 1 km intrusion.

3 Metamorphic grade is a measure of the intensity of metamorphism. Increases in temperature result in increasing grade in contact metamorphism, In regional metamorphism grade is also used to describe environments where both temperature and pressure vary. The growth of metamorphic minerals and textures is controlled by temperature and/or pressure so that particular rock types are associated with different grades of metamorphism.

2.4.6

1 Pure limestone ($CaCO_3$) does not contain the elements needed for the growth of andalusite (Al_2SiO_5).

2 Diagram should include a scale and show, with increasing distance from the contact; hornfels, andalusite slate, spotted rock.

3 The quartz grains in the sandstone recrystallise to form an interlocking mosaic of crystals. This destroys relict stuctures.

2.4.7

1 Paired metamorphic belts form at convergent margins with subduction zones. The zone closest to the trench will have high pressure due to compressive stress and low temperature as no magma is rising. The zone further away has high temperature due to rising magma and low pressure.

2 Recrystallisation/alignment of tabular mineral perpendicular to stress/growth of new minerals.

3 *Marble and quartzite occur in all three grades.

Metamorphic grade	Parent rock	Metamorphic rock	Mineral composition	Texture
Low	shale	slate	clay minerals and muscovite mica with some chlorite and quartz	slaty cleavage fine grain size (<1 mm)
	limestone	marble*	calcite	granoblastic medium grain size (1–5 mm) grain size increases with metamorphic grade.
	sandstone	quartzite*	quartz	granoblastic medium grain size (1–5 mm) grain size increases with metamorphic grade
Medium	shale	schist	muscovite and biotite mica quartz garnet and kyanite	schistosity medium grain size (1–5 mm)
High	shale	gneiss	biotite mica mafic minerals quartz K feldspar sillimanite	gneissose banding coarse grain size (>5 mm)

2.4.8

1 Slate in the chlorite and biotite zones; schist in the biotite garnet and kyanite zones; gneiss in the kyanite and sillimanite zones.

2 Due to their chemical composition clay-rich sedimentary rocks like shale produce a variety of metamorphic minerals as temperature and pressure conditions change.

3 A polymorph occurs in several different forms but all have the same chemical composition. A pseudomorph is a secondary mineral that has a different chemical composition from an earlier mineral that it has replaced, but retains the form of the original mineral.

3.1.1

1 The rose diagram should have nearly all the readings in the right hand side. They do not mirror to the left in this case because flute casts have a single clear direction form round end to open end.

2 The main direction is to the east but slightly NE. The data shows the way the flute casts radiate or fan out so they are not a single linear current.

3 The black shales were laid down in low energy deep sea conditions as clay particles slowly settled out from suspension. The greywackes formed when a turbidity current flowed down the continental slope onto the deep ocean floor and scoured out the sediment to form the flute casts. The sediment carried by the current then settled out to form the beds greywacke. The sequence forms turbidites.

4 As the sediment settles out from the turbidity current it infills the scour marks so that the base of the greywacke bed forms the flute casts.

4.1.1

1 Compaction causes the grains to move closer together. Cement fills in the pore space.

2 Labelled diagram of oolitic limestone: well rounded, well sorted grains, high porosity and permeability, scale 1 mm for oolites. Labelled diagram of greywacke: poorly sorted, angular grains, low porosity and permeability, average grain size 1 mm.

3 5000 mm/day.

4.1.2

1 Must have high porosity and high permeability – well rounded, well sorted grains, little or no matrix or cementation.

2 Labelled diagrams. Unconfined aquifer: open to atmosphere. Confined aquifer: overlain by impermeable rock with recharge zones at edge.

3 Main aquifers: Chalk and Lower Greensand. Aquicludes: Gault Clay and London Clay. Recharge zones: North Downs and Chiltern Hills.

4.1.3

1 Labelled diagram showing cone of depression in water table around well.

2 Description of lowering of water table; subsidence at surface; or salt water encroachment.

3 Rock acts as a natural filter removing impurities; water contains dissolved minerals; water has not been treated/chlorinated.

4 Unconfined aquifers are open to the atmosphere so pollutants can infiltrate into them over the entire area. Pollutants can only infiltrate into confined aquifers at recharge zones.

4.1.4

1 **(a)** Water table – line joining where upper and lower boundaries of the aquifer intersect the land surface.
   (b) Spring – at intersection of boundary of aquifer and either clay layer with the land surface.
   (c) Confined aquifer – area of aquifer to the right of and below the upper clay.
   (d) Spring occurs where water table intersects the land surface at the junction between the permeable and impermeable rock.

2 Spring water is groundwater that has been filtered through rocks removing impurities.

3 Descriptions and labelled diagrams of springs at: boundary between permeable and impermeable sedimentary rocks; igneous intrusion; fault; unconformity.

4.1.5

1 See table in spread 4.1.5.
2 See table in spread 4.1.5.
3 Groundwater will be important in areas with sedimentary rocks and aquifers; in arid areas that do not have a reliable surface water supply.
4 Renewable as part of the water cycle. Sustainable provided rate of extraction does not exceed rate of replenishment.

4.2.1

1 Environment must be marine with abundant plankton, low energy and anoxic sea floor conditions.
2 Source rock is buried, compacted and subjected to temperatures of 50 to 200 °C causing plankton to be converted to kerogen and then petroleum.
3 Descriptions and explanations of any two from: permeability; pressure; density differences; temperature; viscosity of oil.
4 Reservoir rock – highly porous and permeable rock capable of storing and yielding petroleum. Cap rock – impermeable rock overlying reservoir rock.
5 Rocks must have well rounded, well sorted grains; high porosity with oil in pore space; high permeability; grain size 1–2 mm.

4.2.2

1 A geological situation that concentrates petroleum in one place.
2 Descriptions and labelled diagrams of traps: anticline; fault; salt dome; unconformity; lithological.
3 No suitable source rock; no suitable cap rock; oil and gas may have escaped; oil and gas may have been destroyed by igneous activity or metamorphism; quantity of oil and gas is too small.

4.2.3

1 Descriptions of: seismic, gravity and down-hole logging surveys.
2 Advantages – provides actual rock samples; direct evidence; gives precise depth information down the hole. Disadvantages – boreholes are spaced out so may miss information such as faults; geophysical surveys provide continuous data; exploration drilling is very expensive.

4.2.4

1 Reservoir rock drilled into and production well established. Explanation of how oil gushes to surface under natural pressure. When pressure falls oil is pumped to surface using submersible pumps or nodding donkeys. 20–30% of oil recovered.
2 Explanations of variations in porosity and permeability due to variations in grain size, roundness, sorting, matrix, cementation, compaction, presence of structures. Variations in depth, pressure, temperature, viscosity, % gases in solution.
3 Descriptions of: water flood drive; gas cap drive; thermal methods; possible use of detergents, surfactants and bacteriological methods.
4 Thick, viscous oil has high surface tension and sticks to grains.

4.2.5

1 Descriptions of oil spillages; damage to marine ecosystems; pollution of sea water and coastlines; atmospheric pollution caused by fires; disposal of old oil rigs.
2 Description of use of either depleted oil and gas reservoirs or salt caverns.

4.2.6

1 Oil and natural gas are fossil fuels that formed millions of years ago. When burnt they are lost as gases into the atmosphere and cannot be recycled on a human timescale.
2 Environmental conditions, temperature and pressures were suitable for preservation and conversion of plankton to oil and gas. There are suitable source rocks, reservoir rocks, cap rocks and traps.
3 The source rock is coal and did not contain plankton. Gas escaped as the coal formed. There are suitable reservoir rocks, cap rocks and traps.
4 Descriptions of environmental and economic disadvantages.

4.2.7

1 Hot, tropical/equatorial climate and swampy delta top environment. Presence of abundant trees, anoxic conditions and rapid burial.

2 Coalification/diagenesis/compaction – weight of overburden squeezes out water and volatiles, carbon content increases, undergoes thermal maturation.

3 Rank – percentage of carbon in the coal. As rank increases peat becomes lignite, then bituminous coal, then anthracite with the highest carbon content.

4 Suitable labelled axes. Points plotted correctly and joined to give line graphs.

5 Anthracite has a higher carbon content/calorific value; produces less ash, smoke and other waste products/ pollution on burning.

4.2.8

1 Description of opencast coal mining.

2 Longwall mining named and described.

3 Descriptions of: faults; folds and steep dips; washouts; seam splitting; problems of deltaic rock sequences; methane gas build up.

4 Research activity.

4.2.9

1 Labelled diagram(s): exposed – coal-bearing strata outcrops at the surface; concealed – coal-bearing strata is under younger cover rocks.

2 Descriptions of: surface subsidence; spoil heaps; acid mine drainage water.

4.2.10

1 **Either** geothermal aquifer: sedimentary basins with higher than normal geothermal gradient; aquifers interbedded with impermeable mudstones/shales that act as insulators; hot water is pumped up and passed through heat exchanger; cooled waters are re-injected into the ground to maintain water pressure in aquifer.
Or hot dry rock: granites have a higher content of heat producing radioactive elements than other rocks; paired boreholes are drilled into granite; rock is artificially fractured; cold water is pumped down and hot water is pumped up.

2 See table in spread 4.2.10.

3 42.5°C.

4.3.1

1 Ore – rock containing valuable metal(s). Ore mineral – mineral containing valuable metal(s). Gangue – waste minerals.

2 Concentration factor is the amount by which the metal is concentrated above its average crustal abundance to make an ore deposit. Calculated using the formula: concentration of metal in ore ÷ average crustal abundance.

3 Aluminium – concentration factor = 6.17; Gold – concentration factor = 50 000; Tin – grade = 2%

4 Descriptions of: prices and demand; abundance and reserves; mining and mineral processing technology.

5 Gold has a high price and is in demand for bullion, jewellery, industrial uses. Pyrite contains iron but it is difficult, expensive and environmentally damaging to extract the iron from it.

4.3.2

1 Description of origin of hydrothermal fluid and how ore minerals are precipitated in fractures to form veins in surrounding country rock.

2 Explanations of key factors: structures; permeability and composition of country rocks; temperature of fluid; solubility of ore minerals.

3 Research activity.

4 Research activity.

4.3.3

1 Dense (5.2 g/cm³), high melting point, crystallises early.

2 Description and explanation of early crystallisation of dense magnetite and gravity settling to form cumulate layer.

3 Description and explanation of intense chemical weathering removing soluble materials leaving an insoluble residue of bauxite.

4 Factors: tropical climate allows intense chemical weathering; rock must be aluminium-rich, iron-poor; groundwater with pH of 4–10; presence of joints speed up weathering.

4.3.4

1 Labelled diagrams showing placer deposits: on inside of meander bends; in plunge pools; upstream of projections; at confluence of tributaries.

2 Both have high densities but cassiterite can withstand abrasion and attrition because it is hard (6–7) with poor cleavage. Galena is soft (2.5) with 3 cleavages.

3 Research activity.

4.3.5

1 Line graph plotted correctly. Water table marked at 20 m (+/−5); zone of leaching above water table; enriched ore immediately below water table at 20–25 m; primary copper ore below 25 m.

2 See Figure 1, spread 4.3.5.

3 Description of how uranium ore forms as a result of solution, transport and reprecipitation at redox boundaries.

4.3.6

1 Descriptions of: gravity, magnetic and electrical resistivity surveys.
2 See Figure 3, spread 4.3.6.
3 Catastrophic dilution occurs where tributaries meet so metal values are higher upstream of confluences; anomalies can be traced back up tributaries to target area. Most efficient – requires least number of samples.

4.3.7

1 Surface mining likely to have greater initial impact – mainly deforestation, noise and dust, visual and surface water pollution. Underground mining – less visually obvious but problems of subsidence, spoil heaps and acid mine drainage water. Environmental effects of mineral processing are the same for both.
2 Unsustainable as metal ores are non-renewable; take millions of years to form; rate of extraction exceeds rate of renewal; not all metal can be extracted due to technological difficulties; demand for rare metals is outstripping reserves.
3 Research activity.

4.4.1

1 Cement – pure crushed limestone or chalk mixed with clay or shale, gypsum added. Concrete – cement mixed with sand and gravel or crushed rock. Bricks – clay, sandstone or shale; a high carbon content will reduce energy costs during firing.
2 (a) Dolerite – suitable as contains mixture of minerals of different hardnesses, medium crystal size so chippings will contain more than one mineral, hard, low porosity and permeability.
   (b) Marble – unsuitable as monominerallic so will polish, made of calcite which is soft and chemically reactive.
3 Arguments for – we need building and construction materials, super-quarries can provide large quantities, transport costs are low, provide local employment. Arguments against – often situated in areas of outstanding natural scenery, cause pollution, local people do not want a quarry nearby, may conflict with other economic activities such as tourism.

4.4.2

1 Descriptions of: general considerations; foundations; attitude of the strata; geological structures.
2 (a) Leakage of water through the limestone and joints; beds dipping downstream are unstable, slippage and collapse of dam may occur.
   (b) Built on two different rock types – may get differential subsidence; shale is weak with low load bearing strength – dam may collapse; nearby fault suggests area may be prone to earthquakes.

4.4.3

1 Environmental consequences include: flooding of land; damage to aquatic ecosystems; silting up of reservoir; risk of downstream flooding.
   Social consequences include: water supply, agriculture and industry; hydroelectric power generation; flood protection; navigation; possibility of dam failure causing flooding and loss of life; political issues.
2 Weight of dam and water increase load on crust; water acts as a lubricant along faults; infiltration of water increases pore fluid pressure.
3 Research activity.

4.4.4

1 Labelled diagram showing beds dipping into road cutting – possibility of landslips as rocks slide along bedding planes.
2 Weathered rock is loose and weak; has a high permeability and is difficult to drain; some ground improvement strategies can't be used as there are no secure attachment points; needs gentle slope angles to be stable.

4.4.5

1 (a) Granite – hard so rate of tunnelling is slow and expensive; requires drilling and blasting; engineering problems of overbreak and underbreak; possibility of rock bursts; jointing may cause rock falls.
   (b) Limestone – high permeability so possibility of flooding; joints may cause rock falls; may get slippage along bedding planes if dipping; may contain caves and cavities.
   (c) Sand and gravel – high permeability so possibility of flooding; very weak so likelihood of collapse.
2 Description of either grouting or rock drains.

4.4.6

1 (a) Granite – steep, vertical cliff profile.
   (b) Limestone – steep cliff profile with slippage along bedding planes.
   (c) Mudstone – low angle, gently sloping cliff profile with slumping.
2 Research activity.

4.4.7

1 Advantages – ready-made hole in ground so cheaper; area already suffers landscape degradation; ground improvement strategies can be used to prevent leakage of leachate. Disadvantages – limestone has a high porosity and permeability, has bedding planes and joints so leachate may escape; may contain caves and cavities

or be dissolved by acidic leachate; likely to be an aquifer so groundwater pollution may occur.

2 50 days.

3 Research activity.

4.4.8

1 Launching waste into space: advantage – gone forever! disadvantages – expensive, malfunction of rocket may result in radioactive fallout over large area.

Burying in sea floor sediments close to subduction zones: advantage – will eventually be subducted into mantle; disadvantages – expensive and we don't currently have the technology, salt water corrosion of containers may allow leakage of radioactive material into sea water, tectonically unstable areas.

Placing in secure containers on ice sheets of Greenland or Antarctica: advantage – relatively cheap; disadvantage – leakage of radioactive material into environmentally sensitive areas of outstanding natural beauty.

Burying in underground geological repository: advantages – relatively cheap, technically feasible; disadvantages – leakage of radioactive material into surrounding area, rocks are likely to be permeable due to jointing and other structures, some rocks contain naturally high levels of radioactive elements.

2 Descriptions of key requirements: tectonically stable area; dry, impermeable rocks; low water table; free from effects of natural hazards such as flooding.

5.1.1

1 Silicification involves groundwater rich in silica moving through the sediments and infilling or replacing fossil matter. Carbonisation involves heat and pressure and liberation of volatiles, leaving a carbon film. Pyritisation is the formation of iron pyrites by the activities of sulfur bacteria in anaerobic conditions.

2 A mould is the impression of an organism, a counterpart to the real thing. A cast is when a mould is filled with another substance, leaving a copy of the original organism.

3 Increased transport distance increases the fragmentation of fossils due to increased collisions, so they become more damaged. Fine sediments such as clay, infill and mould their particles around the fine detail on the surface of a fossil, preserving this detail. Coarse sediments cannot do this so the preservation is poor. Early diagenesis means there is less alteration to the fossil, once replaced it is more protected from other changes.

5.1.2

1 Exceptional preservation has to have a set of conditions for it to be successful. The most important of these is

anaerobic conditions and some kind of catastrophic event to bury organisms quickly.

2 Quick burial means that there is no breakage, scavenging or decay of the organism. Fine grained sedimentary particles preserve fine detail. Anaerobic conditions means there is no decay. Early diagenesis means that detail is not lost as replacement of original atoms occurs quickly.

3 The Burgess Shale contains organisms that are soft bodied, which is a rarity. This allows us to look at weird forms that are extinct and have not been found anywhere else in the world. It aids our understanding of the evolution of hard parts and allows us to see that soft bodied animals made up a huge proportion of life in the ancient oceans.

5.1.3

1 Trace fossils are the remains of the activities of organisms, but not the organisms themselves. They can be regarded as fossil behaviour.

2 If the animal formed burrows, then the substrate was soft enough to burrow into. Similarly if tracks were formed, the substrate was soft enough to deform. It also tells us that conditions were aerobic within the sediments and at the water interface.

3 Trace fossils on land rarely are preserved as weathering processes and other environmental conditions destroy them.

5.1.4

1 The type of rock gives us information about the substrate where the organisms lived. This in turn gives us an idea of the energy levels involved.

2 A collection of organisms found in the same place and position that they occupied during life is called a life assemblage. A death assemblage is of organisms that have been transported or found with fossils they could not have existed with during life.

3 See the flow diagram on page 226 to check your definitions.

5.2.1

1 Arthropods have jointed appendages (legs), an exoskeleton and advanced sensory systems.

2 Crabs, lobsters, spiders, mites, insects.

3 Facial suture – is the part of the exoskeleton that breaks away first during ecdysis. Pleuron – is an articulated section of the thorax and so allows flexure of the thorax. Glabella – shows the shape of the stomach inside the head. Pygidium – is the fused tail, used for stability.

5.2.2

1 Cephalic fringes spread the animal's mass on a soft substrate to stop it from sinking. It may have been used as a digging tool to excavate shallow burrows.

2 Many pleura/legs/gills. Large crescent shaped eyes.

3 Planktonic forms are possibly blind, and have few thoracic segments. Nektonic forms have many separated thoracic segments and well developed eyes which may be on stalks.

4 Internet research.

5.2.3

1 The main features are septa, dissepiments, columella and tabulae.

2 Rugose – has large corallites which show bilateral symmetry. Tabulate – is always colonial, never has a columella and may have mural pores. Scleractinian – shows distinct radial symmetry displaying 6 major septa.

3 Internet research.

5.2.4

1 Shallow water (<30 m), clear waters, high energy, fully marine and a temperature of between 23 and 27 °C.

2 Zooxanthellae are a type of algae that lives inside the coral polyp. This is a symbiotic relationship as waste from the coral is used by the algae and vice versa. These organisms cannot survive without each other.

3 Internet research.

5.2.5

1 Brachiopods open their valves by contracting the diductor muscles and close them by contracting their adductor muscles.

2 Feeding is by using a lophophore, a fluid filled canal with many sticky filaments lined with cilia. The cilia generate currents which bring in fresh water with particles of food. These particles are trapped by the filaments and then passed to the mouth.

3 See Figure 1 in spread 5.2.5.

5.2.6

1 Thick shells, heavy ribbing and a zig zag commisure.

2 Internet research.

3 Diagram should show the brachiopod attached to the substrate using a pedicle. The pedicle valve should be uppermost and the brachial lowermost.

5.2.7

1 Respiration, movement and attachment.

2 Five-fold symmetry and possess tube feet.

3 Benthonic scavengers on rocky shores.

5.2.8

1 Compare your list with the table in spead 5.2.8.

2 The mouth needed to move away from the centre to enable currents better access for filter feeding. The anus has moved to the side of the animal so that the waste can be deposited into the sanitary tube (part of the burrow where the animal puts waste).

3 The length of the petaloid ambulacra increase (for increased respiration). There was a general increase in size.

5.2.9

1 They filter feed by the extension of siphons (inhalant and exhalent). Water is filtered by the gills and removed from the water.

2 Mussel, clam, oyster and razor shell.

3 Bivalves are symmetrical along their hinge line, and have two equal sized valves. Brachiopods are symmetrical along a median plane (right angles to the hinge line) and have unequally sized valves.

5.2.10

1 The smooth shell is elongate, without any ribbing – this means that they will not cause damage to others in the colony or become damaged themselves when they are moved about in the tides.

2 Growth lines are thickenings of the shell, which gives the animal strength.

3 The part of the organism in contact with the substrate needs to be more robust and heavy to keep the centre of gravity low. This prevents the shells being flipped over in times of higher currents. Smaller right valves mean that the shell is not too heavy for the organism to open the shells, as this is needed for feeding.

5.2.11

1 Elongate, smooth shell, deep pallial sinus, shell may have a permanent gape.

2 They clap their shells together to expel water, directing the currents with the ears close to the hinge line. They do not swim in the strictest sense, but rather do many small hops and come to rest on the seabed. This is a mechanism to escape predators.

3 Burrowers have two adductor muscles whilst nektonic forms only have one large adductor muscle (monomyarian).

5.2.12

1 Deep water dwellers have long siphonal canals (to accommodate long siphons) and may have longer spires than shallow water forms.

2 A cephalopod has a chambered shell, connected by a siphuncle. A gastropod has an unchambered shell.

3 Thick shell for protection, banding or coloured shells to blend into the environment and the secretion of mucus to prevent desiccation.

5.2.13

1 Once plotted, the palaeocurrent direction is ENE (or roughly NE).They are aligned with the pointed end indicating the direction of flow as the heavier part of the guard will be moved less easily in that direction.
2 Five-fold symmetry, tests made of calcite plates and the possession of tube feet.
3 Both are nektonic, swimming in the water column. However, belemnites have a straight guard and ammonites have a coiled shell. Both have siphuncles and can control their position in the water column.

5.2.14

1 It is difficult to extract microfossils with calcareous shells, such as ostracods.
2 They are good zone fossils and so sequences can be dated using them. This aids exploration for oil and gas.
3 They are small and abundant in rocks. They also tend to be better preserved than most macrofossils.

5.3.1

1 The sicula is often pointing in the opposite direction to the thecae. Later thecae may also be larger in size.
2 They are similar to modern day pterobranchs, which do filter feed.
3 They evolved fast, are readily recognisable, have a large distribution globally and are numerous in some rock types.

5.3.2

1 Uniserial, reclined with simple or sigmoidal thecae and probably has two stipes.
2 This may make it easier to 'catch' the particles on which they fed.

5.3.3

1 They could move vertically by controlling the amounts of gas and water in the chambers by using the interconnected tube or siphuncle. Adding gas would allow the animal to move up in the water column as the animal would become for buoyant, whilst adding water would make it sink. The horizontal movement was controlled by tentacles or jet propulsion.
2 Evolute should show an ammonite coiled like a serpent. Involute should be similar to Figure 2 in spread 5.3.3.

5.3.4

1 The sutures – nautiloids show simple, straight sutures (orthoceratitic) and ammonoids show complex sutures (goniatitic, ceratitic and ammonitic). The position of the septal necks – nautiloids have the septal necks pointing towards the protoconch, whilst ammonoids show the septal necks pointing towards the body chamber. The siphuncle is central in nautiloids and eccentric (on the outer margin) in ammonoids.
2 The suture lines of Mesozoic forms would be more complex (ammonitic or ceratitic). The earlier forms would have simple sutures (orthoceratitic or goniatitic).
3 Later forms in the Cretaceous were uncoiled and known as heteromorphs.

5.3.5

1 Lobe-finned fish are primitive fishes that possess gills and lungs.
2 The main similarities between lobe-finned fish and early amphibians are: the fin structure was similar for their four limbs; the limbs are in the same position on their bodies; they lacked claws and nails; and the skulls were very much alike.
3 Skeletal changes (see text) to allow walking in a less dense medium (air). The presence of eyelids to keep the eyeballs moist. Double circulation to increase the efficiency of gas exchange. A tongue to catch prey. Ears to hear in the less dense medium (air).

5.3.6

1 The egg provided an aquatic environment for development (a feature also required for human reproduction as the aquatic environment is in the uterus). The amniotic egg allowed life on diversity on land.
2 Saurischians have hip bones that point forward, a long flexible neck and 'hands' which have only three digits. Ornithischians have hip bones that point forward, a horny beak (duck billed) and some had armoured bony plates.
3 Internet research.

5.3.7

1 Hollow, thin-walled bones; S-shaped curved neck; elongated limbs; large orbits; pubis shifted backwards; and hinged ankles.
2 *Diplodocus* had herbivore adaptations such as peg-like teeth, large size, evidence for gastroliths and a long neck to reach foliage. *Tyrannosaurus* was probably a predator, with the main piece of evidence being large, jagged teeth for tearing flesh.
3 *Iguanodon* had hooves for quick movement and it had a heavy tail which it used as a counterbalance. Both of these would be unnecessary in water.

5.3.8

1 Extinction is when the last member of a species dies out. The species can no longer reproduce.
2 Many dips followed by spikes. Extinction allows diversification afterwards for survivors.

3 A hypothesis is a question or problem that can be investigated in a scientific way. These ideas can then be accepted, rejected or refined.

5.3.9

1 Cretaceous–Tertiary extinctions included: reptiles; ammonites; belemnites; some fish brachiopods and bivalves. Permian–Triassic extinctions included: trilobites; tabulate corals; rugose corals; many brachiopods; and land dwelling plants, tetrapods, amphibians and insects.

2 Volcanism produces poisonous gases which kill animals in the vicinity. The gases and ash can also affect the climate, causing global cooling followed by a global increase in temperature. This can cause animals in their ecosystems to die and upsets food chains.

3 Tektites, shocked quartz, iridium in ash fall and the presence of a large crater in Mexico (Yucatan Peninsula).

5.4.1

1 Many metamorphic rocks form stable, old cratons. The presence of ^{87}Rb in common metamorphic minerals such as muscovite, biotite and K feldspar mean that this method can be readily used as the correct minerals are present in most metamorphic rocks.

2 12.5% = ^{40}K; 87.5% = ^{40}Ar.

3 Sedimentary rocks – dating the fragments not the time of formation, unless you have diagenetic minerals such as glauconite. Igneous rocks – problem as they take a long time to cool and so the date of formation is variable. Metamorphic – problems with overprinting as most metamorphic rocks have more than one phase of deformation.

4 The following half-lives should be plotted and a curve of best fit drawn .

Amount of parent material left/%	Time taken/Ma
100.00	0
50.00	50 000
25.00	100 000
12.50	150 000
6.25	200 000

5.4.2

1 Original horizontality – sediments laid down in beds horizontally. Superposition – youngest sediments always on the top. Way-up criteria – structures only form one way up (e.g. desiccation cracks) and so can be reoriented. Included fragments – fragments from older rocks have to sit in younger ones. Cross-cutting relationships – a feature which truncates other features must be the youngest.

5.4.3

1 Oldest to youngest event on geological map 1. Sediments (clay, sandstone then mudstone) were laid down. The sill was intruded. Folding produced the anticline. Fault F2. Fault F1. Dolerite dyke. Fault 3. Erosion to form modern land surface.

2 Oldest to youngest event on geological map 2. Sediments (mudstone, sandstone then shale) were laid down. The shale contained single-stipe graptolites and was probably Silurian in age. Folding to produce the syncline. Faulting occurred. Emplacement of granite intrusion and microgranite along the faults. Erosion forming the unconformity. Deposition of limestone above the unconformity and then intrusion of the sill. The limestone contains Carboniferous age fauna. Tilting. Deposition of grit. The grit is red in colour with cross bedding and is probably of Permian or Triassic age.

5.4.4

1 This was based on calculating the amount of salt discharged into the sea, dissolved in river water. It is presumed that all the salt in the ocean got there due to weathering. The proportion of salt in the oceans can be calculated and the amount per year can be estimated. Simply divide the amount in the oceans by how much was added each year to get the answer.

2 It did not take into account the fact that Earth is constantly being heated up from within, by radioactive decay in the core.

3 1600 m = 1 600 000 mm (as there are 1000 mm in one metre). 1 600 000/70 000,000 = 0.23 mm/yr. This is more than the calcareous ooze but less than the reef limestone. This does not take into account the amount of Cretaceous rocks that have been eroded or any breaks in sedimentation.

5.4.5

1 Borehole a.

2 Graptolites are more numerous and so more likely to be found. They may be spread over a wider area and so more useful over larger areas.

3 When there is a high level of lateral variation the lithostratigraphic correlation is unlikely to match the others.

5.4.6

1 The Permian–Triassic extinction showed a huge drop in numbers of corals. bivalves, trilobites and graptolites. Other groups were affected but to a lesser extent. The Cretaceous–Tertiary extinction saw the extinction of the ammonites and a drop in the numbers of bivalves and echinoids. Clearly the Permian–Triassic extinction was the biggest extinction event.

2 Internet research.

5.5.1

1 100 000 years ago it was around 3 to 4 °C cooler than at present. 20 000 years ago it was 8 °C cooler than present.

2 Even small changes in temperature can stress organisms and they may no longer be able to survive in the environment that they currently inhabit. This can upset the food chains greatly causing them to break down. An example is modern-day coral that can be affected by a 2 or 3 °C change. Extinction is happening at an alarming rate today due to climate change and humanity's effect on the environment.

3 Internet research.

5.5.2

1

	Eccentricity	Obliquity	Precession
Cycle interval/ka	95 and 123 and 413	41	19 and 23
Wavelength	long	medium	short

2 Internet research on deep sea drilling programme (DSDP) cores.

5.5.3

1 Indicators of higher sea level are raised beach, marine shale with younger fluvial sands above, coral reef terraces, raised cliff line. indicators of lower sea level are submarine forest, marine rocks overlying terrestrial rocks.

2 Eustatic, perhaps due to increased volcanism at mid-ocean ridges.

3 This is the result of global glaciation as water was temporarily removed from the Earth's atmosphere and locked up as ice, causing a lower sea level.

5.5.4

1 The Jurassic is quoted to have lasted 65 Ma. Raise in sea level was 110 m (×1000 to convert to mm). 110 000/65 000 000 = 0.0017 mm/yr. This is very slow indeed. The current raise of 3 mm/yr can be explained by isostatic rebound due to melting ice from the last glaciation. Another factor could also be man's influence on the environment.

2 Large-scale cycles of around 300 Ma are caused by plate tectonic movements. Smaller cycles may be linked to astronomical events.

3 Transgressions alter the conditions on the sea floor, meaning that sessile organisms may suffer first. The continental shelf will then be in deeper water meaning that there are less shallow water habitats available. This in turn would lead to increased competition, and ultimately extinctions.

5.5.5

1 Corals have a symbiotic relationship with photosynthetic algae (zooxanthellae). They need to be in shallow water so that light can penetrate for photosynthesis.

2 Dune bedding (large-scale cross bedding).

3 Birch thrives in cooler conditions, whilst beech survives in warmer conditions. The movement would be south.

6

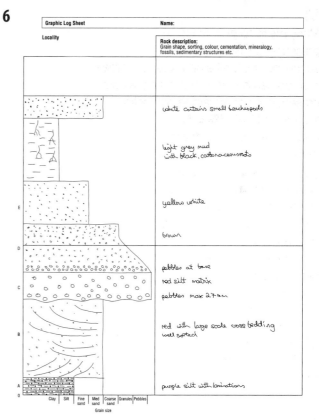

Figure 1 Graphic log of a sequence of beds laid down by a river, showing fining up as the current velocity reduced

Index

Numbers in **bold** indicate figures or tables.